CASSIODORUS:
EXPLANATION OF THE PSALMS

Ancient Christian Writers

THE WORKS OF THE FATHERS IN TRANSLATION

EDITED BY

WALTER J. BURGHARDT

and

THOMAS COMERFORD LAWLER

No. 51

CASSIODORUS: EXPLANATION OF THE PSALMS

TRANSLATED AND ANNOTATED

BY

P. G. WALSH

Professor of Humanity
University of Glasgow

VOLUME I
PSALMS 1–50
[Psalms 1–51 (50)]

PAULIST PRESS
New York, N.Y./Mahwah, N.J.

Library of Congress Cataloging-in-Publication Data

Cassiodorus, Senator, ca. 487-ca. 580.
  [Expositio Psalmorum. English]
  Explanation of the Psalms/Cassiodorus; translated and annotated by P. G. Walsh.
    p. cm.—(Ancient Christian writers; no. 51-)
  Translation of: Expositio Psalmorum.
  Includes bibliographical references and indexes.
  Contents: v. 1. Psalms 1–50.
  ISBN 0-8091-0441-5 (v. 1)
  1. Bible. O.T. Psalms—Commentaries—Early works to 1800. I. Walsh, P. G.
  (Patrick Gerard) II. Title. III. Series: Ancient Christian writers; no. 51,
  etc.
BR60.A35 no. 51
[BS1429]
223'.206—dc20
                                               90-41938
                                                  CIP

Published by Paulist Press
997 Macarthur Boulevard
Mahwah, New Jersey 07430

PRINTED AND BOUND IN THE UNITED STATES OF AMERICA

CONTENTS

NOTES

INDEXES

INTRODUCTION

I

The life of Flavius Magnus Aurelius Cassiodorus Senator, which extended from about 485 to 580 or so, divides neatly into two parts, his career in political administration and secular studies being followed by a religious *conversio* in the late 530s which induced him to devote himself wholly to the service of the Christian Church. His family tradition had fostered in him an ambition for public service. His father, after holding lesser offices under Odoacer, the first barbarian king of Italy, became governor of Sicily and subsequently pretorian prefect under Odoacer's supplanter king Theoderic.[1]

Theoderic (493–526), though an Ostrogoth and therefore of the Arian persuasion, governed Catholic Italy in peace and harmony for a quarter of a century, years during which Boethius was advanced to the chief administrative post of government as *magister officiorum*. But in 519 the restoration of ecclesiastical harmony between Byzantium, under its new emperor Justin, and the see of Rome led Theoderic to fear that the ecclesiastical and political order in Italy might be threatened by interference from Constantinople. When Boethius defended the respected patrician Albinus against the charge that he was conspiring with the eastern emperor, and Boethius himself was arrested and executed in 524,[2] this was an indication that the religious harmony prevailing in Italy was under some strain. The young Cassiodorus had already held the offices of quaestor and consul by 514, and his refusal to implicate himself in this confrontation between Albinus and Boethius on the one side and the royal palace on the other allowed him to gain the position of *magister officiorum* in succession to Boethius in 523–7. In this supreme administrative role at the Ravenna court, he was responsible for imperial decrees and royal correspondence, which he later gathered and published in the twelve books of *Variae* (*epistolae*).[3] His secular career continued to prosper after Theoderic's death; he became governor of Italy as pretorian prefect under Theoderic's grandson Athalaric in 533–7.[4] During his tenure of this office, however, Belisarius, general of the new emperor Justinian, embarked on the conquest of the Ostrogothic kingdom by occupying Sicily in 535, and Naples and Rome in 536. Belisarius finally seized the capital Ravenna in 540. It was during these five years that Cassiodorus decided to transfer his allegiance from the secular world to total participation in Church affairs, a decision recalled in the initial words of the Preface to this *Explanation of the Psalms*.

During his earlier career, Cassiodorus had written panegyrics of personages of the royal household under the title of *Laudes;* twelve books on the history of the Goths up to the year 519 which have been lost but which are summarised in the *Getica* of Jordanes; and a brief summary of Roman history called *Chronica*.[5] This body of writing reflects not merely his earlier secular as opposed to his later religious orientation, but also his eagerness to present the king and his Ostrogoth compatriots in a favourable light to their Italian subjects, and to maintain harmonious relations between the two ethnic communities living side by side in Italy.

It should not, however, be imagined that before 540 Cassiodorus was wholly indifferent to the life of the Christian Church. Already in 535–6 he had attempted, with the support of Pope Agapetus, to establish at Rome a centre of Christian learning which would "train the tongues of the faithful in chaste and eloquent speech" and thus diffuse orthodox Christian teaching in the face of unbelievers and heretical sects.[6] This plan, however, came to nothing, probably owing to the death of Agapetus in 536.

On completion of the publication of the *Variae* at Ravenna, Cassiodorus appended to these twelve books a treatise on the soul,[7] philosophical in its schematic enquiry yet theologically orthodox in its tenets, basing itself on the authority of Scripture and on Augustine in particular among the western Fathers. The twelve chapters investigate the name, the substance, the shape, the moral virtues, the natural powers, the origin, and the location of the soul, and its destiny after physical death. The *De anima* can thus be visualised as a bridge between Cassiodorus' secular and his religious studies. It was after completing this, shortly after retiring from public life at Ravenna, that he embarked upon his detailed study of the psalms, the traditional starting-point in the Scriptures for deeper study of Christian belief.

Cassiodorus' movements during the 540s remain uncertain. After the fall of Ravenna to Belisarius in 540, he may have journeyed directly to Constantinople in the company of the victorious general and the captive king Witigis, and remained there until 554. Alternatively, he may have retired to southern Italy, either to his ancestral estates at Scyllacium (Squillace) in Calabria, or perhaps to Rome. He may have studied in one or in both of these locations between 540 and 547, and then journeyed with Pope Vigilius to Constantinople. (In his *Institutes* he recalls having studied the treatise of Albinus on music in a library at Rome, and this could have been in the 540s, for his *Expositio psalmarum* which was composed then suggests that he was studying musical theory to assist his explanations of some psalms.)[8] But he was certainly in Constantinople by 550-1 in the retinue of Vigilius, for he is cited as *religiosus vir* and *filius noster* by that pope in the letter which condemns two of the papal retinue, Rusticus and Sebastianus, for opposing the pope's support of Justinian in the controversy of the Three Chapters. As the bishop of Squillace, Zacchaeus, was also in the papal retinue, it is tempting to suggest that all three had journeyed to Constantinople together, arriving in January 547.[9] But whether at Constantinople alone or successively in southern Italy and the eastern capital, Cassiodorus devoted the 540s and the early 550s to the concentrated study of the psalms and to the publication of his lengthy treatise on them.

In 555 or a little later, Cassiodorus returned from Constantinople to Italy, and proceeded to establish a double monastery on his estate at Scyllacium, the Vivarium for cenobites on Mt Moscius, and a hermitage for contemplatives on Mt Castellum.[10] He had earlier published a poetic description of the area in his *Variae*, and later in his *Institutiones* he offers further details of the two sites.[11] Similar monastic establishments were being established elsewhere in Italy at this time. It is particularly surprising that Cassiodorus makes no mention of Benedict's monastery, which had been founded a generation earlier; there is no evidence for his having adopted features of the Benedictine rule, nor indeed for any connection with Monte Cassino. Such indications as we have suggest a fluid and experimental regime, loosely based on the outline of Christian life which he read in Augustine's *De doctrina Christiana,* with some respectful regard for the precepts of monastic life laid down by John Cassian.[12] The degree to which Cassiodorus himself participated in this monastic life is disputed. The Conclusion which he attaches to his commentary on Psalm 101 (100) has been cited to claim that he took the tonsure, but this interpretation of the passage has been rightly challenged, for he never describes his own presence there as part of the community.[13]

The early years after the foundation of the monastery are the period during which Cassiodorus composed his best-known work, in two books, the *Institutiones divinarum et saecularium litterarum.*[14] The first book offers a syllabus of sacred reading, with a systematic survey of the books of the bible with recommended patristic commentaries; these are followed by a compendium of Christian treatises and practical advice on how to tackle this reading. The second book outlines a course of study on the seven liberal arts, a knowledge of which he visualises as essential for the proper understanding of the Christian texts prescribed in the first book. In this sense the second book is to be visualised as an ancillary to the first; and we can regard the relationship between the whole of the *Institutes* and the *Explanation of the Psalms* as that of theory to practice, for in the *Expositio psalmarum* he repeatedly makes reference to the seven components of the *trivium* and the *quadrivium* to demonstrate that study of the psalms offers a general education in eloquence. The *Institutiones* provide us with a detailed catalogue of the manuscripts contained in the monastic library at Vivarium.[15]

By the time he had published the *Institutes,* Cassiodorus was in his later seventies. He continued to write for another fifteen years, for in his last recorded work, the *De orthographia,* he informs the reader that he is writing in his ninety-third year. In this same passage he reveals that after finishing the *Institutes,* he "cleansed the stains of the Pelagian heresy from the commentary on *Romans*"; in the *Institutes* this commentary of Pelagius, which takes in the thirteen Pauline epistles, is attributed to Pope Gelasius. He left the task of expurgation of the other twelve letters to the monks of his monastery.[16] The *De orthographia* also informs us that following this labour on *Romans* he composed for the benefit of simple monks a work on etymologies, to which he attached the two *Artes* of Donatus and Sacerdos' book on figures of speech;[17] that in another volume he has catalogued the chapter-headings from Scripture to serve as a work of reference; and finally that immediately before composing the *De orthographia* he had written the *Complexiones*, a simplified explanation by paraphrase, set down verse by verse, of the books of the New Testament other than the gospels.[18] Clearly this group of works is to be visualised as a collection of elementary textbooks composed to assist the monks of Vivarium in their work of reading and transcribing treatises for the library at Vivarium.

II

As was noted earlier, the composition of the *Expositio psalmarum* can be confidently allotted to the period of the 540s and early 550s. The work is dedicated to the author's *pater apostolicus*, who is reasonably identified with Pope Vigilius (537–55), with whom he was on intimate terms, an ascription which allows us to date the first edition of the treatise to 555 or earlier.[19] Certain passages, however, appear to be later additions made after the foundation of Vivarium, and these suggest that a second recension was issued about the same time as the *Institutes* was published. The additions proposed are signalled by Adriaen in the Corpus Christianorum text, and in the notes of this translation.[20]

Cassiodorus' analysis of the individual psalms is preceded by an extensive Preface clearly inspired by Hilary of Poitiers' *Tractatus super psalmos*. In general, Cassiodorus accepts observations of Hilary unless they are in conflict with statements by Augustine. Thus, for example, Hilary's claim that names in the psalm-headings (for example, Idithun or the sons of Core) indicate that there were several other authors of psalms besides David is rejected. But the definitions of psalm, canticle, psalm-canticle and canticle-psalm are all drawn from Hilary; in the definition of the diapsalm, Augustine's explanation is preferred to Jerome's. Other topics raised in the Preface, such as the significance of the psalm-headings, the symbolic purport of psalm-numbers, and the prophetic portrayal of Christ's gospel-activities, can be traced back to the common tradition embodied in the earlier Greek commentaries as well as in Ambrose and Augustine, Hilary and Jerome. But it is notable that Augustine offers no prefatory section, and that those of Ambrose and Jerome are brief; hence Cassiodorus' extensive dependence on Hilary, the structure and verbal echoes of whose introduction are frequently observable.[21]

Cassiodorus' structured discussion of the individual psalms is distinctive. He invariably begins with an explication of the psalm-heading, and then passes to a discussion of the division of the psalm, in which he seeks to identify the speaker (David, or Idithun, or Asaph, or Christ, or the Church, or the synagogue) or the speakers, for some psalms are visualised as dramatic dialogues. He next offers a verse-by-verse explanation of the meaning of the psalm; and finally he appends a conclusion, in which he seeks to demonstrate the lessons which the psalm offers to contemporary Christians. The originality of this fourfold treatment lies in the second and fourth sections. Earlier psalm-commentators in the west, notably Jerome and Augustine, regularly offer only brief comment on the psalm-heading and proceed directly to detailed analysis of the verses. Cassiodorus' second section, the division of the psalm, offers a more general appreciation of the structure and the literary art of each poem. Some psalms are visualised as dramatic dialogues, with different sections allotted to different spokesmen; this is not a wholly original treatment, for individual Greek exegetes from Origen onwards, and Ambrose and Augustine among the Latin commentators, occasionally draw attention to such dramatic features, though not in the systematic fashion followed by Cassiodorus.[22] In his analysis of other psalms, Cassiodorus is content to signal the appearance of diapsalms, where these divisions denote changes of topic within the economy of the whole poem.

The fourth section, the Conclusion drawn from the Psalm, is a wholly original feature. It enables our commentator to take a retrospective view of the main significance of the psalm. As we shall later observe, he is especially eager to exploit the psalms in refutation of the major heresies, and the *Conclusio* is a convenient section in which to underline the need for theological orthodoxy. Another frequent feature of this concluding section is the mystical significance allotted to the number of the psalm. In earlier commentaries of Jerome, Hilary, and Augustine, the significance of particular numbers such as eight or fifty is emphasised, and the connection is duly made with an appropriate biblical context. Cassiodorus claims to be following the practice of his predecessors in this respect: "It remains for us to give credence to the statement of our forbears, that the powers of psalms are in harmony with the numbers allotted to them."[23] In fact he takes the practice much further. In general the decades 1–7 of the psalms typify the sabbath of the Old Testament, and 8–15 point to the Resurrection and embody the New Testament. Within this framework he adduces some obvious and some far-fetched parallels from Scripture for all the numbers of the first twenty-five psalms, but he then at last confesses that his vein of inspiration has run dry at Psalms 27 (26)–30 (29), and thereafter he more soberly contents himself with such occasional allusions to the significant numbers as he had found in his authorities.

III

Cassiodorus states that in his initial study of the psalms he first sought out the authority of Augustine's *Enarrationes*, and their central influence is conspicuous throughout his discussions.[24] In his *Institutes*,[25] he recommends as authorities especially the four Latin commentators Hilary and Ambrose, Jerome and Augustine. We have seen that he based his Preface largely on Hilary's, and in the course of the individual commentaries he frequently cites Jerome[26] as well as Augustine, especially where problems of readings or interpretation of Hebrew are concerned. The influence of Ambrose is much less in evidence, and where he is cited it is his hymns or prose works other than the psalm-commentaries (*De incarnatione, De Trinitate, Super Lucam*) which are quoted. Though Cassiodorus spent some years in Constantinople, the evidence of the *Institutes* suggests that he had not a scholar's confidence with Greek, and we may accordingly assume that he has not studied the Greek exegetes systematically.[27] He is acquainted with some texts of Origen, though this knowledge may be indirect,[28] and in the *Institutes* he warmly commends the *De libro psalmorum* of Athanasius.[29] The Greek influence must in general be accounted slight by contrast with his predecessors who wrote in Latin.

IV

The problem of the Latin text of the psalms on which Cassiodorus based his commentary is complex and disputed. As is well known, versions of Scripture in use before Jerome produced his translations were already numerous; what is conveniently labelled the *Vetus Latina* had in Jerome's words "almost as many versions as manuscripts," because, as Augustine remarked, in the early days "anyone with a smattering of Greek" tried his hand at translation. Augustine urged that the *Itala* be preferred to other versions;[30] this clearly suggests that about 400 there was one generally accepted translation current in Italy, based on the version of the *Vetus Latina* circulating in Africa a little earlier. (Augustine's psalter corresponds with the Verona psalter, a partially retouched version of the *Itala*.)[31] Jerome produced no fewer than three renderings of the psalms. The first, regarded by some scholars as the "Roman" psalter,[32] was a revision in the light of the Septuagint; the second and more thorough revision (the "Gallican" psalter) was made after consultation of Origen's *Hexapla,* and holds pride of place in the Vulgate; and the third, the "Hebrew" psalter, was made after Jerome's mastery of Hebrew enabled him to incorporate corrections of his earlier translations from the Greek.

Cassiodorus did not consistently follow one standard text. It is clear that he constantly had before him a version of the *Vetus Latina* called by some the "Psalterium Romanum";[33] but since he followed Augustine's commentaries on the psalms closely, there are passages where he adopts variant readings which he found in the Augustine text. Moreover, he sometimes prefers to adopt readings from the Hebrew psalter of Jerome,[34] in acknowledgement of Jerome's superior learning in Hebrew. On numerous occasions when he cites the same verse at different points of his commentary, his text varies; some of these variants are doubtless explicable by his having quoted from memory, or by his use of paraphrase, but many citations clearly show that he consults a variety of texts, including Jerome's "Gallican" and "Hebrew" psalters.[35]

V

The ways in which the Scriptures were to be interpreted had preoccupied the Greek and Latin Fathers from the time of Clement and Origen onwards. Two main factors inclined them towards allegorical interpretation of the events of the Old Testament: first, the tradition of such interpretation in the case of Homer was of long standing, and second, criticism of events and characters in the Old Testament by hostile Jewish critics and deviant Christian sects induced them to propound non-literal explanations of them. Thus there developed the thesis of "the four senses" of Scripture: the historical or literal, the metaphorical or figurative, the tropological or moral, and the anagogical or eschatological.[36] The later fourth century was the critical time when the Western Fathers, with Ambrose as bridge, inherited this sophistication of biblical interpretation with its emphasis on allegory.[37] Augustine, who had listened to Ambrose's sermons on Scripture at Milan, and who on his return to Africa devoted himself wholeheartedly to hermeneutics, concerned himself especially with allegorical interpretation, while Jerome his academic contemporary sought to elucidate primarily the literal sense; but both in their exegesis of the psalms sought to present a synthesis of the historical and the allegorical. Other leading Christians of the time like Paulinus of Nola share the enthusiasm for exploring the spiritual sense which lies deeper than the words.[38]

Cassiodorus develops to extreme lengths the allegorical approach which was his master Augustine's leading preoccupation. In his preface, Cassiodorus states that he will try to show the hidden meaning of each psalm, "which varies with the spiritual sense, the historical perusal, and the mystical meaning";[39] but he makes no clear distinction between the "spiritual" and the "mystical." He frequently explains the historical background to a psalm in his initial discussion of its heading, and there is often moral exhortation (the "tropological"

sense) contained in the Conclusion. In the main section, the explanation of the psalm, he concentrates especially on the spiritual sense. His
total ignorance of Hebrew causes him no disquiet; like Augustine
before him, he assumes that the existing Latin versions substantially
represent the sense of the Hebrew, and only occasionally does he
concern himself with the philological issues. His starting-point is the
total conviction that the psalms are a close prophecy of the coming of
Christ and of the ensuing Christian era, and with the self-assurance
induced by this conviction he sets his imagination to work to force out
a Christian meaning from the circumstances, the personalities, and the
exhortations contained in the individual poems. In such interpretations, he sees no need to maintain consistency between a concept or
image recurring in different passages; in one context "arrows" may
represent apostles or evangelists, but in another, diabolical powers.
"Bones" may symbolise moral strength or purblind obstinacy;
"calves" may stand for martyrs at one point, but for antagonistic Jews
at another. There are, however, certain identifications which are consistently made and which are adopted from the earlier tradition of
psalm-commentary; so "clouds" regularly denote prophets or apostles, and "mountains" likewise, as in the earlier Greek and Latin
Fathers.[40]

In such spiritual interpretation, the etymology of names of persons
and places plays a prominent role. Like Augustine, Cassiodorus takes
pains to explain the meanings of the names of persons mentioned in
the psalms, and like Augustine he relies wholly, directly or indirectly,
on Jerome's *Liber interpretationis Hebraicorum nominum*[41] for the elu-
cidation of these names.

VI

We may now address the general question of Cassiodorus' aims in
writing the *Expositio Psalmorum*. Clearly his primary purpose was to
encourage Christians in the west to study the significance of the
psalms as the divinely prophetic proclamation of the future Christian
dispensation. Since he composed his commentary initially in the years
before he founded his monastery, it would be erroneous to assume

that the audience envisaged was restricted to monastic communities; the inference that he is writing for Christians at large is confirmed by several asides. So in his commentary on Psalm(s) 114/115 (113), he addresses all *fidelissimi Christiani,* and again in discussion of Psalm 133 (132) he insists that the message is not merely for monasteries but for the whole Church.[42] The psalms were regarded as the most suitable book of Scripture for initial study; Jerome recommends scrutiny of them before passing on to the New Testament, and Cassiodorus in his Preface offers the same advice.[43]

In his exposition of Christian theology mediated through the psalms, he repeatedly emphasises that the Church is the true and only guide to right belief. In his eloquent address to the Church in his Preface, he states: "Wherever we tread outside your living bark, we encounter certain shipwreck,"[44] a message underlined by repeated condemnation of heretics, pagans and Jews, especially the Jews who refused conversion even when confronted with the miracles performed by Christ and by His apostles. Cassiodorus' attitude to the Jews is of some interest; though his condemnation of their infidelity is vigorous and repetitive, he more than once expresses the conviction that they will be converted and gain salvation before the world comes to an end.[45]

The passionate conviction that the unity of the Church is all-important is reflected in Cassiodorus' vigorous condemnation of the Donatist schism, which is cited on no fewer than ten occasions; there is also an acerbic comment on the Circumcellions, the predatory African peasant mobs who linked themselves with the Donatists. The Donatist schism continued in weakened form in Africa beyond Cassiodorus' lifetime, so that his comments have some contemporary relevance. Moreover, as a devoted disciple of Augustine he eagerly follows the master's example in his attack on this deviant community. A similar judgment may be made about his numerous criticisms of the Pelagians, who with the Donatists had been Augustine's principal opponents in the years following his consecration as bishop of Hippo. Yet here, too, we are to take into account the extraordinary capacity for survival of the Pelagian heresy, for after its condemnation at Ephesus in 431, it remained strong in France and Britain, and had to be condemned again at the Second Council of Orange in 529.[46]

Equally vehement is Cassiodorus' condemnation of other major heresies; though his concern with some of these deviant sects seems anachronistic, it has to be realised that many of them rumbled on for centuries after their initial diffusion, and even when spent they afforded salutary examples of the dangers of dividing Christendom. He is especially concerned to condemn the tenets of Arianism, and there is a certain irony here, since the earlier part of his adult life in the secular world was spent cheek by jowl with his Ostrogoth masters and the Arian creed which they professed. Arius' refusal to acknowledge the true divinity of Jesus Christ is condemned initially in the Preface, and thereafter no fewer than twenty times. Though Cassiodorus does not revert quite so obsessively to the other great Christological heresies, they too appear prominently in the commentary. The teaching of Apollinarius, that in Christ there subsists no human spirit but the divine logos, with the implication that He is perfect in His godhead but deficient in His manhood, had been condemned as early as the Council of Constantinople in 381, but now almost two centuries later is criticised four times. We find a similar number of references to Eutyches and his followers, whose doctrine that after the hypostatic union there was only one nature in Christ was condemned by Pope Leo in his *Tome*, and by the Council of Chalcedon in 451. This monophysite dogma was regarded as contrapuntal to the equally culpable teaching of Nestorius, that there were two separate persons in Christ, the divine and the human; Cassiodorus in this treatise condemns the heresy no fewer than eight times. Finally, the Sabellian doctrine that there is only one Person in God, signified under a diversity of names, and the Manichean rejection of Jesus as the true Son of God, both appear prominently in Cassiodorus' animadversions. Our surprise that he should have concerned himself with these ancient controversies is muted when we read the more articulated criticisms of them in the *De fide Catholica* and the *Contra Eutychen* of Cassiodorus' contemporary Boethius; it seems clear that the controversies aroused by these heresies continued to reverberate for a century or more after Chalcedon.[47]

It is not merely in these negative pronouncements which condemn the Christological heresies that Cassiodorus is concerned to preach the orthodoxy of the Council of Chalcedon. His preeminent concern is that his readers should attain a proper understanding of the doctrine of the Trinity, and especially of Christ's place within it. He visualises

the psalms as clearly divisible into groups which specifically delineate
Christ in His divine and human natures. So he believes that the first
three psalms are given pride of place at the head of the collection to
present Christ in His moral, natural, and reflective aspects.[48] He asso-
ciates eight scattered psalms with each other as disclosing the reality
of Christ's two natures.[49] Four other psalms trace the career of David
in its foreshadowing of Christ's future activities.[50] A further group of
psalms prophesies the Lord's passion and resurrection; these are subdivided into brief allusions[51] and more extended accounts (the first of
this second category he reveals was chanted at the Easter ceremo-
nies).[52] Another group is identified as psalms which depict Christ in
his humanity making prayers to the Father.[53] Another category is visualised as being prophetic of Christ's first coming, and two of them
as foretelling His first and second coming.[54] Other psalms are interpreted as depicting the love of the Church for Christ, and others again
as foreshadowing the Christian sacraments in their description of
miracles which attended the Israelites.[55]

Cassiodorus of course does not attempt to force all the psalms into
such a specifically Christological mould. He is content to present
other groups according to their traditional classification, notably the
penitential psalms,[56] the psalms of lamentation,[57] the Alleluia psalms,[58]
the Gradual canticles,[59] and the psalms describing ecclesiastical discipline; these last are identical with the alphabetic psalms, which Cassiodorus subdivides into those which contain the whole of the Hebrew alphabet and are said to depict perfection in virtue, and those
which omit one or more letters and represent those who have not yet
attained Christian perfection.[60] (The more prosaic truth about this
second class is that letters or verses have fallen out of the texts.)

VII

Cassiodorus' primary purpose, then, is to offer his readers theological instruction, and to encourage them through study of the psalms to
prayer and more committed devotion to Christ. But this aim of spiritual edification does not in itself explain certain curious features of
this spiritual treatise; these appear to be more appropriate to secular

works of literature than to Scripture. Cassiodorus is squarely in the tradition of Christian exegesis, but he is also greatly affected by the continuing tradition of secular commentary on works of literature such as is exemplified by Servius' glosses on Virgil, or those of Donatus on Terence. So, for example, he repeatedly explains the etymology of words to educate his readers in their basic meaning. He draws attention to the numerous figures of speech and thought which are deployed in the poetry of the psalms. He demonstrates too the presence of the various types of definition assembled by the logicians, the numerous forms of argument propounded by the rhetoricians, and the varieties of syllogism which are the stock in trade of both.

It accordingly becomes clear that Cassiodorus deploys the psalms not only for the purposes of instruction in theology and hermeneutics, but also to inculcate a general education in eloquence. In this sense his later work, the *Institutiones*, with its two books on Christian learning and secular knowledge respectively, can be seen to correspond with the *Expositio Psalmorum* as theory to practice, as a theoretical outline of the discipline of Christian eloquence for which the psalm-commentary serves as the ideal text. The suggestion that the psalter is being offered as an educational text-book in the secular as well as the sacred sense may at first sight seem extraordinary. It is as if a modern educationist were to attempt to construct a Christian poetics through the study of the devotional poetry of a George Herbert or a Gerard Manley Hopkins, and to restrict his students' reading to these authors alone.

Yet this is clearly Cassiodorus' important subsidiary purpose. He is implicitly claiming that Christians can gain an education in eloquence solely through the medium of Christian texts and in particular through the bible, without the study of the Classical authors which had survived as the staple of instruction in the Italian schools. As is well known, Jerome (in the account of his famous dream), Augustine in his later years, Paulinus of Nola and others of their age all express the aspiration to excise secular reading from the education of the Christian. The comment of John Cassian, whose influence over Cassiodorus' monastic programme has already been mentioned, is a continuation of that earlier aspiration: "The remedy for a mind infected by poetry is if you are willing to apply the same care and urgency to reading of and meditation on the spiritual scriptures as you claim to have directed to those secular studies."[61]

As always with Cassiodorus, the influence of Augustine is paramount, here exemplified in the connection with the thought of *De doctrina Christiana*. The eloquence of the Scriptures is a passionate preoccupation; hence in the programmatic Preface he includes two long chapters on "The eloquence of the entire divine law" and "The peculiar eloquence of the psalter." That eloquence is mastered by study of the seven liberal arts, and it is Cassiodorus' claim that the psalter provides such an *enkuklios paideia*. So at the close of his commentary he is able to say: "We have shown that the series of psalms is crammed with points of grammar, etymologies, figures, rhetoric, topics, dialectic, definitions, music, geometry, astronomy, and expressions peculiar to divine Scripture."[62]

VIII

In this claim that the psalter provides a medium for teaching the seven liberal arts, Cassiodorus is naturally more concerned with the *trivium* of grammar, rhetoric, and dialectic than with the *quadrivium* of arithmetic, geometry, music, and astronomy. The study of grammar, which in the *Institutes* he calls "the source and foundation of liberal letters," and "expertise in fine utterance,"[63] embraced not only the parts of speech and their syntactical interrelation, but also orthography, on which Cassiodorus contributed a separate treatise late in life, and the figures of speech and thought which were also the concern of the rhetorician. He early provides a definition of figures in general.[64] He is particularly eager to demonstrate that the Scriptures contain all the figures which were classified by the secular grammarians; he has the apologetic purpose of proclaiming that they appear in scriptural eloquence before they are found in secular literature.[65] It is of interest that he draws attention to the examples quoted of such figures (and indeed of syllogisms, definitions, arguments, and other artistic devices practised by the rhetorician and the logician in secular utterance) by distinctive marks in the margin, a practice hitherto unknown to patristic writers, but employed by secular commentators.[66] By his day the classic treatises of Cicero and Quintilian, with their schematic discussions of such literary artifices, had been supplemented by the work of later grammarians. Cassiodorus is closely acquainted with the *Ad Herennium*, the *De inventione* of Cicero (whom he calls in the *Institutes* "the preeminent light of Latin eloquence") and Quintilian's *Institutio oratoria*,[67] but he draws also on a range of later writers, perhaps including the Greek Tryphon and Martianus Capella, and certainly Priscian, Donatus, and Fortunatianus, all of whom receive mention in the *Institutes*.[68] The list of figures to which he draws particular attention is to be found in Appendix D.

Equally striking is the extent to which Cassiodorus seeks to exemplify from the psalms the techniques traditionally assigned to rhetoric. Following the traditional division of speeches documented in detail by Quintilian, he distinguishes between the demonstrative type (the speech of praise or blame appropriate for formal occasions), the deliberative type (which was delivered in political assemblies and offered persuasion or dissuasion on particular courses of action), and the judicial variety (uttered in pleading in a court of law). Examples of all three are offered in the course of the commentary; naturally enough, he equates the greatest number of psalms with the demonstrative category, since they are predominantly expressions of praise to the Creator.[69] Then, in outlining the structure of individual psalms he frequently employs the terminology of the rhetoricians, who prescribe appropriate patterns for the different types of speech; for example, the judicial speech is divided into *exordium, narratio, partitio, confirmatio, reprehensio, conclusio*.[70]

Just as the concerns of the grammarian and the rhetorician overlap, so likewise do those of the rhetorician and the logician. This is clearly the case with discussion of syllogisms, which Cassiodorus repeatedly exemplifies from the psalms; though these are normally regarded as the concern of the logician, Cassiodorus in his *Institutes* includes the *enthymema* and the *epichirema* in the section on rhetoric, the first being regarded as an "imperfect" syllogism, the second as a "rhetorical" syllogism, the expression of which is more diffuse than is that of dialectical syllogisms. Syllogisms in general, however, are regarded as arts of logic, and in the *Institutes* Apuleius' treatise on logic, the *Peri*

Hermeneias, is recommended for study of them. The purest and chief of them is the categorical syllogism, which incorporates an affirmation in syllogistic form; the hypothetical, in which the premiss is expressed in the form of a conditional sentence, is also frequently exemplified. The passages which Cassiodorus offers as examples of categorical, hypothetical, enthymematic, and epichirematic are listed in Appendix B.

Definitions are another leading concern in the area of logic; in the *Institutes*, Cassiodorus lists the fifteen ways in which a person or object can be identified, citing Marius Victorinus' *De definitionibus* as an appropriate text to study. No fewer than eleven of these fifteen are exemplified here, several of them repeatedly.[71] Likewise eleven of the fifteen types of argument listed in the *Institutes* are invoked, some of them repeatedly, and many others fall into the category labelled there as *argumenta extrinsecus*.[72]

Etymologies are another concern of the dialectician in which Cassiodorus shows excessive interest. Greek influence had made etymological study popular at Rome, and the taste for it grew in late antiquity; so, for example, Martianus Capella and Isidore of Seville frequently seek to explain derivations, and Cassiodorus himself composed a treatise on the subject in his old age.[73] It is clear that his main quarry was Varro's *De lingua latina*, as the notes in this volume show. The science of etymology was still at a naive level in Cassiodorus' day, as can be noted from many of the examples cited in Appendix C.

Beyond the three subjects of grammar, rhetoric, and dialectic which formed the *trivium*, Cassiodorus was eager also to educate his readers by demonstrating that the psalms also furnish instruction in the *quadrivium*, the four mathematical disciplines. Arithmetic is the first and foremost of the four, as he makes clear in his discussion in the *Institutes*, where Nicomachus, Apuleius, and Boethius are cited as apposite authors for study.[74] The science of numbers is closely relevant to the Christian mysteries of the one God, the two Testaments, the Trinity, the four Gospels, the pentateuch, the sixth day on which man was created, the seven-formed Spirit;[75] and the numbers of the psalms have their own mystical significance. It is not surprising, then, that on three occasions in reflecting on the meaning of individual psalms, he draws attention to the importance of study of arithmetic.[76] Naturally enough, it is more difficult for him to exemplify the importance of geometry from this book of Hebrew religious poetry, though he adverts to the discipline on two occasions.[77]

Music precedes geometry in Cassiodorus' treatment of the *quadrivium* in the *Institutes,* where he devotes detailed attention not only to its importance in human daily lives, but more especially to its role in religious observance. He treats of the divisions of the subject, the types of instrument, and the various harmonies and tones, citing as authorities Gaudentius, Albinus, and Augustine's *De musica.*[78] It is clear from his discussion of Psalm 81 (80)[79] that he has studied such works as these when writing his psalm-commentary, and there are many incidental references to the importance of the discipline of music in his reflections on individual psalms.

Astronomy, the fourth of the mathematical disciplines, is also given its proper importance.[80] Cassiodorus is especially concerned to distinguish between the scientific study of the heavenly bodies as part of the glory of the Christian God's world, and the debased belief in astrology which was so prominent a feature of the religious consciousness of late antiquity. So he repeatedly condemns the astrologers' attempts to explain the course of the world and the fate of humans as predestined and predictable by observation of the movements of the stars. Here as in so much else Augustine's writings were probably a potent influence upon him.[81]

In this programme of the deployment of the psalms for the teaching of the seven liberal arts and for a traditional education in eloquence, there was a conspicuous problem in the nature of the Latinity. Cassiodorus never admits to the feelings of repulsion to which Jerome and Augustine confessed when they transferred their attentions from the elegance of the Classical masters to concentrated study of the Latin Bible. The uncouth and contorted Latin was especially marked in the psalms. The highly poetic Hebrew originals had been translated literally into Greek, and subsequently from Greek into Latin; and the pedestrian effect of such literal translation was accentuated by the mediocre literary talents of those who composed the *Vetus Latina.* Cassiodorus claims that this biblical Latin is different rather than inferior, and much of his commentary is devoted to explaining the peculiar usages which his readers would probably not have confronted earlier. Such explanations of the Latinity of other books of the Old Testament had been advanced earlier by Jerome and Augustine, so that Cassiodorus in this respect too is following the example of his two formative predecessors.[82]

IX

Though there is general agreement that Cassiodorus' commentary is vitiated by excessive and fanciful allegorical interpretation as by the strained attempt to lend significance to many of the psalm-numbers, there is much that is useful matter for meditation, provided that the reader shares with the author the basic preconception that the psalms represent divinely inspired prophecy of the coming of Christ. Against the dismissive contempt of some modern critics we must set in the scales the experience of numerous Christian scholars of the early and high Middle Ages, some of them individuals of the highest intelligence whose judgment we should hesitate to challenge. In this sense the work has a certain historical importance additional to its intrinsic value, in that it has fostered the spiritual formation of many generations of monastic writers. It is important to remember here that apart from the collected discourses of Augustine, Cassiodorus' *Expositio* is the only complete psalm-commentary composed by any Western Father in Latin. As such, it was a regularly sought acquisition for monastic libraries. We know from library catalogues that there were copies at Reichenau and St Gall in the Carolingian age, at Lorsch and Bobbio in the tenth century, and at Chartres, Bec and Corbie in the twelfth.[83] The most recent editor lists more than eighty extant manuscripts copied between the ninth and the thirteenth centuries, and he is the first to admit that this list is far from exhaustive.[84] A host of distinguished biblical commentators, historians and poets have expressed their debt and in some cases their admiration for the work. The story of the afterlife of the treatise begins with Bede, who exploited it extensively and labelled it *egregia*, outstanding.[85] Bede's noble successor in Britain, Alcuin of York, considers Cassiodorus to be "an outstanding interpreter of the psalms," and another notable member of the circle of Charlemagne, Theodulf of Orleans, quotes at length from the commentary on Psalm 51 (50). It would be easy to document the continuing influence of the work throughout the ensuing centuries; to cite two prominent examples, Abelard shows himself thoroughly conversant with it, and repeated citations by Thomas Aquinas, some from the *Glossa Lombardi* and some (apparently) direct quotations, show the continuing exploitation of it in the thirteenth century.[86]

X

The translation is based on the text edited by M. Adriaen in the *Corpus Christianorum* collection;[87] there is little change from that of Garet in Migne, and numerous typographical errors make it a hazardous edition on which to rely; these and sundry improbable readings are too numerous to record in their entirety. The new edition promised for the *Corpus scriptorum ecclesiasticorum latinorum* by J. W. Halporn is accordingly sorely needed.

Reference to psalm numbers is to the numeration of the New Vulgate, with that of the Vulgate in parenthesis. Cassiodorus follows the numeration of the Vulgate. The reader must accordingly refer to the figure in parenthesis when consulting his commentary on any psalm cited.

CASSIODORUS:
EXPLANATION OF THE PSALMS

PREFACE

Some time ago at Ravenna I thrust aside the anxieties of official positions and the flavour of secular cares with their harmful taste.[1] Once I had sampled that honey of souls, the divine psalter,[2] I did what longing spirits often do, and plunged eagerly in to examine and to drink in sweet draughts of the words of salvation after the deep bitterness of my active life. But I was confronted with the obscurity, familiar to beginners, interwoven in the different personages and shrouding itself in allegories. This obscurity in the words of life is ignored with a disregard that does harm, though frequently we light upon an ambiguity which contains a hidden reference to a great mystery.

Then I had recourse to the highly esteemed commentary of our most eloquent father Augustine.[3] There is such abundance of words gathered there that we can scarcely keep in mind the extensive exposition even after rereading. I imagine that he was eager to satisfy the people's great longing with an ecclesiastical feast, and inevitably his great preaching flowed out in a stream. So mindful of my own weakness, through the grace of God's mercy and in brief summary I turned into shallow streams that ocean of Augustine which wells from the springs of certain psalms; so I have embraced in one volume the wide range of topics which Augustine marvellously unfolded in his fifteen decades. But as a commentator on Homer says, "Removing a part of his thought is like robbing Hercules of his club."[4] Augustine is a preeminent master of all literature and most circumspect in argument, a quality rare in profuse writing. His course is like the clearest of springs, dirtied by no mud. Steadfast in the purity of the faith, he can never offer heretics an opportunity to defend themselves by any grappling hold. He is found wholly Catholic, wholly orthodox. He gleams in God's Church with the sweetest radiance, invested with the brightness of celestial light.

There are some new interpretations framed since the time of that wonderful master;[5] I have inserted these solely through presumption in the Lord, who gives confidence to little ones, sight to the blind, speech to the dumb, and hearing to the deaf. I have divided this book into three sections, each containing fifty psalms preceded by introductions.[6] By this means the clarity of the script will appear clearer to older eyes, and the division of the book's content can meet the needs of the brothers at their reading. So it is left as one volume for library-supervision, but is perhaps more conveniently regarded as divided for study by the community.[7]

So let us trust in the Lord's command, and knock on the closed doors of the heavenly mystery, that He may open His flowering abode to our minds. Then, once we have reached the safety of that heavenly paradise, we may pluck the spiritual fruits without any of the first man's sinning. This is the book that truly shines, the word that brightly gleams, the cure for the wounded heart, the honeycomb for the inner man, the record of spiritual persons, the tongue of hidden powers which brings the proud low before the humbled, subjects kings to poor men, and nurtures little ones with kindly address. In it there is such great beauty of thought, such healing from the drops of words, that Solomon's phrase which he uttered in The Song of Songs is apt here: *A garden enclosed and a fountain sealed up, a paradise full of all fruits.*[8] At one time some psalms endowed with health-giving instruction lead louring and stormy spirits into a bright and most peaceful way of life; at another, they promise that God is to become visibly man for the salvation of believers, and will come to judge the world; at another they warn us to wash away sins with tears, and to atone for faults with alms; at another they express amazed reverence in sacred prayers; at another the power of the Hebrew alphabet gives them profundity; at another they proclaim the saving outcome of the passion and resurrection of the Lord; at another they show deep devotion through the weeping of those who make lamentation; at another their repetition of verses reveals certain mysteries to us; at another they are remarkable for the mounting climax of their song. In short, happily espousing divine praises are rich abundance, indescribable longing, and astonishing depth. The believing mind cannot get too much of it once it has begun to be filled with them.

Finally, the psalms make our vigils pleasant when in the silence of the night the choirs hymn their praise. The human voice bursts into melody, and with words skilfully set to music it leads us back to Him from whom divine eloquence has come for the salvation of the human race. The united voices of the singers become a song which delights ears and instructs souls. In company with the divine angels whom we cannot hear, we mingle words of praise through Him who came from the seed of David, the Lord Christ. As He Himself says in the Apocalypse: *I am the root and source of David.*[9] From Him we have both obtained our saving religion and have come to know the revealed mysteries of the holy Trinity. So the psalms rightly unite the undivided glory of Father, Son, and Holy Spirit, so that their praise is proved to be perfect. They beguile the approaching day with early-morning joy, they dedicate for us the first hour of the day,[10] they consecrate for us the third hour, they make joyful the sixth hour with the breaking of bread, they end fasting at the ninth, they bring to a close the last hours of the day, they ensure that at the onset of night our minds are not darkened. In their own words, *The night is a light in my pleasures, since the darkness will not be your doing, O Lord.*[11] So if a person does not enjoy the sweetness of this gift, he is right to believe that he is a stranger to true life. To put the seal briefly on the virtues of the psalms, God's word is to say in Psalm 70: *But I will confess to thee thy truth in the vessels of the psalms.*[12] Truly they are vessels of truth, for they contain so many virtues, they are suffused with so many odours of heaven, and they are thronged with so many celestial treasures. They are the water-jugs containing the heavenly wine and keeping it ever fresh and undiluted. Their marvellous sweetness does not grow bitter with worldly corruptions, but retains its worth and is continually enhanced with the grace of the purest sweetness. They are a most abundant store, the fecundity of which cannot be exhausted, although so many peoples of the earth drink of it.

What a wondrous sweetness flows from them when sung! When hymned by men's voices they rival the pleasant-sounding organ; when loudly shouted they echo trumpet-sounds; and by the mingling of living chords they produce the sound of the harp. The notes previously observed as issuing from musical instruments are now seen to emanate from the rational bodies of men. But we are not to sing like parrots and larks which seek to imitate men's words but are known to be utterly unaware of what they sing. True, a charming song delights our minds, but does not impel them to fruitful tears; it soothes the ears but does not direct its hearers to heavenly things. But we are pricked at heart if we can heed what our lips say. In the words of the psalter, *Blessed is the people that know jubilation,*[13] and again, *For God is king of all the earth: hymn Him with wisdom.*[14] We recall how the apostle Philip noticed Queen Candace's eunuch reading Isaiah, and suitably explained the Holy Scriptures to him; after the eunuch noted what he had read, he at once sought the grace of baptism, and then received the gifts of perfect salvation.[15] The Lord also says in the gospel: *When anyone heareth the word of the kingdom and understandeth it not, there cometh the wicked one and catcheth away that which was sown in his heart.*[16] This passage allows us properly to grasp that this cannot be the experience of those worthy to listen to the Holy Scriptures with purity of heart. On this issue father Jerome's words are splendid: "Divine Scripture is a pearl, and can be pierced from many sides."[17]

This is why, apostolic father whose holy manners mirror the divine writings,[18] I shall at the challenge of your invitation enter these heavenly heights since God allows it. You correct my mistakes gently; you do not harshly debit me with the faults you amend. But before passing to the spiritual content, I think that I must first offer an *hors d'oeuvre* of topics divided into seventeen chapters, so that when these aspects make their appearance, the draught of this precious nectar may be drunk with the sweetest pleasure. First I must deal in particular with the different kinds of prophecy, so that we may be instructed more specifically on the nature of this prophecy of David. Secondly comes the question why in the psalm-headings different names of apparent authors are found. Third comes the meaning of *In finem,* often found in the headings. Fourth, what is a psalter, and why are the psalms so called? Fifth, what is a psalm? Sixth, what is a canticle? Seventh, what is a psalm-canticle? Eighth, what is a canticle-psalm? Ninth, the five-fold division of the psalms. Tenth, the psalm-headings considered together. Eleventh, what is a diapsalm? Twelfth, should the text of the psalms be divided into five volumes or should they merely be called a single book? Thirteenth, the necessary attitude towards the Lord Christ in the psalms. Fourteenth, the principle of division in expounding the psalms. Fifteenth, the eloquence of the divine law as a whole. Sixteenth, the particular eloquence of the psalter. Seventeenth, the Church's praise. Let us now with the Lord's favour embark on this order of topics outlined.

Chapter 1: Prophecy

Prophecy is the divine breath which proclaims with unshakeable truth the outcome of events through the deeds or words of certain persons. As one writer has well said on this, "Prophecy is the sweet utterance which combines the honeycombs of heavenly teaching with the sweet honey of divine eloquence."[19] So too David himself will remark in Psalm 118: *How sweet are thy words to my palate, more than honey and the honeycomb to my mouth!*[20] The gifts of this grace were proffered in many ways. It was dispensed through the actions of men; to cite a few instances from many, there were Noah's ark, Abraham's sacrifice, and the crossing of the Red Sea. It was dispensed also through the birth of the twins Esau and Jacob, whose actions sacramentally enacted future events; through angels, as when they spoke to Abraham, Lot, Zachary, and Mary; through visions, like those to Isaiah, Ezechiel, and the other holy men; through dreams, like those to Solomon and Daniel; through a cloud and a voice from heaven, as with Moses. So clearly holy David was filled with heavenly inspiration, and not through men's actions, the birth of twins, angels, visions, a dream, a cloud, and a voice from heaven, or any other way of that kind. As the first book of Kings says of him: *And the spirit of the Lord came upon David from that day forward.*[21] The Lord Himself too says in the gospel: *If David in the spirit calls him Lord, how do you say he is his son?*[22] By these words we realise that the psalms were clearly expressions of prophecy through the holy Spirit. We must indeed grasp that every prophecy says or performs something concerning past, present, or future time.

We must also observe that the holy Spirit was assigned to the holiest prophets on such terms that when offended by them through their weakness of the flesh and the opposition of sin He temporarily withdrew and returned at a suitable time when appeased. So St Jerome[23] offered this explanation with such clear reasoning that none dared oppose his view when he explained the evangelist Mark's comment on John: *He saw the heavens opened and the Spirit as a dove descending and remaining on him.*[24] Again in Psalm 50 the prophet after sinning begs: *Take not thy holy Spirit from me.*[25] As blessed Jerome says: "If God's word had always been present in the prophets and had lodged continuously in their hearts, Ezechiel would never have written frequently: *And the word of the Lord came to me, saying....*"[26] Moreover, in Kings the prophet Eliseus says of the woman whose son had died: *Let her alone, for she is in anguish, and the Lord hath hid it from me, and hath not told me.*[27] Then too Paul says: *Concerning virgins I have no commandment of the Lord, but I give counsel.*[28] Paul again says: *This is my instruction, not the Lord's.*[29] In another place he comments: *That which I speak, I speak not according to God.*[30] So the same is the case with the other prophets: the Lord and not the prophets said some things, and the prophets and not the Lord said others. When John the Baptist said: *He who sent me to baptize said to me, He upon whom thou shalt see the holy Spirit descending in the form of a dove and remaining on him, he it is that baptizeth with the holy Ghost,*[31] he would not have been speaking specifically of the Lord Christ, and the additional phrase, *remaining on him,* would not have referred to the Lord Christ, unless it were demonstrable that the Spirit sometimes abandons others. The Spirit remained in Christ because He had no sin, and rightly left others because they experienced the stain of pollution. The holy Spirit can have no communion with sin, for the book of Wisdom of Solomon contains the words: *For the holy Spirit of discipline will flee from the deceitful, and will withdraw himself from thoughts that are without understanding.*[32]

Prophecy is an outstandingly splendid and truthful form of utterance composed not by man's will but poured forth by divine inspiration. As the apostle Peter says: *For prophecy came not by the will of man at any time, but the holy men of God spoke, inspired by the holy Ghost.*[33] The apostle Paul likewise says: *He that prophesieth speaketh to men unto edification and exhortation and comfort,* and a little later: *He that prophesieth edifieth the Church.*[34] Clearly the prophet builds up the Church when through the function of his foretelling he makes wholly clear matters exceedingly vital which were unknown. Those who have been granted the ability to understand well and to interpret the divine Scriptures are obviously not excluded from the gift of prophecy. As Paul says in his First Corinthian: *The spirit of prophecy is subject to the prophets.*[35] Now that we have perhaps acknowledged what Scripture says about the gifts of prophecy, let us carefully examine the remaining questions.

Chapter 2: Why do We Find Various Names of Apparent Authors in the Psalm-Headings?

We read in the first book of Paralipomena[36] that when the prophet David grew old in years devoted to the Lord, he chose four thousand young men from the people of Israel to render the psalms, which he had composed through the Lord's inspiration, so as to attain the great sweetness of heavenly grace by means of pipes, lyres, harps, timbrels, cymbals, trumpets, and their own voices. This sweet harmony clearly comprised a threefold division: a rational part consisting of the human voice, an irrational part comprising musical instruments, and a common part resulting from the fusion of the two, such that the human voice issued forth in fixed melody, and the tune of the instruments joined in harmonious accompaniment. With this performance the sweet and pleasant music presaged the Catholic Church, which by the Lord's gift was to believe with varied tongues and diverse blending in the single harmony of faith.

We often find names of this company of four thousand inserted in the headings, like Idithun, Asaph, the sons of Core, and the rest.[37] Not that they were the composers of the psalms, as some maintain; they were in all probability in charge of the musicians and became the organizers of these affairs, so that by devoting themselves with dedicated minds to their holy task, they might win honour by being remembered in this connection. Above all, their names are inserted because they are seen to reflect a proper understanding of these events; for these men whom I mentioned were not chosen to compose the psalms, but as we read merely assembled to sing them. No historical account maintains that they wrote psalms, and it is rash to assert what no authority proves. There are definite proofs to demonstrate that the psalms are the work of David alone.[38] In fact the author of Revelations, when he wishes his readers to understand the work, makes mention of David alone: *These things saith the holy One and the true One, he that hath the key of David, he that openeth and no man shutteth, shutteth and no man openeth.*[39] Then too in the gospel the Lord Himself says to the Pharisees: *How then doth David in spirit call him Lord, saying, The Lord said to my Lord,*[40] and so on. This proves that the corpus of psalms was the work not of many authors but of a

sole person, who was clearly named by the Lord. Moreover the Catholic Church under the inspiration of the holy Spirit maintains a general and undeviating custom that when any psalm prefaced by another
name is to be sung, the reader must not presume to announce it as
other than a psalm of David. If the psalms were the work of Idithun, or
of the sons of Core, or of Asaph, or of Moses, their names would be
specifically proclaimed, as happens with the gospels, which are cited
under the names of Mark, Luke, Matthew, or John. This view is
adopted also by father Augustine, who properly states that all the
psalms are David's.[41]

Chapter 3: The Meaning of "Unto the End" Which Often Appears in Headings

We use the word *end* in two ways. First there is the common moral
sense, when some guided object reaches the furthest point, from
which it cannot proceed further, and is seen to attain the limit of its
movement. In this sense we say that food comes to its end when
consumed by persistent chewing, or money comes to an end when we
are told that it is spent, and there are other such clear examples. The
second sense of *end* is that perfect and abiding end which we now
seek, and which begins to extend and prolong itself when our dedicated minds attain it.[42] So the end and fullness of the law is our Lord
Christ. As Paul says: *For the end of the law is Christ, unto justice to
everyone that believeth.*[43] When we have attained this End, we shall
seek nothing further; we shall be content in this End of blessedness,
and enjoy the fullest sweetness. Our love of it progresses to the degree
that our understanding is clarified by the Lord's dispensation. So
whenever you find the phrase, *Unto the end*, in psalm-headings, concentrate your mind keenly on the Lord Saviour, who is the End without end, and the full perfection of all blessings.

Chapter 4: What a Psalterium is, or Why Psalms are so Called

Jerome defines *psalterium* as "a tuneful hollow in wood fashioned
in the shape of a letter Δ, with the fat belly in its upper part; when the

strings are taut and plucked with the plectrum at that place in the manner prescribed, they are said to give forth the sweetest melody."[44] Evidently this is the opposite arrangement to that of the lyre, for what the lyre has at the base, the psaltery has at the top. This type of unique and tuneful instrument is an apt image for the body of the Lord Saviour, for just as the sound of the psaltery comes from the upper part, so Christ's body hymns a heavenly message of splendid precepts. As the Lord says in the gospel: *He that is of the earth, of the earth he is, and of the earth he speaketh. But he that comes from heaven testifieth to what he hath seen and heard.*[45] Some people maintain that David's compositions have been called psalms for this reason, because they are known to resound from heaven's height.

You are to realise that the hymns contained in this book are called psalms simply by virtue of their excellence. The prophet Daniel attests that the psaltery is a form of music when he speaks of the sound of trumpet, flute, harp, sackbut, psaltery, symphony, and all kinds of music.[46] Then too Paralipomenon explains it in mention of stairs in the Lord's house and the king's house, and also of harps and psalteries being made for singers from thyine wood, which is commonly called ebony.[47] In Hebrew the psaltery is called *nablum*, a word often found in the book just mentioned. But the word psalm is undoubtedly Greek; some maintain that it comes from Greek *psauein* meaning to touch, for we call the players psalterists when with learned thumb they create musical melodies.

Chapter 5: What a Psalm is

A psalm is a sweet and tuneful melody issuing forth from a single musical instrument, the psaltery.

Chapter 6: What a Canticle is

A canticle is a song sung in God's honour, when a person uses his voice freely without the accompaniment of harmonious melody played by some musician on a sounding instrument; in other words, it represents our present practice in our praise of God.

Chapter 7: What a Psalm-Canticle is

A psalm-canticle was sung by a chorus joining their voices to follow a musical instrument. But the term is restricted to the choir's rendering sacred words.

Chapter 8: What a Canticle-Psalm is

A canticle-psalm consisted of the singing of the choir followed by skilful playing of a musical instrument combining to form a single harmony, so that the combination sweetly sounded forth the words of the heavenly hymn.

Chapter 9: The Fivefold Division

At fitting moments I shall refer to this fivefold division which I have mentioned, wherever any of the five can be found in the psalm-headings, providing by allegorical interpretation some meaning for what follows. But there are other superscriptions of many kinds which I think I should not pass over. I believe that they should be considered briefly together to elicit a single conclusion, so that the reader does not become bored, yet does not chance to pass over necessary information and thus forfeit his understanding.

Chapter 10: A General Consideration
of the Inscribed Psalm-Headings

Some psalm-headings where they make similar allusions must clearly be understood in the spiritual sense, for if you ponder the literal meaning the heading is irrelevant, since you do not find in the psalms the content indicated by the headings. But if a figurative interpretation is applied to them, they seem totally appropriate. For example: *When he fled from the face of Absalom*[48] denotes a historical situation; *When he was in the desert of Edom,*[49] a locality; *On the day before the sabbath,*[50] a date; *For Idithun,*[51] a Hebrew name; *When he changed his countenance in the presence of Abimelech,*[52] a comparison of attitudes; *For the winepresses,*[53] a comparison with similar situations. So in title-headings, whether you chance to find *psalm* or *canticle* or *psalm-canti-cle* or *canticle-psalm* or *Unto the end,* or any example of the sixth type listed, whether you find them alone or whether you find one, two, three or four of them entered there, you must apply them in the senses which I shall explain are present in each psalm. Careful analysis shows that these things are mentioned there to demonstrate some similar but hidden meaning. These expressions hang in front of the psalms like consecrated curtains. By directing your mind's eye through their thin texture, you can easily gaze into their hidden depths. Who would regard all these explanations and these differing expressions as super-fluous? It is wicked to believe that the divine Scriptures contain any idle matter; as we read in Scripture: *Amen, amen I say to you, one jot or one tittle shall not pass of the law till all be fulfilled.*[54]

Chapter 11: What a Diapsalm is

It is acknowledged that a difference of interpretation has arisen between exegetes of the psalms about this term. Jerome, that most learned student of the Hebrew tongue, maintains that it is the continu-ing presence of the holy Spirit, for *diapsalma* means always.[55] How-ever the blessed Augustine, who is the cleverest of researchers into obscure matters and darts between difficulties without coming to grief, is known to have preferred instead the explanation that diapsalm appears to mean a division; he discusses the nature of the term itself.[56]

The fact is that sympsalm is the Greek for the combining and linking of expressions, and diapsalm for a break in the flow of them. Wherever it is found it informs us that a change of spokesman or of situation is taking place. So such a term is aptly inserted where mean-ings or speakers are clearly to be separated. So I too shall divide the psalms appositely wherever a diapsalm can be discovered in them, and I shall investigate others in which authority for the diapsalm cannot be found, as opportunity allows.

Chapter 12: Should the Text of the Psalms be Divided into Five Books, or Should it Rather be Called One Book?

The blessed Jerome thought that the prophecy contained in the psalms should be divided into five books, because on four occasions in the text we find: *So be it, so be it.*[57] Thus with the insertion of this phrase some division seems to be revealed. Subsequent generations agreed, and supported Jerome; my own view is that he judged this to be in his own interest, because wearisome length was thus reduced into several sections. But Hilary, bishop of Poitiers, the sharpest and deepest of students in religious matters, concludes that we ought more aptly to speak of one book of Psalms, because there is one volume in the Hebrew, and above all because in the Acts of the Apostles we read: *In the Book of Psalms . . . .*[58] So on the strength of this great authority we rightly speak of one book.

Chapter 13: How are We to Regard the Lord Christ in the Psalms?

For the instruction of the faithful, the psalms speak of the person of the Lord Jesus Christ in three ways; first, in a manner recognisably referring to His humanity, as in Psalm 2; *The kings of the earth stood up, and the princes met together, against the Lord and against his Christ.*[59] And again, in Psalm 20: *Thou hast given him his heart's desire: and thou hast not withholden from him the will of his lips.*[60] Secondly, he is shown to be equal to and coeternal with the Father, as in the words of the same Psalm 2: *The Lord hath said to me, Thou art my Son: this day have I begotten thee.*[61] And again in Psalm 109: *With thee is the principality in the day of thy strength, in the brightness of the saints.*[62] Thirdly, in connection with the limbs of the Church, whose Leader and Head is Christ Himself, as in the words of Psalm 21: *Far from my salvation are the words of my sins,*[63] and in Psalm 68: *O God, thou knowest my foolishness, and my offences are not hidden from thee.*[64] We must interpret this statement as referring to all individual believers. Wicked deeds are undoubtedly totally alien to Christ; hence Tyconius in his books of Rules has expounded on this carefully and at greater length.[65] If we store all this in our minds, we are not troubled by any confusion. The greatest error arises from the occasion when a statement clearly referring to the one situation is ineptly associated with another. For if our author had spoken only in the one sense, who could have recognised Christ's twin substance, since even with the most obvious distinction made here, some with sacrilegious wilfulness seek to confuse the Lord

Christ's divinity and humanity? Moreover, though much of the admonition He offers is by the letter, equally many of His commands are by the spirit. Quite suddenly He fittingly changes His role, at one moment seeming to speak as Christ God, the Word incarnate made man, the Head of the Church; but at another as a just Man, at another as a penitent Sinner, so that He touches on and incorporates all essential teachings. Everywhere the holy eloquence telling of heavenly matters resounds to the fullest, as with a manifold variety of powers the devoted Redeemer incorporates the adorable mysteries of His kingdom to bestow salvation on the human race.

The purpose of these preliminaries has been to allow the reader when he comes to such passages to be able fearlessly to give ear to what he realises he has now so salutarily learnt. But we must maintain with the strongest belief, on the authority of the Fathers and the witness of Truth itself, that one Member, one Person of the Trinity, God the Word, took compassion on mortals and became Man from the virgin Mary. He did this by His own power and not through compulsion imposed on a servant, for He did not undergo any change to His nature, nor by taking on flesh did He add anything to the Trinity. As one person says, "He washed away our stains with blood, and smoothed our wrinkles with the cross."[66] Since this is the unique protection of our hope, the blessedness of believers, the great bliss of the just, heretics with their profane desires never cease to gnaw at it, for they recognise that it has afforded to the human race the means of salvation.

Chapter 14: How this Commentary on the Psalms is Divided

With the Lord's help I must speak of the wording of headings first; from them issues the meaning of the divine preaching like milk from breasts compressed. Secondly, every psalm must be divided according to its nature, so that our understanding may not be confused either by a sudden change of subject, or by the introduction of different speakers. Thirdly, I shall try to show the hidden meaning of the Psalm, which varies with the spiritual sense, the historical perusal, and the mystical meaning.[67] I shall discuss the fine points and the proper meanings of the words as opportunity presents itself. Fourth, I shall try briefly to expound the power of a passage as it demands, so that the purpose of a poem's division may by God's gift be clear to inner eyes. By the power of a psalm I mean the divine inspiration by which God's purpose is revealed to us, keeps us clear of faults through David's words, and persuades us to lead an upright life. Fifth, when necessary I shall mention the numbers attached to the psalms, for this has been consecrated with a distinction afforded to the most venerable topics.[68] I confess that it has been difficult for me to do this in the case of each and every psalm, because even the authority of the Fathers has left this matter undecided and in the air. The remaining numerations the researcher must carefully work out for himself, for many things in divine Scripture which at present seem hidden become clear with the passage of time. In the final section I draw together briefly a summary of the whole psalm, or say something in opposition to heresies which are to be exstirpated, for true love of the Lord lies precisely in regarding His foes with perfect hatred.

Chapter 15: The Eloquence of
the Entire Divine Law

The eloquence of the divine law has not been fashioned by human speech. Its impact is not doubtful, confused, or ambiguous. So it does not forgetfully contradict what has gone before; it is not in turmoil through confusion of present events; and it is not deceived by the uncertainties of the future. It speaks to the heart, not to the body's ears. It judges everything with great truth and great force of prescience. It comprises the truth of its Author. For this is how the Gospel speaks of the Lord Christ's preaching: *Now he was speaking as one having power, and not as the scribes and Pharisees.*[69] He speaks of certainties, for all things are present to Him, and the outcome of events is seen to be subject to Him.

Now eloquence is the right and fitting exposition of any particular matter. But the eloquence of the divine law is a chaste, secure, truthful, and eternal proclamation. It gleams with the purest possible expression. Its usefulness shines out, the splendour of its power stands out, and its saving work smiles out. As David is to say in Psalm 118: *For thy eloquence will enliven me,* and again; *Thy word is a lamp to my feet, O my Lord, and a light to my paths.*[70] It is truly a light, because it always prescribes what brings life, and forbids what harms; it removes things earthly, and advances things heavenly. This is why the teacher of the Gentiles is a further witness in a letter to the Corinthians: *For the kingdom of God is not in speech, but in power.*[71] In his second letter to Timothy, Paul further recalls: *All scripture, inspired of God, is profitable to teach, to reprove, to instruct, to correct in the discipline which is of justice, that the man of God be perfect, furnished to every good work.*[72]

As the authority of father Jerome attests,[73] divine eloquence among the Jews is composed according to rhythms or metrical law, which the Jews describe as ordered in *fastucia,* a *fastucium* being a fully elaborated concept developed phrase by phrase to draw out the sense.[74] If, careful reader, you wish to examine the force of this, listen to Paul speaking to the Hebrews: *For the word of God is living and effectual, and keener than any two-edged sword, and reaching unto the division of the soul and the spirit, of the joints also and the marrow; and is a discerner of the thoughts and intents of the heart.*[75] Now the holy depth of divine Scripture is expressed in such common language that everyone immediately takes it in. But buried within it are hidden senses of truth, so that the vital meaning must be most carefully sought out. What contributes most of all to our understanding that it is really divine is the fact that ignorant men are known to have been able to explain most subtle things, and mortal men eternal things, but only when filled with the divine Spirit.

Finally, how many successive miracles were performed so that Scripture might become diffused and fill the full extent of the world? As Scripture says: *Their sound hath gone forth into all the earth, and their words unto the ends of the world.*[76] So the greatest proof lies in the fact that the divine law is known to have been received through every part of the world. It exploits its varieties of language in sundry ways, being clothed in definitions adorned by figures, marked by its special vocabulary, equipped with the conclusions of syllogisms, gleaming with forms of instruction. But it does not appropriate from these a beauty adopted from elsewhere, but rather bestows on them its own high status. For when these techniques shine in the divine Scriptures, they are precise and wholly without fault, but once enmeshed in men's opinions and the emptiest problems, they are disturbed by obscure waves of argument. What in the Scriptures is unshakeably true often becomes uncertain elsewhere. So while our tongues sing a psalmody, they are adorned with the nobility of truth, but once they turn to foolish fictions and blasphemous words they are cut off from the glory of integrity. As the apostle James says; *From our very mouths we bless God and the Father, and from our very mouths we curse man who is made after the image and likeness of God.*[77]

Those experienced in the secular arts, clearly living long after the time when the first words of the divine books were penned, transferred these techniques to the collections of arguments which the Greeks call topics, and to the arts of dialectic and rhetoric.[78] So it is crystal clear to all that the minds of the just were endowed to express the truth with the techniques which pagans subsequently decided should be exploited for human wisdom. In the sacred readings they shine like the brightest of stars, aptly clarifying the meanings of passages most usefully and profitably. I shall draw attention to them briefly at the most suitable places, for it will be most convenient to cite the passages in which the expression of the meaning will shine out more clearly.

Moreover, father Augustine in the third book of *De doctrina Christiana* maintained the following: "The learned must realise that our authors have employed the modes of all the forms of expression which grammarians using the Greek term call tropes." And a little later; "Those who know these tropes or modes of expression recognise them in sacred literature, and by knowledge of them are assisted to some extent towards understanding of it."[79] This point he makes very clearly in other books as well; for in the volumes which he calls *De modis locutionum*[80] he showed that the various figures belonging to secular literature are found in the sacred books, and he declared that there are other modes peculiar to divine eloquence which grammaticians and rhetors have not mentioned at all. Other most learned fathers of our number have also stated this, namely Jerome, Ambrose, and Hilary, so that clearly I am in no sense the originator of this idea, but a follower of others. Someone however may say: The premises of syllogisms, the names of figures, the terms for the disciplines, and other items of this kind are not found at all in the psalms. But they are clearly found in force of meaning, not in the utterance of words; in this sense we see wine in vines, a harvest in the seed, foliage in roots, fruits in branches, and trees conceptually in nuts. Moreover, succulent fish though invisible to the human eye before being hooked are caught from the deepest pools. So we rightly proclaim the existence of the techniques which we feel are equally present because of their force. Paul bids us not to be seduced by the empty wisdom of the world,[81] but he does not deny the presence of these techniques in the divine letters. At any rate, let us turn to the psalms, and investigate the reliability of the facts, which is superior to any contention.

The main force of eloquence in the scriptures, previously untried and a pointer to salvation, frequently recounts certain things yet is often explaining matters greatly different from the words heard. This is a simplicity which is at two levels, a guileless form of double speaking such as Joseph employed; though he recognised his brothers by their faces and native speech, he seemed to them to speak as if there could have been absolutely no recognition.[82] The device is not adopted in the interests of deception, but to achieve a most useful effect. It employs the Hebrew language to intimate the deepest of issues. It often uses the one concept in both the bad and the good sense, so that what has a shared name is seen to differ in its qualities. It compares heavenly things with earthly, so that the understanding forbidden by the incomprehensible Majesty can be attained by comparison with objects totally familiar. It has a marvellous faculty of interweaving words, so that suddenly things which are measureless and beyond understanding are expounded in two or three words.

To put it succinctly, often even a single syllable shows the Lord's indescribable nature, as in the phrase: *He who is hath sent me*.[83] Every word of that phrase is subtly sought out, and swarms with numerous meanings. Just as the most fertile land bears perfumed plants to aid our health, so when the divine reading is examined word by word, one always finds there the cure for a wounded heart. (Many of the Fathers have spoken at greater breadth and length on the forms of this eloquence, and I have ensured that their names are mentioned in the introductory books.)[84] But the more constantly the heavenly spring is drunk, the more it knows no drying up. Let us not delay longer on generalities, but with God's help touch on the particular issues of the Psalter, for individual points are clearly recognised when described in particular cases after the preliminary generalisations.

Chapter 16: The Particular Eloquence of the Psalter

The first fact to note is that only the psalms are cited by individual numbers.[85] I have consulted those with the greatest knowledge of Scripture, and after consideration of the psalms and their extent I considered that the practice of those who sing the psalms should be continued, and that they should be set down by their verses, so that the mingling of authorities should not cause confusion in the choice of order adopted. Secondly, there is the fact that no other work with divine authority is divided into a hundred and fifty parts. In what other book do we find so diverse a variety of headings? In one place the votive word *Alleluia* comes first in the titles; elsewhere an allusion to the narrative of the Book of Kings is put at the very beginning, and is seen to denote the powers of psalms. Again, in other places there are merely diapsalms interposed, while elsewhere psalms maintain numerical order following the powers which they possess.

The book starts with Christ's blessedness, runs through the mysteries of the New and Old Testaments, and concludes with sacred praises and holy joy. Hence the Church rightly consoles herself with such a gift, wounded as she clearly is here on earth with the afflictions of many disasters. Weighed down as she is, she can triumph over her disasters by the Lord's kindness, for she grows by persecutions, constantly swells through afflictions, is watered by the blood of martyrs, raised higher by grief, enlarged by want, fed by tears, refreshed by fasting. She thrives on the things which weaken the world.

What will you not find in that book for provision of the means by which the human race must obtain sweet consolation? It is a treasure ever increasing in a pure heart, a great consolation for those who grieve, a blessed hope for the just, a useful refuge for those in danger. One always takes from it what is helpful, yet its stream continues enduring and unfailing. The blessed Athanasius, bishop of the city of Alexandria, in the book which he addressed to his dearest Marcellinus about the peculiar nature of the psalter says: "Whoever recites the words of a psalm seems to be repeating his own words, to be singing in solitude words composed by himself; it does not seem to be another speaking or explaining what he takes up and reads. It is as though he were speaking from his own person, such is the nature of the words he utters. He seems to be expressing the kind of language used as if spoken from the heart. He seems to offer words to God."[86]

A further peculiarity of the psalter is that it is the entry into the divine law. Novices do not begin with Genesis or St Paul; initially we do not knock on the door of the sacred authority of the gospel. Though the psalter is the fourth book authorised by God, it is fittingly the first with which novices begin when embarking on the holy Scriptures.[87]

Chapter 17: Praise of the Church

O truly holy, spotless, perfect mother Church! Through the generosity of God's grace you alone give life, you alone make holy. By your instruction you renew the human race which was brought down by its own sins. To your holy confession nothing can be added or taken away. Through all the psalms and all the canticles you interpose praise of the holy Trinity, so that confession and the sweetest glory might be rendered to the Persons of God to whom belong the consecrated words we utter. You alone sail unceasingly over the salt surge of the world, through the most savage storms of heretics, in the likeness of the famed ark of Noah, which clearly symbolised you; the course of faith does not run aground, nor is there danger from the flood. Though by the sternest necessity you still dwell amidst the world's evils, you take no errors lying down. Wherever we tread outside your life-giving bark, we encounter certain shipwreck.

Though Sabellius goes detestably astray on the issue of the Father,[88] though Arius like a madman is awry on the Son,[89] though Manes sacrilegiously denies the holy Spirit,[90] though others evilly detract from the Old Testament and some do not pursue the grace of the New, you alone by your faithful devotion and through the Lord's gift embrace all teachings without coming to grief; for you teach that the unbegotten Father, the begotten Son, the holy Spirit proceeding from

Father and Son are one God. You preach the holy Trinity coeternal with Itself and equally omnipotent. You confess that the Lord Christ, abiding in His divinity and in the flesh of His assumed humanity, preserves the peculiarity of each nature, yet is one Person. You impart fresh praise to the Old Testament, since you know that the New has risen from the Old. To embrace the whole Truth in a word, you can utter nothing except what it is expedient to believe. For though affected here by diverse difficulties and battered by the opposition of the crafty enemy, your numbers are drawn from the orbit of the whole world, and gleaming like the most beautiful pyramid you are guided to the eternal kingdom.

You are rightly compared to this figure since you raise your precious head over all races, and you transmit the souls of the just like resplendent stars to the kingdom above. You are a pyramid full of heavenly corn, the blessed gathering of saintly men from diverse nations, the shining assembly of bright minds, a structure which cannot be dismantled since it is fashioned from living stones, the eternal happiness of all blessed men, brighter than the sun, whiter than snow, without spot or wrinkle. Of you it is written in the Song of Songs: *Who is she that cometh forth as the morning rising, fair as the moon, bright as the sun, terrible as an army set in array?*[91] And a little later: *Thy eyes are doves' eyes, besides what is hid within, thy teeth as flocks of sheep that are shorn, which come up from the washing, all with twins; and there is none barren among them. Thy lips are as a scarlet lace.*[92] You are a mother yet a maiden, pregnant yet virgin, a mother yet undefiled, whose mouth is fragrant with the odours of all the virtues, of whom her Betrothed says: *And the odour of thy mouth shall be like apples,*[93] and a little later: *The sweet smell of thy ointments is above all aromatical spices. Thy lips, my spouse, are as a dripping honeycomb; honey and milk are under thy tongue.*[94] In short, you deserve Christ's kiss and the continuance of your virginal glory for ever; for these words are spoken to you: *Let him kiss me with the kiss of his mouth, for thy breasts are better than wine, smelling sweet of the best ointments,*[95] and the other verses which that divine book includes with its mystical proclamation.

So now that my listeners are sufficiently amazed and fired through God's kindness with heavenly longing by this entrance or introduction to the work that follows, which is the key to the heavenly mysteries and a herald of sacred language, let us go forward with Christ's

help to discharge what has been promised. O Lord, in whose hands is
all that is helpful, grant that I deserve to be heard with understanding,
joy and profit. I need Your many-sided help that speech may be
granted me, and that I may be able in some degree to explain the words
of Your Majesty. Amen.

Arrangement of Themes to be Treated

Before tasting the honey of the heavenly psalter and before setting
foot with God's help on those fields so famed of the most glorious
passion, there are certain preliminaries or introductory headings
which seem to me to fall into separate sections, and to inform us about
the framework of the actual poems. So I can instruct the reader more
clearly and hasten through the poems without coming to grief.

In the first category the bodily life of the Lord is described.

In the second, the nature of the Godhead Himself is subtly
indicated.

The third enumerates the manifold people who strove to destroy him.

The fourth continues with the same warning, prophetically urging
the Jews to cease to plan and commit evil, since they know that they
must be destroyed by the power of God.

In the fifth, the Lord Christ cries to the Father that His prayers be
heard, and that through His resurrection the Father may grant future
benefit to the world.

Sixth come the words of the penitent throughout a whole Psalm, to
which are appended another six of the same type, these being described at the end of Psalm 50.

In the seventh, Christ humbly asks to be helped by the Father. He is
confident enough to hold a direct conversation more appropriate to
His divinity, but after the fashion of the humanity which He has
assumed He asks for help that the devil may not plunder His soul
through his wicked presumption, and that His glory may not be
dragged in the dust and annihilated.

In the eighth, parables and figurative allusions are gathered, and the
ensuing action is completed with everything referring to the Lord
Christ by allegorical comparison. I mention those figures at the most

suitable places, and draw the clearest attention to them so that all ambiguity is removed for the studious reader.

The ninth has diverse praises beginning with His divinity or His humanity, and then there is a change of speakers and headings with the word Alleluia, which means "Praise the Lord."

Tenth come the psalms of the steps, which lead our minds through chaste and humble satisfaction to the Lord Saviour.

In the eleventh, they once again with verbal variation hymn together the Lord's praises with joyful song. This section proclaims the majesty now of the Father, now of the Son, now of the holy Spirit, so that no-one is in doubt that the holy Trinity is uniquely omnipotent in all that It wishes to perform in heaven and on earth.

The seven remaining psalms form the twelfth group. They celebrate with devotion of heart the entire glory of the holy Trinity in general, with joy in song. So the text of the whole psalter is divided into twelve parts, the number of the apostles, and it comes to a close with wondrous praise in achieving what we know God's followers achieved. There is another more obviously mystical meaning in this number, because the earth was washed clean of its sins in the one hundred and fifty days when the flood covered it; in the same way these psalms were extended to a like number, and aptly absolved the human race of the sins with which it was polluted.

Now let us proceed to explain the words of the psalter in detail.

COMMENTARY ON PSALM I

Why Psalm 1 Has No Heading

The reason why this psalm has no heading is because nothing was to be put before our Head the Lord Saviour, of whom the psalmist intended wholly to speak, for undoubtedly He is the Beginning of all things; as He says in the gospel, *I am the beginning, and this is why I speak to you.*[1] Though other psalms also say much about Him, none of them speaks in this way about His behaviour on earth. Since all that is to be said refers to Him, He is rightly set at the head of the sacred work, since He is known to be Prince of all things. Whatever instruction is given concerning the past, whatever advice about the present, whatever makes us more careful about the future, all that the book has to offer refers to the instruction offered by the blessed Man. Some have said that He has the role of a heading or preface. Though in some commentators' eyes[2] the psalm seems a fitting description of any just man, it can apply most truly only to the Lord Christ. If we say that it can apply to any just man, then the psalm's comment: *Every man is a liar,*[3] does not hold good, nor does Job's comment: *None was pure before thee, not even the child who lived one day on the earth.*[4] Elsewhere we read: "In truth there is no man born who has not acted wickedly, no man of self-esteem who has not sinned"; and there is the statement: "In your case the justice of the just is as the rag of a menstruating woman."[5] Hence the psalm's judgment cannot apply to each and any blessed man, but solely to Him of whom Scripture says: *Who did no sin, neither was guile found in his mouth.*[6] As Christ says of Himself in the gospel: *Behold, the prince of this world will come, and in me he will find nothing.*[7] So it is to the Lord Christ that are rightly applied the words: *Who hath not walked in the counsel of the ungodly, nor stood in the way of sinners, nor sat in the chair of pestilence,* and so on. What a marvellous sequence, a truly heavenly arrangement, since in our interest the beginning of the psalms has sprouted from Him who is clearly the moving Gate to heaven! So let us hasten to enter with the utmost joy where we observe our Advocate himself as the open Gate. As the apostle says: *For we have not a high priest who cannot have compassion on our infirmities,* and a little later: *Let us go therefore with confidence to the throne of his grace, that we may obtain mercy and find grace in seasonable aid.*[8] Now let us insert the keys[9] which can unlock the psalms, so that with the Lord's help we may deserve to enter the palace of our King. So as I said in the Preface, we must split up the psalm; if this division is rightly done, it makes the words so clear and bright to us that before the text of the prayer is read its purpose can shine out before us.

The Division of the Psalm

The entire text of this psalm is spoken by the lips of the prophet. In the first section he explains the life of the sacred incarnation, for should you wish to apply the words spoken of Him merely to Christ's majesty, they cannot be appropriate. The second part recounts the wickedness of sinners who are to incur vengeance at the judgment to come. Its purpose is to enable us to accept the first section of the psalm, since its subsequent part seemed to inspire fear. Look too at the psalm's purpose, which must clearly be closely examined. So initially the Lord Saviour's blessedness is proclaimed so that the human race may be given living examples of how the heavenly Man came and bestowed salvation on us, just as earthly man bestowed death. Initially, man who had been deceived endured the grimmest condition, but later came his glorious redemption. First shameful captivity was imposed, but then followed the freedom which was much desired. Man was expelled from Paradise, but received into heaven. He lost happiness on earth, but will deserve to have the angels as his companions. Grief came forth from the devil, joy from Christ. This is why Paul says: *For as by the disobedience of one man many were made sinners, so also by the obedience of one many shall be made just.*[10] So at the very head of this psalm the definition of the blessed man shines on us like the most beautiful diadem of the shining King. The prayer is short and clear, revealing in various ways the matter expounded. In the first two verses the phrases, *hath not walked, nor stood, nor sat,* is the eighth type of definition which in Greek is called *kat'aphairesin tou enantiou,* and in Latin *per privantiam contrarii.*[11] This is a statement of what He does not do, just as in Psalm 5 the poet is to say: *For thou art not a God that willest iniquity.*[12] But in the third verse the words *But his will is in the law of the Lord, and on his law he shall meditate day and night* form the second type of definition which Greek calls ennoematic, and Latin *notio.*[13] This does not state what it is; instead the object of inquiry is specifically shown to us by what it does. For example, the psalmist will say in Psalm 71: *Blessed be the Lord the God of Israel, who alone doth wonderful things.*[14] Remember that every definition derives either from the matter concerned, that is the body of the thing, or from the species, the nature of the thing, or from both (as in the case of *the man*). The order in which the psalm arranges all that is adduced is remarkable, for if it had first defined what the blessed man was, it need not have said what he was not. The geometrician Euclid reversed this procedure when he said: "A line is length without breadth."[15] First he said what a line is, and then added what it is not. This is what men tend to do when they cite the words of predecessors with some variation, falsely claiming to be the authors of them. Now let us proceed to examine the words, since the sweetest fruit is found at the heart of them, within the shells, so to say.

Explanation of the Psalm

1. *Blessed is the man.* This is a most beautiful and apt beginning; since the holy Spirit was to warn us of the weakness of the human race, he seems to have begun with blessedness so as to entice the minds of the fearful with this hope, so that mortals' frail hearts should not withdraw, for who is not fired to perform difficult tasks when contented blessedness is predicted? So he is called a blessed man, as our forbears' authority tells us, as being well-suited[16] to obtain all that he desires. But in Psalm 143 the prophet reminds us that the adjective has two senses: *They have called the people blessed that have these things: but blessed is that people whose god is the Lord.*[17] So in the worldly sense the blessed man is he who thinks that he is supported by the greatest security, and who continues in abiding joy and worldly abundance. But the psalmist splendidly appended *man* to the second sense of *blessed,* which is deterred from its purpose by no opposition. *Vir* (man) derives from *vires,* strength.[18] In his endurance he admits of no failure, and in his prosperity of no proud self-inflation. Rather, he is immov-

able and steadfast in mind, strengthened by contemplation of heavenly things, and abidingly fearless. This too our forbears called "true statement," for an etymology is a brief exposition which by clear echoes reveals the verbal source of the word scrutinised. You should not doubt that he calls the Lord Saviour a man, for the prophet Isaiah also says of Him: *Behold a man, the orient is his name.*[19] But remember that whenever this definition occurs, the humanity which He assumed is revealed, for *man* describes sex in the flesh which is wholly absent from divinity. Since human nature had to be assumed by the Lord for our redemption, the psalmist aptly called Him *man* so that we might believe Him to be one Person with two natures.

Who hath not walked in the counsel of the ungodly, nor stood in the way of sinners, nor sat in the chair of pestilence. After defining the blessed man, who is the Lord Christ, beginning with the dispensation by which He suffered, the psalmist might usefully have next described Him through His deeds; otherwise the omission in the exposition of the theme is less informative. Men agree that human faults arise in three ways, thought, word, and deed, and these he excludes in turn. First he says: *He hath not departed to the counsel of the ungodly.* So he first excludes any abominable thoughts such as human beings claim intimate acquaintance with, but which had no place whatever in the Lord Christ. We need no extraneous proofs of this, for Psalm 39 fully attests that we must interpret the passage as referring to the Lord Saviour when it says: *Then said I: Behold I come. In the head of the book it is written of me.*[20] *Departed* means forsaking the right path and sliding on to crooked ways.

Next the psalmist excluded deeds of sinful relationships: *nor stood in the way of sinners.* He says this simply because Christ came into the world, which is the way of sinners, but did not halt there since He traversed its wickedness unstained, as He mingled with them. By the phrase, *the way of sinners,* we are to understand the broad way, for clearly the way of the just is narrow. The third phrase which he appended is: *nor sat in the chair of pestilence;* the phrase appears to refer to detestable doctrines diffusing the poisons of harmful teaching.[21] It is rightly denied that such faults lie in Christ, for by His healing preaching He cured the wounds of the whole world. One commentator has interpreted this passage with differentiation of this kind: he says that the ungodly is the person who sins against God, the sinner is the one who wrongs himself, and the pestilential man is presumably one who plunders, oppresses, and harms his neighbour. But reflect on whichever of these you will; you will acknowledge that in the Lord there is nothing of this kind. A *chair* is a form of seating fashioned from some material giving soft support to our bent backs; when we sink into its hollow it encloses us like a well-fitting cover. It strictly belongs to teachers, as the gospel exemplifies in *the scribes and Pharisees have sat on the chair of Moses.*[22] Similarly we say that the tribunal is appropriate for judges, and the throne for kings. The order of phrases must also be studied as a patterned condemnation of Adam; he *departed* when he forsook the Lord's command, *stood* when he took delight in sin, that is, when as lord of Paradise he was gulled into believing that he would obtain knowledge of good and evil, and he *sat in the chair of pestilence* when he left to posterity the precedents of wicked teaching.[23] Note how splendidly the psalmist allotted the individual words, *departed, stood, sat,* to the individual actions; this figure is called *hypozeuxis,*[24] when different words are aptly assigned to individual phrases. So in the case of the Lord Saviour the combination of sins in general is rightly rejected. As Truth Himself says in the gospel: *Behold, the prince of this world will come, and in me he will not find anything.*[25]

2. *But his will is in the law of the Lord.* To have avoided vices would not have been a great glory, but the psalmist further mentioned what was eminently praiseworthy. As he says elsewhere: *Decline from evil, and do good.*[26] The Lord's law, then, is a sacred injunction to eschew the sins which as is well known were imparted to Moses on mount Sinai. The Man of the psalm was truly *in the law* with the purpose of His whole mind, for He was without sin, whereas we may ponder the purpose of the law momentarily, but at the time of sinning our will does not remain in the law. The fitting attitude of the will is to show constancy in unremitting meditation, and if this is doggedly embraced, the weariness of toil is not felt. But so that you do not regard the will itself as idle, the outcome of its activity follows. Benevolence to the holy design was insufficient; it must also satisfy its longing with unbroken and devoted toil. Here a categorical syllogism[27] can be observed. We must not ignore it, for the primary sense must not appear to have been ineptly disregarded. I shall cite the definition and the parts of the syllogism so that none of these matters can remain uncer-

tain to the uninitiated. A categorical syllogism, then, is one which dialecticians greet with the highest praise. It is the reasoning by which from certain premises certain other conclusions necessarily follow because of the premises. It is composed of two propositions and a conclusion, as is clearly the case in this passage. Its first proposition is: "Blessed is the man whose will is in the law of the Lord," and the second is: "No-one whose will is in the law of the Lord departs to the counsel of the ungodly"; the conclusion emerges as proved that: "Therefore no blessed man departs to the counsel of the ungodly." The sedulous students among you will find this feature in various places; I have thought it worthy of less frequent mention because I have many topics to broach which arise from various devices and teachings, in addition to the explanation which is my purpose.

And in the law he shall meditate. One should note that he says for a second time, *in the law,* not beneath the law, for He who spurned sins was within the law, but the rest of mankind are rightly beneath the law for they are bent by the burden of their sins.[28] *Lex* (law) gets its name from the fact that it binds (*ligare*) our minds, and holds us subject to its provisions. But He did not meditate on the law according to the letter, but in the holiness of His purpose. As the psalmist is to say in Psalm 39: *That I should do thy will, O my God, I have desired it, and thy law in the midst of my heart.*[29] Both these aims are demonstrated in this one psalm, for the beginning of the book must be understood with reference to Him, and clearly He has always pondered the Lord's commands. Note too the words of Psalm 77: *I will utter propositions from the beginning.*[30] But when He says: "I will utter from the beginning," He does not wish to express the possibility that His own person may be ignored in other passages. However, following the authority of various Fathers, I have allotted the words both to the Church and the prophet, and have stated that either the justest of men or sinners are speaking. I unfold these clearly in their due places so that the very variety of situations may delight the ear.

Day and night. This connection reveals unbroken time. If you apply the phrase literally, it is quite unfitting to maintain that anyone reads or proclaims the law of God continually day and night, for our bodies are given periods of recreation, and the need for seeking sleep is conceded. But proof of unbroken meditation on the law is shown by the person who has dealt piously with everything, and has in all things comported himself with godly purity.[31] This is truly and undoubtedly apposite to our Head the Lord Christ, though the injunction seems to have been laid also on His members to follow the example of His holiness: *All that you do in word or deed do for the glory of God.*[32] This continuity is also recommended elsewhere, as we read in Psalm 118: *Teach me your testimony, Lord, and I shall always seek your commands in my heart.*[33] Pagans called their days after their divinities, after the gods from whom we know the days got their names; but night (*nox*) is so called because it is harmful (*nocere*) to our sight or to our actions.[34]

3. *And he shall be like a tree which is planted near the running waters.* Next is foretold that most splendid and unique blessedness: just as His wondrous actions have been described, so also His happy fortune is related in a magnificent simile. As I see it, the Lord Christ is well compared to a fruit-bearing tree because of the cross which He took up for the salvation of men. The cross is deservedly called the wood of life both because our Lord Christ, who is our Life, hung there, and because the thief who made this same confession was told: *Amen, I say to thee, this day thou shalt be with me in Paradise.*[35] So today too everyone that believes in the cross wins the gifts of eternal life. Alternatively, as the historical narrative records, the wood truly ensured enduring life in Paradise, had that detestable disobedience not taken place; for how could death have made its entry if Adam had shown devoted love? The most holy Fathers extracted the sweetest honey from the incident when they said that God ordered Adam to enter upon his dominion, but laid down a law to make him more circumspect. But Adam unthinkingly followed the enemy, and unhappily abandoned the Author of life. Then his tearful fate cheated him; he lost the enduring life he was to possess, and rushed into the death which was foreign to him. But to return to the simile which was formulated and its instruction, the phrase, *which was planted,* means that the wood of the cross was implanted by God so as always to flourish and grow in the faith. This figure is called a parable, in other words a comparison between things different in kind.[36] In the same way in later passages Christ is compared to a mountain, a lion, and a worm. Next comes *near the running waters.* The psalmist continues with this pleasant comparison. Just as the running water of the earth is the life of living trees, so spiritual water washes over the sign of the cross which is acknowledged to be the salvation of faithful souls. So

this is the water which is mentioned in the gospel: *If thou didst know who he is who seeks water from thee, thou wouldst have asked of him to give thee living water,*[37] and so forth. It is worth while also to ponder why he said *near* the running waters: it was no doubt so that too violent an inundation should not harm the tree, and on the other hand that it should not become dry because the irrigation was too distant.

Which shall give fruit in due season. Which shall give fruit, in other words, establish churches[38] at the fitting time when He has taken on the mysteries of the blessed incarnation. What wondrous fruit which filled the human race with the sweetest belief! Not to taste it is to sin, and to abstain from such food is a form of negligence, for *fructus* (fruit) gets its name from enjoyment (*frui*).[39] One should also note that he said, *shall give,* because giving is the act of rational thought and of the will of the donor. Though other trees *bear* burgeoning fruits, this tree is rightly said to give fruit because it is seen to bestow eternal rewards.

And his leaf shall not fall off. In other words, under no circumstance does His word abandon the truth. Just as the leaves of a palm-tree are evergreen, so these words implanted in the truth abide with unfailing promises; as the gospel says: *Heaven and earth shall pass, but my words will not pass.*[40] Note that the Lord's words are compared with the leaves of a tree, for just as leaves protect the fruit, so the words guard the promises. These are the waters of the spirit, the leaves of salvation which John mentions in Revelations: *And he showed me a river of the water of life, clear as crystal, proceeding from the throne of God and of the Lamb. In the midst of the street thereof, and on both sides of the river, was the tree of life bearing twelve fruits, yielding its fruit every month, and the leaves of that tree were pruned for the healing of the nations.*[41]

And all whatever he shall do shall prosper. This is most aptly contrasted with the situation of Adam, whose deeds brought a reversal on us, for just as the Lord Christ conferred on the world the sweetness of salvation, so Adam inflicted on the human race the bitterness of death. The shape of this preaching has accordingly been built up in three ways, by stating what He avoided, by recounting what He did, and thirdly by describing the final fruit which He attained. But this is said in a brief and restrained way owing to the lowliness of the humanity which He assumed. But if you wish to grasp His magnificence, listen to Paul's words: *For which cause God also hath exalted him, and hath given him a name which is above all names: that in the name of Jesus every knee should bow, of those that are in heaven, on earth, and under the earth.*[42] And we read in John's Apocalypse: *And I beheld and I heard the loud voice of many angels round about the throne, and the living creatures and the ancients, and the number of them was ten thousands of ten thousands, thousands of thousands saying with a loud voice: the Lamb that was slain is worthy to receive power and riches and wisdom and fortitude and honour and glory and benediction. And every creature which is in heaven, and on the earth, and under the earth, and such as are in the sea, and all that are in them, I heard all saying: To him that sitteth on the throne, and to the Lamb, benediction and honour and glory and power for ever and ever. And the four living creatures said: Amen. And the ancients fell down and adored,*[43] and so on. Divine Scripture is full of such passages, for just as there was humility in the body which He took on, so after the resurrection the Lord Christ's majesty was declared.

4. *Not so the wicked, not so.* The psalmist passes to the second section, where he recounts the future sufferings of the wicked and of sinners, so that by noting their punishment men may avoid doing what those men do. This figure is termed *paradeigma,*[44] a trope arranged with a nicely turned sequence of words, for the paradigm is narration by examples which encourage or deter the individual. The psalmist encouraged him with the words: *Blessed is the man* and the rest, but deterred him when he said: *Not so the wicked, not so* and what follows. This is clearly a most effective type of teaching, which both encourages with success and deters with the opposite, as father Augustine also recounts in his books on Christian teaching: "So the person who handles and teaches the divine Scriptures must as defender of upright faith and conqueror of error recommend what is good and deter from what is evil."[45] This kind of teaching the psalmist powerfully achieves in Psalms 14, 36, 111, 118; the threats of punishment are diverse, but in all of them the rewards are described splendidly. So he says: *Not so the wicked, not so,* because the wicked will not merit the treatment described earlier. So that your faith may be unshakeable, he showed the strength of the denial by repetition. If you seek sedulously to discover the abode of the wicked, listen to the words of John's Apocalypse: *And the devil, who seduced them, was cast into the pool of fire and brim-*

stone, where that beast and the false prophets—the term of course embraces all wicked people—*will be tormented there day and night for ever and ever.*[46]

But like the dust which the wind driveth from the face of the earth. This is a particularly apt comparison. Dust is loosened earth, and the earthly man when puffed up with the seductive wind of pride is cast away like dust from the solid land of the living. Because he could not maintain his stance on the firm ground of the commandments through lack of weight, the wicked man is rightly called dust, for like a thin substance he is tossed in the air by the blasts of vices. But let us not consider that this most stern damnation is compared with the sport of the winds, which with playful pressure transport easily shifted bodies into the breezes of heaven; for at this point the psalmist wishes to reveal the ease with which the man is dislodged, rather than to play down the harshness of his predicament. *The face of the earth* denotes the ground's surface where the thinnest dust can really settle. The Greeks call this *epiphania,*[47] which has only length and breadth, which takes on different colours marked out by differing properties, which is known to admit the imprint of the well-known shapes associated with the teaching of geometry. In short, all that one discerns with the human eye is seen in it.

5. *Therefore the wicked do not rise again in judgment.* The wicked are those who with harshness of mind utterly refuse to confess the holy Trinity, who do not consent to obey the rules of the Old and New Testaments, or who in Paul's words *profess God in words, but in their works deny him.*[48] They do not rise again in judgment because they have already been condemned through their unbelief.[49] The Lord says in the gospel: *He who does not believe in the Son is already condemned;*[50] for if rising again for judgment means that the individual renders an account for his deeds, they are rightly said not to rise again for judgment, for God's sentence has already condemned them beyond doubt. The Catholic faith proclaims that all rise again; in Paul's words, *We shall all rise again, but we shall not all be changed,*[51] for the just man rises to judge, the sinner to be judged, the wicked to be punished without trial.

Nor sinners in the counsel of the just. Sinners are those who proclaim themselves Christians, but are subject to lesser sins. To them is addressed the Lord's prayer that they deliver themselves from evils. But the wicked are those who do not know their Maker, and are polluted by various sins, for example blasphemers, those unwilling to repent, worshippers of idols, and persons fast-bound to the chief vices. So there are two classes of sinners: the first, those who remain in their sins without making any placating satisfaction, and the second, those whose sins are forgiven through the grace of confession. As Scripture says: *Blessed are those whose iniquities are forgiven, and whose sins are covered.*[52] Among these are the saints, because no man is without sin. As the blessed apostle John says: *If we say that we have no sin, we deceive ourselves, and the truth is not in us.*[53] So the psalmist speaks of the first group of sinners who deserved no saving mercy, for they will certainly not judge with the just, which is the reward promised in the gospel-words by the Lord solely to His faithful. *In the counsel* means "at the judgment," for every right judgment is by consultation; counsel (*consilium*) derives from consulting (*consulere*). The expression used earlier, *counsel of the ungodly*, is a misnomer, for they themselves think that they are consulting, but clearly all that they take up they discuss with the trickery that is their bane.

6. *For the Lord knoweth the way of the just: and the way of the wicked shall perish.* The psalmist said that the Lord knows the way of the good, and he maintains that the way of the wicked perishes—as if the Lord did not know both these facts! But the expressions are figurative, meaning that God knows what will remain in blessedness and does not know what will perish,[54] for at His judgment He is to say to sinners: *I know you not.*[55] But if one sought to take this literally, how will He fail to know those whom He created? Similarly He said to Adam after the sin: *Where art thou, Adam?*[56] Not that God did not know that Adam was in Paradise, but rather that Adam is being rebuked as one unworthy to be recognised by God, because he had fallen.

The route of the wicked shall perish. Just as the Lord is the way of the blessed, so the devil is acknowledged to be the route of the wicked; he will undoubtedly perish when with his followers he is condemned to eternal punishment. *Way* (*via*) derives from the journeying (*vehi*) of any traveller upon it;[57] *route* (*iter*) gets its name because it is repeatedly (*iterum*) driven over and worn away (*teri*) by movement over it.[58] Both words one finds used in varying senses according to the nature of the region; earlier the psalmist used *via* for the way of sinners, and *iter* in its turn is used in the good sense, as in another psalm: *And there is the*

way by which I shall show him the salvation of God.[59] Again, the prophet
Isaiah says: *I will give the chief place to Sion, and I will console Jerusalem
on her way.*[60] But now let us embark on the conclusion to be drawn;
this is, so to say, the mirror from which the most beautiful appearance
of the entire psalm can gleam out on us.

Conclusion Drawn From the Psalm

The psalm as a whole is concerned with the moral teaching in
which the good man is steeped, and by which the wicked minds of
sinners are terrified. Moreover, the placing of the Lord Christ at the
beginning of the collection is no idle arrangement. Here is the unique
Oneness, simple and perfect, having need of nothing, and remaining
abidingly within itself. From this Fount comes forth the multitude of
numbers which however multiplied return always to it, and without it
such calculation cannot begin or emerge.[61] So Christ is rightly set here
at the outset of the reckoning, for in Paul's words: *Of him and by him
and in him are all things.*[62] This oneness the Greeks call the monad. If a
substance is incorporeal and unchangeable, it is known to be God; if
incorporeal and changeable, soul; if corporeal and changeable, body.
So this is how the monad is explained by the arithmeticians in such
contexts. Remember that though the monad is regarded as the source
and beginning of number, it cannot itself be called number.[63] Nicomachus says, "Whatever is more than one becomes countable";[64] for
number is the aggregate of units, or the conglomeration of quantity
proliferating from units. The point being made is clarified also by the
evidence of the word itself, for *numerus* (number) is so called from
being numerous. The fathers of our religion have likewise enjoined
that this teaching be not ignored, since it is true and unchangeable and
diffused through all creatures according to the measure of their size.
So we read in Solomon that God made all things *in measure, number
and weight.*[65]

I think that we should note also that all the ensuing psalms mount in
a marvellously prearranged scheme. In the first, the bodily life of our
Lord Christ is described, and next the almighty nature of His divinity
is subtly revealed. Thirdly, the psalmist mentions the numerous people who strove to destroy Him; then seven psalms of penitents purify

the hearts of the faithful. The subsequent action[66] hastens on in parables and figurative allusions, with almost everything pointing by allegorical similes to the Lord Saviour, as I shall duly explain at the appropriate places. Then the prophet celebrates the praise of the Lord Christ with wondrous variation, and to the end of the book never ceases to utter the proclamation of His holiness. So in this sense everything is acknowledged to be a revelation of Him for whose sake this commentary was undertaken.

COMMENTARY ON PSALM 2

1. *A psalm of David.* In some manuscripts this psalm too is seen to lack a heading. Hence we read in the Acts of the Apostles: *As in the first psalm it is said, Why have the races raged,*[1] and the rest. But if you examine the question carefully, no contradiction appears. It is said to be part of Psalm 1, but though we must regard it as such by the criterion of the heading, it is likewise second in order though first in its heading. Numerous works follow this pattern, being literally separate but clearly a unity, as is the case with the very broad field of the gospels which harmonise with each other. So it has become the praiseworthy practice of all the churches that the preliminary headings start where the text begins with the rebuke of the Jews. So it followed that the theme had its own heading since it was known to be separated from the earlier text. Having explained why this section has its own heading, let us now with God's help discuss the words in it. A *psalm* is a hymn composed according to some metrical law. We acknowledge that like the musical instrument already mentioned,[2] it reveals to us a heavenly power. *David* is aptly cited in certain places though he is regarded as the author by divine inspiration of the whole work. Now as we remarked at the outset, the interpretation of names is shown to reveal to us more hidden meanings. Translators of Hebrew names have offered for David the renderings 'brave in hand' or 'much desired.'[3] These meanings can be applied to no-one so aptly as to Christ almighty, who is truly most brave and is to be sought with the utmost desire. So David is to be understood here as the Lord Christ, and the prophet speaks of His passion. The Lord Himself will

speak His own words, a feature found very frequently in the psalms that follow, so that in the title David can be understood as the Lord Christ. A mind that is Christian should believe everything truly and firmly; and so that it may not vacillate through the arguments of heretics I close the definition of the name itself with a brief explanation on the authority of the Fathers. So let us listen to the blessed and most learned Augustine's words in his commentary on John the evangelist: "We must recognise the twin substance of Christ; that is, His divine substance in which He is equal with the Father, and His human substance than which the Father is greater. He is each of these at the same time, but He is the one Christ and not two, for God is Trinity and not Quaternity. So Christ is God, and a rational soul, and flesh."⁴ When this truth is recognised, we fittingly avoid lethal errors.

Division of the Psalm

The beautiful texture of this psalm is fashioned in four sections. In the first, the prophet speaks of the Jews in relation to Christ's passion. In the second come the words of the deranged Jews; in the third, the Lord Saviour's words concerning the all-powerful kingdom and His own indescribable begetting, in so far as our human insignificance can grasp it. In the fourth, the prophet speaks, warning the nations to recognise the Lord's majesty and to be reconciled to the Christian faith, for unless they grasp the most true teaching of the Catholic religion they know that they will perish, separated from the right path. This point is made over and over again by the comments of other prophets.

Explanation of the Psalm

2. *Why have the races raged and the peoples pondered vainly?* This is the figure called in Greek *erōtēma*, and in Latin *interrogatio*.⁵ There are many variations of it. To define a few of them, we ask a question when we wish to learn something of which we are ignorant. An example is a passage in a later psalm: *How many are the days of thy servant? When wilt thou execute judgment on them that persecute me?*⁶ We also express as a question a fact that we certainly know; for example: *Is*

there any among the graven things of the Gentiles that can send rain, or can the heavens give showers without thy will?[7] A further type of question is one of rebuke as in the psalm here, for the prophet chidingly asks the people why they have raged against the Lord Saviour when they had no reasons for anger. Rage is an emotion proper to beasts, and is attributed to men who lose total control and who rejecting reason are fired with bestial madness. Since we must often make mention of rhetorical figures, let me provide a definition at the very beginning so that when one is mentioned it may be clearly identified. A figure, as can be gathered from the term itself, is the shaping of a phrase remote from common use which is always offered like some facial expression to the inner eye; after the example of our forbears we may call it a display or appearance.[8] Father Augustine likewise places figures amongst the techniques of utterance.[9] We need not be exercised that *races* and *peoples* appear to be cited in the plural though the discussion centres on the Jews, for we read in the Acts of the Apostles: *For of a truth there assembled together in this city against thy holy son whom thou hast anointed, Herod and Pontius Pilate with the nations and peoples of Israel.*[10] They *pondered vainly* because they frequently repeated the divine Scriptures without the fruit of understanding, for in countless places which mention the Lord Saviour it was prophesied that the Messiah would come, but they have been deceived by the greatest of errors, and they believe that He has not yet arrived but is still to come. So it is rightly said that they pondered vainly, because they were totally unable to understand His fruitful coming.

3. *The kings of the earth stood up and the princes met together against the Lord and against his Christ. Stood up* denotes not physical presence but intention, for at His passion the Lord was clearly in no way in the presence of kings. By *kings of the earth* the psalmist wants us to understand the Herod who in persecuting the Lord murdered the Innocents, and the other Herod, his grandson who with Pontius Pilate agreed on the death of the Saviour.[11] So they are rightly said to have stood up, for they shared the one crime with the harmony of sacrilegious minds. The psalmist uses the word *princes* with reference to the Pharisees, for the word *principes* sometimes means kings and sometimes leaders, *princeps* literally meaning "he who takes first place." They *met together* not in one assembly but in one desire, for we read that they engineered the crime at different meetings. But to ensure

that it was understood that harm to the Son could have the Father in mind, he mentions both: *against the Lord,* that is, the Father, *and against his Christ,* that is, the Son. As He Himself says in the gospel: *He who honoureth not the Son, honoureth not the Father who hath sent him.*[12]

4. *Let us break their bonds asunder.* These words are spoken by demented Jews. They spoke of bonds which their sins sought to loose, for they thought that they were bursting these bonds if with wicked purpose they sprang on the Teacher of the law and on His apostles. *Their* indicates Christ and His apostles, whose ties to the rule of the Lord are clearly indicated by use of the plural.

And let us cast their yoke from us. They continued this apt comparison of themselves to stupid mules, for they do not cast off the yoke unless they have first broken its fastenings. They are totally deceived by their most vain desire, for though the Lord Saviour's yoke is sweet, and His burden light,[13] they considered His control most oppressive. So because He could restrain and govern them, they unsuccessfully sought to throw it off.

5. *He that dwelleth in heaven shall laugh at them, and the Lord shall deride them.* Heaven here means the saints, for as the psalmist is to say elsewhere; *The heavens show forth the glory of God.*[14] He decided that mention of the saints would be suitable here to confound the bombast and malice of the wicked more emphatically. The words, *He shall laugh* and *He shall deride* and similar expressions, are to be understood as appropriate to our own practice. But the Lord does not laugh with spleen, nor deride with His countenance;[15] rather, He carries out His purposes by His own power in the spirit. The figure is called *metonymy* in Greek, and in Latin *transnominatio,*[16] whenever we indicate the meaning of something in different ways by words foreign and metaphorical. So the prophet rightly maintains that the Jews' perfidy is worthy of derision because they tried to set up false witnesses against the truth, they preferred to crucify the Lord of glory, and they stupidly sealed up the burial-chamber of the almighty Christ. So massive, then, are the accumulations of sins on which they are shown to have embarked madly and foolishly against the Lord's power.

6. *Then he shall speak to them in his anger, and confound them in his rage.* So that we may not imagine that the wicked are worthy merely of derision, the psalmist now states that they are to be sternly rebuked.

Anger and *rage* are in the same category as the expressions previously mentioned,[17] for God judges calmly, and confounds without abandoning His fatherly love. He does not grow heated through some mounting emotion against the wicked, but withdraws from them the impact of His grace. So retribution to sinners is termed God's anger. The blessed Godhead does not experience emotions,[18] but continues always eternal and immovable. But such a change of mood befits human frailty, so that a person becomes sad after being glad, angry after being peaceable, hostile after being well-disposed. *Then shall he speak* marks the time when He shall come to judge the world. So the words *anger* and *rage* are rightly used, since obstinate sinners are accorded all that is appropriate to their deserts.

7. *But I am appointed king by him over Sion his holy mountain.* Up to this point the prophet has spoken in his own voice. Now, by the figure which Greek calls *exallage* and Latin *permutatio*,[19] he relates the Lord Saviour's words; He attests that He has been appointed king by the Father. The word was used of Him also on the inscription at His passion: *King of the Jews.*[20] Even Pilate did not allow this to be effaced, though he consigned Him to the Jews to be nailed on the cross. Again, the Magi by their enquiry confessed His kingship: *Where is he that is born king of the Jews?*[21] The next words are: *Over Sion his holy mountain.* This name stands for many things and is wholly fruitful. At one time it means the Church; at another, the Lord Saviour Himself; at another, the Jerusalem to come. This name is to be found repeated frequently, and so it is more appropriate that fitting explanations be offered in individual instances. Here we must interpret Sion as the Church; the psalmist calls her a mountain because of the eminence of her distinction and the unshakeability of her faith. *Sion* in Hebrew means "a watch-tower,"[22] a suitable name for the Church since she is well equipped to attain future hopes,[23] and she observes the Lord's promises with mental foresight, boasting not so much in present blessings as in future ones. So the Church is rightly called Sion, because her hope is fixed in the strength of her contemplation. Christ is truly her King since she is governed and apportioned by Him.

Preaching the Lord's commandment. He did this by teaching the gospel, to fulfil by His personal appearance the preaching of the prophets.

8. *The Lord hath said to me, Thou art my Son: this day have I begotten*

thee. By *the Lord* He means the Father, but He too is Lord. As the psalmist is to say in Psalm 109: *The Lord said to my Lord, Sit thou at my right hand.*[24] Let us concentrate on this statement, *He hath said to me, Thou art my Son,* a statement He will make again after the baptism: *This is my beloved Son, in whom I am well pleased.*[25] To make us realise that Christ is one Person, in other words the Word made flesh, He added: *This day have I begotten thee.* This is wholly and solely a reference to the only-begotten Son,[26] and the rest have no share in it. The Father had been able to designate and implant Him as Creator of the world. By saying *this day,* He revealed that their majesty was coeternal; with God, today has no beginning and is brought to no end.[27] He was not then, He will not be, but He always abides, always is, and the expression *this day* means any time you mention. So in Genesis He bade Moses say of Himself: *Go and say to the children of Israel, I am who am. He who is hath sent me to you.*[28] So He wanted His eternity to be denoted by the present tense. This use of present time ("today") is acknowledged to be peculiar to the divine Scriptures in this sense of perpetuity. *Have I begotten thee* signifies the nativity, of which Isaiah wrote: *Who shall declare his generation?*[29] He is Light from Light, Almighty from Almighty, true God from true God, from whom and through whom and in whom are all things.[30] Of Him the Apostle says in his Letter to the Hebrews: *The brightness of his glory and the figure of his substance, and upholding all things by the word of his power, making purgation of sins, sitteth on the right hand of the majesty on high: being made so much better than the angels, as he hath inherited a more excellent name than they. For to which of the angels hath he said at any time, Thou art my son, today I have begotten thee?*[31] and the rest of that passage which proclaims the Lord Christ's magnificence. So let empty-sounding arguments cease, let the infidelity of the Arian dogma give place.[32] The Catholic faith and mental sanity understand that the only-begotten Son must be separated from the Father neither in nature nor in time nor in power. It is worth weighing further how the psalmist in these two verses wished to declare to men through the Father's words what He is. He could not establish what is proper to the Son substantially in kind and in species, for this is obviously more appropriate to creatures than to Creator. Since it is clear that He is the Author of all things, how can any genus be established above His nature? So this definition is different from the definition termed substantial, which comes to the particular through consideration of differences. This definition cannot be called substantial because it is altogether impossible to grasp what the substance of God is.[33]

However, in the view of some people God can be defined like this: "God is an incorporeal substance, simple and unchangeable."[34] Now let us investigate minutely the parts of the definition in the psalm here. First He says: *But I am appointed king by him.* But earthly kings too are appointed by the Lord. Then He added: *Over Sion his holy mountain, preaching the Lord's commandment.* But the prophets too were chosen as preachers of the Church. There follows: *The Lord said to me, thou art my son.* But Israel too was called son, as in the words to Pharaoh in Exodus: *I have said to thee, let my first-born son Israel go, and thou wouldst not let him go.*[35] So up to this point He could not have been referring unambiguously to the Person of His only-begotten Son. But then came the addition: *This day have I begotten thee.* It is demonstrable that this was spoken to no other, for only the Son was begotten outside time, the Son through whom all things were undoubtedly created. So this true and most beautiful definition has been appropriated by secular teaching in the schools, when it says that the substantial is that which is beyond the possible establishment of any genus.[36]

9. *Ask of me, and I will give thee the Gentiles for thy inheritance.* This is said with reference to His appearance and form as servant, for He is the Son of a virgin; for whatever Christ received within time, He obtained what He did not possess as man. He is bidden to make requests as a function of His lower nature, and to keep what He obtains; but of course by virtue of His power as Lord, the Son possesses all that the Father has without distinction between them, and it is unnecessary for the Son to request what He is known to possess in common with the Father. *Gentiles* means the nations scattered through the whole world; though divided and separated, a blood-relation embraces them, for the word nation (*gens*) derives from *genus*. Next comes *for thine inheritance.* By saying *thine*, the psalmist shows that Christ's nature is of perfect divinity; the word *thine* reveals the incarnation of the Word, and thus we realise that there is no division, since all things are possessed by the one Majesty. As Christ Himself says in the gospel: *All things whatsoever the Father hath made are mine,*

and all that is mine belongs to the Father.[37] Inheritance (*hereditas*) derives from *herus,* lord, because in an inheritance a lord has control
with untrammelled power.

And the boundaries of the earth for thy possession. Here is demonstrated the future belief of all nations in the name of Christ, through
whom the world has been reconciled to God after the expulsion of
superstitions. The mention here of *thy possession* means that He received with His human nature what He always possessed with His
divine nature; His majesty could not be endowed with what it possessed already. A boundary (*terminus*) is so called according to some
because the boundary-stone is somewhat less (*minus*) than three (*ter*)
feet.[38] I think that we should not pass over the phrase, *boundaries of the
earth,* without attention. They gird and enclose the globe, thus signifying not merely areas of dry land but also the surrounding substance
of the entire air and the unity of all creatures. As Christ summarily and
finally said in the gospel; *All power is given to me in heaven and in
earth.*[39] And Paul said; *In the name of Jesus every knee should bow, of
those that are in heaven, on earth, and under the earth.*[40]

    10. *Thou shalt rule them with a rod of iron.* Next the manner of His
kingship is described; if you concentrate on the literal meaning, it is
hardly useful to note what is shattered and broken.[41] Notice first the
words: *Thou shalt rule them,* so God was removing the power from the
tyrant's control, seeing that those who attain the gifts of salvation are
ruled. *Rod* signifies royal power by which the punishment of His
correction is brandished to sinners. It is *iron,* not because God uses a
metal rod for vengeance, but iron's hardness is apt to describe the
rigour of justice. The rod is that of which the psalmist is to speak in
Psalm 44: *The rod of thy kingdom is a rod of uprightness.*[42] He subsequently explains what He does with this rod; it is the rod which
shatters to bring life, the stick which restrains the weak, the sceptre
which brings the dead to life. As applied to humans, a rod (*virga*) is so
called because it governs by its force (*vi*) and does not allow those
who strain to break loose.[43]

And shalt break them in pieces like a potter's vessel. In other words,
"In Your eagerness to convert them, You will shatter earthly longings
in them, and the life of the old man which is as mud." Notice in the
points of comparison how aptly causes of events are expressed in
individual phrases. The psalmist called the Lord's power *a rod of iron,*

and haughty people *a potter's vessel,* which as soon as it is struck is shattered into the tiniest fragments. So the sinner is well compared to a vase formed of clay, so that the breaking of him might be seen to be easy, and his life worthless. But then he is shaped for the better when with the support of divine grace he is led to become a man of the spirit.

11. *And now, O ye kings, understand.* The third limb of the psalm is reached here, in which the prophet now urges the human race humbly to obey the Creator at the revelation of these fearful mysteries. Here the deliberative type of utterance[44] begins, expressed most beautifully; for when men's hearts are paralysed by the unfolding of the mystery, this most salutary and vital adviser appears, urging us to serve the true Lord with fear and trembling, and showing us that the words spoken are valuable from the viewpoint of the useful and the honourable, motifs extremely effective in deliberative speeches.[45] The useful appears in: *Lest at any time the Lord be angry, and you perish from the just way;* the honourable in: *Blessed are all they that trust in him.*[46] So the deliberative type of speech is achieved by a perfect disquisition. Now let us return to explanation of the words. By *kings* we must understand masters of vices, for they can both *understand* and with the Lord's help fulfill the command. Kings need not invariably denote men in the purple, for the term is applied also to those who have private status, for example, in Paul's description: *Now you reign without us, and would to God you did reign, that we also may reign with you.*[47]

Receive instruction, you that judge the earth. Erudire (instruct) means to teach, for the word denotes the grasping of knowledge, because *rudis* means new. One instructed is raised from an unformed state, in other words removed from ignorance and set in the boundaries of learning. This is a good description for those who have now subdued their faults of the flesh, for they *judge the earth* well when after subjugation of faults they impose the precepts of the law on their bodies with the support of the Lord. *Terra* (earth) is derived from *terere,* to wear away, because the earth is worn by the steps of journeying men.[48]

12. *Serve ye the Lord with fear.* A short but full warning, through which we serve the Lord God with the fear of love, for just as careless complacency incurs faults, so loving fear always keeps sins at bay. Then, so that slavery to God might not be thought exceedingly hard or grim, the prophet added: *And rejoice unto him with trembling,* for fear of the Lord leads not to wretchedness but to joy, for it creates blessed

men and produces saints. But on the other hand, to ensure that this rejoicing does not become negligent, the prophet added *with trembling.* Thus both emotions combined could suitably express reverence for the divine.

13. *Grasp discipline, lest at any time the Lord be angry, and you perish from the just way. Grasp discipline;* what a fine expression, with discipline the defence of a shield, so to say, against harmful vices! The prophet explained most beautifully the usefulness of this action when he said: *Lest at any time the Lord be angry, and you perish from the just way.* He used the phrase, *lest at any time,* to emphasise the Lord's long-suffering which tolerates those who transgress. *And you perish from the just way,* in other words, from Christ the heavenly King who is the Way of those who walk righteously towards life, the Leader of those on the move, the Path of those hastening to blessedness. As He Himself says in the gospel: *I am the way, the truth and the life,*[49] the Way through the incarnation by which He affords an example of living to good men, the Truth through the Judgment, the Life through His Godhead.

14. *When his wrath shall be kindled in a short time.* The metaphor is drawn from fire, which burns the more when it receives fuel to consume. The psalmist said: *In a short time,* because once He passes sentence, He takes vengeance. His dispensation is clearly indivisible from His action; He carries out His decision at once. Note also the earlier statement made to sustain men in this life: *Lest at any time,* whereas the phrase used for the judgment is: *In a short time.* So now the fatherly love of the Almighty is shown, but at that future time His power. At the judgment there is no question of His carrying out the sentence on individuals in turn; just as He made everything in a moment, so also He judges everything. The words, *shall be kindled,* are well expressed, for now the end of that generous patience is proclaimed, beyond which no man is given any ground for hope.

Blessed are all they that trust in him. It is a fitting conclusion after many words to state the end to which the individual must hasten. Trust in Him is now a reward, because the assurance itself comes through God's grace; as Paul says: *From him comes both to will and to accomplish.*[50]

Conclusion Drawn From the Psalm

Now that our explanation is complete, let us briefly ponder this psalm with its abundance of heavenly mysteries, so that now that its sections can be apprehended, its force can be clearly understood. Let us note the strength of divine grace with which the psalmist is endowed. Earlier he preached the Lord's message, and then after recounting his words he begins afresh. In his first utterance he is a prophet, and in what follows an apostle, for with pure faith he foretold what is to come, and with perfect truth he made what follows harmonise with it. The Lord Himself, as though thundering from the sky, openly revealed to us the secrets of His power, so that in our modest fashion we might learn for our salvation both the glory of His divinity and the mysteries of His incarnation.

It is in the number two, so finely composed of two monads,[51] that the two unmingled and perfect natures are most fittingly set in the single Person of the Lord Christ. By one of these He reigns, and by the other He serves. The first is Creator, the second the created; and thus the nature which did the embracing experiences no feeling, whereas that which was embraced does experience feeling. As the Fathers warn us, we must allot the injuries to His flesh, the miracles to His divinity. Let us distinguish the natures with understanding, and avoid harmful errors. His divinity united His humanity with itself in such a way that it can in no sense be mingled with it, for each nature remains unmingled yet united. Though after the resurrection the flesh He had assumed was so ordered as to be glorified, He remained truly human. After the resurrection He said to the apostle Thomas: *Set your hand here, for a spirit hath not flesh and bones as you see me to have.*[52] Again, after the resurrection He took and ate baked fish and honey; and we read in the Acts of the Apostles: *He shall so come as you have seen him going into heaven.*[53] Moreover, the prophet states that even sinners will look on Him whom they pierced[54] (for they cannot gaze on His majesty, since only the blessed will be granted this. As Christ says in the gospel: *Blessed are the clean of heart, for they shall see God.*)[55] So it is utterly fatal not to believe that the two natures abide perfect and united in Christ, since the Truth wished to proclaim them in His own Person by so many examples. This has been stated by Athanasius of Alexandria, Hilary of Poitiers, Ambrose of Milan, Augustine, Jerome, Cyril,[56] and many other Fathers, in order to banish totally the justification of this most pointless objection. Pope Leo and his holy synod at Chalcedon[57] decreed and decided that whoever wishes to be a Catholic should proclaim the one Christ as being of and in two united and perfect natures. If with the Lord's favour we store these facts in our memory, we always abide by the norms of the Church.

COMMENTARY ON PSALM 3

1. *A psalm of David when he fled from the face of his son Absalom.* When Absalom was cruelly attacking his father David, the speed of his mule caused him to collide with a thick oak-tree, and the branches wound round his neck so that he was suspended high in the air.[1] This was a prefiguration of the Lord's betrayer. Just as Judas ended his life in the knot of a noose, so also David's persecutor breathed his last through the pressure on his throat.[2] The history of the kings is evidence that this psalm is later in its event than is Psalm 50, for the persecution by his son Absalom is known to have occurred after David's sins of adultery and murder. Yet clearly the character of the psalm is associated with its apt number, for it was right that the psalm which embraced the power of the holy Trinity and the mysteries of the resurrection on the third day should hold third place. The deliverance of David fittingly signifies the Lord's resurrection, so that the minds of Christians may be strengthened and encouraged in constancy at times of adversity. A similar example of lack of observance of chronological order is in the eight books read before Job, for it is acknowledged that Moses lived many years after him.[3] So for the most part the order of readings is arranged not according to chronology but according to the nature of the writings. Remember that some psalms touch only briefly on the passion and resurrection of the Lord, whilst others recount them more clearly and openly. This is the first of the psalms with brief mention of them.

Division of the Psalm

The whole of this psalm is aptly attributed to the person of Christ the Lord.[4] His person is the strength of the almighty Godhead and the humility of the humanity which he embraced; but the two do not mix through intermingling, but exist in indivisible unity. To begin with, He addresses the Father with chiding of His persecutors who were uttering impious words against Him. Secondly, the faithful people were instructed not to fear death, when He consoles them with the hope of most certain resurrection following the precedent of their Maker.

Explanation of the Psalm

2. *Why, O Lord, are they multiplied that afflict me?* This exordium seems similar to that of Psalm 2, but in that case the query is one of rebuke, whereas here He is surprised that the people are roused against Him since it is known that He has come to save them. By saying: *They afflict me,* He shows that He is considerably grieved at the blindness of those who have rejected His salvation with unbending minds. As He is to say in Psalm 34: *They repaid me evil for good, to the depriving me of my soul.*[5]

3. *Many are they who rise up against me: many say to my soul. . . .* So numerous were they that they included even one of His disciples, the traitor Judas. The repetition, *many,* reveals the bitterly huge number of the wicked, that dense crowd of conspirators which could not thin out. This figure of speech is called *epembasis,*[6] repetition of words out of eagerness to enumerate them, so as to magnify the matter under discussion.

. . . there is no salvation for him in his God. This is with reference to the well-known words of the Jews when they said: *He saved others, himself he cannot save.*[7] They thought that the Father did not love the Son since He allowed Him to be killed in the flesh. What an utterly foolish statement from that evil mob! Was it not necessary for the redemption of the world to be associated with weakness? Insatiable death could be overcome only by Life's entry into the gates of that

tyranny. Darkness cannot persist when excluded by the presence of light.

4. *But thou, O Lord, art my sustainer, my glory, and the lifter-up of my head. Sustainer,* that is, of the form of slave, since the taking up of human nature is the Word made flesh.[8] So it is the flesh which speaks of its glory and the lifting up of its head, for the all-powerful Word assumed it so that the divine and human substance might be one Person without any admixture. This verse is relevant too to the confounding of the Pelagians, who believe that man can by his own efforts achieve something good; for who, pray, could be self-sufficient for performing good without abundance of divine grace? It is through grace by which it is united to God that human nature has taken its place at the Father's right hand. Blessed Augustine has explained this helpfully and in greater breadth, as is his fashion, in his *Enchiridion.*[9] We have here the splendid figure called by the Greeks *auxesis,*[10] which increases and redoubles by appending words in individual phrases. The psalmist says: *But thou, O Lord, art my sustainer, my glory, and the lifter-up of my head.* Paul exemplifies the figure more broadly in the words: *Who shall separate us from the love of Christ? Shall tribulation? Or distress? Or persecution? Or the sword?*[11] and the rest. Close to this is the figure called *climax*[12] or gradation, when praise or blame rises step by step, so to say. The difference between the two figures is that *auxesis* develops without repetition of words for things, whereas with *climax* the final word of the first phrase must certainly be repeated in the following phrase, as in this passage of Paul: *Knowing that tribulation worketh patience, patience trial, trial hope, but hope confoundeth not.*[13]

5. *I have cried to the Lord with my voice, and he hath heard me from his holy mountain.* In saying *With my voice,* He reveals the most sacred purity of His own speech. No mere surface appearance could impair His integrity, which is often removed from other men through weakness of the flesh. The words, *I have cried to the Lord with my voice,* are affirmed by the gospel passage where the Son says: *Father, glorify thy son,*[14] and the rest. The word *my* shows that He has spoken also through the prophets. The following phrase: *And he hath heard me from his holy mountain,* is likewise explained by the gospel passage in which a voice came to Him: *I have both glorified it, and will glorify it again.*[15] *Mountain* signifies in various contexts most aptly the Lord

Himself, His saints, and the Church; here we must understand the word in the sense of the preeminent peak of the Godhead, as in the words of another psalm: *Thy justice is as the mountains of God.*[16] For it was right that the nature which took on humanity, and demonstrated a unique example of patience on earth, should in heaven gain the highest place of all creatures.

6. *I have slept and taken my rest, and I have risen up because the Lord hath taken me up.* The psalmist comes to the second section, in which the hearts of waverers were strengthened so that they should believe that He whom they were to see crucified at the hands of wicked men would speedily rise again. *I have slept,* He said, because He quickly rose again, for in such sleep is the element of life; there is no end to life in it, but temporary rest. *I have taken my rest* denotes untroubled suspension, unlike that of the wicked who are agitated in death and continually disturbed by awareness of their sins. This rest was the blessed sleep of the holy body. Rising up means eagerly getting up again, for the flesh laid aside its mortality and embraced immortality and eternal glory. He clearly explains why He rose up: *Because the Lord hath taken me up.* The nature of humanity could not have risen again by itself and by its own strength; the divine Omnipotence had to bear it up. As Christ Himself says: *I have power to lay down my life, and I have power to take it up again.*[17]

7. *I will not fear thousands of the people surrounding me.* He could not fear the wicked people, for His divinity afforded Him protection. It was written in the gospel that at His passion a great crowd of people surrounded Him.[18] The words, *I will not fear,* do not connote that He will die. He could not fear death, because He foreknew that it would last for only three days, and that it would be of service to the world.

8. *Arise, O Lord; save me, O my God, for thou hast struck all of them who are my adversaries without cause.* Not that God is roused from sleep or rest, but the divine Scriptures in explanation of some matter often make metaphorical statements about God after our manner of behaviour, a metaphor being an expression translated from its own sphere to one not its own. *Save me, O my God:* this refers to the resurrection. The end of His life, which was to be of service to mankind, brooked no deviation. *Adversaries* refers not only to His death, but also to issues which concern heretics, who have no zeal for the truth and assail the Catholic norms with debased doctrines. Such men

are rightly stricken with mental blindness, for they have involved themselves with debased desires.

Thou hast ground down the teeth of sinners. In other words, the biting statements of slanderers, who with wicked beliefs confront the divine power. *Dentes,* teeth, derives from *demere,*[19] to remove. So detractors' tongues are well called teeth, for just as teeth remove particles of food, so these tongues gnaw at men's beliefs through slanderous comment. But the words could also be applied to the Jews, who said: *If he be the king of Israel, let him come down from the cross, and we will believe him.*[20] *Thou hast ground down,* in other words, reduced them to nothing. They are truly ground down, for they know that He whom they strove to kill out of disdain for His humanity has risen in glory.

9. *Salvation is of the Lord: and thy blessing is upon thy people.* This utterance is directed against those whose teeth He earlier said were ground down; for by declaring that *salvation is of the Lord,* He confounded those who believed with despicable complacency that they were depriving Christ of salvation, as though He were an earthly man. Why, evil ones, do you toil to no purpose? How can eternal life be cut off, or the Saviour's salvation be in any way lopped off? *Thy blessing is upon thy people:* by this one sentence He both enjoined on men what they must believe, and promised what they can receive from Him.

Conclusion Drawn From the Psalm

This is a short psalm, but it annihilates the boundless wickedness of pagans who believe that the glory of the heavenly Majesty could not have descended to the humility of suffering. How foolish they are, for their thinking is confounded by the Source of the world's realisation that it has been freed! As Paul says: *Christ Jesus came into the world to save sinners, of whom I am the chief.*[21] Let us now consider how the true order of heavenly wisdom is deployed. Psalm 1 contains the Lord Christ's moral aspect; Psalm 2, His natural aspect, that is, His human and divine being; and Psalm 3, by speaking of His resurrection, His reflective aspect; the rationale of these runs through the whole of the divine Scriptures. So the patriarch Isaac dug three wells, thereby showing that the Lord's commands are contained in threefold teaching.[22] *Wisdom* too warns us to describe them in our hearts *in three ways,*[23] and so on. As you read subsequent psalms you will be able easily to recognise these three aspects, individual or combined, even if you are not reminded of them. You must not demand such notification repeatedly, for I have numerous points to make which are new to you. The holy Trinity teaches the purport of this psalm, for though it has the nature of indivisible unity, it clearly consists of three Persons.

COMMENTARY ON PSALM 4

1. *Unto the end, a psalm, a canticle of David.* Let us examine carefully what these words individually tell us; as I stated in my Introduction, the heading shows most truthfully the content of the psalm. *End* does not mean here the decline of some object but the perfection of things of the spirit;[1] as Paul says: *The end of the law is Christ, unto justice to everyone that believeth.*[2] Christ is the glorious perfection of all good things. So the words, *Unto the end,* remind us that they are to be related to the Lord Christ, or as some prefer, we are to believe that they refer to us: *Among whom the end of the world is come,*[3] as Paul further says. You must realise that the phrase cannot refer to the end of the book, for clearly it is still at the beginning.[4] A *psalm,* as we said earlier,[5] is a musical instrument whose sound issues from its top and by which the divine praises were sung. A *canticle* sounded forth heaven's praise through human voices. The two are seen to be joined here because at the sacred sacrifices they were sounded with harmonious notes both on musical instruments and with choruses of singers. So all these words remind us that this canticle will tell of the Lord Christ.

Division of the Psalm

Throughout the psalm the words are spoken by holy mother Church. She is not a ghostly fashioning of our hearts' imagination, like 'fatherland' or 'state' or something without living personality; the Church is the aggregate of all the holy faithful, one soul and one heart, the bride of Christ, the Jerusalem of the age to come. The Lord Jesus says of her in the Song of Songs: *Let her kiss me with the kiss of her mouth.*[6] And elsewhere: *Who is this that cometh up with white countenance?*[7] And again: *She alone is my dove, she alone my bride.*[8] So it is sacrilegious to harbour any doubt on this score when so great a truth is seen to afford so many evidences. So let us say that the Church, which we know comprises persons emphatically real, here speaks with the figure of *mythopoeia.*[9] In the first section she asks that her prayer be heard, and rebukes the faithless for worshipping false gods and neglecting worship of the true God. In the second part she warns the world at large that it must abandon deceitful superstition, and offer the sacrifice of justice. Then in her attempt to win over the minds of pagans by the promise she has made, she relates that the Lord has bestowed great gifts on Christians.

Explanation of the Psalm

2. *When I called upon thee, thou didst hear me, God of my justice: when I was in distress thou hast enlarged me. Have mercy on me, Lord, and hear my prayer.* Let us examine the nature of this prayer. Mother Church in the one verse says that she has been heard, yet begs to be heard again. She shows that this is the way of perfect prayer; though the requests we sought are granted, we should continually ask to be heard, for our solicitation is always commendable. As Paul says: *Pray without ceasing; in all things give thanks.*[10] The Church rightly speaks of *God of my justice,* for she proclaims the unity and omnipotence of the Trinity in the orthodox sense. We find in our sacred reading that her members say similar things individually. So we read in Job: *Mark my innocence,*[11] and the apostle Paul says: *He will render to me a crown of justice,*[12] and the prophet is to say in Psalm 7, *If there be iniquity in my hands . . . ;*[13] not that these men were wholly sinless, but there are certain actions in which the faithful appear clearly innocent. The next words are: *When I was in distress thou hast enlarged me.* Distress always enlarges the Church, since simultaneously confessors emerge and martyrs are crowned. The whole crowd of the just is ever increased by tribulations. The psalmist added: *Have mercy on me, O Lord, and hear my prayer.* The loving mother said that she must win

pity if her prayer for her children was heard, for what is granted to the members is undoubtedly given to the whole body.

3. *O ye sons of men, how long will you be dull of heart? Why do you love vanity, and seek after lying?* Whereas in the previous verse she prayed for us, here she vehemently bids the human race not to continue with the most grievous sin of worshipping demons, so that the prayer which she has poured out for us may be heard. Otherwise any person who does not renounce association with sinners makes vain the prayers of those who entreat for him. There follows: *How long will you be dull of heart?* Rightly she claimed that too long were they dull of heart who after the proclamation of the truth preferred to adore false idols. As the gospel passage has it: *The servant who knew the will of his lord and did not worthy things shall be beaten with many stripes.*[14] Initially the world was rightly scourged with a few stripes because it was clear that it did not know its Lord.[15] But after the arrival of its Creator it will most justly be beaten with many stripes, since it still pursued the fairy tales of idols. Next comes: *Why do you love vanity, and seek after lying?* Vanity is the general term for vices, but vain in the particular sense means that which is found alien to God. Just as trusting in the Godhead is fruitful constancy, so deviating from Him is the vanity that perishes. In the words of Isaiah: *Through worshipping vain and false things they have forfeited thy mercy.*[16] So those who burned with the most base love of idols are convicted, and the phrase is to be pronounced as a rebuke, as if the words were: "Why do you love the vanity by which you perish?" We ought to love things that are beneficial, not harmful, for it is better to curse the things which cause the punishment of lasting damnation to afflict us. *Why do you seek after lying?* You ought not to have sought it at all, but avoided it. *Lying* here connotes idols, which have rightly obtained this title because they were set up in the face of the dignity of the truth.

4. *Know ye that the Lord hath magnified his holy one. The Lord will hear me when I shall cry unto him.* She continues with her salutary rebuke to turn the hearts of foolish people to experience the true religion and to reject evil, and she announces to them the mystery of the truth so that they may not refuse to accept reverently the sacred incarnation. *The holy one* is the Lord Christ. As the Truth elsewhere proclaims of Himself: *Preserve my soul, for I am holy.*[17] She added: *The*

Lord will hear me when I shall cry unto him. She rightly showed confidence that she was heard, since she was preaching to the nations that the holy Lord was to be magnified. *When I shall cry* means "When I shall supplicate the Godhead with good works," for the cry is that which reaches God in silence, and ensures that those who constantly devote themselves to good works are heard.

5. *Be ye angry, and sin not: the things you say in your hearts, be sorry for them upon your beds.* This is rightly referred to the Jews. If they had happened to be angry, they would at any rate have abstained from forbidden enterprises. But it is fitting for us to interpret the words more generally. The anger which does not effect its indignation is pardonable; in the words of Scripture: *He that conquers his anger is better than he that taketh a city.*[18] So the injunction to control it is appended, so that if we are already angry we do not sin through impulsive rashness. Because of human frailty we cannot govern our hot emotions, but with the help of God's grace we contain them with the discipline of reason.[19] So the blessed prophet permitted what is normal conduct, but forbade what is blameworthy, for if in our anger we are not restrained by reflecting on the Lord, but happen to be frustrated in our purpose by some unavoidable obstacle, it is quite clear that we bear the guilt of the deed even if we cannot achieve what we desired. Some prefer[20] to interpret the passage as meaning that we should be angry at our past sins so as to be able to avoid wickedness in the present, for we cannot avoid fresh faults unless we condemn old ones by laudably cursing them. What is repentance but being angry with oneself, so that one is aghast at one's deeds, and seeks self-torture so that the angry Judge may not afflict us instead?

The next words are: *The things you say in your hearts, be sorry for them upon your beds.* They show that the Lord acknowledges the secret thoughts of men, for the phrase, *The things you say in your hearts,* connotes the sentiments which you think are unheard, and which you accordingly consider hidden because they have not been issued by word of mouth. There follows: *Be sorry for them on your beds.* Strictly speaking, *cubile* (bed) means a haunt of wild beasts, being derived from *cubare*, to lie down.[21] So she aptly labels *beds*, the thoughts of aggressive men. But sometimes we find the word misapplied and used in the good sense, as in the phrase about the saints: *They shall be joyful in their beds.*[22] *Be sorry for* means show repentance for, because the conversion we desire comes from a kind of sorrow in our souls, as if the words were "Abandon your debased thoughts before you commit wicked deeds." There follows here the silence of a diapsalm, and I have suitably indicated the division, for another topic obviously begins here. Having laid aside the old man, we are bidden to make the salutary offering of ourselves as a new sacrifice.[23]

6. *Offer up the sacrifice of justice, and trust in the Lord.* Our most merciful mother had earlier urged men to abandon the old superstitions. So now the second instruction is that as men reborn they should not be eager to sacrifice cattle as victims, but should try to offer themselves as a sacrifice to God, for the gift of sacrificial beasts to the Lord is not commensurate with the offering of devoted human hearts. If Christ Himself was sacrificed for us, how much more fitting it is to offer ourselves as sacrifice to Him, so that we can rejoice in imitating our King! The term she used was: *Offer up,* and in case this was interpreted as sacrificing beasts, she added: *The sacrifice of justice.* In other words: "Live an upright life, and always offer your hearts pure to God." She further added: *And trust in the Lord,* so that more blessed hope may attend a good life. We cannot in this world obtain a full reward even if we offer our good deeds before God's sight, but we are instructed to trust in the Lord so that we may obtain the promised salvation in the time to come. But this trust does not deceive us; such aspiration does not lead to condemnation. As Paul says: *Hope confoundeth not, because the charity of God is poured forth in our hearts by the holy Ghost who is given to us.*[24]

7. *Many say: Who sheweth us good things? The light of thy countenance, O Lord, is signed on us.* In this conflict so to say between adversaries, the hearts of the faithful band together for salvation. The *many,* those still wise in the flesh, say what not even a few ought to have said: *Who sheweth us good things?* The answer is surely the Church, who always preaches that the resurrection is to come at which all just men will obtain eternal rewards. The phrase must be taken as accusing in tone, as if they were saying: "A promise is being made to us which we utterly fail to see fulfilled; we are aspiring to what we cannot obtain here." The reply to them signals the blessing which we possess even in this world: *The light of thy countenance, O Lord, is signed on us.* Just as coins carry an image of the emperor, so the signs of the heavenly Emperor are imprinted on the faithful. This is the protection by

which the devil of many shapes is driven off, and he does not succeed
in overcoming with his deceitful trickery mankind whom he tempted
and held captive through his enticement of the first man. The cross is
the invincible protection of the humble and the means by which the
proud are brought low, the victory of Christ and the annihilation of
the devil, the destruction of the denizens of hell and the strengthening
of the dwellers of heaven, the death of infidels and the life of the just.
On this subject, John, bishop of Constantinople, in his address on the
Cross lit, so to say, manifold stars in defining it in these terms: "The
cross is the hope of Christians, the cross is the victory of the Romans,
the cross is the resurrection of the dead, the cross is the leader of the
blind, the cross is the path of the converted, the cross is the stick of the
lame, the cross is the consolation of the poor,"[25] and the other descriptions of this kind which poured from this man under the influence of the divine Spirit. Observe the genuine gifts, the presents
afforded here and now, by which the tongues of the foul-mouthed are
blocked and their throats condemned. In Greek this figure is called
peusis and in Latin *percunctatio*, when there is both question and ready
answer following.[26] The psalmist added: *The light of thy countenance,
Lord*. When the cross leaves its mark, the light is of God's countenance, for it is known always to shine in those who choose not to
befoul themselves by any wickedness. As Paul says: *Grieve not the holy
Spirit of God, whereby you are sealed in the day of redemption*.[27] What the
cross achieves is embraced by Paul with splendid brevity in another
context: *For the word of the cross, to them indeed that perish, is foolishness, but to them that are saved it is the power of God*.[28] So let us spurn
these sacrilegious words. The presence of the Lord's light upon us is a
great and fitting gift enabling us to withstand the prince of darkness.

8. *Thou hast given gladness in my heart. By the fruit of their corn,
wine and oil they are multiplied*. She continues to number the blessings
possessed by Christians. The gladness she mentions is not that which
we express aloud by laughter. It is the gladness of upright faith which
the Lord habitually bestows on a good conscience. We are truly glad
when we rightly believe, and with the Lord's help live a life of trust-
worthy companionship with each other. This is a short phrase which
embraces the matter perfectly. What do doubters seek beyond the fact

that we are seen to campaign for our King under the sign of His cross, and that by the Lord's gift we rejoice in perfect faith? The next words are: *By the fruit of their corn, wine and oil they are multiplied.* She turns back to those who she knows are preoccupied with the things of the flesh. The addition of *their* to the three commodities of corn, wine, and oil is not idle, for it is the Lord's *living bread which came down from heaven.*[29] So, too, with the wine: *Thy chalice which inebriateth, how goodly it is!*[30] And also the oil: *Thou hast anointed my head with oil.*[31] Sinners, then, do not have these commodities from God; they have their own earthly ones by which the body lives but which the soul does not enjoy. Corn (*frumentum*) is derived from *frumen,*[32] the larynx in the upper part of the gullet, the top of which the ancients called by this term. *They are multiplied* in their most evil deeds, that is, when filled with worldly desire. This illustrates the point I made in the Preface, that often the deepest matters are revealed in a single word, as is the case with *their* here.

9–10. *In peace in the selfsame I will sleep, and I will rest: for thou, O Lord, singularly has settled me in hope.* She has most nobly confronted human disturbances and fleeting joys, which the world regarded as paramount, with that peace of heart which those involved in secular activity cannot attain; for this peace embraces a life of utter calm which does not dispute with itself mentally, but rather enjoys pleasant peace through abiding in the Lord's blessings. Of this peace the Lord says in the gospel: *My peace I give unto you, my peace I leave with you.*[33] But to prevent your thinking that this peace is bounded by time, she continues: *In the selfsame I will sleep, and I will rest.* The words, *In the selfsame,* are used because no alteration in affairs changes it; it continues abiding in itself unchangeably and eternally.[34] *I will sleep* is to be understood as referring to the end of life. *I will rest* clearly indicates future blessedness, when rest and relaxation in glory will be granted to the saints. Next the reason is given why she rests: *For thou, O Lord, singularly hast settled me in hope.* So the hope of the Church residing in her members is singular, because she alone embraces God's kingdom which the people of Babylon cannot attain. When she says: *Thou hast settled me,* she points to the worthy and carefully pondered ordinance which we possess here only in hope, but which in heaven is obtained in reality. Then we shall indeed deserve the gift of tranquillity, if we trust that it comes through the help of the Lord.

Conclusion Drawn From the Psalm

Now that we have run through the words of our mother's preaching, let us consider the beginning, middle, and end of this canticle, and discover with most reverent investigation the purpose of this great mystery. This is how the force of the psalm is ascertained, by examining in that order the text in the round. In the first verse, holy Church begged to be heard on behalf of her members, and to ensure that her prayer was heard she warned the human race to abandon worship of idols, for she knows that her possession is the Lord Saviour to whom this adoration is truly owed. Next she instructed the people on how they should sacrifice, and also advised them what reply should be made to blasphemers. Then she stated the unique happiness which the Lord has promised to His saints. In this way the holy instruction of the entire Christian teaching was completed, so that men could clearly recognise what they should do and what they should hope for. The number of this psalm, which is 4, reminds us that we should envisage it as proclaimed to the world with the force of the gospel,[35] for it was fitting that the whole circumference of the earth, divided as it is into four cardinal points, should be warned to believe in God as Saviour. Thus the Church, summoned from different nations, could be one throughout the world. Then too the year itself is marked out by four seasons. The void over the whole world experiences the breath of the four cardinal winds; and the mind's dignity is attained by the four virtues of prudence, justice, fortitude, and temperance.[36] The Pythagoreans lavished such praise on this number that they maintained it to be sacred.[37]

COMMENTARY ON PSALM 5

1. *Unto the end, for her that obtaineth the inheritance, a psalm of David.* The meaning of *Unto the end* has just been stated in the

previous psalm. *For her that obtaineth the inheritance* signifies the Church,[1] whose person is introduced into the psalm as spokeswoman. She approaches and possesses the blessings of the Lord Saviour. She is said to obtain the inheritance because spiritual goods have accrued to her through Christ's resurrection: these are the invincible foundation of faith, the most certain reward of hope, the sweet bond of charity, and so on. At present she possesses images of these things, but in the future she will obtain their full force for ever. Of this inheritance the gospel says: *Blessed are the meek, because they will possess the earth by inheritance.*[2] Then again, the Church is called the inheritance, as in the words of Psalm 2: *Ask of me, and I will give thee the Gentiles for thy inheritance, and the utmost parts of the earth for thy possession.*[3] She is rightly called His inheritance, since she has clearly been gained by His precious blood. You are not to think there is a contradiction here. Though the two interpretations seem separate in holy Scripture, they merge into a single harmony and truth of meaning.[4] As explained earlier, we must relate the psalm and the words *of David* to the Lord Christ.[5]

Division of the Psalm

The whole of this psalm is uttered by the person of the Catholic Church, who in the first section asks that her prayer be heard, and proclaims that heretics and schismatics must be excluded from the Lord's gifts. In the second part she begs that through her understanding of the divine Scriptures she may be guided by God's kindness on the direct path to that blessed native land, and she asserts that the unfaithful make themselves total foreigners to it. Finally she mentions the rewards of the blessed, so that by this one proclamation prior warning of their punishment may convert the wicked, and promise of rewards fire the just.

Explanation of the Psalm

2. *Give ear, O Lord, to my words: understand my cry.* These words are here, by the figure of *mythopoeia* which we mentioned already in Psalm 4,[6] most aptly allotted to the Church, so that as His beloved she

may seek the Lord and hasten at His summons, so that while journeying with His help through the wickedness of this world, she may always *without spot or wrinkle*[7] cleave to her Bridegroom. At her first appearance here she expounds, through the sections of her threefold speech, that power of the Trinity which it befits holy Church to possess, for by saying: *Give ear, O Lord, to my words,* she refers to the song of her lips. The next words: *Understand my cry,* she uses to reveal the love of her heart; compare Paul's words: *God hath sent the spirit of his Son into your hearts. In him we cry Abba, Father.*[8] The expression, *ears,* is used of the Godhead by analogy with the human body, for a sound enters men's ears when the air is struck by it, the word *auris* deriving from *auditus.*[9] Note also that she wished her cry to be understood. This utterance was not a noise from the lips, but speech from the heart, not heard by the ears but apprehended by the light of the mind.

3–4. *Heed thou the voice of my prayer, O my king and my God, for to thee will I pray, O Lord.* Earlier she said: *Understand my cry,* and now she says: *Heed the voice of my prayer,* so as to make clear that this is the perfect prayer which fires the feelings of the heart. So we must investigate why with this change of words it engages our senses. *Heed my voice,* she says, whereas a voice is usually heard; this is because God does not allot these senses to particular parts of His body, but performs everything by a single power. The things we see He hears; the things we hear He sees. Our thoughts are subject to His gaze within us, and there is nothing which can conceal itself from His eye. This figure is called *metabole,*[10] in other words, repetition of one idea with variation of words, for with triple repetition it denotes here one and the same thing. She said: *Give ear, O Lord, to my words,* then: *Understand my cry,* and thirdly: *Heed the voice of my prayer.* All these centre on a single petition, as if she were saying: "Hear my prayer." The next words are: *O my king and my God, for to thee will I pray, O Lord.* This expression tends to move some people rightly to ask why in the middle of this short verse the blessed Church has cited the Lord of heaven by name a third time. She says: *O my king and my God,* and then adds: *For to thee will I pray, O Lord.* But in addressing these three Persons she said not "Heed Ye," but: *Heed Thou,*[11] for the Catholic Church proclaims the holy Trinity one God, not like Sabellius in a confused manner,[12] but clearly and perfectly. For the Father is God, the Son is God, the holy Spirit is God, and yet Father, Son and holy Spirit are not three Gods but one. Of them none is greater or less except in the debased view of Arians, who after all these centuries still refuse to admit their error.[13] Note too the marvellous arrangement of the titles themselves. First she speaks of *King,* the name often used of the Lord Christ by the divine Scriptures, for He Himself attests this rank in the gospel when He says: *The way to the Father is through me.*[14] Then she mentions God the Father, and thirdly the holy Lord Spirit. Though the names seem to be distinct because the Persons have to be mentioned, she believes in and speaks of the one God in a perfect way, as do the words: *Hear, O Israel, the Lord thy God is one God.*[15] So let this salutary notion be implanted in our minds: we must believe in distinctions in Persons, and unity in nature.

5. *In the morning too thou shalt hear my voice: in the morning I will stand before thee and will see. I will stand* must clearly be attached to both halves of the sentence so that the statement can be seen to be complete. Hence one who prays in the morning is recognised as engaged in bright conversation, for we speak of morning when darkness is dispelled[16] and the clear daylight gleams. The Church, which acknowledges that she has embraced the darkness of sinners, and that she is composed of the darkness of this world, rightly believes that she is heard when she bursts into the light of conversation with heaven. Moreover she repeated the word, *morning,* because she felt that through God's kindness her mind was inevitably shining whenever in her prayers she stood before God. Notice why the word, *morning,* was used. Once the mind is lent brightness at the very beginning of good works, and begins to recognise the truth, you are not to imagine that after the sinning a delay ensues by reason of which she is enabled to be heard. As the prophet Ezechiel says: *On whatever day the wicked man turns from his wickedness, all his wickedness will be forgotten.*[17] *Standing before* connotes a continuing personal attendance, and the expression indicates the unremitting nature of personal devotion, for to stand before God is properly said of the one who can be worthy to appear in His sight. As Elias said of himself: *The Lord liveth, in whose sight I*

stand.[18] In the first part of this verse the Church said: *Thou shalt hear*, and here she adds: *And I will see*, for at the future resurrection she will see Him whom here she entreated with holy prayers.

6. *For thou art not a God that willeth iniquity. The wicked shall not dwell near thee, nor shall the unjust abide before thy eyes.* 7. *Thou hatest all who work iniquity: thou wilt destroy them that speak a lie. The bloody and deceitful man the Lord will abhor.* In Psalm 1 we mentioned that the force of the ennoematic definition is that it seeks to declare its meaning by denying what it is not;[19] and then by defining what it is, it can clearly demonstrate the point being made. Both these effects are obviously achieved in these three verses. She says: "You are a God who are known not to will iniquity," for what can God will other than what He is known to enjoin? In the words of Isaiah: *I am the Lord that speaks justice, that declares right things.*[20] The next words are: *The wicked shall not dwell near thee.* Here she indicates that sinners changed by no conversion are to be excluded from God's kingdom. Those whom guilt has enmeshed merely look upon Him in the flesh; in the words of Scripture: *They will look on Him whom they have pierced.*[21] They cannot dwell near Him, for they are to be condemned to the tortures of hell. She added: *Nor shall they abide.* She shows that they will together attend the Lord's judgment, but they are said deservedly not to abide before the Lord's eyes, for they are to be consigned to eternal tortures. There is nothing that God fails to see, since we acknowledge that He is fully present everywhere. But those who are to be deprived of His grace and gift are rightly said to be least in His presence. So far the Lord has been portrayed in words which indicate what He is not. Now there is a positive statement showing in three other ways what He is. She says: *Thou hatest all who work iniquity;* she did not say: "All who have worked iniquity," because only those who stain themselves by evil sinning to the end of their lives will be condemned at the judgment. Among the specific citations of sins the general term workers of iniquity is used so that by it you may understand all that is clearly alien to heaven's commands. She added: *Thou wilt destroy them that speak a lie.* These statements seem to contain a problem. She says that God merely hates those who work iniquity, but she maintains that those who seek a lie perish, whereas a literal judgment would account it more serious to perform iniquity

than to tell a lie. But here she refers to heretics[22] who by speaking a lie have destroyed their followers' souls, and what can be graver than to err in a way which can destroy another? Finally she says: *The bloody and deceitful man the Lord will abhor.* The bloody man is he who is stained with human blood, but also he who deceives persons still alive. She added: *And the deceitful man,* for many actions are wrong which we do not perform of our own volition. *Deceitful* signifies those who in wickedness of mind seek to achieve the destruction of another. When she says: *He will abhor,* she means all those who she said earlier are to be exiled from the Lord's kingdom, for they are to be abhorred since they do not deserve to obtain His rewards. The ennoematic definitions are rounded off in these two statements which seem to have been propounded for the great benefit of men so that they might come to know in short compass the sinners whom God curses and rejects.

8. *But as for me, in the multitude of thy mercy I will come into thy house.* Since she had said that the wicked were to be abhorred, it followed that she was attesting her own admission into God's house by divine grace. Though in this world the Church herself is the Lord's house, she can still say through the voices of any of the blessed ones who form his limbs that she will enter the future Jerusalem. In the same way we speak of the fatherland or the state, yet the words used to describe them connote their citizens. But because the future Jerusalem must, we believe, be built by the multitude, the living stones which are the saints, she aptly said: *I will come into thy house,* as though she were concluding with the completed building of the fabric.

I will worship toward thy holy temple, in thy fear. One must note that she did not say 'in the temple' but towards it;[23] as has been previously said, even the syllables partake of the mysteries.[24] The *holy temple* is the Lord Saviour's body which the Church rightly worships because through it she has merited veneration; for He said of His body *Destroy this temple, and in three days I will raise it up.*[25] The next words are: *In thy fear.* She brought in mention of fear to announce that her heart was pricked; faith is solid when fear of the Godhead is joined to chaste love.

9. *Conduct me, O Lord, in thy justice: because of my enemies direct my way in thy sight.* After saying that her prayer was to be heard in the

morning, and after mentioning the rejection of sinners that spells death, she next commences the second section, in which she asks the Lord that she may now be guided to eternal joys because of her exhaustion in this world through diverse hardships. She says: *In thy justice*, meaning, "As thou sparest those who confess, and with the justest power of Thy fatherly love absolve those who condemn themselves by repentance." It is just that He who rejects those who war on Him should be willing to accept those who supplicate Him. *Because of my enemies* refers to heretics and pagans, for the former show opposition in debased belief and the latter are always hostile through unbelief. She seeks to be conducted in the Lord's justice *because of* them, for the reason that their opposition pays no heed to her preaching. *Direct my way in thy sight* means "Guide my light to the sight of Thy brightness," for we cannot reach Him by our own resources as we constantly walk on winding paths.

10. *For there is no truth in their mouth: their heart is vain.* Whereas earlier she sought to be guided to the vision of the Lord through His justice, so as to be able to attain the domain of the blessed by His gift, so now she is observed rebuking the deceits of men so as to demonstrate that the obduracy of obstinate heretics cannot win such rewards as the Lord has prepared for His faithful. The phrase, *There is no truth in their mouth*, is rightly used of those whose heart was possessed by vanity. The tongue follows the mind's intent, and by nature's ordinance the movement of the tongue follows the command of the heart.

11. *Their throat is an open sepulchre: they dealt deceitfully with their tongues.* The figure of *parabole*[26] makes the allusion quite apt, for the liar's throat is the dead man's sepulchre because in his jaws he champs that deadly vanity of his which brings the evil of death. She did well to add *open*, for if it were closed the odour would be less evident. Notice that she said, *They dealt deceitfully with their tongues.* Often we merely talk of deceits and they are not shown as having an effect, but to denote more serious sins she added here, *They dealt.* So their wickedness was shown to be not merely on their tongues but also in their accursed action.

Judge them, O God. Let them fall from their devices. It is the mode of prophecy to foretell the future. Since the Church herself is known to be invested with all that is gained from the company of the good, she did not pray for such a result with a solemn curse.[27] But it was necessary to speak of the obdurate persons of whom she had foreknowledge, for she knew that God would condemn them. *Let them fall from their devices*, that is, when they fail to see themselves gaining what they believed they could obtain, for one is said to fall from something when robbed of it through the loss of one's expectation.

According to the multitude of their wickedness cast them out, for they have provoked thee, O Lord. From this statement we learn that the extent of a person's rejection from the Godhead is according to the aggregate of his sins. The extent of his wickedness is the measure of his rejection, for the guilty man is removed further from Him according as he is swollen by the number of sins. The expression *cast out* is used because of their presumptuous thoughts, for their rash desires deceived them, and they thought that they were afforded access to all good things; for we speak of men being cast out when they are expelled from some inner place. The wicked patients have provoked the good Physician when by their unfeeling obstinacy they rejected the remedies for their salvation.

12. *But let all them be glad that hope in thee: they shall rejoice for ever.* Having emphasised the retribution owed to the wicked, the Church next reverted to the blessed. Their happy gathering enabled her to discern that she must not be silent about the rewards for the good which she knew were to come. Reflect on the fact that what she begs for at the beginning of the verse she promises in the later part, so that we might be in no doubt about what she hoped would most certainly come. So that we might not consider the joy to be transitory, she used the words *for ever*. There is no end to the joy, for the rewards obtained are possessed perennially. Notice that she says that those who hope in the Lord *rejoice for ever*, for in this transient life the wicked too seem to be glad, but in the future only the Church will rejoice for ever.

And thou shalt dwell in them. And all they that love thy name shall glory in thee. The previous verse gives rise to the notion which one can touch upon but not clearly explain. If you ask what that earlier promise, *They shall rejoice for ever,* means, listen to the short answer: *And thou shalt dwell in them.* What great and inexpressible generosity by the Giver! Can any gift be commensurate, when we know that the Lord of all the world Himself is bestowed? Any generous man gives his possessions, but God the inexpressible Good bestows Himself as reward. What can rival the moment when the Author of all blessings begins to fill us? *They shall glory,* she says, because they enjoy the end which they desired. *In thee,* because You are the inheritance promised them. So *They shall rejoice for ever* because *They shall glory* in the eternal Lord. By *All they that love thy name* she means that in the happy fatherland all men glory in sharing in the Lord, though the divine dispensation which is beyond explanation apparently allots to each a sacred dignity according to the nature of his merits.

13. *For thou, O Lord, wilt bless the just.* Once the greatness of the reward and the boundless joys are set before us, we are briefly instructed why our human nature is filled with such great good without its being owed. Thus none may attribute to his own merits what has clearly been bestowed by the Creator's blessing.

O Lord, thou hast crowned us with a shield of thy good will. Let us note how sweetly and aptly this psalm ends, indicating with a single word the Lord's kindnesses which no volumes can explain. The Creator's *good will* which fills us with indescribable gifts is called *a shield,* which in very truth protects us, and bestows fine rewards. The shield is the crown set on our heads and fitted there as a defence for our hearts. It is this which protects all the faithful, and covers the Church spread over the whole world; it embraces also the heaven in which all things are concealed. It is a protection which no blow can pierce, an armour which no death can infiltrate; rather, through it death has been conquered and has surrendered, and men's salvation for which hope had been lost has emerged. *Thy good will:* since the Lord's call comes before all merit, and He does not find a thing deserving but makes it so, for that reason it is called gratuitous; otherwise it would be called just. So this is the good will which summons and draws us. We can think or perform nothing which benefits us without our obtaining it from the Author of goodness. As Paul says, *For we cannot think anything of ourselves, as of ourselves, but our sufficiency is from God.*[28] So let the Pelagians' madness fall silent, lest in seeking falsely to ascribe some goodness to itself it is instead deprived of Him who bestows it.

Conclusion Drawn From the Psalm

How sweet is the prayer of holy Church which has been heard! She both begets us in faith and fashions us by religious formation. She teaches the ignorant, cherishes little ones, relieves the afflicted, and gathers to her own breasts for nourishment those who she knows adhere to her doctrine. She makes supplication so that we may learn to make entreaty; she shuns the wicked that we may curse those who are most evil. She trusts in the Lord that we too may feel an obligation to have confidence in Him. So like a revered mother she transmits to her little ones words for them to speak, so that when prayerful feeling grows strong in us, it may make both psalmody a consolation in our human actions and our actions accord with the divine commands. So let us say what she urges, know what she believes, and at any rate love that for which she has affection, so that when we follow her intention we may undoubtedly become her sons. This psalm, as we know, is the fifth, and the number five is to be associated with the Pentateuch which the Catholic Church alone truly knows, for she has received the fullness of the law which was promised and awaited.

COMMENTARY ON PSALM 6

1. *Unto the end, in hymns, for the octave, a psalm of David.* The meaning of *Unto the end* is now known.[1] A *hymn* is praise of the Godhead composed according to the law of some metre. In the opinion of some commentators,[2] *For the octave* denotes the Lord's coming when the seven days of this age are at an end, and He comes to judge the world. So the psalm itself begins with the utmost trembling with the words: *O Lord, rebuke me not in thy wrath, nor chastise me in thy indignation.* St. Hilary in his prologue on the psalms, St. Jerome in his *Commentary on Ecclesiastes,* St. Ambrose in his *Commentary on the Evangelist Luke,* and St. Augustine in *The Lord's Sermon on the Mount,* in which he discussed the eight Beatitudes, have spoken about the eighth day at some length and with precision.[3] So the reader must opt

for the choice which he prefers; let it be enough to have mentioned such men, for if their statements were gathered into a single sequence they could barely be enclosed in a very lengthy volume. With reference to that day the prophet Amos says: *Woe to them that desire the day of the Lord. To what end is this day of the Lord for you? The day itself is darkness, and not light.*[4] The prophet Sophonias says the same thing: *The voice of the day of the Lord is grim and bitter.*[5] That is why the penitent now introduced before us earnestly supplicates in the ordered divisions of his prayer that he may not be convicted for his deeds on that day of judgment. What is more beneficial and farsighted for the man who could have no hope in his own deserts because of the sins which he has committed than to decide to pray to God's fatherly love while in this world, where there is opportunity for repentance? But others say that because of the state of the world this day will come after six thousand years, because we read that the Lord rested from His work when the world was in that state. They compute a thousand years for each day, for we read: *Before his sight a thousand years are as one day.*[6] Others believe that after seven thousand years— that is, when the seven days of the world have passed—that dawn of eternity can be declared on the eighth day, just as our Lord's resurrection is known to have been so regarded.[7] But since in the gospel the Lord himself says that not even the Son knows this day, it is churlish to be too eager to seek what divine Providence has declined to reveal to us in our own interests. So let it be enough to know as explanation of the words of the heading, that that day will come after the end of the world.

Let us now hasten rapidly to understand the words bestowed on us, for if we ask with a pure heart, why should we doubt that we are heard when we approach Him who has instructed us? O Lord, grant that when we make satisfaction we may be pricked wholly by love, since You have shown us the rule for prayer which brings salvation. Remember that this is the first of the penitents' psalms. It is followed by Psalms 31, 37, 50, 101, 129, and 142. We shall discuss each of these in its due place as opportunity allows. Do not believe that there is no significance in this aggregate of seven, because our forbears said that our sins could be forgiven in seven ways: first by baptism, second by suffering martyrdom, third by almsgiving, fourth by forgiving the sins of our brethren, fifth by diverting a sinner from the error of his ways, sixth by abundance of charity, and seventh by repentance.[8] We must further add the sharing of the blood of our Lord Jesus Christ, provided that it is received worthily. Perhaps other ways of forgiveness can be found, for it is fitting that God's kindness should rise higher than the number of our prayers.

Division of the Psalm

In this psalm the man of piety who confesses his sins prays in four ways.[9] In the exordium, he makes the Judge well-disposed to him; the exordium is a prayer which aptly prepares the listener's mind to hear the rest of what he has to say. In other words, he argues from the power of the Judge, because it is He alone whose eternity keeps in being created things; he argues too from his own weakness, since he cannot endure the punishment he deserves to pay; and he argues from God's habitual clemency, for He does not wish to be entreated by the dead, but confessed by the living.[10] In the second section he recounts his own hardships by which he is seen to be afflicted and worn.[11] The narration is the clear and careful explanation of events to have his case approved.[12] Next follows the correction,[13] for he separates himself from the wicked, a gesture which he knew was most welcome to the good Judge, so that his mind might be alienated from those who clearly regarded justice as foreign to them. There remains the conclusion, in which a definite statement is now made that nothing further is being solicited, for he confounds and rejects all the wicked, as he refused in any sense to share with them.

In this sense the case for profitable repentance is completed. It is made appropriate to God by that use of metaphor which is man's habit. So He listens as Judge, is informed as Examiner, learns the facts as if they were unknown to Him. You will find this type of scheme in many places in holy Scripture. The whole of this psalm is clearly composed out of fear of the future judgment, for it is the peculiar mark of the upright mind to fear looming disasters and to dread what it deserves to obtain. If we have before our minds the words spoken in the Book of Malachy the prophet, we always hasten back to the right ways, and we are set right by beneficial fear. He says: *Who shall endure the day of his entry, and who shall endure to see him? For he comes in like a refining fire and like the cleaning husk of those who wash silver, and he shall sit to wash and cleanse the silver.*[14] The advice of Solomon in Ecclesiasticus is similar: *Before prayer prepare thy soul,* and a little later: *Remember the wrath that shall be at the last day, and the time of repaying when he shall turn away his face.*[15]

Explanation of the Psalm

2. *O Lord, rebuke me not in thy wrath.* First we must come to know that the Lord's omnipotence has so enriched his eloquence most fully by various teachings and skills that it shines out with wondrous adornment on those who seek it, and grants them the seeds of diverse teachings when they are diligently contemplated. It is because of this that we find in holy Scripture all that the masters of secular literature have adopted for their own writings; for among other types of argument which orators attached to developing lawsuits they included admission and prayer for pardon,[16] in which the defendant refrains from defending what has been done, but begs for pardon. Though this type of argument seems without resort and bereft of human force in court-trials here on earth, before God it is invested with invincible protection. Only confession of faith can acquit the man whom no arguments defend. Such a course is permitted to those who truly repent, who in seeking pardon for themselves strive instead to condemn their own actions. This is what Isaiah too advises: *Speak first of your iniquities that you may be justified.*[17]

Now we must ponder how apt and salutary is the positioning of these words. He does not pray to the Lord Father to avoid condemnation, as some have thought, but to avoid blame through severity of judgment, for it is wholesome for many to be convicted in this world. So we read in the Apocalypse of John: *Such as I love I rebuke and chastise.*[18] This is what happened to David too, when the prophet's rebuke corrected him.[19] The Son also rebukes, as we read in another psalm: *I will reprove thee, and set those rebukes before thy face.*[20] The holy Spirit also offers rebukes; in the words of Scripture: *When the Paraclete Spirit is come, he will convince the world of sin.*[21] Explain now, you that have turned away, what is the difference here between Nature and Power,[22] when even their words are not at odds? The wick-

edness of Arians must fall silent, lest in seeking to establish sacrilegious divisions in the holy Trinity they are found to tear themselves
from the kingdom of the Lord.

Nor chastise me in thy fury. The wrath and indignation of the Judge
against the defendant are the outcome of the condemnation, in other
words the engaged emotion provoking Him to inflict punishment. But
wrath is prolonged indignation, while fury is a sudden blaze of the
mind. But these sentiments are spoken figuratively in metaphorical
words; in fact the Lord is not maddened with anger or confounded
with fury, but ever continues in one and the same tranquillity of His
glory. In this same sense Moses remarks: *As the Lord rejoiced in building you up and making you grow, so shall he rejoice in afflicting you and
bringing you to nought.*[23] So the psalmist asks that he be rebuked before
the judgment and not at it, for he who is convicted then is undoubtedly
condemned. We must store in our minds the fact that the day of
judgment is called wrath and fury because of fear of its importance. In
the words of Psalm 2: *Then shall he speak to them in his anger, and
trouble them in his rage.*[24] On this matter another prophet says: *That
day, a day of wrath, a day of tribulation and distress.*[25]

3. *Have mercy on me, O Lord, for I am weak.* The confession of
weaknesses arouses the pity of the heavenly Physician, from whom
cures are readily obtained when our wounds are openly shown. The
psalmist did not say: "Since I deserve it," but: "Since I cannot endure
Your justice." How great is the Creator's kindness! From the Judge
we learn the words we are to recite when on trial. We are taught to
seek His fatherly love so that His justice cannot destroy us. Who
would now doubt that He can hear our words, so long as our attitude
in prayer is such as He deigned to enjoin on us?

Heal me, O Lord, for all my bones are troubled. He continues with the
same plea. The devoted Physician is told that the wasting sickness has
reached the marrow, so that He may not dally in aiding him whose
death He realises is imminent. *Bones* we must interpret figuratively
here as mental courage; when it fails, our energy slips entirely away,
just as when bones are shattered they totally cease to contain the body.

4. *And my soul is troubled exceedingly: but thou, O Lord, how long?* He
said that his soul was troubled so that mention of bones would not be
interpreted as the body. *Exceedingly* is a useful addition to ensure that
the kindly Listener does not permit too long a delay, as might have

happened had He not realised that the psalmist was greatly troubled. After *How long?* we must supply: "Are You delaying, for in no way do You disregard the prayers of penitents until the end." An entreaty like this is recommended for times of great hardship, so that recovery of health can be acknowledged as more precious. Note that this penitent always flees from the Lord's justice, and begs for His unremitting kindness.

5. *Turn and deliver my soul: O save me, for thy mercy's sake.* When God is told: *Turn,* a relaxation of His vengeance is being requested, so that His judgment may not demand the punishments which we owe. Alternatively we say to God after our fashion: "Turn," in the way we often entreat men who turn away, when they are either unwilling to look our way or they scorn to help us. *Deliver my soul,* that is, from the imminent punishment owed to sinners; for He diverts from us the punishment which we have incurred, when His kindly indulgence remits it. The word *Turn* is aptly included in the penitent's prayer, for the Lord promises this to those who do satisfaction, saying: *Turn ye to me, and I will turn to you.*[26]

Save me for thy mercy's sake. How splendidly this plea unfolds in words both apt and profitable! He seeks to be saved not according to his merits but through divine mercy. Pardon is more easily obtained when hope is implanted in that mercy.

6. *For there is no-one in death that is mindful of thee: and who shall confess to thee in hell?* This may elicit the question, why does he say that in death no-one is mindful of God, whereas then we can be made to tremble more by the imminent anger of God? But when we speak of those unmindful of God, this properly refers to the unfaithful. Isaiah said of them: *For those in hell will not praise thee, nor will those who are dead bless thee.*[27] When Paul says: *In the name of Jesus let every knee bow, of those that are in heaven, on earth, and under the earth,*[28] the statement should be taken as referring only to the faithless and obstinate, who deserve to have no trust placed in their confession. So the psalmist rightly hastens to gain acquittal here, since once the sun has set nothing remains except deserved retribution. *Who shall confess to thee in hell?* We must mentally add "to win pardon." Compare Solomon's words on impious men: *For they will say among themselves, repenting and groaning for anguish of spirit,*[29] and the rest. Then too we know that the rich man who saw Lazarus settled in peace confessed

his evil plight, but he was not heard praying for help because it is in this world that confession connotes also obtaining pardon. To help us realise that some distinction is being made in the words of the verse, *in death* means passing from life, whereas *in hell* means hugging the place where souls are known to endure what they have deserved. There is total denial that a confession can be made in each of these situations. So far we have spoken of the exordium: now let us examine the narration.

7. *I have laboured in my groaning.* Once the psalmist had most sedulously obtained good will in the exordium, he moved on to an account of his deeds, maintaining that his repentance had been won by great afflictions, for repentance which best wins pardon is achieved not so much by idle words as by suffering which gains approval. The word *groaning* is used also for what befalls men who are bent or wounded, but Christians must pursue the groaning won by being pricked at heart, when we both remember our evils and are terrified at the thought of future punishment; for groaning (*gemitus*) means grief redoubled (*geminatus luctus*).[30] The faithful rightly seek it, for it consoles the mourner, cleanses the repentant, routs the devil, and reconciles us to Christ. What sweet bitterness, what blessed tears, what salutary affliction! The blessed John discoursed on this subject so brilliantly that he deservedly won among Greeks the title of Golden Mouth.[31]

Every night I wash my bed. Should you seek to take this literally, he was right to wash with tears the bed which he polluted at night. But one realises the impossibility of such abundance of tears as was said to have washed not only his face but also his bed. So we should better interpret bed as the physical delight in which we relax with indolent pleasure as though in our bed. A man can wash such delight with tears, however few, if by heavenly prompting he chances to weep. *Lectus* (bed) gets its name from choosing (*electus*)[32] soft grass, for in the old days men's bodies going to rest were relaxed in sleep upon it.

I will water my couch with tears. Watering implies a greater flood than washing. Let us observe why, after having earlier mentioned his bed, he wished to repeat the idea with *couch.* It is because couch (*stratum*) connotes a layer of sins, which he waters with tears so that when this most salutary shower has been released, he may mature into a new harvest of virtue, and become just instead of sinning, joyful instead of grieving, most healthy instead of sick. Should you wish to interpret *stratum* as a gathering of garments, you meet the same impossibility as arose from the washing of the bed. Alternatively, the phrase can be taken as hyperbole, by which things are often magnified and exaggerated, as when the psalmist is to say of voyagers in Psalm 106: *They mount up to the heavens, and they go down to the depths.*[33] Another example is in Psalm 50: *Thou shalt wash me, and I shall be made whiter than snow,*[34] whereas nothing could be whiter than snow. Again, in Deuteronomy Moses bade Joshua: *Let not this book of the law depart from thy hand: and thou shalt meditate on it day and night, that thou mayest know the route of thy path.*[35] Similarly another penitent is to say in Psalm 101: *For I did eat ashes like bread, and mingled my drink with weeping,*[36] and so on.

8. *My eye is troubled through anger.* Since earlier he both asserts that he has groaned and maintains that he has wept, it is foolish to imagine that he is suddenly confounded by his own indignation. It is because of God's anger that he proclaims the eye of his heart to be troubled. What is more terrible than that God should be angry? For if He does not pity, He destroys. The eye (*oculus*) is so called because it is a keener light (*ocior lux*), quickly focussing and training its gaze. Alternatively, it is known to be hidden (*occultus*) by the eyelids which cover it.[37]

I have grown old amongst all my enemies. I have grown old means: "I have remained in the ancient state of the old Adam," who is rightly so called to differentiate him from the new Man who is Christ. *Amongst all my enemies* means among diabolical spirits or among our sins, for they are truly called inimical since they lead souls into hell and continue with their deadly enticements even today. The promised narration is now complete; it is short and clear, well suited for assuaging the Judge's anger. Now we must speak of most salutary self-correction.

9. *Depart from me, all ye workers of iniquity: for the Lord hath heard the voice of my weeping.* Now that he has recounted his troubles, he enters upon self-correction. As one who had sinned through association with the wicked, he seeks to appear most devoted to the Lord's commands by expelling those companions from his presence. This type of argument drawn from persons' attributes is called the argument from the manner of life;[38] he shows that he has attained full

self-correction by seeking to sunder himself from alliance with the wicked, for note what follows.

10. *The Lord hath heard my supplication: the Lord hath received my prayer.* Supplication consists of frequent, devoted prayer; it is unique in its outstanding aptness, and it appeases by its insistence. By *received* he wishes us to understand "taken up," as if something had been accepted by His hands. Observe too the great and secret joy which makes him say that his prayer has both been heard by God's ears and received like some offering; for men who rejoice usually seek the same end in different ways, and this makes them exult with great vehemence. It is not without point that the psalmist says for the third time that the Lord has lent him aid with this one service, for doubtless he wished to reveal that the holy Trinity had attended his prayers.

11. *Let all my enemies be ashamed and troubled: let them be turned back and be ashamed very speedily.* He has hastened through three quarters of the psalm, and now comes to the final conclusion, the outcome and end of the whole prayer. In it he now exults joyfully, in a manner befitting one who has been heard. This is, so to say, the fitting form for penitents, to begin with tears and end with joy, so that by this means we can acknowledge the truth of the passage in which we read: *They that sow in tears shall reap in joy.*[39] Notice too that once the penitent is freed of his sins and obedient to the Church's rules, he then in holy awareness prays for the conversion of his enemies, that his enemies in the flesh may return to God's grace as he himself has gained pardon. When he says: *Let them be ashamed,* he wants them to be enlightened by such contrition as to be ashamed of their previous acts, and to realise that the deeds which they long considered beneficial are wicked. The word *trouble* was used as connoting fear of the future judgment and the awful proclamation of the Scriptures, so that those most wretched of men may not fall into the punishment which the divine law states will visit sinners. By using the word *my,* he dissolved that hatred to which their numerous faults had been exposed. The next words are: *Let them be turned back,* so that they are not allowed to go where they seek, but on retracing their steps may be delivered from the pit of hell. When Peter turned his thoughts to mortal things, he was told: *Go behind me, Satan,*[40] in other words: "Cease to savour the things which you now savour,"[41] for when an

evil person turns back, he is reformed, but when it is a just man, he stumbles. Since, however, the discussion here was about sinners, it was right to desire for them a conversion achieved by prayer. Then, to avoid the possibility of God's deciding to leave them longer, he added: *And be ashamed very speedily*. What an outstanding desire of a holy mind! What man could have pleaded his cause more vehemently than the psalmist pleaded for his keenest enemies? So God takes pity on such men who do not neglect the importance of mercy. As the gospel-words say: *Blessed are the merciful, for they shall obtain mercy*.[42]

Conclusion Drawn From the Psalm

Though we should apply our eager intelligence to all the psalms, since the greatest resources for living are sought from them, yet we ought to pay particular attention to the psalms of the penitents, for they are like suitable medicine prescribed for the human race. From them we obtain most health-giving baths for our souls, from them we are restored to life when dead through sins, from them when grief-stricken we attain eternal joys. They form a sort of judicial genre,[43] in which the defendant appears before the sight of the Judge, atoning for his sin with tears, and dissolving it by confessing it. He offers the best type of defence by condemning himself. Here there is no outside person acting as prosecutor; he is his own accuser. He merits pardon because he does not excuse himself from blame. No other approach is possible before such a Judge, for before Him no man can deny his sins. Here inference[44] gives place, definition[45] is not sought, other aspects of the nature of the case are not in evidence,[46] since the whole situation is exposed by the brightness of truth. So the only approach necessary is that called concession,[47] in which the defendant does not defend what has been done, but asks to be pardoned. How immeasurable is the Creator's fatherly love! The defendant caused sentence to be passed in his favour because he accused himself more fiercely. Yet in vain could the cleverest of orators have sought to obtain from the Judge what the psalmist deserved to get from Him out of the fullness of his simplicity.

It is not without significance that he set the character of the penitent within the number six, which is acknowledged as perfect in the discipline of numbers.[48] On the sixth day God created man; in the sixth age[49] the Lord Christ deigned to come into the world to free him. Moreover, He willed to be crucified on the sixth day for the salvation of men, so that this reckoning seems to embrace most fittingly both man's beginning and the absolution of his sins. The blessed Augustine considered that the question of the usefulness, power and grace of repentance should not be disregarded at any point in his numerous books when opportunity offered; but he handled the topic with his usual liveliness, briefly but splendidly, in one volume.[50]

COMMENTARY ON PSALM 7

1. *The psalm of David which he sang to the Lord, for the words of Chusi the son of Jemini.* Though this topic is unfolded in greater detail in the Second Book of Kings,[1] need for a brief explanation of the title is acknowledged. When David was being oppressed by his son Absalom in harsh war, he made his friend Chusi go to Absalom's camp to discover his plan so that Chusi could inform him in greater secrecy what operations were planned against him. Indeed, the name also reflects the situation mentioned, for as Father Augustine teaches[2] Chusi means the silence which one faithful to David truly showed on receiving from him instructions which would prosper with greater secrecy. *Son of Jemini* is interpreted as "son of the right hand," a phrase apt for Chusi, as he sought the interests of David's safety by a necessary betrayal.[3] Then too our Lord held His silence amongst the Jews when He donned the mysteries of the holy incarnation; in a sense it was silence towards the unfaithful,[4] but clearly a proclamation to the faithful. So the prophet hymned this psalm about the future mystery of the Lord, taking Chusi as model, for just as David endured unjust persecution from his son Absalom whom he had begotten and raised, so the Lord bore the madness of the abominable arrogance shown by the people whom He had freed and nurtured. We should appreciate that this is the first of the psalms in which the Lord's future mysteries are revealed through the deeds of David; others of the same kind that follow are Psalms 26, 33 and 143. The figure called allegory or inversion[5] is apposite to these, for it says one thing and means another.

Division of the Psalm

The prophet fits his subject to the future mystery of the Lord Saviour, who in a mystical sense is aptly conferred with the name of David himself. In the first section, the psalmist speaks in his own person, begging the Lord to be freed from his persecutors through His strength. Now a human person is a rational and indivisible substance,[6] separated by its own qualities from other things sharing the same substance. In the second section, the prophet also asks that the glory of His resurrection should be made manifest and come to his aid. The third section ushers in the Lord as Spokesman, asking in the lowly role He has assumed to be judged according to His justice and truth. He threatens the wicked with vengeance, and promises the good gratuitous rewards. In the fourth part the prophet again speaks, warning the Jews to abandon their intended wickedness from fear of the future judgment so that they may not endure the vengeance they deserve. It is fitting now to investigate this theme with minds engaged, so that by God's gift we may deserve to gain insight into the psalm's power.

Explanation of the Psalm

2. *O Lord my God, in thee have I put my trust: save me from all them that persecute me, and deliver me.* Though the prophet seems to be suggesting the example of his son Absalom, he none the less pleads that he be freed from all enemies, particularly from spiritual evils against which we must zealously guard, for enemies of the flesh attack our bodies, but spiritual foes seek to kill our souls. *Save* from sin, *deliver* from the devil, for we are removed from his power when through God's mercy we are absolved from the filth of our sins. In the preceding words he states why he should be delivered from his persecutors: he maintains that he has hoped in the Lord.

3. *Lest at any time he seize upon my soul like a lion, while there is no-one to redeem or save.* The lion is an image of the devil, but Christ too is often compared with it. The devil drags us to death, but Christ delivers us into salvation. The psalmist has splendidly applied the apt verbs to their agents; he asks the Lord to *save* him so that the devil may

not *seize* him. He added *While there is no-one to redeem me, nor to save,* understanding: "since You have withheld Your help," for it is when the Creator postpones His assistance to us through the hindrance of our sins that the devil can seize us. He who gave His own Son, a prize beyond reckoning, for the human race redeems the faithful. Salvation can come from no other but the Author of salvation. In these glowing words David proclaimed the Lord Christ.

4. *O Lord my God, if I have done this thing, if there be iniquity in my hands . . .* Here he says: *If I have done this thing,* but later he explains what this thing is when he says: *If there be iniquity in my hands.* This figure is known as *epexegesis*[7] or explanation of a preceding expression. This sentence should not however be given general application, for man cannot escape having some iniquity in his hands. *This thing* is the deed in connection with the persecution by his son Absalom, by whom the prophet was seen to be unjustly afflicted. The text of Kings[8] shows how he treated even one who was an enemy: when he was sending an army against Absalom, he ordered his generals to be particularly careful for the safety of his son. When Absalom was dead, he mourned him with the harshest grief. So he was right to speak of iniquity in this case, but it was not *in his hands,* since he had even desired that Absalom should survive him.

5. *If I have rendered to them that repaid me evils, let me deservedly fall empty before my enemies.* The second section describes the patience earlier mentioned, for he was unwilling to avenge himself on his persecutors. Saul too he treated with the greatest filial love, restoring him to safety on more than one occasion when Saul was committed to him for death.[9] This is what the previous verse attests, for Saul and Absalom repaid with evil though they had previously experienced from him dutiful love. No one repays unless he has previously obtained something. But the prophet, filled with God and most steadfast in the virtue of patience, bound himself in the constraints of perfect good will, praying that if he returned evil for evil he might fall empty before his enemies, in other words stripped of the merit of mighty gentleness, and without obtaining from the struggle any glory for the Lord to attach to his crown. If you ponder these words further, marks of the Lord's sufferings are revealed, when the disloyal Jew repaid evils though he gained continual and indescribable blessings from his Maker.

6. *Let the enemy pursue my soul and take it, and tread down my life on the earth, and bring down my glory to the dust.* By *the enemy* he means the devil, who treads underfoot the souls which he seizes, for if he gains the upper hand his gift is death, not salvation. What he does with the souls he most cruelly enchains is to make their actions foul with earthly infection. So the order of the words is well arranged; first taking, and then treading down. *And bring down my glory to the dust,* glory meaning the distinction of having attained the status of man, who we know has been made in the image and likeness of God. *Bring it down to the dust,* which the wind throws up from the earth's surface.[10] So in defining his own condition he recounted marvellously the fall of sinners.

Now that we have explained the three previous verses, we must next state how in them appears the second type of hypothetical syllogism,[11] which as we know can be developed in this way. A hypothetical or conditional syllogism makes an inference from one or more hypothetical propositions, and deduces a conclusion. The proposition of the syllogism in the present passage is of this kind: *O Lord my God, if I have done this thing, if there be iniquity in my hands, if I have rendered to them that repaid me evils, let me deservedly fall empty before my enemies. Let the enemy pursue my soul and take it, and tread down my life on the earth, and bring down my glory to the dust.* According to the rules of the dialecticians, the reciprocal formulation is like this: "If I should not deservedly fall empty before my enemies, if the enemy did not pursue my soul and take it, if he did not tread down my life on the earth, if he did not bring down my glory to the dust, O Lord my God, then I have not done this thing, there is no iniquity in my hands, I have not rendered to them that repaid me evils." The inference from this reciprocal statement develops like this: "However, I shall not deservedly fall empty before my enemies, nor will the enemy pursue my soul and take it, nor tread down my life on the earth; he will not bring down my glory to the dust." And the conclusion drawn from this inference is: "Therefore, Lord my God, I have not done this thing, there is no iniquity in my hands. I have not rendered to them that repaid me evils." For brevity's sake I have touched on these matters summarily and simply, but if anyone wishes to attain fuller knowledge of figures, he should read Aristotle so far as the Greeks are concerned and Marius Victorinus of the Latin writers.[12] In this way he can easily establish on his own behalf what he now perhaps considers to be difficult.

7. *Rise up, O Lord, in thy anger: and be thou exalted in the borders of thy enemies. And arise, O Lord my God, in the precept which thou hast commanded.* He comes to the second section, in which he passes to the comparison he had made with the Lord Saviour. This plea develops in three stages. The first bids Him rise up in anger, in other words to take vengeance. But he does not actually provoke God to anger, for he knew that God is most gentle, especially as he had earlier said of himself: *If I have rendered to them that repaid me evils.* These things are recounted in human and metaphorical language; in fact this vengeance which is called anger ought rather to be attributed to the devil, who is punished whenever a sinner in thrall is rescued from him. *Be thou exalted in the borders of the enemies* means: "Show your greatness within the devil's domain, which he holds among sinners";[13] for the Lord is exalted among them when a confession of praise is offered by those who turn to Him. The second stage is: *Arise, O Lord my God, in the precept which thou hast commanded.* This is identical with the previous phrase, *of anger,* so that you may know that it is vengeance rather than rage. The Lord commanded in precept when in the gospel He said to His disciples: *On the third day I shall rise again, and I shall go before you into Galilee.*[14] When these events took place, He was exalted in the whole world which the devil's power possessed, and He took vengeance on him when He deprived him of what he possessed. Notice too that in the fashion of prophecy he speaks of the future as the past; he says: *In the precept which thou hast commanded,* precisely because He was still to command it. Compare the words of Psalm 21: *They have dug my hands and feet, they have numbered all my bones,*[15] and the rest.

8. *And a synagogue of people shall surround thee, and for their sakes return thou on high.* The psalmist earlier begged Him to come, but now he reveals what can result at His coming. It is as if he were saying: "You indeed will come to deliver, but the Jewish people will persecute you with lunatic hearts." *Synagogue* here denotes a gathering of wicked men, not a group of religious minds, for if the whole Jewish people had believed in Him, they would have received Him before all with devoted hearts. *And for their sakes return thou on high: their* here

refers to the people of the synagogue, who with rigid habits remained unpledged, and He could not dwell in it since He withdrew himself from its infidelity. *Return thou on high* is here because the gospel says: *No man hath ascended into heaven but he that descended from heaven.*[16] Returning means retracing the same path to the place from where you came. In another psalm he is to say of this glorious ascension: *And he ascended upon the Cherubim, and he flew upon the wings of the winds, and he made darkness his covert.*[17]

9. *O Lord, judge the people; judge me, O Lord, according to my justice and according to the innocence of my hands upon me.* He passes to the third section, in which the Lord Christ now speaks in accord with that dispensation by which He suffered. In the words: *Lord, judge the people,* the majesty of the almighty Father is revealed, but in the expression: *Judge me, O Lord, according to my justice and according to the innocence of my hands upon me* the humility of His humanity is being expounded. So in a single verse are enclosed the hidden truths of such mighty matters. Notice how the economy of the whole truth is preserved; for earlier the prophet had proclaimed the innocence of his hands in the single instance, but now it is announced as a general fact by the person of the Lord Saviour, for it is certain that He had no sin whatever. He rightly pleads that He be judged according to His justice, for as the most perfect Teacher He fulfilled the commands of His divinity. He did not render evil for evil; in His holiness He climbed the cross because of others' sins; He prayed for His persecutors with a loving grace beyond reckoning, and He performed the other actions which the most unerring text of the gospel enunciates. But because His inward innocence is especially relevant, the phrase, *According to the innocence of my hands,* is mentioned here. This manner of speaking, in which meanings of words are exchanged, is recognised as a peculiarity of divine Scripture; so, for example, the psalmist is to say in Psalm 10: *His eyelids interrogate the sons of men,*[18] whereas it is not the eyelids but the tongue which interrogates.

10. *The wickedness of sinners shall be brought to nought: direct the just.* He wants the approach of death hastened so that His resurrection may be swiftly made plain, for the wickedness of sinners is fulfilled when the Lord has been crucified. They could achieve no more, however cruelly they raged. He Himself used this word when set on the cross: *It is consummated.*[19] The one who is directed is the just One, when He

rose from the dead and mounted to the kingdom of heaven. Thus by the zeal of His devotion He is seen to seek that which is known to be the means of life for all.

The searcher of hearts and reins is the just God. God has this peculiar power of both examining our hearts and with the light of His strength piercing the vigour of our minds. Though the heavenly powers are much more exalted than we, no created person has been granted the power of full knowledge of the secrets of our thoughts. Only the Judge has perfect knowledge of what is within us; hence, I think, the comment, *Who art thou, that thou judgest another man's servant?*,[20] implying "You, who do not understand his thoughts." We cannot be known so clearly even to ourselves as we appear to God's eyes, for we read, with reference to man: *Who can understand sins?*[21] We must further think of *hearts* in the sense of thoughts, and *reins* as the most unflinching strength of mind, or as bodily pleasures.[22]

11. *My help is from the Lord, who saveth the upright of heart.* The Incarnation undertaken for us speaks to give us strength, for though He seems to say this of Himself because of His subjection to the Father, nonetheless with devotion immeasurable He bestows hope on those who believe in Him. Since He is one and the same Person, God and Man, His humanity says that His help is the power of the Word, which he assigns to the upright of heart as both pardon and salvation. Note also that the prophet in the earlier section begged for his own freedom, but here Christ promises Himself the help of the Lord, for as He says in the gospel: *All that the Father has is mine, and mine is the Father's.*[23] In the one role He asks as Servant, in the other He promises to Himself as Lord.

12. *God is a just judge, strong and patient: will he be angry every day?* We nonetheless come to the fourth section, in which the prophet speaks for himself, and by hymning the Father's praise strikes fierce terror into the headstrong Jews, and promises hope to them who desire to return to Him. He is called *a just Judge* because He ultimately assigns to the individual according to His deeds; *strong,* because no man can resist His will; *patient,* since even today He awaits the repentance of those whom He could have destroyed because of the character of their crimes. *Will he be angry?* These words are to be intoned with surprise, because the inference is that He will not. He is said to be angry as judges are, when with harsh indignation they rise to pass

sentence when they wish to punish crimes. But this does not befit His divinity, for where there is heated vengeance there is no tempered justice. *Every day* means at every moment, whenever any sin is committed; for where would that splendid patience be if punishment followed immediately upon the offence?

13. *Unless you are converted he will brandish his sword: he hath bent his bow and made it ready.* He terrifies the stiff-necked Jews who hold the Lord's law in contempt and enslave themselves to most wicked cults of idols. It is they who are told: *Unless you are converted he will brandish his sword,* in other words He will send His only Son in shining brightness.[24] By the word *brandish* is meant the clear effect of alternating light and flickering shadow, which certainly occurred at the Lord Christ's incarnation, when He revealed darkness to the unfaithful, and the light of His divinity to the faithful. Paul too calls the Word a sword when he says: *And the sword of the spirit, which is the word of God.*[25] So we fittingly interpret the bow as the writings of the New and Old Testaments, which encompass the necks of the committed, as it were, with its two curved ends. It reveals to the faithful their sweet yoke, but to the headstrong fearful weapons. The expression, *He hath bent,* was added so that His patience might not be thought slack; and *Made it ready,* so that the activity of bowmen might be seen to be fully described, for when they have stretched their bows toward the target, they align their arms in preparing to fire the arrow. But let us observe what arrows this bow when made ready has discharged.

14. *And in it he hath prepared the instruments of death: he hath made ready his arrows for them that burn.* The verse reveals the dispensation of the divine majesty. It is through the bow—that is, the Old and New Testaments—that the effect of death comes, and through its arrows life is bestowed. From this bow there came arrows, so to say, in other words the apostles,[26] who with hearts burning (which denotes longing) transmitted their saving precepts like arrows, through which the wicked might be wounded and the faithful might obtain effective healing. *Made ready* means "achieved," a word which father Jerome has invested with authority.[27]

15. *Behold, he hath been in labour with injustice: he hath conceived sorrow, and brought forth iniquity.* Let us carefully investigate these words. The Jewish people were *in labour with injustice* when they beheld the Lord performing miracles for the salvation of men, yet

preferred to take thought for His death. They *conceived sorrow* when He rebuked them in various parables to win them over from their perversity. They *brought forth iniquity* when they said: *Crucify, crucify*.[28] The psalmist rightly wrote *brought forth*, which implies brought forth wicked sons. Every fruit, as is known, resembles its parent; as has been said in another place: *By their fruits ye shall know them*.[29] But though conception comes first and labour later, he rightly mentioned labour first, so that this wickedness should be shown to have originated not from an external evil but from their nature.

16. *He hath opened a well, and dug it: and he is fallen into the hole he made.* *Well* is used of a pit of unknown depth, enclosed and surrounded by a hole. The eyes of men gazing at it are lulled into a false sense of security by its level surface, but its depth cannot be measured. Such was the well of iniquity which the wickedness of Judah dug. It was opened in their wicked initial attempt, and dug when they completed it for their damnation; *fallen into the hole he made* means into the place of death. *Hole* can be most fittingly apt for both a well and a grave; as Solomon says: *He that prepareth a pit for another shall fall into it*.[30] The evil activity begins with himself, and he achieves his own destruction before he can harm another.

17. *His sorrow shall be turned on his own head, and his iniquity shall come down upon his crown.* Here we must interpret *head* as our soul, undoubtedly our higher part to which are sins are kept subject when they are reined under control. But if the soul should be conquered by our faults, they inevitably overtop it, and overflow with a mass of wickedness. The crown (*vertex*) is so called because it turns (*vertat*) the hair right and left, and means the top part of the head. We may rightly say that our top is our reason, for this is the lofty summit of the contemplative soul, and so bears the stamp of our glorious Creator. Now if this is brought down by the onrush of sins, it inevitably comes down on the crown, that is, over the reason, for it will have become swollen by the addition of iniquity. If we consider this word *iniquity* in itself, what mighty secrets it is seen to demonstrate! To begin with, when wickedness is dispatched in headlong descent from on high, it strikes violently. Secondly, it powerfully suggests how the wicked are tortured, for when their own sins have fallen on them, they are consigned to their allotted punishment through their wicked crimes. The word *sorrow* is used in the sense of a dread that can be subdued.

18. *I will confess to the Lord according to his justice, and will hymn the name of the Lord most high.* Now that he has expounded the Father's powers by which He had terrified the Jewish people by revelation of His miracles, he draws his words together in summary, and with eager mind proclaims his confession to the Lord. We use *confess* in two ways; the first when we condemn ourselves and make humble reparation as in the phrase of the prophet Daniel: *I shall confess my sins and the sins of my people,*[31] and the second as in the present instance, when the Lord's praises are hymned with great elation. So we read in the gospel: *I confess to thee, O Father, Lord of heaven and earth, who hast hid these things from the wise and the prudent, and hast revealed them to little ones.*[32] Nothing is said in the second instance about sin; only the evidences of grace are mentioned. In the present passage also the confession is to be interpreted as the proclamation made with glad heart to the powers of the Lord. *According to his justice,* because He both makes the proud endure their sins and deigns to absolve the humble. *To hymn* consists in both performing the Lord's commands by deeds, and singing hymns with voice and heart. The prophet promises to do this because he knew that it was truly acceptable to the Lord.

Conclusion Drawn From the Psalm

In this psalm splendid mysteries are revealed to us if we eagerly contemplate them. In the first section it teaches us fruitful patience, which clearly produces perfect Christians, for patience in a religious person is the willing endurance of all toils and pains in the hope of future possessions and in the love of the Lord.[33] In the second part the Lord Himself promises salvation to the upright of heart. In the third section, the wicked are deterred from being condemned for their errors at the Judgment. How great is the fatherly love of the Creator, so truly abounding in goodness, for You do not wish to abandon those who You know are assembling for Your Judgment, and in the secret course of Your boundless love You spare those who proclaim You, and You withdraw Your presence from the guilty! For who would escape Your justice if Your fatherly affection were not first to lend help? Then too the number seven reminds us to meditate on the eternal rest, towards the hope of which this psalm directs us. Worthily embodied under this number, it can be sung with gleeful joy, for there is no doubt that after the completion of six days devoted to activity, the seventh is given over to rest, and is acknowledged as the time for theological contemplation.[34]

COMMENTARY ON PSALM 8

1. *Unto the end for the presses. A psalm of David.* It has already been remarked in our commentary on Psalm 4 that *Unto the end* signifies the Lord Saviour.[1] *Press* describes how the resistant inside of the grape when squeezed by heavy weights is reduced to pulp, and the sweetest wine pours out from the emptied skins. This seems a most apt image of the Church, when by the salutary pressure of repentance sweet tears are squeezed from unbending habits and swollen pride. Threshing floors offer a similar parallel to this, for by continual rubbing the wheat is separated from the chaff on them.[2] So it is fitting for us to understand this psalm as delivered by the ancient Church as spokeswoman, for in it there is indeed pressure on bodies but a salutary harvest of souls. If we are right to speak of both Old and New Testaments though we are taught that the law belongs to one, why should we hesitate to maintain that the Church old and new was the one bride of the Lord Christ sought by His precious blood?

Division of the Psalm

The ancient Church, most beautifully made clear to us by the image of the presses, gladly sings the praises of the Lord Christ at her first entrance, proclaiming His majesty and lofty deeds. In the second section she turns more openly to the nature of man, which she says has developed to heights of great achievement from that debased state fouled by Adam's sinning. So the Lord Christ is in a saving way unhesitatingly acknowledged as a single Person, formed of and in two unmingled and distinct natures. We must further keep in mind that this psalm hymns the nature of the humanity assumed by the Lord Christ in tones of such praise as most clearly to attest that it has been raised higher than any creature; in the words of the apostle: *For to which of the angels did he say, Sit on my right hand until I make thy enemies my footstool?*[3] And elsewhere: *Who, being in the form of God, thought it not robbery to be equal with God.*[4] And a little later: *For which cause God also hath exalted him, and hath given him a name which is above all names,*[5] and the rest.

Explanation of the Psalm

2. *O Lord, our Lord, how admirable is thy name in the whole earth!* O *Lord* is vocative, found in opposed juxtaposition to *our Lord,* which is nominative. This figure is called *syllepsis,*[6] when different cases are associated with the one meaning. She truly rejoices in saying *our,* for we must glory in the blessings of Him to whom we acknowledge we belong. When she says *how,* she cannot give vent to her feelings; for who could properly acknowledge the creatures of earth, or the wide reaches of the sea, or the broad extent of empty air, or the adornment of the heavens, all of which the Lord has ordered by that power of His wisdom which is beyond understanding? When the Church contemplates all this, she finds herself glued to and preoccupied with the explanation of these things, and she proclaims: *How admirable is thy name,* and the rest. *In the whole earth,* because her holy religion extends through the whole world, and there will be no native region in which the Catholic Church does not rejoice. So Jews or Donatists[7] must cease to claim for themselves uniquely what they know has passed instead to the whole world.

For thy magnificence is elevated above the heavens. In the previous verse she posed the question which she here fittingly answered; for the *magnificence* is the secret of the Lord's incarnation, and amongst its various wonders we acknowledge above all as a gift bestowed on us the fact that God deigned to become man, and endured the cross for the salvation of all. So this magnificence is elevated above the heavens and above all creatures when the Lord Christ, having risen from the dead, sits at the right hand of the Father. As another psalm likewise has it: *Be thou exalted, O God, above the heavens, and thy glory over all the earth.*[8]

3. *Out of the mouths of babes and of sucklings thou hast perfected*

praise. This prophecy is explained in the gospel by the Lord's words when infants were prevented by the Jews from proclaiming the Lord's praises; the Jews thought it a childish trait since it was performed at that early age. Then the Lord replied: *Have you not read, Out of the mouths of infants and of sucklings thou hast perfected praise?* So that you do not misinterpret sucklings as those still nurtured by their mother's milk—for they could scarcely have sung the Lord's praises—the apostle Peter reminds us that even those of advanced age are meant when he says: *As newborn babies, desire the rational milk without guile, that thereby you may grow unto salvation.* So by *babes and sucklings* are to be understood those who because of their noviceship and inexperience do not take the stronger food of the faith, but are nurtured on more delicate teaching. So the sense here is: You are not only worthy of praise from the perfect who know You fully, but You are proclaimed by the mouths of tiros and little ones.

Because of thy enemies: that thou mayest destroy the enemy and the defender. Because of enemies denotes pagans and blasphemers; I refrain from calling them sacrilegious. Men of learning praise God because they are steeped in meditation on the holy books. She claimed that the Lord is proclaimed also by infants who have begun to draw near to the Lord in newness of faith, so that this wisdom might be seen to be imparted from heaven rather than amassed by human effort. By *the enemy and the defender* she specifies particularly the unfaithful Jew who believes that he is defending the Father but emerges as an enemy to the Son, as a result of which after appearing to be God's most conspicuous defender he is exposed as His opponent, for he who does not honour the Son as well does not revere the Father. As Christ Himself says in the gospel: *He who honoureth not the Son, honoureth not the Father who hath sent Him.* This verse aptly fits all heretics too, for in believing that they are defending the Scriptures by their evil interpretation, they are seen to oppose sacred doctrines with hostile minds.

4. *For I will behold the heavens, the works of thy fingers, the moon and the stars which thou hast founded.* The Church rightly says this in exultation about the future, for she was already established before the Lord's coming in the persons of the patriarchs and holy men. She says: *I will behold the heavens* in reference to the gospel-books, worthily called the heavens since they contain the Lord Saviour who said: *Heaven is my throne, and the earth my footstool.* The phrase, *the works*

of thy fingers, offered a brief definition of the identity of these heavens, for since we read in Exodus that the law was written by the finger of the Lord,[14] which many have sought to interpret as the holy Spirit, my view is that *fingers* appears here to denote clearly that the divine books were completed with the cooperation of the holy Spirit. As we read in another place: *He hath poised with three fingers the bulk of the earth.*[15] This must be understood similarly in a mysterious sense, the finger of God meaning the execution of divine activity most fittingly attributed to Father, Son, and holy Spirit, that is, to the one God. The next words are: *The moon and the stars which thou hast founded.* The Church says that she will witness her waxings and wanings which the moon undergoes, so that at one time she swells with the faith of many, at another she seems to some to diminish with the deaths of martyrs. Such comparisons are often applied to the Church because of men's opinions, but in fact she grows under afflictions and is ever increased by griefs. The moon is compared with many objects which differ from it; sometimes with the whole Church, as in the phrase: *Until the moon be raised up,*[16] sometimes to her brightest Member as in the present passage, and sometimes to the fool, as in Solomon's words: *But a fool is changed as the moon.*[17] She added *the stars* as well, the just and religious men of whom it is written: *As star differeth from star in glory, so also is the resurrection of the dead.*[18] She further said: *Which thou hast founded,* so that we might realise that all has been founded according to the decree of His prior determination. Alternatively, the verse is intended to express the divinity of the Word, that He might be believed to have created everything by this general dispensation, for He seems to have embraced everything under these three headings. Compare the statement: *In the beginning God created heaven and earth.*[19] By mentioning these two things the author embraced the totality. He arranged the subjects of his proclamation in a wonderful order, for since he was later to speak of the holy incarnation, he had first to demonstrate God's divinity and omnipotence.

5. *What is man, that thou art mindful of him? Or the son of man, that thou visitest him?* She passes to a second beginning, in which in one verse by means of two questions and replies man is shown to be both tiny and most powerful. This figure is called *peusis* in Greek and *percunctatio* in Latin, when there is both a question and a ready reply

following, as we have already noted at Psalm 4.[20] *What is man?* The question is to be pronounced with scorn, implying the answer "frail and transient," "follower of Adam associated with the sin of old, and involved in the wickedness which he shares." The Lord is mindful of this when He forgives his sins, and bestows on him the gifts of His mercy. As He is to say in another psalm: *But the children of God shall put their trust under the covert of thy wings. They shall be inebriated with the plenty of thy house, and thou shalt make them drink of the torrent of thy pleasure.*[21] In other words, He is mindful, and bestows on sinners the salvation of this great grace. *Or the son of man, that thou visitest him?* At these words we must rise, because they indicate the Lord Saviour who was not born of two mortals like other men, but came forth from the holy Spirit and from the womb of Mary ever a virgin, like a bridegroom from his splendid chamber.[22] Reflect that earlier she said: *Thou art mindful,* and then added: *Thou visitest.* He was mindful when He took pity from heaven on the patriarchs. He visited when *the Word was made flesh, and dwelt amongst us.*[23] We use the word "visit" for a doctor's attendance on the sick, and this was truly and clearly fulfilled at the Lord's coming.

6. *Thou hast made him a little less than the angels: thou hast crowned him with glory and honour.* From this point on the humility and glory of the Lord Saviour is recounted. He made him less not to oblige Him to serve, but by the spontaneous wish of His devoted love; as Paul says: *He emptied himself, taking the form of a servant.*[24] The next words are: *A little less than the angels,* because He took up the cross of salvation for all; it is in this sense that the Creator of angels was made less than the angels. She did well to say *a little less,* because though He took on a mortal body He had no sin. He was *crowned with glory and honour* when after His most marvellous resurrection, God in so far as He was made man was exalted and received the belief of the entire world. *Crown* is aptly applied to the circle of the world, because the entire circumference of the universe was fashioned in its image.

7. *And thou hast set him over the works of thy hands. Thou hast subjected all things under his feet.* Earlier His glory and honour were recounted, and now this power is defined so that the most perfect fullness of the Lord Christ's majesty may be acknowledged, for the words, *over the works of thy hands,* show that every creature is subject to Him. Just as nothing is outside God's work, so it is demonstrated

that nothing is separated from the power of Christ, for He will judge
the world. The expression, *all things*, suggests that she has exempted
neither the earthly nor the heavenly. So on this passage the heavenly
exegete Paul attests: *For in that he hath subjected all things to him, he
left nothing not subject to him;*[25] and in another place Scripture says:
Adore him, all you his angels.[26] She added, *under his feet,* so that every
creature may rightly appear to worship and adore the Creator himself.
Note that everything has been kept in its due place: she had said that
He was a little lower than the angels through the lowliness of His
flesh, but she states that after the Ascension everything *was subjected
under his feet,* so that this glory may remove doubt from waverers and
reveal the glory of His incarnation.

8. *Sheep and oxen: moreover the beasts also of the fields.* In this and in
the following verse the argument called "by enumeration" is used.[27]
But we must interpret this and the other words that follow allegorically, so that she may not appear to have ineptly subjoined cattle and
beasts to rational creatures. *Sheep* denote the chosen Christian people;
as the Lord says to the apostle Peter in the gospel: *Feed my sheep.*[28]
They are compared with sheep because by the Lord's kindness they
restrain themselves, doing each other no harm in their life together,
and because they surrender without any feeling of grief the spoils of
the world. Just as a sheep does not reproach its shearer, so the just man
does not belabour the greed of the one who strips him. *Oxen* denote
preachers who have ploughed human hearts with divine commands,
and made a harvest of virtues shoot up. *Moreover* is no idle word, for
not only these holy ones but also sinners are His subjects, and the
Lord Christ often triumphs with greater glory in the case of such men
who turn to Him. *The beasts* are men who feast in the fertile plains, in
other words in the pleasure of this world;[29] they become the sheep
when they are now enclosed within the folds of the Lord.

9. *The birds of the air and the fishes of the sea that pass through the
paths of the sea. The birds of the air* are the proud who are puffed up
with the wind of boasting and are, so to say, borne through the empty
air, looking down on lowly things as they are raised higher. Birds
(*volucres*) are so called because of their frequent flying (*volatus*).[30] *The
fishes of the sea* perhaps denote philosophers who with roaming curios-
ity survey the nature of this world, for just as fish direct their heads
and open for themselves paths through the troubled waters of the sea,

so philosophers drop their heads and by human reason and unremitting toil seek out the courses of the world. But since rivers also have
fishes, the use of *sea* here was not idle, but is relevant to those who
think themselves wise.[31] These men and their like are happily *subjected
under his feet* when they come to appreciate the Christian religion, for
though all things bow before Him by the right of His overlordship, we
correctly term as subjects those who have deserved to attain His light
burden and His sweet yoke.[32]

10. *O Lord, our Lord, how admirable is thy name in all the earth!* After
holy Church has gladly sung of the Incarnation of the Lord Christ and
of the glory of His resurrection, she repeats the verse of the Lord's
praise which she spoke at the beginning, for it is fitting that the
beginning and end be allotted to Him who said of himself: *I am alpha
and omega,* that is, *beginning and end.*[33] But since God's words are
fruitful they beget other mysteries for us; they indicate that those
whose lives have begun with divine gifts and with religious auspices
have continued with belief in God. So we must store in our minds the
fact that this is the first of the psalms which by repetition of verses
restates its sacred message; we shall indicate this in other cases also
when appropriate in the due places.

Conclusion Drawn From the Psalm

Psalm 2 and the present one have spoken about the two natures of
the Lord Christ, and there are others to follow, namely, 20, 71, 81, 107,
109, and 138, so that in treading the dark road of the world we may
through these numerous blazing torches be able to avoid falling on the
rough rocks of heresy. So let us be aware of the Donor of this great
blessing; He is the one Lord Christ, begotten of the Father beyond
time, and born of a mother within time. First He created the world
from nothing, and later freed it from widespread death, for He became
a link forged between God and man of such a kind that each continues
whole and distinct without any intermingling; for His divinity, impassible as it is, could not be changed, and humanity received only that
which made it always and abidingly better. In this way He became a
true and almighty Mediator, so that being equal to the Father in His
form as God, He might also become like us in taking on flesh. He

caused to remain joined in Him the elements which He wished to be at peace. This is the unique protection of our hope, the gratuitous gift of the redemption, the destruction of death, the life of saints. What kind of fatherly love is it, I ask, by which the Lord of the angels deigned to take the form of a slave so that death might be conquered together with its creator the devil, who with his bonds held the world in thrall? So blessed Ambrose adorned with the most beautiful bloom of his eloquence his hymn on the Lord's nativity, so that the devoted priest could offer a worthy gift for that great feast; he says, "Let him come forth from his chamber,/ that royal hall of virginity,/ a giant of twin substance,/ that he may eagerly run along the way,/"[34] and the rest which that most holy man perfected in a way beyond human talent.

Then too the number eight is recognised in holy Scripture as embracing mysteries of mighty matters. There were eight souls who entered the ark of Noah and were saved at the destruction of the world.[35] David, acknowledged as the Lord's chosen one, was the eighth son of Jesse.[36] It was on the eighth day that the Jews were purified by circumcision.[37] On the eighth day, the Lord's day, the Lord rose from the dead, and on that day the hope of humankind was raised from the hell of the wicked to the heights of heaven. This is the number which arithmeticians call the first cube in action, which Philolaus the Pythagorean calls the geometrical harmony, because in it all the modes of harmony are seen to converge.[38]

COMMENTARY ON PSALM 9

1. *Unto the end, for the hidden things of the Son, a psalm of David.* The meaning of *end* has already been often stated; it signifies not fading but growth, true renewal for us, the beginning of our blessings and end of our ills. The Jews do not attain it, since they fail through their unbelief. *For the hidden things of the Son* signifies the person of the Lord Saviour; for when some name is cited without reference to its owner, one must regard the word as referring to a high dignitary. Earlier, when the psalmist wished us to understand Absalom, he stated who "his son" was, but here,[1] because he wished the reference to be to the most surpassing dignity of the only-begotten Word, he said no more

than *the Son*, for He is almighty, the Son beyond description, coeternal with the Father, doing what He wills in heaven and on earth. Similarly the gospel says: *If the Son shall make you free, then you shall be free indeed.*[2] In that passage, the words "of God" did not follow, because the word itself, pure and without addition, was sufficient. *For the hidden things* is put in the plural because not one but two mysteries are here acknowledged, for the reference is to both the Lord's incarnation and the future judgment, both of which this psalm is to discuss. But Christ's humanity is already manifest and known, whereas His judgment is still to be endured. But when we hear *for the hidden things*, we must make our minds attentive to the reading, so that with the Lord's help what is proclaimed as hidden may be opened to us.

Division of the Psalm

The whole of this psalm is spoken by the person of the prophet. With his first proclamation he says that he will gladly hymn the Lord because He confounds the devil, whose worship He has exstirpated by the loving dispensation of His coming. The second proclamation warns the faithful to hymn the Lord who dwells in Sion, who avenges the blood of the poor and raises them from death's gates. The third says that the end of evils will come for sinners with Antichrist. In the fourth he is troubled by the excessive number of wicked men, and turns to the Lord, intimating that he has abandoned defence of the poor because the wicked are granted freedom for their audacity. The fifth begs that the time of the fearful judgment may come, in order that all these matters may be accomplished with a swift end, so that no man's wickedness may prevail further, for the wickedness of that time will be such that none of the faithful will pray for an extension of time in this world, in which regular acts of such great wickedness are known.

Explanation of the Psalm

2. *I will give praise to thee, O Lord, with my whole heart: I will relate all thy wonders.* The one who praises the Lord with his whole heart is he who vacillates with no worldly thoughts. This is undoubtedly an

attribute of the perfect, who with God's help have conquered the vices of original sin and the perverse intimations of evil spirits. Next comes: *I will relate all thy wonders.* Who, pray, can relate all the divine miracles which His power achieves every day in heaven and on earth? But the procedure of the Scriptures is to express everything through the figure of synecdoche,[3] which indicates a part of the whole since the totality cannot be comprehended. But so that we too may be seen to state one thing out of many, what is more wonderful than that God became human without ambiguity for the salvation of the human race, and that He who was judged on this earth will Himself come to judge the world?

3. *I will be glad and rejoice in thee: I will sing to thy name, O thou most High.* Not in this world, where rejoicing brings death, nor in the ambitions of the world, where bitter sins are sweet, but *in thee,* where untroubled joy always takes increase. Rejoicing goes beyond being glad, for rejoicing means taking joy in the most delightful freedom with greater mental and physical reactions. He promises also to give thanks to the most High, who is acknowledged to be exalted over all things, because He has deigned to free him from his enemies, whether of the flesh or of the spirit, and as has already been said, he promises to sing to the Lord in deeds and in words.

4. *When my enemy shall be turned back: they shall be weakened, and perish before thy face.* Though David had many enemies, here we appropriately think only of Saul. He said *back* because Saul could not get what he wanted, but the more wicked his persecution, the juster David appeared in bearing with that wicked man.[4] Though he referred to the enemy in the singular, he then added: *They shall be weakened,* because the king was a persecutor who sought his desires with many attendants. So the phrase, *They shall be weakened,* is apt, because when God willed it they all became ineffective. *And perish before thy face;* understand "whereas I with devoted mind take refuge in Thee." The wicked man does not appear before Thy face, that is, before Your grace, because he persecutes an innocent one.

5. *For thou has maintained my judgment and my cause: thou sittest on the throne who judgest justice.* When two persons grapple with each other, one must come to grief because the other happens to win. So once the prophet's cause was approved, the odium clearly fell on his opponent. The persecutor could not win support, for the Lord de-

cided to rescue the one who was evilly oppressed. When the psalmist says: *My judgment and my cause,* he attests that the judgment was favourable to himself; in the same way sailors speak of "their" wind when a happy outcome smiles on them.[5] *Thou sittest on the throne* refers to the Lord Christ who now sits at the right hand of the Father, whence He will come to judge the living and the dead. *Thou sittest* is expressed as present instead of future by the power of prophecy. Clearly this sitting has reference to the Lord's incarnation, which had obviously not taken place at that time. *Throne* means the dais of future judgment, on which the Lord Christ will take His seat with the glorious power of His majesty. *Who judgest justice:* here too he has used the present tense for the future, for He will judge justice when after the world's end His light will shine again to pass judgment. This figure is called an *idea*,[6] when we rouse mental emotion by setting before our eyes, as it were, the vision of a future event. This will be explained more broadly in what follows.

6. *Thou hast rebuked the Gentiles, and the wicked one hath perished: thou hast blotted out their name for ever, till the world after this world.* From this point on the most sacred event of the second coming of the Lord is explained, when unbelieving nations will be rebuked and the devil with his tricks will perish for ever; for his stormy subversion will not continue when with the Lord's help everything will be calm. Who would utter the name of the devil or of his followers, once no enmity shakes the Lord's city, and no foe attacks it? The meaning *for ever* has been suitably explained also in *till the world,* the world here signifying the Lord's future kingdom which will be ended by no age or time. So that no confusion may trouble us, the words, *after this world,* are added to connote that which follows the world which we now enjoy. This world is a returning succession, repeating itself in the exhaustion of the seasons and the yearly revolutions, but the future world does not return to its beginning but continues unbroken and without change. So let heretics stop saying that at some time the devil and his followers can be brought back to grace,[7] for they are clearly told that they are to be condemned *for ever till the world after this world,* so that not even a trace of their name can survive.

7. *The swords of the enemy have failed in the end: and their cities thou hast destroyed. Their memory hath perished with a noise.* The enemy is in the genitive case, signifying 'of the devil' whose swords are attested as

having failed. *Framea* is a Hebrew word[8] meaning sword, with which the enemy rages. The phrase *in the end* is inserted to give the sense of the consummation of the world, for the devil's power is shown to be destroyed by that almighty sword of which the psalmist said in Psalm 7: *Except you be converted, he will brandish his sword,*[9] and the rest. The destroyed cities he mentions are the unfaithful peoples condemned at the Lord Christ's final coming; in this world the devil possessed their hearts as the walls of his city. *Their memory hath perished with a noise;* by *with a noise* he means with a very loud cry, as often happens when good fortune comes to the harshest end, so that neither their power nor their name is seen to remain. Note how he continued with that most splendid comparison, attesting that the cities which he had said were destroyed had been overthrown *with a noise.*

8. *But the Lord remaineth for ever. He hath prepared his seat in judgment.* The contrast is extremely fine and apt. Because he had said that the wicked perish, he now says that the Lord remains for ever, because those who opposed their Creator with debased acts of temerity are unwilling to listen. But they must take refuge with the merciful Lord so that they do not suffer Him as a severe Judge. *He hath prepared:* the subject is God-man, so that He who was judged in lowliness here may come to act as Judge in majesty. This is what is mentioned in the psalm-heading as *the hidden things of the Son,* for it is a gift beyond description that the right hand of His power should have raised to the heavenly kingdom man's nature which was grovelling and sunk low.

9. *And he shall judge the world in equity, he shall judge the people with justice.* This is none other than the Lord Christ himself, who by suffering injustice here is truly said to show justice to the wicked there. *The world* we must interpret as holy men, who assemble from the whole Church as from the circlet of a crown. They are to be judged *in equity,* for abundant mercy will be afforded them through the goodness of their faith and humility. They will be told: *Come blessed of my father,*[10] and the rest. So they shall sit on twelve seats judging the twelve tribes of Israel.[11] *The people* must be interpreted as sinners who seem not to have cast off their devilish deeds. They are to be judged with justice and will be condemned according to the wickedness of their deeds. They must be told: *Go into everlasting fire.*[12] Thus by the two terms equity and justice the psalmist described with marvellous brevity the nature of the Judgment.

10. *And the Lord is become a refuge of the poor, a helper in due time in tribulation.* The poor have abundant hope and a large contemplation of joys, since they have as refuge Him who is their Judge. The word *poor* which we heard we must not interpret as all needy men. God's poor is he who is emptied of earthly desire, and longs to grow rich in heavenly bounty. So that the hearts of the faithful might not be fearful through their own weakness, a firm promise of great help follows: *A helper in due time,* for the sweetest help is that afforded in time of need. That due time he clearly restated in the words *in tribulation;* at such a time the minds of the oppressed are more eagerly fired with zeal to show remorse. As the psalmist is to say in another psalm: *Call upon me in the day of thy trouble, and I will deliver thee, and thou shalt glorify me.*[13]

11. *And let all trust in thee who know thy name, for thou wilt not forsake them that seek thee, O Lord.* *Let them trust in thee,* that is, let them not look to the charms of the world, but have confidence in Your promise. *Who know thy name,* in other words, who reverence Your majesty with most holy devotion. Those without faith have also heard the Lord's name, but only those who as suppliants obey His commands actually know it. Next follows the reason why they must hope in the Lord, because He does not countenance abandoning those who He sees have taken refuge with Him. It is certain that the man who is assured that he is endowed with such power always has the Lord at hand.

12. *Sing ye to the Lord who dwelleth in Sion: declare his marvels among the Gentiles.* The blessed prophet comes to the second section, where he ponders the blessings of the present and future, and encourages the devoted people to sing a psalm, so that when such great rewards are bestowed on them, they may not become at all reluctant physically. First he said: *Sing ye to the Lord;* and so that the Gentiles should not think that they were to sing in their superstitious rites, he added: *Who dwelleth in Sion* to designate the Lord Saviour, who appeared in that region in the flesh but who embraces the circumference of the whole world with the religion inspired by His name. The statement is made with reference to His holy incarnation, for where does He not dwell, when He is wholly everywhere? But so that we may obtain also spiritual insight into the mystery of this name, Sion means exploration,[14] because God is truly discovered by the holiest contemplation. We are

rightly told that He dwells in the place where we who are enlightened by heavenly grace behold Him. The psalmist further explains his earlier word *sing*, for true singing to Him involves declaring His marvels to all the Gentiles. So we can realise that in every action all that can be designated as the Lord's praise is aptly called psalmody. We must further note that this is fittingly explained by definition, for he states that the Lord who is to be hymned is He who dwells in Sion.

13. *For requiring their blood he hath remembered them: he hath not forgotten the prayer of the poor.* He had earlier bidden them to preach to the Gentiles, and it is known that many of them were slaughtered. So that none might think that this crime was unavenged, the next section states that the martyrs' blood was sought back from the wicked persecutors, who would thus sustain for eternity what they inflicted for a time. *He hath remembered* has marvellous application to the two aims of terrifying the persecutors with vengeance and of reinvigorating the martyrs with kindly promise. *He hath not forgotten* is said here to strengthen the weakness of those who complain, for because of the remoteness of the future judgment they think that God is in some measure forgetful of His revenge. By *the prayer of the poor* he means the entreaty of the just which he appends below in his own person, so that you may understand that the bounty which the prophet demands for himself applies to all the faithful.

14. *Have mercy on me, O Lord: see my humiliation which I suffer from my enemies. Thou that liftest me up from the gates of death.* This is the prayer of all poor people appropriately denoted as one, because this crowd of holy men is always merged into a unity. He demands that help be lent him in such a way that it seems to come from the most merciful King, for in truth the sight of Him is help, and the shadows vanish as soon as the brightness of that great Light is diffused. So he prays that his humiliation be measured by comparison with the pride of his enemies, because Christ's martyrs are physically brought as low as their persecutors seem to be exalted in the short term. *The gate of death* is the devil or all worldly enticements, for this is the unhappy entrance to eternal destruction. By *thou liftest me up* he means: "You remove me far from such men," for since the gate of death is accursed intercourse with the wicked, he rightly says that he is lifted up from it because he clung to the commandments of life.

15. *That I may declare all thy praises in the gates of the daughter of*

Sion. I will rejoice in thy salvation. This repetition of *gates* is most attractive, since the word is identical but the objects wholly different; in the first case they are the entrance to death, and in the second access to life. So now that he has been freed from the gates of death and is at the gates of the Church which assign eternal blessedness, he promises to proclaim the Lord's praises, by which His glorious name is famed through the whole world. *Sion* begot the other Churches of the world, because in Sion was born the source from which the beginning of our faith clearly came, and which spread more widely through the whole world. The salvation of the Father is the Lord Christ, His Strength and Wisdom, who has given us eternal rest and salvation. So the prophet rightly proclaims that he rejoices in Him, for there is no end of joy there.

16. *The Gentiles have stuck fast in the destruction which they prepared. Their foot hath been taken in the very snare which they hid.* In this and the next verse, retribution against sinners is powerfully expressed because each is tortured by his own wickedness. By *the Gentiles stuck fast* he means those not bound by fear of the Lord but demonstrably fastened by the nails, so to say, of sins, so that they cannot free themselves from the harsh bonds which are seen to restrain them. It is fair to say that this refers to the Jews; they are stuck fast with their own wickednesses, just as they decided to impale the Lord with nails on the cross. *The snare which they hid* refers only to their aspiration, for nothing could have been hidden from Christ, who foretold His own passion in countless intimations. *Their foot hath been taken:* he continued with the metaphor of the noose used earlier. When we talk of persons *taken*, we mean those drawn tight by intricate deceit. *Foot* indicates mental steps and the debased longing which makes them advance towards evil. As Solomon says in Proverbs: *Their feet run to evil, and make haste to shed blood.*[15]

17. *The Lord shall be known when he executeth judgments: the sinner hath been caught in the works of his own hands.* This statement is most true and uncompromising, for the Lord shall be clearly observed to execute judgments when sinners are allotted the agony of eternal torture. In this life their crimes are uncontrolled, and accordingly they may be assumed to be left unpunished, but when the day of His appearance comes, and the Lord Saviour sits on the throne of His majesty, there will be universal recognition that His judgments are in session,

when the human race by His decree will be divided on left and on right. To execute judgments means investigating the deserts of individuals without obfuscation. There follows the open declaration of this statement, for he states how it is known that the Lord truly executes judgments; that is, when the sinner is held tight in the noose of his own deeds, and suffers worthy vengeance according to the nature of his acts. We must wholly avoid the interpretation which maintains that the sinner will be tortured only by recollection of his faults. If this alone were sufficient, why should Scripture say: *Go into everlasting fire, which was prepared for the devil and his angels,*[16] and again: *Their worm shall not die, and their fire shall not be quenched?*[17] He does not say here that no region of torments is allotted to sinners, but that they are tortured according to the nature of their deeds. So let us realise that a place has been prepared for the punishment of sinners. Let us be aware that there is an externally applied punishment which we read is in store for the wicked. So that we may truly realise that blessedness is set apart from damnation by a kind of boundary, let us recall that the rich man raised his eyes, and the poor man Lazarus was beheld in the bosom of Abraham while he himself was delivered to avenging flames. So this schematic statement of the truth would not be mentioned if sinners were tortured merely by recollection of their wickedness. These are the hidden things of the Son foretold in the heading.

Song of the Diapsalm[18]

There is a fresh division in the psalm, at which a song is clearly set. This fact has caused some scholars to state that they do not regard the diapsalm as a silent pause, for a silent song cannot possibly exist. But this fact does not at all preclude the meaning defined in the Preface, for this song does not remove the interval between verses, but seems to denote the joy to come.

18. *Let the wicked be turned into hell, all the nations that forget the Lord.* He comes to the third section, in which with mental eagerness he proclaims that the end will come for sinners. *Let them be turned* means: "let them be parted from their pleasure in this world, so that they cannot any longer rejoice in their delight." Next follows: *Into hell,* so that they may not believe that they are to be dispatched else-

where. *Infernum* (hell) gets its name from the fact that souls are continually borne (*inferantur*) there, or as some maintain, the word is derived from the region below.[19] But here *infernum* has to be understood as everlasting death into which those who have spurned the Lord's commands will undoubtedly pass. To *forget the Lord* is to be involved in errors of superstitions and in the mud of pleasure, for by contrast those not seeking such things are mindful of Him.

19. *For the poor man shall not be forgotten at the end: the patience of the poor shall not perish for ever.* When the prophet sees that in the world the poor are despised by the rich and consigned to the most cruel oblivion, he says that the poor are not to be spurned at the end of the world when the Lord comes to judge it. Rather, they come all the more to the Lord's remembrance when the rich of this world are debarred from the gifts of His kingdom. He explains why those poor are recalled by the Lord when he speaks of *the patience of the poor* which crowns the most faithful, for if patience is lacking in the midst of any hardship, a soul cannot be perfect. So patience is the act of thanksgiving continually maintained in the fear of the Lord amidst the troublesome difficulties of the world until death. As the Lord says in the gospel: *In your patience you shall possess your souls.*[20] Such is the virtue of patience that even the Lord Himself is called patient,[21] though He endures (*patitur*) nothing.

20. *Arise, O Lord, let not men prevail: let the Gentiles be judged in thy sight.* When the prophet was discussing the end of the world, he foresaw the coming of Antichrist[22] in the clear light of his heart, and terrified by the magnitude of the danger he cried aloud: *Arise, O Lord, let not men prevail.* He is indeed a most wicked man whom the human condition cannot endure, who embodies such deceit or power that only God's strength can defeat his wickedness. The psalmist also asks that the Gentiles be judged by the swiftest advent, for in company with the most savage Antichrist they are about to commit great crimes. Whereas in this world the Lord controls all things with hidden power, He is begged to judge everything openly at the judgment, where the arrogant will not be permitted to do further harm.

21. *Appoint, O Lord, a lawgiver over them: that the Gentiles may know themselves to be but men.* He speaks now more clearly about Antichrist himself, so that sinners may be awarded a leader not to govern them but to perish with them. Finally he adds: *That the Gentiles may know*

themselves to be but men. These are the words of one who threatens, so
that men overconfident of impunity in their crime may instead be
turned towards conversion. Now the true lawgiver is God alone, and
because Antichrist is to give many orders against the Lord's commands, he is abusively described. So they are allotted a giver of wicked
law, because he achieves not the safety but the destruction of villain-
ous men.

22. *Why, O Lord, hast thou retired afar off? Why dost thou slight us in
our wants, in the time of trouble?* After the insertion of a diapsalm,[23] he
comes to the fourth section, in which he discusses the evils of that
time, and in his concern for the afflicted he says to the Lord in the
fashion of human weakness: *Why hast thou retired afar off?* Not that
God leaves a place and passes to another district, for He is wholly
everywhere; but He is imagined to have retired, so to say, when He is
slow to lend help. But after saying earlier: *For thou wilt not forsake
them that seek thee, O Lord,*[24] he now adds: *Thou slightest us in our
wants.* Clearly, however, the first statement is true and definitive,
while the second has been uttered in the troubled spirit of persons
who grieve. We consider ourselves slighted if we are put off even for
the shortest time, but His help is all the more fruitful when He accords
us the consolations of great patience.

23. *While the wicked man is proud, the poor is set on fire: they are
caught in the counsels which they devise.* This statement is to be analysed
with greater care so that it may not be thought that the just man is
burned because the sinner is apparently exalted in this world. Rather
we must interpret *the wicked man is proud* as meaning "When he has
had his fill of the realisation of his wicked will." Then the poor man is
further fired to espouse virtue, for when he sees the sinner raised too
high, he knows that he will easily fall, and he himself strives more
eagerly for the lowly place from which he trusts that he may instead be
exalted. But the harvest of the wicked and the proud is damnation;
they are caught by the punishment which is their due as if by hooks
which prevent them from emerging into the light, for they are together consigned to toil in darkness. Good God, what terror to fear
what we cannot escape, and yet to hate in this life the gifts which Your
command bids us avoid!

24. *For the sinner is praised in the desires of his soul, and the unjust
man shall be blessed. The sinner hath provoked the Lord.* Here is given

the reason causing sinners to be bound by their own thoughts. When the evil man is praised, he is in high spirits, and the man who finds a fawning eulogizer does not think of self-correction. Next comes the exaltation of wickedness, so that the man known as an evil-doer is blessed. Such a person is beguiled by spurious adulators, and puffs himself up with the lofty pride of tyranny. This we must take as referring especially to Antichrist, who is so inveigled by bands of deceivers that he proclaims himself not only as earthly king but also as the God of all things; in Paul's words: *So that he sitteth in the temple of God and lifts himself above all that is worshipped and called God.*[25] But such conduct avails him for destruction; indeed, he provokes the Lord, so that as a false God he is consigned to avenging flames.

25. *According to the multitude of his wrath he will not seek him: God is not before his eyes.* He continues with the account of the purpose of Antichrist, for he will not seek the Lord because of his sins. The words, *according to the multitude of his wrath,* reveal that all his actions will be disturbed and cruel. An apt reason for this wickedness is offered, namely that *God is not before his eyes.* What depths of blindness not to have God before one's eyes! If it is considered the worst misfortune not to see the light of the sun, surely those who in their blindness fail to see the Author of sacred light endure a hell in the world above. Daniel the prophet also refers to the most wicked Antichrist with the words: *The king shall be lifted up against every god, and he shall be magnified over every god, and he shall speak proud words to the God of gods.*[26]

26. *His ways are filthy at all times. Thy judgments are removed from his sight: he shall rule over all his enemies.* Just as the psalmist will say of the just: *Blessed are the undefiled in the way, who walk in the law of the Lord,*[27] so now Antichrist is said to have all his ways filthy, in other words to have foul thoughts and foul deeds. It is inevitable that they be contaminated and foul, because they are begrimed by the leadership of the devil, who carries disease. Also mentioned is another wicked crime: when he sees that his punishment has been postponed, he believes that God does not seek to impose justice. For God's judgments are removed from the heart of the wicked man when he sees that what he had deserved to suffer immediately is rather slow in coming. He is said to have dominion over all his enemies, and this brings his destruction nearer, since he is a slave to vices. Borne along by this success, he

will be more inclined to sinning since he will know that none can confront him. Later he is described so aptly that he seems already present rather than soon to emerge; this trope is called *characterismos*[28] when a person is either described by his appearance or implied by his actions.

27. *For he hath said in his heart: I shall not be moved from generation to generation, and shall be without evil.* With these words the psalmist indicates the thought peculiar to Antichrist or to those who serve his rule. In Scripture's words: *They follow him that are of his side.*[29] Under the impulse of malice he will say to himself, "I shall leave no race untouched, but avenging myself over one nation I shall pass to another to take revenge." Thus by his energy he hopes to be able to afflict all who appeared to oppose his efforts. He defined his actions with a single term when he said that he would do nothing *without evil.*

28. *His mouth is full of cursing and bitterness: under his tongue are labour and sorrow.* His wickedness is described as embracing twofold perversion, for on his lips he shall have blasphemous cursing when he shall falsely claim to be the Son of God, and bitterness when he shall proclaim the death-penalty for those who resist him, and shall order those who refused to adore him as deity to proceed to execution. On his lips will lie his public utterances, but under his tongue, as the psalmist says, he will keep the most savage thoughts, so that since he himself is destroyed he may hasten to destroy everything; these thoughts are described as *labour and sorrow,* labour when he afflicts the innocent with various calamities, and sorrow when he makes martyrs, since the crown of martyrdom cannot be achieved without labour and physical sorrow, so all that he says or thinks is befouled with the same filth.

29–30. *He sitteth in ambush with the rich in private places, that he may kill the innocent. His eyes are upon the poor man.* When the psalmist says: *He sitteth in ambush,* he has compared the actions of Antichrist to the habits of footpads, who stealthily blockade roads to kill the innocent. This trope is called *phantasia,*[30] when the listener's mind is enticed to imagine future scenes. The psalmist says that Antichrist's kingdom is that known to have been established for martyrs to win the crown, and for the unfaithful to be destroyed. There follows: *With the rich,* which means a crowd of evil men, for often in holy Scripture *rich* has a pejorative sense, just as *poor* has a good sense. To *kill the innocent* means to make a religious man sacrilegious, and to condemn his soul to perpetual death. The words, *His eyes are upon the poor man,* mean not that he eyes him to care for him, but that his aim is to kill him.

He lieth in wait in secret, like a lion in his den. By the lion in his den he means the Antichrist just mentioned, who will rend Christ's people savagely and craftily. Initially the persecution of the Church was merely violent, when pagans attempted to force Christians to sacrifice to idols by use of proscriptions, tortures and beatings. The second kind of persecution is by guile, which is now employed by heretics and false Christians. The final form is still to come, and it is predicted here that it will come through Antichrist. Nothing will be more dangerous than this, for it will be extremely violent through the power of that unique kingdom, and through miraculous events it will mislead *so as to deceive,* as the Lord says in the gospel, *if possible even the elect.*[31] So the word *lion* denotes violence and the expression, *in his den,* guile, and thus both Antichrist's vices are suggested by the individual expressions.

He lieth in ambush that he may catch the poor man: to catch the poor man while he draweth him to him. In his net he will bring him down. The repetition of *ambush* indicates the crafty persecutor's excess. *To catch the poor man* points to the sudden peril of the soul to which that most sacrilegious man strives to entice the innocent. There follows a fine repetition, for purposes of explanation, of what has gone before. So that you may not think that the poor man has been seized on account of a public debt or civil lawsuit, he repeated the words, *to catch the poor man,* and then appended the reason for the persecution, *while he draweth him to him,* in other words while he strove to attract him from the true religion to adore his own name. Then, so that you could have no doubt about the phrase, *draweth him,* he added: *In his net he will bring him down. Net* implies the guile by which the hearts of simple people are trapped, and to their sorrow drawn tight by the knot of false faith. *He will bring him down* is a good phrase, because those enticed to unsound doctrines undoubtedly fall from the true religion.

31. *He will crouch and fall when he shall have power over the poor.* This now refers to the tyrant himself who will be given the chance to attack God's servants. *He will crouch* means "when his mind relaxes from large-scale acquisition of the damned, and he is drunk with a surfeit of

evils, and he attains a kind of leisure after punishing and afflicting holy men, he will then through his presumption tumble in his great wickedness when sudden death overcomes him and his followers." He is ignorant of the end of the world, for the Lord has him fixed in His power.

32. *For he hath said in his heart, God hath forgotten, he hath turned away his face not to see the very end.* A most foolish thought; will he imagine that the Lord, whose glory he sacrilegiously tries to seize, pretends not to notice? Will he believe that He is unwilling to keep an eye on the faithful when they are schooled to endure all their sufferings for His sake? Unaware of the truth, he will be motivated by suspecting the opposite, and will not understand the words which follow: *Forget not the poor unto the end.* He does not say that they will suffer nothing, but that they are certainly not to be abandoned *unto the end.*

33. *Arise, my Lord God, and let thy hand be exalted: forget not the poor unto the end.* Having completed four sections, the prophet is now inspired and turns to a fifth, begging that what he knew was to come should now occur. *Arise* means rise more quickly, or come speedily. *Let thy hand be exalted: hand* spells action, but this action of God is the judgment, whose coming we await. The psalmist sought the coming of the judgment, when that arrogant man could be brought low. *Forget not the poor unto the end:* the wicked man said the opposite, for *He hath turned away his face not to see the very end.* Now the psalmist asks that he should not fulfil the prayer of Antichrist and forget the poor unto the end of the world, when there will be retribution according to men's deserts.

34. *Wherefore hath the wicked provoked God? For he hath said in his heart, He will not investigate it.* In this verse a question is put, and a fitting answer follows with marvellous brevity. The words: *Wherefore hath the wicked provoked God,* must be expressed as a question, and the following words: *For he hath said in his heart, He will not investigate it,* as the answer. It is clear that the Lord is irritated because the wicked man did not believe that He could investigate his deeds. But he will find that He who he hoped was forgetful is mindful, and he will come to the realisation that his innumerable actions, which he thought were not remembered because his sins were so many, are taken into account.

35. *Thou seest it, for thou considerest labour and sorrow: that thou mayest deliver them into thy hands.* These words are to be addressed to the Lord in thanksgiving, when the issue is already known. *Thou seest, for none will mock You.* Earlier the psalmist had said: *Under his tongue are labour and sorrow,* and now he repeats these words: *Thou seest it, for thou considerest labour and sorrow.* While that treacherous man had them under his tongue—in other words, while he turned them over in his thoughts—he did not believe that they could be detected at all. But You certainly take thought for them when he is in Your hands, in other words when he is consigned to judgment and does not escape, but incurs a punishment commensurate with his deeds, since He did not think that he should refrain from wicked acts. So all power is declared to be with God, who consigns sinners to himself and punishes them. What is achieved by His servants is undoubtedly fulfilled by His power. When pursued by such power, where can he take refuge? He can commit crimes and feast on the ruin of different persons, but all that he does will not go unpunished when he is tortured in eternal damnation.

For to thee is the poor man left: thou wilt be a helper to the orphan. Now that the wicked have been exposed and condemned, the psalmist returns to the just, so that as the wicked receive treatment consonant with their deeds, so the just may obtain promised rewards. When he says: *For to thee is the poor man left,* he shows that the person consigned to Him is robbed of no advantages, for being left to the devoted Prince is the same as being exposed to all blessings. The poor man (*pauper*) gets his name from having a tiny abode (*a paululo lare*).[32] So he states that the poor man is left to God that all may see what blessings they may gain from His judgment. By *orphan* he means not one whose bodily father has died, but one whose father is the ruinous world. You will find many orphans without visible fathers who are blasphemers, spendthrifts and voluptuaries, a particularly frequent feature at that age; these are known to be alien to the Lord. But God's aid cannot be withdrawn from those orphans whose father Satan is known to have been snuffed out as he committed his crimes. Mark his words: *Thou wilt be a helper,* so that when you see them afflicted in the flesh, you do not doubt that they must be freed.

36. *Break thou the arm of the sinner and of the malignant: his sin shall be sought and shall not be found.* The wickedness of Antichrist again

passes before the prophet's eyes, and he asks that he be allowed no longer to revel in the bloodshed of the blessed. *Break* implies reduce to nothing. The *arm* of Antichrist suggests the power which sinners wickedly exploited, for he performed conspicuously wicked deeds, and accordingly uniquely deserved the title of sinner, since he will have no peer in wrongdoing. He is *malignant* because he will wickedly urge men away from their duty; in this way those whom he cannot pervert by fear, he will at least try to divert by harmful rewards. *His sin* refers to his misdeeds, for though only one transgression is mentioned, undoubtedly countless sins of his will be prominent. The psalmist adds: *And shall not be found,* for there is no doubt that his wicked power must perish, since its author must be condemned.

37. *The Lord shall reign to eternity, yea, for ever and ever: ye Gentiles shall perish from his land.* Once the universal calamity has been expunged, the psalmist passes to the order of future events, for once Antichrist has been slain, the eternal, holy, generous kingdom of the Lord will come. Wicked evil is allowed to run far ahead so that the Lord's kingdom for which we long may be more welcome when attained, for in it the blessed now become untroubled, and take rest. The traps which the holy man is compelled to endure in this world are no longer feared. By *Gentiles* he means sinners and wicked men whose life is death and who disobey the Lord's laws. *From his land* refers to the kingdom of the Lord Saviour which only the blessed enjoy.

38. *The Lord hath heard the desire of the poor: thy ear hath heard the communal longing of their heart.* The prayers of the just are well expressed in fitting words, for he speaks of *the desire of the poor.* Desire always follows love, so that they desire to see Him clearly in heaven, where they are now transported by the mind's eye. There follows: *The communal longing of their heart.* This expression, *communal longing,* is clearly stronger, for it describes how something is sought by a kind of mental eagerness by men in concert. Next comes: *Thy ear hath heard.* We must regularly note that in God there are no physical parts, but the effect of the power by which He hears is called His ear, that by which He sees His eye, that by which He performs His hand. Let these words be stored in your memory, that we may not seem to weary you by repeating them if they have often to be restated.

39. *To judge for the fatherless and the humble, that man may no more*

presume to magnify himself on earth. See how we are informed by the prophet's authority that not only any fatherless child but also all those who are fatherless and humble are most pleasing to God. When the prophet says: *To judge for the fatherless and for the humble,* he is pointing out that the verdict can be passed on his own behalf. But when the word *humble* is used, this is praise of the most just man. There also follows the binding promise that the hardships mentioned take place in such a way that no-one is allowed to exceed them. For them all evils must be ended, since the author of all sins will be condemned with his tribe. These are *the hidden things of the Son* which the heading of this psalm prophesies; for though they appear to have been frequently announced by certain signs, men fail to recognise them when they come. The Lord says of that day in the gospel: *But of that day and hour no man knoweth, neither the angels in heaven, nor the Son, but the Father alone.*[33] On this passage the most blessed Fathers Hilary and Augustine, sacred lights of the Church, have passed numerous illuminating comments.[34] They account it impious that the almighty Word in human form should be thought to have been ignorant of the future on any matter which He proclaimed that His Father knew. Peter in the gospel says: *Lord, thou knowest all things; thou knowest that I love thee,*[35] and the Lord himself says: *All things whatsoever the Father has are mine.*[36] But surely He would not possess all things of the Father if He did not know what the Father knew. Hilary and Augustine taught that for salvation and truth the passage was to be understood through the figure of *metonymy* or *transnominatio.*[37] This is found quite often in the sacred Scriptures, and by it we must realise that God makes His subjects ignorant to their advantage. In Genesis God says to Abraham: *Now I know that thou fearest the Lord thy God,*[38] in other words, "Now I have made you know." So in the present passage the words: "I do not know" mean "I have made you not to know." The Lord himself elsewhere says similarly: *I know you not,*[39] when He could not possibly have been ignorant of those He condemned. Finally when questioned on this very matter He says: *It is not for you to know the times or moments.*[40] He did not say: "It is not for me," or "It is not for us," but *It is not for you to know.* So both points are observed here. Men did not realise what they should not, and the Son of God was not in any sense unaware of this through weakness of the flesh. But if we were to suspect that the divine Majesty cloaked ignorance (a thing it would be impious to say), then that ignorance would be found stronger than the divine nature, and could—to speak foolishness—bring down the providence by which all things were created. But since we are taught that this is quite ridiculous, we must believe that the whole Trinity, whose nature is one and all-powerful, has always an unfailing knowledge of all things.

Conclusion Drawn From the Psalm

The promise proclaimed by the prophet is fulfilled, the hidden miracles of the Son are revealed. What good and wonderful issues appear to be explained, yet are still undoubtedly hidden! When proclaimed they are not considered unknown, but since they are unknown when they come to be, they are demonstrated to be still hidden. In this sense what is spoken and what is not left unannounced to those who seek it is secret. So let us beg God more profusely that He deign to bestow on us a most salutary change of ways, for he who is warned that retribution for sins will come has no excuse for sinning. We must also store in our minds that this is the first psalm in which the coming of Antichrist is prophesied. The number of this psalm also obviously reveals a hidden truth, that the Lord gave up the ghost at the ninth hour. Since this psalm has spoken amongst other things of His passion, its number too rightly announces the hour of that passion, for it is acknowledged to have recounted also the mysteries of the cross itself.

COMMENTARY ON PSALM 10

1. *Unto the end. A psalm of David.* Though the expression, *Unto the end,* often appears in these headings and invariably concentrates our minds on the Lord Christ, it is undoubtedly set there to denote different marvels. At one time it points to the glorious passion, at another to the triumphant resurrection at which all nations wonder. But here it declares the holy faith through which most faithful Christians experience mortal combat with heretics.[1] So it continually reaches to Christ but is found joined to Him in different senses. If you concentrate your

mind you realise that this must be the case with the other psalms as well. So far as *psalm* and *of David* are concerned, it must be enough to recall what we said earlier, as you remember it. But realise that this psalm has been developed to undermine heretics.

Division of the Psalm

The whole of this psalm is to be allotted to the person of the prophet. In the first section he tells of heretics in ambush who strive to seduce Catholics into their own wickedness. In the second he speaks threateningly of the Lord's judgment, clearly revealing what they are to endure at the time of retribution, so that they may fear the Lord's justice and abandon superstitious falsehoods.

Explanation of the Psalm

2. *In the Lord I put my trust: how then do you say to my soul, Get thee away to the mountain like a sparrow?* This figure is called *caenonema*,[2] the divulging of a plan; it frequently occurs when we join words with foes or allies. These words are in fact addressed to persuasive heretics who wish to utter evil to seduce innocent souls with vicious argument. So to them the faithful man says: "Since I am established on the fixed peak of religion, how is it that you seek to persuade me, saying: *Get thee away to the mountain,* in other words, have recourse to the wickedness of heretics, falsely claiming that Christ is where Truth is known to leave no trace?" In the divine Scriptures, *mountain* is ambivalent, being applied in comparison to very different things. It is often used in both good and bad senses. When it is used in a good sense, its strength and notable height are regarded; when in a bad sense, its inner stolidness and lofty pride. So the one term is aptly applied to different objects after reflection on their qualities. There are also several types of sparrow. Some take pleasure in holes in walls, while others make for dewy valleys, and others haunt scaly mountains. But here the psalmist speaks of those whose most random inclination bears them off to the loftiest region of earth. So those who in fickleness of wavering mind turn to most wicked doctrines are rightly considered similar to them.

3. *For lo, the wicked have bent their bow.* We must interpret the bow as the divine commands which the heretic wields and orders according to his own wickedness. He strives to inflict a wound on the soul, not to prick it to enable it to attain salvation, but to pierce it with eternal death. It is good that the bow appears in the most sacred scriptures, because it unites the two Testaments, and offers defence or destruction. As Paul says: *To some indeed we are the odour of death unto death, but to the others the odour of life unto life.*[3]

They have prepared their arrows in the quiver, to shoot in the dark the upright of heart. He continues with the analogy of the archer, for just as the archer has arrows in the quiver, so the heretic carries poisonous words in his heart. *In the dark* signifies either when the Church is troubled with persecutions, when men of the flesh are thought to change their allegiance more readily through fear of danger, or with a hidden plan believing that they can deceive Christians more opportunely, when they imagine that the Christians cannot observe their purposes. When he says: *the upright of heart,* he shows that the heretics' traps are futile and empty, for men are not upright of heart unless they cannot be deceived by any wicked words of persuasion.

4. *For they have destroyed the things which thou hast made: but what has the just man done?* He is saying that the heretics themselves have destroyed the Lord's law when by false interpretations they strive to rend the holy Scriptures, which are prophetic utterances from the Lord for our salvation. A defence of the Lord Christ is further subjoined, for the psalmist says that if men have wished to subvert justice by wicked interpretation, why do they accuse Him who spoke justly? They do not derive their errors from His precept but from their own most wicked will.

5. *The Lord is in his holy temple: the Lord's throne is in heaven.* Having rebuked those who have false ideas about the most true religion, the prophet passes to the second section. Here he says that the Lord's judgments are soon to come, so that human wickedness may amend itself if only by reflecting on the Lord's severity. So that no-one may believe that one deceives the innocent unpunished, he says that the Lord resides in any religious individual; in Paul's words: *If any man violate the temple of God, him shall God destroy, for the temple of God is holy, which you are.*[4] Thus the heretic may know that he can be destroyed by the God who is recognised to possess the hearts of right

believers. *Heaven* here signifies the holy men in whom the Godhead deigns to dwell with the presence of His majesty. How beautifully the praise rises from a mind[5] untainted! What honour, what fame it is to take up the Creator, who certainly ever dwells in the good!

His eyes look on the poor man, his eyelids examine the sons of men. Just as those from whom God turns are unhappy, so they upon whom He looks with kindness become blessed. His gaze is a benefit because those visited by such great brightness are not submerged by the darkness of sins. Even Peter after falling was given the chance to make amends and return when the Godhead's mercy looked upon him. Note that the psalmist first said *eyes* and later *eyelids*. Eyelids (*palpebrae*) get their name from *palpitare*,[6] to flicker. They are, so to say, envelopes of the sight, bags for the eyes which we close in sleep so that we can renew our poor bodies when wearied. So because the functions of the limbs are often allegorically applied to the Lord's actions, the psalmist says that it is not only when He gazes with His eyes that He seeks us out. He also takes thought for the sons of men when He is thought to be asleep and to have no care for such matters.

6. *The Lord trieth the just and the wicked: but he that loveth iniquity hateth his own soul.* We must not consider this as a repeal for the wicked when the Lord examines both just and wicked, for He distinguishes all things in the light of truth. The statement is made so that foolish beliefs may not cause men's longings to go astray, so that the individual may contemplate his guilt which he knows is the sole criterion on which the Lord passes judgment. There follows a brief and clear apophthegm: what does loving iniquity mean? It means to hate one's own soul. This is the way in which the person who follows the devil persecutes himself as he seeks to journey on those paths which lead to the region of punishments which are to be avoided.

7. *He rains snares on sinners: fire and brimstone and storms of winds shall be the portion of their cup.* *Rains* refers to preachers' words pouring from heaven which serve as showers for the truly devoted but become fiery snares for the unfaithful. The first group yield fruit through understanding well the words, the second choke their souls with the noose of perversity by interpreting them wrongly. *Fire* signifies the blazing anxiety which consumes them, so *brimstone* is mentioned because their thoughts are foul with an abominable odour; *storms of winds* describes how they were disturbed with troubled

minds. *The portion of their cup* means the measure by which they are intoxicated by defiled deeds. *Cup,* however, is used also in the good sense, as in: *Thy chalice which inebriateth me, how goodly is it!*[7] For the cup is the measure by which souls are intoxicated. *Cup (calix)* is so called because it frequently contains hot *(calidus)*[8] drinks. Then too Theodosius Macrobius in a work of his[9] says that there was a race of the Cyclicrani established near Heraclea whose name was formed from the Greek *kulix,* a kind of cup which with the change of one letter spells *calix.* So because of this their name is obviously implanted in the memory.

8. *For the Lord is just and hath loved justice: his countenance hath beheld righteousness.* There is added an apt conclusion about the justice of the eternal King. He says that the just Lord loves justice because He can look only on those who can maintain justice. The psalmist added: *His countenance beheld righteousness,* that is, the righteousness which He himself grants in His kindness, for humanity of itself possesses nothing worthy; it has only what it has obtained from the Lord, the Bestower of all things. *Countenance* here signifies the Lord's kindness; as we read in another psalm: *But the countenance of the Lord is against them that do evil things.*[10] But here he said that *it hath beheld righteousness,* so through righteousness the Lord has made His grace comprehensible.

Conclusion Drawn From the Psalm

How well this psalm with marvellous brevity has embraced the wiles of heretics and the penalty which they incur, so that we may be restrained from the wicked deeds of those whose future punishments we descry! In the number of the psalm there lies the sacred power of the Decalogue,[11] which has come to be the most splendid instructor of human life. Just as the ten commandments condemn men's vices, so this psalm wars on the interpretations made by wicked preaching. It frees men from danger which is the greater according as it is worse to fail in faith than to sin through physical frailty. So this psalm too rightly bears the number ten, for by its perfect instruction it strengthens our understanding in orthodox belief. Moreover, in the gospel the good servant who rendered ten talents was praised and received as reward dominion over ten cities.[12] Then too Paul wrote the Lord's word to ten churches to indicate a great mystery, thus showing that this number's dimension embraces the fullness of the sacred teaching, for the number itself has been interpreted as indicating great virtue and praise. Though it stretches to an extended and infinite number, it ever circles upon itself with mounting sum; though receiving no external addition, it is seen greatly to increase within itself.[13] For this reason it is rightly called a glory (*decus*), as having derived its name *decem* from *decus*.[14]

COMMENTARY ON PSALM II

1. *Unto the end, for the eighth day, a psalm of David.* As has already been explained in Psalm 6, *eighth* refers to our eternal rest, for this world does not experience an eighth day. Once the seventh day is finished, it always returns to the first. In these seven days, the number is plural, but eighth is taken as singular because it does not change with any successor. So the psalm's purport must be explained so that the words of the heading can be more easily understood by realisation of its purpose. The prophet, then, begs that this world's wickedness be destroyed, so that the great truth of the future promise may be attained. That undisturbed kingdom is denoted when its blessedness is unceasingly sought. So the eighth day is aptly associated with this psalm, for then this world's flawed manners are left behind, and the advent of the innocence of the next world is demanded. The rest of the heading is well understood from earlier explanations.

Division of the Psalm

In the first section, the prophet begs to be saved from the depravity of this world, because crafty and proud men were denying the Lord's power with wicked contradiction. In the second, he proclaims that the Father's promise is to be made through the all-powerful Son. He briefly praises the Lord's utterances, just as earlier he has rebuked irreverent words.

Explanation of the Psalm

2. *Save me, O Lord, for the holy man has now seceded: truths are decayed from among the children of men.* Let us carefully examine the beginning of the psalm, for it is fashioned with the beauty of expressive figures. The prophet suddenly cries out to the Lord so that the magnitude of the danger is clear from his fear itself. Then by the figure of *synathroismos*[1] he assembles the many objects of his fear up to the division of the psalm. This figure is regarded as one of the most violent, since many things and many changes are united. Since he saw this world oppressing souls in many ways, he asked the Lord to be saved. He knew that true healing could be found with Him, when He said that no saintly man in the world was where such a crowd of evil men was known to be. These words have reference to men, but the Lord is known to be present everywhere; so that we would not interpret it ambiguously, he followed: *The holy man has now seceded,* with: *Truths are decayed from among the children of men.* If there had not been decayed truth, the holy man could not have seceded. This is called "Proof from the consequence,"[2] when a premise is confirmed by the words that follow. But when he says *decayed,* he obviously shows that God's gifts have been befouled by men's sins, for by their perversity they stain the benefits bestowed on them. We should notice too that *truths* are mentioned in the plural, though there is one Truth; but since by heavenly dispensation His power is assigned through each individual, we witness that there are many truths. So we often speak of the prophecies of David and of Jeremiah, of the gospels of Matthew and of John, and of the others whose fame has flourished in this way. In the same manner we speak of truths when by the Lord's generosity the nature of truth is afforded to human minds in facets which cannot be separated. This verse can be aptly applied also to the Jewish people, who stripped themselves of their gifts from heaven, and refused to believe in Him who was prophesied by the crowd of so many who beheld Him.

3. *They have spoken vain things every one to his neighbour: with deceitful lips and with a double heart they have spoken evil words. Vain things* means falsehoods, a sense consistent with his previous words: *Truths are decayed from among the children of men,* when they sought evidence against the Lord Christ and bestirred themselves with evil whisper-

ings. *Neighbours* here denotes not so much kinship as association in wickedness; as for the words: *With a double heart,* whenever we wish to describe cunning men we mention their duplicity of heart. As Solomon says: *A double-minded man is inconstant in all his ways.*[3] But when we wish to characterise simple men, we maintain that there is one heart in them. As the Acts of the Apostles says: *The multitude of believers had one heart and one soul.*[4] In the same way we say that people are two-tongued if they never continue in the same opinion. Look at the statement which follows the points we have discussed: *They have spoken evil words.* It was inevitable that people with duplicity of heart should speak evil words.

4. *May the Lord destroy all deceitful lips, and the tongue that speaketh proud things.* A general judgment follows, just as frequently when an individual errs the sanction of law is applied and the announcement of a severe measure condemns the evil in general. *May he destroy* is with reference to the union of the Jews, so that those who had gathered in the one wickedness might perish in sundry places. *The tongue that speaketh proud things* is that which takes upon itself some great faculty without the realisation that it has been conferred by the Creator, being under the impression that the outcome of events is under its own control. So the Apocalypse says of Antichrist: *I saw in the horn which was the higher, a mouth speaking great things*[5] and the rest. He earlier spoke of *deceitful lips* so that you could not take in a good sense: *The tongue that speaketh proud things.* Note his piety as he says this, for he inveighs not against men, for many of them were to be converted, but against the vices themselves.

5. *Who have said: We will magnify our tongues: our lips are our own. Who is lord over us?* He describes those who in time of success are swollen with overfondness for words and who presume to extol their own glory and to attribute to their own powers what in their madness they fail to realise they have received from God. I pause for a moment to inquire of them why they do not so chatter when overwhelmed with cares and stupefied in silence; they cast their eyes to the earth, they clamp tight their lips, they are dumb with minds confused as though they have lost their tongues. Consider too the various mishaps of sickness, resulting in a person's inability to take food, in spite of his apparent boasting about what his lips can do. Then let them say, if they can, *Our lips are our own. Who is lord over us?* In these words: *Who*

is lord over us? the words of sacrilegious men are being echoed. The figure is called *antisagōgē*⁶ or contradiction.

6. *By reason of the misery of the needy and the groans of the poor, now will I arise, saith the Lord.* In these two verses we must carefully examine the persons of Father and Son, so that confusion in our understanding may be dispelled. After the psalmist has condemned those who proposed shedding the Lord's blood, he comes to the second section in which he promises the Lord Saviour's resurrection in the prophetic voice of the Father, for we can cite the words of another without abandoning our own lips' utterance. Let us understand the nature of the Creator's devotion here, when *by reason of the misery of the needy and the groans of the poor* the Lord Christ achieved glory, so that His faithful were not oppressed with lengthy tribulation. *I will arise* is a metaphorical statement to the effect that He who knows no human weakness of prostration rises up; but *I will arise* means I shall appear and be manifest in the Son, for their strength is one and their majesty undivided. The Father appears and is manifest in the Son; as Christ Himself says in the gospel: *He that seeth me seeth the Father also.*⁷

I will set over my deliverance, I will deal confidently in his regard. By His *deliverance,* the Father means His Word made flesh,⁸ through which life came to men, since every believer attains salvation through His abundant generosity. What does He set over Him? Surely consolation, which He earlier said belonged to the needy and poor; for when the Lord Saviour rose again it was clearly proffered to the faithful. *I will deal confidently* declares the power of the Father's omnipotence, for truly the One whose will no man can confront *deals confidently.* In the same way the gospel says of Christ: *For he was teaching them as one having power, and not as their scribes and Pharisees.*⁹ But the power of the Father is the confidence of the Son, as the confidence of the Son is the power of the Father, and it is certain that this applies to the whole Trinity, in accord with the unity of its nature.

7. *The words of the Lord are pure words.* After the psalmist has spoken the Father's words, he confirms them by praising them, for everything happened as was known to have been promised. What the words of the Lord are is briefly stated: namely pure words, words of utter purity and virginal integrity, such that no lying pollutes them and no stains of falsehood mark them. Just as purity knows no pollution, so

the Lord's words know no contamination of any foulness. Do not accept this statement passively. It is made by contrast with what was said earlier of the wicked: *They have spoken vain things, every one to his neighbour,* so that by examining the diversity of situations we might be detached from evil manners. This figure is called *syndesmos* in Greek and *collatio* in Latin,[10] when persons or cases are contrasted as opposites or compared as similar. Here divine utterances are praised, whereas earlier human words are rebuked.

As silver from the earth, tried by the fire, purged seven times. He is still defining the nature of the pure words by comparing them with a bright metal. *Silver from the earth, tried by the fire,* is usually most pure when cleansed by frequent baking. *Tried* or *purged* is in contrast to what he says about sinners: *deceitful lips in duplicity of heart.* And to enable you to acknowledge the vast gulf between them, he added: *Purged seven times.* The number may refer, it seems, to the seven forms of the Spirit, namely, fear of the Lord, piety, knowledge, fortitude, counsel, understanding, wisdom.[11] Through them the divine Word remains as it were in a fired furnace, shining with the ruddy glow of truth.

8. *Thou, O Lord, wilt preserve us: and keep us from this generation for ever.* Just as earlier he said: *May the Lord destroy all deceitful lips,* so here he promises that the Lord will preserve those who have believed His utterances with a pure heart. Observe with what control the sacred rules are maintained. When he says: *Thou wilt preserve us,* he excised presumption from our transient humanity so that none might think that they should have any trust in themselves. *From this generation* denotes the Jews or sinners of this world from whom we cannot be guarded by our own strength, but protected only by His pity. The psalmist added: *For ever,* because He consoles us here in our tribulations and in heaven sets us in everlasting freedom from anxiety. He helps us here, and glorifies and crowns us there. So the most devoted Creator both preserves us in this world lest we perish, and blesses us in the next so that we can be wholly free of wretchedness.

9. *The wicked walk round about: according to thy highness thou hast multiplied the children of men.* Having in the first section condemned the words of the wicked with appropriate malediction, and in the second having praised the Lord's utterance with wonderful commendation, he passes to the conclusion of the psalm, in which in a single

verse he again attaches to each section the apposite words. In the briefest of statements he says: *The wicked walk round about,* so that they can never reach the right path, for circuitous routes are always invested with evil manners; as Solomon says: *They have left the right ways to walk on wicked ways.*[12] So they cannot attain the repose of the eighth day, for they are always revolving backwards like wheels. The next words are: *According to thy highness thou hast multiplied the children of men.* This refers to those who have genuinely believed the chaste and most pure utterances of the Lord. Note how much is promised in this statement, for he says: *According to thy highness thou hast multiplied the children of men,* not according to their merit, but according to that which has no experience of human trials. We often call high what we cannot grasp; the Creator does not square with the measurement applied to all creatures, and there can be in Him none of the measures which allot to all things their number, weight and size. *Thou hast multiplied the children of men* refers to the promise made to Abraham in the words: *Multiplying, I will multiply thy seed like the stars of the sky.*[13] It is clear that He has performed this, and that He daily performs it in the persons of His saints.

Conclusion Drawn From the Psalm

Let us reflect that this psalm has expounded to us most beneficial mysteries. It has told us how men are seized by empty, superfluous talk, with the result that they seek to attain not the truth by which they live, but the falsehood by which they die. Then he explained in due order the nature of the Lord's utterance, so that each of us by realising how utterly pure are the Lord's words may healthily regard our own as foul. This is the remedy granted for our condition, for it is certain that the sons of men can be freed by the power of the Lord. Then, since the strength of the number eleven, to which this psalm is assigned, is acknowledged as revealing to us a sign of the gospel, let us beg the Father of the household in His great mercy to admit us into the vineyard even at the eleventh hour,[14] so that He may deign to bestow on our actions a reward not due to us, but gratuitous. Blessed Prosper too, in the second part of the book entitled *Before the Law, Under the Law, and Under Grace,* says: "Not without this mystery was the tabernacle shrouded from above with eleven curtains of haircloth. It was to show by it that the whole world is guilty before God, and lives in repentance. The psalm bearing this number has as its beginning: *Save me, O Lord, for the holy man has now seceded: truths are decayed from among the children of men.*"[5]

COMMENTARY ON PSALM 12

1. *Unto the end. A psalm of David.* Since the words of this heading are now familiar from earlier comments, it is fitting to say something instead about the content of the psalm. In sum it speaks of the charity of the Lord Christ, in which resides the perfection of the entire law. If a man has it, he relegates all the enticements of this world, for when it alone is sought with the whole heart, its opposite ceases to be loved. The love of God is, so to say, a spring shower of virtues, beneath which a blessed longing germinates, and holy action bears fruit. In this world it is patient in adversity and controlled in prosperity, powerful in humility and most joyful in affliction, kindly to enemies and over-coming evil men with its blessings. Even creatures of heaven are fired by it, becoming a renewing flame, a longing which swells and brings salvation. To embrace the entire theme in the words of Paul: *God Himself is charity.*[1] So it is fitting that we seek it and long for it unceasingly, so that because of our inability to be filled with it here we may at any rate in our future reward obtain full satisfaction from it. As we read in Psalm 118: *My soul hath fainted at my salvation.*[2] This fainting in fact means participation in blessed immortality.

Division of the Psalm

When in the first section the prophet noted that the human race was obsessed by deadly superstitions, and was not hastening in chaste thoughts to worship of the true Lord, with great longing he prays that his faith may be fulfilled by the advent of the holy incarnation, so that then at any rate confused heathens might for their own good abandon wayward errors. In the second section he earnestly asks that his faith be enlightened, so that our petitions may be effectively presented, and he may not fall by any deceit of the enemy. He says that he has always trusted in the Lord's mercy.

Explanation of the Psalm

How long, O Lord, wilt thou forget me unto the end? As has been stated, the prophet is full of the Lord's abounding charity, through which he eagerly awaited His becoming man. Trustingly he blurts out the message that he is being frustrated too long in his expectation, for delay comes very harsh to every man who has longing. Though he believed in clarity of faith that He would come, he complains about the slowness of Him whose arrival he still hoped for, but did not deserve to see. When God postpones granting a request, He does not forget but is thought to be overcome with forgetfulness by the one suffused with longing.[3] On this occasion, *Unto the end* refers to the time at which he foresaw that the Lord's incarnation would come. Such a complaint strikes the souls of the faithful, so that they both ever long for heavenly things and have enduring trust in the Lord's promise. Also worth noting is the fact that in these four verses he everywhere expresses sentiments of most unfailing patience. He says: *How long? Till when? For what length of time?* and indeed He asks: *Till when?* twice over. This figure is known as *epimone,*[4] when there is duplication of similar words by frequent repetition.

Till when dost thou turn away thy face from me? He asks for the appearance of Christ, whom he had long foreseen in spirit. For His *face* is that which could appear before bodily eyes, which that holy man uttering this general sentiment rightly desired to see, for that face by its manifestation from heaven deigned to save the world. In this way both his longing for God's love was shown and his charity towards his neighbours was clearly fulfilled, since he continually begged for what he knew was beneficial to all. Both are joined in partnership with each other; God cannot be loved without neighbour, nor neighbour without God.

2. *For what time shall I take counsel in my soul?* His most zealous longing as he waits is expressed here. He says he sees no way of being

able to lessen his desire to behold Christ, for his eagerness to desire the good and to await His coming for longer is immeasurable.

3. *Sorrow in my heart all the day. How long shall my enemy be exalted over me?* He continues further with his pious complaints. *Take* is to be carried over from the previous verse, so the full sense is "Shall I take sorrow in my heart?." *All the day* means every day, so that we can understand here the passage of time in an absolute sense. Notice the first word of this verse. By now it is not longing but the greatest sorrow which is aroused and experienced as this beautiful petition swells up; this happens especially when a long-held hope is drawn out. *My enemy* refers to the devil, who before the Lord's coming was raised high and took joy in the enslavement of mankind. *Over me* means "cover my belief," for the devil was eagerly worshipped all over the world, since the heavenly religion did not then win devoted faith.

4. *Consider and hear me, O Lord my God. Enlighten my eyes that never sleep in death.* He comes to the second limb of his prayer for escape. But what tears are we to think that his devotion shed here, lest the whole world through the long delay be trapped in errors and perish! When he says *me,* his petition is not for himself alone; rather he begs help for all the faithful, out of love for whom a universal remedy was being sought. *Consider* is to be joined with his earlier words: *How long dost thou turn thy face from me?* and *hear* with the comment at the beginning of the psalm: *How long, O Lord wilt thou forget me unto the end? Eyes* we must here interpret as those of the heart, which sleep in death when the light of faith is buried, and they are closed through pleasure of the flesh; for this is the sleep in which the enemy delights.

5. *Lest at any time my enemy say: I have prevailed against him. They that trouble me will rejoice if I am moved.* He says this with reference to the devil and his angels, whose custom is to jeer when they seize, for they believe that their victories entail the destruction of those who follow them. What he is saying is: "If I am parted from you, I shall give joy to them who in their despicable way become glad once they know that the persons they have deceived are in their hands." The words: *If I am moved* refer to the fickleness of the disloyal soul, for a man must step into the devil's trap if he withdraws by a single step from the Lord's strength.

6. *But I shall trust in thy mercy: my heart shall rejoice in thy salvation.* Though filled with great longing, he none the less expressed the force of his patience by saying that though his wishes continue to be postponed, he himself with the support of divine mercy can be found most steadfast in the hope of that mercy; as Paul says: *But hope confoundeth not.*[5] *In thy mercy* is inserted because anyone who thinks otherwise makes vain all the hope of his belief. O the strength of faith, the great steadfastness of the believer! He rejoiced at the absence of Him who was actually present. The inner man had already sighted the salvation of the God whom the outer man still longed to behold with the eyes of the body.

I will sing to the Lord, who giveth me good things: yea, I will hymn to the name of the Lord, the most high. Whereas at the start he repeatedly complains that he has had his desire delayed, here he joyfully proclaims the kindnesses of the Lord bestowed on him. This is either because he says through the power of prophecy that he has gained what he clearly knew would come, or because to have believed this was already his reward. As Scripture says: *Abraham believed God, and it was reputed to him unto justice.*[6] So the psalmist rightly says that he has obtained it, for such great steadfastness of faith has been bestowed on him. Notice that he first said: *I will sing,* and then: *I will hymn. I will sing* is from the heart, where he was filled with boundless joy; *I will hymn* lies in good works, as the Godhead chiefly demands.[7] As *I will sing* has reference to the contemplative life, so *I will hymn* refers to the active.[8] The two are most beautifully allied like twin eyes, and make the Christian exceedingly bright.

Conclusion Drawn From the Psalm

Let us view the prophet engaged in blessed contemplation, and note with what longing he anticipated the glorious incarnation of the Lord. Then from this let us realise what a gift it is which we have obtained, when we observe that a powerful king and a holy prophet desired with such enthusiasm to behold it. But we must beg the Lord not to commit us to the devil to be abandoned and tested, and to allow us, however unworthy of such kindness, to serve faithfully, now that He has come, the One to whom the prophet most devotedly ministered when He was still to arrive. The apostles, twelve in number, bid us recall the number of the psalm. By their most perfect teaching of the commandments they both loved the Lord before all things and treated their neighbours with the same charity as themselves. So this psalm has rightly yielded to us these mysteries, for it is clearly consecrated by bearing the number of the apostles. Then too we know that the Hebrew people was divided into twelve tribes. Moreover, the Lord promised the apostles twelve seats at the judgment to come. The year itself is divided into twelve months. The careful reader will find other parallels of this kind so that you may realise that the number abounds in many mysteries.

COMMENTARY ON PSALM 13

1. *Unto the end. A psalm of David.* Since these words are now wholly familiar from previous explanations, recollection of these must be sought from me rather than further explanation. In the headings, *end* is often rightly repeated so that the listener's mind is made attentive to Christ almighty. But the word end, as I said before, expresses our attitude towards our Lord in different senses: now it is confession from the afflicted, now the joy of the exultant, now the attitude of the teacher, now the threat of judgment. However, the present psalm rebukes the Jews' madness with fierce condemnation. It is harsh in its onslaughts, terrifying the impious and hard towards unbelievers. So this attack is rightly assigned to holy Church, against whose purposes lunatic disbelief attempts to unleash debased plots.

Division of the Psalm

The Lord's appearance, sought with prayers of longing in Psalm 12, is depicted here as having arrived. So first the Catholic Church rebukes the Jews who looked on Christ but had not the slightest belief in Him. In the second place, she says that those who were unwilling to acknowledge fruitful fear of the Lord are disturbed by empty anxiety. Their conversion is finally prophesied at the end of the world,' when nations shall have the abundance awaited over long ages, so that when the Lord's devotion to them is revealed, they may more easily be enticed into seeking the cure of proclaiming Him.

Explanation of the Psalm

The fool hath said in his heart, There is no God. When the Jewish people saw that Christ had come in a lowly condition in the flesh which He had assumed, they foolishly said: *There is no God.* They failed to understand that it was He who had been foretold by the prophets. The sin was the greater because they said it not with the lips but in the heart, so that to their evil utterance was joined the unbelief which was worse.

They are corrupt, and are become abominable in their desires: there is none that doth good, none even to one. They are corrupt because in abandoning the sanity of the Scriptures they have demonstrably fallen into sinful thoughts. The punishment for sin follows next; disfigured by their most wicked reluctance to believe, they became abominable to the Lord through their errors. *Voluntas* (desire) derives from *volatus* (flying),[2] because the mind rushes where it wills with great speed. Next comes: *There is none that doth good.* But what about the patriarchs? Did Noah not do good when he was obedient to the Lord's commands, and entered the ark to be saved? Did Abraham likewise not do good when in obedience to heavenly instructions he offered his son for sacrifice? Surely Job did good when he was afflicted with grim suffering, yet repeatedly he thanked the Lord throughout? There is no need to mention prophets and apostles who followed the Lord's commands and offered themselves to glorious deaths. Even today through the Lord's kindness good things are done through the action of just men. But so that this denial may become wholly meaningful to you, ponder the words that follow: *None, even to one.* In fact that only One is Christ, without whom human weakness has not the strength either to begin or to complete any good thing. So the statement was justified that no man can do good unless through His mercy we have gained Christ. When we reach Him and do not abandon Him, every good is undoubtedly performed. So this is *the end* promised in the heading.

2. *The Lord hath looked down from heaven upon the children of men.*

How did the Lord look down? Surely in sending His only-begotten Son, through whom the true faith could be more clearly recognised. *Upon the children of men* can be understood of the Jews.[3] As the Lord says in the gospel: *I was not sent but to the sheep that had been lost of the house of Israel.*[4] So with greater honour he called them *the children of men,* because by contrast with the Gentiles they worshipped one God. As we know, that people was uniquely presented with the gift which they sacrilegiously rejected and made foreign to themselves.

To see if there be any that understand and seek God. To see means to cause to be seen; this figure is called *hypallage*[5] or exchange, when an expression is lent a different meaning. So here it is said that He who knows all things before they come into being gets to know something in the course of time. In the same sense the Lord said to Abraham: *Now I know that thou fearest the Lord thy God,*[6] and He will say to sinners at His judgment: *I know you not,*[7] and so forth. One often finds this type of expression implanted in holy Scripture. He mentioned *any that understand* with reference to Christ's assumption of humanity, for when He showed by many miracles the coming of His divinity He ought to have been recognised as God. He meant *seek* in the sense of their following His commands, for the one who seeks God is he who does not depart from His will. So in a single verse the mystery of the holy incarnation was revealed, so that through it men's faith could be grasped, and the remedy of the desired gift obtained.

3. *They are all gone aside, they are become unprofitable together: there is none that doth good, no, not one.* All are said to have turned aside, though quite a crowd of them believed. But the whole is to be understood from the part, for there were so many impious ones that almost all were considered to be perfidious and to have perished. So they went aside from the grace of God and became unprofitable to themselves.

Their throat is an open sepulchre: with their tongue they acted deceitfully. These five verses to the beginning of the second section are not found in the Hebrew copies.[8] But since by long custom they have been admitted to Church use, we shall explain them individually as permitted. This particular verse appeared also in Psalm 5,[9] but because it was the same nation and a similar case, the apophthegm was obviously apt in repetition. So their throat was well called a sepulchre, for they spoke death-dealing words. Just as when sepulchres lie open they emit foul odours, so these men's throats poured out baneful words, and so that they alone should not perish they scattered deceits abroad with their tongues. But bear in mind that in these five verses the psalmist denotes the fools, of whom he earlier said that they ponder sacrileges in their hearts, by the second type of definition which in Greek is called *ennoematike*, and in Latin *notio*.[10] This type does not specify its nature in terms of substance, but clearly suggests what men are by the nature of their deeds.

The poison of asps is under their lips: their mouth is full of cursing and bitterness. Asps are known to be a monstrous species of serpent. It is said that through their natural obstinacy they do not carry through magicians' spells, and because they can be softened by no charm they cannot be diverted from their aim. The Jews are most aptly compared with this species, for in the face of the words of salvation they have wretchedly affected a fatal deafness, and have chosen to follow poisonous purposes rather than be drawn to practices which bring salvation. So these words seem deservedly to be used of them: *They chose darkness in preference to light*.[11] *Venenum* (poison) is so called because it seeps through the veins (*venae*).[12] This is the path taken by the prayers of malignant men in secret thoughts. The words that follow quite beautifully continue with the analogy of the asps, for while enticing tunes are played to them they continually threaten death; in the same way the mouth of the Jews was full of cursing and bitterness, when instead of giving useful advice to each other they blasphemed the Lord Christ and discussed His death.

Their feet are swift to shed blood. Feet denotes progress in plans by which we proceed from inception to outcome. As for *swift*, it shows that their plans lacked moderation. *To shed blood:* understand this of the Lord Saviour, so that the monstrosity of the deed grows with the speed of the operation. So when the blood of the spotless Lamb was shed by the Jews, it rendered them most guilty, but when it reached us it consecrated us for blessedness.

Contrition and unhappiness in their ways: and the way of peace they have not known. The way of the wicked is well described as *contrition*, for it both rubs and is rubbed. *Unhappiness* is cited because only illomened punishments are attained by this path. Yet a man can walk the way of sinners and still return to the path of justice; but the psalmist says that they are not freed by any conversion when he comments: *The way of peace they have not known,* for they have totally failed to deserve to apprehend the Lord himself, who is the Way of peace, since they are blinded in heart.

There is no fear of God before their eyes. To the preceding points is subjoined a judgment to round off the discussion splendidly. They did such dreadful deeds because they had *no fear of God before their eyes.* As Paul says of them: *For if they had known, they would never have crucified the God of glory.*[13] In this sense we truly say that the God of glory was crucified, though we know that He was slain only in His fleshly and not in His divine nature.

4–5. *Shall not all they know that work iniquity, who devour my people as they eat bread? They have not called upon the Lord.* Holy Church, whose voice speaks in the psalm, passes to the second section in which she threatens all wicked men with God's judgment. She says that those who now freely do evil acknowledge their punishment at that general retribution. The order of words is: *Shall not all they know who work iniquity,* and from the following verse we must attach the words: *For God is in the just generation. They shall know* refers specifically to the future judgment, when they see the divine invitation to good men to enjoy eternal rewards, but themselves led to never-ending punishments. *Who devour my people:* she speaks of those who devour simple Christians by savage teaching. *As they eat bread* seems appropriate to the purpose of sinners. Just as hungry people believe that their hunger is sated by the most succulent food of bread, so these men hasten to be filled by deceiving Christians. Appended is the reason why their death is deepened, because they were unwilling to call upon the Lord. Those who with arrogance of mind refused to call on the Lord Saviour had to do desperate deeds.

There they have trembled for fear where there was no fear. For God is in the just generation. Just as fear at the fitting time is prudence, so it is certainly a species of madness to be troubled by some groundless panic. In the first case it is clearly caution, but in the second cowardice is always condemned. So it was right that those who expelled from their minds the fear of the Lord, which is salutary in this world, were shaken with groundless trembling. The Jews said: If we believe in Him, the Romans because of this new cult will take away our place and nation.[14] So it happened that through not fearing the Lord they were afflicted by superfluous apprehensions. She added: *For God is in the just generation.* This assertion followed to correct the unfaithful to enable them to remember that the Godhead is not present in them when they view themselves rising in empty prosperity. All this is foretold with devoted mind so that the sacrilegious purpose of the wicked may be corrected.

6. *You have confounded the counsel of the poor man, since the Lord is his hope.* The attack is directed at the Jewish people, who are told in riddles: *You have confounded the counsel* of Christ, in other words, you would not receive Him who had come to free you, so that He who had arranged to bestow salvation on those who believe in Him, imparts vengeance when He is spurned. *The poor man* represents the Lord Saviour, who though rich in Himself became poor for us. We must read the whole of this verse with wonder: *You have confounded the counsel of the poor man since the Lord is his hope.* Where He ought to have been an object of greater reverence, He was seen instead to be spurned and to suffer insults. It should not trouble you that God from the viewpoint of His assumed humanity is called the hope of His holy incarnation; the humility of His humanity, which He assumed for men's salvation, could not be indicated in any other way. Similarly He is to say in another psalm: *O God, my God, look upon me: why hast thou forsaken me?*[5]

7. *Who shall give out of Sion the salvation of Israel, while the Lord turns away the captivity of his people?* After holy Church has spoken about the Lord's coming, she now turns to wonder at this great kindness with the words: *Who shall give out of Sion the salvation of Israel?* When she asks, *Who?* she wishes us to understand none save the Lord Father, who deigned to send and provide the Lord Christ for Sion, that is, Jerusalem. He is indeed the salvation of Israel, the eternal salvation and boundless safety of all good believers. There follows: *While the Lord turns away the captivity of his people,* that is, when He has condemned the devil, who with wicked cruelty persecutes and strives to enslave God's people.

Let Jacob be glad, and Israel rejoice. To the earlier questions is appended a consoling reply: *Let Jacob be glad,* signifying the people of Jews and Gentiles now gathered or soon to be gathered through the gift of grace, but at one time wandering away through their infidelity; for *Jacob* must be understood here as the ancient people of the Jews, though his name has apparently been allotted after the manner of the

Scriptures to the new people as well in later times. But *Israel* was properly understood as the universal Church gathered from all parts of the world. It must inevitably rejoice when through the Lord's pity it attains the kingdom of heaven. Observe how apt words have been assigned to the different cases: Jacob will be glad because he has gained a healing beyond his hopes; Israel will rejoice, in other words, will be filled with indescribable joy, when he sees in actuality what he longed for most ardently in hope.

Conclusion Drawn From the Psalm

If we meditate on the words with devoted minds, the virtue preached to us in this psalm is that as far as we can we should with kindly hearts consult the interests of our enemies, so that they do not harden in blind obstinacy and be subject to ineluctable error. The Church rebukes a sinning people, urging them not to hasten to their own destruction; thus they can abandon their wickedness and cast off the vices which can cause them wholly to perish. So let us also as best we can follow this plan so worthy of respect. Let us urge on heretics the true faith, let us preach to the proud holy humility. If we deserve to be helpful to such people, we bestow these qualities rather on ourselves. We must realise that this is the first of the psalms composed for the reproach and conversion of Jews. On the number of this psalm, this speculation we do not consider foolish: holy Church, introduced as spokeswoman, takes in both the Pentateuch of Moses and the eight days' mysteries for the Lord's resurrection.[16] So she seems rightly to embrace the number thirteen because she grasps the mysteries of Old and New Testaments. Alternatively, the number can be ascribed to the fact that there are known to have been thirteen days from the Lord's birth to His epiphany. So the calculation is rightly the outcome of things heavenly.

COMMENTARY ON PSALM 14

1. *Unto the end. A psalm of David.* Since this heading regularly directs us back to the Lord, and there is nothing new for us to say

about its words, let us rather investigate the most appropriate features of the psalm. It is not, like some of the psalms, wrapped, so to say, in profundity, but the Lord replies to the prophet's questioning following the mode of the decalogue, saying that one reaches the hall of His blessedness through ten virtues. Do not look for these in individual verses, for they are grouped in ones, twos and threes in each and every minor verse. We shall advise you at the appropriate places how they are to be distinguished and understood. Observe that this is the second psalm which instructs the faithful. In the first the psalmist defined the blessed man in a fivefold division with the words: *Who hath not walked in the counsel of the ungodly, nor stood in the way of sinners, nor sat in the chair of pestilence: but his will has been in the law of the Lord, and on his law he shall meditate day and night.*[1] In this psalm, however, he says that such a man excels in ten holy virtues. So the power of the Pentateuch is shown in the first psalm, and that of the decalogue here.

Division of the Psalm

The division of this psalm is seen to consist solely of question and answer, but the question takes one short verse, while the answer is contained in six verses. Now let us pass to explanation of the words.

Explanation of the Psalm

Lord, who shall dwell in thy tabernacle? Or who shall rest in thy holy hill? The prophet longs to know whom the Lord has judged worthy of the Church, and like a devoted priest standing before Him, he seeks a reply and desires to be informed about his query. This figure is called *erotēma*,[2] when an apt reply is given to a questioner. He asks who could dwell in His tabernacle. We must ponder rather more carefully why *tabernacle* is used. Our ancestors called poor people's homes taverns (*tabernae*) because they were not yet tiled, and roofed only with beams (*trabes*), and were so to say *trabernae*. Because they dwelt and dined in them—it was the custom of the ancients to take food only once in the day—one word was developed, so it is said, from the two words, *traberna* and *cenaculum* (dining-room), to form *trabernaculum*. From this the euphonious form *tabernaculum* emerged;[3] we mean by it *ad hoc* dwellings erected on expeditions. Now in the Old Testament the Lord ordered a tabernacle to be made for Him when the people of Israel were in camp, so that in this way a house of God could be moved along with the Hebrews' abodes. So it happened that the Catholic faith which has been spread through the Churches all over the world is called God's tabernacle. Josephus, in the seventh chapter of the third book of his *Antiquities,* has described it in careful narrative, and we have had it painted and placed at the beginning of our larger Pandect.[4] *The holy hill* means the Jerusalem to come. Note how splendidly suitable words distinguish different senses: *Who dwells in thy tabernacle?* refers to the person still struggling in the contest of this world; *Who rests on the hill?* refers to any of the faithful who after this world's toils are renewed by the calm of eternal peace.

2. *He that walketh without blemish.* He comes to the second part, from which issue replies as from an oracular sanctuary. The words are spoken from the mouth of the Lord Christ, both to satisfy the questioner's longing and to reveal the venerable secret of His incarnation; for His own initial glory was to enter the tabernacle *without blemish,* when He entered the temple at Jerusalem free from sins. Whereas others had entered the house of God for purification, He was the only One to enter in such a way as to stand before the Father's face without blemish. So the law did not bestow anything upon Him, but as the best Legislator He fulfilled the law.

And worketh justice. This is the second virtue which the Lord manifested, when He cast the buyers and sellers from the synagogue, and forbade men to trade in God's temple. He says *My house shall be called the house of prayer, but you have made it a den of thieves.*[5]

3. *He that speaketh truth in his heart.* The third virtue is that fulfilled by our Saviour in a unique way. *Truth* is that which happens or has happened or is shown as going to happen in no way other than is asserted. He spoke truth in His heart silently when He did not reveal the mysteries of His words to those who craftily questioned Him. When hard-pressed by the Jews' falsehoods and by the chief priest's words, to the surprise of all He answered him not a word,[6] but spoke within His holy consciousness the words which those who were seen falsely to question Him did not deserve to hear.

And hath not used deceit with his tongue. He passes to the fourth virtue. He attests in the gospel that He was without guile in all He said by the words: *Whatsoever I have heard from my Father I have made known to you.*[7] What could be more pure and simple than that the unchangeable truth should pass to men's ears untainted by any addition or suppression in its unadulterated integrity?

Nor hath done evil to his neighbour. He embarked on the fifth virtue, again demonstrated in the Lord: He not only harmed no man but also endured all things patiently. *Neighbour* denoted the Jewish people from whom He derived His physical origin, and for whom He prayed even when fixed to the cross, with the words: *Father forgive them, for they know not what they do.*[8] You observe that no evil was done to His neighbour, for even His prayer was that they be forgiven.

Nor hath taken up a reproach against his neighbour. This is the sixth virtue, a pointer to Judas Iscariot. Though He knew that He was to be betrayed by him, He refrained from embarrassing him with a public rebuke, contenting Himself with the general statement: *He that dippeth his hand with me in the dish, he will betray me.*[9] So it came about that He did not hide the power of His divinity from those with understanding, yet He did not revile the reputation of His neighbour with a savage wound. *Nor hath taken up* means He did not welcome it. If we take something up, we say what we show is welcome.

4. *In his sight the malignant is brought to nothing, but they that fear the Lord magnify him.* This is the seventh response, in which He brought the malignant devil to nothing in His sight when He said to him: *Get thee behind, Satan; thou shalt not tempt the Lord thy God.*[10] To whom else can this be appropriate save Him who is known to govern all spirits by His power? There follows the splendid addition of the second part. Just as *In his sight the malignant is brought to nothing,* so *They that fear the Lord magnify him* always with pure hearts. This figure is called *paradeigma,* as we have already remarked at Psalm 1.[11] It entices us with success, and deters us with adversity.

He that sweareth to his neighbour and deceiveth him not. The eighth virtue is enunciated. The Lord embodies this when He made the promise to the apostles with most indubitable truth: *You are my friends if you do the things that I command you. I do not now call you servants.*[12] But let us examine what this statement says at its beginning: *He that sweareth to his neighbour.* Swearing in human terms means promising something by calling God to witness. But when God Himself also makes the promise, it is more appropriate to say that the swearing lay in His promising, for *iurare* (swearing) is actually *iure orare* (pleading rightly),[13] that is, speaking justly. Now a person speaks justly when what he promises is fulfilled. God's swearing, then, means promising and fulfilling. As He says elsewhere: *The Lord hath sworn truth to David, and he will not deceive him.*[14] And again: *The oath which he swore to Abraham our father.*[15] You will find this often in the divine reading.

5. *He that hath not put his money out to usury.* The ninth virtue is touched on, and we must ponder it more carefully. In the holy Scriptures money is clearly understood in two senses. One is the metal money which we are absolutely forbidden to put out to usury, because it is the vice of greed to seek to demand what you know you have not lent. The Lord Christ had this money, and He gave it to Judas to be paid out to the poor. This He has not put out to usury, since with devoted generosity He donated it to the poor for our instruction. The other kind is that which we are persuaded through the gospel-teaching to put out to usury, namely most holy preaching and divine teaching. He says: *Thou knowest that I am a hard and unbending man. Surely thou oughtest to have committed my money to the bankers; and at my coming I ought to have received at any rate what is my own with usury.*[16] So this ambivalent word is interpreted according to the nature of the passage.

Nor taken gifts over the innocent. The remaining virtue, the tenth, is fulfilled. Here *over the innocent* has the meaning of against the innocent. Not only is it certain that the Lord did not do this; He is known also to have offered Himself for the salvation of all; as He says in the gospel: *The good shepherd giveth his life for his sheep.*[17] He took gifts from the Magi, but not against the innocents;[18] every day He accepts offerings on the sacred altars, but not against the innocent. So let us realise that pious and small offerings made in the zeal of charity are not to be wholly spurned. If He had wished every gift to be rejected, He would certainly not have added the words: *against the innocent.*

He that doeth these things shall not be moved for ever. Having outlined the ten virtues not inaptly attributed to the Lord Christ Jesus, He briefly offers a general reply to the prophet's question. He that does these things dwells in the Lord's tabernacle and rests in His holy hill.

Note that He says *doeth*, not singeth. He wished to attach us to the active virtue by giving prominence to the law, so that we might not merely hymn emptily the secrets of the great mystery, concentrating solely on singing. *Shall not be moved:* in other words not moved from Him, a privilege granted only to the saints and the blessed. Every impious man will be removed from Him for ever, since He will be deprived of a sharing in His kingdom. This figure is called *zeugma* or joining,[19] when a number of dependent statements are enclosed with a single verb or expression. Here it is with an expression; when it occurs with a verb I shall not pass over it in silence.

Conclusion Drawn From the Psalm

This is the great divine decalogue, the spiritual psaltery of ten chords. Here is the truly crowning number which only He could fulfil who with His Father laid low the sins of the world. Let us continually pray to His omnipotence that we who cannot of ourselves perform such acts as are enjoined on us may do them by being enriched with His gift. Meditation on the number too should not be skimped, for the arrival of the Lord Saviour shone forth in the fourteenth generation after the transmigration from Babylon. Thus He who deigned to come in the generation bearing this number seems rightly to have spoken in this psalm.

COMMENTARY ON PSALM 15

1. *The inscription of the heading: they themselves to David.*[1] All the inscribed headings attached to the beginnings of psalms are dedications, but this has a mystical connotation, and is reckoned to be the first to contain this in a special way. We recall that when the Lord suffered, this inscription was framed over His head: *Jesus of Nazareth, King of the Jews.*[2] *They themselves* are to be understood as the Jews who serve Christ with pure devotion. Because our Saviour-King is to speak of His passion and resurrection, mention is rightly made of this inscription which was to appear through the Lord's dispensation so

many centuries later. To help you realise that this inscribed heading must have referred to the Lord Christ, the words: *They themselves to David* were added. We have explained in several places[3] that David aptly signifies the Lord Saviour. We should realise that this is the second psalm[4] to touch briefly on the Lord's passion and resurrection.

Division of the Psalm

The person of the Lord Saviour is introduced throughout the psalm. In the first theme, in accord with His acceptance of human form, He addresses the Father to ask to be saved, because He has always put His hope in Him. By this He does not in any sense lessen His divinity, but reflects the nature of His humanity (by nature I means the source and strength of the substance of anything). He further adds how His saints are chosen not through desires of the flesh but by spiritual virtues, and claims that all His sufferings have been directed towards the glory of His inheritance. In His second theme He gives thanks to the Father, who by appearing at His right hand has by the power of His omnipotence overcome the wickedness of this world. He maintains that because of this His soul has been freed from hell, and He recounts that after the glory of the resurrection He has been set among the delights at His right hand.

Explanation of the Psalm

Preserve me, O Lord, for I have put my trust in thee. Since He is to come among human dangers and the wicked attitudes of Jewish obduracy, He prays that once He has taken on human nature He may be preserved by His Father's protection. So that the result of this prayer may follow more easily, He says that He has always put His trust in the Lord. This figure is known as *ethopoeia,*[5] when the words of an individual are given; here it is the Lord Saviour, the enduring Christ with two distinct and perfect natures, man and the one God.

2. *I have said to the Lord: Thou art my God, for thou hast no need of my goods.* He has *said* not with the lips but with the heart's feeling, so it was His holy conscience that spoke. *Thou art my God:* the Son speaks to the Father in the role of servant, so that we may realise clearly that

in the one person of the Lord there are two natures, the one lowly matching our weakness, the other wonderful in accord with His power. Hence you can grasp that it was in the flesh that He suffered and rose again by virtue of His most powerful majesty. Then, to destroy the pride of the human race, which is sure that it can achieve some good by its own strength, He added: *For thou hast no need of my goods.* Let the Pelagians[6] hear this, for they think that certain goods are to be attained by their own powers. With the words of His humanity He cries that God has no need whatsoever of His goods, and He attributes all things to Him who has bestowed them, and not to himself who received what was bestowed.

3. *To the saints who are in his land he hath made wonderful all my desires amongst them.* First we must arrange the word-order so that by removing obscurity of expression the meaning may shine out more easily. *To the saints who are in his land he*—the Father—*has made wonderful all my desires.* To enable you to realise that the Lord Christ is to be loved by His chosen ones, He added: *Amongst them,* meaning the holy men who are in the land of the living; not among any who boast in the ambition of the world, but only among those predestined for the kingdom of heaven.[7] He means the innocent and just, among whom the Lord Saviour's desires were made wonderful when He made eternal the mortals who were obedient and who did His just works. Through the kindness of His devotion, he made them heavenly from being earthly.

4. *For their infirmities were multiplied: afterwards they made haste. I will not gather together their meetings for blood-offerings.* He refers to the holy men who under the Lord's eye were freed from the beguiling pleasure of the world through most salutary affliction. Earlier they experienced a multiplication of the weaknesses of the flesh through the harshness of the law, so that they might with greater longing attain the liberating grace of the New Testament. He says that these saints were not to be gathered at the bloodshed of cattle or at the ritual slaughter of victims, but at the sacrifice of His body and blood which is celebrated over the whole world and has saved the human race. The expression, *blood-offerings,* refers to the blood of cattle shed in profusion at sacrifices at that time. Later when the Lord Christ came this

custom was changed. The expression, *de sanguinibus* (*for blood-offer-ings*), contravenes the grammatical rule by which the plural of this word is not used. We must accordingly number this among the idioms peculiar to divine Scripture.

Nor will I be mindful of their names by my lips. He says that the ancient names possessed by infidels were altered by the grace that ensued. Earlier they were called sons of anger, sons of the devil, sons of the flesh, but after the coming of the Lord they were reborn by the sacred waters and called Christians, sons of God, friends of the Bride-groom. So He was not *mindful of their names,* since as we know new names were bestowed on these new men. We must interpret Christ the King's lips here as the two Testaments by which we know His wishes were declared. The term *lips* is apt for them because both proclaim God's kingdom, and they harmonise with one sound just as lips are controlled when mindful of the heart's instruction. He says here: *Nor will I be mindful of their names by my lips:* we must take this as an expression peculiar to divine Scripture, as has already been stated in the cases of Psalms 7 and 10.[8]

5. *The Lord is the portion of my inheritance and of my cup: it is thou that wilt restore my inheritance to me.* It was truly a blessed thought to choose the supervision which He knows never experiences any change. It is as if He were to say: "Let others choose for themselves worldly desires and a life like scurrying winds; *the Lord is the portion of my inheritance and of my cup.*" Inheritance denotes genuine member-ship of a family, the cup His revered passion, which when drunk with sobriety bestows the most glorious resurrection. One should note that the desire for and distribution of the Lord is often termed the cup. Cup (*calix*) is so called from a hot (*calidus*) drink,[9] for just as a hot drink when quaffed makes the heart glad, so the cup when drunk continually delights souls that are holy. *It is thou . . .:* here the Son preserves love's obedience; though not inferior in divinity, yet subject in humanity, He addresses these words to the Father. As the apostle says: *Whereas indeed he was the son of God, he learned obedience by the things which he suffered, and being consummated he became to all that obey him the cause of eternal salvation.*[10] *Thou wilt restore* is said because the human race had perished through the action of the devil, and there

is in truth restored to Him His inheritance bestowed on Him by predestination before the world existed. Inheritance (*hereditas*) is from *herus*, a master, in other words, appointed by a lord.

6. *The lines are fallen unto me in goodly places: for my inheritance is goodly to me.* After the ancient fashion, an inheritance was meted out by lines on the earth, so that an individual could obtain an amount of land by measurement, in accordance with the amount bestowed and the person's status. So in the Old Testament Moses is said to have ordered Joshua to distribute the land-inheritance to Israel's sons of promise by means of lines." So He now aptly used the word *lines*, because He was relating the breadth and glory of His inheritance. *Lines* can be interpreted also as the winding sorrows of this world, for *funes* (lines) derives from *funera* (deaths),[12] because they were burned like wax candles before corpses. Undoubtedly the sorrows were transformed to become goodly when they attained the eternal rewards of the resurrection. The inheritance of Christ is the predestined multitude of saints. The words: *Unto me* are added here because He glories not in himself as man but in the Father. But when He uses the word *goodly*, it is reasonable to ask why he says that such an inheritance has *fallen* to Him, for the word fallen is usually employed for adverse situations. But the divine eloquence uses it also in cases of good fortune. In the Acts of the Apostles it says: *The lot fell on Matthias*[13] precisely when the description is of the honour of becoming an apostle by God's choice.

7. *I will bless the Lord who hath given me understanding: moreover my reins also have rebuked me until the night.* We have come to the second section, in which the sacred preaching is to be understood more subtly: with what great foresight already at this time He debarred the heresies to come, so that the Lord's flesh pronounced that understanding was conferred on it by the Lord, the understanding, that is, by which it discerned everything true and holy. So human weakness could not bestow anything on itself, for what could bring benefit to it was afforded not by any earlier merits but by the generous gift of grace. Next comes: *My reins have rebuked me*, as if He were saying: "Over and above the evils which the whole kindred of the Jews inflicted on me, those of the tribe of Judah"—from which the Lord

Christ is known to have had physical descent—"are seen to have rebuked me." *Until the night* means until death. *Reins* indicates the relationship by which the seed of human generation is regularly sown.

8. *I set the Lord always in my sight; for he is at my right hand, that I be not moved.* By explaining His action, He passes on to the unique remedy by which to avoid sins, for the person who with mental eye always gazes on the Lord in no way turns towards sins. So when truth dwells in the mind, it chastises the entry of falsehood. He mentions also the reason why He is not moved: since the Lord helps at His right hand, evils on the left do not prevail, but with total constancy He continues in the purpose which the Lord protects. It was fitting for Him to speak of the Lord as being at His right hand, for if the Lord does not occupy that place the devil will at once seize it for ambush. As was written of Judas, *Set thou the sinner over him, and let the devil stand at his right hand.*[14]

9. *Therefore my heart hath been glad, and my tongue hath rejoiced: moreover my flesh also shall rest in hope.* *Therefore* implies because the Lord has stood at His right hand, and He testifies that delight has arisen in His thoughts and joy on His tongue. Perfect joy is that which is both conceived in a joyful heart and brought forth in eager speech. Just as He used the word *moreover* of His evils,[15] so He repeated the word of His blessings, so that humanity might be thought to have received heavenly joys according to the measure of His human troubles. For He says that His joy has welled over His gladness because the suffering flesh which He took up for the salvation of all of us has merited the truth of the glorious resurrection without suffering corruption. This figure is called *aetiologia*[16] or explanation of a cause, when the proper reason for something previously mentioned is appended.

10. *Because thou wilt not leave my soul in hell: nor wilt thou give thy holy one to see corruption.* Where are the misguided Apollinarians who say that the Lord Christ had not a rational soul?[17] See how He himself cries out and gives thanks to the Father because His soul is not in the usual way left abandoned in hell, but is glorified by swift resurrection, and has passed to the kingdom of heaven. This is attested in the gospel in various passages: *My soul is sorrowful even unto death,*[18] and else-

where: *I have the power of laying down my life and of taking it up again.*[19]
You must not think that this is to be accepted complacently, because
you find in Psalm 29 what seems to be the opposite view: *What profit is
there in my blood, whilst I go down to corruption?*[20] The objection is
resolved by this reasoning: in that passage He says that He goes down
to corruption when pierced by the impact of the impressed nails and
lance, for transfixion of solid flesh is reasonably accounted corruption. But in the present passage He says justly that the corruption of
putrefaction which ravages the generality of human flesh does not
take place, for when on the third day it happened that His flesh was
given fresh life, it was demonstrated that it could not have suffered
corruption.

11. *Thou hast made known to me the ways of life: thou shalt fill me to
the brim with joy with thy countenance: at thy right hand are delights
even to the end.* When He had completed all He had to say on the
sanctity of His body, this verse, which is appropriate also to the just
who choose to obey His commands, introduces the conclusion. *Thou
hast made known to me the ways of life,* in other words, "Through Me
You have brought the human race to a knowledge of the path of life, so
that by walking humbly in Your commandments they might avoid the
poison of deadly pride." *Thou shalt fill me to the brim,* that is, quite full.
Filling to the brim is adding to fullness, and he who does so pours into
a vessel already full. That joy fills in such a way that it is all preserved
for ever. The verse also shows that all just men in that blessed state
will be filled with the joy of the Lord's presence, and He attests that
He can be filled among them because He is the Lord. But let us
examine a little more carefully why He says here that He will be filled
with delights at the right hand of the Father, whereas earlier He said:
For he is at my right hand, that I be not moved. The fact is that in this
world, in which He suffered scourgings in the flesh which He assumed, was struck with slaps, and was spattered with spittle yet defeated by none of its hardships, it was fitting to say that the Lord was
always seen at His right hand. He overcame the opposition of the
world because He moved not an inch from contemplation of the Father. There He has now laid aside the hardships of this world; and His
humanity is filled with the glorification of His whole majesty and
rules united to the Word with the Father and the holy Spirit for ever.

Even to the end signifies perfection and eternity, for His glory abides in its perfection, and will be limited by no season.

Conclusion Drawn From the Psalm

Let us meditate on the immensity of the gift of salvation which this psalm offers for our instruction. It gives us confidence in sufferings and promises eternal glory in hope, so that through this teaching of our future happiness we do not fear the hardships of the present. This is heavenly schooling, learning for life, the lecture-hall of truth, and most indubitably a unique discipline which occupies its pupils with thoughts that bear fruit, not with the flattery of empty words. It is appropriate also to examine the significance of the number fifteen; in our opinion it denotes the fifteen steps by which one mounted the wonderful dimensions of the temple at Jerusalem, thus demonstrating that when we overcome the five bodily senses through the grace of the Trinity,[21] we attain by this blessed gift the basilica of holy Church. This gift will be granted also by this psalm, if with the Lord's protection we hug close His most salutary preaching.

COMMENTARY ON PSALM 16

1. *The prayer of David.* Since many of the psalms contain prayers within their texture, this appears to raise the question why the psalmist set this heading here. But whereas other psalms contain brief prayers for help mingled with various topics, this is a supplication through virtually the whole of its composition. Hence it is rightly designated as such beforehand, since its purpose is wholly directed towards zeal for prayer; but it must be termed *prayer* while still preserving the name of psalm, for we find nothing in this book undeserving of this title, especially as we read it as a book of psalms. The word *prayer* is used in two senses. When delivered among men, it is called *oris ratio*,[1] "reasoning of the mouth"; but when poured out to the Majesty, it is salutary supplication and life-giving humility. Note that

this psalm, together with Psalms 85, 89, 101, 141, is prefaced with the title *prayer*. We shall conveniently state the distinctions between, and peculiarities of, these at the last of them, Psalm 141. *David*, as has been said, signifies the Lord Christ, by whose voice the whole psalm is uttered for the instruction of the human race.

Division of the Psalm

A threefold prayer from the humanity of Christ emerges in this psalm. The first part is when He prays that He be treated according to His justice, the second is that His purity be freed from the treachery of the Jews, and in the third He prays for a most swift resurrection, so that the perverted Jewish people could not continue to insult Him. Then, so that the crowd of the faithful might have no doubt of His majesty, He proclaims that He will abide in eternal blessedness.

Explanation of the Psalm

Hear, O God, my justice: look to my supplication. It is certain that justice has a voice before God, who knows things unspoken through the power of His understanding. His prayer is perfect, for His cause and tongue, His deeds and words, His life and thoughts cry out: *Look to my supplication.* It is not for nothing that these words are attached to the sense organ with which they do not harmonise, looking being a function of the eyes, whereas hearing prayers is the task of the ears. But these words are joined so that the single outcome of both may be grasped: for whatever the ear hears, the eye sees, the hand strokes, the palate tastes, or the nose smells, is wholly known to God solely by the power of His contemplation.

Give ear unto my prayer, which proceedeth not from deceitful lips. He refines on His earlier words, for giving ear means not momentary attention to something, but listening to men's prayers with the most expansive indulgence. *Not from deceitful lips,* like the lying statement emanating from the Jews, among whom He was condemned when innocent, and a thief, as we know, was acquitted.

2. *Let my judgment come forth from thy countenance: let my eyes behold justice. Let judgment come forth from thy countenance* is an ex-

pression peculiar to divine Scripture and unfamiliar to us, for a judgment usually emanates from the mind. But it is aptly applied to the
Lord in metaphor, for He sees what He judges as witness of His
scrutiny; he does not seek testimony from another's action, for He
alone knows most truly all men's secrets. *From thy countenance* therefore signifies: "From Your look in accord with what You see and
know in me." Christ rightly prayed for this, knowing that He had no
pollution of sin. Next comes: *Let my eyes behold justice*. We must
interpret justice here as the Godhead; He prays that He may ever
discern it without delay so that by training His eye on it in its true
appearance He may have no stain of sin. The words in the previous
psalm were similar: *I set the Lord always in my sight: for he is at my right
hand, that I be not moved.*[2] What a saving gaze, what wholly clear eyes
that behold that justice! They can certainly not be blinded by the
darkness of this world, since they deserve to be filled with such great
brightness.

3–4. *Thou hast proved my heart, and visited it by night, thou hast tried
me by fire: and iniquity has not been found in me, though my mouth
speaks no word.*[3] He maintains a splendid order. First He says He was
proved, then *visited*. The proving points to the passion, the visiting to
the resurrection. He was proved when He displayed proofs of marvellous patience among the Jews' wickednesses and among mortal
hazards. He was visited by night when His soul was not abandoned in
hell, but attained that marvellous resurrection with the brightness of
eternal glory. *Thou hast tried me by fire, and iniquity hath not been
found in me.* Here is introduced the metaphor of furnaces blazing with
fire, which regularly cure faults in metals which they take in and
devour, and restore them when cleansed to their natural purity. Similarly the Lord Christ was tried by fiery hardships, but no iniquity was
found in Him for any burning to melt off. He then added the fine
words: *Though my mouth speaks no word,* in other words, "even if I
were silent, you judge me pure." What need was there for Him to say
anything of the worth of His manners, when it is certain that all things
are known by the Father's majesty? Men's ignorance is to be instructed by words, but the Godhead knows all things with utter certainty, even when what has been done is unspoken.

*The works of men: for the sake of the words of thy lips I have kept hard
ways.* This section of the verse requires the word-order "The works

of men, that is, hard ways, have I kept for the sake of the words of thy lips." *The works of men* are briefly defined as *hard ways*. As the blessed Job says: *The bird is born to fly, and man to labour.*[4] The path of avoidance of sins is hard, and the ascent is always difficult, whereas when we slip towards vices, it is an easy downhill path. But the Lord Christ, set before men's eyes in this world, demonstrated the canons of total meekness and self-discipline, so He rightly says that by reason of the Lord's commands He has walked with spotless feet on the hard ways of men. It is not that they could be hard for Him, for Psalm 90 declares: *For he hath given his angels charge over thee, to keep thee in all thy ways, lest thou ever dash thy foot against a stone.*[5] But they are called hard ways because they are known to be hard for the human race to imitate. This verse contains the figure of *parenthesis*[6] or insertion, for in the middle of the sentence, as has been remarked, words are inserted which seem to disconnect the flow of the sentence.

5. *Perfect thou my goings in thy paths: that my footsteps be not moved.* *Perfect* has the sense of "preserve to the end," when merits and reward are wholly complete. Our beginning is when we live in this world in commendable association with each other, but when our dutiful observance reaches its end we are then perfected, wholly fulfilled and entire. As the gospel says: *He that shall persevere unto the end shall be saved.*[7] *Goings* means the human actions by which we proceed in this world, stepping out, so to say. *In the paths,* that is, 'in Your commandments'; these are the truly right ways, and if we follow them as dedicated people we attain the rewards of our heavenly land. But why does He mention paths first, and at once add *footsteps?* By paths we signify the means of passage from one place to another. Human acts are aptly compared with these, for they lead us from one business to another, transporting us through life's stages which differ in their nature. *Footsteps* signifies the marks of our soles which we leave behind as we pass along. So the Lord Christ asks for protection for both his *goings,* or human actions, and his *footsteps,* which we can fittingly interpret as the faithful apostles[8] in whom after His glorious ascension He left the marks of the Catholic religion. So the meaning is of this kind: "Guard me by Your commandments, so that those who imitate me may be dislodged by not so much as a fraction from You." He

follows faithfully in the footsteps of Him who shows the example and walks straight.

6. *I have cried, for thou, O God, hast heard me: O incline thy ear unto me, and hear my words.* He commences the second section of His holy prayer. But we must examine why, whereas the usual formula is: "Thou hast heard me because I cried," this sentence seems to have the reverse order. He who cries is acknowledged as especially pure, innocent, and spotless, because He is heard. He prayed with confidence because He presumed that He could be heard by reason of the purity of His conscience. Let us realise that He says: *Incline thy ear,* since human weakness cannot approach the Father by its own power. The Father hears when He mercifully shows His indulgence, and bestows His clemency beforehand so as to receive the prayers of suppliants.

7–8. *Make wonderful thy mercies: thou who savest them that hope in thee from them that resist thy right hand.* He prays that the greatness and outstanding nature of His mercies should justly develop within himself, for it could not arouse wonder unless observed in some new guise. He refers to the wonders which He was to perform in the flesh, and which the Jewish people regarded with astonishment though they did not all believe. *Thou savest them that hope in thee,* that is, "You will set them in eternal life," for often those who believed in His name were slain in this world and not saved. His phrase: *From them that resist thy right hand,* is splendid, for the right hand of the Father is the Son, whom the Jews tried to resist when they voted to crucify Him.

Keep me, O Lord, as the pupil of thy eye. Protect me under the shadow of thy wings. By the figure of *icon,*[9] in Latin *imaginatio,* the Lord compared himself with the pupil of an eye, the pupil being the conspicuous part of the eye set at the centre which enables us to distinguish the colours of objects of different kinds. It is called a pupil (*pupilla*) because it is small (*pusilla*).[10] The comparison of Christ with it was apt, for His allotted task at His judgment is to separate the just from sinners; hence it is most fitting for Him to be guarded as the pupil of an eye, for it is through the pupil that we discern visible objects, and no more excellent faculty is found in our bodies. There follows: *Protect me under the shadow of thy wings.* Another figure is introduced here, in Greek *parabole*[11] and in Latin *comparatio,* when things dissimilar in kind are joined in some relationship; for the Father's protection is compared with wings. Mercy and love are, as it were, the Father's wings by which He fittingly demands to be protected. The comparison derives from birds, which guard their dear brood by spreading out their wings.

9. *By the face of the wicked, who have afflicted me, my enemies have surrounded my soul.* This verse is to be examined with rather greater care. *By the face of the wicked* refers to the demons who roused and drove the Jewish people with headlong passion to murder the Lord. Their *face* was their harsh presence. As the gospel says with reference to Judas: *Satan entered into him.*[12] So it happened that the Jews had sought to snatch away His soul, that is, His life in time, through the instigation of demons. The word *surrounded* itself expresses the truth of the gospel narrative, for a crowd of madmen encompassed him with swords and clubs.

10. *They have enclosed their fat: their mouth hath spoken proudly.* People enclose their fat when they grow stout from gluttony; in the same way the Jews were fattened with excess of wickedness, and forfeited the sharpness of true understanding. It remained that those swollen with this obscenely fat wickedness should speak proud words. He well remarked that they spoke only from the mouth not the heart, for it is the tendency of the wicked often to defend with words actions which they are known to condemn when conscience is their witness.

11. *They have cast me forth, and now they have surrounded me: they have set their eyes bowing down to the earth. Cast forth,* in other words, expelled from the city. *Now they have surrounded,* not in obedience but in madness, for we know that He was nailed to the cross. *Now* designated the present for the future, as we know is common in the prophets. Next comes: *They have set their eyes bowing down to the earth,* referring to the tendency of wicked people to look down at the ground when sunk in evil thoughts.

12. *They have taken me as a lion prepared for the prey, and as a young lion dwelling in secret places. They have taken me,* that is, the Jews took Him from Pilate when he said to them: *Take him and crucify him according to your law.*[13] They greedily accepted the offer and implemented their cruel desire, so that they are rightly compared with savage beasts. We have said that *lion* is used for the devil, but is quite

often compared with Christ; this ambivalent manner of speaking is to be regarded as one of the peculiarities of divine Scripture. Here, however, it clearly denotes the devil, for the Jews' leaders are justly compared with him. Under his guidance they raged and were made much worse than he, for whereas the devil tempted the Lord, their cruel madness nailed Him to a cross. The *young lion* denotes the rest of the Jewish people who made themselves sons of the devil. Of them it is said in the gospel: *You are of your father the devil.*[14] *Dwelling in secret places* means remaining in ambush, for it is the tendency of execrable men to hide their evil aspirations so that their designs can attain their end by stealth.

13. *Arise, O Lord, disappoint them and supplant them: deliver my soul from the irreligious one, thy sword.* The third section of the blessed prayer is begun. *Arise* means "arise against sinners," so that they may know that He whom they believe to be inactive after the human fashion is awake, preventing the extension of their wickedness. *Disappoint,* that is, so that they can be overthrown before they can perpetrate their sins. In earlier psalms I have demonstrated that this meaning is well suited to the wicked when they are not permitted to involve themselves in unlawful pursuits. They too are happily overthrown who are brought back to the right path from debased vices. *Deliver my soul from the irreligious one,* none other than the devil, who is rightly called irreligious because he is always hostile to pious persons. *Deliver,* that is, cause to rise again, which clearly came to pass. *Thy sword:* the closing phrase briefly explains the nature of the Lord Saviour's soul. It is the sword of the Father, since by it He conquered the devil, and by it cleansed the world of foul superstition. By it the captivity which possessed the offspring of the human race was overcome. We have said that *framea* (sword) has many meanings:[15] at one time a club, at another a breastplate, at another a two-edged sword, but all definitely relate to the use of weapons. Remember that in this verse we have the fifth type of definition which is called in Greek *kata tēn lexin* and in Latin *ad verbum,*[16] for by this one expression He has defined the nature of Christ's soul as the Father's sword.

14. *From the enemies of thy hand, O Lord, by means of the few scatter them from the land, and supplant them in their life.* Once again the prayer refers to the Jews, who were enmeshed in the power of the

devil and were to be roused to wicked assaults. For the enemies of the Lord's hand are the devils who savage the human race, their will ever hostile to the Lord. He also prays that unbelievers may be divided by the few, that is, by the apostles; when they are separated from the wicked land of this world, they are converted to the Lord. It was by the apostles' preaching with the Lord's help that Israelites as well as Gentiles were separated from the wicked territory of this world and followed Christ as their leader. *Trip them* is here meant in the good sense, for those who condemn their sins and pass over to right ways are tripped to be accepted. The additional phrase, *in their life*, means in this world while they are alive, when there is a chance to repent, when a cry is raised to the Lord not from the lips but from the heart, when they are accepted because their entreaty was wholly unsullied.

Their belly is filled from thy hidden stores. They are filled with swine's flesh, and they have left to their little ones the rest of their substance. The hidden things of God we can aptly interpret in both a bad and a good sense. Every sin is odious to Him and foreign to His gaze, though obviously they do not in any way escape His observation. As Psalm 5 has it: *The wicked shall not dwell near thee, nor shall the just abide before thy eyes.*[17] So too Scripture says of Cain: *Cain went out from the face of the Lord, and dwelt as a fugitive on the earth.*[18] So He says that the Jews are filled with the uncleannesses which were hidden from the Lord, in other words, those which are acknowledged to be forbidden. But if you take this when you read it as meant in the good sense, as in the passage: *How great is the multitude of thy sweetness, O Lord, which thou hast hidden from them that fear thee, and which thou hast wrought for them that hope in thee,*[19] His kindnesses are being listed so that the offence of ungrateful men is shown to be the greater. *From thy stores,* that is, from the law of the Old Testament and from the miracles which the Lord Christ was to perform in them by His glorious dispensation. *Their belly* conveys their wholly fleshly feelings, in which the Lord's commands are stored as in the belly. Their feelings are well compared to the belly, for from them spiritual foods are expelled like the meanest dregs, as they slip out from those whose hearts are corrupt. But when these men were filled with heavenly things so that they ought to have admitted nothing earthly, note what follows: *They were filled with swine's flesh.* What accursed wickedness! Their minds heard God's commands, yet they were befouled by the dirt of sins, and in unprecedented fashion after being fed on heavenly blessings they were filled with the dregs of evil things. *Swine's flesh* bears the sense of things polluted and, among other precepts of the Old Testament, it is designated as impure.[20] They transmitted the rest of their sins to their children when they cried: *His blood be on us and on our children!*[21]

15. *But as for me, I will appear before thy sight with justice: I shall be filled when thy glory shall appear.* He says that He appears with justice before the sight of the Father, since He had fulfilled His will when by the shedding of His blood He saved the world from the death of sin. *I shall be filled:* this phrase is seen to be aptly repeated. Earlier He said that the Jews were filled with swine's flesh, in other words, with their uncleanness. Now He says that He is filled with the belief which the human race embraces, when the number of the saints will be filled out at the union of the blessed. The glory of the Father shall appear at the judgment held by the Lord Saviour, when each person will receive according to his deeds. As the Lord himself says to the apostles: *On that day you shall know that I am in the Father, and the Father in me.*[22] So in this way the proclamation is being announced of the one nature, the one power, the one glory of the Father, Son and holy Spirit.

Conclusion Drawn From the Psalm

Let us meditate, dearly beloved, on what great mysteries of our faith this psalm has embraced, so that he who hears this Man at prayer must note that He is to be praised also as Creator. He who chooses to believe that even today there are in the Lord Christ two uncompounded and unchangeable natures cannot be deceived by any falsehood. This is why the blessed Cyril stated in one passage, marvellously but briefly: "So if we note the manner of the incarnation, we see that two natures have come together in indivisible unity without intermingling and without the possibility of change. For flesh is flesh and not divinity, though it has become God's flesh; likewise the Word is God and not flesh, though by that dispensation He made flesh His own."[23] All this He fulfilled without sin, for He found no bonds of error in Himself. The aggregate of the prophets has adorned the number of this psalm, so that the Lord's incarnation is seen to be worthily proclaimed by this number, in which the chorus of the prophets is seen to be assembled.[24]

COMMENTARY ON PSALM 17

1. *Unto the end, a psalm of David the boy of the Lord, who spoke to the Lord the words of this canticle on the day that the Lord delivered him from the hands of all his enemies, and from the hand of Saul, and said.* . . . The three expressions, *unto the end, of David, the boy,* can undoubtedly be applied to the King our Saviour, for we read in the prophet also the word *boy: A boy is born to us.*[1] After these words what follows: *Who spoke to the Lord the words of this canticle,* are to be added so that a fuller and total context appears. *Canticle* clearly means a meditation on heavenly things, so that our gaze may not rest merely on the history of king David. *On the day that the Lord delivered him from the hands of all his enemies, and from the hand of Saul, and said.* This event is very well known from our reading of Kings,[2] where there is a more extended description of how David was freed from subjection to his enemies. In parallel to this the Lord's resurrection and the deliverance of His body from the devil's power are proclaimed.

Division of the Psalm

This psalm cannot be allotted to a single spokesman. In the first section, the prophet speaks, giving thanks because God's devotion has deigned to free him from serious dangers. In the second, the Church speaks. Before the Lord's coming she endured countless calamities, and subsequently He took pity on her. He granted her the healing of the holy incarnation, and by the gift of baptism He gathered the Christian people from the whole world. In the third part, the voice of the Saviour glides in like the dew of mercy. Here His strength and power are described with most beautiful allusions. In the fourth, the words of the Catholic Church again emerge, and the gifts of the Godhead are praised with great joy.[3]

Explanation of the Psalm

2. *I will love thee, O Lord my strength.* He loves the Lord, for he obeys His commands devotedly. As Christ says in the gospel: *He that*

heareth my commandments and keepeth them, he it is that loveth me.[4] *Diligo* (I love) derives from *de omnibus eligo* (I select from all).[5] Note that the love promised for the future is such as is seen never to have failed. *My strength:* the prophet is freed from his foes, and rightly proclaims the Lord as His strength, for by His gift he was made to appear stronger to his enemies. This is the twelfth type of definition, which Greek calls *kat'epainon* and Latin *per laudem.*[6] His proclamation announces God's nature in individual and varying words: now *strength,* now *firmament,* now *refuge,* now *deliverer,* now *helper,* now *protector,* now *horn of salvation.* All these terms beautifully denote what the Lord is.

3. *The Lord is my firmament, my refuge, and my deliverer: my God is my helper.* He justly calls the Lord his firmament, for He enabled him to stand firm in the line against his enemies, and to fight with lively spirit. *And my refuge.* Precisely so, for when he needed advice he took refuge in the Scriptures, and found what could help him through the prompting of the Godhead. He rightly proclaims the Lord as his Liberator, for He freed him from the anger of Saul the most savage king as if from the mouth of hell. *My God is my helper:* charmed by the sweetness of what has been granted him, he repeats in summary the earlier things he has said, for God was everywhere at hand, and guarded him with the protection of His strength. But note that he runs through all the epithets in such a way as not to presume that gifts have been bestowed on his own deserving merit.

And in him will I put my trust. My protector and the horn of my salvation, my helper. He now makes a trusting request, as one who after seeing examples of the Lord's kindnesses is confident of His grace, for he says that he has trusting hope for the future, having experienced the Lord as Helper in the past. *My protector* expresses his being guarded when ambuscaded by his enemies. The description of the Lord here as the horn of his salvation refers to the scattering of the enemy, for horns are beasts' weapons by which they maintain their safety in crafty contention. *My helper:* the sweetness of the kindness made him repeat the phrase, for earlier he called Him by the same word *helper,* which he repeats here.

4. *Praising, I will call upon the Lord, and I shall be saved from my enemies.* After the catalogue of His virtues, the holy man did not glorify himself with any pride, but since he had to rejoice because of

the gladness of the events themselves, he said that he was calling on the Lord with praise, and attributing everything to Him who deigned to bestow all things. And he says that he must be preserved from his enemies, because he was seen to assign his victory not to himself but to the Lord. He who does otherwise is made captive by his vices, though he is seen to have overcome the enemy.

5. *The groans of death surrounded me: and the torrents of iniquity troubled me.* After the joy which the prophet experienced with holy devotion, we come to the second section, in which is introduced a spokesman[7] for the just men who certainly existed at that time. He devotedly prays to avert the disasters of the human race. This just man rightly maintained that he was *surrounded* with *groans,* for there was a countless multitude of superstitions, whilst the devotion of the faithful was rare. Then, so that you would not think that the groans were uttered through loss of opportunity or some such, he added: *Of death,* for there was truly death where the devil's dominion reigned. *Torrents* we often use of rivers swollen by winter rains; so here the simile of torrents is applied to iniquities running swift, and thus when they roared with the din of threatening waters, they justifiably troubled the anxious people.

6. *The sorrows of hell encompassed me: the snares of death prevented me.* The words of this part of the verse should be joined in reverse order, so that the sense here can be better revealed to us. *The sorrows of hell encompassed me* is applicable to pagans who will be the sorrows of hell, or to those who are to be tortured in hell with the pain that is their due. We say that we are *prevented* when something is known to go before us, like the guilt of original sin which makes us guilty from our very conception, before we are born. So the prophet is to say in Psalm 50: *For behold, I was conceived in iniquities, and in sins did my mother bear me.*[8] The just man rightly said that he was prevented, for he knew that his guilt had preceded him. But he later explains how he was freed from these things.

7. *And in my affliction I called upon the Lord, and I cried to my God.* Among the many evils which he had recounted, he proclaims that there is one unique remedy, to call on the Lord in his afflictions, for obviously what we long for in time of need we seek with all our strength. Note that he first addressed the Lord, but so that you would not think it was some foreign lord, he added: *I cried to my God. Cried* is

stronger than *called upon;* his language intensified as his longing grew, and his spirit when fired to prayer eagerly leapt to cry out.

And he heard my voice from his holy temple: and my cry in his sight came into his ears. *Temple* we aptly interpret either as heaven or as the Lord's body which the prophet foresaw was to come. So he says that his words were heard when he continually offered them for the Lord's coming. But we must examine how his cry in God's sight could make its entry. This cry is the justice of his cause, which could enter into God precisely because he prayed on behalf of the world's calamities. The next words are: *Came into his ears.* The words are used metaphorically after our custom, for his cry came into the Lord's ears as though they were something physical, though God's senses are purely spiritual, knowing all things before they come to pass. The nature of our acts is always before Him as if before His gaze, and what is hidden from us is made clear to Him.

8. *Both the earth shook and trembled, and the foundations of the mountains were troubled, and were moved, because God was angry with them.* Having discoursed on the sadness which the blessed people were enduring as they waited for the Lord's coming, he passes with the spirit of prophecy to the secrets of His incarnation, and recounts its dispensation in a wonderful description. This figure is called an *idea,*[9] when we set before our eyes so to speak a vision of some future thing, and thus rouse our emotion. Clearly this is achieved both here and in the verses that follow. So let us now hear the mysteries of the Lord Saviour; for *the earth shook* is apt for Christ's coming, because it was right that sinners should tremble at the Judge's presence. The prophet preserved the order of events, for first he showed that the world was shaken, and then said that it trembled. *Foundations of the mountains* means the preoccupations of the arrogant, the riches, distinctions, and other human things on which they concentrate and depend as though they were enduring foundations. All these were moved because the world's false hope was removed when the true Lord came. The words progress in a most fitting sequence. First *the foundations,* the hope of the arrogant, were dislodged; then he says they were shaken. He also added the reason why the foundations were moved: *because God was angry with them,* that is, precisely because human vices are demonstrably hateful to the Lord. Subsequently it is revealed that those who pursue them will certainly be punished.

9. *There went up a smoke in his wrath, and a fire flames from his face; coals were kindled by it.* Smoke appears here in the good sense, for just as earthly smoke causes aimless tears, so the smoke fired by heat of repentance pours out fruitful streams of tears. *In his wrath,* that is, when He troubles sinners here with fear of the future judgment, to draw them towards the remedy of conversion. The *fire* is love of God, which spreads by advances in the virtues; the more it is desired, the more effectively it increases. The phrase, *from his face,* is well turned, because by its illumination love is granted to those who abandon sins. By kindled coals he means sinners, who like dead coals lie shadowed in the darkness of this world, but come to life again when repentance fires them. From being dead fuel they become living coals. Next follows how they were kindled, namely at the coming of the Lord Redeemer.

10. *And he bowed the heavens and came down: and darkness was under his feet.* A great mystery is enclosed in these words. The Word so humbled Himself as to assume, admittedly without sin, the likeness of sinning flesh. His coming down was His coming to us; in Paul's words: *He emptied himself, taking the form of a servant.*[10] *Darkness* here is the devil, who clouds men's minds, making those whom he possesses unable to see the brightness of truth. *Under his feet,* because undoubtedly the accursed wickedness of devils is trodden underfoot by the majesty of the Lord Saviour. As the prophet is to say in Psalm 90: *Thou shalt walk upon the asp and the basilisk, and thou shalt trample underfoot the lion and the dragon.*[11]

11. *And he ascended above the cherubim, and he flew: he flew upon the wings of the winds.* This figure is known as *hyperthesis* or *superlatio,*[12] when we maintain that something notable in the estimation of all is in our opinion surpassingly outstanding. For example, there is the phrase in Psalm 50: *Thou shalt wash me, and I shall be made whiter than snow.*[13] *Cherubim* is interpreted as a mass of knowledge, or knowledge multiplied;[14] elsewhere we read: *Thou that sitteth upon the cherubim, appear.*[15] So He ascended above the cherubim when in the sight of the apostles He mounted to the kingdom of heaven. He now sits above the cherubim, set at the Father's right hand. He reigns in heaven and on earth with the Father and the holy Spirit, both manifestly transcending the whole limits of knowledge or wonder, for what creature could sufficiently plumb the hidden depths of this great mystery, which set

earthly, mortal flesh in the eternal glory of heaven, and made the flesh which endured earthly sufferings the object of all adoration to all creatures? Next comes: *He flew: he flew upon the wings of the winds.* The repetition aptly denotes the extreme speed with which He swiftly rushed through the space of the world, when as He lay in the manger the brightness of the star announced Him to the Magi. What can be called swifter than He who as soon as He was born was seen in another part of the world? So on that occasion the speed of the winds was overtaken, though nothing in the world is known to be swifter than they. The repetition of the same word without a connecting particle in *he flew, he flew,* is the figure *epizeuxis,* which in Latin is called *coniunctio;*[16] in subsequent psalms the prophet is to say: *Day to day uttereth speech,* and: *O God, my God.*[17]

12. *And he made darkness his covert, his pavilion round about him: dark waters in the clouds of the air.* *Darkness* alludes to the mystery of His incarnation, whereby the most devoted Redeemer who could not be visible in the nature of His divinity appeared before human eyes under the covering of the flesh which He assumed. So the blessed John, bishop of Constantinople, made this wonderful and orthodox observation: "If He had come in divinity unclothed, sky, earth, seas and no creature could have borne Him; yet the unravished womb of a virgin bore Him."[18] Remember also to take *darkness* in the good sense, as in the following passage from Solomon's Proverbs: *He understands also a parable and dark sayings.*[19] All the divine things of which we are unaware are dark to us, in other words, deep and obscure, even though they enjoy undying light. His *covert* is the hidden seat of His majesty, which He reveals to the just when they are allowed to gaze face to face on the glory of His divinity. *His pavilion round about him:* here is expounded the splendid dignity of the blessed, whereby those who faithfully continue in His Church dwell close to Him. *Round about him* signifies proximity, for He goes round and enters all things, and is not encompassed by anything, for He cannot be confined in any place. The phrase, *in circuitu eius* (round about him), can be understood also as designating not locality but the defence and the protection of the pavilion.[20] *Waters* denotes the Lord's utterance, which is *dark in the clouds of the air,* in other words, in the prophets who preach the word; for though a person thinks that he understands their sayings, he cannot attain full comprehension of their force in his present condition.

As Paul says; *We see now through a glass in a dark manner, but then face to face.*[21] Once he sees the object of his belief, he is seen to gaze on the object of his hope.

13. *Gleaming clouds passed in his sight, hail and coals of fire.* We must not pass over this verse without reflexion. *Praefulgorae* (gleaming) is one word, nominative plural, agreeing with clouds. Now as we said earlier, *clouds* is to be understood as the preachers of God's word. The meaning is something like this: "The clouds containing God's waters (that is, the divine utterances) seem to be dark (that is, obscure) in this air, but gleam in God's sight where the truth is always clear." The meaning is not sought by use of prepositions, nor cloaked in parables; it is stated in clear daylight. So these clouds, the proclaimers, abandoned Israel's people and passed to the Gentiles. It is known that this happened when the Jews' obstinacy failed to merit the message which had come for their instruction. *Hail and coals of fire* explains in allegory what these clouds contain, saying one thing, but intending a different meaning; the divine eloquence is known to teem with numerous tropes. *Hail* expresses metaphorically the rebukes with which the Jews' extreme hardness of heart was assailed. *Coals of fire* are the flames of love with which the minds of the faithful are rekindled with heavenly fire. As we have said, these passed to the Gentiles in the clouds which represent the preachers.

14. *And the Lord thundered from heaven, and the Highest gave his voice.* He was about to utter mighty mysteries. As the voice of the almighty Father says in the gospel: *I have both glorified and will glorify again.*[22] So many believed that thunder sounded, as we read in that passage. *The Highest gave his voice* with the words: *This is my beloved Son, in whom I am well pleased.*[23]

15. *He sent forth his arrows, and he scattered them: he multiplied lightnings, and troubled them. Arrows* denotes the evangelists flying across on straight paths with the aid of the feathers which are the virtues; not their own, but His by whom they were dispatched. *And he scattered them,* that is, those to whom they were sent, for He admitted the faithful but rejected the impious. As Paul has it: *To some we are the odour of life unto life, to others the odour of death unto death.*[24] He *multiplied lightnings,* in other words, performed many miracles which affected the hearts of witnesses, just as the sight of repeated lightning

often causes terror.²⁵ *Troubled them,* referring to those who were troubled when they realised by the clear evidence that He had risen again.

16. *Then the fountains of waters appeared: and the foundations of the earth were discovered.* In other words, the truth of the prophets, who from their saintly mouths poured forth fountains of eternal life; the Lord's coming revealed what the darkness of their divine utterance was shrouding.²⁶ *And the foundations of the earth were discovered:* the prophets who had not been understood were made plain. Upon them the world was fashioned into the shape of the Church by holy construction; remember that here *the earth* is used in the good sense as the land of the living.

At thy rebuke, O Lord, at the blast of the spirit of thy wrath. At thy rebuke points to the words of the prophets, who with just rebukes chided the sinning people. *At the blast of the spirit of thy wrath* reveals the preachers of the word who were fired by the holy Spirit, and rebuked the sinning people. So by these glimmering parables and verbal representations the psalmist announced to the faithful people, in other words holy Church, the coming of the Lord, but as yet in the spirit of prophecy.

17. *He sent from on high, and took me: he received me out of the multitude of waters.* From this point on mother Church speaks of Christian times. The Father *sent from on high* the Lord Saviour; thus men may understand that He boasts divine power since He came from on high. The Church uses the apt words, *He took me,* for she rejoices in her marriage to Christ as Bridegroom. Two interpretations are possible for *the multitude of waters;* they are either the countless nations of the faithful among which the Church is known to have been composed after the impious Jews were rejected (in the Acts of the Apostles, the most blessed Paul shakes out his clothing before the Jews as they gainsay him and blaspheme, and he says: *Your blood be upon your own hands; I am clean. From henceforth I will go unto the Gentiles),*²⁷ or alternatively they are the sacred waters when the Catholic Church gathers the multitude of her sons in the rebirth by baptism.

18. *He delivered me from my strongest enemies, and from them that hated me: for they were too strong for me. Strongest enemies* is with

reference to the harsh persecutors who oppressed Christ's people with tortures and buffetings. She says that she has been delivered all the more because her enemies were too strong for her; it was when the enemy oppressed her that she was given power from above, and deserved to increase. It is truly God's providence that the foe is destroyed through his own onslaughts; the greater the harm which he thinks he inflicts, the greater is his need to be unmatched in the most savage persecution.

19. *They prevented me in the day of my affliction: and the Lord became my protector.* The first words refer to the time when false apostles sought to forestall the true preachers, and tried to subvert the hearts of simple people. Next comes: *In the day of my affliction,* when the martyrdom of Christians won renown. *And the Lord became my protector* because men assailed her; both proceedings so dissimilar to each other, momentary onslaught and eternal protection, occurred simultaneously.

20. *And he extended me in breadth: he saved me because he wanted me.* No member of the Catholic Church is unaware that it is regular for the faithful to extend the boundaries of the faith, as the saying goes, according as pressure of persecutions increases. It is then that through God's grace spirits rise unconquered, and then that the fire of charity blazes forth. They form a column, and gladly rush upon hostile swords because they long for the rewards of eternal life. So the Church was *extended in breadth* since the number of her faithful is known to have swollen through the savagery of persecutors. In the phrase, *He saved me,* the fact that the Church is described as masculine[28] need not trouble us; the male designation does not seem ridiculous because she is composed of men. So this column of the blessed is right to say with joy that they have been saved, because they have deserved to attain the heights of the Christian faith. *Because he wanted me,* in other words, because He who calls all men without seeking any return chose me. He does not obtain a benefit before deigning to bestow one; as He Himself says in the gospel: *You have not chosen me, but I have chosen you.*[29]

21. *And the Lord will reward me according to my justice: and will reward me according to the innocence of my hands.* The Church did well

to maintain both points. Earlier she said before she was adopted: *Because he wanted me*, and now she says: *He will reward me according to my justice*, in other words, "according to my will," which she demonstrated after His kindnesses in the depth of her holy heart. *The innocence of hands* seeks to express the work of devotion practised by the saints' virtue through the divine beneficence. The repetition of *He will reward me* must be attentively observed so that the Pelagian heresy[30] may not deceivingly beguile you.[31] St Paul says: *As for the rest, there is laid up for me a crown of justice which the Lord the just judge will render to me in that day.*[32] It was not that in his humility he attributed anything to his own merits, but rather that he was sure that the reward could be due to him because of the Lord's prior kindnesses. The apostle James makes this very point: *Every best gift and every perfect gift is from above, coming down from the Father of lights.*[33]

22. *Because I have kept the ways of the Lord, and have not done wickedly against my God.* The *ways of the Lord* are love of God and charity for one's neighbour, both of which are most zealously observed by those not wishing to forsake the Lord's commands. She added: *And have not done wickedly against my God.* The term wickedness here denotes those who presume to reject the Lord's commands. The Church with dedicated spirit says that she has properly shrunk from the cause of her giving offence to the Creator.

23. *For all his judgments are in my sight always, and his justices I have not put away from me.* She now explains the reasons why she has kept the ways of the Lord, and not done wickedly, according to her earlier claim: it was because she was continually meditating on His terrible judgments. She added: *And his justices I have not put away from me.* Such rejection is the act of those overcome by frailty of the flesh. After long observing His justice, they fail, and sometimes forsake the right behaviour which they had begun to keep. But the blessed people has never rejected the Lord's justice, for it has always lingered in their hearts.

24. *And I shall be spotless before him, and shall keep myself from my iniquity.* She recounted here the fruit of her blessedness, the advantage gained from not having put away the Lord's justices, namely her spotlessness. But she is not spotless like the Lord, but like the person

whose suppliant tears have cleansed him from the foulness which he has incurred. All this is to be understood in the way which we explained previously, when she used the words, *He will reward,* twice over. Her holy humility may presume on divine kindnesses, but not, heaven forbid, on her own efforts. Next comes: *I shall keep myself from my iniquity.* Here the life of the blessed man is subtly described. When he knows that he has attained some of the Lord's grace, he takes precautions that he does not again implicate himself in the disasters of his former wickedness.

25. *And the Lord will reward me according to my justice, and according to the innocence of my hands before his eyes.* Here she explains her earlier words: *And I shall be spotless before him.* Once people become spotless, it undoubtedly follows that He renders to each according to his justice which He actually deigns to bestow, and that He compensates them in a way worthy of the purity of their acts. *Before his eyes* is a splendid addition, for this experience can specifically befall only the blessed. Just as they always behold the Lord in their heart, so the divine power continually gazes on them.

26–27. *With the holy thou wilt be holy, and with the innocent man thou wilt be innocent. And with the elect thou wilt be elect, and with the perverse thou wilt be subverted.* Whereas earlier she was saying that heavenly justice renders to each individual according to the nature of his deeds, now she explains how the injunctions of the law can be fulfilled. Our behaviour is modelled mostly on that of our elders or their leaders; each of us rejoices in the mentality with which his leader is endowed. So we have been given as the law of our salvation and behaviour the possibility of being holy with the holy Man, who is the Lord Saviour; this is His gift; as He Himself says: *Be ye holy, because I the Lord your God am holy.*[34] It is also laid down that we should deserve to be innocent with His innocence; the words: *The innocent in hands and clean of heart*[35] refer to Him. The third point added is that we are chosen as He is, for Isaiah too speaks of Him in this way: *My elect, my soul delighteth in him.*[36] This is our portion, when we obey His commands in salutary fashion. Next comes: *With the perverse thou wilt be subverted,* in other words, "You will be subverted with the devil, who is perverted through his wickedness." Those whom he wins over to the dominion of his obedience he makes most wicked. This most notable form of argument is one of the basic ones, and is labelled "that attributed by a person externally,"[37] when a man is condemned because of wicked friends, or is praised for associating with good men.

28. *For thou wilt save the humble people, but wilt bring down the eyes of the proud.* Note how aptly this matches the verses preceding. The one who is devoted to holiness and innocence, and to the Lord's choosing, will likewise be saved, for at the day of judgment he will be set on His right hand. *The eyes of the proud* are to be brought down because they will be subverted with the devil their perverse sponsor, when they are set on the left to be consigned to eternal torture. The phrase, *Thou wilt bring down the proud,* is fitting as contrast, for the boastful drop as far down into hell as they thought they were going to rise upwards.

29. *For thou lightest my lamp, O Lord: O my God, enlighten my darkness.* It is still the Church or the blessed people speaking with wonderful words of beauty. The Church's lamp is John the Baptist, of whom the Lord says in the gospel: *He was a burning light, and you were willing to rejoice in his light.*[38] The Lord also says in the gospel: *No man lighteth a lamp and putteth it under a bushel.*[39] So the sense is something like this: the Church says to the Lord, "*Since thou lightest my lamp*"— meaning John the Baptist and the other apostles or those known to shine with heavenly brightness—"by means of them *enlighten my darkness,*" meaning by this the remaining members of the believing community who still dwell in the darkness of the flesh. The lamp is a nocturnal light aptly given to those who stray, so that by the light of the Word they may avoid the darkness of sin. So remember that it says here that the Father enlightens. The Son too enlightens, for we read in another psalm: *The Lord is God, and he hath shone upon us.*[40] The Spirit also enlightens; in the prophet's words: *I will hide my face no more from them, for my spirit has shone on the whole house of Israel.*[41] Who, then, is so darkened with clouded heart as to fail to understand that the holy Trinity has one nature, one coeternity, one power?

30. *For by thee I shall be delivered from temptation: and through my God I shall go over a wall.* She has here given notable instruction in the rule of faith; she said: *By thee,* not "by me," *I shall be delivered. Temp-*

tation means the devil, who at every moment attempts to seduce us from right behaviour. *Through my God,* in other words, with the support of His strength, *I shall go over* the obstacle of sins which the wickedness of mortals has erected between God and men. This is the wall of death, not salvation; it is not raised as protection, but is the preliminary to eternal death. She did well to say *I shall go over,* and not "I shall burst through" or "shall destroy," for that wall remains immovable for the human race, even when holy men with divine help manage to leap over it.

31. *My God, his way is undefiled: the words of the Lord are fire-tried: he is the protector of all that trust in him.* It is notable that this verse has embarked on one topic, but has moved to another. With *My God,* it embarked on some prayer, and then appended to it as unexpected close: *His way is undefiled.* If the beginning were in harmony with what follows, *My God* would be in the genitive.[42] This figure is called *para prosdokian* (in Latin *inopinatus exitus*),[43] where one topic is introduced but a second is developed. *His way is undefiled* means that His path is most pure, or it refers to the incarnation of the Word which certainly contained no defilement of sin. Next comes: *The words of the Lord are fire-tried.* The flame of faith, the heavenly law, is being examined, when the divine utterances are under scrutiny in longing for knowledge. In a similar way the prophet Jeremiah incorporated an utterance of the Lord in this marvellous definition: *Are not my words as a fire, saith the Lord, and as a hammer that breaketh the rock in pieces?*[44] A general promise was also appended to lighten human hearts, so that we may not think that the person subject to sin fails to merit protection; for the phrase, *all that trust in him,* excludes none except the one who has neglected to hope in Him. This verse is developed in the most staccato formulations of praise.

32. *For who is God but the Lord? Or who is God but our God?* This is an utterance against the madness of pagans, who with diverse stupidities have fashioned gods for themselves. She spoke of *the Lord* because we are His servants, of *God* because we most rightly adore and worship Him; but our God is the inseparable Trinity, with separation only of Persons and not of substance. Praise of the Lord was suitably passed over briefly here, since He is to speak in the next section.

33. *God who hath girt me with strength: and made my way blameless.* We have reached the third section, in which the Lord Saviour describes His power. His statement: *He hath girt me with strength* denotes both His status and His power; it is clear that both befit Him since He is to judge the world by the force of His strength. The words, *made my way,* aptly follow, for they mean "stabilised and strengthened my way," so that he was unaffected by worldly ambition. He calls His way *blameless* to denote a most pure life without the foulness of sin; He alone trod it, for He had no sin. But all these allegorical and metaphorical expressions already used or coming later we aptly allot to the Lord's incarnation.

34. *Who hath made my feet like the feet of a hart, and who setteth me upon high places.* In the divine Scriptures this animal is often introduced in a good sense, as in the passage: *As the hart pants after fountains of water.*[45] It is cited there because of its excessive thirst, but here because of the speed of its running. Harts can leap over briars[46] and jump over hazardous chasms, just as the Lord passed over the sins of the world which afflict men's salvation, and over the deepest pits of sins with His holy steps. Note too how the passage continues with the comparison with harts, for when they shun the plains they climb the mountain-heights. He means that He is set above every rank of creature; as Paul says: *And God has given him a name which is above all names: that in the name of Jesus every knee should bow, of those that are in heaven, on earth, and under the earth.*[47]

35. *Who teaches my hands to war, and has made my arms like a brazen bow.* To be taught means to become watchful of looming traps, and *hands* denotes activities. *War* refers to the struggle with the devil, with whom we are locked in spiritual conflict, and against whom we are ever armed for unceasing struggles. The *arms* are Christ's prophets and apostles, through whom He achieved what He longed to do. He compares them with a brazen bow because the servants of God acknowledge no slackening in their preaching. They persist by divine strength, and fire the words of salvation like arrows shot from afar which prick the hearts of committed men.

36. *And thou hast given me the protection of thy salvation: and thy right hand hath held me up. And thy discipline, the same shall teach me.*

The protection of salvation alludes to the glory of the resurrection, when He laid aside His mortal flesh and took it up again, incorruptible and glorified. The *right hand* is the power of the Godhead, which set in eternal majesty the humanity which had been assumed. He did well to say that He would be taught, for He was seeking to express the nature of His true humanity.

37. *Thou hast spread wide my steps under me: and my footsteps are not weakened.* He says that the most glorious acts of His incarnation, which were to be demonstrated in His most holy life, were *spread wide*. *Footsteps* indicates the path of His teaching, which He left in most explicit form to the apostles, when He planted His steps and advanced with holy deeds. Accordingly He rightly said that these footsteps would not be weakened by enemies, for though the hurricane of the world arose, it could not divert His steps, which He implanted firmly so that Peter would not be drowned in the sea.

38. *I will pursue after my enemies, and overtake them: and I will not turn again until they fail.* 39. *I will afflict them, and they shall not be able to stand: they shall fall under my feet.* Undoubtedly these two verses must be understood of those who initially rise against the Lord, and are later converted and lie at his feet. They had incurred death when arrogant, but they gain life when they submit, for He pursues His enemies when they are wearied by calamitous afflictions of various kinds, and He overtakes those whom He converts from perverse pursuits. But wholly happy is the one who is caught, who does not succeed in escaping those hands, for when such captivity overtakes him he is given greater freedom. Next follows: *And I will not turn again until they fail.* When the Lord does not turn again, the booty is then seized; the man overcome for his salvation ceases from his wicked pursuits. He added: *I will afflict them, and they will not be able to stand,* for when afflicted by sundry disasters they cannot continue in their obstinacy, since they have lost strength of wickedness in their rash deeds. Then, as the next phrase says: *They shall fall under my feet.* The man who falls under the Lord's feet does not oppose Him further, and is now defended by His protection, but he is raised back on his feet when by humble satisfaction he submits himself to Him.

40. *And thou hast girded me with strength unto battle: thou hast*

subdued under me them that rose up against me. This refers to the unclean spirits which initiated wicked strife against Him through the Jews' opposition. He is *girded with strength* when through the strength of patience He has overcome the confrontation of wicked men. But those who puffed themselves up against Him with mad plotting will undoubtedly be subdued at His judgment, so that with their prompter they will perish for refusing to believe in their Maker.

41. *And thou hast made my enemies turn their back upon me: and hast destroyed them that hated me.* This verse has taken in twin mysteries of the law. The first is that the back denotes the conversion of those who after resisting His name were put to flight towards the victory that brings salvation, and they suddenly emerged as Christians. For example, the apostle Paul after being the harshest of persecutors after the Lord's rebuke suddenly appeared as His disciple. The second is that He announces that those who hate Him will be destroyed for continuing in the obstinacy of their infidelity, as is observable in the case of the Jews who in wicked tones said: *His blood be upon us and upon our children.*[48]

42. *They cried, but there was none to save them: to the Lord, but he heard them not.* He means the vain cries which the wicked will utter at the judgment. As He says in the gospel of those to be condemned: *There shall be weeping and gnashing of teeth.*[49] Their cries cannot save those who resolved that the Author of salvation should be spurned in this world. *There was none to save them:* he means because of the devil, at whose instigation they had sinned: for who will save such men, when their tempter and leader is to be the first to be condemned? But when these men see that their hope in the devil has crashed, they will cry to the Lord, but He will not hear them because as their condemnation is now just, their repentance is acknowledged to be fruitless.

43. *And I shall beat them as small as the dust before the wind: I shall bring them to nought like the mud in the streets.* Where now are their fine-speaking tongues and windy arrogance? Let those who with wicked minds seek to gainsay the Lord understand that they will be beaten *as small as the dust.* So that no individual may imagine that he can rest immobile though pounded to dust, He added *before the wind,* so that they cannot rest after being fragmented. He does well to com-

pare sinners to mud in the streets, for it is befouled with the most malodorous filth, and does not escape people's feet, so that its smell is constantly worsened. *I shall bring them to nought,* that is, remove them from circulation like the mud in the streets. Observe too the actual force of the comparison. He says: *Like the mud in the streets,* which is easily removed because it is found to be very soft.

44–45. *Thou wilt deliver me from the contradictions of the people: thou wilt make me head of the Gentiles. A people which I knew not hath served me.* Clearly He was delivered *from the contradictions of the people* when the disloyal Jews were rejected, and He was translated to the faith and devotion of the Gentiles. The contradictions refer to the hostility which the criminal mob repeatedly heaped on Him. His words: *Thou wilt make me head of the Gentiles,* denote the sign of Christian faith, for it was on the foreheads of the Gentiles that they made the ensign of the cross shine forth.[50] *A people which I know not:* in other words, "to which I did not come, a new, unschooled, formerly excluded people." *Hath served* means "has believed," for whoever believes also serves, and this was what the Gentiles did, for they had not been sought out by Christ in the flesh. Yet what is there that Christ does not know, with His insight into the passions and hearts of men?

46. *At the hearing of the ear they have obeyed me. The children that are strangers have lied to me.* This praise of the Gentiles is a great rebuke to the Jews, for those who did not see still served, and those who did not hear one most sacred word from His mouth none the less listened. As Scripture says: *For they to whom it was not told of him will see, and they that heard not will behold.*[51] But understanding of the verse prompts an addition. The Jews who saw and heard, as He says later, showed a totally opposed disposition. Isaiah foretells this also: *Blind the heart of this people, and make their ears heavy, and shut their eyes: lest they see with their eyes or understand with their heart and be converted, and I heal them.*[52] This figure is called *aposiopesis,*[53] a statement of which the end is left unsaid, so that the listener is either frightened or roused to longing. *The children that are strangers* are the devil's children, to whom Christ says in the gospel: *You are of your father the devil.*[54] *They have lied to me,* that is, when they said: *Master, we know that thou art from God and teachest the way of God in truth.*[55] Lying (*mentiri*) means speaking against the mind (*contra mentem*),[56]

and saying with the tongue what the individual does not believe in his mind.

Strange children have faded away, and have limped from their paths. He did well to say that strange children have limped, for the Lord's sons are known to walk with straight steps. We use *limp* correctly of those lame in one foot, and this was clearly the experience of the Jews, who observed in the flesh the precepts of the Old Testament, but rejected the grace of the New, with the result that they limped on one side of their minds and became lame.[57] Some maintain that this was foretold in the famous struggle of the patriarch Jacob with the angel, when after his sinew was touched, one foot went lame.[58] The addition of *their* is not otiose, because they abandoned understanding of the Law and were moved by their own superstitions, with the result that they did not accept the promise of the Lord Saviour, and unleashed their lunatic lies about the washing of hands and cups.[59] They were indeed foul, but could not be cleansed by observance of this kind. They could have been purged of their filth if they had sought the bath of sacred baptism.

47. *The Lord liveth, and blessed be my God: and let the God of my salvation be exalted.* Here the gate of the fourth and remaining section is opened, in which the Catholic Church spread through the whole world again speaks, briefly both recounting the Lord's kindnesses and uttering a hymn with sweet delight. She rightly said: *The Lord liveth,* for with abiding contemplation she beheld Him in her own heart. By *liveth* she means: "He is seen with firm belief here present." *Blessed be God* means when praise is offered Him with the most concentrated devotion of the mind. As we read elsewhere: *Blessed is he who comes in the name of the Lord. Hosanna in the highest.*[60] A right understanding of *blessed* implies "because He kindly blesses all things," just as *the Lord liveth* implies "because He imparts life." These and similar observations, as we have often stated, are clearly made with allegorical allusions. The sense lent to *let him be exalted* is: "Let him be believed through the whole world," for in what other way could He who is rightly called "most High" be exalted?

48. *O God who avengest me, and hast subdued the people under me.* In this world the Church is honourably avenged when the blasphemers and the unfaithful are brought to the sanctuary of the true religion, so

that those who previously stood out as men of arrogance may subject themselves with profitable devotion to her. That is truly devoted avenging, salutary punishment, glorious vengeance. Those persons are subject to the Church who are known to be free from vices, for those who part from her soon run into the noose of harmful captivity.

49. *My deliverer from angry nations. And thou wilt lift me up above them that rise up against me: from the unjust man thou wilt deliver me.* By saying *angry* she enhanced praise of the Deliverer. It is a lesser achievement to deliver one in danger from lukewarm enemies, but much more splendid to deliver him from those seething with burning ill-will. A picturesque variation follows. The higher her enemies rose in anger, the more splendidly she who endured them was exalted. *The unjust man* denotes the schismatic who walks in the wickedness of evil belief.

50. *Therefore will I confess to thee, O Lord, among the peoples, and I will sing a psalm to thee among the nations. Therefore* indicates the reasons stated earlier. *I will confess to thee* means: I will proclaim your praise through the Christian people," whose tongue is none other than the voice of the Church. *A psalm,* as has been said, denotes an active work. So she says that thanks is to be offered to God by works of the faithful, and the Godhead is known to hearken to such thanks more than to mere words. *Among the nations* denotes universality, for the Church was to be extended through the multitude of nations.

51. *Glorifying the salvation of his king, and showing mercy to David the Christ and to his seed for ever.* She expounds the nature of the psalm earlier enunciated, for it glorifies His Son through the whole world. *Christ* was earlier the term for every person anointed for kingship. So it was said of Saul: *Why didst thou dare to put out thy hand against the Lord's Christ?*[61] He showed mercy to David because, as the psalm-heading states, He freed him from the savagery of his persecutors. *And to his seed:* she denotes the Lord Saviour who came in the flesh from David's line. So she speaks of *mercy shown to his seed* with reference to the time when after three days He rose from the dead, ascended into heaven, and sits at the Father's right hand. *For ever* means for eternity, like the phrase, *Unto the end,* earlier in the psalm; for these words mean the same, though clearly varied for pleasant diversion.

Conclusion Drawn From the Psalm

With what remarkable interweaving of words is the action of this psalm enacted, retaining its impact by variation of speakers, as alternating speeches replace and succeed each other! Let us realise how mighty is this glorious alliance of the chorus. Even the Lord Himself has deigned to add His words of salvation on behalf of those for whom He did not refuse to assume the lowliness of the incarnation. Even the number of the psalm encloses the Law's great mysteries: the ten refers to the decalogue of the Old Testament, the seven to the seven-formed Spirit. Brought into a single partnership, they form seventeen, so outstanding mysteries of the holy Law are embraced by the number of this psalm.

COMMENTARY ON PSALM 18

1. *Unto the end, a psalm of David.* This heading is often deployed because it attributes the words of the psalm to the Lord Christ, of whose first coming the prophet is to speak. That coming was the cause of the enemy's fall, and of a unique protection for the human race. It was through Him that the tyrant Satan groaned in bonds, and it is man instead who has been freed, after being subjected to the constraint of lethal chains. Bear in mind that this is the first psalm on this topic; four others follow, Psalms 79, 84, 96, and 97.

Division of the Psalm

Throughout the psalm the words are the prophet's. His initial account praises those who proclaim the Lord, and with most beautiful comparisons he appends words about His incarnation. The second section praises the precepts of the New and Old Testaments. In the third, he begs the Lord to be cleansed of secret vices, asking that He make the psalmist worthy in His eyes. Through these words we realise that only they who refuse to dissociate themselves from His teaching truly sing the praises of the Lord.

Explanation of the Psalm

2. *The heavens show forth the glory of God: and the firmament declareth the work of his hands.* The phrase, *The heavens have shown forth the
glory of God,* can be understood literally. As the Wise Men came to
Bethlehem, a star went before to guide them, and poised over His
cradle it revealed the coming of the Lord Saviour. However, we apply
the statement more aptly to the apostles and prophets,' who by discussing His coming filled the world with sacred admonitions. God
dwelt in them as though in the heavens. He embraces all things far and
wide, entering them not partially but with the entire fullness of His
majesty. In God there is no part, but He is wholly and fully everywhere. Whereas the wicked man is told: *Who are you to tell of my
glory?²* Next comes: *And the work of his hands,* in other words, man
himself, who was made by His hands. This is said in praise of the
prophets so that as His work they may deserve to announce the venerable mysteries of their Creator. He added: *The firmament declareth,* in
other words, those who preach His incarnation through which the
stability of our faith is unshaken and develops. Note that here it is said
that man was made by God's hands. Again, we read: *And his hands
formed the dry land.³* The allusion here is to human action, which
cannot fashion anything without hands, whereas God created all
things by the dominion of His will. So we read: *He spoke, and they were
made: he commanded, and they were created.⁴*

3. *Day to day uttereth speech: and night to night sheweth knowledge.*
Day to day uttered speech when the Lord spoke to the apostles, for He
Himself, shining out with heavenly brightness, divulged words of
heavenly light to those most pure in heart. He uttered speech when
from the deepest sanctuary He brought His words to the knowledge
of His saints. *Night to night shewed knowledge* when Judas betrayed
Christ to the Jews,⁵ and handed Him over to execution. Shewing
implies betrayal, for they made an arrangement between them to arrest
the Person whom that most wicked man kissed. What a most criminal
traitor, isolated justly from the companionship of the blessed! He
brought on the onset of death with a kiss, which for the human species
is a means of expressing affection. As for the confrontation of day
with day and night with night, this is the so-called argument from

equality;⁶ as the psalmist is to say in Psalm 41: *Deep calleth on deep at the noise of thy flood-gates.*⁷

4. *There are no speeches nor conversations in which their voices are not heard.* By saying that there were no speeches nor conversations from which the apostles refrained, he seems to proclaim that by divine inspiration they were to speak in the tongues of all nations, for their conversations and speeches resounded through the whole world with freedom of utterance. *Conversations* means shared discussions, *speeches* exhortations in public; it is undoubtedly true that the apostles exploited both.

5-6. *Their sound hath gone forth into all the earth, and their words unto the ends of the world. He hath set his tabernacle in the sun.* Earth we must here understand as man, for he can both hear and believe. The *sound* is the report of miracles, which by its very strangeness raced through individual peoples with most favourable rumour. *The ends of the world* are the kings, who like boundary-stones in fields protect their kingdoms, so that we may claim that the gospel-words have reached not only the lowly but also the princes of nations. Next comes the prophet's holy teaching concerning the incarnation of the Word, so that he too might be seen to have done what he praises others for doing, for he passes from the apostles to the person of the Lord. This figure is called *exallage* or substitution.⁸ *In the sun* means in the clear gaze of the world; *tabernacle* means the dwelling-place of His body. I think the phrase, *set in the sun,* is used to indicate that the man whose inner eye is most pure can both bear and behold the brightness of that mystery, whereas the person bewildered by heretical perversity is blinded by the brightness of His incarnation, and cannot gaze on the Lord's holy light because of the rheum of his sin.

And he as a bridegroom coming out of his bride-chamber hath rejoiced as a giant to run the way. He means the Lord Christ, who as Bridegroom of His Church came *out of his bride-chamber,* that is, the virginal womb. With this great simile he unfolded the mystery of His incarnation. By this miraculous dispensation, He came forth from a virgin womb to reconcile the world to the Godhead, and with a Bridegroom's love to join himself to the Church. So He was rightly born of a virgin, for He was to be joined to a virgin in holy wedlock. Christ is aptly termed a Bridegroom, for the Latin word⁹ derives from *spondere,* to pledge, and He was promised by the prophets on numerous occasions. Our Christ is now well compared with a giant, for He transcended human nature with the greatness of His power, and has brought low all the world's vices together with their harsh begetter. By saying *to run the way,* he reinforced his words of Psalm 1: *Nor stood in the way of sinners.*[10] The way signifies here the course of the life which the Lord led when He was born a man—His birth, growth, teaching, suffering, resurrection, ascension into heaven,[11] and His place at the right hand of the Father. The expression, *He ran the way,* is apt, for His actions could not stumble over any ambition in this world. All this is fittingly expounded in allegorical similes, which say one thing but persuade us that another meaning is intended.

7. *His going out is from the top of heaven, and his advance even to the top thereof: and there is no one that can hide himself from his heat.* If we examine this statement more carefully, the majesty of the whole Trinity is revealed. *From the top of heaven* refers to the Father, *His going out* to the Son, a birth not in time but coeternal with the Father and before all beginnings, since the Son Himself is known to be the beginning. His *advance* expresses the human dimension, for after His taking on flesh, Christ continued in both natures, and advanced to the abode of His Father's majesty. *Even to the top thereof* returns to the divine dimension, in which the Son is always equal to the Father. When He left the top, He was in no sense the lesser; when He returned to the top, the God-man continued as He had left, equal to the Father in His divine essence since His human lowliness took nothing from Him. The statement: *There is no-one that can hide himself from his heat* seems to point to the holy Spirit, whom He sent to the disciples after His ascension, for we read in The Acts of the Apostles[12] that fire appeared, and when it settled over them individually it gave them the power of speaking with the various tongues of the nations. So the heat from which no man can be hidden is He who by the power of His divinity knows the heart of every individual. So in this one short verse the great mysteries of the holy Trinity are expounded. Observe too how while alluding to the three Persons he still maintained their consubstantial unity; for by saying *his* he speaks of one, because the holy Trinity is one God. As Scripture says: *Hear, O Israel: the Lord your God is one Lord.*[13]

8. *The law of the Lord is blameless, converting souls.* We have reached

the second section, in which for six verses[14] individual aspects are recounted with separate praise. This is the seventh type of definition which the Greeks call *kata metaphoran* and the Latins *translatio,*[15] when we reveal the nature of something with brief commendation. Let us now proceed to the individual points. That law which He conferred through Moses is indeed blameless, for it comprises perfect truth which was not censured by the Lord Saviour but rather clearly fulfilled. As He says in the gospel: *I am come not to destroy, but to fulfill.*[16] So that we should not feel destructive despair at its rigour, he added *converting souls;* for fear of its sternness corrects the sinner, and makes him hasten back to Christ's grace, once he has begun to have no confidence in his own merits.

The testimony of the Lord is faithful, giving wisdom to little ones. Here he speaks of the Father, for all the testimonies which He gave to the Israelite people were especially faithful because they were recognised in their explicit truth, and they gave wisdom to little ones, specifically not to the proud or to those boasting with swollen arrogance, but to little ones. The little ones are the humble and innocent; as Paul reminds us: *Do not become children in sense, but in malice be little ones.*[17] The Son also gives testimony; as Paul says to Timothy: *I charge thee before God who quickeneth all things, and before Christ Jesus, who gave testimony under Pontius Pilate.*[18] Paul says the same about the holy Spirit: *For the Spirit Himself giveth testimony to our spirit.*[19] You see how in the case of the holy Spirit, divine Scripture does not wish us to distinguish lesser or greater, so that it does not even allow words to be separately allotted.

9. *The justices of the Lord are right, rejoicing hearts.* They are truly right, because He is known to have acted precisely as He taught, whereas those whose actions differ from their words manifest no right justice. *Rejoicing hearts;* supply "of the just, who take joy in God's judgment," for they know that they will attain the rewards of the Lord's mercy. As Paul says: *As to the rest, there is laid up for me a crown of justice which the Lord, the just judge, will render to me in that day.*[20]

The commandment of the Lord is lightsome, enlightening the eyes. Lightsome indeed, for it is immaculately pure and spotless, such as fittingly[21] emerges from the Father of all light. It enlightens the eyes, not the eyes of the flesh which even the beasts share with us, but specifically the inner eyes which are spiritually brightened by the divine gift.

10. *The fear of the Lord, enduring holy for ever and ever.* Let us see the point of this definition. The fear of God is not panicky consternation but untroubled commitment, the terms of which are changed by no transient alteration, but continue to concentrate upon it with the sincerity of a good conscience. Human fear changes with time, and is not holy because it cannot be productive, whereas fear of God contains no disturbance. Though he rightly fears his Maker, he knows that the Judge is truly merciful to those who beseech Him; so the person who is found both to fear and to love dwells in all holiness. Fear of the Lord is love mixed with apprehension; in secular contexts it is called reverence.

The judgments of God are true, justified in themselves. I think that the judgments of God refer to the commands assembled in the Old and New Testaments, because they are truly promulgated in accordance with the Judgment. The singular form judgment is used when the good are separated from the wicked. The expression that follows, *desirable*, forbids us to apply this verse to the time of the future Judgment, for Scripture says: *Woe to them that desire the day of the Lord.*[22] These judgments of both Testaments which have been mentioned abide in unchangeable truth, and there is so much good in them that when welcomed by devoted minds they make men truthful and blessed. They impart what they contain, for what makes men just must abound in justification. The conclusion is now reached of the praise proclaimed in sixfold diversity, with praise of the Lord's law, the Lord's testimony, and God's judgments; this number is acknowledged as perfect in the discipline of arithmetic.[23] The works of the Lord are demonstrably sung in eager praise with the individual verses fused like reeds of a pipe so as to teach the perfection and appropriateness of the praises proclaimed by this number. What astonishing profundity in such mighty matters! Who could have sufficiently charted or proclaimed the Lord's works if they had not palpably issued from the holy Spirit? Only one who can fully know himself can speak worthily of himself.

11. *Desirable more than gold and many precious stones, and sweeter than honey and the honeycomb.* As has been stated, the desirable judgments of the Lord are the commands of the New and Old Testaments.

More than gold refers to the commodity which human longing seeks to possess most eagerly, and for its sake often despises even the welfare of souls. But because this description is insufficient for so important a matter, he added: *And many precious stones,* which have the greatest value in the smallest pearl, and which with a tiny weight of metal are worth more than a huge amount of money. But since men of restraint could be found to grind underfoot harmful greed with praiseworthy parsimony, he appended: *Honey and the honeycomb,* since their taste is pleasant by their outstanding sweetness. No person is unaffected by this, however apparent his self-control, for their sweetness transcends that of honey in the Old Testament, and that of the honeycomb in the New; for whereas honey and the comb sweeten only the palate, God's judgments bring total sweetness to men's minds. This figure is called *auxēsis* in Greek and *augmentum* in Latin,[24] for the sentence gradually rises to higher things.

12. *For thy servant too will keep them: in keeping them there is great reward.* When he says: *Thy servant,* he means the just and committed man; with *will keep them,* understand "enticed by that sweetness," for the Lord's judgments are always bitter to the most wicked minds. Observe the significance of *will keep them,* for apparently the view of these matters is not only adopted for the moment, but continues with such devotion to the furthest limit of life. After obedience, prizes follow, the *great reward.* So great are the gifts of God's clemency that they cannot be apprehended. Of them Paul says: *Eye hath not seen, nor ear heard, neither hath it entered the heart of man what things God hath prepared for them that love him.*[25] So they are rightly labelled *great* because they could not be grasped in entirety.

13. *Who can understand sins? From my secret ones cleanse me, O Lord.* See how the gate of the third section swings open, in which the prophet begs that all his sins may be wiped clean, so that his mouth's utterance may be made acceptable in the eyes of the Lord. But whereas human errors transgress in three ways, by thought, word, and deed, he confines this boundless sea of sins to brief compass, and attests that it wells forth from two sources. Secret sin is that termed "original," in which we are conceived and born, and by which we sin with secret longing, as when we desire our neighbour's property, or long for vengeance on our enemies, or wish to become more eminent than the rest, or seek more succulent food, or commit similar sins which sprout

in and steal on us in such a way that they seem hidden from many before they take effect. If they do become obvious to anyone—and Solomon warns: *Go not after thy lusts*—[26] we must yet realise that there are many sins of which we are wholly ignorant, whose sources and deceptions we cannot realise. So in the phrase, *Who can understand sins?* we must additionally interpret this as all sins. Since the psalmist is to say in Psalm 50: *My sin is always before me,*[27] and in another place: *I have acknowledged my sin to thee,*[28] how can the sinner fail to understand the sins which he is constrained to confess? But if one adds "all," then this objection clearly falls.

14. *And from alien sins spare thy servant. If they shall have no dominion over me, then shall I be without spot: and I shall be cleansed from my greatest sin.* In the previous verse, *secret* was explained as original sin; now we must explain the meaning of *alien.* Alien refers to the sin committed at the behest of evil men or the devil which becomes our own because we lend culpable consent; for as a result of that inheritance, the mass of mankind was corrupted, and without divine grace was swiftly undermined by our spiritual foe, for they were shown to be flawed through the disobedience in the first man. How easy it is for the ancient plotter to persuade tainted men to do what is forbidden, when by his cleverness he could deceive those who were free and uncorrupted! So the prophet begs to be purified from original sin, from which no living man is exempted until the end of the world, on the grounds that he is not completely cleansed of bodily vices. But when he says: *Thy servant,* he shows that he is now rightly a slave to the Lord's law. Sins are our master when through our fallacious will we are presumptuous in their regard; but they forfeit their dominion when men are separated from them by God's grace. So the prophet rightly trusts that he will become spotless once he becomes free of their control. Now the greatest sin is pride,[29] by which the devil himself fell and dragged man with him. Its great power for evil can be understood from its having made the devil out of an angel, from its having brought death to man, and having emptied him of the blessedness he was granted. It is the mother of evils, the source of all crimes, the spring of wickedness. As Scripture says: *Pride is the beginning of all sin,*[30] but the Lord at His coming brought it low by His humility.

15. *And the words of my mouth shall be such as may please: and the*

meditation of my heart always in thy sight. O Lord, my helper and redeemer. He explains when the words of his mouth can please the Lord, namely, if he becomes a stranger to the sins he earlier mentioned, because of what is said to the sinner: *Why dost thou declare my justices?*[31] But what is the meditation of heart which can reach God? It is the hope, charity and faith which are particularly worthy of attaining Him. The things which He is known to approve deserve to mount into His sight. He calls God his Helper in goodly things and his Redeemer from evil ones,[32] so that none may attribute to his own merits what he has obtained from the generosity of heaven.

Conclusion Drawn From the Psalm

With what marvellous economy has our most splendid prophet sung the entire psalm! He praised those who proclaimed the Lord, and he himself preached the coming of the most sacred incarnation, praising its great features by different kinds of definitions. Then, returning to the recollection of his own frailty, he begged to be cleansed of his sins so that he might become a worthy expounder of such great mysteries, for he taught that the Lord's Scriptures should be declaimed with a most pure conscience. Then too the number of this psalm is seen to proclaim its power. In the gospel a woman who had been crippled for eighteen years was delivered from her infirmity at Christ's command;[33] in the same way the prophet in this psalm seeks to be freed from his sins, thus showing by the psalm's number the most appropriate time at which he too deserved the benefits of the Lord which bring salvation.

COMMENTARY ON PSALM 19

1. *Unto the end. A psalm of David.* Since the words of the heading are now well-known, let us say something of the texture of the psalm, so that once its purpose is clearly recognised in sum it can be greeted with greater gratitude. Well then, the prophet is filled with insight

into the future, and by use of the optative mood he prays for the prosperity of holy Church, which he knew would most certainly come to it through the arrival of the Lord. Filled with boundless love, he prays for success for her whose member he knew himself to be; for saintly men always have longings such as indicate that their blessings reside in the shared joy of the prayers of the truly deserving.

Division of the Psalm

At the outset the prophet prays for blessings for holy Church, so that in her weariness at the diverse affliction imposed by the world, she may be heard, and may receive Christ the Lord. Secondly, he prays that through the devoted love of His omnipotence, the Lord may strengthen her entire plan of life and upright faith. He promises that the faithful people will be exalted not by worldly force but by divine power.

Explanation of the Psalm

2. *May the Lord hear thee in the day of tribulation: may the name of the God of Jacob protect thee.* By the figure of *prolepsis* which in Latin is called *praeoccupatio,*[1] the prophet is fired with the zeal of great love, and desires that the Catholic Church may obtain what he saw could come to her a long time later. We are known to be heard when we obtain something in its totality; by saying, *In the day of tribulation,* he denotes the time of greatest affliction in which we beg the Lord with great longing. We do not pay lip-service, but rather beg from clean hearts for what we ask to be granted us in those circumstances. We must also examine why the name of the patriarch Jacob is seen to be appended. It was he who sought the grace of the entire blessing, and stole it from his elder brother, so that Esau as well as the rest of the people should be subject to himself.[2] This parallel of the blessing is aptly applied to the Christian people, who came after the Jewish race but transcended them in the devotion of their committed hearts, and so by the gift of grace became first through the Lord's generosity. When the psalmist says: *May the name of the God of Jacob protect thee,* he wishes the Lord to understand a parallel of this kind, and he wants

the new people to be granted the blessing which that holy patriarch obtained in such a prefiguration.

3. *May he send thee help from the sanctuary, and defend thee out of Sion.* In his prayer he says: *May he send* to show that the Son was sent by the Father. But this is an expression of love and not subjection. As Christ Himself says of the holy Spirit in the gospel: *It is expedient to you that I go. For if I go not, the Paraclete will not come to you. But if I go I will send him to you.*[3] As for Sion, as I have often said, it is a mountain, and it signifies "meditation," which is appropriate to the Godhead, for all these matters are known to Him not by their outcome, as they are to us, but by the glorious secret of His dispensation.

4. *May he be mindful of all thy sacrifice: and may thy holocaust be made fat.* The *sacrifice* of holy Church is to be interpreted not as the offering of cattle, but as the rite now celebrated with the customary immolation of Body and Blood, which the psalmist foresaw would come and which he knew must not go unmentioned. Next comes: *May thy holocaust be made fat.* With the expression *holocaust* he continues with the parallel of the sacrifice preceding, for holocaust means "whole burnt offering," but now it is to be used for the most sacred purity of our communion. The holocaust in itself is burnt up and dry, but becomes rich and pleasant when received by the grace of the Godhead.

5. *May the Lord give thee according to thy own heart: and confirm all thy counsel.* After the break in the psalm inserted here,[4] he comes to the second beginning, in which he is still praying for blessings for the Church which he knew would continue with constancy in the orthodox religion. He says: *May the Lord give thee according to thy own heart,* in other words, according to the understanding which you gained from the Lord Saviour, that you may believe that He alone of the Trinity suffered in the flesh and hung on the gibbet of the cross for the liberation of the world, that He rose again, that He sits at the right hand of the Father, and that He will come to pass judgment. He further added: *And confirm all thy counsel,* that is, so that you may despise the enticements of the world once you have pondered the Lord's promise, and so that you are not troubled at the dangers of the present world as you continually await the glad rewards of the resurrection to come. This is the counsel of holy mother Church, to believe that Father, Son, and holy Spirit are the one God by whom all things

were made and ordered in their entirety. The prophet prays that this doctrine, by which he knows he will attain eternal rewards, may be well maintained among the faithful people.

6–7. *We will rejoice in thy salvation: and in the name of our God we shall be exalted. The Lord fulfil all thy petitions.* When this most holy man sought spiritual blessings for the Church, he fittingly joined his own person with her to show that he was a member of her body; for he announced that he would rejoice in the salvation of the Church, the salvation which is the Lord Christ, and he attests that he will be exalted in His name, because Christians were to get their name from Christ. To be exalted means to become great, since the name bestowed on the servant is adopted from the name of the heavenly King. Next comes: *The Lord fulfil all thy petitions.* Here he happily reverts to the Church, so that the frequency of the prayer may demonstrate the greatness of his conspicuous good-will.

Now have I known that the Lord has saved his Christ. From here to the end of the psalm he speaks in his own person. This figure is called *apostrophe* or switching, when we often assign words to different persons.[5] By saying: *Now have I known,* he reveals the great power of prophecy, for he said that he knew in his day what could be established only after many ages. The Father *has saved his Christ* the Son by the glorious resurrection, when He also ascended into heaven.

He will hearken to him from his holy heaven: the salvation of his right hand is amongst the powers. The Father *will hearken* to the Son in the flesh which He assumed after the resurrection, when He sent to the apostles the holy Spirit, whom He had promised to send when on earth. Then, to demonstrate that the Son is almighty in His divinity, there follows: *The salvation of his right hand is amongst the powers.* So the salvation established by the Son is recognised as our power, for that salvation is neither weakened by diseases nor wounded by pains, but it makes us powerful by guarding us with its everlasting existence. So the sense is something like this: The Father will hearken to the Son from His holy heaven, because salvation is in the Son's right hand; the Son by His own divinity possesses what He is seen to seek in the flesh.

8. *Some trust in chariots and some in horses, but we will be exalted in the name of the Lord our God.* The prophet puts trust in the purity of

his faith which has been bestowed by God's gifts, and he rejoices, despising those who ride in stately chariots and prefer to put their trust in worldly distinction. There were two types of triumph among the ancients: one was the greater, celebrated in chariots and called a laurelled triumph, the other, the lesser, called an ovation.[6] But the psalmist leaves such things to worldly men, and maintains that he has been exalted in the Lord's name. It is not chariots or the horse that exalt, though they are seen to glorify with distinctions in this world, but the Lord's name which in the end leads to eternal rewards. This figure is in Greek called *syncrisis* and in Latin *comparatio*,[7] when we demonstrate by some comparison that our cause is juster than that of an opponent.

9. *They are bound, and have fallen, but we are risen and are set upright.* He has powerfully revealed the outcome of what goes before: those who trust in human distinctions have been caught in the noose of their base desires, and have fallen into the pit of death. Because he intended to say that they have fallen, he preceded it with *they are bound*, for this inevitably happens to those seen to bind themselves in knots of errors. A Christian is said to rise again in two senses; first, when in this world he is freed by grace from the death of vices, and he continues being justified by God; in the words of the most wise Solomon; *A just man falls seven times, and rises again.*[8] Secondly, there is the general resurrection, at which the just will attain their eternal rewards. Here both meanings are clearly appropriate, and he used the words: *We are set upright,* because in any resurrection the faithful rise from humility and are exalted to divine rewards. This argument is one of the grounds of proof and is called "the argument from the issues themselves,"[9] when we say that our opponents have *fallen,* and we attest that we are set *upright.*

10. *O Lord, save the king, and hear us in the day that we shall call upon thee.* The prophet is enticed by longing for the future, and again asks that what he knew would happen should come to pass. The Father is urged to save the King, in other words, "Let Christ the Lord rise from the dead, ascend into heaven, and intercede for us." Thus our prayer may no longer waver; rather, we may presume to pray with Him as our Advocate who taught us to pray to the Father that the noose of death

may not bind us tightly. Finally there follows: *Hear us in the day we shall call on thee,* a blessing which emerged for the human race when they firmly believed and joyfully beheld the Lord's resurrection.

Conclusion Drawn From the Psalm

The most holy prophet has taught us with what devotedness we must serve Christ the Lord. He seeks for Him the blessings which he knew would come to pass, for it is the habit of right believers to pray for what we long to happen. So in the Lord's prayer we are likewise forewarned *Thy kingdom come,* which will come to pass even if we did not pray for it. But the prophet in his devotion does not wish to cease desiring what he believes will come. So let us be oppressed at His passion, and rejoice at His resurrection, for we can be called His if we deserve to be associated with His dispensation.

We cannot establish any mystical meaning for this number taken as a whole, though sections of it will perhaps have significance for us. The number twelve is doubtless applicable to the apostles, and seven to the week clearly indicating the initial creation of the world; when joined together they encapsulate the mysteries of both laws. In this way the prayer of this psalm uttered to the Father contains venerable mysteries of both New and Old Testaments.

COMMENTARY ON PSALM 20

1. *Unto the end. A psalm of David.* The heading is the same as that in Psalm 19, for this psalm too is to speak of the Lord Saviour, but in a different fashion. The earlier one contains the prayer of the prophet and the trust by which the Christian people is to be freed from this world's disasters. Here a kind of panegyric is recited about His incarnation, and later the deeds of His divinity are recounted so that all may understand that the Son of Mary ever a virgin is identical with the Word of the Father. Our belief which is conducive to salvation is that there are two natures, divine and human, in Jesus Christ, and they continue in one Person unchangeably for ages without end. This state-

ment should be repeated frequently, because regularly hearing and believing it brings life.

Division of the Psalm

In the initial narrative of this psalm the prophet's words are addressed to God the Father concerning the Lord's incarnation. The second describes His various virtues and glory, beginning with His suffering and continuing to the point at which by His own gift He attained the dominion and peak of all things. In the third, the prophet also turns to the Lord Christ, and here like those who yearn He prays that what He knows is to come will take place at the judgment.

Explanation of the Psalm

2. *In thy strength, O Lord, the king shall joy: and in thy salvation he shall rejoice exceedingly.* The prophet says to the Father: *Lord, in thy strength,* in other words, "In the omnipotence of thy majesty in which Thy Son also reigns"; as He Himself says: *All the Father's things are mine, and all mine are the Father's.*[1] *The king shall joy* means Jesus Christ rejoices. Of Him we read in another psalm: *Give to the king thy judgment, O God, and to the king's son thy justice.*[2] Then too there was written on the inscription of His passion: *King of the Jews.*[3] Next comes: *And in thy salvation he shall rejoice exceedingly,* that is, "Your Son who is Saviour will rejoice because through Him You have saved men." He added *exceedingly* so that the greatness of His joy is as considerable as His bounty in giving.

3. *Thou hast given him his soul's desire: and hast not withholden from him the will of his lips.* The prophet recounts how great and how glorious are the things bestowed on Christ the Lord in the flesh. *His soul's desire* was as He describes it in the gospel: *With desire I have desired to eat the pasch with you.*[4] This figure is called tautology,[5] the repetition of the same word, as in: *Blessing I will bless thee,*[6] and: *Multiplying I will multiply thy seed.*[7] But He is the only one who with desire desired to die, when He offered Himself for execution for the salvation of all so that His precious blood might redeem the world, and the devil might not continue to ravage it with wicked arrogance. *The*

will of his lips was when He gave orders to unclean spirits, healed different illnesses by the command of His word, and implanted His preaching in committed minds. It is certain that His will was *not withholden* in anything, for all that He ordered to be done was fulfilled. In the words of Scripture: *Whatever the Lord pleased, he hath done in heaven and in earth.*[8]

4. *For thou hast prevented him with blessings of sweetness: thou hast set on his head a crown of precious stones.* After the pause of a diapsalm,[9] he passes to the second section in which he describes with wonderful clarity the power of His incarnation. By saying: *For thou hast prevented,* he shows that humanity is ever adorned by the anticipatory grace of the Godhead, since no man offers Him anything first; for all that is good has been granted him by the kindness of heaven. The Pelagian should blush to claim as man's own what the spotless incarnation of the Word, as we read in Scripture, clearly received. The *blessings of sweetness* refer to the words: *This is my beloved Son, in whom I am well pleased.*[10] *Thou hast set* is a metaphorical expression deriving from those who receive the worthy reward of a crown after most extensive labours. It refers in its entirety to the nature of humanity, which received from the Godhead what it did not possess. *On his head* we must also note as metaphorical, in so far as the word refers to physical substance; the Godhead does not have physical parts, for He is everywhere whole and perfect. The crown seems quite aptly to allude to the assembly of disciples ringing Him, for as He taught, a circle of apostles seeking Him out surrounded Him. This was the crown of His head, this was the kingly diadem, which was not laid on Him to adorn Him, but rather gained its adornment from the Lord Christ. We can rightly observe in this crown the circle of the entire world, by which the Church at large is denoted. This figure is called *characterismos,*[11] in other words, explanation or description which brings some absent thing or person before the mind's eye. It often occurs both in praise and in blame.

5. *He asked life, and thou hast given him length of days for ever.* Life denotes resurrection, which He sought with the words: *Father, glorify thy Son.*[12] *Length of days for ever* means unfailing perpetuity brought to a close by no end. But bear in mind that these and similar expressions are uttered with the passion in mind.

6. *His glory is great in thy salvation: glory and great beauty shalt thou*

lay upon him. The initial words formed a statement subsequently explained: for great is the glory of His incarnation in what brings salvation, namely the Word of the Father. But human thought could not appreciate this glory if he did not explain it in the following words with marvellous exposition. This figure is called *epexegesis,* or in Latin *explanatio.*[13] *Glory and great beauty* seems to point to the time of the judgment, at which the All-highest will appear in His divinity with glory from the judgment and beauty from His majesty.

7. *For thou shalt give him to be a blessing for ever and ever: thou shalt make him joyful in gladness with thy countenance.* Step by step he passes on to declare the glory which the Lord Christ received in the flesh when glorified by the Father. He says that He will be given as a blessing which cannot be cut short by any end. These words must be weighed with devoted scrutiny, so that the mystery of this important subject can shine out for us. We have already stated on many occasions that what cannot be applicable to the Lord Saviour himself must be understood as referring to part of His members, and our forbears are said to have expounded passages similarly. So: *Thou shalt make him joyful in gladness with thy countenance* is to be understood of each and every individual of the faithful, of whom another psalm is to say: *And the upright shall dwell with thy countenance.*[14] When united with the Word in this way, they are undoubtedly regarded as a single person. To take joy in the Lord's countenance is acknowledged as the emotion of some other, and the Catholic Church does not allow this to be understood of Christ.

8. *For the king hath hoped in the Lord: and through the mercy of the most High he shall not be moved.* He explains the reason why He has received so great a gift, for this King (He was so described in an inscription legible in three languages)[15] hoped in the Lord in His human role, so that we may recognise that we cannot attain His mercy except by suppliants' prayers. There follows the likely reason for this enduring status: he who continues to hope in His glory cannot be detached from the Father's mercy. As Solomon says: *Who hath hoped in the Lord and been confounded?,*[16] and in another psalm we read: *He is the protector of all that trust in him.*[17] We defined the categorical syllogism in the first psalm, and the hypothetical syllogism in the seventh;[18] it now remains for us to explain *enthymema,* rendered in Latin as *mentis conceptio.*[19] It is a syllogism consisting of one proposition and a con-

clusion, which dialecticians call a rhetorical syllogism because orators often deploy it to attain the brevity they seek. This one unfolds in this way: "All who hope in the Lord will exult and rejoice in His mercy; therefore I will exult and rejoice in His mercy." This is the third type of syllogism by which dialecticians demonstrate in the cleverest arguments what they seek to prove. The fact that in these sections words fashioned by dialecticians after long experience for the instruction of pupils are not employed, should not trouble us, for in the proclamation of the sacred message the proof itself is established, but freely expressed. Now let us examine the rest.

9. *Let thy hand be found by all thy enemies: let thy right hand find out all them that hate thee.* He passes to the third section, in which he begs the Lord Christ to do what he knew He would achieve, for he says: *Let thy hand be found,* in other words, "Let Your action be recognised; convert Your afflicted enemies who through the pleasure of the world dissent from Your laws." Of them Paul says: *For if, when we were still enemies, we were reconciled to God by the death of His Son, much more, being reconciled, shall we be saved by his life.*[20] But these people are called enemies only so long as they are beguiled by the enticements of the devil. Once they return to the Lord Christ they are called servants, sons and friends. Next follows: *Let thy right hand find out all them that hate thee.* Here the time of the judgment is indicated, when the Father's right hand, the Lord Saviour, will judge the world, and those who hate Him are to be condemned in undying punishment.

10. *Thou shalt make them as an oven of fire, in the time of thy anger.* An oven is a fashioned vessel of bronze, circular in shape, for baking loaves. When thrust into blazing flames it is hot inside. Sinners are aptly compared with it, for at the judgment to come they will be tortured with both mental grief and the pain of punishment, for having lived in opposition to the Lord's laws with unbending minds. The time of the Lord's anger is the day of judgment when the Son of man will be visible to all, but only the just look on Him as well by contemplation of His divinity. Remember that earlier the psalmist in praising the Lord Christ used the figure of *characterismos,*[21] by which he described the Lord's distinction and glory in the diverse nature of graces. Now by the same figure he says that the Lord's enemies will be afflicted by various punishments, so they were to be rendered as grisly as He was to be made marvellous.

The Lord shall trouble them in his wrath; and fire shall devour them.
The proceedings at the judgment are described in a most splendid
account, for he says that sinners who torture themselves because of
the wickedness of their deeds will be troubled by the Lord's wrath
when they hear the words: *Go into everlasting fire.*[22] The sentence they
will receive is to be devoured by undying flames. No delay ensues at
the Lord's command; His decision is no sooner made than it is carried
out. But this fire consumes in such a way as to preserve, and preserves
so as to torture. The lot of those wretches will be mortal life and
punishment that preserves.

11. *Their fruit shall thou destroy from the earth: and their seed from
among the children of men.* Their fruit would have sprouted in the land
of the living if they had believed in God's Son, but because they
resisted His commands with obstinate demeanour they deservedly lost
that fruit of blessedness. *Their seed* denotes the prayers or deeds of
sinners, well-termed seeds because from them sprouts a retribution
for each individual worthy of his deeds. *Thou wilt estrange them from
the children of men:* in other words, "from the saints whom in the
generosity of Your mercy You will consign to their eternal
inheritance."

12. *For they diverted evils against thee: they devised a plan which they
were unable to establish.* We use the verb divert to express the idea of
repelling evils which threaten some group into a different sector innocent of any wickedness which might merit such a fate. This clearly
happened in the case of the Lord's passion, for since the Jews believed
that the Roman empire would encompass their destruction if they
accepted the Lord Saviour as king, they are seen to have diverted upon
Him the evils which they thought would befall themselves from Roman vengeance. *They devised a plan* with the words: *It is expedient that
one man should die for all.*[23] *Which they were unable to establish:* in other
words, to complete their design. All unknowingly they spoke the
truth; it was necessary that one Man should die for all. The words
were true, but they were uttered with evil aspirations, and so they will
suffer punishment for such a deed because their consciences were not
pure. This figure is called *amphibolia*,[24] or ambiguous expression
which leaves the meaning uncertain or in the air. *A plan* is some
pondered design for action or for avoidance of action.

13. *For thou shalt make them turn their back: in thy remnants thou*

shalt prepare their face. The Jews were made to turn their back, because through their own fault they were wise in earthly things, but did
not deserve to behold the heavenly. *Their face,* in other words, their
evil intention, is aptly related to the Lord's *remnants,* which denote
His passion. Whereas they believed that they were inflicting the penalty of death, the result was salvation for the whole of mankind.

14. *Be thou exalted, Lord, in thy own strength: we will sing and praise
thy power. Be exalted* means "be glorified by the resurrection," for He
is seen to be exalted from the lowliness He assumed when He clearly
rose again in His glory. *In thy own strength,* that is, in the divinity of
the Word, through which You said: *I have power to lay down my life,
and I have power to take it up again.*[25] Singing entails uttering the
Lord's words with the lips, and praising means fulfilling with constancy the divine commands by good works. These are the two things
demanded of us in every way: faithfully to sing the Lord's praises with
our lips and to carry out His commands by our deeds.

Conclusion Drawn From the Psalm

In a marvellous description of the actuality, the shape of the heavenly King is revealed to us, so that the world through the evidence of
the ear could believe in the arrival of Him whom the Jews did not
deserve to recognise in the flesh. Let us remember that this is the third
of the psalms which we have suggested have spoken more clearly
about the two natures.[26] But note that the precept has been observed
throughout that in these psalms both the two natures and the single
Person have been affirmed. This is so that in brief and salutary summary both those who lyingly claim that there are two Sons, and those
who with clever perversity falsely maintain that there is only one
nature in the Lord Christ, can be broken down. You who consider
yourselves the wisest of men explain the words of the apostle which
he wrote to the Hebrews: *Then the Son also shall himself be subject unto
him that put all things under him, that God may be all in all.*[27] If one
nature had been created from deity and humanity, as you believe, what
sort of substance, pray, can be subject to the Father for ever? It remains for you to be sucked into the Arian heresy. One must admit that
the Word can be subject to the Father, though some of the Fathers

have thought that this statement can be applied to Christ's members. Did it not seem sufficient, then, to be seized in subjection to the error of Eutyches?[28] Had you also to be submerged by the Arian disaster[29] and its additional burden? Authors have condemned their errors individually, but what are they to do with you, convicted by twofold guilt? As soon as you engage, you call the follower of Nestorius orthodox.[30] We have your own judgments to deploy against you. You impute as a charge against others the argument of which you are known to have convinced yourself.

This psalm embraces the companionship of the number of two tens. Just as this equality connotes the one round number, so this psalm proclaims the one Lord as author of both laws. There is outstanding strength in these units of ten, and each time they are redoubled they announce the mysteries of mighty matters.

COMMENTARY ON PSALM 21

1. *Unto the end, for the morning raising, a psalm of David.* The meaning of *unto the end,* and *psalm,* and *of David,* has been explained several times. We must explain the remaining phrase, *for the morning raising,* which we acknowledge as new. The morning raising is the time of the resurrection; as the gospel states, *On the first day of the week Mary cometh when it was still twilight unto the sepulchre,*[1] and the rest. The raising was when the Lord Christ in brightness laid aside the condition of the old man, and raised His mortal body to great glory. Before Him *every knee bows, of those that are in heaven, on earth, and under the earth.*[2] *Morning* was used to express early morning, the hour known from countless passages to be apt for the Lord's resurrection. But since He will clearly have much to say in this psalm about His passion, let us see why its heading sought to mention only the resurrection. Often what has gone before is intimated by what follows. So when we speak of something done in the early morning, we realise that the night too has passed. Likewise when we speak of a freed individual, we realise that he has been a slave, and so on. This figure is called *synecdoche,*[3] when we can understand what precedes from what follows. So there is no doubt that mention of the resurrection indi-

cates also the blessed passion. The power and clarity of the psalm we can wholly grasp from the fact that the psalmist designated it with the heading of morning light; for it is certain that the Lord Christ's passion which it recounts was granted for the salvation of the human race.

Division of the Psalm

The Lord Christ speaks through the whole of the psalm.[4] In the first section He cries that He has been abandoned by the Father, that is, He has undertaken the passion assigned to Him. He commends the great potency of His humility brought by the degradation imposed by men. In the second part He foretold the sacred passion by various comparisons, praying to be freed by divine protection from His savaging enemies. Thirdly, He advises Christians to praise the Lord for having looked on the Catholic Church at His resurrection, so that having heard of this great miracle they may continue in the most salutary constancy of faith. This was so that men's weak hearts might not be in turmoil, if the passion alone had been foretold. Let us listen to this psalm with rather more attention, for it abounds in admiration of mighty events. In this way we can ascertain what we must spurn in this life, and what we must hope for in the next, by the admonitions of our Head Himself. Though many of the psalms briefly recall the Lord's passion, none has described it in such apt terms, so that it appears not so much as prophecy, but as history.

Explanation of the Psalm

2. *O God, my God, look upon me: why hast thou forsaken me? Far from my salvation are the words of my sins.* Christ the Lord who foresees and ordains all things, who sees all future events as present, cries out as though impelled by a passion close at hand: *O God, my God.* But these words are to be interpreted as coming from His human nature; by nature I mean strength and power of substance. The repetition itself indicates the emotion of compulsive prayer. The Son most dear in a double address invoked Him who He clearly knew would afford Him not safety in this world, but the brightness of eternal majesty. *Deos* is a Greek word rendered in Latin by *timor,* fear. This fact inclines me to

the view that our forbears decided that God's name is derived from fear; so one of the pagan poets says: "Fear was the first to create gods in the world."[5] When He says: *Look upon me*, He begs that the aid of the resurrection may appear most swiftly for Him. Next comes: *Why hast thou forsaken me?* The word *why* is known to introduce a question; so the Master of consubstantial wisdom, the Spokesman of the Father is so confused by the impending death of His flesh that in apparent ignorance He asks the Father why He has been abandoned by Him. These and similar expressions seek to express His humanity, but we must not believe that divinity was absent to Him even at the passion, since the apostle says: *If they had known, they would never have crucified the Lord of glory.*[6] Though He was impassible, He suffered through the humanity which He assumed, and which could suffer. He was immortal, but He died; He never dies, but He rose again. On this topic, Father Cyril expressed this beautiful thought: "Through the grace of God He tasted death for all, surrendering His body though by nature He was life and the resurrection of the dead."[7] Similarly blessed Ambrose says: "He both suffered and did not suffer, died and did not die, was buried and was not buried, rose again and did not rise again."[8] In the same way we say that man too even today suffers, dies and is buried, though his soul is not circumscribed by any end. So He attests that He was forsaken when He was interrogated, though in fact He could not have been consigned to the hands of wicked men if the power of His majesty had not allowed such things to happen. In the gospel-words: *Thou shouldst not have any power against me, unless it were given thee from above.*[9] He also broadcasts the experiences of the humanity which He assumed, repelling words of blasphemy and impious mouthings, for He says that words begotten by sins are far from Him. The *salvation* of His sacred soul was not to embrace the speech of sinners, but gladly to endure by the virtue of patience what He suffered through God's dispensation. As He Himself says in the gospel: *Father, if it be possible, let this chalice pass from me.*[10] Then He added: *Nevertheless, not as I will, but as thou wilt.* He also speaks of *the words of my sins* when they belong to His members. He who was without sins called our sins His, just as in another psalm He is to say: *O God, thou knowest my foolishness, and my offences are not hidden from thee.*[11] So let us hear from the Head's lips the words of the members, and realise that He has rightly spoken in our name, for He offered

Himself as victim for the salvation of all. Hence Paul says: *Him who knew no sin, he hath made sin for us.*[12] For in the law too offerings for sins are called sins.

3. *O my God, I shall cry by day, and thou wilt not hear: and by night, and not as folly in me.* The humanity of the Word cried out *by day,* for the darkness of sins did not engulf it; clearly it was not heard, though no transgression was seen to block it. So the grumbling human race should heed this in their desire to have their requests fulfilled at once. As has been said, the Word made the plea in His human capacity. He deserved to be heard, but was clearly so far from being heard that the world's wicked sins were washed clean by His sacred blood. The same lesson is taught by further examples. Paul begged that the flesh's prick be removed from him, but was not heard by the Lord.[13] The devil prayed that he might smite holy Job with the harshest of disasters, and we know that this was subsequently granted him.[14] But Paul was denied the fulfilment of his prayer for his glory, whereas the devil was granted his for his pain. Thus it is often an advantage not to be heard even though postponement of our desires depresses us. The psalmist further stated that He cried *by night,* in other words, at time of tribulation, when even sinners are often heard. Then He added: *Not as folly in me* (we must supply 'are you to regard this'); for there are two kinds of petition. When we ask for distinctions, riches, vengeance over enemies and other things of this kind, our requests are foolish because we long for worldly things. But when we demand to be freed from dangers so that eternal life may be granted us, our request is not stupid; rather, our prayer is appropriate. So Christ, Mediator between God and men, petitioned not foolishly but wisely, yet clearly went unheard because this was how the world's redemption was to come through the Lord's dispensation.

4. *But thou dwellest in the holy place, the praise of Israel.* After saying that He had not been heard, He wished to prevent anyone from assuming that God the Father did not love His own Son in pretending not to hear Him. The Father Himself said in witnessing to the Son: *This is my beloved Son, in whom I am well pleased.*[15] So He added an indication of His great love with the words: *But thou dwellest in the holy place, the praise of Israel. Thou dwellest in the holy place* made His incarnation explicit, just as elsewhere He says: *Preserve my soul, for I am holy.*[16] *The praise of Israel* indicates the Father's identity by the definition: *The*

praise of Israel, for He who grants to His saints all splendid things is truly the praise of them that see God.[17] This is the third type of definition, called *poiotēs* in Greek and *qualitativa* in Latin;[18] by stating what a thing is like, this type of definition clearly shows what it is.

5. *In thee have our fathers hoped: they have hoped, and thou hast delivered them.* So that none would ascribe the claims of the Son not to have been heard to the Father's hardness, as has been stated, the Son briefly touches on the deeds which the Father performed. He delivered the people of Israel from the land of Egypt: He rescued the three boys from the furnace: He freed Daniel from the lion's den, and there are countless other incidents which occurred or are recorded. But though He granted or grants these great concessions in answer to men's prayers, *He did not spare his own Son, but delivered him up for us all,*[19] clearly so that the scriptures might be fulfilled and that through His passion the salvation of the world might emerge. The fact that the Lord Christ speaks of His fathers should be understood from His calling the apostles His brothers; for example, in the gospel He said after His resurrection: *I ascend to my Father and your Father.*[20]

6. *They cried to thee, and they were saved: they have hoped in thee, and were not confounded.* The belief which expresses the outcome leaves no room for doubt; he who cries to the Lord is invariably heard for his advantage. Think of the stature of the martyrs who infidels thought were not being heard while physical torment was consuming them; on the contrary, they were indeed heard, for they deserved to obtain the crown of martyrdom. So the Lord always listens to His just ones, but with awareness of their interests. The psalmist's frequent repetition of: *They have hoped,* is not idle; this is the figure which in Greek is called *epembasis* and in Latin *iteratio,*[21] and is used when words are repeated for the most handsome effect in individual phrases. *They were not confounded,* specifically those who will undoubtedly attain their reward. It is the person who can clearly realise an aspiration that is good who is not confounded.

7. *But I am a worm, and no man, the reject of men and the outcast of the people.* These words embody the figure of *tapeinōsis,* which in Latin is called *humiliatio,*[22] employed whenever wondrous greatness is compared with most lowly things. As Paul says: *The weak things of the world hath God chosen, that he may confound the strong.*[23] The worm seems contemptible through utter lowliness, but incorporates the

sacred symbols of a great mystery, being born without intercourse,[24] creeping low, and moving without noise. If you ponder these facts, you will realise that it is not without justification that the Lord Christ is called a worm. So He is a worm as being mortal man, born of the flesh without mingling of human seed, and because His ways appeared silent and lowly. The Creator compares himself to the lowest of His creatures so that you may regard nothing as despicable which is known to have been fashioned by His agency. As Scripture has it: *God made all things very good.*[25] Thus David too followed his Teacher, and compared himself with the humblest flea;[26] for the real power of religion is that the more an individual humbles himself after the model of the Creator, the more splendidly he is exalted to glory. *No man,* in other words, no sinner, for sin could not reside in Him. So He is called a man in so far as He partakes of human nature, and also *no man* because He had no sin, for sin is the mark of a man. Even the devil is called a man in the gospel, as in the phrase: *A man who was his enemy came and oversowed cockle.*[27] So clearly the term *no man* is a homonym. He was *the reject of men* when Pontius Pilate gave the mob the power of choosing whom they wanted to acquit; they chose Barabbas, and preferred to reject the Lord Christ instead.

8. *All they that saw me spurned me: they have spoken with the lips and wagged the head. All* is to be understood only of the wicked, for if you include the faithful, the statement cannot stand. This figure is called in Greek *synecdoche,* in Latin *a toto pars.*[28] So the Jews spurned the Lord Saviour when they said: *He saved others, himself he cannot save,*[29] and the rest. He aptly said: *They have spoken with the lips,* for such men converse with mouth rather than with heart, since no opinion emerges from them strengthened by meditation. But what was it that they spoke with the lips? It was: *If he be the son of God, let him come down from the cross.*[30] It seems clear that their lips alone proclaimed this, and that their minds did not concur; and so that one could demonstrate that it was said in anger, not with reason, He added: *They wagged the head.* Men do this when threatening, not when judging a situation.

9. *He hoped in the Lord, let him deliver him: let him save him, seeing he delighteth in him.* This was spoken by the Jews using the figure which in Greek is called *ironia* and in Latin *irrisio,*[31] its surface-meaning being at variance with what it seeks to say. These words are in fact an exact gospel-text, for when Christ hung on the cross the Jews said:

He hoped in the Lord: let him deliver him, since he will have him.[32] How unchanging is the divine dispensation! We surely seem to be reviewing the gospel here rather than a psalm, since these things were fulfilled so authentically that they seem already enacted rather than still to come; and rightly so, as traitors could have no excuse, nor the faithful be left in doubt.

10. *For thou art he that hast drawn me out of the womb: my hope from the breast of my mother. Out of the womb* (that is, of the Virgin, already then exempted from the stain of original sin) He came forth *as a bridegroom out of his bride-chamber.*[33] He says that He was drawn from the place where humanity was held in subjection; or alternatively we must understand Him as rightly saying that He was drawn from His mother's womb to show that the birth was accomplished by the Lord's power, so that birth from a virgin should not seem incredible as long as it was brought to fruition by the Lord's action. To manifest His perfect humanity, which He deigned to assume and to demonstrate, He says that He has put His hope in the Lord from the beginning of His life. But here too is demonstrated a holiness which we cannot grasp, and a unique greatness, for what other was granted the power of acknowledging God's divinity when His mother's breasts were still giving Him suck? So His first years uttered words which others' mature years could scarcely attain.

11. *I was cast upon thee from the womb: from my mother's womb thou art my God.* He spoke these words as man, for when He says that He was cast on the Lord, He shows that He was sequestered from the wickedness of men. The next words, *from the mother's womb,* refer to the sin of the synagogue, from which as is known He was driven by the Jews' infidelity. Yet that very conception did not take place without God. Just as a man is conceived amidst wickednesses, so at the very fount of the Lord Christ's incarnation God's substance was declared joined and united to humanity. So too the angel prophesied to Mary ever a virgin: *The holy Ghost shall come upon thee, and the power of the most High shall overshadow thee: therefore the Holy which shall be born of thee shall be called the Son of God.*[34]

12. *Depart not from me: for tribulation is very near, and there is none to help me.* These words were uttered in fear of death, for He was also to say: *Father, if it be possible let this chalice pass from me.*[35] By *tribulation* He means the thought of death which became imminent many

generations later. He proclaims it to be *very near* so that His taking on of true flesh might reveal the grimness of the passion. Or because to Him everything in the future is near; as the prophet says: *For a thousand years in thy sight are as yesterday which is past.*[36] Or He says that tribulation is very near because He is to suffer in His own flesh, for when a man suffers loss of faculties, bereavement of children, loss of possessions or other things of this kind, he is recognised to endure ills at a distance from himself, whereas when a man suffers in his own flesh the tribulation imposed on him is very near. In His words: *And there is none to help me,* the integrity of the Suppliant and the power of the Godhead are revealed, for if God did not lend help there would be none to snatch Him from peril. So let us contemplate whether we should at any time be separated from Him, for we cannot be saved by anyone's pity but His.

13. *Many calves have surrounded me: fat bulls have besieged me.* He has completed the prayer with which He always prefaces His sufferings (just as He did at the time of the betrayal, as the evangelists' words attest) so that the faithful may not utter vows presumptuously and perhaps thoughtlessly. He now comes to the second part, in which He reveals the secret of His crucifixion by allegorical comparisons. Note that He treats future events as past to establish the guilt of the most hard-hearted Jews, as though the truth is already established. This is the figure known as *prolepsis,* in Latin *praeoccupatio,*[37] when something believed still to come is ascribed to time past. It was all enacted so that the unbeliever might not perish, whereas he who after so many warnings scornfully refused to follow was proved guilty in his own sight. *Many calves* are clearly the Jewish people, who do not experience God's yoke, and sport with heedless wantonness. They are also shameless and foolish, for they do not guide their steps with any sense of control, but with wandering and fluid course skip and bound towards wicked designs. By *fat bulls* He designates the Jewish leaders, who like bulls raised their heads high, and puffed out their wickedness and pride, and with savage horns spilt the blood of the guiltless One.[38] The addition of the adjective *fat* is apt; for that beast becomes exceedingly restless when it bulges with surplus fat, and after being tame it becomes fierce once it is incited with the arrogance of excessive flesh. If we weigh more carefully as authoritative phrases the expressions *have surrounded* and *have besieged,* the first can be

ascribed to those who surrounded Him with swords and cudgels, the second to those who guarded His tomb so that He would not be secretly carried off by the disciples; for a siege means investment by force, in other words, an enemy blockade.

14. *They have opened their mouths against me, as a lion ravening and roaring.* The metaphor is drawn from the behaviour of wild beasts, which greedily open their mouths when seeking to devour something. By *against me* He meant in opposition to me, when with odious unanimity they said: *Crucify, crucify.*[39] Their mouths were truly their own, because wisdom did not open them for the Jews, but their own wicked thoughts unbarred them. Let Pelagians[40] hearken to both these statements; when the Jews uttered wickedness, they themselves opened their mouths, whereas in the case of what is good we read: *O Lord, thou wilt open my lips, and my mouth shall declare thy praise.*[41] As for His words: *As a lion ravening and roaring, ravening* refers to the lunatic disturbance when they seized and dragged Him to be heard at the judge's tribunal, and *roaring* to the blasphemous words with which they cried: *Crucify, crucify.* In both cases comparison with wild beasts is appropriate, since that mad people squandered a reasonable plan of action.

15. *All my bones are poured out like water, and scattered.* The comparison contains a quite important hidden meaning. *His bones are scattered* refers to the steady and faithful apostles, when He said to them: *Behold, I send you as sheep in the midst of wolves.*[42] Then they were *poured out like waters;* when water is poured out, it moistens and cleanses. In the same way the apostles abundantly watered the world with heavenly rain, cleansing it of the foulness of sins.

My heart is become like wax melting in the midst of my bowels. By His *heart* He means His will, which in the heavenly Scriptures remained covered and concealed, but once His passion was fulfilled the whole truth of His coming was revealed as promised. The mysteries of the law are well compared to wax, which shows its glories when melted and dissolved by heat to provide light.[43] By His *bowels* He means the Catholic Church, in which when the fullness of time came, the hidden words of the proclaiming prophets became clear. Hence too the fact that the temple-veil is known to have been rent at the Lord's passion;[44] by this event were revealed the secret things which were hidden.

16. *My strength is dried up like a potsherd, and my tongue hath cleaved*

to my jaws: and they have brought me down into the dust of death. Let us not consider the comparison of Christ's strength to a potsherd as unfitting, for just as the potsherd hardens in a furnace and is strengthened when baked by fire, so by His passion the Lord's strength was hardened, whereas earlier it seemed to unbelievers as soft as mud. His *tongue* denotes the apostles as preachers, who cleaved to Christ's jaws in maintaining His commands; for the one who with God's help continues to proclaim Him remains in the Lord's jaws. But how can He say that He has been *brought down into the dust of death,* when His flesh did not endure corruption? We are to understand this as expressing the longing of the Jews, who believed that they had inflicted on Christ the death shared by all men, through which He was believed to have been reduced to dust. Alternatively, He may be saying that He has been brought down to dust in His limbs, in other words the Church, as this fate was seen to be common to the human condition.

17. *For many dogs have encompassed me: the council of the malignant hath besieged me.* Here He describes the mysteries of His passion with marvellously apt words. The nature of dogs is such that they cannot relax at all in the presence of unfamiliar people, but they drive off with aggressive and unremitting barking any whom they do not know from the familiarity of domestic acquaintance. So the Jews are most justly compared with them, for they totally spurned the Lord's new teaching, and barked against Him with the fiercest growling. The teaching is indeed new; as the evangelist says; *A new commandment I give unto you, that you love one another.*[45] The prophet Isaiah also attests this with the words: *The old things are passed away. Behold, all things are made new.*[46] The Jews' proceedings are openly described, for *the council of the malignant* planned to arrest the Lord Jesus by guile and to consign Him to death; for by *malignant* He means having malicious intentions. He rightly proclaims Himself *besieged,* for in Him lay the city of Jerusalem which the enemies of the Christian faith were seen to besiege in His person.

They have dug my hands and feet. Before coming to the beginning of the passion itself, we must examine why He chose for himself such a death, whereas He said: *I have power to lay down my life, and I have power to take it up again.*[47] A first reason is that the setting of the cross is such that its top points to the heavens yet its base does not quit the earth. When implanted it touches the depths of the realm below, and its breadth, with arms so to say extended, stretches towards the regions of the whole world; when flat it marks out the four points of the earth. Thus in tiny compass it seems to have embraced the totality. I speak of the Lord's cross, which from being the punitive source of ill for sinners became their blessed redemption. What had for long brought death later bestowed the blessing of salvation. It is the gibbet of salvation, the death denoting life, the lowliness announcing God's loftiness. So by the figure of the cross you may realise that Christ is in heaven, on earth, throughout the world, and even in the realms below. But if He had been hacked by the steel, destroyed by fire, brought down by stones, submerged by waves, or encompassed by any other destruction, by what sign, pray, would the devil be routed? By what mark would the foreheads of Christians have remained unharmed? By what sign would the weakness of body and soul be strengthened? No death save that which bequeathed to us the signs of attained salvation could have been better suited to such great Majesty. To aid our belief, care was taken to have it set higher, to be seen by many and believed by most. So that none would doubt that He in whose passion so many miracles of such power had assembled was God, *there was darkness over the whole earth, the earth quaked and the rocks were rent,*[48] so that the world could clearly witness that its Maker had suffered. Thus it was appropriate that this crucifixion, which welcomed the temple of the holy Redeemer, should contain all that is wondrous. So Christ did well to choose the cross, both to die upon in unique fashion and to expire by the common lot of mankind.

Though there seems to be here simply and literally an account of the Lord's passion, this action indicates something which we should interpret also on the spiritual level. The Jews did violence to Christ's *hands* when they preferred to disbelieve totally in His miracles, for *hands* points to the actions which the heavenly Physician performed when various people were sick, so that the Jews' stiff-necked obstinacy could be softened by the power of the signs. They also *dug* His *feet*, when they thought that the apostles, through whom the Christian faith walked abroad among the nations, should be torn asunder. So in the crucifixion of the Lord future events were foretold. We must not take *dug* in its literal meaning, for the earth gives life to various offshoots when known to have been ploughed by the eager work of men. This happened in the case of the Lord Saviour's body, for when it was fastened with nails and pierced by a lance, it yielded for us fruit which would abide for ever. So we do not now fear to say that God suffered in the flesh, that God died for the salvation of all. So Father Augustine in his usual brilliant manner preached these words: "It was a long-standing fact that man should die. But so that it should not always happen to man, a new event occurred, that God died."[49] So too Paul says: *But we preach Christ, and him crucified.*[50] So that you might not think, as some madmen believe,[51] that the Virgin's Son was some other, he added: Christ, *who is the power of God and the wisdom of God; for the foolishness of God is wiser than men, and the weakness of God is stronger than men.*[52] For what seems so foolish and feeble to unbelievers as when they hear that God, God's Son, was both crucified and buried? *But it pleased God by the foolishness of our preaching to save them that believe,*[53] for the Lord's incarnation is the wondrous height of His mercy, a gift beyond calculation and a mystery beyond understanding. From it either salvation sprouts for right-thinking minds, or death is begotten for perverted intelligences.

18. *They have numbered all my bones. And they have looked and stared upon me.* The shape of the cross is described with wonderful aptness. The whole body is said to be stretched on it, so that His bones seemed easily counted by human eyes. Thus what the covering flesh had concealed showed through in the excessive stretching of the body. But let us see whether this must be labelled punishment or tribunal, condemnation or enquiry. He was set there, so to say, on a royal throne; He abandoned the guilty thief who rebuked Him, but at once acquitted the one who confessed belief in Him. By this action He who outstandingly pitied the human race revealed through the thief's sudden confession what He was to grant to His saints. *His bones were numbered* refers to the apostles or the other Christians, when they were sought out for destruction by the mounting of persecution by the savage Jews to prevent their swelling to greater numbers. There follows the abominable obduracy of Jewish unbelief, enabling us to observe that they did not act in a momentary or offhand way. He says rather that they *looked and stared,* and that their stony hearts were not softened by miracles. Rocks were rent, the earth trembled, the sun hid itself in the garb of darkness so as not to witness so great a crime, yet sadly enough their wickedness remained immovable in its sacrilege, and their eyes unbending.

19. *They parted my garments among them, and upon my vesture they cast lots.* Though the Lord's entire passion contains great mysteries, some greater secret is brought forth here. He says that some of His garments were to be parted, yet lots were to be cast for the rest of His vesture. The garments which were to be parted signify the writings of the prophets or other divine readings, which heretics have split by their debased interpretation, thus associating themselves by such wicked rending with Pilate's soldiers. The shirt for which lots were drawn, which compassed His holy body and which the evangelist says was *woven from the top throughout,*[54] is clearly the Catholic Church, which is certainly not allowed to be torn apart at human discretion, but by God's kindness is always bestowed whole and inviolable as if by lot on every man. It is woven from the top because no man parts or tears it. With the greatest strength of enduring firmness, it abides with the power of its unity. Of it Truth itself says: *Thou art Peter, and upon this rock I will build my church, and the gates of hell shall not prevail against it.*[55]

The evangelist testifies that this happened when he says: *After they crucified him, they divided his garments, casting lots.*[56] The word *lot* is mentioned so often in the holy Scriptures that it seems to have some important secret sense of the divine judgment. In Leviticus it is written that one lot was offered to the Lord and one to the emissary, the person who was to carry it out.[57] Again, Moses divided land by lot amongst certain tribes across the Jordan.[58] Joshua too the son of Nave distributed the land promised in return to the sons of Israel after casting lots.[59] The lot also betrayed Jonah as he lay hidden;[60] and in Solomon's book we read: *The lot suppresseth contentions, and determineth between the mighty.*[61] In the New Testament too in the Acts of the Apostles the lot designated Matthias as apostle.[62] Again, the apostle Paul himself when writing to the Ephesians says that he was *called by lot, according to the purpose of him who worketh all things according to the counsel of his will.*[63] Moreover, in writing to the Thessalonians he says: *Giving thanks to God the Father, who hath made us worthy to be partakers of the lot of the saints in light.*[64] Since we read that many things in the Old and New Testaments were divided by lots, none has dared to deny that the lot has been God's way of manifesting what devoted hearts sought with prayerful petition.

20. *But thou, O Lord, remove not thy help to a distance from me: look*

towards my defence. Here he now prays for a most speedy resurrection, so that the evil belief of the wicked may be nullified by the onset of such glory. *Help* denotes the resurrection itself, which was certainly not removed to a distance, since He came forth on the third day. Next comes: *Look towards my defence;* what this defence is He next expounds.

21. *Deliver my soul from the sword: my only one from the hand of the dog.* He asked to be delivered from the death which He was to undergo, that is, when the aid of the resurrection was bestowed. *Framea* (sword) is a noun with a cluster of meanings such as spear, sword, or any weapon; by it He wished the future destruction on the cross to be signified, for it is through this weapon that death usually follows. But first He said: *Deliver my soul.* He is now asking for deliverance for the Church, which in His eyes is the *only one,* the Catholic Church. Thus we are to realise by this word denoting unity that He has rejected new teachings and the councils of the wicked. Here He compares heretics to dogs which have been cruelly tamed by a kind of family savagery, for when they leave our inner sanctum they hasten to bite and rend God's Church. So that you may know that dogs are most aptly cited in comparison to such men, He used the words: *From the hand of the dog,* a phrase appropriate rather to a man than to a dog. Or as some have it, the hand of the dog refers to power in this world, which ever hastens to rend God's Church with a wickedness both biting and deceitful. But numerous passages attest that dogs are cited to illustrate not only evil but also good features.

22. *Save me from the lion's mouth, and my lowness from the horns of unicorns. From the lion's mouth* means from the devil's power, for he is well compared to wild beasts since he always takes delight in the destruction of men. But so that some people may not have doubts arising from the fact that the same image is often attached to both the best and the worst of people, we are to say that it is to be compared to similar characteristics. Obviously each and every object must have different qualities; for example, the lion which we are now discussing shows courage, on account of which it is called the king of beasts. But it also manifests harsh savagery, for which it is labelled fierce. So its courage and power are reasonably compared to Christ's, as in the passage: *The lion of the tribe of Juda hath prevailed.*[65] But its fierceness is aptly associated with the devil; in the words of the apostle Peter: *Be*

sober and watch, because your adversary the devil as a roaring lion goeth about seeking whom he may devour.[66] So the one animal is rightly on consideration of its qualities compared with things quite different from each other. We may reasonably say that this kind of usage is perhaps peculiar to divine Scripture; thus the explanation of the present passage holds good also for other comparisons. *From the horns,* in other words, from the arrogant, who strike with the strength of their heads. But note what He appended, *of the unicorns,* those who raise themselves unaccompanied. As they rise in excessive pride they cannot endure any partners, thinking that they alone must do whatever is their pleasure. For such animals equipped with a single horn are much stronger than those assigned twin horns; the Greeks call them *monokerōs* (one-horned). He demanded that His lowliness, which if unsupported could be easily overwhelmed, should be rescued from the intolerable arrogance of unicorns.

23. *I will declare thy name to my brethren: in the midst of the church I will praise thee.* After His sacred passion He says that the fame of His divinity should be noised through the whole world. He says: *I will declare,* that is, I cause to declare. *Brethren* means those who love and are loved; since He had come to suffer for the salvation of all, which of them would He fail to call brother? On this subject the Apostle says clearly: *For it became him for whom are all things and by whom are all things, who had brought many sons into glory, to perfect the author of their salvation by his passion, for both he that sanctifieth and they that are sanctified are all of one. For which cause he is not ashamed to call them brethren, saying: I will declare thy name to my brethren.*[67] Similarly he says in the gospel after the resurrection: *Tell my brethren,*[68] and elsewhere: *Whoever shall do the will of my Father that is in heaven, he is my father and mother and brother.*[69] Next comes: *In the midst of the church he praises the Lord;* yes, for He lived devotedly among men. Purity of manners when maintained is praise of the Lord, for the flesh can do nothing good unless God's mercy is seen to have endowed it with worth. *In the midst* means openly and in intercourse with many, where the activity of an upright mind affords an example to the rest of the faithful.

24. *Ye that fear the Lord, praise him: all ye the seed of Jacob, glorify him.* Now that He has recounted the Lord's passion at considerable length, He passes to the third section, so that the hearts of the faithful

should not be dismayed by enduring sadness. Here He addresses His devoted ones, asking that they acknowledge the Lord's ordering of events and praise Him, thronging to proclaim Him with universal joy, for through His passion has come salvation for the faithful and life for the just. Now let us observe how sweet is the declaration of feeling in the fear of the Lord. Human fear brings forth not praise but abuse, but fear of the Lord is just and right, and so it begets praise, confesses love, fires the flames of charity. So He says: *Ye that fear the Lord, praise him,* in other words, "You that have reverence for His name." No man deserves to proclaim Him unless He is known also to fear Him. Take *all* as connoting the good, for He wants us to understand only those who share Jacob's faith and devotion, who in religious feeling transcend the original offspring of the old man.

25. *Let all the seed of Israel fear him.* By *the seed of Israel* He does not signify the people of a single nation. It denotes the full complement of all nations, so clearly the Church is to be understood here. Because He had earlier said: *Ye that fear the Lord, praise him,* those to whom this fear is relevant are here proclaimed, and especially the Israelites, those who behold the Lord;[70] for those blinded by the wickedness of heretics, or those who with depraved minds are slaves to idols, do not know fear of the Lord.

Because he hath not slighted nor despised the supplication of the poor, as men who boast of their distinction in this world are wont to do; they are contemptuous of the poor, despising beggars, assessing a cause by the quality of clothing worn by the pleader, so that if he is smartly clad he is considered truthful, but if his clothing is shabby, he is regarded as a complete liar. But it is totally different in the eyes of God, who does not judge by clothing, and who does not honour wealth; He hears and aids the prayers of the faithful poor. The needy man is precious to Him, provided that he is most wealthy in holiness.

Neither hath he turned his face away from me: and when I cried to him he heard me. Let us understand this verse, and offer the greatest possible thanks to God with devoted minds. When He said that thanks are to be rendered by one and all because the Godhead deigns to hearken to the poor, the Lord Christ intruded himself with the words: *Neither has he turned his face away from me.* In this way, then, He made the cause of all men His own; in this way He eliminated the sins of the world through the holiness of His body, so that by His drawing human weakness to himself the devil might lose the prize he held. But why did He cry, and why did He say He was heard? Precisely so that our death might be bounded by His destruction, so that the sin of the old man might be redeemed at the price of His most holy passion.

26. *With thee is my praise in the great church: I will pray my vows to the Lord in the sight of them that fear him.* *With thee* means 'concerning Thee'; *In the great church,* that is, the Catholic Church spread through the whole world, for it is rightly called *great* in glory and distinction. *My vows* He wishes us to interpret as the sacraments of His body and blood,[71] offered in the presence of those subject to Him in holy fear. Finally observe what follows.

27. *The poor shall eat and shall be filled.* These are the vows which He spoke of earlier. Realise that by *poor* He meant those who scorned the enticements of this world with the richest contempt; not the wealthy, stuffed with this world's happiness, but the poor, those hungry for God's kingdom. So He added: *And shall be filled;* only those possessed by such hunger could be filled.

And they that seek him shall praise the Lord: their heart lives for ever and ever. He stood by His previous words, for when the poor have been filled, they *shall praise the Lord.* The poor praise the Lord, the rich exalt themselves. The rich accumulate treasures on earth, the poor grow rich with heavenly abundance. Their resources differ, but their mentalities are totally at odds. In short, the rich derive their wealth from the world, the poor from God. How very different are the vows which they have fulfilled! The poor possess what they can never lose; the rich hold what not only the dead but even the living often lose. Next comes: *Their heart lives for ever and ever.* Their heart lives, in other words, their hope immovable is renewed; for we say that what continues in the grace of the Godhead truly lives.

28. *All the ends of the earth shall remember, and shall be converted to the Lord.* We use *remember* in the strict sense of those who after suffering the harm of forgetting, have returned to the healing of the memory. But how can this be understood of pagans who before their conversion did not partake of any of the sacraments of the faith? Yet we do well to say that they too remember, because every man confesses that God is his Maker. Now when God is faithfully acknowledged as almighty, He is rightly held to be remembered by such men, so that they truly return to Him after having neglected Him with

perverted will. Next comes: *They shall be converted to the Lord*. This prophecy appertains to the whole Church, now known to extend through the whole world.

And all the lands of the Gentiles shall adore in his sight. So that none might consider it doubtful how He is to be adored by all nations, He inserted the words, *in his sight*, where none without prior convictions about the genuineness of the faith adores. For *his sight* takes in only the most faithful and the most blessed. By using the words, *all the lands of the Gentiles*, He omitted nothing and included everything, so that even the very lands are considered pious because of their inhabitants.

29. *For the kingdom is the Lord's: and he shall have dominion over the nations*. Let us observe what this reversal of order of the verses compels us to understand: God shall have dominion over the nations, for the kingdom is the Lord's. Kingdoms belong not to nations but to the Lord, who both changes and preserves kings by His power, and He who is known clearly to be the Lord of this world is to be adored everywhere. On this subject, Father Augustine in his book to the priest Honoratus said in marvellous words: "He who was mocked and crucified and abandoned obtains this kingdom, and will at the end hand it over to God His Father, but not so as to lose it Himself; what He sowed in faith when He came as one less than the Father, He is to carry through to the glory in which He remained with the Father, whose equal He is."[72] By these words the universal Church was signified. So men must cease to be disturbed by the empty words of the Donatists. The devil's deceit cannot prevail over the Christian religion. It is necessary to refute the wickedness of heretics by unearthing such a passage, for we strengthen our awareness of the Catholic faith when through God's kindness we bring them low.

30. *All the rich ones of the earth have eaten and have adored*. Why does He earlier say that the poor are filled with the Lord's body, but maintain here that only the rich ones of the earth have eaten and have adored? Undoubtedly you are to understand here not the humble but the proud, who do not set their hope in the meekness of proclaimed teachings, but presume on their wealth. Though both groups have taken up the mysteries of the proclaimed message, there is not the same dedication in them. The humble eat until they are filled, that is,

until they reach perfection, while the rich eat but are not filled with great longings. It is one thing to wish to lay hold of something in a restrained way, and another to seek it out with total zeal of the mind. So these men are called not Christ's poor but *the rich ones of the earth*.

31. *All they that go down to the earth shall tumble in his sight: and for him my soul shall live.* Because He had earlier said that *the rich ones of the earth* were tepid Christians, He now speaks of them as tumbling or falling before God, for through the frailty of their flesh they *go down* to earthly desires and cannot appear visible to men. *Go down* is well said, because all sin is clearly at a lower level. While the assembly of the Church takes in all people without distinction, those separated by the nature of their merits are known to *His sight*. He says that His soul lives for God because He passed through this world living a spotless life.

32. *And my seed shall serve him: there shall be declared a generation to come to the Lord.* *Seed* means the works which He revealed on the earth at the time of His incarnation in order to instruct peoples, reveal the secrets of religion, and establish the apostles as preachers to proclaim holy religion with pure faith. *Shall be declared to the Lord* means, as some suggest, by the angels who are said to carry human prayers back to the Lord. As it is written in Tobias, *I offered the memorial of the prayer to the Lord.*[73] But the words, *shall be declared to the Lord,* are used figuratively, for He knows and foresees all things. In the words of Scripture: *For your Father knoweth, says the Lord, what is needful for you before you ask him.*[74] So the angels declare to the Lord to serve rather than to inform Him. *A generation to come* means that which is to be begotten through the Lord's generosity of water and the holy Spirit. To show that this generation is just, He says that it will come to the Lord; for a generation of evil men is seen to come on its own behalf rather than to the Lord.

And the heavens shall show forth his justice to a people that shall be born, which the Lord hath made. In other words, the evangelists will proclaim the Son of God, for He is the justice of the Father. So justice is to be preached to the people who are to believe in God, who abandon the death brought by sins and advance to life, who by God's kindness are born of faith in such a way as to deserve to live for ever. So the statement that the Lord has made the Christian people is especially apt. He created them when He brought them forth from their mothers' wombs, but then He freed them from sins when He made them Christians by the water of regeneration. So we must store in our hearts the fact that this and other psalms which speak of the Lord's passion find their outcome above all in the hope of Christians. In this way we may recognise that by this wonderful ordering of events, salvation has been bestowed by such a mystery on those that believe.

Conclusion Drawn From the Psalm

This is the psalm which the Church solemnly chants at the paschal service, so that we obtain the salutary teaching that in human affairs even the blessed are for a time abandoned by the Lord to some degree, though by the strength of His protection He leads them to eternal joys. As we listen to it, we happily weep, for we can be refashioned by it if after fixing our minds on it, we merit a similar affliction. How hard were the hearts of the Jews, how foolish their minds, bereft of all belief! Ought not this psalm alone to have been enough to inspire belief in the passion which Truth so obviously proclaimed about himself? So that no excuse should be left to those of extreme hardness of heart, among succeeding psalms are others composed on this subject in clear and most obvious prophecy, namely, Psalms 34, 54, 68, and 108. So what was proclaimed by heralds of such eminence ought to be doubtful to none.

The number of this psalm, however, contains other mysteries of heavenly matters; for after the prophet Daniel had continually offered prayer to the Lord for three weeks so that he could ascertain what would become of the people of Israel, the reply came by the voice of an angel. He said that he had been sent at Daniel's first prayers, but had been delayed by grappling with the devil, and had been able to come down to him only on the twenty-first day to be able to answer his prayers.[75] So this psalm too is seen to have been appropriately endowed with this number, for having destroyed the devil's malevolence it unlocked the gifts of the healing passion, by the benefit of which the human race was freed from eternal death, and attained the gifts of enduring salvation.

COMMENTARY ON PSALM 22

1. *A psalm of David.* Where there is no new information to be sought, it is fitting to pass on. I need mention only that we must apply this heading's words to their spiritual sense, as we said initially. Through the whole psalm it is the most faithful Christian, reborn of water and the holy Spirit, who speaks; he has laid aside the old age of the first man. He gives thanks that through the Lord's generosity he has been led from the desert of sin to the region of pasture and the water of rebirth. We must also observe that just as previously he accepted the ten commandments of the law, so here he rejoices that he has been enriched by ten kindnesses. They are not reported in separate verses but recounted in brief phrases.

Division of the Psalm

This is admittedly a short psalm, but clearly consists of many parts. The divisions lie not according to the spokesman but by topics. So fittingly, I hope, we have not indicated divisions here as in other psalms, but denoted the particular number in each section.

Explanation of the Psalm

The Lord ruleth me, and I shall want nothing. That most holy man, who was renewed by the grace of baptism, and having cast off the pomp of this world, recognised himself as the Lord's poor, delightedly rejoices on the couch of his good conscience, and with the sweetest pleasure proclaims himself protected by the Lord. He says that he is ruled by the Lord, in whom there is strong protection and great safety, for no man fears an enemy in that role, and none is apprehensive through his weakness. Through the addition: *I shall want nothing,* that poor man acknowledges his riches, for he believed that the Lord would none the less bestow substance of the spirit upon him. But let us hear in what follows how rich this poverty is, for it is filled with such blessings as kings' treasuries do not deserve to possess. This figure is called in Greek *sunathroismos,* and in Latin *congregatio,*[1] when many things are gathered into one, and are offered to listeners' minds as a weighty package. This figure is usually regarded among orators as the most forceful, whether used for praise or for blame.

2. *He hath set me in a place of pasture.* The faithful man we mentioned joyfully explains the first of the gifts, which we rightly realise refers to Christ's universal Church; so he claims that he is established in a place of pasture, such that flesh and body cannot be fattened from it but the soul can be refreshed with heavenly food, and grow fat with the sleekness of spiritual joy; for God's pastures are those which do not vanish with digestion by the stomach, nor does an unseasonable hunger again ensue. When once the soul has begun to be filled, it continues so by the gift of heaven. What is called here the place of pasture is the divine reading. Just as cropping a field makes cattle fat, so the divine word when pondered over can fatten the soul in faith. It was from these pastures that the man was filled who burst out to the Lord: *How sweet are thy words to my palate, more than honey and the comb to my mouth,*[2] and so on.

He hath brought me up on the water of refreshment. He reveals the second gift which profits him, and he compares the divine blessings to the pleasures of this world from which human weakness is wont to derive much joy. But let us ponder the further message which he wishes us to grasp through these comparisons. *The water of refreshment* is the baptismal font[3] by which the soul, barren through the parching effect of sin, is watered by heavenly gifts to bear good fruits. He did well to add: *He hath brought me up,* in other words He gradually nourished as it were the babes and reborn; as the apostle Peter says: *As newborn babes, desire the rational milk without guile, that you may thereby grow unto salvation.*[4]

3. *He hath converted my soul.* He passes to the third kindness, in which he claims that his soul has been converted by divine favour. He says *converted* because after baptism it became just after being sinful, most pure after being polluted, unwrinkled after being lined. As Paul says: *That he might present it to himself a glorious church, not having spot or wrinkle or any such thing.*[5] So he is right to boast that his soul has

been converted to Christ after being known to be for long captive to the devil. But this conversion is salutary only if we do not again slip back into sins through the stimulants of vices. But note what follows this conversion.

He hath led me over the paths of justice for his own name's sake. He relates the fourth benefit which must be investigated more earnestly. Since it is an act of pride to transgress the paths of justice, why does the holy man rejoice that he has been led in a direction apparently opposed to the Lord's commands? But *over* here is to be interpreted as if the expression were: "He has been set over the correction of the people whom he must instruct on the paths of justice." In the words of another prophet: *He sets me over the high places that I may conquer in his brightness.*[6] In his phrase, *for his own name's sake,* Christ's servant rejoiced that he had obtained such knowledge as to be able to publicise the Lord's commands; for the path of justice lies in the two saving precepts in which the law and the words of the prophet are fulfilled: *Thou shalt love the Lord thy God with thy whole heart and thy whole soul, and thy neighbour as thyself.*[7] So he rightly rejoiced that he had been led over the paths of justice, for he had achieved this by mental contemplation. He added: *For his own name's sake,* so that none could say that what he showed was granted by God's grace had been bestowed through his own merits.

4. *For though I were to walk in the midst of the shadow of death, I will fear no evils, for thou art with me.* The fifth kindness follows, which is bestowed with true certainty on every really staunch Catholic. He means: "Even if I were to walk among heretics and schismatics" (they are rightly called *the shadow of death* since they have the form of death as they lead us to hell) "I will not fear their foul enticements, for You defend me with the protection of Your presence." In the prophet's words: *I will not leave thee nor forsake thee;*[8] for in this world the Church walks among the wicked, until He who separates the good from the evil shall come on Judgment Day. As the prophet says: *The breath of our mouth is Christ the Lord, under whose shadow we live among the Gentiles.*[9] Alternatively, the shadow of death is simply the devil, who sets snares for us in the darkness so that we may lose our way in the fog which he draws around us, and fall headlong into eternal death.

But this fate is not feared by him who is truly faithful, even if in his reliance on divine mercy he presumes to walk amidst those snares; for why should the just man fear those who stand in awe of holy men and unwittingly serve them?

Thy rod and thy staff, they have comforted me. He now takes joy in the sixth generous gift. The *rod* denotes the justice and strength of the Lord Saviour. As he says in another psalm: *The sceptre of thy kingdom is the rod of justice.*[10] *Staff* indicates a support for men, with the aid of which the foot is firmly planted and the whole body of those who lean on it from above is poised. The patriarchs employed it, for Jacob says: *With my staff I passed over the Jordan.*[11] Again, in Exodus the Lord says to the sons of Israel: *You shall gird your reins, holding staffs in your hands, and you shall eat in haste.*[12] You will find such references in many places in the divine authority. So the faithful man says that he has been consoled by these two things; one is the punishment which represses the wicked, the other the guidance which supports most faithful Christians. *They* he makes plural, alluding to rod and staff just mentioned. But let us note how both objects, though utterly different from each other, will be able to console us. There is no doubt that the staff consoles, for it is always used to aid human weakness, but what shall we say of the rod which strikes, beats, and corrects our vices through the Judge's severity? Obviously this too consoles the faithful when it brings improvement and leads men to the Lord's path. We rightly say that everything that helps us consoles us, even if it brings passing pain for our correction. So the apostle says to the Hebrews: *For all chastisement for the present seemeth not to bring with it joy but sorrow, but afterwards it yields much fruit.*[13]

5. *Thou hast prepared in my sight a table against them that afflict me.* The seventh act of thanksgiving is added when he says: *Thou hast prepared in my sight,* in other words, "You have made prior arrangements for a holy altar which the whole Church sees, which the Christian people surrounds." *Mensa* (table) is formed from *mensis* (month), because feasts were celebrated on the same day, after the fashion of the Gentiles.[14] But the Church's table is a blessed feast, a happy banquet, the fullness of faith, the heavenly food. It is indeed clear that this table is prepared against them that are plunged into some wickedness,

and who oppressively sadden God's Church with their error. Paul says of them: *He that eateth unworthily, eateth and drinketh judgment to himself, not discerning the body of the Lord,*[15] which is given for the remission of sins and for the possession of eternal life. Remember, however, that *table* bears a good and a bad sense; as Paul says: *You cannot be partakers of the table of the Lord, and of the table of devils.*[16]

Thou hast anointed my head with oil. The eighth act of generosity is defined. The *head* of the faithful is the Lord Christ, rightly described as anointed with oil since He does not dry up through the aridity of the sinner. So he claims that his Head has been anointed with oil, doubtless so that the other limbs can take joy from this. But why is it that this kind of sacred blessing is often applied in anointing prophets and consecrating kings? It is rightly done, for the olive also afforded a sign of peace, a gift acknowledged to be especially divine. The juice of the olive is the oil of gladness and the favour of great distinctions, and its foliage continues in the beauty of its greenness. It was the olive which announced to Noah by means of the dove that salvation was restored to the earth,[17] so that it rightly seems able to bestow so great a blessing since it enjoys both great beauty and usefulness in its fruit. As another psalm says of it: *Therefore God, my God, hath anointed thee with the oil of exultation above thy fellows.*[18]

And thy cup which inebriateth me, how goodly it is! The ninth gift is the Lord's blood, which inebriates in such a way that it cleanses the mind, preventing it from wrongdoing, not leading it to sins. This drunkenness makes us sober, this fullness purges us of evils. He who is not filled with this cup fasts in perennial need. The word is found also in the bad sense, as in Isaiah: *And I have received from thy hand the chalice of destruction, the cup of anger and my wrath.*[19] He added: *How goodly it is!*, especially as He bestows such gifts to lead us to heaven. The gospel says of this cup: *Whoever drinks of the water that I shall give shall not thirst for ever, but it shall become in him a fountain of water springing up into life everlasting.*[20]

6. *And thy mercy will follow me all the days of my life.* The tenth part of the division which we promised is now completed here, where the greatness of his longing finds fulfilment in boundless joy. Though the Lord's mercy always goes before us, he says here that it *will follow me.*

It follows particularly to protect, but it precedes to bestow grace. If it merely followed, no-one would observe its gifts, and if it merely preceded, none could keep what is bestowed. The ambuscades laid by the devil in our rear are quite formidable, and without the presence of the Lord's mercy our human frailty is most easily deceived. It is precisely when a person believes that he has outflanked a vice that he is more easily lulled by rash ignorance. So it is vitally necessary that the Lord's grace should precede us and His mercy follow us always.

And that I may dwell in the house of the Lord unto length of days. This conclusion is linked to the previous sections; he claims that those gifts had been granted him that he might reach the goal of dwelling in the house of that glory. This is the full perfection of all blessings. As he says in another psalm; *Blessed are they that dwell in thy house: they shall praise thee for ever and ever.*[21] *The house of the Lord* denotes the Jerusalem to come, which continues without uncertainty *unto length of days,* for it is lasting blessedness and joy without end. Remember that in the first verse of this psalm: *The Lord ruleth me and I shall want nothing,* he has stated briefly what he has recounted at greater length in the later verses. This figure is called *epitrochasmos*[22] or "going round" the subject, when it briefly summarises what will subsequently be expressed in greater detail. In the final verse: *That I may dwell in the house of the Lord unto length of days,* there is set the exceedingly noble figure of *epiphonēma*[23] or acclamation, which after the account of the subjects briefly bursts forth in acclamation and finally closes with a heightened climax. Thus beginning, middle, and end of the psalm are brightened with the beautiful light of differing figures.

Conclusion Drawn From the Psalm

Let us store in our minds the song of this heavenly pipe, close packed with its ten virtues, and note how sweet a lay it has sung with health-giving delight to the soul. In this way through rejoicing in the divine mystery we may acknowledge not our ears' pleasure but the gaining of health for our souls. The number of this psalm also points to the perfection of wisdom; for we know that there are twenty-two books of the Old Testament by the Jewish reckoning, and they were clearly bestowed on the human race for a full understanding of the knowledge of God. So in different ways the heavenly mysteries are acknowledged as assembled in this psalm.

COMMENTARY ON PSALM 23

1. *A psalm of David on the first day of the week.* Let us with the Lord's help eagerly remove the veil of this title, so that the inner sanctum may become clearer to us. *The first day of the week* indicates the Lord's day, the first after the sabbath, the day on which the Lord rose from the dead. It is rightly called the Lord's day because of the outstanding nature of the miracle, or because on that day He stabilised the world, for by rising again on it He is seen to lend succour to the world and is declared also its Maker. Because the whole psalm is sung after the resurrection, this heading has been set before it to inform the hearts of the faithful with the appropriate indication.

Division of the Psalm

After the Lord's resurrection the prophet becomes more joyful, and addresses the human race which was in thrall to various kinds of superstition. In the first section he defines the whole world as the Lord's, so that no man might either claim that he was exempt from the Lord's power or regard himself as a stranger to belief in Him. In the second part he lays down the powers with which those established in the Church are endowed. In the third, he addresses those whom superstition has made mad, so that they may become servants of the true Lord, and abandon the wickedness that harms them.

Explanation of the Psalm

The earth is the Lord's and the fullness thereof: the world and all they that dwell therein. Though we are aware that *earth* is often used in both a good and a bad sense, we must recognise it here as the Church which with pure heart serves the Lord in a special way. Though all things

have been created by Him, we maintain that what worships Him as its
Maker belongs to Him in a special sense. So we rightly identify the
Church here with the earth fruitful in blessings, because it nurtures
and contains Christ's people. Next comes: *And the fullness thereof,* in
other words, the holy multitude with which the Church is filled. So
that we may not regard the earth earlier mentioned as perhaps connoting a confined area, he now speaks of the *world,* that is, the whole
Church bounded by the limits of the entire globe. Note that he says:
They that dwell therein; in other words, not those who gather and then
retire, but those who continue with unwavering constancy of mind.
By *dwell* we mean remain, which is not the practice of vagrants since it
does not befit their capriciousness. Only he who continues until his
death in the most upright faith dwells in the Church. As another psalm
has it: *That I may dwell in the house of the Lord all the days of my life.*[1]

2. *He hath founded it upon the seas: and hath prepared it upon the
rivers.* What does founding on the seas mean except establishing the
Church in the firmest belief on the shifting waves of this world's
vices, so that when faith's anchor is lowered she may not tremble at
the storms of any hazard? So the apostle too says: *Which we have as an
anchor of the soul, sure and firm.*[2] Similarly he says that it has also been
prepared upon the rivers, since it is certain that the Church is equipped
to face the turbulent desires of her persecutors, so that their evil
wishes cannot harm her, though they rise against her in the headlong
lunacy of their minds.

3. *Who shall ascend into the mountain of the Lord, or who shall stand
in his holy place?* Once he has briefly taught us that all creation is the
Lord's since He established it, he now begins the second section with
a question, and in answer explains the necessary character of those
who wish to call themselves His. This is the figure called *exetasmos* or
scrutiny,[3] when we investigate with questioning a number of separate
issues, and apply an appropriate answer to each. So he first asks questions so that an apt reply may ensue. He asks: *Who shall ascend?* because he intended to speak of the mountain signifying justice and the
other virtues; we make our way towards them only with great effort,
since we are hindered by sins which confront us. Then having said:
Who shall ascend? he next asks: *Who shall stand?* for it is much more
beneficial to stand in the holy place than to mount to its summit.

4. *The innocent in hands and clean of heart, who hath not taken his*

soul in vain. This is the reply which was awaited: *The innocent in hands and clean of heart,* the person whose activities hurt no-one, and who strives to lend succour to the best of his power. So that you might not think that being *innocent in hands* is enough, he added *and clean of heart,* because we often seek to harm but we lend aid unwillingly, and likewise we desire to do good things but abandon the performance of them. So he says that only the person in whom both qualities can be discerned mounts to that place. The man who thinks that passing or transient things are desirable does indeed take his soul in vain; but that person has not taken his soul in vain who knows that he has been begotten to understand the Godhead, to guard the Lord's law, to ponder on eternal life and all that can win heavenly grace.

Nor sworn deceitfully to his neighbour. By saying *deceitfully,* he seems to allow oaths that are sacred. As Scripture says: *The Lord hath sworn, and he will not repent,*[4] and we also read that the most holy patriarchs swore oaths. Why then does the gospel say: *You will not swear by heaven or by the earth,*[5] and what follows? Swearing truthfully was certainly not forbidden in the Old Testament, but because a pretext for perjury often occurs to human beings through mental weaknesses, in the New Testament it states that it is more profitable that we should not swear at all. This is the case too with other things acknowledged as being worthy of circumspection rather than forbidden. In the gospel, for example, the Lord Himself states: *It has been said by the ancients an eye for an eye, but I say to you not to resist evil.*[6] So a man swears deceitfully if he intends to act differently from his promise, not regarding it as perjury if he wilfully misleads one who makes the mistake of trusting him.

5. *He shall receive a blessing from the Lord, and mercy from God his saviour.* Earlier he offered expressions of devotion; now he enumerates also the rewards. *He shall receive a blessing from the Lord* Himself, not from anyone else. It is the future Judge who blesses; He who could have imposed irreversible damnation forgives. So he wanted us to acknowledge the deserving kindness of this magnanimous concession of the Lord. Amongst orators this line of reasoning is called *a persona.*[7] Next comes *mercy,* so that the blessing may appear to have come not through human deserts but through the Lord's kindness, for there is no person who does not need pity to be shown him. Sins are conceded so that a crown may ensue, just as freedom cannot be bestowed unless

slavery has first been removed. So our Lord Christ is the Saviour by whom blessedness is granted and also sins are loosed. We should not be disturbed because he first said: *He shall receive a blessing from the Lord* and later added: *And mercy from God his saviour,* whereas in the order of events He would first pardon our sins and then the gifts of His blessing would follow. You frequently find this variation with mercy placed first; for example: *May God have mercy on us and bless us.* Then he reverses it: *May he cause the light of his countenance to shine upon us; and may he have mercy on us.*[8] This figure is called *anastrophe* or inversion,[9] when we express an idea in the reverse order.

6. *This is the generation of them that seek the Lord, of them that seek for the face of the God of Jacob.* Because he had earlier used the singular in: *Who shall ascend to the mountain of the Lord?* he would not have you think that this is to be applied merely to the Lord Christ, so now it is acknowledged as valid for the Christian generation. When he says: *This is,* he means: "Such is that generation which seeks the Lord, which is reborn from the spring of holy baptism, and which recommends its faith through devoted works." Next follows: *Of them that seek for the face of the God of Jacob.* What is the point of the repetition of the word *seek* and the addition of the final words *of Jacob?* Initially he had spoken generally of: *Them that seek the Lord,* who do not canvass for prior position, but who are content with their role and final disposition as long as they deserve to obtain even the smallest place in Christ's kingdom. But because there are others whose zeal of faith is outstanding, and who by the goodness of their works seem to be preferred to others, he added *of the God of Jacob;* so in their case he can do what he is said to have done in the case of Jacob, who was born later but who obtained the primacy belonging to his brother.

7. *Lift up your gates, O ye princes.* He comes to the third section, in which the prophet, having announced the Christian religion, gives commands with great joy to various sinners, so that with fitting faith they may unfasten the bars earlier locked, and deserve to admit the Lord King Himself into their hearts; for he bids them remove the gates of death known to have been set there by the prince who is the devil. They are called *portae* (gates) because men pass through them transporting their business and carrying provisions with the greatest care.[10]

And be ye lifted up, O eternal gates, and the king of glory shall enter in. Eternal gates are aptly set against the gates of death, to show that the

second are transient but the first perennial. What Adam lost by trans-
gressing the law through the work of the devil, the Lord Christ renewed by fulfilling the law. The eternal gates are *lifted up;* this signifies the grace of baptism, the glory of the chrism, the salvation of
preaching and the other gifts granted at Christ the Lord's coming.
They are rightly called eternal gates since the King of glory deigned to
enter through them.

8. *Who is the king of glory? The Lord who is strong and mighty, the
Lord mighty in battle.* The prophet asks: *Who is the king of glory?* in
order to condemn the infidelity of the Jews. The reply is made by the
third type of definition which in Greek is called *poiotēs* and in Latin
qualitativa:[11] *The Lord who is strong and mighty, the Lord mighty in
battle.* If you examine this statement, it will be shown to be appropriate to Christ alone. The princes of earth can also be called glorious,
but none can be found to be the King of glory save the Highest alone.
So to this question, as has already been said, the reply is appended, and
here the wicked presumption of the Jewish people is well proved by
each word. *Strong* is set against their belief that He could be arrested
by swords and clubs. He is *mighty* whom they consigned as powerless
to Pontius Pilate. The additional phrase, *mighty in battle,* was added so
that they should not believe that they had won any victory in their
concerted action. In short, when they came to arrest Him, they heard
the words: *I am he,* and on the testimony of the evangelist John all at
once fell backwards.[12] Thus the Lord Saviour has been as clearly announced to us by His powers as if He were revealed by His own name.

9. *Lift up your gates, O ye princes, and be ye lifted up, O eternal gates,
and the king of glory shall enter in.* 10. *Who is this king of glory? The Lord
of hosts: he is the king of glory.* Here too there is the use of that most
splendid figure which in Greek is called *anadiplosis* and in Latin *congeminatio dictionis,*[13] and which is achieved either by changing or repeating expressions. Since we have already discussed this subject, our
earlier explanation must be more than enough here also. To confound
the Jews, he earlier expounded the Lord's magnificence word by
word, as was appropriate; but now he has briefly added the climax to
the entire encomium and truth, for he now says that He is not only
strong and powerful and great in battle, but also the Lord of the hosts
themselves. Indeed, the King of glory is none other than He who
makes glorious those who glorify Him—in the Lord's own words:

Those who glorify me, I will glorify[14]—and He who assigns power and strength and the other gifts to each individual as He will. *Glory* implies praise from the throng, eulogy from the crowd. Now through the Lord's gift the angels—Powers, Thrones, Dominations, and other most powerful creatures—are glorious, but the only King of glory is He who created and controls these lofty ones. What astonishing praise, what a marvellous conclusion! Nothing worthy could be said by anyone save Him who alone can tell His power. You masters of secular literature, realise that from here have flowed forth your figures of speech, your proofs of different kinds, your definitions, your teachings about all disciplines, for in such writings you find enshrined what you realise was said long before your schools existed.[15]

Conclusion Drawn From the Psalm

The whole of this psalm is concerned with the teaching of manners, for it warns us to abandon superstitions and faithfully to serve the true and holy God. What is juster than to abandon him who made us subject to death in Adam? What is more blessed than to follow Him who enabled the human race to escape the death imposed on them? Now grant, Lord, that we who have entered the gates of Your mercy by the font of sacred rebirth may not depart from them with sins hounding us. The number of this psalm may have reference to the twenty-three letters of the Latin alphabet which form the style of true eloquence. Hebrew has twenty-two letters, Latin, from which we have our speech, has twenty-three, and Greek twenty-four, but none the less in the comprehension of any language there is an appropriate number of letters to be employed. Likewise we breathe the odour of perfection in the numbering of this psalm.

COMMENTARY ON PSALM 24

1. *Unto the end, a psalm of David.* Since the words of the heading are now familiar, and this is the first psalm set in the frame of the Hebrew alphabet, a word must be said instead about its point. Through the

whole book there are two types of these psalms. The first is that clearly containing the whole alphabet, like Psalms 110, 111, 118; in my view, these show that the just sing the Lord's praises by His kindness through the perfect devotion of their meritorious deeds. An example was Nathaniel, of whom the Lord says in the gospel: *Behold, an Israelite indeed, in whom there is no guile.*[1] There is also Jeremiah the prophet, of whom the Lord also says: *From the belly of thy mother I have called thee, and in the womb I have sanctified thee.*[2] Job too was likewise praised by the Lord's words, for He says: *Hast thou not considered my servant Job, that there is none like him in the earth, a man just and simple and upright, fearing God and avoiding evil?*[3] And there are others who are known to God alone. When we reach these psalms, a clearer explanation will be given. The second type deletes certain letters; these show that there are men singing in the Church on whom good works in their entirety do not smile to the same degree; examples are the present psalm, and Psalms 33, 36, 144, on which we shall speak at greater length and with greater clarity in their due place.[4] Here we must be aware that this psalm omits the sixth and nineteenth letters; I have decided that the rest be inscribed in ink in the text of the psalter, so that readers of it may not find them confusing and obscure. These letters of the alphabet and the words which they connote have been assembled in summary by the labours of father Jerome.[5] The alphabetic arrangement is found to be not unusual in the divine Scriptures, for Jeremiah bewailed the captivity of Jerusalem by lamentations extending over the alphabet four times,[6] thus teaching us that the sacred use of letters unfolds for us also mysteries of heavenly matters.

Division of the Psalm

Throughout the whole psalm the Church prays in marvellous supplication with the figure known as *ethopoeia*[7] that she should not appear before God's eyes as a figure despised by her enemies. In the first section she demands that she may know the Lord's intentions and His ways; this part contains five letters of the alphabet we mentioned. In the second section, she asks for His kindnesses which He bestowed on the holy fathers from the beginning of the world; this embraces six further letters. In the third place she says that those who keep the

Lord's commands deserve eternal rewards, and she attests that she remains constant in this one desire; here the remaining nine letters are incorporated. So the whole psalm is expressed under the headings of the letters which I have mentioned.

Explanation of the Psalm

2–3. ALEPH. *To thee, O Lord, have I lifted my soul: in thee, O my God, I put my trust: let me not be ashamed, neither let my enemies laugh at me.* By lifting we mean raising upwards. So the psalmist says that the Church has lifted her soul from earthly intercourse and faults of the flesh to God, that is, to contemplation of heavenly matters by which the devoted mind gazes on the Lord; for the person who has once sighted things divine readily despises things human. Being ashamed means being troubled with sudden anxiety of mind, and suddenly observing an eventuality other than was expected. So she begs that she should not become less in His sight, since she has trusted in His devotion. Enemies laugh when they see that the trust of just men is not fulfilled, if things turn out differently from their predictions. So mother Church hopes that the Lord may carry out His promises so that her foes may not have the chance to laugh at her. Laughing is usually the characteristic of one well-disposed, but laughing at an individual is always the trait of a foe.

4. BETH. *For none of them that wait on thee shall be confounded: confounded let wicked men be who do vain things.* Waiting on God in manly fashion entails expecting Him while enduring evils, so that when He comes at His judgment He may render what the spirit of the committed person was seeking. In the same way another psalm says: *Expect the Lord: do manfully and let thy heart take courage: and wait thou for the Lord.*[8] Notice that through the figure of *anadiplosis* (in Latin called *congeminatio dictionis*)[9] she repeats an expression for beautiful effect. In the previous psalm this was done with whole verses,[10] but here with single words. She added: *Let them be confounded.* The very word set at the end in the case of the faithful has provided the beginning so far as the wicked are concerned. But in the first case the prayer is that it may not come to pass, whereas in the second there is an entreaty that it may happen. *Who do vain things,* that is, things

known to be foreign to the Lord, for we call vain that which is fruit-less and empty.

GHIMEL. *Make known to me, O Lord, thy ways, and thy paths teach me.* There is no small difference between *ways* and *paths*. By ways we mean the roads over which travellers in general wander freely; the word *viae* (ways) comes from *vehere* (to travel)." But paths are routes by a narrow track not generally familiar, but the means of private journeys; *semita* (path) is so called because it is half a road (*semivia*)." So let us say that *ways* relate to the course of life traversed both by the learned in their manner of life and by the crowd of the ingenuous, whereas *paths* we must interpret as understanding of the law, familiar to few and known to be narrow because of their difficulty. This is clear from the words that follow, *Teach me,* an expression obviously suited to the law rather than to a track.

5. DALETH. *Direct me in thy truth, and teach me: for thou art God my saviour, and on thee have I waited all the day long.* This verse embraces higher meanings in each word. *Direct me* relates to life, *teach me* to knowledge. The following words, *For thou art God my saviour, and on thee have I waited all the day long,* instruct us briefly but per-fectly. There are two factors which make good Christians: the first that we believe that God is our Saviour, the second that we must await His recompense with patience all our lives. *All the day long,* as if she were saying: "every day"; that is, an extended period without in-terruption in time, but with the sense of unbroken life.

6. HE. *Remember, O Lord, thy bowels of compassion, and thy mercy which is at the beginning of the world.* She comes to the second section, begging with her most devoted humility that she may obtain the Lord's mercy as His kindness permits. He is bidden to remember by the human convention; in fact He can never forget anything. As for the person who longs to gain help, she believes that the Donor is forgetful of His kindness when He has been detained by some delay. She added: *And thy mercy, which is at the beginning of the world.* In these words a noble and orthodox sentiment seems to shine forth on us, for no man attains God's grace by his own merits. By speaking of *thy mercy, which is at the beginning of the world,* she continually praises the Lord as the donor of mercies who does not as a prior step take up men's deserving deeds, but grants first His own gifts. Truly all here-sies have taken their origin from an execrable notion, and we are given

to understand here how destructive the Pelagian evil is from its being clearly refuted with such insistence. *At the beginning of the world (saeculum)* means when time began to exist, when the world began to be ordered, for *saeculum* means the continuing order of the world which extends into the future and quits the past. Some have thought that this time is to be divided into units of seven years, after the manner of the seven days, whereas others have suggested that they were called *saecula* because of the periods continually recurring.[13] So that we may not seem to omit distinctions of meaning between words, *bowels of compassion* refers to kindly acts, and *mercy* is concerned with a clement nature. So she asks that the Lord be mindful of both His attributes.

7. ZAIN. *The peccadilloes of my youth and my ignorance do not remember: according to thy great mercy remember me, O God.* Some would hold a peccadillo (*delictum*) to be a lighter sin, and to be so called from the fact that it leaves (*linquere*)[14] the path of justice, but does not participate in the worst criminal wickedness. It is a peccadillo to take food too greedily, to burst into unseemly laughter, to pay heed to idle words, and to do other things of this kind which are obviously not very serious sins but are none the less certainly forbidden. By *youth* she meant not only her green years, but also the boldness of the impulse most readily embraced at that age when our mental heat outweighs moderate behaviour. Many young persons show maturity by seriousness of manners, but equally some old men are marked by the sin of levity. She spoke of *ignorance* because we do many things which we do not realise are evil. Often we lend advice which harms our neighbour; we offer as a remedy to a sick man foods causing severe pain. We often transgress the law too through ignorance; yet we ought not to be ignorant of it since the Godhead has wished it to be learnt and ever preserved by the mass of mankind. Others state that the peccadilloes of ignorance refer also to small children, whose feeble senses are dormant but who are still subject to original sin. So she begs that He should not reserve for vengeance the peccadilloes of youth and ignorance; that He should not allow her to be haled to judgment, but regard those faults as vanishing before Him. So the Church prays that He should not remember her peccadilloes, but rather be mindful of her according to His great mercy.

Because of thy goodness, O Lord. By saying: *Because of thy goodness, O*

Lord, she made it clear that it was not because of her deserts. So it is not lawful for anyone to be presumptuous at any time except the person who happens to sin seriously. This figure is called *emphasis* or exaggeration, here of the kind which suggests what it does not state.[15] So His goodness is truly proclaimed of whom it was written: *None is good but God alone.*[16]

8. HETH. *The Lord is sweet and righteous: therefore he will establish a law for sinners on the way.* The Lord is sweet because while excelling all in kindnesses He still awaits the conversion of the sinner, for *He raineth upon the just and the unjust,*[17] granting life to those who deserved to be blotted out. So He is deservedly called sweet, for sweet things are forthcoming from Him. As another psalm says: *O taste and see that the Lord is sweet.*[18] The expression *sweet* derives from its association with sweetmeats which so greatly delight the human race. He is righteous because after numerous rebukes and extremely long delays He opposes evil men, humbles the proud and wicked, so that they may finally become wise and repent of their having sinned. As for His establishing a law, this was a particular mark of sweetness and righteousness, for He did not wish those men to sin whom He preferred to correct by the proclamation of the law. But so that none might believe that this came as a punishment emanating from harshness, He expounded the purpose of the law which He introduced, the law of goodness and sweetness. *On the way,* that is, in the present life, where the law by which we are warned to live righteously is established.

9. THETH. *He will straighten the meek in judgment: he will teach the mild his ways.* In other words, He ensures that the peaceful in heart reach the promised blessedness. One who is straightened is made upright after being bent. The term *meek* excludes the proud and the puffed up; as the gospel says: *Blessed are the meek, for they shall possess the land.*[19] *The mild* are the converse of the proud, who with a freedom harmful to themselves kick against the soft yoke and the light burden; He will teach those who do not grumble, but do what they acknowledge as commands. The difference between mild and meek seems to be this: the meek are those untroubled by any flame of wildness, constantly abiding in gentleness of mind, whereas the mild (*mansueti*) are so called because they are tamed by hand (*manu sueti*), in other words, bearing injuries and not returning evil for evil. She spoke of *His ways,* and next expounds what the Lord's ways are.

10. JOD. *All the ways of the Lord are mercy and truth, to them that seek after his testament and his testimonies.* Though the ways of the Lord are beyond understanding, she assembles them most aptly in brief compass, for who could have the resources to tell of His works, of the extent of the power by which He controls things heavenly and earthly? But though those ways could not have been detailed, they are sufficiently summarised: *All the ways of the Lord are mercy and truth. Mercy,* because He outstrips every creature in goodness; *truth,* because He makes His judgments with integrity. But so that we may not think that this is to be a general gift, those who can be fitting recipients follow: *To them that seek his testament and his testimonies.* When testament is used in the singular, it connotes either the Old or the New; here then we must interpret it as the New. But *testimonies* is used of the prophets who went before,[20] for they were witnesses of the sacred promises which the Lord fulfilled with the manifestation of His coming.

11. KAPH. *For thy name's sake, O Lord, thou wilt pardon my sin; for it is copious.* We do well to apply this to the person of the Church, whose assembly as we know is the gathering of diverse sinners. *For thy name's sake, O Lord:* Jesus, whose name is translated as "saviour" in our language, was to be cited since the name itself is acknowledged as a claim to salvation. Next comes: *For it is copious;* in other words, it is such that You could not spare in itself, but only because of the holiness of Your name. When sin is termed copious, it is known to be most abundant, since it ever increases with the course of time, and if help is not lent by divine mercy for the period of one's life, one sins solely through human frailty. Store in your memory also that the Church speaks for part of her members in saying that her sins are abundant. So those who proclaim themselves pure, like the Catharists,[21] can realise that they do not have their lot with holy Church.

12. LAMED. *Who is the man that feareth the Lord? He hath appointed him a law in the way he hath chosen.* She passes to the third section, where there is particular emphasis on who it is that fears the Lord, or with what gift the Lord felicitates him. But after her fashion she asks a prior question, intending to make the fitting reply: *He hath appointed him a law.* This is the man whom she wished to emphasise. She says that the man has accepted the law to which the Lord wished

to attach fear so that he could not sin in the security of ignorance. *In the way he hath chosen:* in other words, in the holiness of his plan of life.

13. MEM. *His soul shall dwell in good things, and his seed shall inherit and possess the land.* When just men strip off their bodies, the perfect blessedness promised to saints at the resurrection is not immediately granted; however, she says that his soul can *dwell in good things,* for even if there is still a postponement of those rewards which *eye hath not seen, nor ear heard, neither have they entered into the heart of man,*[22] they still at this time feast on the unshakeable delight of hope in their future reward. Next comes: *And his seed shall possess and inherit the land.* She now indicates without conditions the future reward, since *his seed,* or his good works, will be taken into eternal safe-keeping, and his possession will not be troubled by any further expulsion; for the man who holds something through inheritance boasts a most secure possession.

14. *The Lord is a firmament to them that fear him, and his covenant shall be made manifest to them.* In this short verse she carefully strengthened the spirits and minds of believers. To begin with, because human manners are fickle she says that the Lord will be *a firmament,* so that man should not have doubts on his own account, since he is shored up by such a promise. But notice her words: *To them that fear him;* she does not make this promise to the arrogant and reckless. Note also the force of the arrangement of the words. Fear of man breeds lack of confidence, but fear of God yields the support of hope. The second point to be grasped is really vital, that His law is declared to us as a gift, without which we can neither understand anything good nor achieve praiseworthy deeds.

15. SAMECH. *My eyes are ever towards the Lord: for he shall pluck my feet out of the snare.* After earlier enunciating the rewards of the blessed, she now says that her gaze has ever been on the Lord. The varying statements here yield a most beautiful sense. The man who does not watch the ground before his feet is likely to run into snares or fall into open wells. But the statement here is remarkable and true, that we shall walk circumspectly and guide our feet if we continually raise our eyes to the Lord, for such gazing makes us strangers to all stumbling.

16. AIN. *Look thou upon me, and have mercy on me: for I am alone*

and poor. Her response incorporates a splendid comparison; previously she said: *My eyes are ever towards the Lord*, and now she says: "*Look thou upon me*, as I look on You, *and have mercy on me.*" He who always looks to the Lord asks that He should look with pity on himself. She appended most compelling reasons for His mercy, since a lone person wins more love, and a very poor man attracts more sympathy. The Church uses these words aptly of the persona of the Christian people, which is *alone* in His eyes, for it alone guards the mysteries of the true faith, and *poor* because it is isolated from the world's enticements, and is not filled with worldly ambition.

17. PHE. *The troubles of my heart are widened: deliver me from my necessities*. The Church's troubles are widened when she spreads her thoughts over the disasters of the world where she is set, for one afflicted on behalf of many is inevitably bent low under a massive burden. The necessities mentioned are those endured from the snares of persecutors and heretics, for these are people seeking to bring slaughter on Christians. She was right to call these necessities hers, for she had shouldered them in the zeal of her love.

18. ZADE. *See my humility and my labour, and forgive me all my sins*. *See*, in other words, regard with kindness. The *humility* of the Church is when in her teaching she endures the undisciplined and debased, and permits them to be kept concealed and hidden for God's judgment. Her *labour* is because she is wearied by many persecutions and much strife; though always assailed by the reproaches of the wicked, she does not in this world take relaxation in the rest of the peace she desires. So after such great sufferings she rightly begs that all her sins be forgiven her, for the truly grinding toil of her devoted endurance ever awaits the mercy of the Judge.

19. RES. *Look on my enemies, for they are multiplied and have hated me with an unjust hatred*. In saying: *Look on my enemies*, she prays for their return, for He converts without delay those whom He looks upon; for example, in the gospel the Lord looked on Peter, and he wept. She appended the reason why they should not perish: *For they are multiplied*. One might perhaps believe that a few could be held of

little account, but the loss of many could not be endured without the greatest grief. Next comes: *And have hated me with an unjust hatred.* They did indeed hate the Church with an unjust hatred, for while she poured out prayer for them, they did not interrupt or cease their persecution. So she added: *With an unjust hatred,* for hatred can apparently also be just, as in the passage: *I have hated them with a perfect hatred.*[23]

20. SIN. *Keep thou my soul, and rescue me: I shall not be confounded, for I have called on thee.* The Church asks that her faith be guarded in its most upright form, so that saved from schismatics she cannot be disturbed by any perversity, but may be offered without spot and wrinkle, and adorned with the virtues of the faith, to her Bridegroom. There is appended the praiseworthy reason why she ought to obtain her prayer, since she has called on the Lord. Because she is known to have set her hope on such great virtue, she truly does not deserve to feel shame; for she chose to call on Him who cannot discard those who entreat devotedly.

21. TAV. *The innocent and upright have adhered to me, because I have waited on thee, O Lord.* By *the innocent* some understand the little ones reborn by sacred baptism, who are as yet uncontaminated by any intercourse with the world, but pass through it in the holiness which they have deserved to attain. They wish *the upright* to be interpreted as those converted at a mature age and freed from the snares of sins by God's gift. But since we have said that the Church is made up of differing human manners, how is it that here she merely says: *The innocent and upright have adhered to me,* as if she does not contain intermingled with the others those contaminated with wicked morals? But ponder the force of this expression, her saying that the innocent and upright have adhered to her, as though they were joined and glued to her, a result apparently ensured by the worthy manners in both, whereas the remainder have been sustained with pain rather than have adhered. *I have waited* means: "I have endured like a man the regular hardships in this world, but I had one consolation, to wait on thee, O Lord." Examine the force of this verse. She says that the innocent and upright have adhered to her because she waited on the Lord; otherwise she could not love such people if she was not seen to be confident of such strength.

22. *Redeem me, God of Israel, from all my hardships.* When she says:

Redeem me, she demands the coming of the Lord Saviour, by whose blood she is redeemed and freed from the devil's confinement. *God of Israel;* in other words, God of those who behold you,[24] because He finds truly grateful those to whom He grants a glimpse of His own thoughts. By adding *from all my hardships* she expresses the longing that no stain be found in her, for she cannot be joined as a holy bride to Christ unless she is *without spot and wrinkle,*[25] as Scripture has it.

Conclusion Drawn From the Psalm

Let us listen to how the Church, set among the hardships of this world, cries to her Liberator throughout the whole psalm, and let us cease to bear our sufferings with impatience, for it is clear that the mother herself endures most weighty hardships on our behalf. With the Lord's help let us bear adversity like men; let us constantly hope in His dutiful love, for if we remain within the fold of His bride, we shall by God's generosity attain eternal joys in company with her. The number of this psalm, twice twelve, declares heavenly mysteries to us, because twenty-four elders with unwearied voices sing together praises to the Lord in sweet melody,[26] reminding us to imitate them and to sing this psalm with repeated devotion.

COMMENTARY ON PSALM 25

1. *A psalm of David.* Since *psalm* signifies the harmony of spiritual attributes in our actions, and *David* means "brave of hand" and "one to be desired,"[1] the whole of this text is to be applied to the theme of the perfect Christian who by the Lord's generosity continues with committed mind in His Church, winning praise for his different merits, and consoling himself with God's kindnesses. But since the hymn is described as such, we must ascribe it to Christ the Lord through the power of our understanding.

Division of the Psalm

The holy man whom we have mentioned prays in the first theme of the psalm that his innocence be observed, because he has not shared the lot of wicked men. In the second he prays that he should not be set among heretics or schismatics at the Lord's judgment, because he has claimed to have loved His house.

Explanation of the Psalm

Judge me, O Lord, for I have walked in my innocence, and I have put my trust in the Lord, and shall not be weakened. The request for judgment seems indeed to be hazardous, but separation from evil men, which takes place at the Lord's scrutiny, is acknowledged to be fittingly sought by one who is truly deserving. So we have here not pride in what he deserves, which is execrable, but a just request from a faithful servant asking to be separated from the exceedingly wicked, so that he may not share the portion of evil men. The holy man demands judgment because he is certain of the Lord's mercy. As Paul has it: *As to the rest, there is laid up for me a crown of justice, which the Lord, the just Judge, will render to me in that day.*[2] He walks in his innocence because, as he says later, he puts his trust in the Lord, and the presumption he shows is not in his own powers but in God's generosity. There follows a beautiful proof of this assertion, for he maintains that he is not weakened in his trust in the Lord. This is in fact the *innocence* of which he spoke earlier, in other words, confidence in the Lord's power that no weakness of sin can weigh on him.

2. *Prove me, O Lord, and try me: burn my reins and my heart. Prove and try* is said not out of presumption, but as a demand that it be done to bring about an improvement; for when He examines and tries us, He makes us aware of our sinning, and helps us attain the reward of repentance. Otherwise, were He not to warn us by any adversity in this world, we would leave neglected the things for which we ought to make satisfaction. He himself later explains why he asked to be proved and tried: precisely so that his reins and heart should be burned, that is,

in order that human pleasures and thoughts might be purged by the heat of the Lord's word, for he removes the foulness of vices after the manner of furnaces, and draws men's souls to the cleansing which brings the most perfect beauty. But we must examine why he prays to be tried, whereas in the gospel-prayer it is stated: *Do not put us to the test.*[3] Well, there are two kinds of trial. The first is the Lord's, by which He tries good men to train them fittingly; as we read in Genesis: *The Lord tried Abraham.*[4] Or again, there are the words of Moses: *The Lord your God tries you.*[5] The second type of trial is the devil's, which always leads to death; with regard to this, we pray that we may not be led through blindness of mind into his domain. So the prophet does well to pray with the words: *Prove me, O Lord, and try me* in this the Lord's sphere, so that he might not be led into the other trial which is the devil's, for which the ensuing words are: *But deliver us from evil,*[6] that is, from the devil himself.

3. *For thy mercy is before my eyes: and I am approved in thy truth.* This was the reason why he did not fear the hazards of temptations, because he could not forget His mercy; he continually regards this as an aid to him, because he always sets before his eyes the kindnesses which have been bestowed. Because of this he also says that he has been *approved* in the Lord. To be approved means to deserve the Lord's eternal grace in company with the saints. *In thy truth* means "In thy Christ," for He says: *I am the way, the truth, and the life.*[7] Otherwise he cannot be pleasing to the Lord unless he has been strengthened by such belief.

4. *I have not sat in the council of vanity: neither will I go in with the doers of unjust things.* In this very fine statement he maintains that he has been pleasing to the Lord, for he tries to show his innocence in two verses by his avoidance of what is wicked, and then in two further verses by performing what is right. In the *Topics*[8] this argument is called "from opposites," for *the council of vanity* and the gathering of innocents are utterly opposite to each other. He now lists what he has achieved through the Lord's kindnesses, for this was the basis of his claim that he was approved. *I have not sat in the council of vanity;* he does not lend assent to the discussions of the wicked by any association with their plans. It can happen by some chance that a holy man attends a council of the wicked at which unfitting or empty proposals are made, yet while he has cognizance of these he does not associate

himself with them, nor linger with any delight in them, but instead either argues against an evil proposal or quits it. So whereas earlier he said that he had not sat with the wicked, now he claims that he has not gone in with those who are very wicked; first he avoided their discussions, and later he forsook their actions. *Going into* crime means beginning some reckless action, for the going in signifies the commencement of the activity which the holy man claims is alien to his moral sense.

5. *I have hated the assembly of the malignant: and with the wicked I will not sit.* It would not have been enough for the holy man to have avoided the evil council without also hating the assembly of those who are cunning in every way. Hatred connotes division, just as love connotes partnership. Just as he said earlier that he had not sat in the council of vanity, so now he claims that he does not sit with the wicked, for both must be utterly forsaken. The vain and the wicked are different from each other. The vain are those concerned with transient interests who spend their time in empty discourse; but the wicked are the heretics who seek to devalue the divine Scriptures with treacherous questions. As the apostle Peter says: *Wresting them to their own destruction and perdition.*[9] So he rightly warns that both groups be avoided, because the first loves empty things, and the second implants weapons of subversion.

6. *I will wash my hands among the innocent, and will compass thy altar, O Lord.* The man who follows Christ his Head, and who despises earthly things through longing for things heavenly, can say such things. As Paul has it: *But our conversation is in heaven.*[10] Whoever makes spotless his own deeds through eagerness for a goodly life with others washes his hands among the innocent. He did well to add *among the innocent,* because guilty men also can wash their hands, as Pontius Pilate did when in fouling his soul by wicked betrayal of the Lord he washed his hands in the water of this world. But whoever washes his hands in the tears which render satisfaction, washes his hands in the spiritual sense. He said: *I shall compass,* in other words, visit frequently, to show the diligence of his most pious devotion. *Altar* gets its name from altitude,[11] since altars on which there is sacrifice to the Lord are lofty so that the gifts of His mercy may be laid open to the sight of nations.

7. *That I may hear the voice of thy praise, and tell of all thy wondrous*

works. He journeys to things heavenly, and in spirit compasses that altar to hear the harmony of the Lord's praise. Perhaps he says this because in his presence there is singing with unwearied voices before the throne: *Holy, holy, holy, Lord God of hosts.*[12] Once he heard these words and acknowledged them with the greatest devotion, he would recount to the nations all the wonderful things which even today the blessed Church sings when celebrating holy masses.

8. *I have loved, O Lord, the beauty of thy house, and the dwelling-place of thy glory.* The most blessed man whom we have mentioned commences the second motif of his prayer. He begs that since he has loved the beauty of the Lord's house, he should by no means be mingled with those who are foreign to it, but should continue in His Church. *The beauty of thy house* means not splendour of walls or most expensive tableware, but the most blessed nature of those actions in which the whole Church rejoices: namely, the glad rendering of psalms, the piety of prayers, the most humble devotion of the Christian people. Previously he spoke of the Church as a whole, and now he comes to the saints in whom God's glory is known to dwell. Of them Paul says: *For the temple of God is holy, which you are.*[13] By his mention of *the dwelling-place*, he was pointing to the secret region of the human heart; and he adds the wonderful phrase, *of thy glory,* for wherever He dwells there is glory, since He makes glorious whatever place He deigns to dwell in, and the majesty of the lodging grows with the merits of the Guest.

9. *Take not away my soul together with the wicked: nor my life with bloody men.* He justly asks that his soul should not perish with the wicked at the judgment to come, for he has not joined in action with them. He deservedly sought to be separated there from the persons from whom he separated himself here; for *bloody men* are those who live according to the flesh, and who long for no commands from heaven. So such men are dispatched to death from the Jerusalem to come, for they are to be condemned because of their wickedness.

10. *In whose hands are iniquities: their right hand is filled with gifts.* He expounds the nature of bloody men, association with whom we see involves wicked actions. Our hands signify general activities which we perform in this life; *right hand* here has the special connotation of the venality of a judge which he says is filled with gifts because it is weighed down through being offered much money. Realise that he

curses the class of judges who accept this; for he who sells justice fills his right hand with gifts, and he who acquits the guilty likewise fills his right hand by receiving gifts. So both statements are in my view to be aptly applied to men of blood.

11. *But as for me, I have walked in my innocence: redeem me, and have mercy on me.* This is the figure of *syncrisis,*[14] when a man tries to make his case better by reference to his opponents. Whereas when they receive money they rejoice that their right hand is filled with gifts, he says that he himself has made his way into the riches of innocence. Having entered into spiritual treasures, he consoled himself much more genuinely than they could have rejoiced over worldly riches. *Redeem me,* in other words, free me with precious blood at Your coming, for by it the world was delivered when held subject to sins. *And have mercy on me,* that is, in this world, where You spare those who faithfully entreat You.

12. *For my foot has stood in the upright way: in the churches I will bless the Lord.* Among the shattering heresies and oppressively fierce hardships of the world, the Catholic well proclaims that his foot has remained immovable, for though tossed in grievous tribulations it cannot be shifted by any compulsion from its commitment to the faith. This claim can be made by men such as this and those like them. The Lord himself testifies to them, as in the statement: *I have left me seven thousand men who have not bent their knees before Baal.*[15] *In the upright way,* that is, in Thy commands which are upright, and which make the upright obedient. Whenever churches are mentioned in the plural, the Christian people of the world is indicated. They are known to be gathered from different nations; the one and perfect Jerusalem to come will be cleansed by the exclusion of the wicked. So this blessed man of whom we have spoken says that he will sing to the Lord not in the Church, but in the churches, because the name Catholic is known to exist throughout the whole world.

Conclusion Drawn From the Psalm

Let us consider the nature of the pattern of life which the religious man has passed on to us. He says that he has in this world avoided the very wicked, so that he cannot be associated with evil men at the

Lord's judgment. He warns us that by shunning association with the unjust, we may be ever joined to Christ's faithful in spiritual love, because we always derive the nature of our behaviour from prolonged intercourse with men. Psalm 6 likewise reminds us of this when it says: *Depart from me, all ye workers of iniquity.*[16] Likewise the words of Psalm 17: *With the holy thou wilt be holy, and with the innocent man thou wilt be innocent. With the elect thou wilt be elect, and with the perverse thou wilt be perverted.*[17] The frequent warnings on what we must avoid are to ensure that we realise the immensity of the evil. So let us most eagerly seek out the most glorious and appropriate partnership which can school us in virtues and fire us with longing for divine love, so that we may not deservedly be joined with the very wicked as retribution for our evil deeds, since we chose to associate with the ill-disposed here in this world. If we examine the matter with some care, the number of the psalm itself is not otiose; the authority of the gospel points out to us that at Jerusalem[18] there were five porticoes in which a crowd of invalids lay sick. When the number is multiplied by five, the total becomes twenty-five. So the hearts of the faithful are refreshed in the depths of this psalm, just as in those porticoes the sick bodies of those who lay there were healed by the waters of the pool called Probatica.

COMMENTARY ON PSALM 26

1. *The psalm of David before he was anointed.* The history of this heading is revealed in greater detail in the book of Kings. When Saul sinned before God, David was anointed into the kingship in the presence of his father by the holy prophet Samuel.[1] But the heading does not refer to that anointing, but is seen rather to commemorate a second anointing, when after Saul's persecutions he was advanced to the kingship by the prayer of the people;[2] for it is clear that he wrote this psalm in witness of those events. If you care to concentrate your attention on the first anointing, you read that he composed no psalm before it, so it remains for us to understand the reference here as to the second anointing.

Division of the Psalm

The prophet speaks throughout the psalm of his being delivered from most oppressive enemies on numerous occasions before his kingship. In the first section he says that he fears the Lord and trembles at no other. He attests that among the hardships of the world he has one refuge, that though tossed by physical dangers he has dwelt in the Lord's house with the most steadfast commitment of mind. In the second part he gives thanks in diverse ways after being freed from manifold disaster, and with the breath of prophecy promises himself the hope of future blessedness. We are in fact to realise that this is the second of the psalms pointing through the deeds of David to the future mysteries of Christ the Lord.[3]

Explanation of the Psalm

The Lord is my light and salvation: whom shall I fear? The Lord is the defender of my life: of whom shall I be afraid? 2. Whilst the wicked draw near against me to eat my flesh, my enemies that trouble me have themselves been weakened, and have fallen. Let us listen a little more attentively to these three verses. They are enclosed in the form of the great argument called by the Greeks *epichirema*,[4] and by the Latins *exsecutiones* or *approbationes;* we employ this argument when we wish to prove a matter at issue with some example. Here the case was advanced in one and a half verses. He said *The Lord is my light and salvation: whom shall I fear? The Lord is the defender of my life: of whom shall I be afraid?* In the other one and a half verses, he attached an example of why he ought not to have trembled, since those known to be persecuting him fall instead. He says: *While the wicked draw near against me to eat my flesh, my enemies that trouble me have themselves been weakened and have fallen.* So the shape of this *epichirema* has been attained in small compass. Now let us return to our exposition. The prophet, then, says joyfully that he fears no man since he has been enlightened by the Lord. He shows that fear always brings its darkness, for against it is set the light of heaven. Next comes: *And my salvation.* In this expression he encloses everything, both health of body and safety of soul. Both are indications of salvation, since they undoubtedly endure most severe sufferings. *Whom shall I fear?* means "I shall fear no man"; fear of the Lord had ensured that he could fear no other. There follows: *The Lord is the defender of my life: of whom shall I be afraid?* Through wicked deeds many have lost God's gifts which they received, but those whose defender was the Lord have lost absolutely nothing. *Of whom shall I be afraid?* These words must be uttered as a question, implying "Of no-one," just as earlier he asked *Whom shall I fear?* Undoubtedly such questions are to be understood as denials. He added: *While the wicked draw near against me to eat my flesh.* Here the aspirations of harsh enemies are exposed, for they desire not only to destroy but in the greed of madness even cruelly to devour human flesh. Such barbaric behaviour of enemies is recounted so that the grace won by freedom may be redoubled. He added: *My enemies that trouble me have themselves been weakened, and have fallen.* This verse is linked with the earlier statement. It is proof of how he ought to have feared no man, for if his persecutors who could have inspired dread have collapsed, what fear, I ask, will there be when his apparent assailants fall down instead? The verbs are placed in sequence; first weakened, then falling; and notice here that the benefits experienced by the faithful are briefly recounted, so that it is not so much those oppressed by sufferings but rather those who hasten to gulp the blood of the innocent who collapse instead.

3. *If enemies in camp should stand together against me, my heart shall not fear.* Now that the proof of his salvation is complete, the prophet joyfully enthuses, with beautiful *emphasis*[5] or exaggeration, that even if the great crowd of an encampment assembles against him alone, his mind's constancy must not be alarmed, even though men are usually terrified by the attack of a great number. A *camp* is a strong fortification which the onset of an attacker cannot easily storm. But he says that all such things are trivial in his eyes, since he is protected by divine help.

If a battle should rise up against me, in this I will be confident. A camp could remain inactive and not assemble for battle, but now he appends the savage conflict itself, so that he should be seen to fear none of the things which humanity considers frightening. If it should *rise up*, in other words if a sudden concerted attack like a seething storm should burst out against me, *I will be confident* of victory in such a battle. When battles are joined, the glory of the victor is always in evidence, for his underlying courage which has not been tested in battle is now proved. As the psalmist said earlier: *When I was in distress, thou hast enlarged me.*[6] One must note that this verse has a beginning identical with the preceding one. This is the figure called *anaphora*,[7] when a word is repeated at the beginning of phrases. This effect is clearly achieved at the beginning of the psalm, with *the Lord . . . the Lord.*

4. *One thing have I asked of the Lord, this will I seek after.* He says that he has asked one thing of the Lord, and he expounds it later. But let us examine if he has asked for one thing rather than for everything. It is indeed one in number, but numerous in the various objects for which it is useful. The request is restricted, but the reward extended. The plea is in few words, but the response is on a large scale. So it is the habit of good men to beg merely for the Lord's house, because all good things are contained in it, whereas evil men are torn in their earthly wants, and in seeking health of body, in begging for riches, in demanding the destruction of enemies they weary in their pleading and sometimes seek things which will not endure.[8]

That I may dwell in the house of the Lord all the days of my life: that I may see the will of the Lord, and may be protected by his holy temple. This is the one request for which he begged earlier. Note that he who has walled himself in with such a defence must fear no camp, no battle; for what state is comparable to, what army is stronger than dwelling in the Lord's house, where nothing human or devil-sent is clearly to be feared? And this is for no short period, but for all the days of his life. So when, I ask, is he to fear, when his entire life is safe? He who sees the will of the Lord understands His commands, for he has surrendered himself with all his mind to His purity. The prophet asks to be protected by the temple of Christ's body, from which we obtain support for faith and invincible strength of protection, for through virtue of mind he had attained what he did not yet behold in appearance.

5–6. *For he hath hidden me in his tabernacle on the day of evils: he hath protected me in the secret place of his tabernacle. He hath exalted me upon a rock.* Let us analyse this verse with a little more care. He says, as we see: *For he hath hidden me in his tabernacle on the day of evils,* meaning the time when during persecution by Saul he continually lay hidden in many regions in foul caves and on desolate mountains. This was truly for David a *tabernacle,* because his mind never abandoned its religious duty. Next comes: *He hath protected me in the secret place of his taber-*

nacle. Earlier he said: *He hath hidden me;* now he says: *He hath protected me*. Being *hidden* means not being exposed to the eyes of seekers; being *protected* means being freed from all fear and danger. He said: *In the secret place of his tabernacle,* in other words, in the depths of His divinity, towards which the spirit of this committed man always hastened; it seemed to him to be in the place where his attention was concentrated. As for his words, *He hath exalted me on a rock,* this refers to the Lord's incarnation, for from his seed was born Christ the Cornerstone[9] uniting peoples.

But now he hath lifted up my head above my enemies. After he mentioned the rewards to come from the Lord's incarnation, he now speaks of present rewards, since it is clear that he has been freed from his enemies whether of the flesh or of the spirit. *My head* we seem to interpret correctly as the mind's eye, which is truly our head, for when it is fresh we can have clear sight; we often call it the head because the head stands out. *Above enemies* refers to the sinful appetites over which our mind is appropriately set when kept pure by God's kindness.

I shall go round and offer up in his tabernacle a victim of jubilation: I will sing, and recite a psalm to the Lord. After having discoursed on the kindnesses, future and present, which he knew he had received, he now describes his joy in marvellous narrative. He says: *I shall go round,* in other words, mentally survey the power by which He made the heavens, created the stars, put limits on the seas, steadied the earth, and filled the whole world with diverse praise of the virtues. After mentally traversing all these, he says that he is offering up *in his tabernacle a victim of jubilation,* in other words, he is offering in His Church the sacrifice of praise. We speak of *jubilation* because we take delight in praise when in our joy we hasten to give thanks with the utmost pleasure. Earlier we said that it was one thing to sing, another to recite a psalm. Singing means uttering praises with the voice alone, whereas reciting a psalm means proclaiming the Lord's glory by good works. Singing and reciting a psalm are themselves *the victim of jubilation*.

7. *Hear, O Lord, the voice with which I have cried to thee: have mercy on me, and hear me*. He has reached the second section, so that in his thanksgiving he might demonstrate his gift of psalmody as he promised; thus he joins the present theme with the previous one. He *cried*

when he said: *That I may dwell in the house of the Lord all the days of my life.* Whereas he earlier said that he was offering a victim of jubilation, because he had obtained diverse gifts, he now again asks to be heard. He does not yet satisfy his longing unless he makes this request with repeated supplication, doubtless because he cannot have enough of things divine, but the more the Lord is tasted the sweeter is our seeking Him. As he says in another psalm: *Taste, and see that the Lord is sweet.*[10]

8. *My heart hath said to thee, I have sought thy face: thy face, O Lord, I will seek.* The heart reveals its silent longing, to which the Godhead listens more than to the most thundering voices of nations. He said to Moses: *Why criest thou to me?*[11] although we do not read that Moses had said anything. So the faithful man said that his heart was speaking to the Lord, since he seemed to offer his thoughts by this means. The man who lives a holy life seeks the face of the Lord; of such men Scripture says: *Blessed are the pure of heart, for they shall see God.*[12] He duplicates his statement with the words: *Thy face, O Lord, will I seek.* The content is the same but the prayer is repeated, for he knew how precious was the fact of his praying so many times with fervent zeal.

9. *Turn not away thy face from me: decline not in thy wrath from thy servant.* He catalogues his wants with appropriate care. In the previous verse he claimed that he sought the Lord's face with longing, and since it is not in man's power to attain his desire, he prays that the Lord should not turn away His face which he eagerly demanded, for it lies within God's discretion to afford a sight of himself to the most faithful. Next comes: *Decline not in thy wrath from thy servant.* We have often said that by wrath is meant the time of judgment when He separates the bad from the good, for He is thought to be angry with those condemned by unhappy sequestration. So he asks that the Lord should not *decline* from him on the occasion when He grants the face of His majesty to His holy ones. The man of the flesh fears God in case he should lose his substance, or be orphaned of his sons, or have his store of gold or silver diminished through the weight of his sins; but the holy man fears only that he may become a stranger to the Lord's face.

Be thou my helper, forsake me not: do not despise me, O God my saviour. Where are those who claim that something can be achieved through human merits? Here a king and a prophet, full of grace and heavenly blessing, asks that he be not abandoned by the Lord, for he knows that if the Lord forsakes him no power will be able to guide him. Nor is it enough for him to have made the prayer once; he must redouble and repeat it. Being despised is always the condition of the bondsman, and he cannot be relieved of care unless the kindly eye of the Judge gazes upon him.

10. *For my father and my mother have left me: but the Lord hath taken me up.* By his *father* he means Adam the first man, and by his *mother,* Adam's wife Eve, from whom the human stock descends. So these left him with his mortal condition, and could not nourish him since they had been removed from this life. But this verse could be understood also of David's parents, because he left the house of his father and mother when he was raised to the dignity of kingship by the Hebrew people. Next comes: *But the Lord hath taken me up,* that is, in place of a true parent. He is a Father as founder and ruler, a Mother because He nurtures and feeds with milk the weak and tiny. His phrase, *hath taken up,* means He established him in the kingship from the status of private citizen.

11. *Set me, O Lord, a law in thy way, and guide me in the right path because of my enemies.* He begs that the Lord Saviour's law be preferably set before him, for we know that by means of it he freed debtors through favour. By that time the law had already been given to Moses, but there was hope that the Lord's law was coming, and he asks that it be established for him. *In thy way* means "in thy Christ," for He is *the way, the truth, and the life.*[13] He rightly presumed that since Christ was coming, he could both teach the law and guarantee that it could be fulfilled. We have already said that the *path* refers to understanding of Scripture. So the prophet prays that he may rightly understand the books of the Old Testament, and recognise in them that the Lord is to come. *Because of my enemies* is added to denote heretics or the unbelieving Jews who strove with foul purpose to topple them.[14]

12. *Deliver me not over to the will of them that persecute me: for unjust witnesses have risen up against me, and iniquity hath lied to itself.* This can be understood in the historical sense[15] of Saul, who persecuted him with the keenest hatred. But since Saul was king and could not carry out his orders alone, the plural is aptly used here. In similar fashion the plural, *unjust witnesses,* is employed to denote when Doeg the Edomite in the scriptural account betrays him, for when Doeg accused

him before the king, he probably wished to prove his allegations through other witnesses. But the plural is seen to be aptly used because such a person could not be readily accused through one individual only. So the unjust witnesses were Doeg the Edomite and those like him who revealed to Saul that David had been received by the prophet Achimelech, and that a sword and victuals had been given to him; the king revealed this through the death of the priest and his sons. They lied when they said that David had been entrusted with a conspiracy against Saul, and that Achimelech prayed to the Lord on David's behalf. The text of Kings reports this at greater length. *To itself* is most beautifully said, because he who hastens to bear false witness suffers punishment for his lie. Or, as others state, it is a peculiarity of divine Scripture that the plural is employed for the singular; one finds it as a feature of other passages. For example, we read the statement about the dead Herod: *They are dead that sought the life of the child.*[16] Or the declaration made to Moses about Pharaoh: *For they are dead that sought my life.*[17]

13–14. *I believe to see the good things of the Lord in the land of the living. Expect the Lord.* After having begged the Lord in many ways not to betray him to persecutors, he returns to the help afforded by his trust, and promises himself *to see the good things in the land of the living,* that is, in the future life where the good things are everlasting. That land is rightly termed *of the living,* for this earth belongs to the dead. Amongst the orators this is the basis of the argument termed inferential,[18] when what is not stated is inferred from what is, so that one is instructed through it just as if it had been written down. So here he believes that future rewards will come to him because of the kindnesses which have gone before. Divine Scripture appropriately speaks of *the land of the living;* appended is: *Expect the Lord,* that is, Him who does not deceive when He promises, who does not submit an account when He bestows. As the apostle James says: *Who giveth to all men abundantly, and upbraideth not.*[19]

Do manfully, and let thy heart take courage: and sustain the Lord. Since in the previous verse he believed *to see the good things of the Lord,* he now states how he can see them. We must believe that the word *manfully* is attributed not only to men but also to women. When men grow soft they have a womanly spirit, and women become manful when they continue with strength of mind in a good course of action.

Next comes: *And let thy heart take courage,* so that you may not grumble through weariness, and despair through exhausting fatigue. Instead he says with a hopeful and carefree mind: *Expect the Lord,* who cannot take away what He promises. *Sustain* and *expect* are spoken to the perfect Christian, as if he were advising him: "Sustain what you suffer, and expect what you believe."

Conclusion Drawn From the Psalm

The most venerable prophet has revealed what we should particularly long for amidst manifold and savage hardships, namely that we should seek in every way to dwell in Christ's Church. Let us open our ears to this, and listen and pray with diligent supplication; nothing could be stated more briefly, no broader gift could be obtained. But in the number of this psalm, and some which follow it, we could find no striking reason for the figure. That is to say, we could not elicit the nature of any created object mentioned in Scripture connected with the numbers 26, 27, or 28. We leave this to studious readers to emulate the examples already offered. When they do not find any significance in each individual number, they must search for similarities in divisions of them, whether divided by two or three. For example, they can divide 26 into 20 and 6, or again, 27 into three nines. When the total has been split, perhaps an appropriate explanation can be advanced, for what difference does it make if the vessels of the psalms contain two or three measures? But if you do not discover anything apposite by this means either, it is right to believe that the Creator of heaven and earth has divided His actions and His words without ambiguity through the powers of different numbers; for we read that He has perfected all things in weight, number, and measure.[20] Because drops of rain, stars in heaven, or grains of sand on the seashore cannot be numbered by us, this does not mean that they are not clearly numbered in His eyes. Things known to be hidden to us are none the less known to the power of God. It remains for us to believe the statement of our forbears, that the powers of the psalms harmonise with the numbers allotted and designated.

COMMENTARY ON PSALM 27

1. *A psalm of David himself.* We have said that David means "strong of hand."[1] When should such a name be mentioned except when the glorious struggles of the Lord's passion are recounted? He is indeed strong of hand, for by His enduring He laid low the prince of darkness. He overcame death by dying, He freed the captive human race by the dispensation of His crucifixion. When the psalm is said to be of *himself,* what is stated is that no other can be meant except the Mediator Christ the Lord Himself, who speaks through this whole psalm, praying in the lowliness of the flesh which He had assumed, and revealing the punishment owed to persecutors, not out of malevolent zeal but as witness of vengeance. We must note, then, that this is the third of the psalms which briefly commemorate the passion and resurrection of the Lord.[2]

Division of the Psalm

In the first section, the Lord Christ prays in His human capacity that His prayer be heard at the time of the passion to come. Secondly, He gives thanks because His prayer has been heard in the events which He asked should take place; and He appends at the end of the psalm the request that just as He was raised up by the power of His divinity, so may the people who believe in His name be saved.

Explanation of the Psalm

Unto thee have I cried, O Lord: O my God, be not thou silent to me. Christ the Lord cries to the Father at the time of the passion that He should not be silent to Him; in other words, that He should not refuse to assent to His prayer, but should reply. A most beautiful contrast of words is achieved. Man cries that God be not silent, because when we are silent the Lord says nothing, and when we are indifferent we are not kept in mind. On the other hand, if through the Lord's generosity we look to Him, He looks to us. If we cry, He hearkens; if we love, we are also loved.

And I shall be like them that go down into the lake. In other words, "If you are silent, I shall be like those who dwell in the depths of this world"; for this world is a sort of lake which is thought to be pleasant and calm, but we do not know what depths and drownings it manifests. A lake (*lacus*) is so called because earth lurks (*lateat*)[3] below it. So in His humanity the Word prays that He may not be like other men, for though He took on the general condition of the flesh, He has deserved to excel all creatures because He is united with God. Of Him the apostle says: *To which of the angels has he said at any time, Thou art my Son, today I have begotten thee?*[4] Alternatively *lake* signifies the tomb in which He was placed after the passion was ended.

2. *Hear, O Lord, the voice of my supplication when I pray to thee, when I lift up my hands to thy holy temple.* He alludes to the time of His most sacred passion. He prays that the prayer which He made before He was betrayed may be heard; for He left the disciples and retired, and prayed in these words: *Father, if it be possible, let this chalice pass from me. Nevertheless not as I will, but as thou wilt.*[5] His words, *to thy holy temple,* He wishes to be taken, I think, as that custom of the Hebrew people by which it was enjoined that in whatever region they were they should always pray towards the place where they knew Jerusalem lay. We read that Daniel too did this three times a day at Babylon.[6] It was necessary that the Lord Christ should do it because He had come to fulfil the law, not to destroy it.[7] Or He wishes *thy holy temple* to be understood as heaven, for this is what men are wont to do when they pray. Though people who supplicate have no doubt that God is everywhere, they are eager to believe that help comes to them from heaven; so we say in the Lord's prayer: *Our Father, who art in heaven.*[8] So it is not foolish to interpret temple as heaven, for the divine reading shows heaven to be the Lord's abode.

3. *Consign not my soul with the wicked, and with the workers of iniquity destroy me not.* Because He knew that He would die, He rightly asked that His soul should not be consigned to hell and mingled with the wicked, and that He have no share with *the workers of iniquity.* But this separation is sought by Him in most salutary fashion so that our own hope may be roused to similar aspirations, and in truly achieving this He prays that man should not become a foreigner to Himself.

Now where are those who believe that Christ did not have a soul? They seem to me not to read these words, or wholly to forget what they have read.⁹

With these who speak peace with their neighbour: but evils are in their hearts. He is discussing the Jews, who to try Him said to Him: *We know that thou art come a teacher from God.*¹⁰ So there was peace on their lips but malice in their hearts. This figure is called irony or mockery, when something masquerading as praise clearly connotes abuse. By *their neighbour* He means Himself, because He was kin to them in the origin of the flesh. They were justly reviled because they made haste maliciously to destroy their neighbour.

4. *Give them according to their works, and according to the wickedness of their pursuits.* The Jews wittingly performed evil, but unwittingly did good. They inflicted death on Christ, but by this death itself was ended. They shed His blood, but by this the world's sins were cleansed. So He asks that it be given them according to their works, that is, according to their wish, for every man does what he wishes. Those who strive to do harm often do good, as the devil does, for in inflicting the punishment of death on the innocent he affords martyrs a path to a heavenly crown. He underlined His earlier words when He said: *According to the wickedness of their pursuits,* that is, according to their evil aspiration to harm the innocent. They preferred to consign to death Him who had come to save them.

According to the works of their hands give thou to them: render to them their reward. There are four types of reward. One is when men render evil for good, as the Jews did to Christ; though He had come to save them, they voted to crucify Him. The second is when good is rendered for good, as when God will say to His chosen: *Come ye, blessed of my Father, possess you the kingdom prepared for you from the foundation of the world.*¹¹ The third is the future repayment of evil with evil, when He shall say to the wicked: *Go into everlasting fire, which was prepared for the devil and his angels,*¹² on the principle that *with the same measure that you shall mete withal it shall be measured to you also.*¹³ The fourth is when He repays good for evil as He states here, so that former persecutors become converted, and subsequently praise Him. But all this which He foretells of His enemies is not malevolent supplication but a presaging of the future, for in the gospel He says: *Father, forgive them, for they know not what they do.*¹⁴ But both statements are loving; here

He threatens to frighten so that they may not perpetrate their crimes through despairing fatalism; in the second case, in His passion, he prays that He may guide their hearts to repentance. The frequent repetition of the terrifying sentiment is not idle; He strives to break their stony hearts with the fire of His great threat.

5. *Because they have not understood the works of the Lord, and have not given thought to the operations of his hands, thou shalt destroy them, and thou shalt not build them up.* He cultivates the higher meaning, for He says that retribution is owed them *because they have not understood the works of the Lord.* His work was to teach the people the path of truth and faith, and to reconcile man to God by the mystery of the holy incarnation. Thus through the gift of the Lord's visitation our flawed nature could make its way to the heights to which it had not been able to rise. Then, so that pig-headed minds would not withhold belief in the true teaching of the Son of God, He strengthened it by the additional force of mighty miracles, so that the Jews might clearly realise that it was the power of the Godhead which was achieving what they knew the ordinary man could not do. But in their lunacy they believed that He was only a man, and they were outraged that He was called the Son of God. Next follows: *And have not given thought to the operations of his hands.* If they had given thought, they would certainly have feared rather than despised, lamented rather than spat, adored rather than crucified. Such a sacrilege could have sprung only from those who lost the understanding of truth, for God destroys some for their correction, but brings low others for their destruction. He destroyed Paul to build him up better, and to make an apostle out of a persecutor; but the most High drowned the wicked Pharaoh so that he might perish, because he did not believe such great wonders. So He says that they are destroyed in such a way that they are not to be rebuilt. As we have often warned, the word is an indication more of the prophecy than of the character of His anger.

6. *Blessed be the Lord: for he hath heard the voice of my supplication.* He knows that all He was seeking is to be fulfilled, so He passes to the second section, and gives thanks that He has been delivered from His enemies, though they had not as yet made their appearance. This figure is called *prolepsis* or in Latin *praeoccupatio*,[15] when things to come are regarded as past. But let us examine the significance of this verbal arrangement: *Blessed be the Lord, for he hath heard,* for He is

blessed whether He hears or not. But we use the words *bene dictus* (blessed) properly of the person whom we thank, in other words, when we speak well of him. So *blessed* is appropriate here, since He deigned to hear.

7. *The Lord is my helper and my protector: and in him hath my heart confided, and I have been helped. And my flesh hath flourished again; and with my will I will give praise to him.* *Helper* refers to the dangers to life which He overcame with the Lord's help, *protector* because the Lord shielded Him by His protection against the ambush of the devil. It is after these events that He says that He has faithfully hoped in the Lord. When He speaks of His heart He points to the secret region of the soul, which is assuredly *the sacrifice of justice.*[16] He again added: *I have been helped,* so that the extent of the help might grow with the degree of holy devotion which He imparted. He did well to say: *My flesh hath flourished again,* for it flourished initially when it gleamed forth from the sinless Virgin like the unique glory of a most beautiful blossom. As Isaiah says: *And a flower shall rise up out of his root.*[17] So *flourished again* means "rose again," for He burst out into the air of heaven with wondrous beauty. Next comes: *And with my will I will give praise to him,* that is, after the resurrection when His human nature had been freed from corruption, and abiding in the unity of the Word He had been brought to immeasurable glory.

8. *The Lord is the strength of his people: and the protector of the healthy of his anointed.* This is a short but powerful definition. What is the Lord? *The strength of his people,* and rightly, since all obstacles are overcome with his help. He is also *the protector,* since He shields them and frees them from impending ills. *Of the healthy,* as if He were saying of the just, whose health is the Lord. He did well to add: *Of his anointed,* so that one ought to have noted the reference to the Son of God; for others were called anointed when either royal anointing or priestly glory adorned them.

9. *Save, O Lord, thy people, and bless thine inheritance: and rule them and exalt them for ever.* The Word in His human form prays for the Christian people, for whose sake He is known to have been raised up, so that by making faithful satisfaction they may be saved in this world, where they were known to have been exposed to dangers from the Jews. *Bless thine inheritance* refers to the future Judgment when the words are to be pronounced: *Come ye, blessed of my Father, possess ye*

the kingdom which was prepared for you from the beginning of the world.[8] And to show clearer approval of the love which He enjoins, He asks again that the Lord rule His devoted people in this world, so that they do not long for the things of the flesh, nor choose base paths; but rather, being enlightened by His guidance, they may have no experience of association with the most wicked. He added: *Exalt them,* so that they may advance through praiseworthy effort in understanding of the Scriptures and in holy deeds; thus when they have been cleansed of earthly vices, they may be raised up and led to eternal rewards. He asked that this should be done *for ever,* that is throughout the course of this world, where ages ensue until that eternal age which is succeeded by no other, because it is everlasting.

Conclusion Drawn From the Psalm

You have heard the devotion with which this psalm is brought to a close. He who is entreated by angels supplicated on our behalf. The Judge of all creatures was called our Patron. He chose to be killed so that we should be snatched from death. In this psalm too was foretold the pattern of the Lord's passion. He spoke of His own crucifixion and resurrection; finally He prayed for the faithful, so that those who have deserved to believe in Him must rejoice in perennial blessings.

COMMENTARY ON PSALM 28

1. *A psalm of David at the finishing of the tabernacle.* Since the first words are now familiar, it remains for us to investigate rather more carefully the words: *The finishing of the tabernacle.* The phrase connotes the perfection of the Catholic Church, now known to be established throughout the whole world. By the term *tabernacle* the Church is said to have been founded in the world; as it wages war on the vices of the flesh, it has deservedly won the title of "expedition-dwelling."[1] So the prophet sings this psalm, so rich in the glory of Christian teaching, in praise of the holy Spirit, once he has hymned the perfection of the Church as a whole; since so important a subject as the

Church's perfection has been fulfilled by prophets and apostles in their blessed teaching, he wants it to be adorned fittingly with the Spirit's praises. The whole psalm is teeming with praise of the holy Spirit, and by various allusions it issues proclamations of His majesty. This is what orators call the demonstrative type, when someone is revealed and acknowledged by description of this kind.[2] But what could anyone say appropriately about Him, except what He deigns to utter about Himself?

Division of the Psalm

The blessed David realised that the territories of the whole world were to be drawn to the Catholic faith by prophets and apostles through the gift of the holy Spirit. In Peter's words: *For prophecy was brought not by the will of men at any time: but the holy men of God spoke, inspired by the holy Ghost.*[3] So first he addresses the whole Church, bidding them perform sacrifices to Him with committed mind. Secondly he recounts in sevenfold narration[4] the powers of the holy Spirit by various allusions in mighty praise, which in numerous passages is said to be especially appropriate to Him. But to ensure that you realise that the power of Father, Son, and holy Spirit is one, he says in the third section that the Trinity dwells in baptism, and that the Lord gives strength and a blessing to the Christian people reborn in it.

Explanation of the Psalm

Bring to the Lord, O ye children of God: bring to the Lord the offspring of rams. Bring to the Lord glory and honour. Since the prophet had the spiritual vision to realise that the multitude of nations, as had been foretold, would come to belief in the true faith, and that the whole world's praise was to be joined in unity with them, it was right to advise the people who were so to say believers to show an expression of their faith by devoted sacrifices. He invites *the children of God,* in other words, those who have become His children by the grace of rebirth; as the evangelist John says: *He gave them power to be made sons of God, to them that believe in his name.*[5] Though the whole Trinity is one God, and there is no separation of His majesty or nature, we find mention in sundry places of what is known to be attached to individual Persons. Here we must interpret *Lord* in the special sense of the holy Spirit, whom he begins to praise in connection with the perfection of the tabernacle. Notice that through his refraining to say initially what they are to bring, they are being ordered to offer themselves, in other words, their hearts shining with holy purity, an offering known to be acceptable to the Lord beyond every sacrifice. Next comes: *Bring to the Lord the offspring of rams*. *Rams* is to be interpreted as the apostles,[6] who as leaders of the flocks have led the Christian people into the Lord's fold. By *the offspring of rams* which are to be offered he means those whom the apostles have begotten by true preaching, rather than those found to be strangers through debased belief. The apostles are well compared to rams, since these animals are extremely strong in the forehead, and always bring obstacles down by butting. The apostles are known to have done this by their preaching, for they shattered diverse superstitions and the most entrenched idols with the forehead, so to say, of the heavenly word. *Aries* (ram) gets its name from *a fronte ruens*,[7] rushing head-on. He added: *Bring to the Lord glory and honour*. Here we are especially reminded that the holy Spirit suffers no injury, for he who says that the Spirit is less than the Father or Son clearly does not bring Him glory; it is no-one's glory to be told that he is the lesser. So we offer to the Lord, that is, to the holy Spirit, pure, full, true glory when we say that He is both consubstantial and coeternal with the Father and the Son, and when we proclaim Him almighty without any separation. In this way all heresies are destroyed in different passages of holy Scripture through the proclamation of the holy Spirit.

2. *Bring to the Lord glory to his name: adore ye the Lord in his holy hall.* Earlier he said: *Bring glory to him;* now he says: *To his name.* So he who makes the holy Spirit more widely known brings glory to His name when he converts the hearts of unbelievers and extends His name amongst the mass of common folk and crowds of the people. This seems to imply more a warning to teachers. Do not think it idle that he has repeated *bring* four times. This figure is called *epimone*, in Latin *repetitio crebra sermonis*,[8] when it gathers many things discussed with the repetition of a single word. There follows: *Adore ye the Lord in his holy hall*, that is, worship Him with your conscience at its purest; for

this is the royal hall, the dwelling of the holy Spirit. As Paul says: *You are the temple of God, and the Spirit of God dwelleth in you.*[9]

3. *The voice of the Lord is upon the waters: the God of majesty hath thundered: the Lord is upon many waters.* He comes to the second section, in which by the figure of *epimone* which we have mentioned above he frequently uses the one word at the beginnings of verses, and hymns the praises of the holy Spirit with His sevenfold power. With the Lord's help I shall try to explain this in the appropriate places. This is the first of the verses devoted to the same topic: *The voice of the Lord is upon the waters,* in other words, the Spirit of wisdom; for He established the law by which the crowd of believers was to be governed. The tablets of the testament which are read were written by the finger of God,[10] by which we understand specifically the holy Spirit. His words: *Upon the waters,* signifies the nations; as another psalm says: *Save me, O Lord, for the waters are come in even unto my soul.*[11] And in the Apocalypse we read: *The city which sitteth on many waters.*[12] So it is clear that these allusions show that the Spirit of wisdom established the law for nations. Next comes: *The God of majesty hath thundered.* This too refers to the Spirit of wisdom; he tells of when He has announced the day of judgment, when He has foretold the pains of hell with their fear beyond measure, so that He seemed not so much to speak as to thunder. He further added: *The Lord is upon many waters,* in other words, over the people of different nations which He won over by the preaching of prophets and apostles. So in this phrase too he denoted peoples, just as he wished us to understand them in the phrase used earlier.[13]

4. *The voice of the Lord is in power.* What remarkable brevity, three words[14] expressing so great a thought! By the voice of the Lord in power he means the Spirit of understanding, who casts down and lays low all opposition. As Scripture says: *And there is none who can resist thy will.*[15] So the voice of the Lord is rightly said to be in power, for it is blocked by no obstacles.

The voice of the Lord is magnificence. Here the Spirit of counsel breathes its fragrance. What is more magnificent than He who illuminates the heart, and brings the realisation that good things are to be sought and all most wicked things avoided, who makes provision that the impious man becomes pious, the captive free, the slave a son?

There is no doubt that this accrues to those in whom the holy Spirit dwells with the power of His majesty.

5. *The voice of the Lord breaketh the cedars: yea, the Lord shall break the cedars of Libanus.* Here the Spirit of courage shines out, breaking the pride which has confidence in itself, and raising up the humility which has prior confidence in His goodness. The *cedars* we must interpret as pride which raises itself high and apes the lofty summit of this tree, especially as the wood itself is useless unless it is felled. No-one cleaving to his roots bears useful fruit; this was true of the detestable arrogance which brought sin into the world. It is this pride which the Lord's voice breaks when He says: *God resisteth the proud, but giveth grace to the humble.*[16] He says a second time: *Yea, the Lord shall break the cedars of Libanus.* But though this seems similar to what went before, with the further addition: *Of Libanus,* it seems to denote a considerable difference. Cedars which grow elsewhere are not at all high, but on Libanus they are seen to appear to overtop all other trees. So divine power breaks the nobles and kings of this world who despise other men as if they were lowly shrubs, when it chooses the poor and humble. The poor and humble are inferior in power, but nobles and kings amidst their riches either groan in their thoughts or are loosed from their base ambition. *Cedars* is used also in a good sense. As the Psalmist says: *The cedars of Libanus which the Lord hath planted.*[17]

6. *And shall lay them low as a calf of Libanus, and the beloved as the sons of unicorns.* This verse refers to the Spirit of power. Men in antiquity often used to offer calves of Libanus at sacrifices, for owing to the luxuriance of the sweet grass they were quite fat and beautiful. He wishes to compare them with the highest worldly positions, which were to be laid low like the calves seen to be offered at sacrifices; for such men are also sacrificial victims when they are converted and offered with their sleek minds to Christ the Lord. But so that men should not complain that a hard law had been imposed on them, he says that even *the beloved,* the Son of God, will die, of whom Scripture says: *This is my beloved Son in whom I am well pleased.*[18] Through the incarnation He became as a son of unicorns,[19] in other words of the Jews, who exalt themselves alone. Alternatively, the Jews are called unicorns because they are seen to accept one Testament alone. So he says that Christ will die in the flesh like the Jews' sons, for with a

devotion beyond reckoning He embraced our condition in death to prove to us His immortality.

7. *The voice of the Lord cutting off the flame of fire.* He points to the Spirit of knowledge, who demarcates good from bad by cutting off every plan or hot impulse opposed to Him, in other words, by separation. By the knowledge of His majesty He quenched the fiery and flaming disturbances of the Jews, so that what those wicked men had done in seeking to deny the one Man might be turned to the salvation and glory of all mankind.

8. *The voice of the Lord shattereth the solitude: and the Lord shall shake the desert of Cades.* This verse denotes the Spirit of piety, who shatters the deceiving thoughts and foolish prayers of men, and draws them when corrected towards zeal for the truth. He did well to call their errors *the solitude,* for they do not have God dwelling there; and they cannot remain longer in their wicked deeds since they either abandon them in tear-inducing death or quit them by a blessed conversion. Next comes: *And the Lord shall shake the desert of Cades.* This still refers to the Spirit of piety. The account in Numbers carefully explains this reference when it tells how the people of Israel came to Cades, and were suffering from excessive thirst because of the aridity of that place. Moses struck a rock at the Lord's command, and suddenly provided abundance of water for them. In a remarkable way the earth which lay foul with unwatered dustiness was irrigated.[20] By this comparison the prophet says that the most obdurate hearts of sinners can be liquefied into waters of wisdom, and that exemplar of Cades must be reenacted in human hearts. The term *desert* is often used of places where unfaithful people are known to gather; as the gospel says: *The voice of one crying in the desert.*[21] John could not have preached in the desert where none could hear; rather, *desert* is used to describe those who had not as yet apprehended the gifts of faith.

9. *The voice of the Lord prepareth the stags: and he will expose the thick woods: and in his temple all shall speak his glory.* He speaks of the seventh Spirit, the Spirit of fear of the Lord. Stags are timorous, it is true, but they imbibe poisonous draughts.[22] They are rightly compared with those who both fear the divinity and swallow down all that is opposed to Him. They cannot be deceived or harmed by those known to oppose the Church of God with gall-steeped dispute. As we said

earlier, the seven-formed Spirit has been denoted here, as you easily infer by calculation and recognise by His activity. But we must regard this holy Spirit as one and the same as Him whose virtues are known by Isaiah's witness[23] to be the same seven which we have mentioned: the Spirit of wisdom, of understanding, of counsel, of courage, of knowledge, of piety, of fear of the Lord; and He distributes these to each as He wills. It should not trouble you that everywhere he ascribes the words to the voice of the holy Spirit, for clearly *voice* is associated with the whole Trinity. We read of the Father's voice when He says: *This is my beloved Son in whom I am well pleased,*[24] and again of the Son's voice in the words: *Saul, Saul, why persecutest thou me?*[25] Likewise in the Acts of the Apostles we read of the holy Spirit: *Separate me Paul and Barnabas, for the work whereunto I have taken them.*[26] The most holy Augustine gathered together this sharing of words usefully in one book which he composed against the Arians,[27] so that every judicious person could recognise the equality of substance or power of the undivided Trinity when he proves that their very words are shared in common. The fear of the Lord also exposed *the thick woods* when devoted people laid aside their ignorance and assembled for an understanding of the divine law. In return for this, all declare His glory in His Church, according as each individual receives the gifts of the seven-formed Spirit already mentioned, for *glory* is praise rendered by the celebration of many, a definition which we often recall.[28]

10. *The Lord dwelleth in the flood: and the Lord shall sit king for ever.* 11. *The Lord will give strength to his people, and will bless the people with peace.* Having run through the powers of the seven-formed Spirit, he passes in this third stage by marvellous organization of topics to the connection with the Trinity. By speaking three times in these two verses of the Lord, he shows that the holy Trinity *dwelleth in the flood,* that is, in the waters of baptism. As the gospel says: *Go and baptise all nations in the name of the Father and of the Son and of the holy Ghost.*[29] But let us ask why the word *flood* is used here for the holy waters; rightly so, since what was done under Noah's leadership bore the image of sacred baptism. Just as baptism cleanses souls of the foulness of sins, so the flood destroyed the wicked sins of the world. So the term flood is rightly used for baptism, since it was brought about to achieve a similar purpose. As for the fact that he repeated *Lord* twice

without distinguishing persons, we can realise that first he refers to the holy Spirit: *The Lord dwelleth in the flood.* Next follows: *And the Lord shall sit king for ever;* this we rightly identify as the Son. *The Lord will give strength to his people* we note is appropriate to the Father. *His people* denotes the Christian people whom He sought out for the gift of sacred baptism. He also added: *And will bless his people in peace.* He did not say "They will bless" but *He will bless,* because the Lord our God is one. *In peace,* because of those words of the gospel, *My peace I give you, my peace I leave to you;*[30] for the peace of Father, Son, and holy Spirit is one.

Conclusion Drawn From the Psalm

Let us recall how this psalm thundered forth from a great trumpet, so that those who depreciate the holy Spirit cannot be defended on the pretext of ignorance. His power was praised in the sevenfold distribution, so that we might realise that nothing in it is inferior or divided, since the unity of the holy Spirit is stated at the close. The mad disloyalty of heretics must cease to stir up empty calumnies. They should read Didymus, blessed Ambrose,[31] and the other Fathers who have discussed this subject with most perfect argumentation. Let them proffer to the undivided Trinity glory and honour, and not establish a separation in equality, unless they choose to be led to destruction.[32]

COMMENTARY ON PSALM 29

1. *A sung psalm for the dedication of David's house.* The meaning of *sung psalm* is already known. Now let us examine why it is defined as: *For the dedication of a house.* *House* denotes the temple of the Lord's body, and *dedication* the resurrection of that same Lord of ours, Jesus Christ; for then His body was conducted to eternal glory and power. As Christ Himself says in the gospel: *All power is given to me in heaven and on earth.*[1] We use the term dedication when some new house is put to the most crowded use. It is called *David's house* because of David's

seed, from which our Saviour derived his bodily origin; this is the house which now gladly sings from the opened doors of parted lips: *I will extol thee, O Lord.* The house was built at His birth, but is known to have been dedicated at His holy resurrection.

Division of the Psalm

In the first section the Lord Christ our King gives thanks to the Father after His glorious resurrection, because the Father freed Him from the hostility of this world. He orders the saints to announce praise of the Lord, since all things lie in His power. In the second section He says that He is not to be shifted from His steadfast purpose, and further adds that praise of the Deity is to be discharged by the living and not by the dead. In the third section He joyfully and delightedly returns to His resurrection, for having laid aside the frailty of the flesh He continues in the undying glory of His majesty. In his usual fashion He describes as past what He knew would come.

Explanation of the Psalm

2. *I will extol thee, O Lord, for thou hast upheld me, and hast not made my enemies to rejoice over me.* The Lord Christ thanks the Father in the ordering of events by which He rose from the dead. *I will extol* means I make more widely known what was fulfilled by the holy incarnation of the Word and by the glorious resurrection; for how many before this time could have come to know the Lord spiritually if at His coming the truth already promised had not become celebrated? As a Man He could extol the name of the most High because He was clearly raised up by Him. How could He either have revealed the hidden things of God, or have told the future judgments of God, except by the heavenly power by which He succeeded in revealing His own secrets and those of the Father? A problem now follows in *Thou hast not made my enemies to rejoice over me.* How did His enemies fail to rejoice when they buffeted Him and said: *Prophesy unto us, O Christ; who is he that struck thee?*[2] And again, when they stood before the cross, and said: *Vah, thou that destroyest the temple, and in three days dost rebuild it!*[3] How did they fail to rejoice again when they cast

lots over His garments?[4] But this fleeting and empty joy turned into repentance and sadness for them when they saw Him rise again after three days, whereas they had hoped that He had experienced the death common to all. The word *delectasti* has the force of "Thou hast made to rejoice"; this is the figure called *hypallage*, when either the gender or the declension of a word is changed.[5] *Over me* means when He passed from this world, for then His enemies were saddened, and His devoted ones abounded in great joy.

3. *O Lord my God, I have cried to thee, and thou hast healed me.* How was He healed when there is no mention of His having fallen sick? He was secretly sick when at His incarnation He shouldered the whole of humanity which was subject to both diseases and deaths; because we were healed in Him, He proclaims that He was healed. The Lord Christ was saved when by rising again He set our frail flesh into the joys of eternal life, and all who faithfully believed in Him were saved.

4. *Thou hast brought forth, O Lord, my soul from Hell; thou hast saved me from them that go down into the pit.* What are we to say of them that do not believe that the Lord Christ had a soul? See how on numerous occasions He cries that under the human condition He was led to hell, and that His soul was brought forth from there by the power of His divinity. Note that He says *brought forth;* that is, when the bars of hell were broken, it was conducted all the way to heaven. *Them that go down into the pit* are those enmeshed in the wickedness of this world. He did well to say: *Go down,* to express the idea that those oppressed by the weight of sins descend into the depths and are swallowed up by the deepest abyss. But how was He saved, when it is clear that He was killed? He was saved precisely from such men (in other words, freed from association with them) when He rose from the dead and death could harm Him no further.

5. *Sing to the Lord, O ye his saints, and give praise to the memory of his holiness.* After His resurrection He fittingly orders His saints to sing, so that the members might rejoice at the resurrection of the Head, most of all since their hope was strengthened by such a dispensation; for clearly they too rise again in joy who have chanced to believe in His teaching. He said: *To the memory of his holiness* because He deigned to be mindful of us lingering in the shadow of death, that is, in the thick cloud of our sins. We were not mindful of Him who created us; rather, He was mindful of us whom He created. As He says in the

gospel: *You have not chosen me, but I have chosen you.*[6] So *the memory of his holiness* is to be both praised and glorified, for it brought the human race to remembrance of Him, and thus achieved the possibility of our salvation.

6. *For wrath is in his indignation: and life in his good will. In the evening weeping shall have taken place, and in the morning gladness.* Let us understand this verse section by section; in it He recounts vengeance on the wicked, rewards to the just, the sadness of His passion, and the joys of the resurrection. Thus once they have been separated they do not experience the injustice of being confused. But since our anger, as Scripture says, imposes death,[7] the first phrase says of God metaphorically that His indignation actually spells death for the sinner in particular. His deigning (*dignatio*) is when He mercifully takes us up, His indignation (*indignatio*) when He casts us angrily off. Not that He is angry; death ensues from His turning away, which follows on human anger. Next comes: *And life in his good will.* Nothing more splendid can be said; as there is death in His indignation, so there is life in His good will, but it lies not in our merits but in His wish. This mode of argument is called in the *Topics* the *Ex contrario.*[8] He added: *In the evening weeping shall have place.* We speak of evening when the sun sets, the daylight is over, and the darkness of night follows; clearly this happened to the Church when Christ the Lord was killed. Then there was truly an occasion for weeping, when for three days the crowd of the faithful mourned, and the natural world was shaken, so that the world itself seemed to lament the end of the Lord in company with the human race. We speak of *morning* when the darkness departs and the gloaming begins to gleam forth. At this time the resurrection was noised abroad, as the gospel attests; clearly the *joy* of the blessed undoubtedly swelled from this quarter. Thus in a single verse the mighty completion of such great events is unfolded.

7. *And in my abundance I said: I shall never be moved.* After He had given thanks for His resurrection, and had enjoined a sung psalm on the saints for their welfare, in the second section He returns to the most glorious reason for His passion, and as a devoted Teacher He explains His inward thoughts at that time. Let us now see what this abundance is by which He claims that He is in no way to be moved. The Son always had abundance from the virgin Mary, because: *The Word was made flesh, and dwelt amongst us.*[9] What is more abundant

than that grace which deserved to possess the fullness of the God-head? As Paul says: *In him dwelt the fullness of the Godhead corpore-ally,*[10] in other words, most truly, substantially and perfectly. So He rightly stated that He could never be moved, for His majesty gave Him gifts of confidence.

8. *O Lord, in thy favour, thou gavest strength to my beauty. Thou turnedst away thy face from me, and I became troubled.* In this verse He clearly explains the source of the abundance which could not be moved, for He does not say that He had *strength* from His human nature, but claims that it was bestowed on Him from above. As for His beauty, the passage, *Thou art beautiful above the sons of men,*[11] affords proof. But this unspotted beauty of humanity, brighter than the sun, received strength when it was joined to the Word, and by that strength performed many miracles, as Christ Himself attests in the gospel with the words: *As the Father hath life in himself, so he hath given to the Son also to have life in himself.*[12] There follows the proof of the previous statement in: *Thou turnedst away thy face from me, and I became troubled.* It is as if He said, "You gave me what I have in the flesh, so that when You turned away I was troubled." With these words He cuts short men's wicked gestures of arrogance, for how can a sinner dare to show presumption in his own regard when spotless Holiness confesses that strength and beauty have been afforded Him by the Lord? This argument is called in the *Topics* the *A consequenti-bus,*[13] for when the Godhead turned away His face, the result was that the weakness of the flesh was troubled.

9. *To thee, O Lord, will I cry, and I will make supplication to my God. O Lord* in the first phrase and *To my God* in the second are identical statements, for making supplication to God means crying to the Lord.

10. *What profit is there in my blood, whilst I go down to corruption? Shall dust confess to thee, or declare thy truth?* The unspotted Word incarnate continues with the prayers already begun with the words: *If I go down to corruption,* in other words, to the putrefaction to which all flesh is subject through our general condition, what will be the hope of the faithful who believed that I was rising again speedily within three days? So He is asking not that He should not die, but that His flesh freed from corruption should show some sign of its promised majesty because of what He says elsewhere: *Nor wilt thou give thy holy one to see corruption.*[14] He fears that there may begin to be no profit for

the world in the blood of the Lord's passion that brings salvation. Confession here means praise, which men certainly cannot offer if they dissolve into dust by a common death. Next comes: *Or declare thy truth?* the truth which He spoke to the disciples after the resurrection: *Go ye, preach the gospel to every creature. And he that believeth and is baptised shall be saved: but he that believeth not shall be condemned.*[15]

11. *The Lord hath heard, and hath had mercy on me: the Lord became my helper.* He comes to the third section, in which He is now exultant about His resurrection, and is soothed with the delight of eternal blessedness. How the Lord became a Helper He next explains; our explanation must not be appended, so that instead the sequence of words may form their own explanation. This figure is called *epexegesis*, in Latin *explanatio*,[16] when earlier words are explained by those which follow.

12. *Thou hast turned for me my mourning into joy: thou hast cut my sackcloth, and hast girt me preeminently with gladness. Mourning* belongs to death, *joy* to resurrection; it is clear that both have now been fulfilled. *Sackcloth* is a very thick and rough texture employed for the use and toil of men, and is aptly associated with the human flesh. So *the sackcloth is cut* refers to His body when He deigned to die for us. Before His end, death gripped us with twisted bonds, and held us enclosed in rigid confinement as though we were a measure of corn. But to enable you to understand that sackcloth has been inserted to denote the sadness of death, to balance it He says of the resurrection: *Thou hast girt me preeminently with gladness.* Consider the expression: *Thou hast girt preeminently;* it denotes the girdle appropriate to the dignity of a judge. The "girt" power is seen to be established in the word itself; we say that a judge is girt when we announce his office and distinction. He says not "Thou hast girt" but *Thou hast girt preeminently,* in other words, "Thou hast raised me over all powers and virtues," because in Paul's words: *He hath given him a name which is above all names.*[17]

13. *To the end that my glory may sing to thee, and I may not be pierced: O Lord my God, I will give praise to thee for ever.* This short verse is connected with those before it. He said that He was girt with gladness so that His humanity which is His glory might sing to the Godhead.

We have said that singing reflects mental gladness, properly speaking. Christ's *glory* is the Father's *majesty*, from whom He heard: *This is my beloved Son in whom I am well pleased.*[18] And because He was once *pierced* for the salvation of the world, in other words, crucified, He recounts that He does not subject Himself further to any suffering, for He has laid aside the frailty of the flesh and continues in the glory of His majesty. As Paul says: *Christ rising from the dead dieth now no more. Death shall no more have dominion over him.*[19] But so that you may not think that the song which He mentioned is transient, He says that He gives praise for ever. *I will give praise* is here to be interpreted as applying to His members, as though it were "I shall speak in unison," that is, "I shall praise you with the saints in tones unending." The belief is that this will come wholly to pass when the city of Jerusalem is dedicated, when the singing of psalms without end is promised to all just men. Christ often promises that He does precisely what the Christian people will do, as in the verse: *I will give thanks to thee, O Lord, in a great Church: I will praise thee in a strong people.*[20]

Conclusion Drawn From the Psalm

This is a short psalm, but one full of the fecundity of heavenly teaching, having in its verses the grace of brevity, and in its meanings the most extensive breadth; for here is mentioned the grace of the sacred resurrection, here is recounted the glorious passion of the Lord, so that no tribulation of suffering may frighten those gladdened by the great hope of resurrection. Notice that here with novel charm the order was reversed, so that it began with the resurrection which obviously occurred after the Lord's passion.

COMMENTARY ON PSALM 30

1. *Unto the end, a psalm of David.* We have often said that the words contained in the heading are to be ascribed to Christ the Lord, with

whom the whole of this psalm is to be associated, since it sings of His passion and resurrection. He deigned to speak from the level of our lowliness, and even endured a human body's suffering. The good master schools us by his eloquence, so that by imitating that teaching in things heavenly we too may with humility and devotion follow the words of our Head. We must note that the psalm is the fourth of those which make brief mention of the Lord's passion and resurrection.[1]

Division of the Psalm

Throughout the psalm the words spoken are those of the Lord Saviour. Initially He begs the Father that He may be freed from over-hanging ills, and then He rejoices that He has undoubtedly been heard. In the second part He returns to His passion, and in a splendid narration by means of diverse allusions He describes what occurred. Thirdly He offers thanks in general for Himself and for His faithful people, since God has bestowed the gifts of His mercy on the whole Church. He also warns the saints to continue in the Lord's love now that they have earlier heard both the rewards of the good and the punishments of the wicked.

Explanation of the Psalm

2. *In thee, O Lord, have I hoped: let me not be confounded for eternity. Deliver me in thy justice, and rescue me.* We should observe how expressions like this are often repeated with pleasant variety. Christ begs the Father, in accordance with the human nature which He assumed, that He may not be disappointed in His hope, and suffer the revilings of men's scorn. He adds: *For eternity,* in which His thoughts remain implanted and unchangeable. *In thy justice,* in other words, "where You are accustomed to aid those who ask it, those who have the strongest confidence in Your majesty." *Deliver* means the dispelling of this world's dangers; *rescue,* the speed of the help, so that the resurrection so salutary for the world may not be long delayed. *Eripe* (rescue) is known to be formed from *rapere* (snatch).[2] So He rightly implored the Lord's justice, for He knew that He was to suffer through unjust men. What a truly marvellous, heavenly exchange! He

accepted death, and gave salvation in return. He endured injustices, and conferred distinctions; He shouldered pain, and bestowed safety. He is both unique and wholly devoted, for He proffered sweetness when He obtained bitterness.

3. *Bow down thy ear to me: make haste to deliver me: be thou unto me a God, a protector.* He said: *Bow down thy ear* because of the lowliness of His members. Since His human condition by its nature could not attain divinity, he asked that the Godhead should bow down and descend to it, and this occurred through the incarnation of the almighty Word. So what was known never to have happened previously was rightly requested. Next comes: *Make haste to deliver me,* in other words, "Hasten to grant Me a most speedy resurrection," not the lugubrious one which the mass of mankind is hitherto known to endure. The numerous occasions on which this prayer is made teach us that we ought not to interrupt our praying even when we think that something can be granted to us. He also asks that He be protected by heavenly power from the harsh plotting of this world, so that His simplicity may not lie abandoned and exposed to His enemies. As the prophet Isaiah writes: *As dumb as a lamb before his shearer, he did not open his mouth.*[3]

And a house of refuge, to save me. The *house of refuge* is the glorious resurrection, once debilitated by no weakness, but enjoying majesty uncorrupted, for He was safe when death could not prevail further against Him. So His fear springs from concern for us; His confidence is the mark of His divinity. Some say that the house of refuge refers to the Catholic Church in which He seeks safety for His members, because every Christian truly achieves safety in it, just as when the flood rose only they were saved who happily deserved to enter Noah's ark.

4. *For thou art my strength and my refuge, and for thy name's sake thou wilt lead me and nourish me. Strength* refers to the endurance of what He suffered, *refuge* to the end of His ills, when He overcame the injustices of this world with the climax of a glorious death. Next follows: *And for thy name's sake thou wilt lead me.* For His name's sake the Lord led humanity, for through the diffusion of that most salutary preaching He made that name more widely acknowledged through all nations. Or this is to be understood as referring to His members, as has already been said. He is rightly called our Leader since we follow

Him and do not avoid the tracks of His teaching. He also said He
was nourished until the Catholic Church could attain perfection by
His gift.

5. *Thou wilt bring me out of this snare which they have hidden for me:
for thou art my protector, O Lord.* The snare was indeed hidden by the
enemy, but it was not to be hidden from Christ, for He did not fall into
death by deception but knowingly undertook it to free us. So the Jews
hid the snare for Christ because they thought that He was only a man,
and they plotted to destroy him by secret ambush. So He says that He
is to be brought out of it, in other words, swiftly raised to the realms
of heaven by the kindly gift of the resurrection. But He says that all
the Jews' plans are to be foiled, for if the Lord offers protection, no
opposition can prevail.

6. *Into thy hands I commend my spirit: thou hast redeemed me, O
Lord, the God of truth.* Let us consider why the words which the
gospel-text utters are set here, for the gospel too says: *Into thy hands I
commend my spirit; and bowing his head he gave up the ghost.*[4] Undoubtedly this is so that you may realise that here too the same Man was
speaking who was to say the same words when set on the cross many
centuries later. *Into thy hands* means "Into Your truth, where You
always perform kind and just deeds." So He commends to the Father
that treasure beyond reckoning, that soul which did the Father's will
with equal dedication. So it was right that such a spirit be commended
to One so great to raise it. Then He attests that He was redeemed. But
let us see at what price; it was that stated by Paul: *He emptied himself,
taking the form of a servant.*[5] You see how great the price was, that He
lowered His majesty to the level of human flesh. He emptied Himself
to fill things human with things heavenly. But so that you might
clearly realise that this was the Lord, He added His identity, *the God of
truth.* In a unique sense He is the God of those who love truth and are
not compounded with any falsehood.

7. *Thou hast hated all them that regard vanity most emptily: but I will
hope in the Lord.* Elements demonstrably opposed are always hateful to
each other; so Truth rightly hated vanity because vanity dwells in
falsehood. He himself expounds this when He uses the phrase *most
emptily,* for vanity is labelled not just empty but most empty, and
rightly so, for by removing fruitful understanding it becomes foreign

to the Lord. And whereas first He says that the Lord hates vanity, He now says that He loves what is most true. What is it that is most true? *I will hope in the Lord,* in whom there is nothing empty, nothing most empty, but everything remains secure and whole. But what cause follows on this?

8. *I will exult and rejoice in thy mercy, for thou hast regarded my humility.* In this and the previous verse a categorical syllogism is again issued; we have already explained the definition and the parts of this in Psalm 1.[6] It is compiled in similar fashion here too: I have hoped in the Lord; Every man who hopes in the Lord will exult and rejoice in His mercy; so I will exult and rejoice in His mercy. It is indeed a fine technique of speech to knit together in small compass what cannot be prised apart by any opposition. Now let us deal with the words of the psalm. Exulting means taking joy with great alacrity of mind; rejoicing means being charmed with a controlled mental affection. But let us note how frequently we are warned to put no trust in human strength. As was said earlier, how should anyone show presumption in his own case, when we read that He who was sacredly incarnate refrained from it? So the attempt of Pelagian wickedness must be accursed, for it seeks to be presumptuous in matters which it should have realised the holy Spirit has so often condemned earlier.[7] Let us also be aware of who says that His humility has been regarded. It is He who both created and keeps in being heaven and earth, He to whom the heavenly powers minister. But there was humility in the most High because humanity perfected at the very conception was truly joined to Him.

9. *Thou hast saved my soul from necessities, and thou hast not shut me up in the hands of the enemy.* Necessity (*necessitas*) is so termed because it is set in slaughter (*in nece*),[8] in other words, placed in the toils of death. When we are entangled in the nooses of sins and we cannot be loosed from them by our own strength, this is called necessity. So on that occasion the soul of our Lord Saviour was freed from *necessities,* for it was delivered from the sins to which it was in every way a stranger. Next comes: *And thou hast not shut me up in the hands of the enemy.* This was the very necessity which he earlier mentioned, the prospect of being consigned to and subject to the devil's power through sinful deeds; for men are *shut up,* so to say, in a penal gaol if

they are encompassed by the hands of the most savage Satan. *Thou hast not shut me up* means that He has been freed from the devil's power. As He Himself says in the gospel: *Behold, the prince of this world will come, and in me he will not find anything.*⁹

10. *Thou hast set my feet in a spacious place. Have mercy on me, O Lord, for I am afflicted.* After registering His exultation at being freed, He passes to the second topic, in which He is to speak at length of the passion, so that by frequent recollection He can most devoutly remind us that He undertook it for the salvation of all. *Thou hast set* means "You have strengthened," for He who had no earthly sins could not have slipped down. *In a spacious place,* that is, a place of freedom perpetually safe from the devil's power, for a place is safe when the enemy does not lie in ambush before it, and it is spacious when he does not occupy it. Notice that he did not say "on the way," but *in a spacious place,* in other words, in the homeland of the virtues, in the region of the blessed; for we read that the way of the just is narrow.¹⁰ His *feet* denote the moral virtues by which He walked through the world with certain steps, which the devil's enmity could not hinder. But though He walked through the world without fault, it was essential that divine grace should aid His weaknesses, so that His feeble flesh might not desert the integrity of His heavenly purpose. So there follows: *Have mercy on me, O Lord, for I am afflicted.* He asks that aid should be lent to His affliction because of the condition of the human body; so he says in the gospel: *My soul is sorrowful even unto death,*¹¹ and the like. Alternatively, His feet denote the apostles, who took their stand through the whole Church on the most unswerving steadiness of faith.

My eye is troubled with wrath: my soul and my belly. Throughout these four verses the figure of *diatyposis,* in Latin *expressio,*¹² appears, in which the shapes and appearances of things or persons are described. He begins to recount the nature of the great danger. It is as if He were saying: "My spirit was troubled, since the rage of persecutors sought me out"; He expressed the ire of enemies by the word *wrath. Eye* denotes the understanding, which we always *trouble* and disturb when we fear looming dangers. Our *belly* is the hollow in which we store swallowed food. It is aptly comparable to the memory, for just as the belly takes in the foodstuffs passed to it, so the recess of the memory aptly houses our acquaintance with things. So He speaks of His troubled belly with reference to His memory, in which He kept stored the Lord's promises to Him of His glorification. But when the flesh saw that dangers threatened it, the result was that it was troubled with panic. Note that He often says that He was troubled, but nowhere that He despaired; this was said by Him so that the heavenly Master could show us this formula for imitation. Anxiety cultivates the human race in close acquaintance, but despair could not emanate from divine sanctity.

11. *For my life is wasted with grief, and my years in groans.* The cause of that trouble and physical fear is the fact that His life was wasted with griefs. This word *wasted* implies long and most heavy sufferings; wasting implies being gradually less active, and reaching one's end through loss of some of the constituents of good health. Clearly this can happen to human life, which is invariably brought to the end imposed by death. In making this first declaration, He then adds *And my years in groans,* thus signifying a large number of days. Note that He said *groans,* for it was no light grief when His groaning resounded uninterruptedly. Alternatively, the phrase refers rather to the sufferings of martyrs, who since they are Christ's members are rightly considered as belonging to the Head. Note too that He said *in groans,* not "in words"; thus what seemed hidden from men was better known to God.

My strength is weakened through poverty: and my bones are disturbed. Strength of spirit is weakened through poverty, for human frailty lacks all that is good. What could be poorer than frailty, which is known to have in itself no fitting possession? *Bones* are the strength by which the body's frame is sustained. Both these expressions, *strength* and *bones,* are nobly used here to express the weakness of our human substance, for there should be no presumption in strength of spirit, nor hope in the flesh. As the prophet says: *Cursed be the man that trusteth in man, and placeth hope in the strength of his arm, and whose heart departeth from the Lord.*[13]

12. *I am become a reproach above all my enemies, and very much to my neighbours: and a fear to my acquaintances.* The phrase, *Above all,*

rather than "among all," is not idle; *Above all my enemies* is said by way of amplification. Whilst the enemy were indeed a reproach, Christ the Lord though innocent and stainless was regarded as a reproach among those who contaminated themselves with wicked sin. Next comes: *I am become a reproach;* not "I was truly a reproach," but "I was thought to be what I was not by those who erred through being deceived by baseless persuasion." Reproach (*probrum*) means "opposed to the worthy" (*contra probum*),[14] that is, dishonourable and unfitting. A reproach suggests an extremely loathsome deed, which was clearly ascribed to the Lord Saviour among the wicked Jews when they said: *This man is not of God, who keepeth not the Sabbath,*[15] and elsewhere: *Thou art a Samaritan, and hast a devil.*[16] *Neighbours* He calls those close to Him in proximity of faith, men who as yet had not believed, but were disposed to believe. But when they saw that He hung on the cross, they were shifted from their proximity to belief once they saw the suffering of Him who they thought should be adorned. Though they saw inevitably come to pass what was foretold in faith, they remained unaware of it, and then they were all the more withdrawn from firm belief. Note that He spoke first of enemies, and then of neighbours; next he advances to *acquaintances.* This denotes the apostles, thrown into utter confusion by His passion. Of them Scripture says: *I shall strike the shepherd, and the sheep of the flock shall be scattered.*[17] In this way the figure of *diatyposis* is fittingly carried through in these four verses, as we have said.

13. *They that saw me fled out from me: I have fallen from the heart as one dead.* In this and the next verse occurs the figure of *metriasmos,* in Latin *mediocritas,*[18] the expression of an important matter in modest terms. Here He says: *They that saw me fled from me,* that is, those who did not believe the Scriptures beheld the Lord nailed to the cross and retired from His divine presence, hoping that their expectation was ended by His death. Or it denotes heretics, who hear the divine Scriptures in the Church and see glorious events, but break away to wicked preaching, fleeing from the truth in which they wholly refuse to allow themselves to continue. The next phrase is splendid: *I have fallen from the heart as one dead.* Ponder what *as one dead means;* the faithful do not call Him dead, for His divinity is rightly held to be incapable of suffering. *I have fallen from the heart* means from the minds of the

faithless. This usually happens to those who in burying their dead obliterate with their bodies all memory and recollection of them.

14. *I am become as an abandoned vessel, for I have heard the blame of many that dwell round about.* An *abandoned vessel* is one that is broken and without essential use, and is always thrown away; so when Jesus died He was believed by the faithless to be disposable like an abandoned vessel. What more humbling statement can be made than that the almighty Majesty should be compared to frail jars? But realise that this was the belief of madmen. In fact there always existed in Him a unique omnipotence and a marvellous divine fullness. As Paul says: *In him dwelleth all the fullness of the Godhead corporeally,*[19] that is, substantially and openly, for the Godhead cannot be corporeal. Next comes: *For I have heard the blame of many that dwell round about.* He means the faithless Jews who dwell round the synagogue and not in it. *Circum* (round) is from *circuitus;* He wishes us to catch a reference to sinners, of whom He says elsewhere: *The wicked walk round about (in circuitu).*[20] So such men are rightly called dwellers round about, for they have preferred to attend to God's law not in the spirit but in the flesh. So through these shining words the dark crimes of the Jewish people are subtly denoted.

15. *In this while they all assembled together against me, to receive my life they consulted. But I have put my trust in thee, O Lord.* Let us restore the natural order of the words so that the expressions which go together may be followed more easily: "While all together they assembled against me, in this they consulted to take my life." *In this they consulted* denotes the greater part of the Jews plotting to consign the Lord to execution, for every crime perpetrated by the design of numerous people is the more serious. By saying: *All together,* He wishes it to be understood that it was not a few of them, so that due vengeance may attend that accursed crowd. *To receive my life* means to take it away, to remove it. The order of the phrases is marvellous and most sacred. When His enemies dwelt round the synagogue and put their hope in their strength, He says that He trusted the Lord, for He knew that their power was non-existent, and that they were attempting to kill themselves rather than Him by such plots.

16. *I said, Thou art my God: my times are in thy hands.* The Lord Christ says: *Thou art my God,* but He speaks from the standpoint of

the humanity which He assumed, and which as He later says was subject to both time and death. He does not, as His enemies thought, state that His life was to be ended by their persecution, but He places His life's times in the Lord's power; for we exist through His creation, wax strong through His dispensation, and also pass on at His command. So it was necessary that He kept His hope implanted in the Lord, for He knew that His life and death were in His power.

17. *Free and deliver me out of the hands of my enemies, and from them that persecute me. Make thy face to shine upon thy servant.* He prays to Him who can destroy the lives of His adversaries and win over men's hearts in accord with His marvellous dispensation; for He spoke first of His enemies, that is, the Jews, and then attaches the phrase, *and from them that persecute me,* that is, pagans or the various heretics who attack God's Church with their deceitful frauds. Next comes: *Make thy face to shine upon thy servant,* that is, "allow men to see that You deign to attend on Me, so that as they despair at My death they may also believe in My resurrection." Do not be troubled at hearing the words *Thy servant* spoken by the Lord, for all such statements are to be attributed in particular to His humanity, just as elsewhere He says: *I am thy servant, and the son of thy handmaid.*[21] Where are the people who refuse to admit that there are two natures in the Lord Saviour? How else can this diversity be reconciled save by your realising that in one and the same Person are both the Lord of heaven and He who was subject to the passion?

18. *And save me in thy mercy. Let me not be confounded, O Lord, for I have called on thee.* By saying: *Save me in thy mercy,* He denies His own merit. He continually says the same things for our instruction, and is never sated with the confession which He loves, for the sweetness of the truth knows no satiety. He further adds: *Let me not be confounded, Lord, for I have called on thee.* What a wonderful, perfect proclamation, containing as it does both a prayer of humility and the impenetrable constancy of belief! So He asks that He be not ignored and confounded. But how does He believe that He is heard? *For I have called on thee;* calling in faith is an act deserving rather than injurious, since He can in no way be deceived because of His presumption that He is heard by Him.

19. *Let the wicked be ashamed, and be brought down to Hell: let deceitful lips be made dumb.* In the previous verse He said: *Let me not be confounded, for I have called on thee;* here by contrast He begs that those who invoke idols *be ashamed,* and likewise the rest who stain themselves with similar impiety. It is fitting that those confined for torture in eternal punishment should be ashamed, for as they do not believe in God's promised judgment, their *deceitful lips* blaspheme and prattle. But when they acknowledge the manifestation of the resurrection and note that they are subject to grave peril, they swiftly become dumb and no longer explode into wanton words, which are silenced by considerable fear.

Which speak iniquity against the just with pride and contempt. He explains the *deceitful lips* which by His power of knowledge He earlier prophesied would grow dumb; they *speak iniquity against the just,* that is, against Christ, in this world. He is rightly called *the just,* a worthy and apt title, for He is known to be *the way, the truth and the life.*[22] Now in opposition to this great and noble title He beautifully sets *iniquity,* for as light is opposed to darkness, so iniquity is seen as opposed to justice. Falsehood combats truth, when the Jews proclaim that the Messiah is still to come, when the Arians state that the Lord Creator is a creature, when pagans foolishly proclaim that Saturn, Jupiter, Venus and other monsters are heavenly powers. He added: *With pride and contempt,* because they argue with pride about Christ's lowliness when they say that the Lord of heaven could not have assumed the substance of the flesh, and they show contempt when they eschew belief in the passion of the immortal Lord; for when they hear that He was cut with scourges, beaten with blows, and consigned to the hands of the wicked, they at once burst into blasphemous words, wholly failing to understand the strategy of salvation. It was not that the most High could not have been seen at His most splendid in the stately distinctions of the world, but He suitably declined the means which caused the human race wickedly to despise their Creator.

20. *O how great is the multitude of thy sweetness, O Lord, which thou hast hidden from them that fear thee!* He comes to the third exordium, recounting in different ways the mighty benefits bestowed by the Lord on them that fear Him, reminding us that all holy men should

love the Lord, who is known to be both our Judge and Donor of all
future blessings. But let us consider what the words of the verse
contain. *The multitude of sweetness* is mentioned because the Lord's
sweetness is revealed by many rewards. He is sweet when He
corrects, sweet when He spares, sweet when He promises eternal
rewards to believers. But you must realise that He is sweet only to
those who taste His savour; the sweetness cannot reach those who
have not deserved to taste Him. As another psalm says: *Taste and see
that the Lord is sweet.*[23] Next comes: *Which thou hast hidden from them
that fear thee.* It is not that the sweetness is hidden from the saints, so
that they fail to attain it; rather, that what we experience as hidden
here is promised as perceptible at the Judgment to come. But we are
right to interpret *hidden* as meaning that human desires seek it the
more, because all that lies beneath our gaze is usually despised, and
what is forthcoming without any difficulty is usually regarded as
worthless. But this word *hidden* is a homonym, for it means also
"denied," as in: *I thank thee, Father, Lord of heaven and earth, because
thou hast hidden these things from the wise and prudent, and hast revealed them to little ones.*[24]

*And which thou hast wrought for them that hope in thee, in the sight of
the sons of men.* The sweetness which He had hidden from them that
fear Him He achieves in those who seek it with longing and an unflag-
ging mind. This is what true hope is, if we maintain some aspiration
with constant integrity of mind. He further added: *In the sight of the
sons of men,* that is, at the universal resurrection, when He shall render
to His saints the promised rewards, and make all nations realise that
His words were wholly accurate.

21. *Thou shalt hide them in the secret of thy face from the disturbance
of men. Thou shalt protect them in thy tabernacle from the contradiction
of tongues.* 22. *Blessed be the Lord, for he hath shown his wonderful mercy
in a surrounded city.* He passes to a recital of the blessings which the
Lord in His abundant mercy bestows on His saints. This most noble
figure is called *synathroismos* or in Latin *congregatio,*[25] when many sins
or many blessings are gathered into one passage; it is regarded as one
of the most forceful figures, because concentration of topics brings
the point to a climax; for in continuing to expound the Lord's sweet-

ness, He first says: *Thou shalt hide them in the secret of thy face from the disturbance of men;* secondly, *Thou shalt protect them in thy tabernacle from the contradiction of tongues;* and thirdly, He elaborated on His teeming kindness with the words: *Blessed be the Lord, for he has shown his wonderful mercy in a surrounded city.* Now let us proceed to explain the words. He says: *In the secret of the face of the Lord,* that is, at the resurrection, when all just men will attain the rewards of gazing on Him. As Scripture says: *Blessed are the clean of heart, for they shall see God.*[26] *From the disturbance of men,* meaning evil men; He says that the most faithful are to be hidden from them. This will be when they are set in eternal blessedness, where no-one disturbs the wholly spotless truth with his filthy desires, but the goodness of things abides in all their splendour. What a noble expression He uses when He speaks of the sight of the King *in secret,* because the impious will not behold that contemplation of Him which the just will enjoy! *Men* here means all persecutors and schismatics, who often terrify Christian people on this earth. He says that when men reach the next world, disturbances by wicked men will have no further role in oppressing God's servants, for the wicked are to be separated from Him. They are dispatched into eternal punishment, but the just are called to eternal rest.

But to ensure that frail hearts are not troubled by this mere promise of a future reward, under the second heading He says that they are to be protected. We have often remarked that by *tabernacle* is signified the Catholic Church, which endures struggles in this world and is often signalled by the title of a "dwelling on the march."[27] Earlier He said: *Thou shalt hide:* here: *Thou shalt protect.* In the next world they shall be hidden where wicked men will not see them; in this world they are protected in a place where the malevolence of evil men is allowed to inflict no harm whatsoever, for the souls of the just are preserved unharmed, no matter what the oppression suffered by their bodies. In the third place the divine Man, the Mediator Lord Christ, rejoices with a spiritual joy, because through the incarnation of the Word the gifts of salvation have sprouted forth to the world. By *the surrounded city* we must understand the physical Jerusalem, set in the midst of nations and known to exist as the temple of faith. The nations which lay round her deserved to obtain from her the guidelines of

Christian teaching; it was as though the clearest of springs had been opened up, and they were irrigated with the gifts of heavenly life. So in this city the Lord *hath shown his wonderful mercy,* for it was there that He deigned to teach, to perform miracles, and to suffer for men's salvation. There too He revealed the glory of His resurrection, so it was rightly said that He shows His wondrous power in Jerusalem, where He decided to reveal such mighty mysteries.

23. *But I said in my fear: I am cast away from the face of thy eyes.* The Son in His role of servant addresses the Father: "I despaired[28] because Your grace was abandoning Me when the depression of the passion waxed strong, particularly in the fear of death." *From the face of thy eyes,* that is, from the sight of Your mercy. It was a fine touch to give His eyes a face, because the eyes especially reflect the desires of men's hearts. *Vultus* (face) is so called because it reveals by its reactions the wish (*velle*) of the heart.[29] So the eyes of the Godhead promise His grace when they have regard for us.

Therefore thou hast heard the voice of my prayer when I cried to thee. He states that He has been heard by the Lord because He said as men do that He was despised, but in humility, not in despair. Grace could not be withdrawn from Him of whom His Father's voice was to say: *This is my beloved Son in whom I am well pleased.*[30] *When I cried to thee,* that is, when He said in a loud voice at the passion: *My God, my God, why hast thou forsaken me?*[31] It is certain that these cries of His were heard, for He gained the glory of resurrection, and was clearly set at the Father's right hand.

24. *Love the Lord, all ye his saints.* When He has sung this hymn in return for the kindnesses bestowed on Him, He urges the saints to love the Lord, so that His members may love the Donor of such great kindness by acknowledging that it has been bestowed on their Head. He bids them love as friends now, not as servants; it is the role of servants to fear, of friends to love. As He says in the gospel: *If you do the things that I command you, I will not call you servants, but friends.*[32] But this instruction is to the saints, for it is their nature to love the Lord because they do not love the world.

For the Lord will require truth, and will repay them that show pride in gross excess. So that we may not believe that the Lord can ignore the blasphemies of heretics, He says: *The Lord will require truth,* which those men shackled by errors of falsehood do not know. Next comes: *And will repay them that show pride in gross excess.* He shatters to take vengeance, He seeks out to punish. *In gross excess* is aptly added; He will not punish those who reform themselves with swift improvement. But the proud, whose sins are abundant and who despise the Lord's instructions with wicked presumption, are to be undoubtedly cut off. Here we must not take *pride* as a single sin, because from pride springs every fault involving wickedness of behaviour. As Scripture says: *Pride is the beginning of all sin.*[33] Such a label is rightly pinned on all vices, for He punishes not only the arrogant but also all who war on the routine of holy living.

25. *Do ye manfully, and let your heart be strengthened, all ye that hope in the Lord.* Herein the power of the whole psalm and the usefulness of the sacred passion is summarised. After He had said: *"Love the Lord, ye his saints,* for He bestowed on your Head both the crucifixion and the glory of the resurrection," He finally said as the decisive sentence: *"Do ye manfully, and let your heart be strengthened,* and hope in the Lord." In other words He urged the hearts of the faithful not to be frightened by the sufferings foretold, but to strengthen themselves for that glorious imitation which they knew had been inaugurated for the healing and salvation of the world. This figure is called *epiphōnēma*[34] or shouting, when after the narration of certain matters it bursts summarily forth with an exclamation. So this is an exhortation to good men, urging them not to withdraw themselves from a good course through weakness of the flesh. *Do ye manfully,* in other words "continue most resolutely in good works, and do not fail through womanly softness if you offer your hearts with constancy to the Lord." Those who sustain their spirits are lent strength if they fortify their hope in the Lord's power. This precept is common to both men and women; both sexes *do manfully* when they refuse to change their ways through a most cowardly malleability. Observe how He preserved throughout the psalm the divisions of His passion. First He spoke the prayer, and then the passion followed. Finally He warned the faithful in their joy and resolution, so that after they received such kindness, delay which is hostile to faith could not prevail further.

Conclusion Drawn From the Psalm

The health-giving, beautiful texture of this psalm is now completed. In it the weakness of humanity is described, and God's kindnesses demonstrated, so that no-one can be proud when pondering his frailty. But when he thinks of God's mercy he is far from afraid. The number of this psalm represents the peak of lofty numeration, and promises rewards for faithful marriage;[35] thus when the soul has united with this preaching in blessed behaviour, it can grow rich on a payment thirtyfold. Other mysteries also square with this number. We read that Joseph was thirty when made lord in Egypt;[36] our Saviour too was thirty when He was dipped in the waters of the Jordan, and thus consecrated life-giving baptism.[37] The holy Trinity too, which bestows on our faith a rule not to be broken and salvation, is present in three units of ten.

COMMENTARY ON PSALM 31

1. *The understanding of David.* All the psalms in general are addressed to the understanding, so that our minds may acknowledge them to ensure that they do not remain unaware of the rules for living. So it seems reasonable to enquire why the psalmist put the words, *The understanding of David,* in this title.[1] To begin with, he recalls David because of the Lord Christ, for whatever the repentant David is to say has reference to Him. Then *understanding* is added because if we do not with the aid of the Lord's mercy understand our sins, we cannot attain zeal for repentance; as another psalm has it: *Who can understand sins?*[2] This is what understanding means: once the Godhead has allowed us to understand our sins, we may most zealously pray to have them washed away. A man does not pray about a fault of which he is wholly ignorant. The Lord Christ too in the psalm's fourth section starts the first verse with *I will give thee understanding,*[3] so that *understanding* was inserted in the prefatory heading through the merit of this penitent, who is promised it also in God's words. Though there are other psalms of penitents, they are marked by a different significance in the titles, to express a subtle distinction. The first of them, set

in the sixth psalm, contains the words: *Unto the end, in hymns, for the octave, a psalm of David,* for the whole of that psalm has reference to fear of the Judgment to come. But this psalm is rightly prefaced with a heading like this because[4] he realised too late that he had degenerated, for he admitted that he had left unsaid for too long the sins which ought to have been laid before the Lord at once. The essential point of this plea is the concession granted to all who repent; such a concession is granted when the whole case is conceded to opponents, and the guilty person is defended by tears of supplication alone.[5]

Division of the Psalm

In the first section of the psalm the penitent speaks, openly admitting his sin and declaring that the punishment served on him is deserved, for he thought that his baneful deeds should be kept hidden. In this section, both exordium and narration are included.[6] In the second part there is nothing but correction, for since he has condemned himself by his own admission he believes that the Lord must spare him. In the third part the psalmist praises the blessings of repentance, and maintains that even the saints in this world entreat the Lord. He attests that his refuge lies justly in Him, where the words of the penitent likewise find their goal. In the fourth part the Lord Christ replies to his words, and promises to invest with mercy those who hope in Him, so that none may believe that the purity of the suppliant is being disregarded through any indifference. These four sections are separated by diapsalms[7] lying between them. Clearly we must take these sections one by one.

Explanation of the Psalm

Blessed are they whose iniquities are forgiven, and whose sins are covered. The penitent knows what he has done, and like the publican who beat his breast and did not raise his eyes to heaven,[8] he sighs in humility of heart, and without presuming to call on God's majesty he says with all the force he can muster: *Blessed are they whose iniquities are forgiven.* In this he longs for absolution of his sins, but does not dare to demand such a gift. So he rightly calls blessed those who have previously obtained this boon. This is the eighth type of definition which in Greek is called *kat' aphaeresin tou enantiou* and in Latin *per privantiam contrarii*,[9] for sins are opposed to the blessed man. Since he says here *forgiven,* clearly the blessed man is aptly portrayed under this type of definition. Saint Jerome[10] makes a distinction in this psalm between iniquities and sins, saying that iniquities are committed through ignorance or through knowledge before the faith is embraced, whereas he defines sins as those committed after acknowledgment of the faith or the grace of baptism.

2. *Blessed is the man to whom the Lord hath not imputed sin, and in whose mouth there is no guile.* This man too is embraced in the same type of definition. But we ought to realise that there are some to whom sins are ascribed. Paul for example was told: *Saul, Saul, why persecutest thou me?,*[11] and in the gospel Christ said to the woman in adultery: *Go, and sin no more.*[12] It is clear, however, that there are others to whom He does not ascribe sins, like Job of whom it was said: *Hast thou not considered my servant Job, that there is none like him in the earth, a man upright and simple and fearing God?*[13] Or again Nathaniel, of whom He says: *Behold, an Israelite indeed, in whom there is no guile.*[14] So by his prayers he chose the role in which he would be afflicted by no anxiety. All men attain these gifts by the grace of divine mercy. As the apostle John says: *If we say that we have no sin, we deceive ourselves, and the truth is not in us.*[15] Next comes: *To whom the Lord hath not imputed sin,* that is, him *in whose mouth there is no guile;* in other words, the man who does not become complacent after any forgiveness. Since he is a sinner, he does not proclaim himself to be most holy, a sickness to which human nature is especially addicted, but acknowledges his sins and continually perseveres in making humble satisfaction. He who is displeasing to himself pleases the Lord, for when we impugn ourselves we seek the truth, but when we seek to praise ourselves our words are falsehood. The exordium ends at this point. In it the psalmist sought to obtain the good Judge's mercy through abundant humility. But we do not make a division in this section, because we observe the diapsalms, the separations known to exist through the silence of the holy Spirit. We can note the exordium, but by no means ignore the diapsalms.

3. *Because I was silent, all my bones grew old: whilst I cried out all the day long.* Having completed his exordium in an aptly brief way, the

penitent now passes to a highly abridged narration, which some have well described as the heart and others the soul of the judicial plea, for in the course of the narration we acknowledge whatever strength lies at the heart of a case. He says: "Since I have not confessed my sin to You, all my resolution has become enfeebled in weakness," like a wound in a body which if not exposed for healing remains hidden and festers. *Bones,* as we have often remarked, signifies mental resolution. They are rightly described as having grown old because the sore had not been opened to the Physician of salvation. Next follows: *While I cried out all the day long.* Whereas earlier he says that he was silent, here he claims in turn that he cried out. But he was silent towards the Godhead whom he ought to have entreated continually, whereas he cried out in justification of himself during the lapse of a considerable time. So he did not say what it was right for him to say, and he said what he ought to have left unsaid. So both actions were culpable, though they appear different. But remember that the whole power of this psalm is known to be opposed to this accursed failing of the human race. No man should think that what he stores away hidden in the depths of his conscience is concealed from the Lord.

4. *For day and night thy hand was heavy on me.* The hand that scourges is oppressive to the sinner, and the avenging hand is weighty. *Day and night* denotes continuous time, so that hand was rightly felt to be heavy since it did not cease from oppressive punishment. He would not happily have been humiliated if the hand of the Godhead had not oppressed him. *Hand* metaphorically denotes work, because it is the practice of men to work with their hands. The Godhead does not do anything by hand, but arranges and completes everything by the power of His will.

I am turned in sore straits while my spine is broken. This is a repetition of the previous phrase, *Thy hand was heavy upon me. In sore straits* means being brought to total ruin, *ruina* being so called because it falls to the lowest level (*repetens ima*).[16] He was *turned in sore straits* because he had tumbled from his pride. So he who earlier cried out in elation now confessed to the Lord in humility; hope of salvation returned to him because he acknowledged that the deeds which he performed were fatal. *The spine* is what keeps the whole body upright and holds it in place; it is rightly cited here to denote pride, the breaking of which does not cast us down to death but rather raises us to salvation.

This argument is termed *from necessity*,[7] when most recent causes are advanced so that the mind may be corrected and brought to a profitable confession.

5. *I have made known my fault to thee: and my injustice I have not concealed.* Just as earlier he explained why he had been wounded, so now as he comes to the second section he tells the source of his anxiety bestowed by the Lord. What crafty naïveté, a purity more careful than that of a thousand laggards! His sin is said to have been revealed to Him from whom nothing is hidden, to whom the plea cries louder than the tongue. Even if He does not hear it from the man, he knows all with greater certainty than the perpetrator. *Making known* means making confession of sins; *concealing* is cloaking something wholly in silence, or hiding something with the heart's dissembling. This is what foolish people do who believe that God can remain ignorant of their actions. On the other hand, those who are aware that He knows all things clearly abase themselves to humble confession and prayers of repentance so as not to suffer a hostile Judge when they could have Him as merciful Advocate. Some have considered a *fault* to be a minor sin committed through some carelessness; *injustice*, however, is the perpetration of some monstrous and savage deed. Here the purity of the confessor is revealed; he did not bear to hide even what was thought to be a venial error.

I said: I will pronounce against myself my injustice to the Lord, and thou hast forgiven the wickedness of my heart. Here is revealed the great devotion of the Godhead, for at the mere promise of dedication He suddenly absolved his sins, for He regards the piety of a prayer as if it were the outcome of an action. The penitent said in his heart that he would not keep silent before the Lord about his past deeds; then, just as if he had revealed all, he was absolved of what he wished to confess, and rightly, since it is the will alone which absolves or punishes anyone. *I will pronounce* means "I will state publicly, that my devoted and faithful confession may draw others to imitate me." From his self-accusation follows the saving remedy, for since the guilty man did not spare himself, the Judge spared him. His *wickedness of heart* was his former decision to be silent, for he believed that he lay hidden from Him who can know with utter certainty all things before they come into being.

6. *For this shall everyone that is holy pray to thee in a seasonable time.*

Now that he has completed the exordium and the narration or satisfaction, he comes to the conclusion of his prayer for pardon, in which he commends his request for forgiveness in such a way as to claim that it is shared even by all holy men; and rightly so, for he who is not a stranger to sins ought to involve himself in prayers of entreaty. What a saving cure! To withstand all sinners' diseases, different remedies are offered them when sick; but if this one antidote is taken with a pure heart, the poisons of all sins are overcome. He added: *In a seasonable time*, that is, in this life of the world where it is permitted to attain conversion; for in hell, as was said earlier in Psalm 6,[18] no-one confesses to the Lord with profit.

And yet in a flood of many waters they shall not come nigh unto him. Whereas earlier he attests that holy men continually pray, he now says that this devotion is not to be granted to various superstitions. The *flood of many waters* is the error of the worst of men adrift on various evils who set up for themselves manifold teachings which they have certainly not received from the true Master. This statement confutes above all the heretics, who in the flood of their perversity produce problems which cause storm and shipwreck. These men *shall not come nigh unto him*, for they abandon true religion. This figure is called metaphor or *translatio*,[19] when a term or word is transferred from the subject to which it belongs to one in which its strict sense is absent, or in which the transferred sense is better than the strict one.

7. *Thou art my refuge from the affliction which hath encompassed me: my joy, redeem me from them that surround me.* A *refuge* is a place to which people flee to avoid dangers. But this penitent did not flee to trackless deserts, to a fortified camp or to human help, but to God, who could scatter the spiritual foes surrounding him. Then he calls the Lord his *joy*, for he knew that he would be spared by Him. As for his statement, *Redeem me*, the Lord surely does not give gold to obtain his freedom? No, He gave His precious blood, comparable with no wealth or resource. But let us investigate a little more carefully what these words tell us. When he says: *My joy*, this seems to be confession of kindness received. When he adds: *Redeem me*, he reveals the fear of one still in danger. But since he was now rejoicing in hope and still fearful in fact, the two are aptly combined; we can rejoice mentally when we know that our present ills are to be ended very speedily. He added: *From them that surround me*, denoting either sins of the flesh or

impure spirits which hasten with headlong speed to destroy us. The penitent's conclusion ended with fear for the present and hope for the future. Come now, you public speakers who handle men's affairs with the craftsman's sophistication; observe this man on trial absolving himself with tears, hark to the sinner who is acquitted on a confession, realise that the President's sentence does not seek the defendant's acquittal but instead condemns his sins. This is the judgment which no man procures by purchase, this is the sentence in which nothing is pronounced with ambiguity. You should prefer to defend your cases in this way, for you are accustomed to mingle your faults with crimes by denial of the truth. Change the manner of secular cases, begin your speeches with the peroration, recount with tears your disordered wretchedness, at once truthfully make known your amendment, and thus deserve to complete in joy what you happily commenced in tears. By this means you will understand how this saving procedure differs, for what culminates in joy cannot endure the opposite. Now let us examine in the next section what reply the Lord makes to him.

8. *I will give thee understanding and I will instruct thee in this way in which thou shalt go: I will fix my eyes on thee.* He comes to the fourth part, where the Lord's speech bedews him like a shower of honey. But let us ponder how suitably, how mercifully Christ is introduced as spokesman, so that hope might manifest itself more clearly to penitents when the Judge Himself makes the promise. But what does He say particularly? *I will give thee understanding.* You observe that sinners do not have understanding except when the Lord grants it in merciful kindness to the converted, for understanding spells good action and the directing of one's prayers to the Lord's commands. This is the very understanding which the truth of the psalm-heading revealed, and which the Lord's power mercifully poured upon repentant men. He added: *And I will instruct thee,* as if to say: "I shall teach you in your ignorance," or "I shall gird you with the sword of life's salvation, for you are unarmed." Previously when he refrained from telling the Lord his acts of guilt, he had been bereft of counsel, but now he is instructed, being advised at the Lord's prompting to denounce himself. What healing of repentance beyond reckoning, for it not only absolves sins but also grants the blessed rewards won by holy men! The road on which he had entered is the Lord's service, after condemning the evil of his earlier behaviour, a road which embraces

no error unless one leaves it. It is the road of peace and truth on which blessed virtues travel, on which no wrongdoing makes its appearance. Next comes: *I will fix my eyes on thee*, that is, "I will direct on you the light of My intelligence"; for the person who is truly wise and performs the Lord's commands with a pure mind is justly said to have the Lord's eyes upon him, So let us observe with what glory the lowliness of penitents is exalted, so that they may hear that the Lord's eyes are fixed on them when they speedily desire to give satisfaction to Him.

9. *Do not become like the horse and mule in whom there is no understanding. With bridle and bit bind fast their jaws.* At this point He now gives a general warning to the human race not to surrender itself to wandering errors. But let us examine why these comparisons are made. A horse serves its rider's will undiscriminatingly, and gallops off, whoever mounts it; a mule patiently accepts baggage with which it is laden. In this sense neither has understanding, for the horse does not choose the one it obeys, and the mule is unaware of the burdens with which it is laden. So He bids men of this kind not to be mounted by the devil's deceits and weighed down by burdens of vices, so that they may not be consigned to the role of arrogance through disobedience. But what does He say that we should do with such people? Surely what we do with foolish animals, for by these comparisons He harnessed stupid men against their will to the truth. *With bridle* has reference to the horse, for *frenum* (bridle) gets its name *a fero retinendo*[20] (controlling a beast), since the ancients called a horse *ferum*. *With a bit* refers to the mule, so these restraining implements hold back the two animals mentioned. As a result they proceed at their master's will, so they do not rush along according to their own inclinations. *Jaws* aid animals to chew their food so that their bodies' life may be maintained. By the figure of allegory he says that these jaws of disobedient men must be bound fast, in other words, supplies of food must be given to them quite sparingly, so that restrained by the need to fast they may surrender themselves to the dominion of the Creator. Allegory, as we have often said, occurs when the words used are at variance with the meaning.[21] We have said that in this section the Lord Christ speaks; He tells the Father to *bind fast* because the holy Trinity has one wish, one power, one joint activity.

10. *Who come not near to thee, many are the scourges of sinners.* He continues with the comparisons just made. It is necessary that un-

tamed animals accept the bridle and endure whipping until they can become accustomed to follow a road by the direct path. The order of words is: *Many are the scourges of sinners who come not near to thee;* but by saying *who come not near,* He shows that some sinners come near to the Lord, and though they sin through weakness of the flesh, they do not abandon devoted prayers. Those who depart from the Lord in a spirit of obstinacy as though fearing obstacles before them, and do not proceed on direct paths, endure many scourges so as to be compelled through the administration of whippings to fulfil what they refuse to do willingly. But these are the scourges which swiftly heal us, which quickly free us and lead us to the path of truth.

But mercy shall encompass them that hope in the Lord. In fact, God's justice promises scourges to those without hope but mercy to those who hope in Him. As the prophet Ezechiel says: *I am the Lord who am not mindful of evils, but seek only that man turneth himself away from his wicked life and from all the iniquities which he hath wrought, and he shall live.*[22] He did well to say *shall encompass,* so that no place should remain from where the devil's enmity can find a way into them.

11. *Be glad in the Lord, and rejoice, ye just: and glory, all ye right of heart.* Here a categorical syllogism[23] can be framed, so that like runaway slaves the rules for dialectic can be put to some use for the divine Scriptures. Every just man rejoices in the Lord: every man rejoicing in the Lord is of upright heart: so every just man is of upright heart. Let us remember, however, that we are not to take cognizance of syllogisms too often, because the careful reader most frequently finds in the sacred Scriptures passages from which he can draw them out for himself, and set them down after the fashion we have shown. It is enough for us to have demonstrated, admittedly somewhat infrequently, that the divine Scriptures undoubtedly contain amongst the arts of logic this facet as well, in effect if not in form. He frequently warns us that the just must *be glad in the Lord,* not in themselves, for he who is joyful in himself is deceived by false presumption, as has often been stated, whereas he who is glad in the Lord enjoys delight without end. *Being glad* means being soothed by sweetness in the heart's silence, *rejoicing* means showing joy with the warmth of an excited spirit. Next comes: *And glory, all ye right of heart.* Here, by the figure known as *apo koinou* or *a communi,*[24] we must also append: "Glory in

the Lord, you who are subject to Him, and entrust your freedom or distinction to His service, realising that you attain rewards of eternal blessedness by that means." We must also note that for the sake of variety he earlier spoke of the just, but here of the *right of heart*. All who are just are right of heart, and in turn those who are right of heart are undoubtedly most just. So since the two terms are inseparable, there is no doubt that they are set side by side for the sake of variety, for frequent repetition of the same words is cloying. But let us ponder why this penitent deserved to obtain in clear tones a reply from Him to whom he prayed with his whole strength. The man who a little earlier was bent low and weighed down by the burden of sins is numbered among the just and welcomed among the upright of heart; thus his exaltation after being pardoned is as great as was his earlier abasement in rendering satisfaction. So he is now blessed, for he is clearly absolved by the decree of the most devoted Judge.

Conclusion Drawn From the Psalm

Let us now consider the power of this psalm, the fact that by supplication in ten verses it obtained God's response without any delay. Perhaps it reminds us of the working of the ten commandments; just as observance of the decalogue invites us to a reward, so this prayer poured out from a remorseful heart leads us to supplicate for mercy. So let us read it carefully, and let us lament through remorse of heart, for what psalm is to be pondered over more eagerly than that in which sins are forgiven by the words of so great a Judge? The psalm has this outstanding and unique feature, that whereas other psalms of penitents in their peroration exult through the impulse of heaven-sent remorse, in this one the Lord who is addressed with great longing Himself promises mercy and joy. So we are continually to beg Him with an insistence which He welcomes, for He promises what was likewise recounted in the gospel-parable: *Ask, and it shall be given to you: seek, and you shall find: knock, and it shall be opened to you. For everyone that asketh, receiveth: and he that seeketh, findeth: and to him that knocketh, it shall be opened.*[25] So who, I ask, should now lack confidence in most devoted supplication, seeing that the love of the King has deigned to strengthen us with this triple promise?

COMMENTARY ON PSALM 32

1. *A psalm of David.* This heading is thoroughly familiar, and so the reader should seek our previous explanation of it. But we offer this necessary advice, that in this psalm the prophet urges the faithful Church by means of certain comparisons to sing the psalms. He recounts the power and deeds of the Creator, so that the Church may hasten more eagerly to praise Him when she recognises His power and devotion.

Division of the Psalm

The prophet speaks throughout the psalm. In the first section he warns the just that they should rejoice with all eagerness of mind in the Lord, who is known to encompass His creatures with marvellous power. In the second section he cries out that the one who has deserved to engage in His worship is blessed; he is pointing to the Christian era, in which the great crowd of nations was to believe.

Explanation of the Psalm

Rejoice in the Lord, ye just: joint praise becometh the upright. The blessed David dissociates the Catholic Church from the contagion of heretics, and advises upright Christians to rejoice not in earthly delights but in the Lord, where their joys are perfected in unbroken sweetness. Though this world's afflictions are appropriate to the faithful, the just are told *rejoice.* But with what joy? It could only be that of which the Lord advises us: *When men persecute you and speak all that is evil against you untruly for my name's sake, be glad and rejoice, for your reward is very great in heaven.*[1] In the same way Paul mentions that we must rejoice unceasingly, for he says: *Rejoice in the Lord: again I say, rejoice.*[2] This repetition makes the point that we should rejoice here in afflictions, and be glad in the undying peace of the kingdom to come. This is why the Lord says in the gospel: *I will see you again, and your heart shall rejoice, and your joy no man shall take from you.*[3] The psalmist added: *Joint praise becometh the upright.* Who these upright are he is to tell us in the second part. In this phrase, *Joint praise becometh the upright,* he shows that such praise does not become debased heretics. As another prophet has also said: *Praise is not seemly in the mouth of a sinner.*[4] *Joint praise* is the same praise uttered in the mouths of many; the expression is used to denote the unity of the Church, which he proclaims is preserved everywhere. When he says *becometh,* he demonstrates that it is appropriate and suitable that one who sings the praise of the Lord is likewise pleasing to Him both in uprightness of faith and in worth of deeds.

2. *Give praise to the Lord on the harp: sing to him with the psaltery, the instrument of ten strings.* Those instructed are the just previously mentioned, who sing the Lord's praises in devoted melody by their holy deeds. The harp, as we have already said in our Preface,[5] consists of a hollow set in the base of a wooden belly, across which the strings stretch upwards; when strummed it emits the sweetest sounds. It has obtained its name of *cithara* because it is strummed with swift repetition (*cita iteratione*).[6] With it are rightly compared deeds which extend from earthly things to heavenly grace; in other words, when we feed the hungry, clothe the naked, visit the sick, and perform those other works which though apparently concerned with the flesh are done for love of the Godhead. We also play the harp when in time of suffering or loss we say in untroubled and joyful tones: *The Lord gave, and the Lord hath taken away. As it hath pleased the Lord, so it is done. Blessed be the name of the Lord.*[7]

We said that the psaltery has ten strings. The harp's arrangement is reversed here, for it has its belly in the upper part, and from it the tuneful strings go down to the lower. The commands of the decalogue are aptly associated with it, because the arrangement of the instrument is re-enacted when we receive the Lord's commands issuing from the upper regions. Note too that this is the only musical instrument which because of its excellence is called the decachord; we do not recall the word being used of the harp or of other instruments of the kind.[8] The ten-stringed psaltery, as men of old have said, reveals to us this further mystery. Three of the commandments we relate to God who is the Trinity. The first consists of His words: *Thou shalt not have strange gods before me;* the second: *Thou shalt not make to thyself a graven thing;* and the third: *Thou shalt not take the name of thy God in vain,* to which He subjoins the command about the Sabbath. But the seven which follow these, as men have stated, refer to love of our neighbour: *Honour thy father and thy mother, Thou shalt not kill, Thou shalt not commit adultery, Thou shalt not steal, Thou shalt not bear false witness against thy neighbour, Thou shalt not covet thy neighbour's house, neither shalt thou desire his wife,*[9] and the rest. So the power of the entire ten-stringed psaltery is revealed to us in its perfection and distinction. We also hymn on ten strings when we involve ourselves in praiseworthy behaviour through the five bodily and five spiritual senses. But these matters of which we speak are not detached from us as is the case with the teaching of music; for the harp and psaltery lie within us, or rather we ourselves are the instruments when like them we sing through the quality of our actions by means of the Lord's grace. We are granted understanding of this by that other example when the psalmist says: *In me, O God, are vows which I will pay, praises to thee.*[10] These and like expressions are, as we have often said, spoken with metaphorical allusion.

3. *Sing to him a new canticle: sing well to him in jubilation.* The new canticle means the Lord's incarnation, at which the world was filled with the exultation of salvation and the angels sounded forth with tuneful voices, praising and saying: *Glory to God in the highest, and peace to men of good will.*[11] So he advises us that we should both state and believe these same things. Next comes: *Sing well unto him in jubilation,* that is, invoke God by good works; *jubilation* is joy expressed with warmth of spirit and the cry of intermingled voices. In this jubilation only he who shows eagerness for goodly living can sing well. Ponder the salutary teaching which forewarns us that we must sing with innocence before the Lord, who knows our passions and our hearts; this is to prevent our sinning more seriously by appearing to approach such great mysteries with wickedness and guile.

4. *For the word of the Lord is right: and all his works are done with faithfulness.* From this point he begins to hasten through the praises of the Lord by different statements made in the demonstrative genre,[12] so that all His deeds and commands may grow sweet in our eyes. So *the word of the Lord is right,* that is, for the guidance of men. It is truly called right for it makes men right; a marvellous epithet, a true-spoken word. Since we are corrected by the divine law, we are detached by it from our wickedness, and then we live according to the law since we obey its commands. This is the fifth type of definition, called by the

Greeks *kata tēn lexin* and in Latin *ad verbum;*[13] for one part of the prayer defines what the word of the Lord is, namely *right*. He attaches the phrase, *And all his works are done with faithfulness;* this is especially so when He works in those who by His gift have gained the merit of fidelity. As He says in the gospel: *Thy faith hath made thee safe.*[14] That woman would not have deserved the Lord's help if faith bestowed through gratuitous generosity had not preceded it.

5. *He loveth mercy and judgment: the earth is full of the mercy of the Lord.* In this and the ensuing verses, by means of the third type of definition which is called in Greek *poiotēs* and in Latin *qualitativa,*[15] he praises the Lord by recounting what He has done or what He does every day. We say that we love the things that we perform regularly; so here it is said of the Lord that He loves mercy and judgment, as if He did not love both prudence and temperance! But because He frequently grants us mercy, He is said to love it utterly. So in this world *He loveth mercy,* for here He spreads it far and wide, obviously when He is forbearing with sinners, when He patiently waits on blasphemers, when He grants life to the unworthy, and performs such actions clearly to be attributed wholly to divine kindness. He also loves *judgment,* when He separates the godly from the ungodly, sifting their merits by the quality of justice. Wherever He bestows the mercy earlier mentioned, what ensues is that *the earth is full of the mercy of the Lord.* It is precisely this which supports us in our wretchedness, when we struggle under the devil's attack, when through weakness of the flesh we abandon the divine commands; for what mercy can we ask for when we are not oppressed by any needs? So let us seek here the mercy of which the whole world is full.

6. *By the word of the Lord the heavens were established: and all the power of them by the spirit of his mouth.* Though this verse appears to refer to the condition of the natural world, it is appropriate to interpret it in a spiritual sense. *By the word of the Lord,* that is, by the Son of God, *the heavens were established,* in other words, the apostles or saints were set in place to fill the earth with the preaching which brought salvation. Next comes: *And all the power of them by the spirit of his mouth;* just so, because their teaching came from the holy Spirit. *Power* refers both to the miracles which they performed and to the Lord's law which they preached to the nations. If we examine the passage more carefully, we see that it signifies here the holy Trinity. By

speaking of *the word* he announces the Son, by adding *of the Lord* he mentions the Father, and *by the spirit of his mouth* he wishes to be interpreted as nothing other than the holy Spirit, who came forth from the Father before time began. And so that you might grasp the manifest unity in three Persons, he spoke of His mouth, not of their mouths.

7. *Gathering together the waters of the sea as into a skin: setting abysses in storehouses.* His words, *Gathering together the waters of the sea as into a skin* means, if you wish to take it literally, the sea enclosed by shores. But if you wish to acknowledge a spiritual sense here, a skin is the hide stripped from cattle which serves human needs for gathering certain liquids. This skin is compared to the Church, for just as a skin holds water or similar liquid poured into it, so the Church too encloses the unity of believers. *The waters of the sea* denotes the Christian people shaken in the salt surge of the world by the alternating onset and ebbing of the waves. We use the word *abysses* to express something extremely deep which because of its depth does not allow human eyes to plumb it. So in His storehouses, that is, of wisdom and knowledge, He sets boundless depths to try out who seeks the Scriptures with devoted zeal.

8. *Let all the earth fear the Lord: and let all things and all the inhabitants of the world be moved by him.* The *earth* here denotes the sinner who is unyielding in all things. He is rightly termed the earth for he is robbed of the gift of heavenly grace. So this earthly sinner who knows not how to love must fear the Lord, so that if he does not refrain from sins through desire for rewards, he should at least be recalled through pondering the punishment. With the words, *by him,* the psalmist shows that they are moved also by the devil, of whom Isaias says: *This is the man that troubled the earth.*[16] So the prophet rightly asks that all things be moved by the Lord, because all that is arranged by His dispensation is always applied to useful ends. But though he had spoken first of all things in general, he passes now to men, for though all things need to be administered by His command, the human race in particular is known to be subject to sins because it has degenerated from its nature through the vices that creep into it.

9. *For he spoke, and they were made: he commanded, and they were created.* He gives the reason why all things should be moved by the Lord: it is because He is their Creator, and it is necessary that He

should dispense their existence, since He consented to create them through grace. *He spoke and they were made* points to the world's beginning, when bidden by His Son's command all things burst forth. *He commanded, and they were created:* it was through the prophets in particular that He laid down the law by which the faithful were created at the Lord's wish. You see how salutary it was that the prophet sought that all things be moved by God, for He alone can be merciful to His creatures.

10. *The Lord bringeth to nought the counsels of nations: and he rejecteth the advice of the people, and casteth away the counsels of princes.* He does indeed bring to nought the counsels which are wicked, or rather most wicked, for He ever aids and strengthens those which are good. Most fitting words are used to describe the issues. He *brought to nought the counsels of nations* when He did not allow them to continue worshipping idols any longer. He *rejected the devices of the people,* for though the Jews' wish was fulfilled in the wicked murder of the Lord, they were clearly rebuked at His resurrection. Because he had spoken of nations and of the people, and did not wish to leave anything unmentioned, he later speaks also of *princes,* whether they are tyrants who with savage persecutions attacked the Lord's law, or the impure spirits whose counsel is always wicked.

11. *But the counsel of the Lord standeth for ever: the thoughts of his heart for all time.* Just as he said that the debased plans of men are to be made vain, so now he says that the dispositions of the Lord remain for ever; for whereas the sinner and the mortal man experience transient things, the eternal Lord established what will never be blameworthy. As Isaias says: *All my counsel shall be enduring, and all that I meditated I shall achieve.*[17] Jeremiah too says the same thing: *If my covenant were not under guard day and night, I should not have issued the laws of heaven and earth.*[18] We do well to understand His counsel as the secret of the incarnation, known to have been granted in the interests of the human race. It is dissolved by no period of time but *standeth for ever,* because the Lord's triumphant death has blotted out for ever the destruction imposed by the devil. *The thoughts of his heart* denote the predestination in which all things have been set, whether they are past or are still to come in future generations. This predestination sustains that order of events which abides *for all time.* Those men who falsely state that there is one nature in Christ the Lord rightly yield before this declara-

tion; for if His counsel is enduring, and His heart's thoughts abide for all time, and His thought and counsel were the secret of the incarnation, it is inevitable that through the shape of the humanity which He assumed, He always continues as the one Son in two distinct natures, perfect and united, just as He began in the unity of one Person.

12. *Blessed is the nation whose God is their Lord: the people whom the Lord hath chosen for his inheritance.* He passes to the second section, in which he is to state who are *the upright whom praise of the Lord becometh,* as propounded in the first verse. So he talks of the nation as being the heavenly Jerusalem which we know is gathered from all nations. It is indeed blessed, for God is truly worshipped and the Lord of all adored by it, the Lord who protects and guides them. *Inheritance* refers to what is both left to another and acquired. But the Christian people is an inheritance gained, not bequeathed, for their Creator possesses those whom He sought by His holy preaching and precious blood.

13. *The Lord hath espied from heaven, and hath looked on all the sons of men.* Here the future coming of the Lord is explained by the figure which in Greek is called *idea* and in Latin *species;*[19] when we set before our eyes the representation, so to say, of a future event, and stir our mental aspiration towards an eagerness to listen. *The Lord espied from heaven* when He bestowed the advent of His own Son; man did not look to the Lord, but the Lord looked to man. Espying means beholding at a distance him who had been truly cut off by sins and had been set at a distance by his Creator, a thing which it is sacrilegious to say. The words, *And hath looked on,* denote the grace of the pitying Lord, for we say that we look on those to whom we claim something has been granted. Notice that he does not mention the sins which He looked on, but *the sons of men.* When He looks on faults, He punishes, but when He gazes on man He pardons. As the psalmist is to say in Psalm 50: *Turn away thy face from my sins,*[20] and elsewhere: *Turn not away thy face from me.*[21] So we must realise and remember this difference.

14. *From his habitation which he hath prepared he hath looked upon all that dwell upon the earth.* He was speaking at that time of the future body of the Lord; for since all that comes to pass as the due sequence unfolds was decided by predestination,[22] how much more certain it is

that the miracle of the incarnation was arranged before time began, for it could bring aid to the endangered world which He had decided to create.

15. *He who hath fashioned individually the hearts of them, who shows understanding unto all their works.* He has *fashioned the hearts* of those on whom He has bestowed the gifts of His understanding. We say that modellers *fashion,* for they create certain shapes to achieve the purposes of their work. In the same way the Lord forms and arranges the minds of the just to lead them to the gifts of His mercy. *Individually,* that is, separately and distinctly. *The hearts of them,* namely, of holy men living in fear of the Lord. Next comes; *Who shows understanding unto all their works.* He understands particularly when He gives worthy rewards in return for the deeds of good men. When he says: *Unto all their works,* he means the thoughts, words, and deeds by which we always perform good and evil.

16. *The king will not be saved by abundant strength: nor shall the giant be safe by his own great courage. King* means the man with self-control; though he rules his body by God's mercy, he cannot be saved from the vices of the flesh when he presumes upon his own strength. Human strength is justly forsaken when the good and perfect gift is attributed not to the generous God but to one's own powers. *Giant* likewise is to be understood as one strengthened by greatness of virtues, who wars with the monstrous nature of the devil in a continual struggle. He is rightly said to be a giant since he confronts such spirits. But even he who with the aid of God's grace now puts to flight many spirits will not be able to be safe if like a giant he is raised high by the vice of pride, by which our frail humanity is snatched up, and becomes presumptuous about the nature of his merits. Though giant (*gigas*) is in Latin *terrigena* ("earth-born"), the word is clearly used in a good sense as well, for we read of Christ: *He hath rejoiced as a giant to run the way.*[23]

17. *Deceiving is the horse for safety: neither shall he be safe in the abundance of his strength.* He deploys *horse* for worldly happiness, which supports men as though they were conveyed by the movement of horses. This human hope deceives like a deceiving horse. He who advances in self-boasting suddenly experiences an unexpected fall. He explains why the horse deceives; when it makes for the plains and gets

its feet entangled in precipitous haste, it cannot maintain the safety of its rider. Overeagerness spells carelessness, and one who does not proceed with self-control is always liable to fall disastrously. The horse is called *deceiving* because it usually tricks those who put trust in it.

18. *Behold, the eyes of the Lord are on them that fear him and hope in his mercy.* The eyes of the Lord represent the divine will, for when we find people likeable we rest our eyes on them without distrust, whereas we remove our gaze from those alien to our hearts. So *the eyes of the Lord are on them that fear him;* His devotion protects those who He knows fear Him. Since he has spoken of those who fear, He aptly continues with those who love, for both feelings are combined in love of the Lord. He who fears the Lord well also loves Him, and he who loves Him also fears Him. These feelings are separated in human activity but united in heavenly devotion. He explains the identity of them that fear Him with the words: *And hope in his mercy.* This is called the argument "from what is added."[24] The addition is "fear the Lord and hope in Him," and these are joined in a reciprocal and unbroken alliance.

19. *To rescue their souls from death, and feed them in hunger.* These are the two prayers of the most faithful Christian, that at the future judgment he may be rescued from perpetual death, and that on earth he may live his life with spiritual nourishment. The Lord rescues the souls of the just from death when He removes them from the power of the devil, when by His kindness He sets free those whom the dominion of sin had held captive. He feeds them in hunger when in this world, where there is a shortage of good things; He does not cease to nourish with spiritual food those whom He has redeemed. By feeding here is meant nourishment of the mind, for those in hunger are the people who perpetually burn with longing for heavenly things. How abundantly satisfied is that hunger, ever worthily greedy and without need~! The blessed are hungry not because they fast at the Lord's feast but because they continually burn in their quest, for they progress in their search for the Lord. As the evangelist says, *Blessed are they that hunger and thirst after justice, for they shall have their fill.*[25]

20. *But our soul waiteth for the Lord, for he is our helper and protector.*

The psalmist's word *sustinet*[26] reflects the patience of the Christian so that the just enticed by future rewards may persevere in constancy of mind. But let us understand the nature of this virtue which we are so often advised to observe. Patience is what makes glorious martyrs, what guards the blessings of our faith, what conquers all adversity not by wrestling but by enduring, not by grumbling but by giving thanks. Patience represses the extravagance which beguiles us. It overcomes hot anger, it removes the envy which ravages the human race, it makes men gentle, it smiles becomingly on the kind, and it orders men who are cleansed to attain the rewards that are to come. Patience wipes away the dregs of all pleasure, patience makes souls pure. Through patience we soldier for Christ, through it we conquer the devil, through it we blessedly attain the kingdom of heaven. As Scripture says: *In your patience you shall possess your souls.*[27] Next comes: *For he is our helper and protector.* He is our Helper when we try to reach Him with the aid of grace, our Protector when we confront the enemy. So the person who depends on such a promise *waiteth for the Lord* untroubled. Note that he puts patience after all the precepts, so that we who have confidence in the bestowal of so great a reward may endure everything in a manly way.

21. *And in him our heart shall rejoice, and in his holy name we have trusted.* So that none may grumble about the patience which has been proclaimed, so that none may be disturbed by a will that grows weary, there follows a gift which is magnificent and most sweet, for the waiting itself has a reward, since the one who waits rejoices in the Lord. He adds: *And in his holy name we have trusted,* that is, in Christ's name, for it was He whom the most holy prophet awaited, rejoicing at His future coming. *We have trusted* reveals a continuing time, because it is not right to stop trusting at any point at which the weary soul can gain refreshment.

22. *Let thy mercy, O Lord, be upon us, as we have hoped in thee.* With these words he was longing for the fulfilment of the Lord's incarnation, which he eagerly awaited with burning spirit. Notice how abundant is the gift which enriched the human race, which filled the bands of angels with the sweetness of joy, and which even the regions of hell experienced. He seeks that his longings should be fulfilled so that he

can be found to be most perfect. He added: *In thee* so that he might exclude all superstitions and all debased activities by praying to the true Lord.

Conclusion Drawn From the Psalm·

How honey-sweet are the words which we have heard! The heavenly psaltery has indeed played for us a song of salvation. The chords of the resounding commands are such that if we hearken to them with our inner ear, we too shall be cleansed by the healing of David's lyre in them. That purification which Saul experienced will take place also in us, so that once we have routed the unclean spirits we may serve the Lord with minds made clean. The saints have their own music which comes to the ear of the faithful soul, and the sound of it does not fail, and its impact does not grow feeble. So you who love shows, abandon the pleasures which bring death. Instead, assemble for these joys, these mysteries, in which harp and organ arouse virtues rather than stimulate desires for debased pleasure.

COMMENTARY ON PSALM 33

1. *A psalm of David when he changed his countenance before Abimelech, who dismissed him, and he went his way.* Since the history of this heading is revealed by reading the Book of Kings,[1] it is superfluous to divert the abundance of that source into this short account. We wish to avoid filling and covering the area of a whole page with an extended account of that one passage. When Saul was pursuing David, David fled to king Achis, and since through the motive of jealousy he was suspected there, he carefully *changed his countenance,* covering his face with spittle so that he would be thought to be diabolically possessed and thus released unharmed as an object of pity. But these and other deeds were accomplished by David as evidence of a great mystery, for he showed that the spittle, which represented the holy Scriptures, was running down his beard, that is, had great strength. The significance of these things led to the substitution of the name of Abimelech, meaning "kingdom of my father,"[2] for Achis, to whom David had fled.

Clearly this incident aptly refers to the Lord Christ, through whom the glorious Father with most holy devotion undertook service to the world. The expression, *who dismissed him*, refers to king Abimelech; *and he went his way* means that David departed to another region because, as we have said, he had begun to be suspected. This is the third psalm of those in which the signs of the future concerning the Lord Christ are denoted through the deeds of David,[3] though we see that it is the second alphabetic psalm.[4]

Division of the Psalm

Throughout the psalm the words are spoken by the prophet, who sets the letters of the Hebrew alphabet, minus the sixth,[5] in sequence at the head of the verses. In the first section he promises to bless the Lord, and warns the meek to join with him in continuing with His praises; this section embraces four letters of the alphabet already mentioned. In the second section, devoted to the conversion of the faithful, the rewards for deeds of deserving merit are not omitted; this section contains six letters. Thirdly, he warns mankind, as if they were his sons, from what sins they ought to refrain; this has four letters. The fourth part says that the just are to be delivered from all tribulations, and that the wicked will suffer their allotted punishment, to ensure that the Jews may not entertain some doubt and grow soft in their dangers; here the remaining seven letters are marked before the verses. Remember, as has already been stated in Psalm 24,[6] that this incomplete alphabet denotes those who cannot sing the Lord's praises with the fullest purity of good works.

Explanation of the Psalm

2. ALEPH. *I will bless the Lord at all times: his praises shall be always in my mouth.* We know that times differ for men, being at one moment harsh in tribulations, at another pleasant with joy. So the prophet announces that the Lord is to be blessed at all times, both when we suffer reverses and when we rejoice after happiness is bestowed on us, as the just have done and as those who burn with the love of the Lord do. But though it is always right and profitable for a creature ever to

praise his Creator, none the less it seems virtually impossible for us to make the praises of psalm-singing resound continually to the Lord, because of the different activities which men have. But the Lord's praise is always in the just man's mouth when he either ponders or speaks thoughts which cannot be criticised by any rebuke, for all that we speak or ponder in mind as a result of patience, love, simplicity or the other virtues is justly assigned to God's praises. To have honourable thoughts on lips or at heart is praise of Him who bestows them. The word praise (*laus*) derives from the laurel[7] which used to crown victors. This is the spittle, allegorically speaking, foretold by that parallel in the heading; these are the words which seemed to express the strength of the divine Scriptures.

3. BEHT. *In the Lord shall my soul be praised: let the meek hear and rejoice.* The servant's love is stated most beautifully in a single phrase: he says that it is not in himself or in riches that his soul is to be praised, but in the Lord. The faithful servant exults when he is known to have a lord who deserves praise, for he knows that a blessing redounds to him when his lord is lauded by the lips of many. If today someone detracts from the merit of a lord, with what rage and indignation is his devoted servant fired and afflicted! It is the part of faithful servants either to resent hostile gossip against their lords or to be delighted if people speak well of them. Next comes: *Let the meek hear and rejoice.* He did not speak of persons learned in the law, nor of those who fast or sing psalms, but the meek are to rejoice, for through their special charity they are used to self-restraint in all things.

4. GIMEL. *O magnify the Lord with me, and let us extol his name in turn.* Our bodily interest longs to enjoy what it desires with greedy pleasure, but spiritual grace does not wish to perform alone what profits the salvation of many, in case abhorrent envy mingles with it as it transacts holy works. This is what the present verse now explains, for it summons the obedient people to magnify the Lord's name in splendid fellowship. Next comes: *And let us extol his name in turn.* This is a sweet exchange, a most just requirement, that all should do together what is seen to be offered to the holy Unity. *In turn* denotes the arrangement of the choruses when they respond to the Lord's psalmody alternately. This figure is called *enargeia* or *imaginatio*,[8] bringing the action of something before the mind's eye.

5. DALETH. *I sought the Lord, and he heard me: and he delivered me*

from all my troubles. So that the persons whom he has invited should hasten to celebrate the Lord in psalms, he now states what blessings have come to him from this activity. *I sought the Lord,* not over massive tracts of lands or broad and far-flung regions, but in the heart, for if we ponder His majesty there, we find it present in every way. Observe what he says: *I sought the Lord, and he heard me,* for His understanding embraces all things, and it works not by physical senses but by spiritual powers. Next follows how profitable it has been to have sought the Lord, since He has delivered him from all hardships; who would be able to seek one by one all the great benefits which he has succeeded in obtaining at the one time? For by saying: *From all,* he leaves no possible remaining obstacle still surviving.

6. HE. *Come ye to him, and be enlightened: and your faces shall not blush.* To begin with he uttered praises and arranged the choruses; now in the second part he encourages the people to come to communion, so that as spiritual adviser he might set before us the rite of the Church to come. *Come ye* is addressed not to drunkards, adulterers, or the arrogant, but to sober, chaste, humble Christians who deserve to be enlightened by reception of the sacrament. As Paul attests with regard to communion: *Whoever shall eat this bread or drink the chalice of the Lord unworthily, eateth and drinketh judgment to himself, not discerning the body of the Lord. But let a man prove himself, and so let him eat of that bread and drink of the chalice.*[9] So one must ensure that the person who comes to Him so governs himself in making humble satisfaction that he seems capable of being enlightened rather than blinded. *Face,* as we have often said, means presence, and it can often experience confusion and change colour if heavenly gifts are withdrawn from it. So the faithful do not blush, since they obtain these gifts; blushing is the mark of one who is frustrated by not being able to achieve his longings. Some people make a big issue of this passage, and think that we must interpret it in this way: since Paul says: *Only he that has immortality and inhabits inaccessible light,*[10] how can the psalmist say here: *Come ye to him, and be enlightened?* But the problem is solved by this brief statement of the truth: His light is said to be inaccessible when the unique and almighty nature of its substance is described; but when the grace of the sacred Godhead pours forth, we both approach Him and obtain blessed enlightenment. So elsewhere it is stated: *Which enlighteneth every man that cometh into the world.*[11]

7. ZAIN. *This poor man cried, and the Lord heard him: and freed him from all his troubles.* This denotes the poor in spirit who is empty not only of worldly wealth but also of abundance of vices. This is the poor man who comes to God and is enlightened, whose face does not blush, whose cry to the Lord gets a salutary and appropriate hearing; and then he emerges to be freed not from a single affliction, but from all worldly difficulties. This often happens to the just when they devote their souls to a holy manner of life, and pass from the anarchic disaster of this world to enduring freedom from care. You must also reflect here that a letter of the Hebrew alphabet has been leapfrogged; the seventh letter is set down in the place of the sixth. I believe that this is to be explained by my previous observation that the psalm denotes persons who are holy but shown not to be perfect in all their works. I have not found any stated opinion of the Fathers to this effect.

8. HETH. *The Lord will send an angel² round about them that fear him, and shall deliver them.* So that we might not believe that the Lord can neglect His faithful, He consoles them with this divine message. Examine the healing word which He speaks: *He will send,* for because of the arrogance of human frailty He does not act openly but works by hidden directives, so that you can receive what can aid your salvation without your knowledge. *An angel* is an agent of God's will; so if you wish to become an angel, do what He enjoins, so that you may free a person in danger, help the troubled, rescue the innocent, and perform the other commands prescribed by divine authority; for we are angels in the spirit when we are made agents of the will of heaven.

9. TETH. *O taste and see that the Lord is sweet: blessed is the man that hopeth in him.* He comes back to the most holy communion of the Lord, and never stops repeating what he knows is the source for men of the joys of eternal life. *Taste* refers not to the palate but to the sweetest emotion of the soul, which is fattened by contemplation of the Godhead. So that you may understand what *taste* means, *see* follows, and this refers specifically not to the mouth but clearly to our contemplative nature. So when we receive this Body, we may be confident that the grace of life is being granted to us. He does not wish you to relate that communion to the body which all men share, so he says: *The Lord is sweet,* for by this communion He grants salvation to mankind in accord with His devoted love. Our Life who is truly God, who united to Himself the flesh assumed from the virgin Mary and

made it His own, claimed that it brings life; as He says in the gospel: *Amen, amen I say to you, except you eat the flesh of the Son of man and drink his blood, you shall not have eternal life in you.*[13] Though that flesh has been assumed from human nature, we must not account it as belonging to one of us or as stained by the contagion of any sin, but flesh worthy of adoration, which brings salvation, gives life, and forgives sins through the Word to which it is joined. As the Lord himself says in the gospel: "*That you may know that the Son of man hath power on earth to forgive sins,*[14] and leads us to the kingdom of enduring life." The psalmist next appends this unconditional and strong statement, that the man who does not cease to hope in the Lord is blessed. This is a leading theme, for it is so frequently repeated in order that we may never cease to seek what we know is proclaimed with such constancy.

10. IOD. *Fear the Lord, all ye his saints: for there is nothing wanting to them that fear him.* He enjoins fear of the Lord on all saints, so that no individual however well-deserving may stray from that most salutary resolve. He shows the usefulness embraced in fear of Him with the subsequent words: *For there is nothing wanting to them that fear him,* a short statement but what a mighty promise∼! Those who are assigned riches, bodily health, kingdoms can be lacking something;[15] the only man short of nothing is he who is enriched with fear of the Lord.

11. CAPH. *The rich have wanted and have suffered hunger, but they that seek the Lord will not fall short of any good.* In a single verse with splendid contrast he has distinguished the earth's rich from Christ's poor. He says: *The rich have wanted, and have suffered hunger.* When are the rich in want? When they do not have right faith. When do they suffer hunger? When they are not even slightly filled by the Lord's body. Such rich men are in want, and though their bellies are filled they are always hungry in spirit, for what can men possess if they do not have God? Next comes: *But they that seek the Lord will not fall short of any good,* because those who enjoy spiritual desires do not fall short of any good. When we love the Lord, we find everything in Him. He who is sought is One, but in that One all things are contained. What marvellous gain, what unique profit! Why should we weary ourselves with diverse pursuits? So let us hasten to Him in singleness of mind, for after attaining Him we seek no further for all blessings, but possess them. As Paul says: *We know that to them that*

love God all things work together unto good.[16] This argument is called in *The Topics* "the converse,"[17] for the statements that the rich want and that the poor do not fall short of any good are converse to each other. An argument (*argumentum*) is the mark of a clear (*argutus*) mind,[18] for it wins belief in a doubtful case by persuasive researches.

12. LAMED. *Come, children, hearken to me: I will teach you the fear of the Lord.* Having recounted the solemn rites relating to the Church's sacraments, he now comes to the third part, in which he addresses those who undertake their first instruction in the faith. By saying: *Come,* he shows that they were not within the Church; this is what is said nowadays to those who confess when they come to the Christian faith. The Father's voice sounds forth, the voice of dutiful love warns us to listen to Him as He speaks unasked, for we ought to have sought Him when He was silent. But how sweet, how useful is the fear to which the child is invited! When he says: *I will teach you,* he is advising us not to be afraid at hearing the word *fear.* This is not fear which induces dread, but that which induces love. Human fear contains bitterness, but this contains sweetness. The first forces us to slavery, the second draws us towards freedom. Finally, the first fears the bars that exclude us, the second opens up the kingdom of heaven. So he rightly claimed that this fear is useful, so that we should learn of it with eager mind.

13. MEM. *Who is the man that desireth life, and wishes to see good days?* The question propounded is such that general assent follows. What man could say either "I do not desire life" or "I do not wish to see good days"? Would that we sought eternal life in the same way as we set our hearts on this transitory life! *Good days* does not mean those on which we are busy with transient pleasures, but those which are truly good, occupied with the greatest holiness.

14. NUN. *Keep thy tongue from evil, and thy lips from speaking guile.* This expresses the desire to see good days if only our tongues refrain from uttering anything unfitting. *Evil* is anything forbidden; whatever wars on truth is marked by such a description. Notice the more subtle point that he says the tongue is kept from evil before we begin to move it when we wish to speak. He added: *And thy lips from speaking guile.* The lips at once attend on the movement of the tongue; a kind of harmony is joined by the euphony of both, and thus human speech is achieved. *Guile* is when we deceive the listener, so that what is be-

lieved to be helpful actually is seen to cause a hindrance. This is
rightly forbidden since it is clearly and always opposed to an unblem-
ished conscience.

15. SAMECH. *Turn away from evil, and do good: seek after peace, and
pursue it.* To see good days it is not enough merely to refrain from evil
deeds; we must also be induced by devoted love to carry out good
works.[19] The first step to virtue is not to seek other people's possessions, but the second and higher step is not to refuse one's own to
those in need. By this action we avoid blame, by it we win the palm of
brotherly love. Not to have done harm to a ward, not to have robbed a
poor man shows restraint, which in itself is not enough for rewards.
At the Judgment, the only people who hear the words: *Come ye, blessed
of my Father, possess ye the kingdom which was prepared for you from the
beginning of the world,*[20] are those who have purchased the Lord's
favour at His inspiration by various acts of giving. So you see that the
words, *And do good,* are necessarily added, for this is what frees and
commends us. However, the prophet knew that in this struggle with
the body in this world, even the most faithful do not have peace, and
that they have a perpetual struggle with their vices. So he said most
beautifully: *Seek after peace,* so that though they do not obtain it here
they may still search for it most eagerly. He did not promise that it
could be attained in any sense here, but He commands us to seek after
it as if it lies before us; why is it to be pursued except that it evades us
here? It is to be hoped for in the future, for it lies in the enduring
continuity which exists there. So let us seek it diligently, let us follow
it zealously, for we cannot find it there unless we search for it more
sedulously here. We shall be permitted to grasp these things when we
behold the Author of peace Himself.

16. AIN. *The eyes of the Lord are upon the just, and his ears unto their
prayers.* He passes to the fourth section, and from here to the end he
strengthens the people with a double proclamation. Now he relates
the rewards of the just, and now he rebukes the sins of the wicked, so
that the people he has won over may be warned by both injunctions
and learn to serve the Lord. This figure is called a *paradigm,*[21] a most
effective kind of trope because the example we are to follow is enjoined as being doubly useful. When he says: *The eyes of the Lord are
upon the just,* he shows the uninterrupted favour of the Godhead, so
that His gaze on them seems to be unmoving. He further mentions His

most swift speed of hearing when he recounts that the Lord's ears are trained on their prayers. What delay could they encounter in obtaining a request, when the One who can hear them resides in them? But though He often listens to sinners, much more is promised to the just, since He is known to have His ears open to their prayers.

17. PHE. *But the countenance of the Lord is over them that do evil things: to cut off the remembrance of them from the earth.* Having explained the favour granted to the just, he now turns to punishment of the wicked. So that the most evil of men may not say: "He pays heed to the just, but ignores us, and we are now untroubled in our actions, for we do not merit His eyes on us,"[22] he proclaims that the countenance of the Lord, which is His understanding, is upon the wicked. He observes them but ignores them; He ignores them but takes note of their deeds. So we must be afraid to do evil, because we know that we do not escape His awareness. Note that the expression used with regard to these men is *over them that do evil things,* so that His close proximity cannot be deceived. Be aware that He sees both groups, but the outcome of His gaze is different; He hears the just, but destroys sinners. When he says: *From the earth,* he means from the native land to come, which only those pleasing to God will possess. Their *remembrance* will die because there will be no recollection of them among the just, for we keep in our memory those to whom we are eager to lend support. Those who pass from the Lord's remembrance undoubtedly go to eternal punishment.

18. ZADE. *The just cried, and the Lord heard them, and delivered them out of all their troubles.* He returns to the just, and speaks of them at somewhat greater length, so that the account of their rewards may give heart to people terrified by punishment of the wicked. He says that the just cried out to the Lord, and claims that they were always heard. What are we to say, then, of martyrs who cannot be shown to have been delivered from the execution of tyrants? They were indeed delivered when they were escorted to the kingdom of heaven; they were clearly rid of all their troubles. The cry of the just is always heard above all for their profit in eternity, not merely for their passing benefit.

19. COPH. *The Lord is nigh unto them that are troubled in heart: and he will save the humble of spirit.* This verse too refers to the blessings of the just. The Lord's ways and men's practices are different. The man

seeking to draw near to higher things raises himself up, striving to be
able to attain lofty heights; whereas the Lord, the most High, cannot
be reached except by lowly acts of humility, and we cannot attain His
joys except by bitter tears. Others interpret *nigh* not in the sense of
proximity, but in the help He lends. We must also note the fact that he
speaks of *them that are troubled in heart;* many are troubled, but not in
heart, like grumblers and silly people who do not lament their sins, but
are saddened by worldly losses. But the troubled in heart are those
who make others' ills their own misery, who mourn for the world and
are oppressed by the calamities of the community at large. So He will
save those who have subjected themselves to the greatest humility in
their dealings with others. Notice too that he does not refer to the
humble of speech, for the wickedness of sinners often affects such
humility, but *the humble of spirit.* As the gospel says: *Blessed are the poor
in spirit, for theirs is the kingdom of heaven.*[23]

20. RES. *Many are the afflictions of the just, but out of them all has
the Lord delivered them.* This and the next verse further recount the
blessings of the just, for it was appropriate to dilate on this topic so
that men's frail hearts should not surrender too often through the
repeated approach of fear. Truly the afflictions of the just are many,
because on the one hand the devil attacks them more powerfully, and
on the other men often oppress them through jealousy. Then too the
wicked man, if he suffers a reverse in solitude, can be troubled, but the
just man both is afflicted by his own sufferings and through charity
shares those of others. When the statement is added: *But out of them
all has the Lord delivered them,* the power of the Creator is revealed, for
the crowd of afflictions cannot hinder His deliverance. From this we
realise that every just man is burdened by many tribulations, but is
undoubtedly freed from them all.

21. SIN. *The Lord keepeth all their bones: not one of them shall be
broken.* Bones means the constancy of the faithful; in other words, their
patience, meekness and other virtues which cannot die in the persons
of the saints because they are preserved by God's keeping. Though
their bodies' bones are broken, these virtues cannot be shattered. If
you interpret this phrase literally, large questions seem to arise. How
were the bones not crushed of that thief to whom the Lord had said:
This day thou shalt be with me in Paradise,[24] when we read that they
were broken by the soldiers? And you find that many martyrs' bones

were physically damaged. But all this removes the shadow of doubt if we interpret *bones* as the virtue of faith and strength of soul.[25]

22. *The death of the wicked is very evil: and they that hate the just shall be guilty.* By *the death of the wicked* he means the death which men cannot gaze upon, and which he proclaims as not merely evil but *very evil;* it is truly very evil, for eternal punishment attends it. If you identify this death with the death visible to our eyes, you often see a rich sinner borne to burial with stately and seemly splendour, and households mourn him in such a way as to mislead the ears of men with the impression that he was holy.[26] His friends too attend him with floods of tears, so that you would really believe that a man seen to be mourned with such great grief was one of the good men taken from us. We need not mention the costly perfumes with which their bodies are entombed so as to be preserved even after death; all this is performed with such zeal and pomp that such men survive with life restored at their own funerals. Where then is the very evil death of the wicked? Undoubtedly in hell, where those admitted suffer eternal punishment. In what state, we imagine, was the rich man in purple escorted to the tomb who begged for a drop of cold water from the pauper Lazarus?[27] Observe that in this expression the harshness of death itself is unfolded, for *pessima* (very evil) is equivalent to *pessum data* (sent to the bottom). He added: *And they that hate the just shall be guilty,* in other words, those who regarded the Lord Saviour with sacrilegious hatred were unwilling to accept His commands; the death of these men too is very evil, just like the death of those of whom he spoke earlier.

23. TAU. *The Lord will redeem the souls of his servants, and he will not abandon all that trust in him.* How appropriately this psalm ends with the hope of the good, so that they may abandon the gatherings of the wicked and may instead be directed towards future blessings! *The Lord will redeem,* that is, with His precious blood; for the man who has truly believed in Him will be redeemed from the captivity of sins which is his due. Scripture often substitutes *souls* for men, as in Exodus: *There went down to Egypt seventy-five souls.*[28] The whole man is to be understood from his better part. But observe that he says: *Of his servants,* not "of those who live in debased freedom." He added: *And he will not abandon,* like the good shepherd who guards his sheep with

faithful devotion. But he redoubled the note of caution in his promise. He does not say that none are abandoned, but that He does not abandon *all that trust in him*. He will abandon those who put their trust in their own strength or in the presumption of some individual.

Conclusion Drawn From the Psalm

The sacrosanct mysteries of this psalm are at an end. In them the order of the Mass is fulfilled in such a way that you would believe it to have been composed in Christian times. At one point the order of hymns is summarised, at another the devoted people is ordered to come to communion, at another those who undertake their first instruction in the faith are invited to attend. The result is that we feel that nothing is missing from this great ceremony, though we know that at that time none of these things occurred. Here too the human race is both enticed by the blessings accorded to the just and deterred by the vengeance exacted from the wicked. This is what the heading foretold in song: *When David changed his countenance before Abimelech.* So we too must usefully change the nature of our pleasure, and take refuge with the bastion of the Lord's Catholic Church. The number of the psalm represents the age at which the Lord endured His passion, at which according to the reading of the Fathers we are believed to rise again; on this matter father Augustine has written carefully from many aspects, as is his wont, in his *Enchiridion*.[29] So no-one doubts that a psalm hallowed with such great virtues must by frequent meditation be stored in the luggage of our memory as a heavenly treasure.

COMMENTARY ON PSALM 34

1. *For David himself.* It is no trouble briefly from time to time to repeat points already made, so that the mind of the reader may be summoned back to necessary study of what he has stored in memory. As we have said, *David* embraces two meanings, "strong in hand" and

"desirable."[1] Both these senses are certainly appropriate to the Lord Saviour. He is strong in hand because He laid low our captivity to death, together with the wicked one who caused it. He is desirable because His coming promises us blessings beyond telling. So this psalm is sung in the person of the Lord Saviour, who seeks to be freed from the persecution of enemies. When the word *himself* is mentioned in the heading, it warns us that Christ is meant; He is aptly called David because the entire significance of the name is rightly applied to Him.

Division of the Psalm

Throughout this hymn the words are spoken by the Lord Christ in reference to the order of His passion. In the first section of the psalm He demands that retribution be exacted from His persecutors, seeking for them the reverses which would none the less assist their conversion. In the second He rejoices in His resurrection. He rebukes the Jews' wickedness and explains the course of His passion. In the third He promises to utter praise to His Father's power throughout the whole world through His members, for the Father has freed Him from His enemies by the blessing of the resurrection. He prays that His persecutors may be routed, and that the faithful may rejoice in great glory.

Explanation of the Psalm

Judge thou, O Lord, them that wrong me: overthrow them that fight against me. It is the weakness which He assumed for us that cries out that those who wrong Him should be condemned; He means the devil and his agents, and He knew that this would come to pass. To judge the wicked is to condemn them, for those shown to have been ever involved in debased activities cannot be freed at the Judgment. As has been said, this has reference to the devil and his followers, through whom sprouted the evil of the Jews' wilfulness. Since He Himself commands us: *Pray for your enemies,*[2] this statement cannot aptly be referred to men. So He begs that they be damned who by the power of His prescience He knows cannot attain the remedies of repentance;

for in what follows when He turns to men, He begs that they be converted rather than perish. He further added: *Overthrow them that fight against me.* He who fights against you seeks to overcome you; he who is overthrown is totally conquered. So unclean spirits are rightly called aggressors, because though they cannot overcome holy men they do not cease to struggle with them in wicked wilfulness. The Lord *overthrows,* for He alone can achieve what He wishes; His struggle is a triumph, and every fight a victory.

2. *Take hold of armour and shield, and rise up to help me.* Arma (armour) derives from *arcere*[3] (to ward off), for by using armour we ward off the most violent enemies. So this statement is made in accord with the custom of men, which sets arms in the hand to lay low the enemy. But armour and shield are nothing other than the Lord's will, by which He protects one in danger and takes the enemy by storm. Paul too uses this metaphor: *The shield of faith and the helmet of salvation and the sword of the spirit.*[4] The word *scutum* (shield) is as it were *sculptum*[5] (fashioned), because men of old used to depict their deeds on it. As for His words, *Take hold,* does God take hold of a means of defence alien to Him for the use of the moment? The outcome of events is always in His hands, for He is known to be almighty; nor do we believe that He rises up from rest, as it were, since He has manifestly never lain down. *Armour,* then, denotes the iron corselet by which a man's safety is protected, and the *shield* is for repelling the enemy's blows, so that his darts seeking human destruction may fall without effect. So the Lord Christ's prayer is made in His human capacity. He asks that His human safety may be protected, and that the enemy's will be frustrated by His efforts.

3. *Bring out the weapon, and shut up the way against them that persecute me: say to my soul, I am thy salvation.* In the divine Scriptures, *framea* (weapon) has many meanings, for it denotes sword, royal spear, pike, and punishment.[6] Here however, He wishes us to understand it as His soul, which was truly a weapon against adversaries. Through His soul the sacrilegious cult of idols died out, the devil's wickedness was overcome, the power of death itself was shattered and surrendered though previously it ruled with free rein throughout the world. Already in another psalm we read: *Deliver my soul from the wicked one as thy weapon.*[7] So *bring out the weapon* means "Enlarge my soul by granting the gift of Your fatherly love." *Shut up,* that is, "when

My passion and Your law which you foretold through the prophets are fulfilled." He also asks that the Lord say to His soul: *I am thy salvation,* because He knows that His words are fulfilled without any difficulty.

4. *Let them be confounded and show reverence that seek after my soul. Let them be turned back and be confounded that devise evil against me.* When at this point He turns to men, no abuse is uttered but correction is demanded. To be *confounded* means to blush at their deeds, and to change so as to obtain a better judgment, for men are said to be confounded when sentenced to punishment. So that you should understand the word rather in the sense of conversion, He added: *And show reverence,* in other words, become changed and worship the One who they thought should be persecuted. *Those that seek after my soul* expresses a derogatory sense. They seek in such a way that they do not desire to revere it, but hasten to separate it from the body. Seeking after Christ's soul is an expression used also in the good sense, when He says: *Flight hath failed me: and there is no-one that seeks after my soul.*[8] To be *turned back* is spoken only of those judged worthy of correction; when He said to the apostle Peter, who in the human sense defended Christ's safety: *Go behind me, Satan,*[9] He said it not so that Peter should perish, but that by a happy improvement he might follow the Lord's will. So those whom He wishes to get behind Him He desires not to carry out the most wicked intention of their will, but rather to follow Him in the place where they clearly do not wander. *They that devise evil against me* can be taken to denote the Jews or the heretics or the pagans; for all who with debased intention hasten to make assertions untrue to the Catholic religion devise evil.

5. *Let them become as dust before the wind, and let the angel of the Lord afflict them.* Dust is an earthy but exceedingly dry and thin substance which when the wind blows is not permitted to remain in its place, but is raised into the bright air. So the desires of sinners, once admonished by inspiration of the truth, are raised from earthly vices, and through the Lord's help led to heavenly virtues. So here the wish is expressed for wicked men that by blessed self-improvement they may attain heavenly life. By *angel* we mean a messenger of heavenly power by whom the divine commands are carried out. So the angel afflicts the converted so that by the gift of humility they may be

brought to the blessed fatherland. This affliction is a kindness, for the prayer that it may come to pass is expressed as if it were a great gift.

6. *Let their way become dark and slippery, and let the angel of the Lord pursue them.* He demanded that the situation of sinners be wholly arduous, so that *their way,* which seems to them clear and firm as they linger pleasurably upon it, may become *dark and slippery* so that they cannot stand on it any longer. As the prophet Jeremias says: *Therefore their way has become slippery in the dark: and they shall be thrown down and fall thereon.*[10] But if they decide to linger further in their evil ways, He asks that the Lord's power pursue them, so that He may not cause them to cleave to their sins as they hasten to aspire after their own destruction. What a blessed proliferation of so many obstacles! How vehement is the prayer in this verse that the most salutary opposition be afforded them!

7. *For gratuitously they have hidden from me their net unto destruction: to no purpose they have upbraided my soul.* Gratuitously indeed, for He had done them no evil. This figure is called *syncrisis,* when by a kind of comparison we show that our case is juster than that of an opponent.[11] We say that a thing is gratuitous when it is not offered to counterbalance something else. *They have hidden from me,* as they imagined, because they did not believe in the power of His divinity. Yet what can be hidden from Him from whom nothing can be concealed? He both pointed out His betrayer at supper, and told of His passion before it occurred; there was nothing hidden from Him because He endured everything by the sequence of events sanctioned by His own will. The phrase, *their net unto destruction,* is well expressed, because it was not the net of one who died but the destruction of one who sinned. The following words, *to no purpose they have upbraided my soul,* mean that the Jewish people made a false accusation when they ascribed to the Lord Saviour words of truth as if they were a crime. In their madness they lyingly cried out: *This man said, I will destroy this temple,*[12] whereas He actually said: *Destroy this temple and in three days I will raise it up.*[13] What in their zeal for sinning is more foolish than to seek to apportion for blame what was proclaimed to all for their salvation?

8. *Let the snare which they know not come upon them, and let the net which they have hidden catch them: and into that very snare let them fall.*

What holy retribution, what salutary punishment! Because they had laid the snare which they thought could not be detected, they fell into the noose of which the sinner's consciousness was unaware; and thus held fast by the cord of truth they could be liberated instead. Next comes: *And let the net which they have hidden catch them.* What is that net other than the death of the Lord Saviour, known to have been contrived by their secret plotting? *Catch them* bears the sense of immediately catching up with them as they flee, and achieving the entire purpose of enabling them to avoid being abandoned and buried by their wicked deeds. Note that He uses *snare* in the good sense here, so that caught by the Lord's commandments they may through heavenly grace continue to advance to the kingdom. This is the prayer of Him for whom the destructive snare was gratuitously hidden. He did not render evil for evil, but when He hung on the cross He prayed for His persecutors.

9. *But my soul shall rejoice in the Lord, and shall be delighted over his salvation.* After fittingly announcing what was to overtake impure spirits, and after praying in His devoted fashion for sinners, He comes to the second section, in which He recounts the joy of His heart and also recounts the sequence of the passion with the clearest truth. It is the prime blessing of a pious spirit to rejoice in the Lord, for in Him everything is sought when the unspotted mind seeks its destination there. The joy of the person who rejoices in the Lord never fails at any time, and he will find nothing sweeter to love. So what follows this rejoicing? Surely that it *shall be delighted over his salvation.* That salvation is the Lord's majesty, the majesty of the Word from which it comes and by which life is conferred; the fount of mercy, the healing of those who make supplication, the remission of their sins.

10. *All my bones shall say: Lord, who is like to thee?* Clearly bones have neither feeling nor voice. As we have often stated, they must be interpreted as strength of spirit and constancy of mind. These are rightly compared with bones, for just as bones hold the body together, so these qualities strengthen pious intentions. So the bones, that is, firmness, not the flesh which is slackness, must utter this mystery, for only courage of mind can speak such praise. *Who* bears a negative sense, for none can be like to Him, since He is uniquely the holy Trinity. The creature differs greatly from the Creator; in short, the first is slave, the second, Master.

Who deliverest the resourceless from the hand of him that is stronger than he: the needy and the poor from them that plunder him. In this verse He has expounded the earlier question: *Who is like to thee?* When the devil held almost the entire human race in his hand, we know that it was freed by the incarnation of the Word from the power by which it was held in subjection. He further added: *The needy and poor,* so that the three gathered into one could show the condition of the human race afflicted by disasters. Man is called *resourceless* because he was made mortal, *needy* because he sought his bread by toils and sweat, *poor* because he was cast down from the wisdom and purity which he earlier had, and now possessed only an unsubstantial and faint shadow of reason. Who could say that men were really wise when they were shown to have no knowledge of their Creator? But how remarkable, how unique in every way is the fact that Christ by His incarnation freed such men as this! We may rightly say: *Lord, who is like to thee?* And remember that the earlier words, *from the hand of him that is stronger,* denote the devil who was certainly stronger than man. The later phrase, *from them that plunder him,* He wishes to be interpreted as the impure spirits who with wicked commitment war in company with the devil's power.

11. *Unjust witnesses springing up have asked me things I know not.* After He has mentioned the manifold disasters with which the human condition was afflicted, He did not wish to distance himself from it, so He now relates His own passion which through His devotion He deigned to shoulder for us. So the witnesses who spring up with bestial onslaught and are not constrained by self-control to take an impartial stance are undoubtedly total liars, and He powerfully categorises them with the one word: *unjust.* They were truly unjust, for they were to speak against fairness and justice. He adds: *Things I know not,* in other words, "Things of which I was wholly unaware of having said." We say of a man who through the Lord's kindness governs himself by upright behaviour, "He does not know lying, he does not know robbery, he does not know repression." The Lord was unaware of the blasphemy which the chief priest imputed to Him as he rent his garments. Christ said: *You shall see the Son of man sitting at the right hand of the Father,* and the Jews' leader responded with: *He has blasphemed. What further need have we of witnesses?*[24] But the next words showed the nature of the testimony. He did not say that the witnesses

had convicted Him; he asked Christ a question, as though he did not trust in his own integrity but was troubled by the statements of the others. On this episode the evangelist Matthew says: *Last of all there came two false witnesses, and they said: We have heard this man say, I am able to destroy this temple,*[15] and the rest.

12. *They repaid me evil for good: and barrenness of my soul.* Nothing could be expressed more briefly or more elegantly. The Lord's kindnesses and the Jews' deeds are unfolded in one word for each, *evil for good.* To elaborate, whereas He had bestowed life on believers, they preferred to offer death in return. This kind of repayment as we know is the worst of all evils. Barrenness of soul occurred when the good Master could not find the fruit of faith in them. Their breasts did not yield seeds of belief, for they were hardened into rocklike stupidity. So that the Jews might not take too lightly their being consigned to barrenness, the gospel attests that He cursed it also in the case of the fig-tree on which He found no fruit whatsoever.[16]

13. *But as for me, when they were troublesome to me, I clothed myself in haircloth.* Haircloth is the rough and bristly goats-hide; goats are rightly associated with sinning, for by the Lord's judgment they are set on the side of sinners.[17] So the Lord relates that He clothed himself in haircloth because He took on sinning flesh. If one takes this in the historical sense, one never reads that He wore haircloth. So while the Jews were being troublesome with insults and traps, He hid His divinity with the covering of the flesh from their blinded minds, because they did not deserve to recognise Him whom they treated with such impiety. This figure is called *metriasmos* or *mediocritas,* when we play down some important matter with a humble prayer.[18] The careful reader will recognise this figure in both this and later verses. Note too the tone of divine patience. He does not say: "When they persecuted me" but *When they were troublesome to me,* a phrase which we habitually use in minor matters, when we undertake with resigned assent some inconvenient provision.

I humbled my soul with fasting, and my prayer returned into my bosom. The Lord's fasting took place when He could not find men to bear up to His spiritual banquet because they were hardened with wicked obstinacy. This was *the barrenness of his soul,* which is also the fasting. *Ieiunium* (fasting) is the same as *inedium* (not eating),[19] because if men fast too long it induces starvation. So the Lord fasted because the unbelieving crowd had withdrawn from Him. Fasting of the physical kind can also be ascribed to the Lord, for He fasted on the mountain for forty days and nights[20] with the perfect fasting of which Isaias speaks: *Loose every band of wickedness, undo the ties of oppressive changes. Let them that are broken go free, and break asunder every wicked retribution. Break thy bread for the hungry, and bring the needy and the harbourless into thy house. When thou shalt see one naked, cover him, and despise not the household of thy seed. Then shall thy light break forth as the morning, and thy health shall speedily arise. And let thy justice go before thy face, and the majesty of the Lord shall surround thee. Then thou shalt call, and the Lord shall hear thee. While thou art still speaking, he shall say: Here I am,*[21] and the rest which that marvellous text promises with divine generosity. So the good Master in His human role revealed with clear examples what He had foretold in the books of the prophets. He broached in addition a more hidden matter well clarified by a parallel in the gospel. The Lord said to His disciples: *But when you come into the house, salute it saying: Peace to this house. And if that house be worthy, your peace shall come upon it. But if it be not worthy, your peace shall return to you.*[22] The present speech also poured out by the Lord is of the same kind. Since the accursed Jews were wholly unworthy to receive it, it made its way back into His bosom, that is, to the hidden region of His breast from which it had emerged. If it had acted in men's hearts, it would have been said to issue forth and not to return, which is the precise term used.

14. *As a neighbour and as our own brother, so did I please: as one mourning and sorrowful, so was I humbled.* So far as Latin usage goes, we say "He was pleasing to a neighbour and a brother," but here the case of the nouns is changed, accusatives replacing ablatives.[23] This figure is known as *antipsōsis*,[24] when one case replaces another. He means: "I showed myself favourable as towards a neighbour, as towards our brother;" in other words, "I rejoiced in the kinship of those who attacked me as enemies." It is a perfect requital if favour is extended in return for hatred, if kindness is offered in return for injury. The Lord was pleased in their case when He taught them not to sin, when He prayed for them to the Father as He hung on the cross. Next comes: *As one mourning and sorrowful, so was I humbled.* The Lord's holiness and devoted charity, which He taught, attest that He loved the Jews as brothers and neighbours, but He justly relates

that He is sorrowful because He could not find in all of them the faith which He earnestly sought. If a person wishes us well, he must be saddened when he cannot find in us what he seeks.

15. *But they rejoiced against me, and came together: scourges were gathered together on me, and they knew not.* When Christ the Lord was saddened out of devoted love, the Jews were rejoicing in a freedom which was impious. But the repayment will be different. Christ will rejoice after His sadness, and the Jews will be tortured after their rejoicing, for those who grieve for justice's sake are blessed, and those who wax proud in foolish elation are wretched. He also expounds the occasion of their most wicked blindness: they were preparing against their Lord the tortures which were to rebound upon themselves through the scales of justice. This is what He means by *and they knew not.* He caused to be turned back on them what they seemed to be heaping physically on that innocent Man.

16. *They were scattered, and repented not: they tempted me, they scoffed at me with derision: they gnashed upon me with their teeth.* He relates what happened to the Jews after they abandoned their wicked rashness. They were indeed scattered when at the Lord's passion the sun suffered eclipse, the earth shook, the veil of the temple was rent. Yet though these mighty miracles were revealed to them, they were not converted because of the effect of their obduracy. *They tempted* when they said: *If thou be the Christ, tell us.*[25] *They scoffed* when they charged Him as He was pinned to the cross with the words attested by the evangelist Matthew: *In like manner also the chief priests, with the scribes and Pharisees, mocking said: He saved others, himself he cannot save.*[26] The manner of speech is employed here which uses abundance of words to show that some event is seen to have been fulfilled. For example, "I shall bless you with a blessing," "I shall curse you with a curse," "I shall build you up as a building," and the like. This argument is called *notatio,* when the verb entices a word of similar sense to follow.[27] Next comes: *They gnashed upon me with their teeth.* This is what savages do when defeated by reason. When words fail them because of the truth of an issue, they lose patience and gnash their teeth, revealing their wishes by silent threats. All this is aimed at the great pride of the human race, so that His members may not think it burdensome to suffer what they realise their Head has suffered.

17. *Lord, when wilt thou look upon me? Restore thou my soul from their*

evil deeds, my unique one from the lions. When wilt thou look upon me? is said in the way of human weakness, for which all that is to come is melancholy. As soon as it desires something, it hastens to fulfil it. *Restore* is used with the sense of "Rescue what has been snatched away," in other words, "Let it emerge again from evil deeds," for we know that He was unjustly executed. *From the lions* means from the bloody and cruel powers. Some have wanted *unique one* to have reference here to the Lord's flesh, for though this is shared with men it was none the less uniquely created because it was from a virgin without sin, and because it was joined to the Word, the Son of God. Alternatively,[28] by *unique one* we can understand the Catholic Church which is one through the whole world, and which is called unique in its great love, for gatherings of heretics are wholly excluded from it. The following verse will speak of the Church, and this gives grounds for accepting that it is called unique. Note too that the order of events has been most beautifully preserved. First He prayed for His resurrection, which has now truly occurred. Next He prayed for the freedom of the Church, which at the time of the Judgment will be protected from all anxiety.

18. *I will confess to thee in a great church: I will praise thee in a laden people.* He comes to the third limb of the psalm, when having now observed the gift of the resurrection He proclaims that He confesses the Lord through the whole world. We have stated that there are two forms of confession, one of praise and one of repentance.[29] Here the words which immediately follow, *I will praise you,* compel you to take it in the sense of praise. *The great church* is the Christian people who hold firmly to the right path and who with their girth embrace the extent of the whole world. Next comes: *In a laden people,* in the precise sense of a people bearing a harvest, for we know that it is composed not of flying chaff but of ears of corn. When the wind of temptation comes, it does not blow it away from Christ's threshing-floor, but by such winnowing it is cleansed rather than blown away. So the Lord is praised *in a laden people,* but is blasphemed by those who are fickle and wholly empty of faith.

19. *Let not them that are my enemies wickedly insult me: who hate me without cause, winking with the eyes.* The order of words is "Let not them insult me who wickedly are my enemies, winking with the eyes, and who hate me without cause." Those who insult are heretics, after

holy Church deletes certain people from the roll of the faithful. They are *my enemies wickedly* when they rejoice in the error that causes them to perish; the Lord's loving intercession demands that this should not happen. Next follows: *Who hate me without cause,* implying "I have done them no harm"; the cursing is pointless if no reason for doing harm is advanced. *Winking with the eyes* is what we do when we declare our wish with a silent and crafty gesture; and when we do not wish to betray our presence with words, we warn an individual with a wink of the eyes.

20. *For they spoke indeed peacefully to me: and in addition to their anger they devised guilefully.* The sacrilegious cunning of the Jews is foretold; it is proclaimed not by our words but by those of the gospel. They seemed to speak peacefully when they said: *Master, we know that thou art a true speaker, and teachest the way of God in truth. Is it lawful to give tribute to Caesar or not?*[30] Even a man who does not plan murder can devise guile; for example, if one plots to steal money or a possession from a neighbour. But He here added *anger,* so that their guile might be exposed as deadly. This refers to the time when the Jews set in motion a guileful trick: *it is necessary that one man die for all,*[31] and the rest.

21. *They opened their mouths wide against me. They said: Well done, well done, our eyes have seen it.* They opened their mouths wide when they shouted: *Crucify, crucify,*[32] not winking with the eyes any longer, not devising guilefully, but condemning Him openly and freely. What a wicked crime! The judge said that the deed the people demanded should not happen. The Jews' words follow with deadly rejoicing; it is as if they were saying: "Good, good, we see that what we wanted to achieve we are achieving in Your case, that having failed to appease the mob You are to hang on a cross in the company of thieves." What wonderful patience in One whose majesty was the greatest! Could He not have descended living from the gibbet of the cross to confound His enemies, since after dying He could rise again from the tomb on the third day? But it was not appropriate for God's power to react to the words of abusive men, for they were to blush all the more when all that was foretold came to pass. Though we do not read in the gospel that the Jews said: *Well done, well done,* they did speak insults of a similar kind, so that the simple facts are seen to have been truthfully recounted by a different form of words. *Well done, well done* exempli-

fies the figure of *epizeuxis*, when words are repeated in a single verse without any interposing expression.[33]

22. *Thou hast seen, O Lord, be not silent: O Lord, depart not from me.* The three verses which we see related above apply here. *Thou hast seen*, in other words, "You have approved the fulfilment of what You had seen would be devised against me." This is what we say when we want to offer a reminder of something, as in "You have seen how cruel he has been to me," "You have seen the extent of the damage that wicked robber inflicted on me." *Be not thou silent*, that is, "Do not postpone passing sentence," a procedure to be carried out by speech, not by silence. As for His saying: *Depart not from me*, we must interpret this as spoken in His human guise, which submitted to the passion.

23. *Arise, O Lord, and be attentive to my judgment, to my cause, my God and my Lord.* We often in our human fashion say, *Arise* to Him who in fact is always awake and always attentive, and since He continually supervises all things, He is considered to have paid attention when He punishes. *To my judgment*, which He suffered from the Jews, a judgment without law, a torture for no crime, a death without sin. *My judgment* was well expressed, because He had truly endured it. The expression, *Be attentive to my cause*, was well turned, in place of "to my punishment"; His punishment appeared to be like that of the criminals, but such a cause could be shared with none. What is this cause which the Lord was asked to observe? It was that He who had come to grant salvation to the human race was seen to be executed by mad and faithless men.

24. *Judge me, Lord, according to thy mercy, my God: and let not my enemies be abusive to me.* Though He who had committed no sins had an excellent cause, He none the less asks to be judged according to the Lord's mercy, to show an example of prayer to us who could not undertake a like activity. Next comes: *And let not my enemies be abusive to me*, that is, "Let them not say what the wickedness of abusive men can aver: we achieved it, we did it, we carried it through." But He prays that they may sorrowfully and salutarily lament their evil deeds rather than rejoice that they have performed them to their own destruction.

25. *Let them not say in their hearts: Euge, euge, to our mind: neither let them say, We have absorbed him.* He elaborated upon the abuse

which He had earlier said was to be experienced. *Let them not say Euge, euge*, that is, "It is well, it is well." These are the words of men rejoicing within wicked hearts; they cannot speak the words openly while affected by pricks of remorse. So let them condemn their evil intentions, so that they may not suffer the sentence of punishment. How great and boundless is the Creator's love~! He does not allow them to be left for a time in their joy, so that they may not be overthrown by eternal disaster. Being *absorbed* means being suddenly fused with the body of some other. This happens to those swallowed whole by certain superstitions, who abandon the living power of the true faith. He asks for this to instruct the faithful; such things could not befall His own purity, which is beyond description.

26. *Let them blush and have reverence as well who rejoice at my evils. Let them be clothed with shame and reverence who speak great things against me.* The revenge is worthy, the punishment sufficient. He who blushes at his own deeds is condemned on his own assessment; he who is enchained with the bonds of embarrassment is tortured by the vengeance which he exacts from himself. Yet a man can blush and still not have reverence; here however He added: *And have reverence as well*, so that He might announce the signs of their conversion. *Reverence* is fear of the Lord mingled with love. It springs up in men who through most pure desire obtain the gifts of confession. Next comes: *Let them be clothed with shame and reverence*, as though with the hair-cloth of repentance and with garments of mourning. He speaks of shame in contrast to the daring which they showed in their madness, and *reverence* in contrast to the shamelessness of their falsehood, so that by the two virtues they may heal what they perpetrated by the two sins. By *speaking great things* He means the proud words which exceed the bounds of uprightness; as blessed John says in the Apocalypse: *I saw a mouth speaking great things against God.*[34]

27. *Let them rejoice and be glad who are well pleased with my justice: and let them say always, The Lord be magnified, who delight in the peace of his servant.* Now that enough has been proclaimed about His perse-cutors, He turns to the role of the faithful. He wishes persecutors to be tortured with wholesome repentance, and the faithful to be filled with the greatest joy of blessedness. Note that the very words make their deserts conspicuous. The persecutors often say: *It is well, it is well to our mind*, a transient joy and a fleeting happiness. But the

blessed say always: *The Lord be magnified,* which is eternal and endur-ing. Persecutors bestow worldly pleasures on their own souls, but the faithful turn their prayers to the Lord, and place their joy not in themselves but in His praises. The words *of his servant* have reference to His human form, for there is lowliness in the flesh He assumed, but power in His majesty. Each is perfect and most genuine; there is the one Lord Christ. So *who delight in the peace of his servant?* Surely those who are made strangers to vices, and who by God's gift dwell in peace of mind in the blessing of continence.

28. *And my tongue shall meditate thy justice, thy praise all the day long.* His tongue meditated justice when He preached the New Testa-ment to the people. *All the day long,* as has often been stated, points to the whole time of one's life. But because it seems impossible for human beings to praise God with unceasing voices, let us transfer the sense to connote good deeds, for the one who believes that the divine commands reside in every intention always praises God.

Conclusion Drawn From the Psalm

Let us ponder the importance of the sequence by which the Lord Christ has deigned to speak to us throughout the whole psalm. He started with a prayer, as in other similar psalms. Then He recounted the future events of His passion and resurrection. Finally He finished with the great hope of the faithful, so that there is no doubt that this psalm has also ended with the pattern which we mentioned at the outset. So let us rejoice in our disasters and let us trust in our dangers, for why should faithful servants shun what the Lord of creation en-dured for the salvation of all? We must further observe that this is the second of the psalms which are known to communicate the passion and resurrection of the Lord at greater length.[35]

COMMENTARY ON PSALM 35

1. *Unto the end, for the servant of the Lord, a psalm of David.* All these expressions are appropriately understood of the Lord Jesus. *Unto the*

end points to Him; *For the servant of the Lord* is spoken of Him who *taking the form of a servant became obedient unto death.*[1] As the prophet Isaias says of Him: *Behold my servant: I will uphold him.*[2] *Psalm* and *David* are now familiar from numerous explanations; they are seen to refer to the Lord's person, since the explanation of the expressions themselves show that they are appropriate to Him.

Division of the Psalm

The whole psalm is spoken by the person of the prophet. In the first section he fiercely accuses those who despise the law. He says that they do not dwell with the Lord, and recounts their wicked desires. It should not trouble us that after the initial heading he chose to make a start with foolish men, for he praises the role of the good with greater vehemence after first setting down what painfully disgusts him. In the second part under the Lord's praises are gathered and described the rewards of the blessed, and he says that they are filled with the abundance of the Lord's house. This psalm ends briefly with the destruction of the wicked, so that none may think that they should perhaps try out what they knew had been condemned with such malediction. So let us examine its subtlety a little more sedulously, for it contains a certain difficulty of coherence.

Explanation of the Psalm

2. *The unjust hath said within himself that he would sin: there is no fear of God before his eyes.* There are two types of sinners.[3] The first believes Scripture, but cannot fulfil its commands because of the weakness of the flesh. Solomon says of these: *The corruptible body is a load on the soul, and the earthly habitation presseth down the mind that museth on many things.*[4] The other type is bold, irremediable, blasphemous and plans to commit evil of its own free will. It despises everything, and whispers to itself, believing that God does not tend mortal affairs. So such a man as this has said within himself the wicked thing which he did not dare proclaim openly. He thinks this way so as to seem to bestow on himself the liberty to commit sins, that he may sin without measure since he has decided that fear of the Judge should be

dismissed. Next comes: *There is no fear of God before his eyes.* He refers to the thoughts of the wicked that fear of God is not witnessed by Him, in other words that God does not trouble that men should fear Him. They believe what erring philosophers have stated, that the world is governed by chance rather than arranged by the ministrations of heaven.[5] Alternatively, *there is no fear of God before his eyes* has reference to the unjust man, who presumes to make such a statement with sacrilegious intent. Next follows:

3. *For in his sight he has done deceitfully, that he might find his wickedness and hatred.* This accursed man, of whom it was said: *There is no fear of God before his eyes,* did not bother to heed the law in order to realise that his belief was wholly false. Spurning those salutary words, he eagerly sought in every way to avoid knowing the truth.[6] So *He has done deceitfully in God's sight* to shrink from *finding his wickedness and hatred.* He believed that he could defend himself on grounds of ignorance of the law. Our sins are well defined as wickedness and hatred, for we must hate the things through which we deserve eternal punishments.

4. *The words of his mouth are iniquity and guile: he would not understand that he might do well.* The speech of the wicked is aptly given summary definition; their words are iniquity and guile. So what were beyond counting are expounded in two words. *Iniquity* refers to blasphemy, *guile* to deceit against one's neighbour. What is left, I ask, for him to do when he does not refuse to sin against God and his neighbour? When the psalmist says: *He would not understand that he might do well,* he refers to those who have in some degree apprehended the spark of wisdom, but who through their own faults have abandoned true understanding and corrupted themselves with base errors. This charge is aptly applied also to the totally demented Jewish people, to whom the Lord came but who spurned His healing with accursed obstinacy. Pardon is often granted to lack of wisdom, but just vengeance always visits the evil-doing which is deliberate. This is called the argument from mental disposition,[7] when people sin not through ignorance but through their malicious will.

5. *He hath devised wickedness on his bed: he hath set himself on every way that is not good: but evil he hath not hated.* The psalmist continues with his explanation of the man of great wickedness. He says: *He hath devised wickedness,* in other words, has devoted extended thought to

error by writing perverse books, so that not only should he himself sin, but also, through his writing, posterity after him. *On his bed* means in his heart;[8] for *cubile* (bed) is derived from *cubare* (to lie),[9] when the mind that lies within us ponders good and evil. The phrase, *He hath set himself on every way that is not good,* means in the life of this world, which he did not traverse like those who proclaim that they are leaving it behind, but lingered in it and was absorbed by it. As the climax to his sins the prophet made the charge: *Evil he hath not hated.* Here he wishes evil to be understood as the mother of all serious sins, summarising in a single word what is seen to be diffused more widely abroad. To pursue it is wickedness, for we are not only commanded to avoid it but also forced rightly to hate it, so that we may condemn an abomination so great with continual curses. Bear in mind that from the beginning of this psalm throughout the four verses the psalmist has employed the figure of *synathroismos*,[10] which encloses many sins in one consideration and compass.

6. *O Lord, thy mercy is in heaven, and thy truth reacheth even to the clouds.* Now that he has assessed the thoughts of wicked men, in this second section he passes to praise of the Lord. Though his mercy is on land, sea, and everywhere, here he specifically states that it is in heaven; that is, in the creatures of heaven and in the saints,[11] amongst whom the divine gifts have flowed more abundantly. He further mentions the *truth* of the just, who are involved in the struggle of this world. We said earlier that *the clouds* are an image of the prophets' preaching.[12] Just as the clouds pour down nourishing water on the earth, so the prophets send forth a shower of salvation on faithful souls to give the fruit of faith to those which had become barren through the shrivelling effect of sin. In this way we may come to realise that He who brought the truth to the human race through the apostles and prophets truly grants His mercy to the heavenly virtues. Observe that this praise is introduced as a general statement to contrast with the abuse heaped on the wicked, so that the psalm might more clearly appear as the demonstrative type, with both aspects explained.[13]

7. *Thy justice is as the mountains, O Lord: thy judgments are a great deep: men and beasts thou wilt preserve, O Lord.* The common reading is: *Thy justice is as the mountains of God,* but Jerome's faithful translation which replaces *Of God* with *O Lord* is much more correct.[14] *Thy*

justice means the blessed apostles, who with committed attitudes emerged able to embrace the Lord's justice. The psalmist rightly compared them with the mountains, for upon their summit they drank in the light of truth at the very source, and poured it on lowly peoples by their holy preaching, like mountains which at sunrise receive rays of new light and transmit it to the valleys with reflected brightness. He speaks of *the deep* here in the good sense, comparing its depths with divine judgments. A deep is a depth of waters which we can neither measure nor wholly plumb with our eyes. Who could either descry the depths of the great ocean or embrace its huge extent? In the same way we can neither embrace in mind the divine judgments, nor define them by any rational explanation. As Paul says: *How incomprehensible are his judgments, and how unsearchable his ways!*[15] A single word, *deep*, is used to express all these ideas; in other words, a depth which cannot be gauged. He also explains why he called the judgments depths; rightly so, since He bestows the kindnesses of His devoted love on sinners even though they deport themselves with the disordered wilfulness of mules. But what mind, what reason could grasp that the entreaties of those who repent attain the rewards of the just? So you see that the Lord's judgments are most aptly compared to boundless depths.

8. *O how thou hast multiplied thy mercies, O God! But the sons of men shall put their trust in the protection of thy wings.* He now expounds by varied recapitulation what he earlier stated briefly: *Thy judgments are a great deep. How* is an adverb used by one expressing wonder; in other words, "how loftily, how powerfully hast thou bestowed thy mercies with wonderful generosity, both to help sinners attain rewards and to bind the just to anticipate their promised gifts." Note that earlier he spoke of men, but now uses the expression, *Sons of men.* The description *men* is used for those who have not yet laid aside the old nature of the first man and who continue in original sin; for since Adam himself came first, he is called man, not son of man. *The sons of men* are those who have obtained the grace of baptism, and are reborn to become a new generation through the Lord's help.[16] Christ Himself was called the Son of man, so that those who attain His rewards may be adorned also with His name. The Lord's *wings* are the commands of the New and Old Testaments, under the protection of which as we know every just man has hope, as long as he is seen to obey them. The parallel is

fittingly derived from birds, whose tender young are wont to place their trust in the protection of their mother's wings. By this example is revealed the simplicity of the person with hope, as well as the security of the Lord's most soothing kindness.

9. *They shall be inebriated with the plenty of thy house, and thou shalt make them drink of the torrent of thy pleasure. Inebriated* is adopted from the sinful habit of men afloat with too much wine, who become sluggish, when their minds are afflicted; but here it describes the role of good men.[17] This heavenly inebriation cuts off recollection of worldly matters, and thus makes the things of the flesh depart from the mind, just as intoxication from wine divorces men's actions from their senses. There follows the source from which such inebriation can spring, namely, *the plenty of thy house,* in other words, the spiritual store of holy mother Church. She is the house which cannot but disburse its store to some effect; she has sufficient for the whole world, so that she is always full to overflowing. That inebriation is sober, that drunkenness is splendid in which the drinker sins if he spurns its further embrace. We have said that *a torrent* is a swift river descending after a sudden cascade of rain; the wisdom of Christ is well compared with it, for it is both sudden and so swift-moving that it attains the end which it seeks without further delay.

10. *For with thee is the fountain of life: and in thy light we shall see light.* In what salutary and powerful fashion does he reveal and expound the meaning of that earlier phrase, *Thou shalt be inebriated!* He says to the Lord Christ: *For with thee is the fountain of life,* that is, the beginning of all blessings and the source of virtues from which we are most completely filled when we accept any gift from His devotion. This life which we can drink inebriates us when we drain from the sacred preachings an enthusiasm for their goodly words. As Isaias says: *You shall draw waters out of the Saviour's fountains.*[18] But in human usage light and fountains are different things;[19] in fact they are antithetical, because a fountain of water extinguishes the light of flames. But with God they are one, for whatever term you employ is true but still inadequate. We say that God is the Light, because *He enlighteneth every man that cometh into the world;*[20] a Fountain, because He fills the thirsty and empty; a Mountain, because He is strong and tall; the Way, because He is straight; the Master, because He is the

Teacher of eternal life; the Rock, because we know Him to be the foundation and base of the Church; and the other descriptions in sacred literature likewise. But in each and all of these we grasp the Lord Christ alone; to be able to understand this verse perfectly and carefully, we must know that the term *light* is common to the whole Trinity. For we read, *God is the light, and in him is no darkness.*²¹ So because Father, Son and holy Spirit are one God, we rightly realise that this phrase, *God is light and in him is no darkness,* refers to the whole Trinity. So the verse rightly says of the Saviour, *In thy light we shall see light;* that is, the light of the Father and of the holy Spirit, because through His preaching it happened that the whole Trinity became clear to us.

11. *Extend first thy mercy to them that know thee, and thy justice to them that are right in heart. Extend first,* he said, meaning "give preference," "implant first," "scatter far and wide so that those who know You can walk more safely in the world." *Them that know* the Lord is to be understood in various ways. They know the Lord who proclaim the holy Trinity with most steadfast heart, who do not distort the rules sent from heaven through any defect of their understanding; finally, they alone know God who do not refuse to be fulfilled by the unity of the Catholic faith. The psalmist asks that mercy be first extended to them, so that they may both live in this world under the Lord's loving care, and obtain worthy rewards at the Judgment to come. *Thy justice to them that are right in heart* means that those who through God's kindness have deserved to live here with upright minds will be most justly set at His right hand.

12. *Let not the foot of pride come to me: and let not the hand of the sinner move me.* He prays that he may not leave the just path with his mind's tread, lest he fall from his upright stance into pride, after settling in the safety of a humble position. His use of the singular *foot* is not otiose, for clearly we cannot stand on one foot for long. This is aptly used to signal pride, for pride cannot keep a man puffed up for any length of time. *Foot* is used to denote a mental attitude. Just as our walking takes us from one place to another, so we become separated from the Lord when we cut ourselves off by arrogant thoughts. This is acknowledged to be the greatest of sins by which the angel fell, by which Adam as we know was excluded from Paradise. *The hand of the*

sinner is the activity of one who offers evil counsel which dislodges us from the constancy of faith, when it troubles us with wicked disputation.

13. *There all the workers of iniquity are fallen: they are cast out, and could not stand. There* is the place earlier mentioned, in which *the foot of pride* and the debased counsel of wickedness are. His employment of *fallen* is good. It is as if he were saying "They have tumbled into a deep pit." One who rests on that foot will not stand upright, but fall, for who can doubt that those supported by one foot only, as I have said, can tumble down? Even if no-one pushes such a man, he is most liable to fall through his own weariness. The psalmist however does not identify this foot with one sin alone, but with *all the workers of iniquity;* but though some tumble through cruelty, others from lust, others from greed, and others from the devil's envy, all fall through the sin of pride because they spurn the Lord's commands. Just as the person who obeys many instructions is called obedient, so one who spurns the numerous commands of the Lord is most accurately labelled arrogant. This is called the argument from species,[22] for pride is the species from which all sins are known to take their origin. As Scripture says: *The beginning of all sin is pride.*[23] Next follows a statement concerning these men: *They are cast out, and could not stand.* It is certain that they are cast out, for they will be told: *Go into eternal fire.*[24] They could not stand because they will not be permitted to postpone the Lord's commands, but are immediately cast down by the angels to where the fire of punishment is prepared for them.

Conclusion Drawn From the Psalm

It is pleasing to recall the beautiful way in which the earlier part of the psalm is presented. It enumerates all that divine grace has afforded to its servants, how they attain the fullest sufficiency in blessed fecundity. How very praiseworthy is that inebriation! That drunkenness should be sought in every prayer, for moderation springs from it, and integrity of mind is fully attained from it. It does not cause staggering confusion, mental delirium, or blackouts; the soul is made healthier, according as it is filled with that drunkenness. So let us drink this draught eagerly, not with our bodily lips but with the heart's purest devotion. From it we do not obtain temporal happiness, but seek the joys of eternal life.

COMMENTARY ON PSALM 36

1. *For David himself.* There is no need for us to discourse again on the words of this heading, but there is a great obligation to reveal the purpose of the psalm. Its entire point is the correction of manners, for the Church, here introduced as spokeswoman, instructs the human race by her saving commands not to become involved in deadly errors. She deters the wicked with the punishment, and promises rewards to the good. This type of teaching is extremely effective, causing the arrogant to be humbled, and the humble to gain worthy consolation. There is also the ordered disposition of the Hebrew alphabet minus the sixteenth letter.[1] As we have already said in earlier discussion,[2] we consider this attributable to those deficient in some degree in the perfection of behaviour of holy men. Since all the Hebrew letters have their meaning, it is perhaps right to believe that an alphabet short of a particular letter does not embrace its meaning either. Those who have studied the subject can perhaps discourse better about this. After quite long researches I have not been granted any insight beyond what I have stated. Remember that this is the third of the alphabetic psalms, which reach a total of seven,[3] as we must explain at the appropriate place.

Division of the Psalm

As has been mentioned, throughout the whole psalm the voice of the Church is introduced for the correction of the people. First she warns that none should imitate the malevolent. Whatever blessing we should hope for is to be demanded of the Lord, who can both grant what will aid us and bestow what will abide for ever. Six letters of the Hebrew alphabet are contained in this section. In the second part she says that sinners here are tortured by the most severe suffering of envy, for they realise that in their own actions they evince nothing comparably good. This section contains seven letters. In the third part she proclaims that she has never seen a just man abandoned, and she intermingles the punishments of the wicked and the rewards of the good in profitable interchange. This section contains the remaining eight letters.

Explanation of the Psalm

ALEPH. *Be not emulous amid evil-doers, nor envy them that work iniquity.* The beginning of the psalm, *Be not emulous amid evil-doers, nor envy them that work iniquity, for they shall shortly wither away as grass, and as the green herbs shall quickly fall,* has the character of a categorical syllogism,[4] as follows: Those who are evil-doers and work iniquity will shortly wither away as grass, and as green herbs shall quickly fall. All who will shortly wither away as grass and as green herbs shall quickly fall, are not to be emulated. Therefore we must not seek to emulate evil-doers nor them that work iniquity. Holy mother Church restrains us by the figure of *ethopoeia*[5] from taking pleasure in the acts of evil men and from associating with bands of them in baneful alliance. The wicked troop of sinners entices many, and there is a certain delight in being deceived when we rush to sin in numerous company. The next stage is that we do not imitate these madmen one by one, perhaps believing that those who temporarily enjoy freedom to sin are blessed. Being emulous here means imitating evil deeds, when people think that they have wasted their days in their regretful feeling that licence to do wicked deeds has come too late to them. Paul uses the word *emulous* also in a good sense when he says: *Be emulous for the better gifts.*[6]

2. *For they shall shortly wither away as grass, and as the green herbs shall quickly fall.* A commendable reason is given why we should not follow those who we know will quickly perish. Grass is beautiful while it sprouts, but once it withers it immediately changes colour and fades. So too the wicked, who after glowing with blossoming joy come to a sere and early end. They are first compared with grass in their withering, and then with wild herbs in their falling. The psalmist did not say "garden vegetables," but *green herbs,* to denote instead the worthless plants which grow untended in the countryside. Vegetables

(*olera*) get their name from the pot (*olla*)[7] in which they are assembled and cooked. So let us compare with grass the nobles of the world who sprout forth easily and are clothed in the grace of abundant greenness, and let the green herbs symbolise the mean and lowly, for they grow with sprouting abundance in uncultivated regions, and keep the rustic, bristly quality of their native haunts. The first *shortly withers away,* the second *quickly fall.* Someone may ask: When are we to believe that this happens to them? The answer is at the time of the Judgment when the summer's glory gleams, when every person shows his fruits as the trees do. This world is like the winter, when every seed of our deeds is enclosed within. Judgment cannot be made on them, for they are known to be hidden. So in these two verses that outstanding type of argument is used which is called *epichirema,* or in Latin *exsecutio* or *argumentum,*[8] which confirms by examples the validity of a doubtful case, for it is demonstrated that the wicked quickly fall by the examples cited of grass and herbs.

3. BETH. *Trust in the Lord, and do good: and dwell in the land: and thou shalt be fed with its riches.* After emphatically decreeing that evil-doers must be avoided, the Church here advised us what we must do. First she warns us to *trust in the Lord;* this is the entry to faith, the beginning of salvation. Next comes: *Do good,* for as we read in scripture; *Faith without good works is dead.*[9] *Dwell in the land,* in other words, continue in the heart of holy Church, for it never befits the faithful to leave it. Then, to prevent the question "What advantage will there be if we do these things?," there follows the great reward for everything: *Thou shalt be fed with its riches. Thou shalt be fed* denotes satiety and enduring sweetness; *with its riches* means with the contemplation of Christ the Lord, who is alone as we know the Church's reward beyond reckoning. What marvellous feeding, not the defective renewal of the body, but strength of soul which cannot be excelled! By it the faithful are fattened; the more this food satisfies, the more it ever intensifies our blessed hunger.

4. *Delight in the Lord, and he will give thee the request of thy heart.* Delight is accounted as both physical and spiritual; the first nurtures vices, the second virtues. When she says: *Delight in the Lord,* she wants your recollection of Him to be sweet so that you may love Him whom you fear, long for Him whom you reverence, and strive to attain Him whom you dread. Next comes: *And he will give thee the*

request of thy heart. Note that she said *heart,* not flesh; this usually refers to wisdom; for the heart's request is faith, charity, knowledge of God, and performance of good works. He is accustomed to give merciful approval to what she regularly recommends in her holy preaching. In this way the Christian's spirit is fashioned for eternal life by her each and every statement.

5. GIMEL. *Unveil the way to the Lord, and trust in him: and he will do it.* The thick fog of sins is a sort of veil in which our *way,* that is, our lives, is clothed as by the covering of a cloak of darkness. We unveil ourselves of this when we confess our sins most eagerly. The apostle Paul unveiled his way when he said: *The flesh lusteth against the spirit, and the spirit against the flesh.*[10] He trusted in the Lord with the cry: *Unhappy man that I am, who shall deliver me from the body of this death? The grace of God by Jesus Christ our Lord.*[11] She added: *And he will do it;* He who is all-powerful and strong in hand, whose commands all things truly obey. The nature of the things which He will do she next unfolds in detailed explanation.

6. *And he will bring forth thy justice as the light: and thy judgment as the noonday.* He explains the previous words, *and he will do it.* The light of the sun reveals to us physical colours; God's brightness shows up the nature of our deeds so that our justice, the faith which we have in Christ, may shine forth to be clear to the eyes of the spirit. To *bring forth* means to draw something out of darkness into light, in other words to lead it from the murk of this world to the brightness of the judgment to come, where all things become clear and are no longer hidden in dark hiding-places. So then our justice, which we now possess in faith by God's gift, will be visible to human sight, and will sprout forth like light when Christ our hope is revealed. As Paul says: *When Christ your life shall appear, then also you shall appear with him in glory.*[12] *As the noonday* is hyperbole;[13] it denotes the most clear and pure light, for at that time the sun bathes the earth in the greatest brightness, and traverses all parts of the world with translucent gleaming.

7. DALETH. *Be subject to the Lord, and beseech him. Emulate not the man who prospereth in his way.* Even the man who seems foreign to belief in the Lord is subject to Him, but by the power of His dominion and not by deliberate choice. But so that you would realise that this applies to holy men, the words, *Beseech him,* follow. Only those who serve the Lord with committed devotion can do this, for beseeching

means humbly begging. Note that these two things, behaving well and always supplicating, are regularly juxtaposed. As Paul says: *Instant in prayer, communicating to the necessities of the saints*.[14] She also returns to the advice with which the psalm began: that the man of faith must not imitate the prosperous sinner. The words, *in his way*, were appended so that you would understand not holy men but the wicked; for Christ's is the only way that is good, whereas our way is subject to sins. The next verse also clearly reveals this point.

The man who committeth injustice. She states what she said earlier: *Who prospereth in his way*, in other words, the man who commits wickedness, whose deeds are base, and whose business is impure.

8. HE. *Cease from anger, and leave rage: show no emulation in doing wickedness*. She addresses the word *cease* to the person still grumbling in a mad mental ferment, who with fiery rage and indignation pours out words of blasphemy, complaining that he is denied that worldly happiness which he observes is possessed by most wicked men. As we have said elsewhere, anger is what fires the mind with swift emotion, whereas rage lasts longer. So she bids us abandon both, for through them we can commit serious sin. She adds: *Show no emulation in doing wickedness*. The ancients defined wickedness (*nequitia*) as voluntary evildoing into which we do not fall by chance, but partake of it with willing delight. She often forbids anyone to desire to aspire to it. *Nequam* (wicked) is the same word as *nequaquam*, "not at all,"[15] in other words, appropriate at no time.

9. *For evildoers shall be expelled: but they that wait upon the Lord, they shall inherit the land*. A twofold reason is adduced for wholly shunning imitation of wicked men: fear, and a reward. Man, why do you long to imitate those whom you see perishing? Do you not hear your loving mother asking you why you do not rejoice with the good so that you may not perish with the wicked? *Expelled (exterminari)* means being thrust beyond the boundary, in other words, being deprived of the city of God. But so that fear alone should not disturb men's feeble hearts, she also incorporates hope of the good with the words: *But they that wait upon the Lord, they shall inherit the land;* that is, those who despise the success of the wicked and do not wish to be presented with this world's gifts, but await the coming of the Lord Saviour. They will take joy in His inheritance, the inheritance which comes lawfully, which is secure and eternal. *They shall inherit the land* means they shall

acquire the future city of the Lord which God's devotion promises to the just. So let us ponder the economy of this heavenly guarantee, let us await these promises at their due season. Let us not through our desire to demand these promises in haste be seen to harm ourselves by abandoning our cause. This verse is joined to the preceding words: *Emulate not the man who prospereth in his way;* this figure is called *hyperbaton;* the order of words is held up and developed later.[16]

10. *For yet a little while, and the wicked shall not be: and thou shalt seek his place, and shalt not find it. A little* means something small and tiny which can be grasped with the closed fingers of the hand, for *pusillum* derives from *pugnus,* a fist.[17] The Church promises this short, final age to heal those who toil, so that the period in which the man of faith can become exhausted may be not thought to be too long. She says that the time remaining till the day of judgment is *a little while,* because by comparison with days gone by it is very short. *And the wicked shall not be,* not because the past sinner will not exist, but because he will now cease to sin. *His place* denotes this world, which is indulgent to sinners and is intimate especially with him; clearly sins flourish there as if in their own abode.

11. *But the meek shall inherit the land, and shall delight in abundance of peace.* We term as meek (*mansueti*) those accustomed to the hand (*manu sueti*), that is, the patient and gentle who endure injustices from others without presuming to afflict anyone themselves. But note the great force of this term. Since it is fitting for the Christian to embrace many virtues, clearly the decree is made to explain the perfection of the wholly good man. She says that the meek will possess the Jerusalem to come of which we have now often spoken, a city always filled with sweet blessings, in which its inhabitants do not live by trade but feed on delight in God. None there toils to live, but in tranquillity receives all that his blessed spirit desires. There the inner eye is fattened by blessed hunger, there the soul is renewed by sight alone, for all that it desires is granted by contemplation of the Lord's face. Next comes: *They shall delight in abundance of peace.* This is the peace of the world to come, where there can be no hostility or opposition; the joy begun in the single tenour of its course continues most sweetly.

12. ZAIN. *The sinner shall watch the just man, and shall gnash upon*

him with his teeth. The entire narration of this psalm appears as inter-weaving of sinners and just, but it is not inappropriate to divide it here since we feel the introduction of something new amongst the con-trasts. So let this be our second section. She had earlier said that the faithful should not emulate the wicked; now she says that sinners are tortured at the prompting of envy as they eye the just. It is their divergent will which breeds hatred for the just man, for when the wicked man sees him cultivating good manners, he believes that he himself is being particularly indicted. He gnashes his teeth and rages in mind. He at once tries to take the very life of him whose manners he cannot corrupt. *Shall watch,* that is, shall eye with resentment as if from hidden ambush. Gnashing of teeth is characteristic of raging beasts, which the angry man emulates when he threatens his neigh-bour with death. So it is shameful to imitate those who are envious of others' possessions, since the man indicted by the guilt of envy re-gards himself as the worst of men.

13. *But the Lord shall laugh at him, for he foreseeth that his day shall come.* Wonderful is the nature of the consolation revealed to us, for who should feel delight at the luxury of him whose recklessness he knows is soon to perish? If we do not wish to be confounded by any jealousy, let us follow what the Lord does. Let us laugh at him whose fall we foresee; let us account as unhappy the possessions which we realise are soon to fade. Let us believe most securely in such an out-come, for it has been promised us by the truth. It will come to pass that the sinner will depart as an object of derision, though he earlier waxes proud with a happiness that is fleeting.

14. HETH. *The wicked have drawn out the sword: they have bent their bow to cast down the needy and poor, to kill the upright of heart.* The sword of the wicked is any guile which seeks to harm another. He who attempts to plunder the needy wickedly unsheathes the sword of his design. He who longs to deceive innocent souls with corrupt persua-sion reveals the sword of his most foul intent. *Drawn out* means uncovered, so what was previously hidden in the scabbard of intention became clear when it was unsheathed, and the designs were blatant. Bending the bow does not mean immediately firing the arrow but keeping it aimed and ready, awaiting a moment for a deed of deception when they can defraud the simple and innocent. The next words are:

To cast down the needy and poor. The difference between needy and poor we explained not long ago. The expression *cast. down* is well-turned, for it denotes one who is upright and endures with strength of faith; such people are cast down when dark and deathlike error envelops them. She added: *To kill the upright of heart.* This can be understood of martyrs who are upright of heart but slaughtered in the flesh.

15. THETH. *Let their swords enter into their own hearts: and let their bow be broken.* Whatever seeks to destroy is well called a sword, for a sword is the type of weapon successful in causing death. It is called *gladius* (sword) because it is used for destruction (*clades*)[18] of the enemy. To enable you to realise that the sword here proceeds from their intention, she used the reciprocal expression, *enter into their own hearts;* the sword invaded the wicked ambush from where it had come. We have said that *bow* indicates the hidden malevolence devised against the most innocent; she said that this is broken because it would not harm the faithful in their souls. Note that she repeated the same words in describing the punishment as she used in describing the sins; this is because of the well-known judgment of the gospel: *With the same measure that you shall mete, it shall be measured to you likewise.*[19]

16. *Better is a little to the just than the great riches of the wicked.* The devoted mother as though kissing and embracing her children continues to console them, persuading them that *better is a little to the just than the great riches of the wicked.* But let us concentrate on what *a little* means, for this is what makes us great. A little here is to be interpreted as humility; while our minds restrain themselves with it, they rise above the precious possessions of the world. At the other extreme the wicked have great riches, in other words a mass of sins and an abundance of faults. So let us assess how much better it is to obtain the little of the just and not to have a heap of those great crimes, for the first leads us to the kingdom of heaven, but the second plunges us into hell. This is the proof drawn from contraries;[20] for the little of the just is the opposite of the great riches of the wicked.

17. *For the arms of the wicked shall be broken in pieces: but the Lord strengtheneth the just. The arms of the wicked* symbolise proud actions in which unholy people show their presumption when influenced by no rational thought. She did not say *broken,* which could be the result

of one blow, but *broken in pieces,* or shattered by continual pressure; for it is always more painful to be broken bit by bit than to be wiped out by sudden destruction. Just as she weakens the unholy by such threats, so she strengthens the just by her goodly promise; for strengthening means giving resource to one in mental distress by words of consolation. If you look back carefully, you will see that the power of the whole psalm is expressed in these words. The purport of all these statements is that the sinner's presumption is brought low, and the spirit of the just raised up. This figure is called *paradeigma,* in other words, an example given to encourage or deter.[21] This is what has happened here too, when she entices the just by success and deters sinners by adversity.

18. IOD. *The Lord knoweth the paths of the undefiled: and their inheritance shall be for ever.* Our human ignorance cannot gaze on the paths of the undefiled, for the narrow path of the virtues is invisible to the flesh. But the Lord who created them knows them in their most unalloyed nature and extent. She explains what can be the reward of such as these: *Their inheritance shall be for ever.* Their inheritance is the heavenly Jerusalem most rich in eternal peace, which is so often rightly promised that the uncertainty of the normal promise is removed. *Shall be for ever* is added because inheritances in this world cannot be eternal, whereas that inheritance is granted enduringly since it is accorded without end.

19. *They shall not be confounded in the evil time, and in the days of famine they shall be filled. The evil time* means the day of judgment when all flesh anxiously fears retribution and atonement for its deeds. As the psalmist says elsewhere: *The Lord will deliver him in the evil day.*[22] So at that time the undefiled are not confounded, for their sins are forgiven through the grace of satisfaction. The next words are: *And in the days of famine they shall be filled.* The days of famine indicate the time in this world when the blessed hunger and thirst after justice;[23] for at the resurrection the just experience not a period of hunger but eternal fullness of all blessings. So in this world, where the just can hunger, or seek justice, *they shall be filled;* filled, that is, through the holy Scriptures, through the example set by the Lord, through the promises of rewards so often made. These are the feasts

with which He fills faithful Christians. So total freedom from care is promised to the committed, so that they are not ashamed at the judgment to come, and they obtain the appropriate gifts in this world.

20. CAPH. *Because the wicked shall perish: whereas the enemies of the Lord shall presently be honoured and exalted, but disappearing shall disappear like smoke.* It is worth noting that in this verse one statement of proof is then followed by a second. She says: *Because the wicked shall perish,* and again: *Whereas the enemies of the Lord shall presently be honoured but shall disappear.* This figure is called *epexergasia,*[24] when we attach two proofs to a single issue. At the Judgment, the wicked shall perish since it is clear that they are wholly empty of spiritual food. In this world they account themselves full and wealthy, but their fullness in spite of its abundance is utterly starved and empty, since it leads to their destruction. Observe that she maintains that *the wicked shall perish,* in other words, will be condemned at the Judgment. You will ascertain that they are unholy because they enjoy the world's delights through the whole period of their lives; so why does she say, *Presently?* It is because he who climbs on to a crumbling eminence at once tumbles from the truth, because he begins to perish at the time when he begins to mount what is doomed to fall. *Disappearing:* because they could have disappeared in another way, she added: *Like smoke,* so that no trace of their deeds is seen to survive. Just as smoke issuing from flames rises through the air in curling wreaths, and the higher it ascends the quicker it vanishes, so our dark and unsubstantial sins dissolve with a speed commensurate with the height to which they rise. The expression, *disappearing shall disappear,* is called the argument from related forms,[25] for these words derive from each other, and originating from the same source are harmoniously similar to each other.

21. LAMETH. *The sinner borroweth, and shall not pay again: but the just sheweth mercy, and lendeth.* The sinner borrows when he hears the word of God and does not echo it in his actions. This is the refusal to pay, the total failure to fulfil the commands of the Godhead. He also borrows when he accepts God's kindnesses and gives no thanks in return, but instead is impudent and continually ungrateful, as if he has obtained nothing. The case of the just man is different, for though he

obtains few things, he pays back more with dutiful devotion. He gives abundance of thanks in all cases. He considers the poverty bestowed on him to be riches. He embraces his very pains and misfortunes, for in the hope of his reward to come he grapples even with instances of death by giving scope to patience. Pay heed to the words: *Sheweth mercy and lendeth;* this further refers to bestowing alms, in which mercy comes first and genial kindness follows after. Observe too that she makes an opposing distinction between the just and the wicked man by the figure of *diaphoresis,*[26] by which the difference between individuals is established.

22. *For such as bless him shall possess the land, but such as curse him shall perish.* Just as earlier she distinguished the wishes of sinners from those of the just by the figure of *diaphoresis,* so here by the use of the same figure she has separated their punishment and reward, so that she should not leave intermingled what are wholly disparate and discordant. Those who bless the Lord, that is, those who render thanks in all things and keep His commands, will obtain for their possession the land of the living, of which another psalm says: *My portion is in the land of the living.*[27] But the evil-tongued blasphemers or those who disobey God's laws will be ejected from that native land. I do not say that they are not future victims of the punishment of fire, but that they will lose the promised blessedness of the just.

23. MEM. *By the Lord shall the steps of a man be directed, and he shall be most eager for his way.* Let us understand the argument propounded. The steps of a man in themselves are always tortuous and debased, because we have been conceived in wickedness and born in sinning; but then we are directed by the Father of light, when we accept the rule of faith on which we tread. We are clearly directed when we walk without going astray. But where does this direction lead us? Surely to help us attain perfect faith and eternal rewards. But this Christian who has already been directed in heart will be most eager for the way of the Lord, in other words, he will love above all things the Lord Saviour Himself, who is truly our Way, Truth, and Life.[28]

24. *When the just man shall fall he shall not be bruised, for the Lord strengtheneth his hand.* You must not understand *fall* as falling into sin, because she has spoken of the just man, but rather as falling into the

hands of sinners, into harsh fortune, which often befalls holy men through the devil's ambush. So that you may seem to be satisfied about this, note that after speaking of falling, which has reference to the feet, she speaks additionally of strengthening the hand of him who falls, whereas she ought rather to have strengthened his footsteps to enable him to rise after falling. So it is quite clear that falling here means falling under the sway of the unholy; for He strengthens his hand, that is his design and action. That captive cannot be troubled, for he has decided to undergo fearlessly the hardships of this world.

25. NUN. *I have been younger, and now am old: and I have not seen the just forsaken, nor his seed in need of bread.* We have reached the third section. If you consider that an individual is speaking, a short and restricted period of time is denoted; but you are to believe that the Church's voice is introduced, which proves that the statement is true from the beginning of the world until its end. She was younger when at the commencement of time she received the beginnings of the law in the form of the first man; she is now old, in other words, she has reached the more honoured age when in her final days she deserved to receive the Lord and Redeemer. The evangelist John says in his epistle: *Little children, it is the last hour.*[29] But she says that throughout this time which has outlasted the period of the whole world she has not seen the just forsaken. Thus a long period seems to be denoted by the words of the Church. So what do we say of the just men who fell into the hands of robbers, and of the just Man Himself who cried out on the cross: *My God, my God, why hast thou forsaken me?*[30] But so that we may escape every tangle of contradiction, the just man is not forsaken, but his resources are spiritual and not, as men think, temporal. Through those spiritual blessings rewards were truly bestowed when they could overcome the tortures of the world; as Christ Himself attests: *Blessed are they who suffer persecution for justice's sake, for theirs is the kingdom of heaven.*[31] In similar fashion she says that she has not seen the seed of the just man in need of bread. If you take this literally, what is said cannot stand, for we read that Abraham, Isaac, and Joseph changed their lands owing to hunger, so there is no doubt that they were in need of bread, for clearly they made for foreign regions because of the indigence of their native areas. But let us turn back to the

inner man, and the true pronouncement will become clear to us in a salutary way. We said that the seed was the work of each individual which he sows and reaps, whether good or evil. So the work of the just has no need of bread, that is, of God's word with which he is filled and renewed and by which he truly lives and is inwardly fed. So what seemed to be contradictory is found to be brought into harmony.

26. *He sheweth mercy and lendeth all the day long: and his seed shall be in blessing. All day long* means all the time of his life. *Day* is often used in the singular to denote the era of a lifetime; for example in the words of Psalm 1: *On his law he shall meditate day and night.*[32] So it happens that when we speak of a little we are thinking of a lot. *He sheweth mercy and lendeth:* either she speaks of almsgiving, in which mercy first touches the heart and so opens the hand, for this is the perfect almsgiving which begins within ourselves and so hastens to come to the help of another. Or rather, we may say that he lends the spiritual blessings which God's poor man possesses in abundance. The just man clearly lends that in which he is rich: teaching, piety, justice, patience, and the other blessings which his most holy heart enjoys. But so that you may not think that the just man wishes to lend only occasionally, she stated: *All the day long.* What riches beyond reckoning, bestowing their abundance most generously throughout his life! He rightly gives unceasingly, for he has been accustomed to receive from Christ always. Next comes: *And his seed shall be in blessing.* This passage too is like those that precede. If you wish to take seed in the sense of children, many holy men have begotten children who were degenerate and unholy. But seed denotes action, which by heaven's gift is scattered by a person like seeds of corn. This is received as a blessing, because it is sown with good intent. Paul teaches us that we must understand seed as action when he says: *He that soweth in the flesh, of the flesh shall reap corruption. And he that soweth in the spirit, of the spirit shall reap life everlasting.*[33]

27. SAMECH. *Decline from evil, and do good, and dwell for ever and ever.* Our devoted mother forms our lives in two ways. The first is her exhortation to avoid evils, because a sinner cannot suddenly have an appetite for good things. The second is her encouragement that we do good things because we have abandoned things worthy of rebuke. So

let us avoid the evils which are our possession, and do the good things which are Christ's, for the Lord at the judgment does not call the just to their reward for doing nothing for the poor. He crowns them because they have clothed the naked, visited the sick, and chosen to feed the hungry and thirsty. So you see that it is not enough for the Christian to refrain from evils; he must also strive to do good in some action. But what follows these instructions? *And dwell for ever and ever*, so that the man who trusts such a promise now seems to possess those future rewards in most certain hope. *For ever and ever* suggests the eternal kingdom, which shall not be supplanted by any change.

28. *For the Lord loveth judgment, and will not forsake his saints: they shall be preserved for ever.* When you hear these words, you too must love judgment, that is, do justice so that with the Lord's help you may control yourself with righteous desires and rejoice in your own blessings, for the Author of justice cannot forsake those who choose to fulfil His commands. Notice the promise. He does not say that the just will not be in any sense abandoned in temporal matters, but proclaims that they will be preserved for ever; for those rent by afflictions and punishments cannot be preserved visibly here and now. Those eager for the present life, who are known to beg for a long span of years, should listen: those who strive to please the Lord are to be preserved not in this world but for ever.

But the unjust shall be punished, and the seed of the wicked shall perish. This thought is often repeated so that we may believe more strongly in what is to come; for the divine pity in seeking to enable us to escape the punishment of hell deigns to warn us repeatedly. Just as earlier she said that the seed of the just, in other words, their works, would remain blessed, so here she confirms that the deeds of wicked men perish. They shall indeed perish, for both sinning and the abode of sinners we know is destroyed. That the works of the unfaithful perish we shall prove not so much by our own words but by those of Solomon. Such men will say at the Judgment: *What hath pride profited us? Or what advantage has the boasting of riches brought us? All those things are passed away like a shadow.*[34] You see that all that destroys man perishes; the only things surviving are those that make him abide in the kingdom of the Lord.

29. *The just shall possess the land by inheritance: and shall dwell above it for ever more.* Just as she diligently rebukes to correct, so often she promises gifts to encourage us. Each of these, as we have said, is a most effective technique of teaching: that punishment attends the wicked and promised rewards the good. The land (*terra*) is so called because it is worn down (*atteratur*)[35] by travellers' feet. The land of the future is so called because of its likeness to the land of today; not that it is worn away, for it will remain undamaged permanently, but it does not lose the name, for it will continue with its qualities unchanged. In the same way we believe that both heaven and our bodies are renewed, but though new are still called by the same names. The words: *And shall dwell above it for ever more* were added so that you may not believe that it will ever be abandoned. It is not otiose that she said: *Above it* rather than "therein." We think that she seems to be explaining the secret of that manner of dwelling, and so the words used were *above it,* for it will not be necessary for a spiritual body to grind the earth with heavy tread. As Paul says: *Then we who are alive, who are left, shall be taken up together with them in the clouds to meet Christ, into the air; and so we shall be always with the Lord.*[36]

30. *The mouth of the just shall meditate wisdom: and his tongue shall speak judgment.* This account reveals the time of the blessed resurrection through the figure of *characterismos,*[37] which in Latin is called *informatio* or *descriptio.* She does not say "meditates" but *shall meditate* on what is to come. We must interpret *mouth* here as thinking, because what the tongue says follows after. *Shall meditate wisdom,* then, implies not by reading the Scriptures but by the heart's most clear vision, for in that place wisdom is not garnered from literature but granted without toil by heaven's largesse. *And his tongue shall speak judgment,* because there words will not be at odds with thoughts; rather, as the heart shall meditate wisdom, so the tongue shall speak justice in all things. This is the way of heaven and of the blessed; being themselves unperplexed by any error they are rightly received into partnership with the angels. So the just man's tongue speaks judgment when he is filled with the appearance of the true light. Judgment (*iudicium*) means statement of the law (*iuris dictum*) because the law is expressed in it. The saints will not always judge, for it is certain that

there is only the one judgment of the Lord. But they will speak justly for ever, as God's virtue embraces them most truly.

31. *The law of his God is in his heart: and his steps shall not be supplanted.* You see how the perfection of future blessedness is revealed to us: man receives in his heart nothing but God's will by which he is made blessed, through which he mounts to that great height. To Him he will give thanks without ceasing. *His God* means Him who freed him from this world's calamity. The word *His* denotes the grace of the Lord Saviour, for though He is God of all, He is said to be peculiarly the God of him whom He deigns to free. When she says: *In his heart,* she shows that the entire sense of "blessed" is fulfilled by such possession. So none will be able to *supplant his steps,* since now original sin will not exist, and the devil will not have freedom to deceive. By supplanting we mean setting traps before the feet so that one cannot gain a firm footing. Clearly this cannot be achieved where everything is safe and enduring. As the psalmist is to say in Psalm 55: *Because thou hast delivered my soul from death, my eyes from tears, my feet from falling.*[38]

32. SADE. *The wicked watcheth the just man, and seeketh to put him to death.* These words still refer to the future judgment. Watching means eyeing something with deep thought, penetrating to the utmost centre of things. On the day of resurrection, the sinner weighs the just man, and says in his heart: Is not this the man who was in need, whom we held in contempt and derision? Do we now see him chosen in preference to us, and set in the highest glory? This is the wicked, watching the just man. *Seeketh to put him to death* describes the tendency of criminals to strive to destroy the just man even in the next world, where they are known to have by then no freedom to do harm.

33. *But the Lord will not leave him in his hands, nor condemn him when he shall be judged.* Notice how she has assessed this arrangement in the world to come. She says that the just man is not to be any more consigned to the power of the enemy, as has often happened in this world when martyrs are abandoned to be killed in the flesh at the hands of persecutors. At that future time He will not leave His servants to the will of the wicked, but will set them in eternal peace, and possess them once they are freed of all danger. *Nor condemn him when he shall be judged:* He does not condemn the just man when He judges

the wicked, but when there is separation of deserts, blessedness will embrace the just man, and the allotted punishment will torture the wicked.

34. COPH. *Expect the Lord, and keep his ways: and he will exalt thee to dwell in the land: when the sinners perish thou shalt see.* Having carefully explained the previous matters which could refer to eternal blessedness, she returns to the just man to console him with the words: "You who have already believed in the blessings you can attain, *expect the Lord* with trust," in other words, endure patiently. The nature of this patience does not go unmentioned. The injunction, *expect,* is not addressed to the idler but to the toiler who keeps the ways of the Lord, in other words keeps His most holy commands. Further, she has appropriately allotted the proper fate to the right people. Only the exalted person can possess the land, for it is so great, so holy, so heavenly that none can gain it without deserving it. Next comes: *When the sinners perish, thou shalt see.* The joys of the just are enhanced for a double reason: first, when they realise the extent of the happiness in which they are to be placed, and secondly when they see the punishment of sinners they will be further overjoyed at having been delivered from eternal punishment, for the character of the gift allotted to them becomes more welcome when the hostility of the punishment becomes manifest. So she says: *Thou shalt see;* in other words, what you now believe you will then know totally; and you will rejoice, when they deservedly perish, that you have been set in the greatest happiness by the Lord's grace.

35. *I have seen the wicked highly exalted, and lifted up above the cedars of Libanus.* Here the most abundant remedy is provided for the most serious disease, for some say: "If such things displeased God, such great happiness would be of little avail to sinners." So through the figure of *enargeia,*[39] which imaginatively reproduces the performance of an abstraction, she says that she has seen the wicked grow not towards distinction but rather destruction. Such men are exalted in this world above the just, because the just are humble while those men are proud; but whereas they will fall at the Judgment, the just will be happily raised up. And because she had said: *Highly exalted,* in case you might think that this meant merely raised above the lowly, she added: *And lifted up above the cedars of Libanus,* so that the wicked man might

appear higher even than those tall summits. His advance is praised in such terms so that his inevitable fall may be demonstrated. It is right to take this as referring to the devil as well. Joel the prophet offers evidence about him with the words: *And I will remove far off from you the northern one: and I will drive him into a land thirsty and desert: and I shall expel his face into the nearest sea, and his hinder parts into the utmost sea.*[40] We thank You, Lord, for this arrangement; what would the devil do if free, when he afflicts the world when bound?

36. RES. *And I passed by, and lo, he was not: and I sought him, and his place was not found.* The world is passed by in two ways. Either it is abandoned by seeking better company, or it will be quitted in the end by the dead. So the man who passes to God by a most holy life does not now behold the sinner wielding power, because he sees everything in which humans boast weakened. She says: *I sought him,* that is, I recalled him to mind, for the just recall sinners most vividly when through the Lord's mercy their status is improved, and they grieve because they are unhappily separated from them through their evil deeds. The place of sinners is known to be this world, in which they both commit crimes and are enriched with transitory happiness. But this place is destroyed together with their success when the glory of the entire world, doomed to corruption, is ended.

37. SIN. *Keep truth, and behold justice: for what remains is for the peaceable man.* When she enjoins us to keep truth, she warns us not to care for worldly things. Only he who is always diligent in pondering and saying and reconsidering this, who is never detached at any moment from this preoccupation, is in the habit of keeping truth. But what is this truth? It is precisely God, who said: *I am the truth.*[41] So if you keep watch on God, He undoubtedly keeps watch on you. She also says: *And behold justice,* that is, God's justice, for she next expounds what justice is with the words: *For what remains is for the peaceable man.* Let us ponder how we should understand these words: *What remains is for the peaceable man,* for his hope is gained through the Lord's payment. What is left is that he attains the rewards of eternal blessedness after this life. So what remains for peaceable men is the time when they begin to have most certain hope, at the moment when they gain perception of the Lord's gifts. *Peaceable* describes the

one who in this world makes peace between disputants, who in zeal for gentleness is not involved in unbecoming conflicts. Observe that he to whom this virtue is granted by the Lord's loving kindness is set in the place of the blessed.

38. *But the unjust shall be destroyed together: the remnants of the wicked shall perish.* Appropriate judgments are pronounced on dissimilar groups. Just as the just after this life rejoice in the greatest hope, so the unjust, when the light of their days is ended, are destroyed. Or as some interpret it, *the remnants* points to the recollection of the good which the just man leaves in this world after his death, when praise is accorded to the worthiness of his deeds. This happens particularly in the case of martyrs, who have yielded up their blessed souls in witnessing to the truth. The wicked can in no way attain this, for they leave no worthy trace of their memory, since at death their false glory and frail life are dissolved.

39. TAV. *But the salvation of the just is from the Lord: and he is their protector in the time of trouble.* Holy Church comes back to the customary consolations, that she may not be thought austere through not registering the joys of that goodly promise. That constant pledge, that strong protection relates that *the salvation of the just is from the Lord,* and comes from no other power. At this point the thought of another psalm is worthy of mention: *If I should walk in the midst of the shadow of death, I will fear no evils, for thou art with me.*[42] Next comes: *And he is their protector in time of trouble. Time of trouble* has two quite dissimilar meanings. On earth there are transient troubles which the Lord does not wholly remove from His faithful. They bite rather than devour, prick rather than shatter, afflict rather than destroy. But the trouble befalling the wicked on Judgment-day is evil because eternal, grim because it tortures, intense because it is severe. So in this time of trouble the Lord is *protector* because He rescues the just from it.

40. *And the Lord will help them and deliver them: and he will rescue them from the wicked and save them, because they have hoped in him.* She speaks of faithful servants whom He effectively helps in this world when they are wearied by struggles with the antagonist. He delivers them when He does not allow their faith to be undermined by debased persuasion. *He will rescue them from the wicked,* which simply means

that He preserves them unharmed from opposition in this world. She further added the reason for this liberation, *because they have hoped in him;* not because they have not sinned, but because they have put their hope in the Lord's devoted love. This can be applied also to the Judgment, when He will deign to bestow eternal rewards on His saints.

Conclusion Drawn From the Psalm

How profitable are the words diffused by the holy Spirit's kindness! With what wondrous strength is the Lord Christ's tunic woven by heaven's dispensation; not with threads but verses, not with fibres but pity, not with wool but grace～! This is undoubtedly so that it may encompass His whole body and cover His limbs like a sacred garment. The lunatic wantonness of the soldiers could not part it, and the crowd of heretics through all the centuries cannot tear it, though they tug at it unceasingly. It maintains its strength but protects only those known to be pleasing to the Lord. So let us ask the indivisible Trinity that the garment may protect us as well, and enclose us within the folds of its gratuitous kindness. Here we can borrow the words of Sedulius: "What I ask for is great, but you can bestow what is great."[43]

COMMENTARY ON PSALM 37

1. *A psalm of David, in commemoration.* By the words, *in commemoration,* this heading declares to us that because we cannot escape sinning entirely, we should always have it in our minds. Thus while we are mindful of faults we may restrain ourselves from a multitude of sins. Just so in Psalm 31 the words: *The understanding of David*[1] are set down; and in Psalm 50 he himself proclaims: *And my sin is always before me.*[2] But though the prophet gives the testimony of his name most of all to what is to come, he does not ignore the past either, for he knows that this is relevant to the salvation of the faithful. This psalm, as some have maintained,[3] relates wholly to the most vivid suffering of the blessed Job, who overcame this mortal life, conquered his flesh, and triumphed over his monstrous punishments. This was doubtless

so that those who repent may regard their burdens as light when such examples of most grievous trials are recounted. Divine Scripture regularly recounts the suffering of most experienced soldiers of Christ so that from them the spirits of novices may be more effectively initiated. So let us rejoice in harsh afflictions, let us exult in the torment of our flesh, for the pain which we momentarily suffer here for the Lord's sake frees us from eternal punishment. We must also ponder the fact that in these psalms of penitents[4] we read of none whose sufferings are so great that they are reasonably assessed as measuring up to the nature of the joys later experienced.

Division of the Psalm

Through the figure of *ethopoeia*[5] is introduced the character of Christ's unconquered soldier, as we have said. He is pierced by the pain of wounds, he oozes with worms, and in addition he is wounded with reproaches. Besieged by these numerous disasters he retains total health solely by vigour of faith. I believe with reason that this persona is to be attributed to blessed Job, for he endured similar hardships, and the very words seem virtually to represent him. So we shall give evidence of this in individual passages by quoting from the Book of Job, so that the sufferings may be seen to harmonise with and resemble each other.

This psalm of the penitent is divided into four sections. First there is an exordium in which the penitential life moves the pity of the kindly Judge. Next comes the narration in two parts, in which he relates the affliction to his body by different punishments, and the harsh wounding of his spirit by the accusations of friends. Since no consolation remains in either respect, he prays to the Lord with all his strength. Appended as the third part is the consolation of the saving remedy: this he says is the hope that he has placed in the Lord in the midst of his manifold disasters. Like a wholly devoted servant, he further says that he is ready to endure a whipping, for he thinks that he deserves still more than he is seen to have suffered. After this emerges the joyful conclusion always granted to penitents, in which he is now delivered from all disasters and proclaims God as the Author of his salvation. This is to teach that one enriched by sharing in such joy is clearly in possession of the most certain hope.

Explanation of the Psalm

2. *Rebuke me not, O Lord, in thy wrath, nor chastise me in thy indignation.* This most holy man—the Lord described him as *Simple and upright and fearing God and avoiding evil*⁶—was consigned to the devil's temptations to be tested. In his griefs he was troubled, but he was not so much concerned at his punishment as afraid that he had offended God. So he asked that he should not bear the pains which he suffered as if they were inflicted by an angry Judge; a whipping ordered by a dispassionate mind is for correction. As Scripture says: *Rebuke a wise man, and he will love thee.*⁷ But a whipping ordered by a hostile judge we quite reasonably fear. The first offers correction, the second vengeance; this is why Job asks that he be not convicted in anger, nor punished with lasting condemnation. This is how he speaks fearfully in his book: *His wrath is kindled against me, and he has counted me as his enemy.*⁸ Father Augustine has spoken with beautiful economy about the Lord's anger in his *Enchiridion:* "When God is said to be angry, this does not mean that He is disturbed like the mind of an angry man. The metaphor is adapted from human emotions, and His vengeance, which is wholly just, has received the label of anger."⁹ So far as anger or rage is concerned, our earlier comments on these words in Psalm 6 must suffice.¹⁰

3. *For thy arrows are fastened in me: and thy hand hath been strong upon me.* The case made in these ensuing words is a credible one, that he should not be punished at the Judgment since he has been harshly oppressed by evils already; for when the Lord punishes here, He spares at the Judgment, because His mercy does not demand two acts of vengeance for the one transgression. As Scripture says: *The Lord will not judge the same action twice.*¹¹ But though this most faithful servant knew that he was harassed by the devil's deceit, he knew too that the devil would not prevail against him unless he had received permission from God's instructions; so Job speaks to Him in whose power all things lie. *Arrows* can be taken in both a good and a bad sense. An example of the good sense is: *He has made ready his arrows for them that burn.*¹² But in this passage *arrows* denotes the devil's powers which wound like darts when unleashed with the Lord's permission. *Fastened* is a good expression, for there could be no respite from his pains. The most blessed Job likewise says: *For the arrows of*

the Lord are in me, the rage whereof drinketh up my spirit, and the terrors of the Lord war against me.[13] Next comes: *And thy hand hath been strong on me.* Though God's power always achieves salvation and life for the faithful, Job's long affliction through many disasters is attributed in metaphor to His hands; not that God himself destroyed Job's sons or ravaged his wealth or afflicted him with painful sores, but He was slow to dislodge the devil who was known to have inflicted such trials. Similarly in Job's own book it was written: *Why dost thou not remove my sin, and why dost thou not take away my iniquity?*[14] The request is appropriately made of the power of the Judge, so that His saving good-will may be won.

4. *There is no health in my flesh because of the appearance of thy wrath: there is no peace for my bones from the manifestation of my sins.* He awakes pity because of his personal weakness, for his flesh, which had been struck by so many blows and had collapsed, could not endure the warfare. *The appearance of wrath* is apprehension of future vengeance pondered under pressure of great fear. So he asks to be freed by God from the wrath to come, for he says that he was so utterly terrified of that future anger that he utterly lost his physical health. He is like a servant who is ashamed, and who before he suffers a whipping is already exceedingly depressed by the punishment to come, whereas the one who is hardened in mind does not tremble at punishment even when it is inflicted. He further added: *There is no peace for my bones.* The word used earlier, *health*, is now duplicated by *peace*; and rightly, for health is peace of the humours and a restrained calm in the whole body. In this verse excessive pain is described, for he had said that his flesh was not healthy, and now he says that even his bones were troubled. The punishment which descends into the marrow is heavier; nothing is left untouched since the very foundations of the body are shaken. He refers to the devouring by worms which he was suffering, and which could give no rest to the holy man. They never ceased to consume him; as Job himself says: *They that devour me never sleep.*[15] But over and above the physical pains he says that he is afflicted from *the manifestation of his sins.* This is characteristic of a holy spirit, which in recalling its wicked deeds believes that it will suffer sterner punishment.

5. *For my iniquities are gone over my head: as a heavy burden they are become heavy on me.* To obtain good will a third type of approach is

made. He does not claim that he is afflicted unjustly, but appears to ascribe his suffering to his sins. Now let us resume our explanation of the words. Our iniquities raise themselves over our heads when they claim for themselves more than reason and justice can allow. Our *head* denotes the reason, than which we have nothing loftier among the gifts bestowed on us. By the Lord's gift we are guided by the leadership of reason which leads us to good actions which profit us. If iniquity overcomes it, it is at once defeated and surrenders. But this change of fortune is attributed to such iniquities, so that those who become puffed up in their fickleness are burdened by the heaviest afflictions. The exordium has been built up by the truth in all its beauty. Now we must investigate how the narration has been fashioned.

6. *My scars are putrefied and corrupted from the appearance of my foolishness.* We have reached the narration. This is a useful addition to all pleading, for through it the attitude and action of the accused are clarified. The narration is fashioned in a double pattern. For five verses he describes the tribulation of his body. In the five which follow he recounts his intense mental sufferings, so that everything is included which is seen to be oppressed by grim disasters. This is called "the proof from necessity,"[16] when a person is forced by correction to take a right attitude through the harsh circumstances which earlier befell him. So in the first verse of this section we recognise the figure of *tapeinosis*,[17] for nothing lowlier or more abject can be imagined. *Scars* are the traces of earlier wounds when healed; they are known to trouble us more oppressively when they bear afresh the hazards previously experienced. *Cicatrix* (scar) is so called since it reveals a wound hidden (*caeca*) within it.[18] So often a body is seen to be disfigured with scars so severely that the survivor has barely endured the sufferings which lifeless corpses usually undergo. Job himself similarly says: *Only the grave remaineth for me.*[19] He added: *From the appearance of my foolishness,* that is, "from the presence of my stupidity," for appearance denotes presence. If mind or body is without it, he cannot make an appearance; he says he has been putrefied through this stupidity, for the holy man did not wish to attribute any of these events to God's design. Job too in his own words replies to the Lord: *Therefore I have spoken unwisely, and things which beyond measure exceeded my knowledge.*[20]

7. *I am afflicted with miseries, and am bowed down even to the end; I walked sorrowful all the day long.* He was rightly distressed, since he seemed burdened with such great griefs. It is the man who punishes his soul with griefs and weeping who is *afflicted with miseries.* So Job with reference to his sufferings says: *I have done with hope. I shall now live no longer. Spare me, O Lord, for my days are nothing.*[21] *Even to the end* denotes either the end of life or the Lord Saviour; for each one of the faithful is troubled until pardon is granted and we reach Him. The expression which follows, *I walked sorrowful all the day long,* denotes the lasting nature of the grief. His phrase, *all day long,* includes nights as well, for they were not strangers to the torment of him whose scars are said to have putrefied. But meanwhile sad weeping possessed him, and this—a common experience of the faithful—without in any sense his despairing of the Lord's love.

8. *For my soul is filled with illusions, and there is no health in my flesh.* This was the cause of his sadness all day long. The devil, who had taken in hand his bodily affliction, sought also to weary his soul unremittingly with empty fancies. He speaks of a weakness to which human sickness is especially prone. When we are prostrate in prayer we appear to seek unnecessary things, and when singing the psalms we ponder on earthly things. But I have spoken sufficiently about this illusion which we suffer in the book which I wrote to the best of my poor ability on the soul.[22] Though this experience befalls persons chiefly at leisure, he says that it befell him too in his physical infirmity, so that like a city under siege he was battered by the hostile enemy on all sides. Though his flesh was afflicted by diverse hardships, he did not become immune to the weaknesses of original sin. This is the illusion remedied at the Lord's second coming, when we do not experience the sins of the flesh, nor suffer any more the attacks of the devil.

9. *I was bent and humbled universally: I roared with the groaning of my heart.* He uses the same expressions again, but the impact is more violent through concentration in a single verse. We can bend physically without humbling ourselves mentally; but both are joined here because his manifold calamity leaves nothing unaffected. To these he added something more, the word *universally,* that is, from every side and every aspect, so that abundance of misfortune manifestly surrounded him on all sides. Next comes: *I roared with the groaning of*

my heart. Roaring is properly applied to wild beasts. To show that his roaring is quite intense, he compares himself with animals who declare their will with the loudest din. Note the final words: *With the groaning of my heart.* To show the power of great patience, he claims that he burst into a groan and not words.

10. *And all my desire is before thee, and my groaning is not hidden from thee.* His desire was to deserve presence before God. The one who seeks pardon for his sins, who performs all the acts summarised earlier, places his desire before God. God usually listens to what is before Him; the Lord embraces what He does not reject. The groaning which shows devotion and which is uttered to free the soul is not hidden from God. Many groan when they lose their riches or seek base desires, but that groaning, that weeping is known to be hidden from the Godhead. The word groaning, *gemitus,* is used to express great grief, *geminatus luctus,*[23] redoubled grief.

11. *My heart is troubled within me, my strength has left me: and the light of my eyes is not with me.* After recounting his physical hardships with tearful remonstration, he now passes to the most piercing pains of his mind. He sought to show that besides the numerous sufferings of the flesh, the holy man's mind was still more intensely affected. Observe how beautifully the separate expressions shine together, for one latches on to the other. Because his strength has left him, his heart is troubled. His strength denotes the force of patience, and while it continues it guards our will by its constancy; but if it withdraws, the mind is confused and yields. So he says that the resolve of his patience has been undermined by abundance of evils. Next comes: *And the light of my eyes is not with me.* The light of the eyes is the untroubled reasoning of judgment, which he could not maintain because he endured massive hardships.

12. *My friends and relatives have drawn near, and stood against me.* *Friends* are those not of our blood but those joined to us in affection. *Amicus* (friend) is *animi aequus*[24] (a peer in spirit), for he is joined to us in identity of will; friendship lies in the direction of our will to a person because of the good qualities in that person, whom we love with reciprocated will.[25] *Relatives* are those joined to us by kinship. These are the two groups in whose consolations people habitually rejoice. But now he speaks of those who came to the holy man to console him, as the Book of Job declares, but who instead wounded

his heart with numerous rebukes: *But now the scourge is come upon thee, and thou faintest. It hath touched thee, and thou art troubled,*[26] and the rest. Let us ponder how harsh was this affliction when he endured such words from friends and relatives, so that those who usually remedy numerous calamities intensified his sufferings. So truly *the light of his eyes was not with him,* for affliction came upon him from the source which usually brings men healing.

13. *And my relatives stood afar off: and they that sought my soul used violence. And they that sought evils for me spoke what is vain, and studied deceits all day long.* His relatives were close in blood, but became distant through their loathing of the stench. What he endured in his wounds they could not bear in their noses. Job himself says of his wife: *My wife hath abhorred my breath.*[27] What then was to be the disgust of outsiders, when his own dear wife could not bear his breath? As for his relatives, these are Job's words: *He hath put my brethren far from me, and my acquaintances like strangers have departed from me.*[28] When he says: *And they that sought my soul used violence,* he indicates the devil and his agents, who strove to bring death to his soul the more they witnessed him persisting in love of God. He added: *And they that sought evils for me spoke what is vain.* He refers to his wife who was impelled by wicked spirits, and in her desire that Job be freed of his suffering urged the most holy man to speak of the Lord's injustice. Her words were: *Curse the Lord, and die.*[29] The same people also *studied deceits,* for while they thought that they sought his bodily welfare they were offering counsel deleterious to his soul.

14. *But I as a deaf man heard not, and as a dumb man who did not open his mouth.* Nothing can be braver or more unique than to listen to harmful charges and not to refute them. Though his words were just, he was deaf to suggestions made by those claiming to console him. He added: *And as a dumb man who did not open his mouth.* A dumb man says nothing even when he bawls, though he sometimes murmurs a stuttered response. But he was like a dumb man who did not open his mouth, who did not move his lips with any harsh words or any murmuring against God. What calm that holy man possessed! Outwardly devoured by worms, inwardly he was immune from suffering. He was clearly intent on God's praises as though he were becoming another person.[30]

15. *And I became as a man that heareth not, and that hath no reproofs*

in his mouth. The identical sense is repeated so that this exemplar of great patience may be inculcated in us more strongly. He certainly had truth on his side by which he could have refuted those offering evil counsel. But that man of infinite patience pondered everything within him, and refrained from rebuking them. As Job himself says: *Have I not dissembled? Have I not kept silence?*[31] When he could have refuted those who attacked him with false charges, he chose to be silent, as a man usually does when he is known to have no truthful reply to offer. Consider now the remedies applied in each case. He said earlier in confronting bodily pains: *I roared with the groaning of my heart.*[32] Now against wicked promptings he stated: *But I as a deaf man heard not,* and the rest. So the words of the narration come to an end with their twofold exposition.

16. *For in thee, O Lord, have I hoped: thou wilt hear me, Lord my God.* Having finished the account of his sufferings, he now passes to the aid brought by saving healing, for in the course of his harsh disasters his trust never failed. He continually hoped in the Lord who can transform sadness into joy. So he thinks that his plea will be heard, for he is sure that he has hoped in the Lord. As Job himself says: *Though he should kill me, I will trust in him.*[33] This is what the three boys likewise proclaimed: *He is able to deliver us from the furnace of fire. But if he will not, be it known to thee, O king, that we do not serve thy gods.*[34] Such is the resolve of holy men, such the purpose of their minds so resolute, that they are enticed not by any worldly gain but only by the love of the Lord Himself.

17. *For I said: Lest at any time my enemies exult over me: and whilst my feet were moved, they spoke great things against me.* He now retails the reasons why the Lord deigns to listen. Amidst that crushing tide of evils that unique man was particularly careful that the enemy should not exult over his fall. They exult over a man when they seduce him to the wickedness which is their aim in the belief that their victory lies in the downfall of the faithful. *Feet* here denotes the nature of our actions by which we step forward, so to say, in this life. But when troubled by our humanity's frailty, they at once encounter evil men who sneer at them and rise against them with loud rebuke. As the psalmist says elsewhere: *They that trouble me will rejoice if I am moved.*[35] But devoted men take counter-measures; they are troubled by the misfortunes of others, and they long to bring consolation to the fallen and solace to

those who have been deceived. As Paul says: *Brethren, if a man be overtaken in any fault, you who are spiritual instruct such a one in the spirit of meekness.*[36]

18. *For I am ready for scourges, and my sorrow is constantly before me.* Notice why the Lord deigned to listen to the suppliant. Since he knew that he had erred in his frailty, he appeared to reconcile himself duly to the punishment. This is the attitude of those who always convict themselves, so those who have had the grace to condemn themselves on their own admission in this life may be pardoned at the Judgment to come. *Scourges* here means not thongs for whipping but the most grievous suffering of pains. Next comes: *And my sorrow is continually before me.* That most just man's sorrow was before him when he seemed to have diverged from the Lord's commands, with the result that he lost his saving innocence, and had acquired mortal faults. That grief is worthy of imitation, and the judgment is sound when a just man feels anger against himself, for the wicked man who speaks in his own defence undoubtedly promotes his destruction.

19. *For I declare my iniquity: and I will think for my sin.* He revealed the possible source of the grief which he expressed. If his grief for his sin had been trifling, the radiance of this great confession would by no means have been evident. The virtue of perfect patience is revealed in two ways. First, we proclaim ourselves to the Lord as sinners; as Job says in his book: *I have sinned. What shall I do to thee, O keeper of men?*[37] Note the holy man's proclamation, his true confession, which did not deprive him of life but redoubled the joys of salvation. But to ensure that you would not think that this proclamation alone could suffice for our confessions, he added: *And I will think for my sin;* in other words, "If you grant it I shall perform the things necessary to erase my sin; that is, let me weep and give alms, and you will cleanse me from the sin I committed, if I observe your commands."

20. *But my enemies shall live, and are stronger than I: and they that hate me wrongfully are multiplied.* By his *enemies* he means the spiritual evils which the most holy man endured at the Lord's discretion to test him. *Shall live* is to be proclaimed sorrowfully, for it means that they acquire the freedom to do their will; they do not dread the death which we endure physically. It is not enough for him to say merely: *They shall live,* without adding: *And are stronger than I;* he next added something which made him more aghast still: *They are multiplied.* This figure is

called *emphasis*,[38] which gradually swells to arouse the mind's emotion. Those that are multiplied are they that hate him wrongfully when the number of unclean spirits hovering over him are increased; for one ravaged his cattle, a second slashed his inheritance, others even slaughtered his sons. It was inevitable that his enemies should swell amidst these many calamities, for he undoubtedly endured such numerous dangers. The word *wrongfully* was appended because the most saintly man is always unjustly loathed by wicked spirits. This is intended to describe the devil's wish rather than any debased or empty boasting about his own merits.

21. *They that rendered evil for good detracted me: because I followed justice.* He returns to his friends who were tearing him apart. They imputed harsh errors to the most holy man, and castigated him when they ought rather to have praised his patience in particular. Even his wife cast aspersions on his justice when she said: *Curse the Lord, and die.*[39] His claim to have followed justice is apt, for he was never known to have abandoned it. This is his own witness: *You shall not find iniquity in my tongue, neither shall folly sound in my mouth.*[40] The stated judgment of the Lord witnesses that this claim proceeded from unsullied purity of heart, when He speaks to Job's friends at the end of the book: *My wrath is kindled against you, because you have not spoken the thing that is right before me, as my servant Job hath.*[41] The comparison between Job and the psalmist set up in this third section is now finished. Undoubtedly it prescribes for us the healing that saves. Now let us look at the conclusion, which brings to an end the whole composition.

22. *Forsake me not, O Lord my God: do not thou depart from me.* The most holy penitent is freed from his past dangers by the Lord's kindness, and now joyfully cries to the Lord, whom he begs not to abandon him now that he has been delivered by His agency. A good conscience is more harshly fearful of sinning after being pardoned, for it would incur guilt again when it owes gratitude. For when the Lord departs from us, we leave the path and wander, for it is inevitable that we err when we do not follow the path of greatest righteousness.

23. *Attend unto my help, O Lord, the God of my salvation.* Earlier he begged not to be abandoned by the Lord; now he more zealously prays that the Lord may deign to attend to his help, because he knew that he was engaged in a struggle against the one who said: *I will set my seat at*

the north, and I will be like the most High.[42] By what strength could that most monstrous enemy be overcome unless the Lord attended? If the Lord gazed on him, that enemy could not but perish. So that you might realise that he had discharged his gratitude, he added: *The God of my salvation,* that is, the God who brought him salvation after the numerous wounds of his sufferings, and bestowed safety on his soul such as that tyrant of old cannot snatch away. Observe how the role of the penitent has been fulfilled, how he exults in his salvation, whereas before he had mouldered in the wasting of his sores. This is how the Lord's soldiers when under assault attain victory.

Conclusion Drawn From the Psalm

How courageous, how triumphant over himself this Job described by David became! Among the many agonies of his wounds he did not cease to moderate his cries. His body lay in ordure, but his spirit dwelt in heaven. He was gnawed by worms, but he overcame unclean spirits. His sufferings were small if one ponders his rewards. Thus service to the kindly Lord is profitable, thus we recognise the mercy of the Godhead, for when we offer Him the generous gifts that are His, we exact in return most abundant repayments. How blessed are the untroubled hearts of penitents, how marvellous the height to which self-humiliation soars! By confession he who on his own assessment has condemned himself is restored to grace. At any rate let us understand the dignity of those who repent; even Job was not excluded from it, for he was praised by the words of so great a Judge.

COMMENTARY ON PSALM 38

1. *Unto the end, for Idithun, a canticle of David.* This heading has introduced a name new to us, so let us investigate more carefully the reason for its position, and what its meaning is. It has already been mentioned in the Preface[1] that such men were not psalm-composers, but since they were outstanding singers they are obviously cited because of the meanings of their names. So from such mention they

could gain the glory of their praiseworthy office, and the secrets of the psalms could be revealed from interpretation of the names themselves. *Idithun* is a Hebrew name meaning in Latin *transilitor*, one who jumps over;[2] not in the sense of one who steps over something, or crosses a gap at a leap, but of one poised above the vicissitudes of this world in such purity as to obtain the rewards of future blessedness and no others. So in this psalm a spokesman is introduced whose conversation is holy, one who has surmounted human attractions but has still sought the joys to come. He recounts some of his troubles; but so that you would not think that this psalm like the last is to be ascribed to penitents, he added the word *canticle,* which cannot be especially apt for such people, for singing befits one who rejoices and sometimes one who grieves, but never one who repents.

Division of the Psalm

This Idithun, whom we have called one who leaps over harmful vices, provides for us the embodiment of the just man. In the first section of the psalm he says that in the face of enemies who sought to trap him he remained silent to achieve what was most expedient, and what would cure him. He seeks as his end in life the duty of recognizing whether he deserved to see the Lord's incarnation with physical eyes as well as with mental vision. Secondly, by means of a syllogism in five parts, he proves that men's fear is empty, for all things lie in God's power. Thirdly he asks that pernicious sins be forgiven him, so that his life may reach a happy close.

Explanation of the Psalm

2. *I said: I will take heed to my ways, that I sin not with my tongue.* It is the regular experience of mankind that when you have been involved in praiseworthy discussion you are at once attacked by the traps of vilifying men. So this Idithun, who has incurred the enmity of most evil men through his laudable beliefs, takes thought with himself, and says that it is better to keep silent than to say anything to men of ill-will. What song sung by men is there which if uttered among envious men does not contain a single word attracting some indict-

ment? Now let us look at the individual phrases separately. *I said,* that is, inwardly in my heart, where wise men ponder before they speak. *I will take heed to my ways;* he does not mean "Let me refrain from sinning," for he was already holy, but "Let me refrain from excessive words." Even a self-controlled man can rarely avoid such words; as the apostle James says: *For the tongue no man can tame. It is a little member, but it boasteth great things.*[3] It is a difficult thing for the tongue, set as it is in the slippery region of the throat, to keep control over the unmoving truth, and if its reins are negligently loosed it often contradicts itself. We avoid blame more easily by silence than by speech.

I have set a guard to my mouth when the sinner stood against me. This is the figure of *epexegesis,* or explanation of preceding words. He explains the reason why he may sin with his tongue. The mouth is regarded as the tongue's gate, and the tongue will be enclosed and supervised if the gate is guarded. As Solomon says: *Make a door and bar to thy mouth, and make a yoke and balance for thy words.*[4] (*Sera,* a bar, is so called because it is fastened on doors *sero,* late at night.)[5] After first mentioning this close guard, he next explains when it must chiefly be mounted. This is when some hostile person takes his stand against an individual, with the intention of hearing a possible source of calumny.

3. *I was dumb and was humbled, and kept silence from good things: and my sorrow was renewed.* Those who set the trap were tricked by his foresight. While they insidiously sought to hear him speak, they encountered silence. People whose mouths are often closed through excessive anger can also be struck dumb. He added: *And I was humbled,* so that you may realise that his silence was not crafty but most holy, for *humbled* means prostrate on the ground. He further says that he refrained from uttering good instruction so as not to teach one who had spurned him. It is the habit of wicked men even when they hear a good message not to assent to it, so he says that by necessity he has *kept silence from good things,* since those seeking the seeds of discord could not take salutary advice. The Lord says in the gospel: *Do not cast your pearls before swine.*[6] As for *my sorrow was renewed,* he means that he has experienced the sorrow earlier as well, when he realised by virtue of his understanding the aspirations of those evil men. But now, when he saw that the wicked deeds of these men were being intensi-

fied against him, his sorrow was renewed as he pondered his own piety. He was converting the sins of others into his own affliction.

4. *My heart grew hot within me, and in my meditation a fire flamed out: I spoke with my tongue.* After the silence which he says he endured unwillingly, since he could have uttered most unwholesome words to men, he turned with great warmth of love to address the Lord. But let us hear how powerfully the heat of his thinking is expressed. *My heart grew hot,* he says; in other words, it was kindled on all sides so that this great emotion might attain contemplation of heavenly things. *Within me,* that is, in the inner man, where the reason speaks without words and is deservedly heard by the Lord. Next comes: *And in my meditation a fire flamed out.* So that you would not think that the fire burned hot with crazed emotions, he wrote: *In my meditation,* that is, in counsel or deliberation, in which the mind's ardour is prudently kindled with moderation, and a controllable flame flits round the enlightened mind. What waxes warmer than charity? But this is a tranquil heat, a gentle flame, emotion without guilt, haste under control. So this most holy man both maintained a fitting silence and spoke appropriately as the most perfect people do. He had been silent before enemies' guile, but cried out to the Lord with the truthful tongue of conscience. His words, *with my tongue,* are not meaningless; he means with the pure heart with which he was wont to confess to the Lord, and to seek His coming with the zeal of committed love.

5. *O Lord, make me know my end and what is the number of my days, that I may know what is wanting to me.* It would be ludicrous to imagine, after that boundless patience and outstanding strength of unconquered resolution, that the holy man was demanding to be informed of the sum of his years in this life. But he was full of longing for the Lord Saviour—it was right that he should seek Him out with the whole of his mind—and so he wished to know what limit of days was in store for him, in the hope that his advanced years could live on to see the holy incarnation which he visualised mentally. So he asks to know his end, which is the Lord Saviour, for He is our End; and to have attained Him is life, but life without end, as long as we do not make Him hostile through the faults that attend us. Then he longs to heed the number of his days, that it might become clearer whether he was to deserve the sight of the Lord with his bodily eyes. He added: *That I may know what is wanting to me,* for once he had reflected on his

end he could become aware how much might remain until the Lord's coming. The addition, *what is wanting to me,* is splendid, for his judgment was that there was something truly wanting to his life if he did not deserve to behold the Lord's presence. By the nature of these words the longing felt by his great zeal is obviously expressed.

6. *Behold, thou hast made my days ancient, and my substance is as nothing before thee.* You note that the presence of Christ has been rightly demanded before he proclaims that his days are ancient. Though he conducted himself with converse pleasing to God, his days were none the less ancient since he had not yet attained the grace of fresh rebirth. Days were ancient when they at once consigned the human race to the failure of death; there was no element of newness in them, for the approach of the Lord Saviour had not yet directed the tiniest beam of light. So the prophet says: *The ancient things have passed away: behold, all things are made new.*⁷ Next comes: *And my substance is as nothing before thee.* He speaks not of his acts but of his substance as being nothing before God. How could it be that he who had leapt above the world, and overcome the vices of the flesh, could be regarded as nothing before God? But he rightly states that his substance is nothing before God, for it was condemned when Adam sinned. If the Godhead bestows nothing on it, it has no grounds for trusting to its own actions.

And indeed all things are vanity: every man living. When this man who transcended vices had filled himself with contemplation of the true light, and had beheld with the heart's eye the future coming of the Lord Saviour, he was anxious that none should believe that holy men are not subject to temptation. So he returns to the subject of his weakness, which through the frailty of the flesh he bore in company with outstanding virtues; and he says: "These things which we have said are indeed great, the things which we believe are great, but since we dwell in this mortal condition in which human frailty assaults our minds, and the one eternal force which can make us stand firm in its constancy is not as yet with us, *All things are vanity, every man living.*" Vanity, as I have often said, means changeability; every man except Christ who is clothed in this flesh endures it. The most holy man rebukes the ways of the life of this world, longing to attain the eternal happiness where he knew that he would share his lot with the angels.

7. *Though man walks as an image of God, yet he will be disquieted in*

vain. He stores up, and he knows not for whom he gathers these things.
This is the true mark of the wise. After he had been edifyingly silent
and had then spoken piously, he passed to the second section, where
in a five-part syllogism he proves that the human race after the first
man's transgression is subject to vanity in all except its hope and
expectation of God. By saying: *Though,* he wishes something glorious
and notable to be understood, but though man boasts it he is still seized
by empty desires. However he next explains this outstanding feature:
Man walks as an image of God. The image of God is that which man
gained in that dispensation of the world when it was said: *Let us make
man to our image and likeness.*[8] This statement with its brief division
will become clear to us if we first realise that *image* is one thing and
likeness another; the image carries a likeness of the thing of which it is
the image, but a likeness does not always bear the image of what it is
like. So the inner man, which as Paul says *is renewed day by day,*[9] and in
which lies the understanding of the reason and the recognition of the
truth and the immortality bestowed by the Godhead, is rightly said to
bear God's image since it is more outstanding because of the spiritual
disposition of its acts. But the outer man, which as Paul says *is
corrupted*[10] and weighed down by a varied accumulation of sufferings,
nonetheless bears a resemblance to the Creator in its life, its vision, its
being, its turning to the Mind that controls it—which is said to be its
blessing outstanding among all other creatures—though in God these
faculties are greatly and sublimely different from what they are said to
be among creatures. But what am I to say of the outer man? Compared
to it are the worm, the lion and the stone,[11] not in dignity of substance
but in recognition of a certain likeness. In the same way God is rightly
understood to have made man in His own image and likeness, if only
what has been prised away were restored to its place. Father Augustine in his second book of *Questions* has discussed this with some
sophistication and care.[12] This image is admittedly great, and boasts a
certain likeness to the great Creator in its life, reason and immortality.
Yet since it is made man, it is subject to sins and unlike its first father
before his transgression. It is disturbed and confused by transient
desires, at one moment thinking of food, at another seeking clothing
through the demands of the season, or other quite countless things by
which man is subdued and preoccupied in this world. The phrase, *he
will be disquieted,* is good, because those preoccupied with temporal

longings lose their integrity of mind. He added: *He stores up, and he knows not for whom he gathers these things.* This demonstrates his foolish vanity, since he desires to keep what will perish and to guard what will pass away, and especially since the possession of these things is demonstrably uncertain. The one who thinks he is bequeathing them to dear children does not know whether his greatest enemies may not come into possession of them instead. Notice that though there are many similar points on which man's fickleness may be indicted, greed is singled out in the charges against him. This is so that his signal fault may hear the accusation which his lesser vices know are directed against them too: for as Scripture says: *Greed is the root of all evils.*[13]

8. *And now what is my hope? Is it not the Lord? And my substance is before thee.* Having first spoken of the most evil vanity of the human race, he now returns to his own self, proclaiming his hope of the Lord Christ, and saying that no anticipation of his lies in transient desires. Rather, he awaits Him who is now known to have come bringing salvation to the world. This hope can signify also the Judgment, at which holy men are known to gain joys without end. This outstanding leaper over vices inevitably waited for the time when his eternal rewards would crown him. His *substance* here is not that of Adam which he described two verses earlier. That substance was mentioned in a bad sense, whereas here it is in a good sense; for the word is ambivalent. So here we are to take substance in the good sense as possession of the moral faculty by which he was sustained and nourished, the source of his wealth and position as head of the family. *Before thee* means not in my money-bags, as was said of misers earlier, but in Your sight and not in my hiding-places from which we know that riches cannot be recovered. Of the bad substance it was said it was *as nothing before thee*, but of this good substance *it is before thee*, where nothing can stand except what has been perfected by splendid deeds.

9. *Deliver thou me from all my iniquities: thou hast made me a reproach to the fool.* Although this holy man applied himself with edifying devotion, he none the less asks to be freed by the Lord's pity from all his iniquities. This is so that we may acknowledge that no-one in this life is safe, even if he obtains divine kindnesses. When he says: *From all*, he shows that iniquities are made up of small and diverse parts. As Psalm 18 has it: *Who can understand sins? From my secret ones cleanse*

me, O Lord, and from those of others spare thy servant.[14] Next comes:
Thou hast made me a reproach to the fool. Foolish people tend to jeer at
those who they know espouse good manners. So the holy man was a
reproach to the foolish, because they spurned him for being unlike
themselves. Wicked men praise only the traits which they are seen
to share.

10. *I was dumb, and I opened not my mouth, because thou hast made
me to do so.* He returned to what he said earlier, claiming that he did
not reply to his enemies, and adding: *Since you made me.* He indeed
made him do so because He granted him the gifts of patience. He
would not have maintained this silence so salutary if the generosity of
heaven had not granted it.

11. *Remove thy scourges from me: the strength of thy hand hath made
me faint.* Now that he has pleaded his devotion, Idithun fittingly begs
for pardon. He asks that since he had obeyed the Lord's commands he
should deserve to be heard. *Scourges* are reproofs of the whip by which
we are most justly flogged because of our sins. So the most holy man
longs to have those scourges removed which were incurred for the
faults which he had committed. A strong hand wields the whip
harshly; inevitably anyone struck by a hand raised high was made faint.

12. *In rebukes thou hast corrected man for iniquity. And thou hast
made his soul waste away like a spider: surely in vain is every living man
disquieted.* Here the Lord's devotion is clearly shown. He does not
favour rebukes except for man's correction; for the iniquity of mortal
men would spread without limit like a wasting disease if the healing
rebuke did not excise it in any way. It is when we feel that we are
condemned by the Lord's commands that we are converted, and abandon our evil intention. The spider has a thin body and does not dwell
on the earth, but weaves very slender webs in higher places by spreading out its inner parts; in the same way certain worms are said to
weave silk. So to this tiny frame is aptly compared the soul of the
converted and afflicted man who wearies himself with long observances and vigils, who forsakes things earthly, and who through fear
instilled by heaven wastes himself in performing the most refined
works of the virtues.

After this he returns to the beginning of his thesis to say that though
he is rebuked and wastes away, he is still troubled by a range of
different problems through the frailty of his humanity. From this

disquiet he alone is freed who with pure heart devotes himself to the contemplation of heaven. As I see it, the five-part proof of the rhetorical syllogism termed *epichirema*[15] is now complete. Let us now state it with its limbs and verses as far as we can. His proposition is: *Though man walks as an image of God, yet he will be disquieted in vain.* The proof of the proposition: *He stores up and he knows not for whom he gathers these things.* The minor proposition follows, continuing for four verses: *And now what is my hope? Is it not the Lord?* and the rest. It should not trouble us that the minor proposition appears so long; we have remarked that the length of these limbs of the syllogism was later restricted by secular teachers. We must here search out the traces of the constituent parts which are not so much stated as indicated. The proof of the minor proposition is added: *In rebukes thou hast corrected man for iniquity. And thou hast made his soul waste away like a spider.* There now emerges, if I am not mistaken, the awaited conclusion, appropriately matching the proposition: *But surely in vain will every living man be disquieted.* So the argument of the five-part syllogism is I think completed.

13. *Hear, O God, my prayer and my supplication: give ear to my tears.* The more numerous the mysteries which Idithun had learnt, the more earnest the supplication with which he prostrated himself before the Lord. So he comes to the third section, where he humbly but confidently prays that his sins may be forgiven before he ends his life. Why is it necessary to ponder why he who was said to have leapt over the world's vices seems even yet to lament so grievously? It is doubtless because a victory gained over faults is insufficient for any man unless it is maintained with constant entreaty. So he spoke first of prayer and then of supplication. *Oratio* (prayer) is *oris ratio* (the mouth's account),[16] which we utter bent low as we reveal our wishes; but supplication is repeated, and continual entreaty is uttered from the secret depths of the heart. Listen to what follows: *Give ear to my tears.* We have often said that God hears what He sees and sees what He hears, for no distinction of bodily parts is applicable to Him, performing as He does all things by virtue of His godhead. So that you would not think that the entreaty consisted solely of words, he spoke of *my tears*, which in prayers are always profuse, and which impel the mind of the pitying listener towards healing clemency.

Be not silent in my presence: for I am a cultivator with thee in the land,

and a sojourner, as all my fathers were. He said: *Be not silent,* in other words, "I shall hear you say what the gospel attests: *Thy sins are forgiven thee.*"[17] Or the words of the psalm elsewhere: *Say to my soul, I am thy salvation.*[18] Or; *Come ye, blessed of my Father, possess ye the kingdom prepared for you from the beginning of the world.*[19] Whichever of these you wish mentally to supply is accordingly apt. *Incola* (cultivator) means one who cultivates the land, who comes from the outside world for a time and does not dwell in his native region. This is the experience of every saint received in the heavenly city. Sin has made us all outsiders and has kept us captive in a wicked region. But when His mercy receives us, we become cultivators since we reach that place; in other words the Lord draws us on, and we are translated from Babylon to Jerusalem. He wrote: *With thee,* so that you might realise that he was a cultivator in the Lord's city and not in the devil's. He added: *And a sojourner, as all my fathers were.* He has emphasised what he said earlier, for every man received in blessedness is called a sojourner because he begins to be where he was not before. *Peregrinus* (sojourner) gets its name from *pergens longius* (travelling further).[20] So that you would realise that this was a general condition, he added: *As all my fathers were,* so that none should be considered exempt from this status.

14. *O forgive me, that I may be cooled before I go hence, and be no more.* He is a man of foresight, and filled with the brightness of the Light itself; so he sought forgiveness for himself, so that he could proceed unwavering to the Judgment to come, and obtain some refreshment in the present life when he had obtained the certainty of that kingdom. He claimed that he was afire with an anxiety which scorched him, and he demanded to be cooled with the rain of mercy. As he says of himself earlier: *My heart grew hot within me, and in my meditation a fire flamed out.*[21] So he rightly asked that he be cooled, for he was ablaze with the heat of such great desire. He added: *Before I go hence,* in other words, "Before I leave this life." *And be no more,* that is, in this world where succour is given to sinners' crimes as long as they accept humble correction from the Lord and amend themselves. Or I shall *be no more* means "if You cease to help me"; for *be* does not mean remaining in eternal afflictions, since being is properly used of the blessed. So he justly said that he would not *be* if he thought that he had no portion with the elect.

Conclusion Drawn From the Psalm

Note how this outstanding leaper over vices has with his most healthy and blessed teaching warned us to exercise discipline over the tongue amongst the blasphemers and the wicked, to avoid the conflicts that harm, to quell brawls with most earnest control. That silence wins approval which inclines us least towards sin, which reveals the wise, which makes people highly serious, which nurtures prudence, which shows that speech too is a most pleasant faculty. So let us drain this most health-giving and remedial drink; once we realise that the saints profited so much from silence, we may cease to love the unbounded freedom of the tongue manifested by sinners.

COMMENTARY ON PSALM 39

1. *Unto the end, a psalm of David.* We have often stated that by *end* and *David*, the Lord is denoted; this psalm is to be related to Him. But in the preliminaries His Church, that is, His heavenly bride, the limbs of Christ, the crowd of the faithful, speaks. Then the psalm passes to our Head, the Lord Saviour, so that the texture of the whole psalm is appropriately fitted to the one body.

Division of the Psalm

In the first narration, the Church composed of the Gentiles gives thanks because she is freed from the languid grief of this world and has deserved to attain the joys of the New Testament. In the second, the Lord Christ Himself speaks, and explains the holy Incarnation and the justice of His proclamation. He begs the Father's help to overcome the dangers imposed by the Jews, and asks that His enemies be confounded, and that all who hope in Him may rejoice.

Explanation of the Psalm

2. *With expectation I have expected the Lord, and he heeded me, and he heard my insistent prayer.* The Catholic Church, to be gathered from

the regions of the whole world, proclaims the virtue of patience, which a Christian appropriately considers as one of his highest glories; for how is he to bear his sufferings or escape the burden of dangers if he does not through heaven's kindness depend on the strength of endurance? But we must contemplate the double use of the same word here, for this beautiful repetition is not otiose. We can expect even if we are ungrateful, but we expect with expectation only when we meekly endure something with great longing. This is the argument called *a coniugatis,*[1] when one word related to another changes its form; *sapiens* becomes *sapienter, prudens prudenter,* and so forth. *He heeded,* for He anticipates all that is good for us. We cannot possess the light of truth unless we deserve to be made visible by His brightness. *He heard me* is added, so that the Church seems devotedly and successfully to have expected Him. *Deprecatio,* as has been said, means *insistent prayer;* she could not pray merely intermittently when her endurance was endurance for the Lord.

3. *And he brought me out of the lake of misery, and the mire of dregs. And he set my feet upon a rock, and directed my steps.* Just as she instructs the Christian to act in two ways, to avoid evil and to do good, so she says that the Lord grants what will be serviceable to us in two ways. First He leads us out of the most yawning disaster of this world, the malevolent expanse of which is called a pit of misery and foul mire. She appended *mire* to express the physical density of sins; it is enclosed by the lake so that you may not think that sins are being compared merely with water however muddy. Just as mud in a lake is foul-smelling and oppressive, so the sins of men are slimy, for they smell foul and drown us with their weight. Then He sets our feet upon a rock when we walk in the commands of the Lord Christ, for He is our spiritual Rock which does not allow the feet planted on it to sink. Notice that just as sins are opposed to virtues, so the paths of the two are different. Sins, being soft and degenerate, wallow in the muddiness of their route, whereas virtues are stiff and immovable, and take a rocky path where they walk with clean rather than with dirty feet.

4. *And he put a new canticle into my mouth, a hymn to our God. Many shall see and shall fear, and they shall hope in the Lord.* The earlier verses of the psalm refer to God's moving the human race, sunk in the mud of this world, to the stability of the rock, that is to the Christian religion. This verse now makes this clear with the words: *And he put a*

new canticle into my mouth, that is, the most holy proclamation of the
New Testament. *New* is a good description, for no earlier age looked
on the Lord's incarnation with bodily eyes. But for God nothing is
new, since before the foundation of the world He knew all the content
of His dispensation. *Hymn* is a Greek word meaning praise in metri-
cally-composed verses, and since there were hymns which the Gentiles too sang lustily to their idols, the Church added: *To our God.* Thus
we could clearly note what kind of hymn she meant. *Many shall see
and shall fear:* she is referring to the wonders performed at the time of
the holy Incarnation. When the Jews saw such things they were
afraid, and crowds of people believed the preachings of Christ the
Lord. They hoped in the Lord when they began to be Christians, so
that they were converted after their fear of the miracles, and were
known to have the firmest hope in the Lord.

   5. *Blessed is the man whose trust is the name of the Lord.* This blessed
man is described by the second type of definition, called in Greek
ennoematike and in Latin *notio.*[2] This definition seeks to reveal an
object not by what it is but by what it does. The nature of the blessed
man is determined beforehand by the limits laid down, *whose trust is
the name of the Lord. Spes* (trust) stands for *stabilis pes* (stable foot).[3]
People who pray that temporal goods be given them are also said to
put their trust in the Lord; such men are seen to love God not for His
sake but for the objects of their demands. But he truly has trust in the
name of the Lord who desires with greater longing contemplation of
the Lord, and nothing else. So among all others the name of the Lord is
the eternal Saviour, and trust is put in His name by one who believes
that he is to be saved not by his own merits but by the Lord through
grace. Then too in the gospel some are called eight times blessed, as in
the passage: *Blessed are the poor in spirit, for theirs is the kingdom of
heaven,*[4] and the rest. We find a similar passage in Deuteronomy,
when the Israelites entered the promised land.[5] The land is called
"various," because blessedness is afforded in diverse ways. The diligent reader will find all this carefully set down under the individual
types of definitions.

   And who hath not regard to vanity and lying follies. This verse is
appended to the previous statement: she is explaining who it is whose
trust is in the Lord's name, namely, *he who hath not had regard to vanity
and lying follies.* We read in Scripture: *No man can serve two masters;*[6]

this passage too makes the same point. He who has hope in the Lord who has power over all things ought not to have regard for transient affairs. It is *vanity* to be alienated from holy religion by sudden change, and to turn the mind elsewhere through deceptive misapprehension. *Lying folly* consists of having fashioned from rocks a god for pagans to adore, when they sought a false foreshadowing of future events. *Lying* is a splendid epithet for *folly;* for follies deceive the mind since they dissent from the truth. The expression can be applied also to those beguiled by the pleasure of deceiving shows. The plural follies is used so that we should pursue the matter more broadly by seeking parallel instances.

6. *Thou hast multiplied thy wonderful works, O Lord my God: and in thy thoughts there is none like to thee.* When she spoke of the mad works of men, she aptly inserted divine miracles. How much better it would be if those fired by races between charioteers or rendered effeminate by dancing pantomimes[7] were to ponder how heaven and earth are fashioned with most beautiful variety! They have a splendid appearance, and they also elicit quite marvellous reflections. Next comes: *And in thy thoughts there is none like to thee.* She continues to strangle the superstitions which men have devised for themselves for perverted worship, or have fashioned when stirred by some pleasure in attending shows. But surely running with feet extended along a rope is not so remarkable as Peter's treading the sea's surface with implanted footsteps?[8] Surely sporting in the theatre with ignited torches is not so remarkable as when the three boys walked on the fiery furnace?[9] Surely listening to tragedies on the stage is not commensurate with acquaintance with the psalmodies that bring salvation in the choruses of the Church?[10] We should rather feast our eyes by reading these passages of Scripture to which foolishness does not impel us and which are always profitable to hear. By saying: *None is like to thee,* she rebukes those who devise evil things, who wickedly glorify themselves and boast of originating methods of deception.

Up to this point holy mother Church has done the preaching. Now let us listen to the Lord Saviour speaking, so that the words: *None is like to thee,* may be made clear to us in the ensuing explanation.

I have announced, and I have spoken: they are multiplied above number. This is the second section of the psalm, introduced by the figure of *exallage,* which in Latin is called *immutatio.*[11] Words of mystery pour forth from the Lord's person when He makes known His coming and His holy preaching to the nations; for announcing means proclaiming the future, and this He did through the mouths of the prophets. *I have spoken* refers to when He lived among us and preached the gospel, when He embodies the mystery of the blessed Incarnation. He added: *They are multiplied above number,* that is, the crowd of sinners is multiplied above the computation of the blessed. How few are the faithful from such massive peoples! And naturally so, for when many are preoccupied with the follies of this world, you will be able to find few who are truly wise. Note that He says: *Above number,* marking out only those counted in the book of the living, those known to be predestined for the heavenly Jerusalem.

7. *Sacrifice and oblation thou didst not desire: but thou hast perfected thy body for me: holocausts for sin thou didst not require.* This verse embraces the mysteries of the Old and New Testaments. She says that God later spurned the sacrifice and oblation earlier made to honour the Lord by immolation of cattle; from this source the priests obtained food. Earlier He deigned to accept such sacrifices, since through them a kind of prefiguration of Christ's body seemed to exist. But after the Messiah, the Lord Christ who had been foretold, came and revealed Himself as Victim of devoted love for us all, it was unnecessary, now that the truth was fulfilled, for that forerunning type to continue. The apostle expounds these verses to the Hebrews in this way: *In this willing we are sanctified by the oblation of the body of Jesus Christ once,*[12] and the rest. These words are acknowledged to refer to this most splendid distinction.[13] Next comes: *But thou hast perfected thy body for me.* This clearly indicates the holy incarnation, as the apostle states. The body previously promised by the images of sacrifices she now says was fulfilled by His coming. She added: *Holocausts for sin thou didst not require.* Holocausts means things wholly burnt. They were placed on consecrated altars to expiate sins, and were subsequently burnt by fire, so that when they were consumed the sins might be removed. She says that the Lord did not now seek these, and rightly, for He seeks from us what we read in Psalm 50: *A contrite and humble heart God does not despise.*[14] Do you see now that the Church truthfully said: *Who is like to thee?*

8. *Then said I: Behold I come: in the head of the book it is written of me.* *Behold* denotes "at once," promising haste. It gives promise of speed

by every means. Jew, since you do not have your own sacrifices, whom do you await in your beguiled state? He has now come. That Word has been made flesh. He has filled the world with His preaching that brings salvation. But you are still dreaming some strange dream in your bed. What further do you seek? Why are you lost in amazement? In this Book of Psalms He says that *in the head of the book it is written* of Him, so you must believe that the blessed One has already come. His life as it is now befallen is clearly set down. Where are those who realise that they do not have the sacrifices promised here? Since they do not have this statement in their sacred books, they are appropriately silent, speechless at the words which confront them.

9. *That I should do thy will: O my God, I have desired it and thy law in the midst of my heart.* The words are the Son's, directed to the Father. He wished to do the Father's will, for *He hath not walked in the counsel of the ungodly, nor stood in the way of sinners, nor sat in the chair of pestilence.*[15] The words: *I have desired it* made clear the virtue of foreknowledge, so that He announced what was clearly in the future as if it were already past. Further, the divine law remained *in the midst of his heart*, while His *will was in the law of the Lord, and on his law he meditated day and night.*[16]

10. *I have happily declared thy justice in a great church: lo, I will not restrain my lips: O Lord, thou knowest it.* He happily declared the Lord's justice with the words: *Not so the wicked, not so: but like the dust which the wind driveth from the face of the earth.*[17] In a great church, as we have often stated, refers to the Catholic Church which is dispersed through the whole world. In that first psalm there is reference to it in the words: *Which shall bring forth its fruit in due season.*[18] Next follows: *Lo, I will not restrain my lips: O Lord, thou knowest it.* He speaks in his role as Son subject to God. Though it was dangerous to proclaim the truth among obdurate men since He knew that His death would be the outcome of it, He none the less did not cease to warn the people about the men of treachery with the words: *For the Lord knoweth the way of the just: and the way of the wicked shall perish.*[19] Here he called the Father, whom He invokes, to witness that He has feared no dangers when He proclaimed spiritual blessings to a people tied to the flesh. In this way those most authentic verses of Psalm 1 seem to be echoed by the Lord's words here.

11. *I have not hid thy justice within my heart: I have declared thy truth and thy salvation.* It is the just man's wish not to hide the truth when it can be of use, and there is no doubt that the Lord Saviour acted in this way when He chided the crowds, rebuked unbelievers, and preached many messages of this kind which the gospel-words declare. But there was a time when He was silent in his suffering; as Scripture has it: *But Jesus gave him no answer. Pilate therefore said to him: Speakest thou not to me?*[20] He declared the truth when He proclaimed: *I am the way, the truth and the life.*[21] The saving Christ is announced by the confession of blessed Simeon, who said when he saw Him: *Now dismiss thy servant in peace, for my eyes have seen thy salvation, which thou hast prepared before the face of all peoples,*[22] and the rest.

I have not concealed thy mercy and thy truth in the crowded synagogue. He still continues with the exposition of His deeds. He did not conceal the Father's mercy when He said: *If you being evil know how to give good gifts to your children, how much more will your Father from heaven give blessings to them that ask him?*[23] He also spoke the *truth in the crowded synagogue,* that is, in a thick-packed assembly of the people, when He took and read the Book of Isaiah, and then said: *This day is fulfilled this scripture in your ears.*[24] Do you hear, unbelieving Jew, him who was once your prophet harmonizing with our gospel? You would continue to support him by acknowledging that the Lord Christ has now come, if your heart was not cloaked in a noxious cloud.

12. *Withhold not, O Lord, thy tender mercies from me: thy mercy and truth have always upheld me.* Having recounted His holy deeds, He comes to the glory of His passion, so that the unity of His whole life and life-giving death may be made manifest. Here He justly begs His Father not to withhold His tender mercies from Him, for He was soon to die by virtue of the true manhood which He had accepted. As He says elsewhere: *O God, my God, look upon me: why hast thou forsaken me?*[25] The *mercy* lay in rescuing human nature, which was wounded through the sin of transgression, by means of the holy Incarnation; the *truth* lies in His sitting at the Father's right hand through the blessing of the promised resurrection, and from there He will come to judge the living and the dead. They *upheld me,* that is, received me to be glorified. We are said to uphold people in the good sense when we proclaim that they have been received into our favour.

13. *For evils without number have surrounded me: my iniquities have overtaken me.* He says this on behalf of the members of whom Christ Himself is the Head, so that He might proclaim that He was suffering what the crowd of the faithful was enduring. It is the same as in the passage: *Saul, Saul, why persecuteth thou me?*[26] Next comes: *Without number,* meaning so far as men are concerned, for all things are numbered by God, who knows the grains of sand on the seashore, the drops of rain, and the crowd of stars in their complex quantity. He added: *My iniquities have overtaken me.* His manner of speaking is the same as in the previous phrase: *Evils have surrounded me.* The Lord Saviour neither perpetrated iniquities nor was subject to evils; the phrase is aptly used on the part of His members who endure such things. It was characteristic of our Head's loving care that having said so much about Himself, He should deign to mention also the faithful, so that they should not feel they were abandoned when they saw that they were passed over.

And I was not able to see. They are multiplied above the hairs of my head, and my heart hath forsaken me. This is to be wholly referred to His members, for such descriptions cannot befit the Lord Christ. *I was not able to see:* in other words, my iniquities surrounded me, as a faithful person can truthfully state. Though the hairs on a man's head seem innumerable, his sins are clearly known to exceed that number. The comparison of hairs with sins is not made idly, for in the Old Testament priests were shaved because of this similarity, so that when they were purified by such bodily cleansing they might appear to have laid aside their faults. So the heart forsakes us when through sinning it does not seek the things which would avail the sick man.

14. *Be pleased, together yet alone, O Lord, to deliver me: look down, O Lord, to help me.* After recounting these earlier points, He comes to His most salutary conclusion, by which all opposition is confronted, and all harmful agents destroyed. He asks the Lord to be pleased to deliver Him, for He was engulfed by the opposing things of this world. Notice His expression, *be pleased together,* in other words, "be pleased one and all"; for here the harmony of the Trinity is revealed, and what pleases the Father likewise pleases the Son and the holy Spirit. He added: *Yet alone,* so that you might realise that the holy

Trinity is one God. Next comes: *Look down, O Lord, to help me*, that we may realise that His looking down is our protection. As the gospel has it: *And he looked on Peter, and Peter wept bitterly.*[27] Otherwise we could not be freed if the Godhead were not appeased and did not look on us.

15. *Let them be confounded and ashamed together, that seek after my soul to take it away.* He passes to the remaining narration, in which the Lord Saviour prays that confusion and shame may befall the wicked, but He asks that exultation and joy may well forth for the faithful. *Let them be confounded* means "Let them be thrown into confusion by the working of miracles"; *let them be ashamed* means "Let them be corrected by the glory of the resurrection, so that they may confess to that God who they had long believed should be slaughtered." *Together*, in other words, just as they all persecuted Him so all the foreordained may be freed by the gift of conversion. Next comes: *That seek after my soul.* The soul is sought after in two ways, for glory or for death. He added here, to denote those who sought it with hostile intent: *To take it away*, not to love or venerate it, but to seek to separate it from My body by the intervention of death.

Let them be turned backward and be ashamed that think out evils for me. We have often observed that prayers are kindly offered for evil men so that they may turn back from their pleasures and not continue in wicked activity. If they undergo confusion they escape, but if they enjoy the happiness of the world they perish. *Backward* is used in the good sense, as attested in the gospel-passage: *Get you backward, Satan.*[28] As for: *That think out evils for me*, the phrase signifies the Jews' evil wishes; but their purposes were evils not for the Lord but for themselves the originators. The word *cogitationes* (purposes) derives from *cogere*,[29] to bring together.

16. *Let them immediately bear their confusion that say to me, 'Tis well, 'tis well.* It is those who come to recognise that they have wickedly erred who *immediately bear their confusion. Let them bear* implies a massive burden. *Immediately* means after beginning to sin, so that they may not be weighed down to their greater danger by continuing further. *Their confusion*, in other words, their debased thoughts, confuted by the truth. Next comes: *That say to me, 'Tis well, 'tis well.* Here he rebuts lying eulogisers who strive for greater deceit by adulation

than the wounds which they can inflict by censorious words. *'Tis well* is an expression of approval, but when not uttered with a sincere heart it is used to introduce derision—the figure known as irony or *irrisio*.[30]

17. *Let them that seek thee rejoice and be glad, O Lord, and let such as love thy salvation say always, The Lord be magnified.* Just as He sought that His enemies be confounded since they mocked Him with false praises, so He prays that His devoted ones may truly rejoice, since they are known to have set their hope in the majesty of the Lord, for He asks that they may not only rejoice but also be glad. The nature of this rejoicing is next explained: *And may they say always, The Lord be magnified.* This is the proclamation which makes Christians glad for ever; though continually uttered it is none the less perpetually sought. Job feasted on this notion even in this world, when gravely wounded by physical affliction: *The Lord gave, and the Lord hath taken away. As it hath pleased the Lord, so it is done. Blessed be the name of the Lord.*[31] He rejoiced when he was glad in the Lord, in whom all that will avail truly exists. But to prevent your believing that this rejoicing is to be granted to one and all, He added: *Such as love my salvation,* in other words, "Those who seek me with spiritual love and sweetly obey my commands."

18. *But I am needy and poor: the Lord has care for me.* Having said that those who sought to love the divinity of the Word were to be filled with gifts of joy, the Lord God speaks in the role of the humanity which He had assumed, so that none should claim for himself the glory of any merits: *I am needy and poor. Needy,* for humanity always needs for itself aid from the Lord; *poor,* because if not lent glory by divine grace it is found to be utterly resourceless in itself. But so that you would not regard this poverty as cheap and degrading, He added: *The Lord has care for me,* that is, for Him of whom He was to say: *This is my beloved Son in whom I am well pleased.*[32] What poverty, richer than all treasures! He is poor in our possessions but rich in His own, for He assumed the need of human nature to make us sharers in His abundance.

Thou art my helper and my liberator: Lord, do not delay. Untroubled, He asks for the necessary speed in obtaining help and protection. Since it was not right that death be avoided, He prayed that the resurrection should at least follow with haste. When He speaks of helper and liberator, He reveals the endurance of different sufferings from which this psalm began. So the whole of the psalm is rightly devoted to the virtue of patience, for it ends on the same note.

Conclusion Drawn From the Psalm

Splendid and most sweet words entered deep into our hearts when we heard Him whom we adore as our Creator teaching from His own lips. Though we revere all the psalms with great honour, a greater sweetness is audible when some message which concerns the holy incarnation emerges. Every person of faith hears with the greatest gratitude of that through which he is known to have been freed. Observe the order in which the words of this psalm are arranged. First the Church speaks as if instructing the ignorant, strengthening the fearful, and composing the disordered, so that the people thus prepared may listen in salutary spirit and joyful mind to the ensuing words of the Lord Saviour.

COMMENTARY ON PSALM 40

1. *Unto the end, a psalm of David.* These words through their regular use ought now to be very well known to us. To touch upon them briefly, all are directed towards the Lord Christ. What makes this psalm splendid is its acknowledged position under the number 40, a number often associated with cleansing and purifying. It was in forty days that the earth was cleansed of man's iniquities with the spread of the Flood.[1] Moses fasted from bodily food for forty days to deserve conversation with God.[2] Similarly Elias abstained from the remedy of bodily nourishment.[3] The Lord Himself too fasted for the same number of days and nights[4] to show us the manner of blessed purification. Then too we are instructed by the example of Lent itself; a time of fasting is set before us so that we may come to the Lord's resurrection with pure minds, after cleansing away the foulness of our sins. So let us regard this psalm as concerned with those sacred things which

cleanse our souls with heavenly purification, particularly when the prophet speaks of almsgiving, which is specifically known to remove sins, for the Word says: *As water extinguishes fire, so almsgiving extinguishes sin.*[5]

Division of the Psalm

Initially the prophet speaks, proclaiming the blessed man who bestows alms, and hymning him with manifold blessings. Secondly, the Lord recalls His glorious passion. Thirdly, the Lord Christ also foretells His resurrection to strengthen the hope of the faithful.

Explanation of the Psalm

2. *Blessed is he that understandeth concerning the needy and the poor: the Lord will deliver him in the evil day.* Once again the hypothetical syllogism[6] shines out with this reasoning: "If every blessed man has understanding concerning the needy and the poor, the Lord will deliver him in the evil day. But every blessed man does have understanding concerning the needy and the poor. Therefore in the evil day the Lord will deliver him." The hypothetical or conditional syllogism is that which makes an absolute assumption from conditional propositions, and infers the conclusion. Now let us see what follows. The second type of definition, called *ennoematike* in Greek and *notio* in Latin,[7] shows the nature of an individual from his deeds, for it speaks of how sins are expiated by the most salutary working of almsgiving, so that the most glorious blessedness can be attained.

The importance of the subject has persuaded us to digress and generalize; we felt that we had to praise almsgiving as the means of reconciling the human race. But since it has been celebrated by the most holy and eloquent mouths of many Fathers, it must be enough to direct the hearts of my listeners to their books. In this way their needs will be more fruitfully met, and with the Lord's help I can industriously carry through the work which I have begun. But though several of the Fathers have written copiously on this matter, a certain disagreement arises between them about it. We read: *Give to all who solicit thee,*[8] but it is also written: *Alms sweat in your hand until you find the just man upon whom to confer them.*[9] Yet if we seek none but the just man, we restrict the generosity enjoined on us. However, this issue resides solely in our dutiful intention; it is not our task first to analyse people's characters, and only then to lend help to need. For us it is enough to be unaware that we are bestowing anything on evil manners, to refrain from giving alms when puffed up through striving for men's good opinions, to act with the sole motive of offering help, which God has commanded us to attend to above all. He who makes gifts in this way, even if he does not give to just men, will none the less disburse justly to all.

We must however make greater effort to help holy men in any need for the sake of Christ our Lord, who at our individual judgment will say of His poor: *He who did it to one of my least brethren, did it to me.*[10] What can be said more lofty and splendid, when those whom we ignored conduct us into the flames, or those whom we rewarded place us at the right side? But observe the word, *understandeth,* implying the offering of alms even to those who do not request it. He who gives to a petitioner performs a good work, but he who is aware of one silent in need undoubtedly attains blessedness. He added: *The Lord will deliver him in the evil day.* This signifies the day of judgment. Some are troubled because so often he calls it the evil day; everyone says that God's judgment in his case is evil and fearful, anticipating the punishment owed to sinners. Even if we are freed by His pity, we none the less rightly tremble at the power of His judgment.

3. *The Lord preserve him, and give him life, and make him blessed, and cleanse his soul upon the earth: and deliver him not up to the hands of his enemy.* This request of the prophet amounts to a definite promise, for it is inevitable that this will happen if the needy and poor are aided by a holy gift. *Preserve,* in other words, prevent his perishing among the world's evils, and lead him unharmed to his reward through his holy style of living. People are aptly said to have life if they do not cut themselves off from the Christian faith. Of those who dwell in error Scripture says: *Let the dead bury their dead.*[11] So: *Give him life* means "Establish him in his lot, to live among the elect." He added: *And make him blessed,* meaning precisely "Establish him on the right side at the resurrection, and by the proclamation of the great Judge may he be conducted to the native region of the blessed." But then after those earlier words he touches on an extremely vital matter, that while he

remains in this world he must be cleansed by the remission of sins. The pardon for which we long is obtained if we lament with devoted supplication. He further added: *Deliver him not up to the hands of the enemy.* The enemy is the devil, his hands his wicked power—for what hands has a non-physical being? So *hands* are the power by which he punishes God's servants with diverse trials. Note how often he wrote *and* in this verse, to demonstrate the figure of *polysyndeton*[12] by frequent repetition.

4. *The Lord help him on his bed of sorrow: thou hast overturned all his couch in his sickness.* So that you should not believe that this blessed man obtains unshaken repose in this world, he begs that his grief be lessened, so that the crowd of ills may be conquered by kind reduction of them. A bed is given us for rest, so that men's weary limbs may be refreshed. Similarly one who gains an inheritance, or takes a wife, or begets sons, or makes friendships, obtains rest in the blessing of delight as on a bed. But the Lord often makes this state bitter and grievous for His servants so that they may not set their hope in transient things and fail to seek future blessings. So the prophet begs that the Lord console his grief, for he lies wounded in his delight as on a couch. He added: *Thou hast overturned all his couch in his sickness.* He refines on the reason mentioned earlier, why the divine providence is fulfilled by the worldly delight of God's servants being encompassed with hardships and griefs; this is so that by being afflicted by different disasters here, they may obtain the repose of eternal blessedness. This happened in the case of Job, whose worldly blessings were overturned in his sickness; but subsequently he became happier because worldly success withdrew its presence from him. So the prophet begs the Lord to help such griefs, so that his human frailty may not be overcome through being afflicted by hard toils.

5. *I said: O Lord, be merciful to me: heal my soul, for I have sinned against thee.* Since he knew that the afflictions of the faithful occur through God's judgment, the dutifully fearful prophet loudly asks to obtain the Lord's mercy, for since he knew that he had sinned, he rightly feared that he was being subjected to trials. Every sin is a disease of the soul, and when it spreads, the inner man's health is impaired. He who cried out to the Physician realised his sickness, but

he was healthy in understanding when he was aware of his infirmity. So he longs for his soul to be healed, that is, by remission of sins. We are truly healed by this, since the sins that choke us are loosed.

6. *My enemies have spoken evils against me: when shall he die, and his name perish?* So far the prophet has spoken of the tribulation of the blessed. Now in this second beginning the Lord Saviour will speak of His passion, so that when God's servants are afflicted by different misfortunes they may not believe that they have been abandoned by God, once they realise that the Lord Christ endured such things. He said: *If they have persecuted me, they will also persecute you. If they have kept my word, they will keep yours also.*[13] *Enemies have spoken evils* when they uttered falsehoods. It was inevitable that the wicked should ponder lies, for they were maddened by the devil's influence. Next comes: *When shall he die, and his name perish?* These are the words of the crazed Jews, for they said: *If we set him free, the Romans will come and will take our place and our kingdom from us.*[14] Again, Caiphas said: *It is expedient that one man should die for all, and that the whole nation perish not.*[15] Yes, His name did perish, but only for those who refused to believe in Him.

7. *And they came in to see: their heart spoke vain things. They gathered iniquity to themselves, and they went out and held converse.* He describes the famous occasion of the Lord's passion, when Judas came in not to worship the Lord but rather to betray Him craftily. The plural, *they came in,* denotes also those who presumed to lay hands on Him. The Jews *spoke vain things* when they cruelly discussed the death of Him who is known to be the Life of all. Next comes: *They gathered iniquity to themselves.* Their gathering was nothing other than an assembly of sinners, for in their one wicked deed all crimes were committed when they decided to crucify the Lord of creation. *They went out* since they could not remain within, for they were at odds with the hidden mystery of faith. Both journeys were wretched and baneful. They went in to perform an evil deed; then they went out from the territory of truth.

8. *All my enemies buzzed in unison against me alone: they devised evils against me.* Buzzing is a very low sound in the mouth, joined with no vocal differentiation. It is adopted from the bees, whose continuous sound is a buzzing. This is what occurred among those who de-

lighted in whispering in each other's ears, for those associated in a conspiracy of crimes do not dare to proclaim their plans. He added: *All my enemies devised evils against me.* He detailed the madness of a lunatic and stupid people. Those who promote crimes are usually few; here all were said to have devised evils, so that none incurred lesser guilt since all were condemned by equal responsibility in crime. As for the words: *Evils against me,* if you seek the outcome it was to their own harm, but in intention it was *against me.* The punishment is that of the just One who does not suffer, but the odium is the perpetrator's.

9. *They determined against me an unjust word: shall he that sleepeth not rise again once more?* The unjust word refers to when they cried to Pilate: *If thou release this man, thou art not Caesar's friend.*[16] *They determined,* that is, they decreed and defined when they pronounced sentence on the Lord Saviour. Sleeping is respite from physical sensations with mental concentration at rest, so that we return to our life's activity with renewed vigour of spirit. This seems most splendidly apt to the Lord's death. His resurrection was so swift that He is reckoned to have slept rather than died. He lay down weak, but rose up strong. So that heretics may not beguile themselves any longer, let them hear Him who sleeps immediately add that He is rising again. As He says in the gospel: *I have the power of laying down my life, and I have the power of taking it up again.*[17]

10. *For even the man of my peace in whom I trusted, who ate my bread, has made clear his deceit against me.* The man of His peace refers to His disciple Judas, who offered peace to Him when he betrayed Him,[18] for we say, "Peace," when we kiss each other. But if one means tranquillity of soul, peace could not exist in the heart of him who devised an ambush with soothing words. He added: *In whom I trusted,* that is, "in whom I was believed to trust." How could He have trusted a most evil man when He could know his nature before he was born? So that you may realise that He knew that nature beforehand, the Lord Himself says: *Have I not chosen you twelve? And one of you is a devil.*[19] Next comes: *Who ate my bread,* which means either "Who listened to my teaching," from which comes our spiritual nourishment, or that Judas put his hand into the dish with the Lord's, as the gospel-account declares.[20] He rightly said *has made clear,* since Judas himself had

pointed out to the ignorant company the identity of the deceiver. O deaf disciple, what a hard and unteachable heart was yours! Who could believe that his mind had derived any virtue from the Lord's great love when he emerged as a murderer so cruel?

11. *But thou, Lord, have mercy on me, and raise me up again, and I will requite them.* Having expounded His passion, He comes to the third section, in which He begs in His human role that the miraculous events of His resurrection should come to pass. Why do you prick your ears, heretic? Why do you think that you have unearthed something to excuse you infidelity? If you seek His power, hear what He says in the gospel: *Destroy this temple, and in three days I will raise it up.*[21] In this psalm it is His humility which makes the request, whereas in the gospel-passage His divinity makes the pledge. Cease your calumnies; both statements are appropriate to the Lord Saviour, because *the word was made flesh, and dwelt among us.*[22] *I will requite them:* He spoke these words not in the resentment of vengeance but with the prospect of patience, for by bearing with these men even today, He has won over a great number of them by the work of His clemency.

12. *By this I know that thou hast had a good will for me, because my enemy shall not rejoice over me.* He says that He knows the love of the Father by the fact that His glorious resurrection is to follow. *That thou hast had a good will for me*—understand "to glorify, to exalt Me," for both the words spoken and others similar to them are apt to this passage. He added: *Because my enemy shall not rejoice over me.* This is the explanation of His words: *Thou hast had a good will for me,* for His enemy was not allowed to rejoice over Him when they utterly failed to fulfill the plans which they laid; for they wished to kill Him, as has been said earlier, so that they might expunge His name utterly from the earth. But they witness the opposite situation, the Church of Christ spread through the whole world; and they discover that His name is highly famed everywhere. So since the outcome has been so inauspicious for them, they deservedly fail to rejoice.

13. *But thou hast upheld me by reason of my innocence: and hast established me in thy sight for ever.* His holy innocence, simplicity and blessed humility are truly in evidence; in suffering all these ills, He did not defend Himself by any struggling. He went to the cross with a

calm spirit, to die with untroubled mind. With truth unspotted He fulfilled every word foretold through the prophets. He grieved at the misfortunes of those who persecuted Him, and when nailed to the cross He prayed with all compassion for His enemies, for He had decreed that this should be done by all the faithful too. So since He first showed the example, the command that He gave was worthy. Next comes: *Thou hast established me in thy sight for ever.* Here the blessedness of His holy incarnation is already explained. Having laid aside the weakness of a mortal body, the God-man of and in two distinct and perfect natures abides in eternal glory. His name is above every name, His power governs heaven and earth. Before Him *every knee bows, of those in heaven and on earth and under the earth.*[23]

14. *Blessed be the Lord, the God of Israel, from the beginning to eternity. Let it be so, let it be so.* Now that the relevant themes of the passion and resurrection of the Lord had been expounded, the closing encomium followed, beautifully expressed; for He who by the glory of His dispensation has fulfilled our hope, must be blessed at all times. We use the term *blessed* also of a man who wins blessings, but if he is not spoken well of, he is not blessed; in a sense the blessing is dependent for its diffusion on the judgment of others. But God is blessed even if all are silent, for He does not obtain each and every good as something external, since it comes from Him. As for the words: *From the beginning,* they denote the present world from the time when all things began to be ordered; *to eternity* is to be understood as the future when by then all things are everlasting and will not slip away through any changeability in time. Though this world fail, God's blessing remains without change. He added: *Let it be so, let it be so.* The repetition proclaims that all must do it here and now. We must not understand by it that the Lord is considered blessed with the implication that if He were not praised He would not be blessed. *Let it be so* expresses the Source of our progress while we are continually absorbed in His praises. Some scriptural interpreters have thought that the Psalter should be divided into five books because of the unusual use of *Let it be so,* which occurs here and in Psalms 71, 88, 105; but we have made it sufficiently clear in our Preface that we should not agree with them.[24] For in the Acts of the Apostles we read that there is a single book of Psalms.[25]

Conclusion Drawn From the Psalm

In the previous psalm, holy Church spoke in the first section, and the words of the Lord followed after; similarly in this one the prophet precedes the Lord's words. Initially the blessed David has taught us to order our behaviour by almsgiving. Secondly, the Lord by His passion revealed the ways of nature. Thirdly, by the miracle of the resurrection He filled us with clear insight so that the truth of the divine philosophy told in the three parts could be established. If you examine this carefully, you will find it often so ordered in the other psalms. So having obtained the benefit of this psalm, we are to say: *Blessed be the Lord, the God of Israel, from the beginning to eternity. Let it be so, let it be so.*

COMMENTARY ON PSALM 41

1. *Unto the end, a psalm of David, understanding for the sons of Core.* Among the familiar words he introduces a new element, *the sons of Core.* This denotes the singers, not composers, of psalms,[1] as has already been said of Idithun in Psalm 38. These men had been chosen by David for psalm-singing. They seem to have been aptly included in psalm-headings because of the meaning of their name, which we must investigate most eagerly so that the kernel stripped of its shell may appear most clearly before us. *Core* in Hebrew means Calvary,[2] and Calvary is the place where the Lord Saviour is known to have been crucified. So the sons of Core are rightly mentioned for they have deserved to embrace the sign of the cross, the most glorious trophy of the heavenly King. So this psalm is relevant to every Christian who through the Lord's love is fired by the flame of His affection; without this all that is considered of outstanding worth in human affairs is wholly tawdry. This is the first psalm to include this element, followed by Psalms 83–84. As regards these names we must remember what the blessed Jerome says: "As I survey the whole psalter with the eye of understanding, I never find that the sons of Core have sung any melancholy strain, for in their psalms all is joyful and pleasant. They

hold the things of this world in contempt and long for what is eternal and heavenly, as is appropriate when we understand their name."[3]

Division of the Psalm

The son of Core, who we have said is marked with the glory of the cross, says in the first proclamation of this psalm that all the longing of his heart has been directed to the Lord. In the second part he speaks to his soul in a five-part syllogism; he says that it ought not to be troubled in the salt-surge of this world, because God is the refuge on which its thought is trained.

Explanation of the Psalm

2. *As the hart panteth after the fountains of water, so my soul panteth after thee, O God.* Here we have the figure of *parabole*,[4] that is, comparison of objects dissimilar in kind. Man is seen to be compared with a hind. This argument from comparison is called "From the lesser to the greater."[5] Comparison of the faithful man to this animal is not otiose. First, it wreaks no harm: second, it is very swift: and third, it thirsts with burning longing. It attracts snakes with its nostrils; when it has devoured them, the seething poison impels it to hasten with all speed to the water-fountain, for it loves to get its fill of the purest sweet water. The beautiful comparison with this animal fires our desire with longing, so that when we imbibe the poisons of the ancient serpent, and we are feverish through his torches, we may there and then hasten to the fount of divine mercy. Thus the sickness contracted by the venom of sin is overcome by the purity of this most sweet drink. The use of the phrase, *fountains of water,* in preference to "waters" is not idle, for Christ the Lord is the Fount of water from which flows all that refreshes us. Flowing water can often dry up, but a fountain of water always irrigates. So we are rightly told to hasten to the waters of the sacred spring, where our longing could never experience thirst.

3. *My soul hath thirsted after the living God. When shall I come and appear before the face of God?* So that you may realise that the longing previously expressed was for divine love, he says that his soul thirstily

seeks sight of the Lord; the human faculties of the weak are fired especially by this circling of Him. Finally follows: *When shall I come and appear before the face of God?* This is no doubt said because He will appear clearly to us when He gives us appropriate scrutiny at His judgment. So when we have been instructed in these matters we observe that the soul experiences its thirst when moved by heavenly longing, and when it seeks the divine streams which ever pour out in gushing abundance. These waters offer salvation in flood; they do not merely quench the thirst of souls, but also close the door on the poverty of weakness. This thirst always bubbles up from the hearts of the blessed in this world, and does not rest satisfied with any limit, because the discovery of what it seeks is granted only in future blessedness. As the Lord says in the gospel: *Blessed are they that hunger and thirst after justice, for they shall have their fill.*[6] The word *when* is to be uttered emphatically, so that the delay seems oppressive to him.

4. *My tears have been my bread day and night.* Those who do not strive to weep before the Lord should hearken to the message that continual tears have brought satiety rather than starvation. And rightly, for that weeping is the food of souls, the strengthening of the senses, absolution from sins, renewal of minds, cleansing of faults. Through these unremitting tears he shows that the Christian people can be schooled by afflictions. By *day* we should understand prosperity, by *night* sadness, for the whole period of a man's life is delineated by these two.

While it is said to me daily, Where is thy God? The son of Core explains why he has poured out unremitting tears. During the time when Christians were persecuted, these words were continually said to them: "There is none to deliver you; you must certainly endure what we wish, what we command." Who would not under this affliction lament the possession of an upright conscience, and his prostration before wicked men's insults, since it is grief beyond all griefs to witness one loading you with insults who you know is befouled with the wickedness of guilt? Note how the two events accord with each other. Just as he described his sins as continual, so he says that the charges against him were unremitting, so that all the elements in the sacred reading harmonise with each other.

5. *These things I remembered, and poured out my soul in me, since I entered into the place of the tabernacle.* In other words, "As I pondered

these crimes imputed to me, I poured out my soul in weeping as from a full container with a sudden flood, asking God that I should not be tortured any longer by such taunts." Note that all pouring out results in movement towards the neighbouring area; the soul is poured out upon him when it returns to itself with the impulse of remorse. There further follows the reason why he poured out his soul within him: it was because he *entered into the place of the tabernacle,* that is, into the Church there present, for as he entered there, he lamented and grieved the more that the Jerusalem promised as reward by God to His saints was still being postponed. Inevitably longing for what is awaited is keener when we see an outline of it.

Wonderful even to the house of God: with the voice of joy and confession, the noise of one feasting. Here he had to explain what he said in the previous verse, *Into the place of the tabernacle.* He entered the wonderful tabernacle, for he could not yield before such wicked imputations. He was asked: *Where is thy God?* but his longing for God was commensurate with the wicked insults directed against him. He hastened as a holy dweller from that tabernacle even to the house of God which is in the world to come, so that the holy man should not seem to have entertained longings for this world. But how did that man of great devotion seek to go there? *With the voice of joy and confession.* Joy implies psalm-singing, confession laments for sins; the combination of the two moulds the wholly perfect Christian. Next comes: *The noise of one feasting.* The short definition of the voice of joy and confession is the noise of one feasting, for the sound itself feeds the soul and grants it feasting with sweet delight. What is sweeter or more wholesome than praise of God and constant self-condemnation? The section saying that he must thirst for the Lord is now ended, but he repeats this with great and subtle arguments in the next section, so as not to appear to languish out of sadness of mind in the desire which he had kindled with praiseworthy zeal.

6. *Why art thou sad, O my soul? And why dost thou trouble me? Hope in the Lord.* Let us listen to these verses rather more attentively, for they remain obscure if not handled quite subtly. After the taunt of *where is thy God?* which he had heard, and after pouring out his soul, an act performed with harsh affliction, the son of Core reaches the second section. He speaks to his soul words forming a most authentic demonstration of a five-part syllogism extending to the end of the

psalm. He says: "Why, my soul, are you wounded and weighed down by savage taunts of enemies? Why do you trouble me with your affliction? It is inevitable that the sad, lugubrious weakness of men should be troubled." There follows the salutary remedy for this: *Hope in the Lord*, for hope in Him changes everything for the better, and leads to eternal joy those circumscribed by melancholy affliction in this life. As Scripture has it: *Blessed are they that mourn, for they shall be comforted.*[7] It should not seem unusual that the protagonist thus introduced addresses his own soul, for we read elsewhere: *Bless the Lord, O my soul,*[8] and in another place: *Praise the Lord, O my soul,*[9] and in Psalm 42 he repeats the phrase used here: *Why art thou sad, O my soul?*[10]

For I will confess to him, the salvation of my countenance. So that the soul might not chance to say: "How can I hope in the Lord while your weakness often confronts me?," the son of the cross says: *Hope in God, for I will confess to him,* in other words, "I feel repentance for my sins, so that I cannot hinder Your devotion." Next comes the One to whom I will confess, the One who is the salvation of my countenance. The salvation of our countenance is Christ the Lord, who deigned to come without sin in the form of the servant, in which we ourselves live. As the prophet Jeremias says: *The breath of our mouth, Christ the Lord, is taken, under whose shadow we live among the Gentiles.*[11]

7. *My God, my soul is troubled by myself. Therefore I will remember thee, Lord, from the land of the Jordan.* He who was counselling his soul and rationally correcting his mind returns to the human condition and confesses, remarking that his soul is troubled by his own self. And that is true, for if the vices of the flesh failed to act in that way, the mind's purity would continue in its tranquillity. I believe that this reasoning has been quite aptly introduced so that man may clearly acknowledge the different elements in his make-up. But this son of the cross mentioned in the preliminary heading reveals the remedy by which each man can avoid troubles to his soul. He says: *Therefore I will remember thee, Lord, from the land of the Jordan. Therefore* implies "On account of these troubles, with which my soul is sorely afflicted." *I will remember thee, Lord* suggests "I hasten to You with all speed; to arrive there is my remedy, and clearly brings a fitting end to my physical evils." He also announces from where he will remember Him; it will be from the land of the Jordan, the place where the Lord earlier sanctified the blessings of baptism. The name of the river Jordan

means "their descent,"[12] for those who long to renew themselves with
that gift of the sacrament descend into the depth of the waters. Even
today we say of the baptised person, "He descends into the font."
Alternatively this descent denotes the humility which the baptised
person must have to follow the Lord's precepts. So long as we are
mindful of these things, we are not troubled by any disturbance
through the ills that befall us.

And from Hermoniim, the little hill. Hermoniim is a small mountain
situated near the Jordan as we know from reading Deuteronomy: *At
that time we took the land from the hands of the two kings of the Amor-
rhites, who were beside the Jordan from the torrent Arnon to the mountain Hermon.*[13] But let us see what further the meaning of this name
seems to indicate to us. Hermoniim means "anathema,"[14] which a man
pronounces on the devil when he comes to God. *From the little hill* is
well expressed, for God is not sought from the height of arrogance,
but is recollected in modest lowliness. So while we store in our memory the baptism which we have experienced, together with our lowliness, we obtain in a saving way by the Lord's gift the rules of faith
which we have adopted.

8. *Abyss invoketh abyss at the voice of thy cataracts. All thy heights and
thy billows have passed over me. Jordan, Hermoniim,* and *Abyss invoketh
abyss at the voice of thy cataracts* have together fashioned the figure of
sardismos,[15] which is always formed by a mixture of tongues. Jordan
and Hermoniim are Hebrew names, abyss and cataracts Greek words,
while "invoke" and "voice" are clearly Latin. So this figure is here
splendidly fashioned by a mingling of tongues. By the two abysses he
signifies the two Testaments, New and Old, which strengthen each
other by mutual witness when the Old foretells the New and the New
cites passages of the Old. So each invokes the other when by its
affirmation it bears witness to the other. Elsewhere the psalmist similarly says: *Thy judgments are a great abyss.*[16] The Lord's Testaments are
indeed deep, for they dwell in the bosom of Wisdom itself, in the
depth of truth. *At the voice of the cataracts* denotes the prophets and
apostles, for as a mass of water is vomited forth over cataracts, so the
waters of the Lord welled forth from their mouths. We fittingly associate heights and billows with the holy Scriptures; for it is the Scriptures which he earlier termed abysses, in which a billow of parables

sports, one might say, and heights of feelings intensify through devoted scrutiny. So the just man says that these passed over him, for that eager student had immersed himself in knowledge of them.

9. *In the daytime the Lord hath commanded his mercy, and at night hath declared it: with me is prayer to the God of my life.* Let us interpret *daytime* as the leisure-time in which the Lord's precepts are learned. We drink in his law at a time of tranquillity, for there is time to learn when there is nothing to hinder us. Next comes: *And at night hath declared it.* It is precisely what we learn in repose that we utter in tribulation. The words of the Law are learned in leisure, but their fruit is demonstrated in affliction. As we read in Scripture: *The mercy of God is beautiful in the time of affliction.*[7] So what is learnt by day is declared at night. He added: *With me is prayer to the God of my life,* as if he were saying "Within me is a sacrifice for me to offer to God." What is this sacrifice? It is precisely prayer, which God does not scorn, which He prefers to sacrificial victims if offered with the devotion of a pure heart. But this Lord is *the God of my life,* for when we die through our sins we are saved by the indulgence of His clemency.

10. *I will say to God: Thou art my support. Why hast thou forgotten me? Why hast thou rejected me? And why go I mourning while my enemy afflicteth me?* The son of Core had said earlier: *With me is prayer to the God of my life;* now he proclaims that he will make to the Lord the prayer earlier mentioned, which is: "Now that by the divine grace of baptism You have taken me up to be set through Your blessings in that native abode, why do You now allow me to be disturbed by various disasters through the devil's deceit?" The most holy man had realised how sweet that repose would be, and he stood fiercely aghast at the rocky roads of this world. He further says, as men do: *Why hast thou forgotten me?* for the promise which the Lord makes to His saints about the fatherland to come was still being postponed. *Why hast thou rejected me?* He still could not attain the rest which he so eagerly sought. *And why go I mourning while my enemy afflicteth me?* We are particularly morose when we suffer scourgings in this world, when we are tried by the deceitful thieving of our enemy, when we endure the sins of the flesh though our spirit is unconquered and wars on them. This figure is called *erotēma,*[18] when in our chagrin we exaggerate with repeated questions.

11. *While all my bones are broken, those who trouble me have reproached me.* We have often remarked that *bones* refers to strength of mind. So when the strength of our patience is under pressure, it is as if our bones are broken. When our enemies see this they mock at it, and they curse a person as though he were wicked if they perceive that no happiness of this world smiles on him.

While it is said to me day by day: Where is thy God? This is the reproach by which the bones of patience are broken as if by a hammer. Those who persecute and mock afflicted Christians are wont to say: "*Where is thy God?* Let Him deliver you if He can." How often have the martyrs heard this? How often confessors, who refused to yield to various tortures? This is a most famous expression, for it is continually addressed to those who suffer for Christ's name.

12. *Why art thou cast down, O my soul, and why dost thou disquiet me? Hope in God, for I will still give praise to him, the salvation of my countenance, my God.* We must investigate the point of this repetition of words, for it is clear that there is nothing superfluous or confused in this expression. I think that a five-part syllogism is perhaps found here, which Cicero reckons that orators should employ, so it is perfectly clear that they imitated rather than invented such rules.[19] Now let us cite the limbs of this argument one by one. The proposition is: *Why art thou sad, O my soul, and why dost thou trouble me? Hope in God, for I will still give praise to him, the salvation of my countenance.* The proof of the proposition is undoubtedly appended in the four verses that follow. Then the minor premise emerges: *I will say to God, Thou art my support: why hast thou forgotten me? Why hast thou rejected me? And why do I go mourning while my enemy afflicteth me?* The proof of the minor premise follows in two further verses. Finally there is introduced by way of repetition of the first verse the final conclusion of the syllogism which has been propounded: *Why art thou cast down, O my soul?* and the rest. This repetition is now held to be very common in the law of the five-part syllogism. It should not disturb you that the statement in the proposition appears to extend over two verses, but at the close is clearly abbreviated in one. It was appropriate that what is seen to be earlier proposed in more extended form should be summarised at the end.

Conclusion Drawn From the Psalm

This son of the cross at the beginning of the psalm wishes to reveal his notable longing, and so he chose for himself a meticulous parallel, so that we might believe that one known to have desired the Lord with such boundless aspiration loved Him uniquely. But evil manners always block good intentions in the normal way of men; and since the hostile spirit seeks to destroy with crafty abuse the person whom he cannot deceive by flattery, he says that he is moved to incessant tears by frequent insults. So that the sadness of this world should not seize his mind, or his mind undergo the hazards of desperation, he addresses consoling words to his soul so that he may dislodge from his heart that worldly anxiety which is the enemy of the faithful, and so that the weariness of desperation should not grip him. For Scripture says: *For the sorrow that is according to God worketh penance steadfast unto salvation, but the sorrow of the world worketh death.*[20] So he rightly tried to dislodge it from his heart, for he realised that eternal death loomed over him. So even today the Church appropriately sings this psalm, which induces goodly longing and instruction, over those to be baptised, so that once they are removed from the madness of this world, they may hasten to the Lord with total purity of heart. Good King, since there is more than one avenue of Your mercy, grant that just as You cleanse those who are baptised with the water of sacred rebirth, so You may purify us too from the dregs of sins by the gift of Your kindness.

COMMENTARY ON PSALM 42

1. *A psalm of David.* Though some headings contain many words and others fewer, all are directed towards works of divine contemplation in such a way that variation avoids tedium yet does not cease to offer necessary advice. So *psalm,* as we have often said, means a song of heavenly words which we feel re-echoes to us from above. For example, this one will say: *Distinguish my cause from the nation that is*

not holy, and the rest. *David* represents for us the Christ of great strength for whom we long, to whom the psalm is addressed by one who speaks as a most faithful Christian, whose mind and concentration are longingly directed upon Him. Just as the previous psalm teaches us that all things are of little account so that longing for the Lord may be uniquely sought, so this one forewarns us that we cannot be disturbed by worldly affliction, but says that we must rejoice in the Lord's halls. It proves that the medicine so often prescribed by the devoted Physician is most necessary for our ailments.

Division of the Psalm

Each and every one of the faithful will aptly apply the psalm to himself. In the first section he begs the Lord to be delivered from association with the unfaithful when Christ at His last coming arrives to judge the world. In the second part he expresses confidence that he will go to the Lord's altar, where only the blessed are allowed to enter. So he says that his soul will not be troubled by anxieties in this world, for it already glories in the hope of the heavenly gift.

Explanation of the Psalm

Judge me, O God, and distinguish my cause from the nation that is not holy. When the faithful person was troubled by wicked deeds in this world, and while he still mingled in the same dwelling with unbelievers, he suddenly burst into speech, asking that when the Lord passes judgment, his cause may be separated from that of the wicked, when He will set the lambs on His right and the goats on His left. He does not ask to have his sins dispelled, but to be freed from association with the wicked. It would be dangerous to ask: *Judge me*, unless he added: *And distinguish my cause*, that is, "End the intermingling which I endure in this world, and when You have at last separated me from the wicked, set me among the chosen ones of your people." He added: *That is not holy*, referring to those living a perverted and wicked life. His moral sense is truly holy, for he could not even gaze on his neighbour and behold the things known to be opposed to the divine commands.

Deliver me from the unjust and deceitful man. This is indeed a goodly desire, but as yet he has not reached fulfillment; what is now sought by this holy man is obtained by the faithful only at the future judgment. But those known to be peace-makers seek such aims also in this life, so that they long to be isolated from troublesome behaviour so as not to be debased by any wickedness. The unjust man is he who does evil deeds more openly; the deceitful man is he who attacks by devious plotting, like all men known to be strangers to the Lord's commands.

2. *For thou art my God and my courage: why hast thou cast me off? And why do I go saddened while the enemy afflicteth me?* Often the reason precedes the cause, and frequently it follows as an appendage, but here he proclaims his theme at the beginning. Since God is his courage, he wonders why he still seems to be debarred from that coming of the Lord at which He will judge the world, when it is for His sake that he endured with great longing the hardships of the world which he suffered. For courage is the considered endurance of dangers and the unwearied trial of toils.[1] The most holy man knew that he could not be saddened further if he attained the eternal rest of the world to come. It is the habit of those who have an aspiration, that they believe they have been debarred from that which they are not allowed to attain speedily. A splendid elaboration of this point follows: *And why do I go saddened while the enemy afflicteth me?* It is in this world that holy men especially go saddened, since they suffer the most savage scourges of their enemies. When the day of judgment comes, they will cease entirely to suffer such things, for the Enemy with his followers will be totally condemned. So the holy man longingly aspired to the time when he knew blessedness was to be bestowed on him.

3. *Send forth thy light and thy truth: they have conducted me and brought me unto thy holy hill, and into thy tabernacle.* Here he explains the means of dispelling his sadness: that the Father should send His Son, who is the Light and the Truth, to pass judgment. Christ said of Himself: *I am the light of the world;*[2] and elsewhere; *I am the way and the truth and the life.*[3] When this Light and Truth which is the Lord Christ comes, all the grief of disturbance departs from His holy ones, since they will obtain the glory of eternal blessedness. So this faithful man, who we have earlier said is speaking, says that he has been

conducted and brought to the holy hill, that is, to firm belief in the Lord Saviour. He allots all things to the Lord's glory, and attributes nothing to his own powers. With the addition: *And into thy tabernacle*, he refers to the Catholic Church established in its struggle with this world; it is still troubled with the diverse weariness which the Enemy brings. But we have noted the word *tabernacle*; so let us beware of ambush by our Foe, for as long as the Church is in its tabernacles we cannot by any means enjoy untroubled leisure. The words of Exodus depict this tabernacle in a clear description, so that it is presented almost to our very eyes as well as to our ears.[4]

4. *And I will go into the altar of God, to God who giveth joy to my youth. To thee, O God my God, I will give praise upon the harp.* He comes to the second section. But while the Church too has her altar here, it is not otiose that after mention of the tabernacle he says: *I will go into the altar of God.* The altar is something raised high, at present beyond our sight. Only the just are known to approach it, for among the other constituents of the tabernacle which the Lord ordered His servant Moses to build up, He clearly pointed to this with the words: *Look, and make it according to the pattern that was shewn thee in the mount.*[5] This is the altar which is referred to. The undivided crowd of the Church seeks it, but only those pleasing to God can attain to that which the psalmist says that he is to enter in the future. The word *altare* stands for *altae arae* (high altars) or *alta res* (high thing).[6] Next comes: *To God who giveth joy to my youth.* The psalmist writes *youth* here because of the newness of life owed to the Lord Saviour, who renews all things from their defective and decrepit state, and has restored the most powerful strength of youth to believers, See how when saddened by worldly disasters he brought joy to himself by his goodly understanding. He gives praise on the harp, for in enduring this world's hardships he does not abandon the Lord's praise.

5. *Why art thou sad, O my soul? And why doest thou disquiet me? Hope in God, for I will give praise to him, the salvation of the countenance, my God.* Let us recall that these lines were contained also in the previous psalm,[7] where we said there was a five-part syllogism. But we must ponder the fact that he both often warns us and most emphatically persuades us that we must avoid such worldly sadness; and rightly so, for it is always inimical to what is good. Through it the strength of patience is broken, the light of charity is snuffed out, and our hope's

longing and virtue grows soft. Thus the whole of our life is turned upside down when this malevolent wickedness stalks abroad. That truly vital sadness, the peace and continual joy of good hearts which is to be sought by the most vehement prayers of the blessed, is described by Paul: *Brothers, I am glad not because you were made sorrowful, but because you were made sorrowful unto penance. For you were made sorrowful according to God.*[8] The phrase is the same, but the situation is different; the first sadness directs us to death, but the second guides us to enduring salvation.

Conclusion Drawn From the Psalm

In previous psalms we read that many spokesmen have been introduced to lift to the peak of virtue the spirits of those perfected. Now it is the Church, now the penitent, now the prophet, now Idithun, now the sons of Core[9] speaking with great strength of patience. But here the words are modest and more gentle as befits the devoted Christian, so that no individual however weak may lose confidence in his own humble powers, since through God's grace each one finds a target to hasten towards with concentrated mind. The number 42 is appropriately suited to the person who longs to attain the Lord's halls, for the hallowed encampments of the Jews in the desert were of that number.[10] It was in the forty-second generation from Abraham[11] that the Lord Saviour came and saved the world by His coming, so it is rightly believed that this faithful spokesman known to have been associated with this ancient number will attain the Lord's kingdom. So the faithful soul[12] finds here all virtues and all pleasures; thus whoever obtains that spark of divine love can console and renew himself by God's grace.

COMMENTARY ON PSALM 43

1. *Unto the end. A psalm of David for the sons of Core, to give understanding.* The meaning of *sons of Core* has been sufficiently explained, most recently in Psalm 41. But here *to give understanding* appears to

have been added without precedent but with the purpose of reminding us that this psalm must be more carefully studied. We are to hear the martyrs or confessors, who are the sons of the cross,[1] proclaim that while our fathers kept their enemies in subjection without difficulty by God's dispensation, they themselves by divine help sought their victories through the most stern punishments of martyrdom. But here we need a deeper understanding, so that we may reconcile the Lord's deeds with His splendid designs. Initially the wondrous events of the Red Sea and the painless victories over different nations were their lot, so that such a notable miracle could entice the ignorant people to believe in God's power. Then the land of Chanaan was promised specifically to those who lived under the law. But now with the increase of their faith worldly prosperity has been removed from the martyrs, so that human weakness should not aspire too tepidly to the blessings of the world to come; the kingdom of heaven was promised to those known to be subject to grace. So this is the understanding to be sought, this is the grace to be maintained: what happens today is ordained by the Creator of the world for the salvation of all, usually by hidden workings.

Division of the Psalm

Whether you regard the words as those of martyrs or of confessors, you must realise that the psalm has been fashioned with a wonderful structure. In the first part they say that they have heard that their fathers experienced the favour of the Lord, and beheld the victories which they gained over innumerable nations; but they proclaim that they themselves will fittingly witness retribution from their enemies at the Lord's coming judgment. In this way the two kinds of benefits which the Lord deigns to bestow on His servants are recounted separately. In the second section they recount the pains of the different straits which they suffer in this world, but they claim that they have not been so forgetful of God's commands as to refrain from persevering in the virtue of patience. In the third part they pray for aid, so that being harshly afflicted they may be lent help at the time of the resurrection.

Explanation of the Psalm

2. *O God, we have heard with our ears: our fathers have declared to us the work thou hast wrought in their days, in the days of old.* The psalmist put *O God* first, the exordium of either the joyful man or the one wounded with harsh oppression. But so that the words which they are to speak may not be thought dubious, they state that they have heard them with their own ears, so as to obtain greater credence for them. Note that they do not say that young or youthful people have told them of the events that have happened, but their fathers, who by virtue of their title could make a claim to truth. *Our* is attached to *fathers* so that they could tell their children what is wholly indubitable. *Have declared to us:* in other words, have recounted the kindnesses which they wanted to be clearly evident to their descendants for the glory of God. Though God by His daily working maintains the world by His benefits so that the universe runs on according to its established law, we say that He has wrought a work when He has shown us some unprecedented sign. So they attest that their fathers have told them of the work which the Lord has wrought in their days, that is in days of old, when He transported the people of Israel unharmed across the waters of the Red Sea, and made them victorious over their enemies without any toil of their own. This proof is called "From words and deeds of ancestors,"[2] when weight of testimony is strengthened by the most telling authority of our fathers.

3. *Thy hand destroyed the Gentiles, and thou plantedst them: thou didst afflict the people and cast them out.* From here there follows a noble account of the great blessings which God's power accorded to the people of Israel, so that the Lord's kindnesses may shine more clearly in both the successes and the reverses which they are to relate. *Hand* denotes power, an expression often used, for the Gentiles are said in metaphor to have been afflicted by the Lord's hand through which above all we perform our tasks. When the Amorites or the others departed from their lands,[3] we read that the Jews are set in their abodes; they are manifestly *planted*, for in the course of days they swelled by steady growth through God's kindness. He afflicted the people their foes, when at the sound of the priests' trumpets the walls of Jericho broke up and collapsed at the blast; clearly they were expelled from the city, since they could not withstand such great miracles.[4]

4. *For they got not the possession of the land by their own sword: neither did their own arm save them.* So that the Jews should not believe that they triumphed through their own powers, they proclaim that they were not victorious *by their own sword,* nor did they claim the Gentiles' land by their own courage. We use *arm* to denote strength since men fight by engaging their arms; but it was not this arm which succeeded in freeing them from their enemies, but God's power which saved them in a unique way. Thus as the history of the Jews is expounded, teaching is offered which is of benefit to the human race.

But thy right hand and thy arm, and the light of thy countenance, because thou wast pleased with them. We must interpret *but thy right hand and thy arm, and the light of thy countenance* as meaning "jointly saved them." The right hand signifies the successful part, the arm, strength, the light, the plan which the Lord bestows on those in battle when He deigns to grant victory. But so that the people would not say: "Your fathers were pleasing through their merits, and so won such great favours from the Lord," they commented that this was not granted to their merits but because God, who gives freely all that He bestows, so willed it. Also: *He was pleased with them,* since they were chosen from the whole world as the only nation from which the Lord Saviour was to come.

5. *Thou art thyself my king and my God: who commandest the saving of Jacob.* When the sons of Core, the people of the blessed, said: *Thou art thyself my king,* that is, the Lord Saviour to whom the name of King is clearly apt, they added: *And my God,* so that you would not doubt that this is the Lord Christ Jesus, who also mercifully granted salvation to our father Jacob when He made him wrestle with the angel in glorious contest.[5] He commanded the saving of Jacob when Jacob heard through the angel: *Thy name shall not now be called Jacob, but Israel;*[6] for we usually issue through another person any command which is the decision of our will.

6. *Through thee we will push down our enemies: and through thy name we will despise them that rise up against us.* The martyrs have passed on to that glorious species of freedom which we know is to be granted to the faithful at the time of the Judgment. After being exhausted through extreme oppression, they regain their spirits and console themselves with the happiness to come, saying: *Through thee we will push down our enemies.* The enemies are to be pushed down at the time

of God's judgment, when our Saviour separates the straw from the grain when He shakes the threshing-floor with the winnowing-shovel of His judgment. Next comes: *And through thy name we will despise them that rise up against us.* They that rise up, the impure spirits, will be held in contempt when they cannot inflict harm; at present they do the despising, but subsequently just men will presume that they are to be despised. The statement that the Lord's hand destroyed the Gentiles, and planted the Jews in their abodes and allowed them to overcome their enemies without any toil, refers to time here; but the pushing down of the enemy and the despising of the ancient foe belong to the future Judgment, when a victory of such dimensions is to be gained that all contests are known to cease.

7. *For I will not trust in my bow, neither shall my sword save me.* With their usual faith and humility the crowd of saints declares that they will not trust earthly arms. The *bow* is the warrior's protection, and the human mind puts trust in it; but worldly fighters put more faith in the sword. Often an arrow is discharged without effect, but the sword causes most certain death. So they say that what men think is their most effective protection in war does not bring them any help.

8. *For thou hast delivered us from them that afflict us, and hast put them to shame that hate us.* With the confidence of faith they speak of the future as it if were the past; they have no doubts of what they are quite sure will come to pass. So they say that at the Lord's second coming they are to be delivered from the persecution of most wicked spirits, who never cease to afflict them here with wily attacks of various kinds. At that future time they will truly be delivered when they are removed from the power of those spirits, so that they cannot take further joy in exhausting innocent men. This certainly cannot normally happen in this world. Those who hate the blessed are likewise put to shame when condemned to eternal vengeance, whereas the kingdom of heaven welcomes the just.

9. *In God shall we be praised all the day long: and in thy name we will give praise for ever.* Those who say: *Shall we be praised* claim that they will be hymned in the future, but they point to their glory without arrogance, for they witness that their praise will be *in God. All the day long* denotes continuing time which has no night, which will come to be in that eternity when the proclamation of the blessed is known to be uninterrupted. But so that you may not think that those who said

they would be praised in God will be idle, they maintain that they also continually utter praises of the Lord; for this is the happiness of the just, to praise the Lord unceasingly. This is the fullness which can never know satiety, the hunger not brought forth by abstinence, the greed which does not spring from fasting.

10. *But now thou hast cast us off and put us to shame: and thou, O God, wilt not go out with our armies.* After mention of that indescribable reward in the age to come, the devoted martyrs passed to the second section. In these eight later verses they tell of the sufferings they endured at the present time, yet they never abandoned in the least their reverence for the Lord. This figure is called *emphasis* or *exaggeratio*,[7] when we make some claim by assembling many griefs so as to obtain the judge's indulgence by recounting our disasters. The words, *but now*, indicate that earlier they have been speaking of the future era. Notice how the whole sequence runs on in admirable order. *Thou hast cast us off* denotes the delay which holy persons undoubtedly experience because perfect blessedness is promised them not here but in the future. *Thou hast put us to shame* refers to that glorious shame borne by the martyrs when afflicted with injuries, beaten by clubs, constantly exposed to charges and consigned to death. It is of such persons that the apostle also speaks: *Of whom the world was not worthy.*[8] But observe that martyrs are put to shame among wicked men in this life, whereas the unholy will endure burdens of everlasting censure before the true Judge; the shame of this world will lead to glory, but that of the next to unending destruction. But now God does not go out with His armies of martyrs, when He subjects them to afflictions and consigns them to diverse sufferings. Earlier He went out with His armies of the Jews when those who tried to withstand the chosen people were brought low without a struggle. Undoubtedly this is germane to the consolation of a holy people, that none should be resentful that their fathers have been most blessed, whereas they themselves are afflicted with the Lord's permission.

11. *Thou hast made us turn our back before our enemies: and they that hated us plundered for themselves.* They attest that they were routed in this world before their enemies, when they avoided dangers at the hands of pursuers. Turning one's back means avoiding a physical enemy; so we are enjoined, *if they persecute you in this city, flee unto another.*[9] Next comes: *And they that hated us plundered for themselves.*

This is usually the fate of those put to flight; they become loot and plunder, since they have not been able to show the least resistance to their foes.

12. *Thou hast given us up like sheep to be eaten: thou hast scattered us among the nations.* When they say: *Thou hast given us up,* they indicate that everything is allotted by divine power, for they recount that they have been consigned to the Gentiles as if to wolves which habitually devour the tender flock. The tame simplicity of the sheep, the food of the wolves, is aptly compared with the martyrs who resign themselves to being killed by their persecutors without a struggle. Next comes: *And thou hast scattered us among the nations.* They designate here the various faithful persons whom the martyrs' piety now laments; they were consigned to the Gentiles, and lost their freedom with their inheritance. This has happened through God's dispensation to the Christian people at various times so that they may attain eternal blessings of glorious happiness through the ills of transient tribulations.

13. *Thou hast sold thy people for no price: and there was no multitude received in the exchange of them.* We must not interpret this as a rebuke but as an utterance with the usual mystical allusion. God seems to receive a price when He subjects infidels to His deserving people. He consigns unbelievers to them to obtain most devoted followers. But God sells *for no price* when some foreigner consigns the Christian people to affliction, and this happens often by His secret decision so that we may attain the merit of being tried, or may achieve correction. Note that this mode of speaking is numbered among those peculiar to divine Scripture; the word *sold* is used though clearly no price was paid. He added: *And there was no multitude received in the exchange of them.* Men who deal in exchanges obtain things equal to those which they impart, but in this case no multitude is gained by God as a price to compensate for the great loss when Christians are betrayed, for their persecutors are seen to be unacceptable to God. How could they be welcome to the true God, enclosed as they were in their unholy superstitions?

14. *Thou hast placed us as a reproach to our neighbours, a derision and contempt to those that are round about us.* They recount the degree of affliction by which they were shattered, so that the nature of their devotion might be increased amidst these numerous hardships. The affliction which we suffer from neighbours is oppressive, for charges

continually laid by bystanders are not said to be fleeting. The phrase, *Thou hast placed us,* shows that the suffering does not pass; if a person is known to be placed anywhere, he is thought to be there for a long time. Reproach is the antonym of the honourable; as all honourable things are fitting, so all reproaches are unfitting. But this reproach was not in God's sight but before the eyes of neighbours, who were able to make judgments which a depraved intuition was trained to observe. *Derision* is the inarticulate noise of joy indicating its insult with unrestrained amusement; *contempt* denotes that most abject condition of scorn which the Lord's martyrs when betrayed endured with diverse sufferings. *They that are round about us* denote the unfaithful and traitorous who always walk on every side and are not in step with us in right beliefs.

15. *Thou hast placed us likewise before the Gentiles: a shaking of the head among the people.* Notice the figure of *anaphora,* which in Latin is called *relatio,*[10] the repetition of the verb, *Thou hast placed,* already used at the beginning of the previous verse. The frequent repetition intensifies the force of their suffering, for it is clear that the martyrs like Christ were set before the Gentiles, when the Gentiles inflicted equal pain and tortures on them. Head-shaking by enemies befell the martyrs, just as it took place at the Lord Saviour's passion, for we read that *they spoke with the lips and wagged the head.*[11]

16. *All the day long my shame is before me, and the confusion of my face hath covered me.* Shame usually floods in momentarily, and within a short time is quietened and departs; but this shame was most oppressive, since it remained continually. The unbounded shame and fierce confusion of the holy ones was apparent to them, when they saw the men they knew to be impious continually insulting them. Observe how fine is the ensuing description of the shame. They say that their faces are covered, so to say, with a cloak of confusion, for they were ruddy and aflame with a blood-red glow. But when they say: *Hath covered me,* this denotes not only a change of countenance but the bristling of the whole body.

17. *At the voice of him that reproacheth and detracteth me: at the face of the enemy and persecutor.* The description of the confusion continues up to this verse, and now is recounted the cause of that rosy blush clothing the naked appearance of their complexion. To reproach is to abuse face to face, to launch graceless criticisms; to detract is to pull a

person to pieces in his absence, and to afflict him with crafty and biting words. *At the face of the enemy,* in other words, while eyeing at close quarters one who feels mortal hatred for them. So that you would not underrate this foe, they added: *And persecutor.* This is known to be the keenest hatred, for such men seek not only to kill the body, but by their wickedness to slaughter the very soul.

18. *All these things have come upon us, yet we have not forgotten thee: and we have not done wickedly in thy covenant.* The sons of Core have come to the expression of the most splendid constancy of their faith, to show us that no ills whatever ought to separate us from Christ's grace. As Paul says: *Who shall separate us from the love of Christ? Shall tribulation or distress or famine or nakedness?*[12] and the rest. By saying: *All these things,* they gather together what they have said in the previous discussion, so that if their impact was less weighty when fragmented, the effect may be powerful when accumulated. This argument is called "From tortures,"[13] since the spirit of the faithful could be in no way affected by all these ills. *Have come upon us,* that is, like a fearful beast or stormy river. Because heavy affliction usually drives out of men's minds what they previously seemed to believe, they add that they have not forgotten the Lord among such diverse hardships. Rather, the persecution by wicked men moved them to demand help continually from the Lord. Next comes: *And we have not done wickedly in thy covenant.* This is the same claim as *we have not forgotten thee.* Those who keep Him in mind cannot forget His covenant. Whereas the normal Latin form is *Obliti non sumus tui,* it is peculiar to divine Scripture to have *Obliti non sumus te.*[14]

19. *And our heart hath not turned back: and thou hast turned aside our paths from thy way.* Those who despair of the Lord's goodness, and think that He does not help them though begged to do so, experience a turning back of the heart, for He is known to aid even those who do not ask. But the sons of Core certainly did not experience this turning back; they were shown to have hope in the Lord. The psalmist used *paths* here in the bad sense, calling them *ours* as being the shadowy and pleasurable tracks which frail humanity treads. We journey on them when we are remote from the Lord's commands. Way (*via*) gets its name from violence (*violentia*);[15] it is rightly called Christ's way because His faithful walk as He did in trials and tribulations. So human paths are most appropriately said to be separated from the way to

heaven because they lead to execrable death, whereas the heavenly way undoubtedly bestows the salvation we long for. So the sons of Core were truly the sons of the most holy cross when they had such thoughts as these.

20. *For thou hast humbled us in the place of affliction: and the shadow of death hath covered us.* They offer the reason why they have maintained that the *way* and the *paths* were separated; it was because they attest that they were *humbled in the place of affliction,* that is, in the world, which is for the faithful a place of affliction from which remorse is born and repentance follows. Next comes: *And the shadow of death hath covered us.* They speak of the passage of this life, known to be shared by holy men and sinners; but the true death is that by which the wicked are punished with eternal damnation.

21. *If we have forgotten the name of our God, and if we have spread forth our hands to a strange god.* This is the understanding of the faithful which the psalm-heading mentioned baldly, that they should acknowledge no strange god, and that they should not forget Him to whose name they have been dedicated with the mark of the cross. With *and if we have spread forth our hands to a strange god,* they describe a person at prayer who with hands outstretched refashions with his body's posture the cross which he receives on his forehead. The truly faithful performed this not for a strange god but for none other than their Lord, so that perseverance should maintain the fidelity of those unaffected by so many adversities.

22. *Surely God shall search out these things? For he knoweth the secrets of the heart. Surely* is to be emphasised forcefully, since the Lord regards as most serious any sinning in His religion. We usually *search out* when we desire to ascertain things which we realise our knowledge does not possess. But God searches out with knowledge, not so that He may Himself learn anything, but to make us learn things buried in oblivion. So Abraham likewise was told: *Now I know that thou fearest thy God,*[16] as though God at that moment had learnt something, whereas He foreknew it before all time began. The following expression, *These things,* refers to what was previously said: *If we have forgotten the name of our God, and if we have spread forth our hands to a strange god.* And since religious feeling was under discussion, and this is evinced not only by bodily devotion but even more in the recess of

the heart, they hastened to mention God's knowledge, towards which all purity of heart strains, with the words: *For he knoweth the secrets of the heart.*

Because for thy sake we are killed all the day long: we are counted as sheep for the slaughter. Those most blessed men explain their secret words; they were dying not for committing some crime but for love of God, so that most salutary belief in the Trinity might be increased among the nations. To be visited by death means ending the present life through extended sufferings, and this is what perfect Christians do when oppressed by distracting observances. To force you to notice this all the more, *all the day long* is added, so that this could describe not instantaneous death but that extermination of the faithful which is drawn out through the whole period of life. Note the following words: *We are counted as sheep for the slaughter.* Because a sheep does not have the weapons to fight back, it is known to be despised by its plunderers; it does not possess strength of horns, and does not battle with its teeth or take anticipatory flight, but it patiently remains quiet in the robber's hands, not struggling to defend itself. In the same way Christ's servants were thought to die like sheep, for they were seen to be slaughtered without any resistance.

23. *Arise, why sleepest thou, O Lord? Arise, and cast us not off to the end.* Once they had recounted their long list of sufferings, the sons of Core came to the third section, in which they seek aid with such ardour that they even state that the Lord has fallen asleep. This is the figure called *catachresis,* which we rightly call "wrong use," for it attaches an inappropriate label to things.[17] To say that God rises is inapposite, for He is known never to sleep. But because of our human usage we say that He is asleep when our hope is deferred by divine dispensation. If you investigate the power of His majesty, you come upon the clearest of statements: *Behold, he that keepeth Israel neither sleeps nor nods.*[18] The word *arise* is repeated so that He may not refuse to help those whose dangers He sees increasing. Next comes: *And cast us not off to the end;* that is, "Even if You think that You should put us off now, do not reject us at the last, for then the total perfection of Your gift is evinced, and the rewards of the blessed appear, and crowns are prepared for martyrs."

24. *Why turnest thou thy face away, and forgettest our want and our*

trouble? Weighed down as they are by their present ills, they continue their tearful entreaty as the blessed do with the words: "Why do You consider that we must be put off for so long, so that men think You ignore us, since You have postponed Your help?" Next comes: *And forgettest our want,* the sense being "You were accustomed to assist that want which You love so much in others that You proclaim yourself to be in need; for You who are most rich came to aid our poverty." He added: *And our trouble,* for He always looks on it with kindly eyes. As He is to say in Psalm 50: *A contrite and humbled heart God does not despise.*[19] Such pleas have the greatest efficacy with that devoted Judge, though known to be held in contempt by human arbiters.

25. *For our soul is humbled down to the dust: our belly cleaveth to the earth.* After a pause so that they may be heard, these devoted minds had recourse not to the recklessness of desperation, but to the salutary aspirations of continual prayer, for here is expounded the satisfaction gained by diligent intercession. They prostrate themselves in the dust; in recalling their sins they torture their souls by sprinkling ashes over themselves. Next comes: *Our belly cleaveth to the earth.* Those who prostrate themselves in prolonged prayer and stretch themselves out to the full length of their bodies do precisely this. Cleaving to the earth denotes lingering longer in the prayers by which sins are effectively overcome. The great armoury against the devil is not confidence in one's own powers, but supplication to God, for He can repress the enemy.

26. *Arise, O Lord, to help us, and free us for thy name's sake.* Appended to the great afflictions is a most sweet close. They ask to be freed by the glory of the Lord's resurrection, when as we know the hope of all Christians is answered. *Arise* is to be understood as referring not to sleep but to the resurrection; for earlier, when they wished so to say to rouse Him, they asked: *Why sleepest thou?* But here the word is merely *arise,* so we must understand it as the resurrection in which the abolition of human slavery is visible. By His resurrection we are aided, and by His ascension to heaven we are freed. He bestowed all this on us not for our merits but for His name's sake. The Saviour is mentioned because He saves the weak through the grace of His devoted love.

Conclusion Drawn From the Psalm

See how the saving words of the sons of Core have shone on us; see how the Church's dispensation has enlightened us with God's revelation. We see that our fathers were miraculously and visibly freed from their enemies, but now we the faithful have learned to attain our eternal rest through physical suffering and sadness of soul, and so each experience at its own time is seen here to have been profitable to the human race; no-one will complain at seeing himself oppressed by this world's hardships. Moreover, the martyrs' voices swell with the freedom of innocence, when God is said to be asleep and forgetful; this statement should not be taken as a rebuke but as one uttered with the deliberation of deep feeling. We find this very often also in the Book of Job, so that unless you subject it to careful examination you will interpret it as complaints rather than entreaties. But this modest presumption of just men seems to proclaim the purity of a sincere heart, so that simplicity of spirit may appear to express the weight of suffering imposed on them. So whenever we find some such expression in the divine Scriptures, the mercy of the Lord and the purity of the suppliant are being revealed.

COMMENTARY ON PSALM 44

1. *Unto the end, for them that shall be changed, for the sons of Core, for understanding, a canticle for the beloved.* Let us see what these words when weighed individually bear for us, because the psalm-heading is prolonged with the accumulation of many words. *Unto the end* is often used to signify perfection, in other words, the Lord Saviour. *For them that shall be changed, for the sons of Core* has this sense: the sons of the cross who remain within the Church will pass from the sadness of this world to enduring glory. *For understanding, a canticle* explains the text of the psalm, which is to be drawn out to obtain that heavenly understanding in which are contained the spiritual mysteries of future events. *For the beloved* is to be understood as the Lord Christ; the

Father's resounding words; *This is my beloved son in whom I am well pleased,*[1] referred to Him. The spiritual marriage of Christ is now described, and prayers to Him are celebrated with the praise of the marriage-song. His virtue is above all virtues, His beauty above all beauties, His power indescribable, His devotion unique. O blessed bride, known to be joined to such great majesty not in the alliance of the flesh but in the unbreakable bond of love! When will you be seen to be joined to Him who has invested you with His own most radiant light? So let us pray most devotedly to His divinity, so that when we have sailed out with the greatest purity of heart towards that contemplative light, we may turn our ears of the spirit to the marriage with His holy bride.

Division of the Psalm

The prophet is surfeited with His heavenly feast and filled with the nature of his future joy. He promises that He will belch forth the Lord's praise so that the faithful people may obtain most abundant food from the source from which he himself was filled with heavenly generosity. He celebrates a kind of heavenly epithalamium, as has been remarked, with the joy appropriate to marriage. Now *epithalamium* means "praise of the marriage-chamber" offered to the heavenly Bridegroom after the manner of human beings. The first part of it contains praise of the Bridegroom, the Lord Saviour, in four modes. In the second part the bride, the Church, is praised for her mystical virtues with the same number of four sections. The most wise Solomon has also described this in a very well-known passage in the book called Song of Songs. So we append exemplary passages from the Book in this psalm as the occasion demands; thus those who praise, though separated by their eras, may appear to have spoken the one message with the harmony of prophecy.

Explanation of the Psalm

2. *My heart has belched forth a good word: I speak my works to the king. My tongue is the pen of a scrivener that writeth swiftly.* Since the prophet knew that his understanding was pervaded by the brightness

of God's gift, he was impelled by the greatness of his very joy to utter
prior praise of his future words, and this not through joyful zeal but
because he was moved by a feeling for the truth. We use the word
belched when the abundant food which we have eaten emits vapour
which allows the healthiest digestion. But how great was the spiritual
feast with which this man had been so filled that he belched forth the
secret source of so goodly an odour~! Understand by *my heart* the
recess of the mind. By *a good word* he means the Son of God of whom
the evangelist John said: *In the beginning was the Word, and the Word
was with God, and the Word was God.*[2] The Truth itself says of itself:
None is good but God alone.[3] *Works* means the prophet's little composition, his offering of the fine texture of this psalm through his voice's
ministry, his making the divine words resound by the organ of his
tongue as if he were penning them. He was eager to speak to the King
his proclamation which he had composed about His marvellous renown. But so that none would think that he was saying anything
which he himself had willed, he compared his tongue to a scrivener's
pen; it will faithfully express the words of the holy Spirit as a pen
depicts on paper the aspirations of our thought. He added: *That writeth swiftly.* We ought to interpret this scrivener rather as a stenogra-
pher who speedily understands words, and more speedily transcribes
what he has heard. We must realise that the virtue of prophecy is
revealed here. It does not order its thought painfully in a human way,
but reveals the commands of the Godhead with no spite. Let us now
listen to the prophet, who is to utter without flattery his laudatory
marriage-song. It amplifies nothing but the truth; it charms, but without loss of integrity; and though it utters great things, it still falls short
of the reality.

3. *Thou art beautiful above the sons of men: grace is poured abroad in
thy lips: therefore hath God blessed thee for ever.* Having completed the
exordium, and having suitably aroused the people to eager listening,
he has begun his praise of the Lord's incarnation. Just as through this
we have deserved to learn the secrets of the Godhead, so we must also
through it hear the praise of such great majesty. The orators call this
type of praise the *a forma.*[4] But since in Isaiah we read: *We have seen
him, and he had no sightliness or beauty, but his look was without honour
and despised before all men,*[5] can we elicit why He is here described as
more beautiful than the human race? It is not because His beauty

gleamed out from the glory of a milky complexion, or shone from blonde hair, or was outstanding for noble bearing; the truth is that He was more beautiful than the human race because He was sinless. We rightly call beautiful that which is adorned with the grace of the most unspotted purity, though father Augustine says[6] that the beauty of the Lord's body merited praise. But the passage of Isaiah quoted earlier referred to the time of His passion, when we read that He was buffeted by blows, crowned with thorns, and rained with spittle. We read in the Song of Songs of the Church which bears the image of the Lord Saviour: *I am black and beautiful,*[7] that is, black physically and beautiful in heavenly merits. He demonstrates why he used the word beautiful: as Christ put it, the world was reconciled to God through grace.[8] What could there be in the human race comparable to the vision of Him incarnate, through whom the whole world received the gift of redemption? The book of Solomon which has been mentioned speaks of Him in these words: *Thy lips and thy speech are sweet.*[9] Next comes: *Therefore hath God blessed thee for ever. Therefore* means "because of your outstanding preaching and devotion in all respects unique"; for He has bestowed nothing on anyone according to merit, but rather has granted all things by His goodness. He is blessed for ever because His kingdom will have no end. *God hath blessed thee* well described His role as servant, which both endured the passion and attained the kingdom of heaven.

4. *Gird thy sword about thy thigh, O thou most mighty, with thy comeliness and beauty.* Here is introduced the second mode of praise of the Lord Saviour; it is called a *potestate.*[10] The prophet is exalted to joy unknown, and begs the Lord to make his delayed and most salutary appearance as the nations await Him. He says: *Gird thy sword;* the metaphor is adopted from the warrior who is girt with the sword when about to fight to bring the enemy low. But here we must interpret *sword* as the words of proclamation. Christ himself attests this in the gospel: *I came not to send peace but the sword.*[11] And Paul speaks of *the sword of the spirit, which is the word of God.*[12] The sword means God's word, for with the force of its strength it bursts into the hearts of men which are gross with sins; man's weakness cannot resist where the glory of that strength deigns to enter. *Thigh* signifies the incarnation of the Lord Saviour. As we read in Genesis: *The ruler shall not be*

taken away from Juda, nor the leader from his thigh.[13] Moreover, in that divine mystery Abraham made his servant take an oath, and the servant was bound to him by swearing the oath after touching his thigh.[14] The psalmist joined to *thigh* the words, *O thou most mighty,* so that you would believe that the Incarnation taken on by the power of the Godhead was to be reverenced. In the same sense that wisest of men said: *The sword is on the thigh.*[15] He added next: *With thy comeliness and beauty.* Here we clearly identify the description of two natures, comeliness referring to His humanity, and beauty to His divinity. *Comeliness* is a good expression for His saving appearance in the world, and beauty is most appropriately used for the source of all beautiful and seemly things.

5. *Observe and come forth prosperously, and reign; because of truth and meekness and justice; and thy right hand shall conduct thee wonderfully.* So far the event of the most holy Incarnation is explained, and the power of the miracle is proclaimed by each and every word. *Observe* means that He should look down with pity from heaven on man who is close to death. In the words of Psalm 13: *The Lord hath looked down from heaven upon the children of men.*[16] *Prosperously,* because He was to provide the benefits of liberation to the human race. *Come forth,* as the Bridegroom from the maiden's womb; in the words of Scripture: *And he as a bridegroom coming out of his bridechamber.*[17] *Reign,* that is show the power of Your majesty amongst men that believe; but the Son, even before the foundation of the world, undoubtedly reigned with the Father and the holy Spirit. *Because of truth* indicates that truth sprang from the earth to cleanse our false nature with its brightness. *Meekness* was demonstrated when He prayed for His persecutors as He was nailed to the cross. *Justice* has reference to the fact that the devoted Teacher poured into us saving precepts. *Shall conduct thee,* that is, will guard you through the course of your life in sinless behaviour. *Wonderfully,* because in contrast to the usual way of the world which withheld belief He was to rise from the dead on the third day; this miracle swept through regions of the whole globe. *Thy right hand* means the thrust of Your will; for if He does all things by His power, as He clearly does, how can He have someone greater? But the remedy for unsound minds must be applied to this diseased belief;[18] *All the Father's things are mine, and all mine are the Father's.*[19]

6. *Thy arrows are sharp, most powerful: under thee shall people fall, in the hearts of the king's enemies.* The sharp arrows are the words of the Lord Saviour piercing the hearts of men for their salvation. They wound to heal, they strive to free, they lay low to raise up. But let us note the likeness by which this weapon is compared to God's word. The wood of an arrow is armed with iron, and its extremity is feathered; likewise the word of God emerges from the wood of the cross, and has both the power to penetrate and the speed required to reach its goal. Earlier he mentioned the sword that wounds at close quarters, but here the arrows aimed from a distance, in order to point out by this simile His inconceivable power. *Sharp* has reference to speed of penetration; *most powerful,* because no substance however hard is known to resist them, since it is their nature to attain the outcome of their will. *People shall fall* indicates the conversion of men, when believers who previously remained upright through the vice of presumption happily tumble into humility. This happened to the apostle Paul who was pierced by the arrow of God's voice. As persecutor he fell on his face, but the Lord's right hand immediately raised him to be an apostle. *In the hearts* explains the earlier expression, *shall fail;* it has reference not to the feet by which bodies are supported, but to hearts by which the soul's infidelity is aided. The penitent who falls in his heart rises again. Dislodged from his wickedness, he is shifted to the moving commands of the Lord. *Of the king's enemies* denotes the enemies of Christ, who with opposing will dissent from the heavenly law. The title-heading of this psalm foretold this with the words: *For them that shall be changed, the sons of Core.*

7. *Thy abode is God for ever and ever: the rod of thy kingdom is a straight rod.* He passes to the third mode of praise, rightly termed *a causa iudicii;*[20] for here God's abode signifies the coming judgment, in which the eternal Ordainer examines and passes judgment on all things truthfully. *For ever and ever,* for whatever He has decided cannot be dissolved at any succeeding time. *Rod* means the rule of divine equity which is truthfully termed *straight* because it is bent by no wickedness. This rod rules the just, smites the wicked, and confines suppliants in truth. But this rod does not come from the excrescence of a tree but from the power of the Godhead himself. It is uncon-

quered courage, the most upright fairness, unbending discipline. Another psalm is to say of it: *The Lord will send forth the sceptre of thy power out of Sion: rule thou in the midst of thy enemies.*[21] The ancients gave the name of sceptre to this rod, which is the mark of regal distinction, denoting by it the Lord Saviour who is King of the virtues.

8. *Thou hast loved justice and hated iniquity: therefore God, thy God, hath anointed thee.* This is what the straight rod is: loving justice and hating iniquity. No-one loves justice perfectly except the person who also abominates most evil deeds; there is no place for different natures in the one person at the same time, and black cannot be seen there at the moment when whiteness has made its home. Just as the presence of light denotes the absence of darkness, so love of truth means hatred of falsehood. Hence the excellent definition by some authorities: "A substance can embrace contraries, but not at the same time."[22] Next he explains the rewards for these practices: *Therefore God, thy God, hath anointed thee.* The anointed Christ signifies both king and priest, for these offices were assumed by most sacred anointings; the very name of Christ comes from the holy chrism. He is called the anointed One because of the dispensation by which Christ is truly said to have been born, to have died, and to have risen again; but His divinity needed the resource of no award of honour. The repetition of *God, God* reveals the proclamation of great love.

9. *With the oil of gladness above thy fellows: myrrh and stacte and cassia from thy garments.* He shows that this bodily anointing emerged in a twofold way. The oil of gladness means having no stain of sin; hence He cheers himself with this abiding knowledge since He is bitten with no harsh remembrance of sin. *Above thy fellows* is said because He is known to have received the blessing above all humankind; being uniquely anointed He had to anoint the rest. In Him is the source of the blessing, and from Him, as He saw, it fittingly flows through all the chosen. All this aptly denotes the flesh to which the most devoted and glorious Word was united for the salvation of all. Next comes: *Myrrh and stacte and cassia from thy garments.* We have often remarked that the kinds of earthly objects give signs to us of the heavenly virtues; for we could know nothing of that Majesty unless some notion were revealed to us through similarities in the world. So

we explain the later words of this verse first so that the preceding ones may shine out more clearly. The holy body of the Lord is known to be the garment, so to say, of the Godhead. As the limbs of mortal men are covered by clothing, so too the majesty of the Word seemed to be hidden from the eyes of the unfaithful by the covering of the flesh. So from this garment, the secret of the incarnation, myrrh, stacte and cassia are aptly said to come. Myrrh signifies death which He undertook for the salvation of men. Stacte, the term for a resinous gum, is the cure for callous conditions incurred under some harsh necessity; this is splendidly compared with the Lord's incarnation because it dissolves the hardness of the human heart by its holy proclamation. By cassia, which our countrymen call *fistula,* is signified the redemption of the human race by the water of baptism, since this type of plant is said to be found in marshy places. From these plants also comes a sweet smell, so that the comparison is apt between the holy incarnation and the power and sweet odour of the plants. As the bride in the Song of Songs says: *We run after the odour of thy ointments.*[23]

10. *From the ivory houses, out of which the daughters of kings have delighted thee in thy glory.* In the fourth mode Christ's praise takes its rise from the person of His bride. The prophet mentions the source of her most glorious beauty. She takes her position at the Lord's right hand from the ivory houses, which denote those adorned palaces faced with abundant ivory. Let us realise that ivory signifies more than mere riches. The elephant to whom these tusks belong is said to be most chaste; among quadrupeds he is endowed with the highest intelligence, his intercourse with his mate is disciplined, and he enjoys no second spouse. This is fittingly applicable to chaste women, for they are acknowledged to have found their homes in ivory houses, since they have followed the Lord Christ's precepts through chastity. The most learned fathers Jerome and Augustine[24] have stamped their approval on this figurative sense. *Out of which they have delighted* suggests not "They have hastened to You by their own decision" but "have been led to You by delight in You." *The daughters of kings* may indicate the faithful who keep their bodies chaste, and rear as daughters those begotten by holy baptism; or it may refer to children of ruling families who, as often happens, abandon their lordly life in the palace and choose God's service. He added: *In thy glory,* to denote by

such designation religious intention; they took delight not in the glory of their fathers but in the glory of the Lord Saviour.

The queen stood on thy right hand in gilded clothing, surrounded with variety. The whole scene is enacted in a remarkable description. This figure is called *characterismos*, and as I have often said its Latin name is *descriptio* or *informatio*,[25] for it offers to the eyes of understanding what is not visible to bodily eyes. First the Bridegroom's beauty is praised, then His virtue declared. Thirdly, His abode and power are recounted. Because the joy of marriage is described, the manifestations of the sweetest fragrance with their mystical meanings are seen to be appended. Fourth, the source of the queen's remarkable beauty is also stated. Then she is set at His divine right hand, adorned with precious virtues, so that every faithful soul stretches out in heavenly contemplation, beholds its divine longings, and is aware that it must show Him that reverence on earth which it knows is His glory in heaven. The queen is she who says in the Song of Songs: *Let him kiss me with the kiss of his mouth*,[26] and the following words expressed in that text with mystical riddles. Observe that he earlier praised the abode of the Lord Saviour, whereas here he says that the queen stood on his right hand, for the right of the Bridegroom, who we know is the Church's Head, is the side of honour. Next comes: *In gilded clothing.* We must connect the gold with the brightness of love, with which holy Church gleams in her halo of virtue. So that you might realise that it is not love alone which is there, he spoke not of golden but of gilded clothing. We use the term gilded when the appearance of gold is superimposed and adheres to some material; the beauty of love has appeared on top of other virtues because its brightness outshines all things. He added: *Surrounded with variety.* Let us examine why God's Church is praised for the variety of her garments when it is appropriate for her to be unvarying and one. *Variety* here denotes manifold tongues, because every nation hymns the Creator in church according to its native region. Or it denotes the most beautiful diversity of virtues, for it is adorned with the gold of the apostles, the silver of the prophets, the jewels of virgins, the crimson of martyrs, the purple of penitents. So this is the variety of unity woven together from all nations to please the Lord's eyes with their devoted lives.

11. *Hearken, O daughter, and see, and incline thy ear: and forget thy*

people and the house of thy father. Now that the Bridegroom's praise has been sung, the bride is proclaimed in the same number of modes, but in a markedly more subdued and humble manner. It was appropriate not to leave her unpraised even though she comes second, for she has deserved the joy of such splendid and great marriage. The first mode of this praise, then, is that of her beauty, declared in the next verse. Now let us pass to an explanation of the words. He says to her, as she stands at the Lord's right hand, the place of the blessed: *Hearken*, that is, to the prophets, who with truthful promise prophesied the Lord's incarnation, so that she might believe what she heard, and later behold what she believed. The prophet rightly calls the Church his daughter, for the Christian people was begotten by his holy proclamations. *And see* must be spoken in tones of felicitation, for the Bridegroom promised to you has come; in Him is your love, glory and joy. Next comes: *And incline thy ear*; the Church had to lend an ear with due honour to the prophet's words. *Forget thy people*, he said; in other words, abandon and regard as foreign to your spirit the pagans' assemblies or the Jews' most lunatic superstitions. *House* denotes Babylon, which rejoices in its most wicked inhabitants in opposition to Christ's Church; in possessing the affections of its confused folk in the world, it appropriates to itself the faction of the wicked. *The father* refers to the devil, who is known truly to possess that home of confusion in accordance with the interpretation of its name.[27] But realise that the Church was lingering there at the time when she did not have the favour of her heavenly Spouse; so we read that she is swarthy.[28] But she was adorned with outstandingly glorious beauty when the Lord deigned to select her from among the nations.

12. *For the king has greatly desired thy beauty: for he is the Lord thy God, and him they shall adore.* This is the mode of praise which we earlier labelled *a specie*, in beauty. So the Lord Saviour is the King who desired the Church when she was consigned to the devil's lot through the sin of transgression. He did not find her beautiful, but made her so. She was foul when the adversary possessed her; she became beautiful when she returned to her Creator. Of her we read: *Who is this that comes up and is become white?*[29] Observe that the bride is initially praised in words similar to those which describe the Bridegroom:

Beautiful above the sons of men.[30] But he was said to have a unique beauty by His own appearance, whereas she is beautiful because the Bridegroom has joined her to Him. The whole description is varied and distinguished in this way, though the bride is praised for her garments as well. Next comes: *For he is the Lord thy God,* not "He whom you called Father," not "He who had made you dark," but "*He is the Lord thy God,* who removed your earlier foulness and bestowed on you your nuptial beauty." Also added here is the saving statement: *And him they shall adore,* in other words, all the peoples who by their assembly have made you a holy Church will adore not you but the Lord; for your glory lies in Him, and your blessedness is His everlasting fame.

13. *The daughters of Tyre with gifts shall entreat thy countenance, all the rich among the people.* He comes to the second mode, in which earlier he said of the Bridegroom: *Observe, and come forth prosperously, and reign;*[31] but here the Church's honoured role is that her devoted people should supplicate the Lord. Just as in the first passage the power of the Bridegroom is described, so here the glory of the bride is proclaimed as concerned with Christ's honour. Tyre is a city established not far from Jerusalem; he prefers to denote the souls of the faithful by the expression, *Daughters,* of this city. It is not Tyre alone which has brought forth faithful daughters, but also the diversity in unity of the whole world. So this figure is called "the whole from the part." The daughters of the nations, then, entreat with gifts the countenance of the Church when they distribute alms with religious zeal; the gifts are known to be exceedingly acceptable to the Godhead. We direct our gaze on the countenance of the Church, that is, on the face of the Christian people, when we beseech Christ's majesty with holy tears. We must join *all the rich among the people* to what precedes, so this is *hyperbaton* or *transcensio;*[32] "The daughters of Tyre, all who are rich among the people, will entreat thy countenance with gifts." The order of the words is clarified here by placing the final expression first.

14. *All the glory of that daughter of kings is within: in golden borders clothed round about with variety.* You note how he continues with praise of the Church, for it is the Church's glory when the daughters

of princes, or of just men, are converted to the Lord and desire to devote themselves in sequestered consecration. *Within* denotes the hidden region of the thoughts as opposed to the clacking of the lips; it is the region in which the inner man with silent thought ponders what is clearly related to the divine mysteries. This is how the Church is described in the Song of Songs: *The king has brought me into his chamber.*[33] You must regard the Latinity of *filiae regum ab intus* ("of the daughter of kings within") as peculiar to the divine Law; you do not find it in general use. Next comes: *In golden fringes, clothed round about with variety.* Fringes are edges of garments bound together by spinning, hanging down like stalks in fibres; they signify the end of human lives. He states that these are not as previously gilded,[34] but she has them now of gold; for at the end lies total perfection, and love is then seen not as gilded but with the fullness of gold. *Clothed round about with variety* indicates the various virtues of the faithful clearly explained earlier. Since the Catholic Church is clothed in such different robes, she is necessarily clad in multicoloured clothing. The garments of Aaron likewise denoted this, for they were woven in gold, purple, fine linen, crimson and violet.[35]

15. *After her shall virgins be led to the king: her neighbours shall be brought to thee.* Just as in the third mode the Bridegroom was praised at the Judgment,[36] so here the Church is praised thirdly in her members. See how powerfully he maintains the due order; *after her,* he says, *shall virgins be led,* specifically after the Church because she came first so that her unity could be made clear and then the separate enumeration of her parts could emerge. Observe that he said: *Shall be led,* so that the Lord's grace may be emphasised. That grace leads us to Him when He has gazed on us with pity. As the gospel has it: *No man comes to me unless the Father draw him.*[37] But what virgins are led before the Lord's sight? Undoubtedly faithful ones, those who deport themselves with chaste hearts. What profit will any individual have in maintaining a virgin body if she does not have inviolate faith? Next comes: *Her neighbours shall be brought to thee. To thee* means "to God." The Church's neighbours are the widows and chaste women who are joined to her at the lower level; whereas virginity obtains fruit a hundredfold, these glory in fruitfulness sixtyfold. Note that there is a

considerable difference in the expressions themselves. He said that virgins are *led*, for they are strong with inviolate bodies, but widows are *brought*, for they are usually afflicted by various troubles and wearied by physical weakness.

16. *With gladness and rejoicing they shall be brought into the temple of the king.* To show the abundant gifts to be bestowed on holy Church, he says that she will be conducted by the ministry of angels with gladness and rejoicing—not only to behold the King, but into His holy of holies, that is, in the Jerusalem to come. Arrival there is blessed joy and freedom from care. The words: *Shall be brought with gladness and rejoicing*, are well chosen, for the frail sex has overcome the sternest of bodily passions.

17. *Instead of thy fathers, sons are born to thee: thou shalt make them princes over all the earth.* He passes to the fourth mode, in which as was earlier described the Church mounted from steps of ivory to stand adorned at the King's right hand.[38] But now comes a powerful explanation of the great increase marking the progress of this bride, for instead of her ancient fathers (that is, worshippers of idols), sons have been born to her in the persons of the apostles, whom she has sent through the whole world as princes of preaching. The huge contrast is seen to bring praise to the Church, for those fathers were men who diverted people into error, whereas these sons are masters of truth. The fathers sowed deaths, the sons urged men to life. What praise, worthy of such joy attendant upon escaping the enemy's clutches and attaining marriage with the God of thunder![39] This motif is aptly called praise from offspring, since holy descendants are proclaimed here.

18. *They shall remember thy name in every generation and progeny: therefore shall people praise thee for ever, yea for ever and ever.* By those who remember he meant the Christian people, who continue with His praises in devoted aspiration through different generations of mankind. It is wonderful fame, the highest praise never to accept the final plaudits amidst such numerous generations. Next follows: *Therefore shall people praise thee for ever.* When every Christian utters the mysteries of the Creed, he makes confession before the face of the Church; this confession becomes eternal because it is truthful and

devoted. The addition: *For ever and ever*, signifies the future when all opposition ceases and justice alone rules, for the devil's hostility will have been eradicated.

Conclusion Drawn From the Psalm

So the splendid marriage-song concludes with the delight of the psalmist. See how praise of Bridegroom and bride is hymned with marvellous variety; their spiritual union, their marriage continuing in the virginity of individuals, their chaste love, eternal charity, their bonds dissolved by no end. Here the prophet's timbrels resound with holy delight, here the apostles' instruments echo in sweetest harmony, here the martyrs' harps sound forth not from strings but from virtues, here the saints' chorus with their spiritual pipes charm the ear most pleasantly, here such music is made that all human joy is transcended by it. We have feasted, good King, and drunk heavenly delights at your wedding-feast. Wondrous Bridegroom, grant that we who have here rejoiced in hope may be filled with the most perfect joy in the life to come. Blessed Jerome, in writing to the maiden Principia, has also discussed this psalm with his usual wonderful elegance.[40] I have thought it desirable to mention him so that what I have perhaps failed to make sufficiently clear can be filled out by the explanations of that most learned man.

COMMENTARY ON PSALM 45

1. *Unto the end, a psalm for the sons of Core, for the hidden.* We know how *unto the end* can be referred to the Lord Christ. We have said that *the sons of Core* signifies Christians,[1] in whose persons this psalm is sung. *For the hidden* denotes the coming of the Lord Saviour, which he has ordered in a wondrously secret way for the salvation of men.

Division of the Psalm

The sons of Core, who are to be understood as faithful Christians, proclaim in the first section of the psalm that they do not fear the troubles of life, because God is known to be their refuge and strength. In the second part they state that Christ appears in the midst of His Church and has deigned to build it on Himself as on the firmest of rocks. In the third section the mass of believers is invited to gaze on the great things of God. They say that almighty God shatters the arms of wickedness, banishes wars, and transforms the sadness of the faithful into eternal joys.

Explanation of the Psalm

2. *Our God is our refuge and strength: a helper in troubles, which have found us exceedingly.* At the very beginning of the psalm a categorical syllogism[2] smiles on us. What he says is: "In the troubles which have found us exceedingly, our God is our refuge and strength and helper. In troubles we shall not fear when the earth is shaken. So in troubles which have found us exceedingly, we shall not fear when the earth shall be shaken." Now let us discuss the words in detail. How fine and succinct is the connection! As if they were being asked: "What is our God?" they reply: "Our refuge and strength and helper." This is the fifth type of definition, which in Greek is called *kata tēn lexin* and in Latin *ad verbum,*[3] when we show the nature of anything by individual words. The word *our* was added to distinguish us from the most untrue Christians whose God is not wont to be a refuge. He is the refuge of the faithful when He frees them from danger to the soul, and their strength when He protects their minds firmly from the harmful error of the world. Next comes: *A helper in troubles;* here by different definitions is expressed the mercy of the heavenly Majesty, which both receives us and defends us. Any trouble in which we show devotion makes God merciful to us, and discharges our guilt. He helps us especially when He realises that we wish to trust in Him. As Paul says: *For the sorrow that is according to God worketh penance steadfast unto salvation.*[4] So that you may not consider these troubles mild, he added: *Which have found us exceedingly,* so that you would not believe that any of your severe experiences were light. The dangers were suitably heightened so that He who destroyed them should appear as most powerful.

3. *Therefore we will not fear when the earth shall be troubled: and the*

mountains will be removed into the heart of the sea. The time of the
trouble previously mentioned is being explained, when at the coming
of the Lord Saviour holy men who presumed on His name and
strength could not feel fear, whereas the hearts of the Jews were
confused at the strangeness of so great a miracle. Next comes: *And the
mountains shall be removed into the heart of the sea.* This happened at
that moment when the mountains, in other words, the apostles, abandoned the unbelieving Jews and crossed over *into the heart of the sea,*
that is, to preach to the Gentiles. As we read in the Acts of the Apostles: *To you it behoved us first to speak the word of God: but because you
rejected it, and judged yourselves unworthy of eternal life, behold, we
turned to the Gentiles.*[5] We note that following the example of these
spokesmen, the mountains jutting out with their holy peak and most
secure in the firmness of their faith, were removed to the heart of the
sea, that is, to instill belief in all nations. And we should note that he
has compared the Jews' perfidy to the dry earth, and the Gentiles'
readiness to believe to the salt waters, so that you might realise that the
Jews' hearts had hardened into evil, and truthfully assess that the
Gentiles were seasoned with the salt of the gospels; for a sea does not
have a heart, but men do.

4. *They roared, and his waters were troubled: the mountains were
troubled with his strength.* He continued with his earlier thought. The
trouble which arose from the Lord Christ's coming is still being explained. He says that the apostles roared their preaching like a most
loud report of some thunder, which sounded not only in men's ears
but also in their minds. At this time he claims that the waters were
troubled; he means the innumerable nations of this world, which were
terrified by such wonders. This figure is called *parabole* or *comparatio,*[6] when we associate things dissimilar in kind by comparison of
their natures. But it should be noted that the point is made with a
splendid, most beautiful comparison. Waters are disturbed with the
greatest turmoil when a massive pile of masonry is thrown into the
depths of the sea, and they make a mighty noise when waves beat on
each other with imposing weight. This is precisely what happened
when the whole world trembled with the resounding preaching of the
apostles, and later summoned itself back to belief in the Lord with
purified heart. Next follows: *The mountains were troubled with his*

strength. Here he speaks of mountains in a different sense, namely worldly powers; for mountains can be interpreted in a good and a bad sense. The mountains of God are steady and beautiful, the mountains of the devil fickle and ugly. The mountains of the world were troubled when pagan leaders introduced sacrilegious laws against God's religion.

5. *The force of the river maketh the city of God joyful: the most High hath sanctified his own tabernacle.* Earlier he spoke of the terrors experienced by the world from the new preaching; now the benefits are enumerated which were bestowed on the Church at the Lord Saviour's coming. So the change of sense aptly inserts the division of a diapsalm here. Observe what is said and the special significance with which the words are distinguished. The city of God is made joyful by the force of the river, and it finds rest; to make you realise that this river irrigates souls, he does not say that it has saturated the city, but has made it joyful. For this is the river of which Truth Itself says: *Whoever believes in me shall not thirst for ever, but there shall become in him a fountain of water springing up into life everlasting.*[7] He did well to speak of the force of the river, since its course allows nothing marshy or sluggish since it has steeped itself in the power of the Godhead. Next is added: *The most High hath sanctified his own tabernacle.* The tabernacle of the most High is either the Church or His glorious assumption of a human body; clearly both of these were sanctified when *the word was made flesh, and dwelt among us.*[8]

6. *God is in the midst of it, and it shall not be moved: God will help it with his countenance.* God is not said to be in the midst as though He were confined by the limits of a place. He is not circumscribed by any space, since He is wholly everywhere in equal measure, showing no disproportionate kindness. He is said to be in the midst because He always has regard for the faithful. So God is rightly described as in the midst; this refers to His justice, for He gazes on all men with uniform will. No person will be robbed of His gaze except the one who has alienated himself from Him. *It shall not be moved* is said of the Church, to whom that unique promise was given: *Thou art Peter, and upon this rock I will build my church, and the gates of hell will not prevail against it.*[9] The Church cannot be moved as it is seen to be founded on the most solid rock which is the Lord Christ. Next comes: *God will help it*

with his countenance, that is, with the presence of the incarnation, when His saving face dawns. *Will help* means "will help it when it struggles with the opposition of the world."

7. *Nations were troubled, and kingdoms were bowed down: the most High gave his voice, and the earth trembled.* Nations were troubled precisely when they were most devoted to idols and suddenly heard the rules of a religion unknown to them. The working of miracles converted many, the fear of the Judgment which was preached overwhelmed many; and though they were guided towards the good, they could not escape having troubled minds. Next comes: *And kingdoms were bowed down,* that is, they were brought low to adore and not to fall, for every man is raised up in so far as he bends to make satisfaction. He added: *The most High gave his voice, and the earth trembled.* He did not say "uttered," but *gave* as a wonderful gift and blessing of a reward. *Voice* refers to the holy preaching which the almighty Teacher made to resound through the whole world with the strength of thunder by His own lips and those of the apostles. It was inevitable that sinners should tremble at it; for they heard the fearful commands of the eternal Judge.

8. *The Lord of virtues is with us: the God of Jacob is our protector.* This is a brief explanation of how Christ is almighty: He is Lord of virtues, for the heavenly Virtues attend Him, and all power serves Him. Listen, you men with hard hearts, listen, you who are unhinged: Why do you seek utterly to perish by presuming to sin in the face of such great majesty: Next comes: *With us,* for He took on flesh and dwelt on earth. The words, *the God of Jacob is our protector,* are added. He is a Protector, for He deigns to join His power to the infirmities of others. The God of all is truly called our Protector, for He took on[10] flesh for the salvation of the faithful. The sons of the cross do well to call him *ours,* for He is the Protector only of them who have deserved to attain belief in Him. *The God of Jacob* is to be understood as meaning that He will bestow on His faithful believers as much as He conferred on Jacob. God is not the God of Jacob only; but of all who show commitment with similar faith.

9. *Come and behold ye the works of the Lord, what prodigies he hath set upon the earth.* After the break of a diapsalm, he passes to the third section, where he invites the people to behold the Lord Saviour's great works which He performed through the wonderful dispensation of

His incarnation. When he says: *Come,* he urges them to draw close to the Lord in faith, for they could not see Him at a distance. His additional words, *the works of the Lord,* are an invitation to all to a great spectacle, so let us approach with eager spirit, for when we behold such things in faith, we lay hold of what can lead us to eternal joys. He used the word *set* as if He placed certain signs which the world could behold and hasten to the remedies of its salvation. The word prodigy is so called because it is a forward statement (*porro dicat*),[11] when the revelation of some future novel happening is declared by certain signs. This happened at the Lord's nativity when the Virgin bore Him; a star shone more brightly, and the chorus of angels proclaimed the birth of their Lord.

10. *Making wars to cease even to the end of the earth.* See how these promised works of the Lord were proclaimed. Inevitably such a great promise expounds some great and hidden meaning. There was a rebellion against God when paganism with manifold superstitions adored sculpted statues which fell with their worshippers at the Lord's coming. So He made wars of belief cease even to the ends of the earth when they were being waged over the whole world. He restored to His peace those on whom He bestowed the gifts of true religion. Or this can be understood as true historically, because we read that the world was pacified at the Lord's nativity in the reign of Augustus. This is known to have been achieved not by human powers but by the bodily presence of the Lord Christ.

He shall destroy the bow, and break the weapons: and the shield he shall burn in the fire. The bow represents the ambush of the infidels trodden underfoot by the power of truth, when their mad aspirations are reduced to nothing. *Weapons* here signifies superstitious conflicts of pagans burnt by the flame of heavenly fire for man's liberation. This soldier whose bow is trodden underfoot, whose weapons are broken for man's salvation and whose shield are burnt in the fire, belongs to the devil. He could not have escaped other than by losing the arms which he thought were his protection. Alternatively all the arms mentioned, as some believe, can be interpreted as provoking vices. Strip us, good King, of the arms of the devil, by which we are not defended but oppressed, and gird us with the sword of the spirit, which bestows on us both salvation and protection.

11. *Be still, and see that I am God. I will be exalted among the nations,*

and I will be exalted in the earth. The sons of Core in the midst of their utterance are translated by the spirit of prophecy, and speak this short verse in the role of the Lord. This figure is called *apostrophe,* or in Latin *conversio,* when we turn with a sudden shift to another matter.[12] They are rightly told: *Be still,* for they were armed with worldly deceits and were serving in the devil's army in a struggle deadly to themselves. In short, they could not hear unless they laid aside their most wicked arms, and with minds still and tranquil gathered to listen to the message of salvation. His words are: *I am God* and not he who armed you, not he who led you to wicked struggles, but the God who shall be exalted among the nations. His religion is true, and His eminence not frail. And so that you would not think that He would perhaps be exalted among some nations but not also among the race of the Jews which he earlier compared to the earth,[13] he added: *And I will be exalted in the earth,* that is, in the Jewish nation. As Paul promises: *For I say to you—that you should not be wise in your own conceits—that blindness in part has happened to Israel until the fullness of the Gentiles should come in, and so all Israel should be saved.*[14] So you see that the Lord is exalted and will be exalted both among the nations and in the race of the Jews.

12. *The Lord of armies is with us: the God of Jacob is our protector.* The sons of Core return to their own identities, and the psalm has a fine ending with the repetition of a verse. They repeat this claim a second time so that they may make it clear that liberation has been granted us by means of it. *The God of Jacob* is repeatedly introduced so that the victory of the Christian people may be asserted; though they emerge later in time, they excel the earlier people in faithful devotion.

Conclusion Drawn From the Psalm

How brightly this short and healing psalm has gleamed forth! If we take confidence from it by the Lord's kindness, we surmount with strength of spirit the thorns of this world, and in the proverbial phrase we obtain help from tribulation. For in it all hope lies in the coming of the Lord Christ, through whom on our behalf the Church was founded and great wonders became manifest. He who said: *My peace I give to you, my peace I leave to you,*[15] removed the wars caused by superstitions.

COMMENTARY ON PSALM 46

1. *Unto the end, a psalm for the sons of Core.* All the words in this heading have been explained and are stored in our minds. But you, eager reader, must always ensure that you understand the meanings attached to the incidences of these expressions in the psalms. If you examine the text of psalms more carefully, you will realise that not one word of them can be idle. So it happens that at one place variation in headings and at another similarity both appear to denote the Lord Saviour. When they vary, it relieves the tedium; when identical, they strengthen the eyes of our understanding with unwavering stability. So both are clearly issued for the salvation of all, and are acknowledged to be beneficial. In this psalm again the sons of Core, whom mother Church signs with the emblem of the cross, are the spokesmen.

Division of the Psalm

Though this whole hymn is sung by the sons of Core as spokesmen and is assembled in most welcome brevity, it is still divided by the pause of a diapsalm. In the first part nations are warned that praises should resound to the Lord, for the devoted Judge has subjected all things to the possession of His people, and set them in His inheritance. In the second part the ascension of the Lord and His kingdom which His saints are to attain without end are briefly recounted.

2. *O clap your hands, all ye nations: shout unto God with the voice of exultation.* People living a dissipated life usually make a din by beating their hands together, and by this means produce some melody to delight the ears without recourse to words. So we must interpret this clapping in a spiritual sense such as the sons of the cross could bring themselves to express and such as we should listen to. Thus people who give alms, pity and serve the sick, conduct some precept by worthy acts, or do some such thing which can attract God's grace, are clapping their hands. *Shouting* means rejoicing; *iubilare* derives from *iuvare*, to delight,[1] when we express our joy not in articulated speech but in mingled sounds. So that we should not confine ourselves to such joys alone, he added: *With the voice of exultation,* signifying

psalm-singing addressed to God in the majesty of His name. So he gives us the most perfect advice that our hand should perform praise of God to the same degree as our human tongue utters His glory. It is fitting that both the tongue sings and the hand performs the precepts of their Lord.

3. *For God is the highest, terrible, a great king over all the earth.* He offers reasons why we ought to clap and shout to the Lord. This figure is called *epexegesis* or explanation of foregoing words.[2] First, God is *highest; terrible,* for He will personally judge the world; *a great king,* since His is *King of kings and lord of lords.*[3] He is the One of whom it was written over His passion: *King of the Jews.*[4] It is true that he was King of the Jews, but He is also King of all nations, for He is Creator and Administrator of all things. The psalmist says that He is King of all the earth so that He would not be thought to have been merely King of the Jews. Let Jews observe the Lord's power, which has spread far and wide from their narrow bounds, and let them not cease to worship Him since they hear that His domain is everywhere.

4. *He hath subdued peoples under us, and the nations under his feet.* This has reference to all Christians deserving to possess God's grace. *Peoples and nations* denotes those known to lurk outside the Church. In a spiritual sense they are subject to all the just, for they cannot equal their merits; we must prefer this spiritual interpretation so that holy men may not appear to be affected by pride—God forbid! *Feet* signifies the holiest preaching to which peoples are rightly said to be subject, since they were bound by the rules which that preaching laid down. As the prophet Isaiah says: *How beautiful are the feet of them that proclaim peace.*[5]

5. *He hath chosen for us his inheritance, the beauty of Jacob which he loved. He hath chosen for us*—understand "to grant us," so that He who had come to save the people of Israel granted this with kindly generosity instead to the Gentiles. We must set this parallel before our eyes so that the truth of the matter may be recognised more clearly. Esau was enticed by the attraction of bodily food, and demanded lentil soup of his brother Jacob; Jacob answered him that he would grant this if the glory of being first-born were allowed him by his brother.[6] Esau was an eager hunter of earthly things, and yielded his distinction; through

this event Jacob by blessed interchange offered bodily gifts to obtain spiritual possessions. This is the beauty of Jacob which the Lord greatly loved; He wishes his faithful servants to do the things which Jacob by that mystical sign forewarned us to emulate. We are truly called Christians if we seek heavenly things by offering earthly ones in their stead.

6. *God is ascended with jubilation, and the Lord with the sound of the trumpet.* The sons of Core come to the second section, in which with devoted praise they together hymn the time when the Lord's glorious ascension was truly witnessed by bodily eyes. *With jubilation* is the phrase used, since the apostles stood amazed at such a miracle and were filled with indescribable joy of heart; their blessed eyes were privileged to behold the Lord Saviour going to the heavens. We have said that jubilation is extreme joy not expressed in words. *The sound of the trumpet* denotes the words of angels thundering forth with might din as the air was shattered with crashing sound. Then the angels said to the apostles standing hypnotised at such a sight: *Men of Galilee, why do you stand amazed? This Jesus who is taken up from you shall so come as you have seen him going into heaven.*[7] This was so that the world might believe more firmly what was proclaimed by heralds such as these.

7. *Hymn to our God, hymn ye: hymn to our king, hymn ye.* The frequent repetition of the word is not idle; we recognise how useful and salutary is the act which he sought to repeat so frequently. This figure is called *epembasis,*[8] when words are repeated to duplicate their beauty. To *hymn* is to sing praise to the Lord by good actions; if it is carried out well, we are known to share it with the angels as well, for they continually in harmony celebrate the Lord's praises with spiritual exaltation. Next comes: *Hymn to our king.* By *our king* he meant no outsider, but the Lord Christ. This praise befits Him, since He is the only one deservedly to receive praise, for He both creates all things and continues to govern them after they have been created.

8. *For God is the king of all the earth: hymn ye wisely.* This is said on account of those people who created for themselves diverse divinities in individual places—Venus at Paphos, Mars in Thrace, Jupiter in Crete;[9] for the almighty King must be worshipped everywhere, since He is known to be the sole Creator and Deliverer of all. He added:

Hymn ye wisely, so that we must not only sing but also understand what we hymn. No-one does anything wisely if he does not understand it.

9. *The Lord has reigned over all nations: God sitteth over his holy throne.* The sons of Core have come to the enduring blessedness of the age to come, in which they now say that the Lord will reign over the nations. Though even now He reigns over all, He is said to reign in a proper sense when shown to dwell more evidently among His faithful. *Over all nations* signifies the heavenly Jerusalem which is the unity of all nations. Next comes: *God sitteth over his holy throne;* he means the Lord Saviour, who sits at the right hand of the Father and reigns for ever and ever. Observe that he calls the throne itself holy, so that you may not understand by it things lacking feeling or reason; rather he refers to the Virtues and Thrones, over which the glorious Ruler presides. It can be understood also of the saints, for if a person possesses the blessing of a good life, he too undoubtedly becomes a royal throne. If you study this more deeply, the whole statement is uttered against those who are unfaithful. So those who think that humility is to be despised surrender when they hear of His power.

10. *The princes of the people have gathered with the God of Abraham.* The princes of the people connote leaders of different nations, of whom the opening of the psalm sings: *Clap your hands, all ye nations.* *Have gathered* is the equivalent of "have believed," for gathering means the coming of many to one. *With the God of Abraham,* that is, to Christ who is the God of Abraham. For after the expulsion of the unfaithful Jews, sons of Abraham only in the flesh and not by works, He admitted the Gentiles in their fullness to possess the blessedness of the promise which He had made to Abraham and his seed, for though they were not Abraham's sons by the seed of the flesh, they became such through their holy faith.

For the strong gods of the earth are greatly exalted. The sense here depends on the previous phrase. The princes of the people gathered with the God of Abraham because the strong ones of the earth, the people of God, are greatly exalted. This is because the Jews, who had been granted power among the nations, raised themselves up against God, and were swollen in mind. Through their pride they became the last, when by humility they could have become the most outstanding.

Conclusion Drawn From the Psalm

Let us examine the text of this psalm, which is brief in words but not in virtues. The number itself declares great mysteries to us; in its mystical interpretation we read that the Lord's temple at Jerusalem was completed in the forty-sixth year.[10] These years were set down by the ancients for the number of days, for when multiplied by the perfect number six they amount to the two hundred and seventy-six days during which our Lord is known to have dwelt in the Virgin's womb in the likeness of the human species, from March 25th to December 25th. So the whole of this psalm is rightly regarded as descriptive of the Lord in a special way, since by its number as well it is appropriately joined to the mystery of His conception and birth in the way prescribed.

COMMENTARY ON PSALM 47

1. *A psalm-canticle for the sons of Core at the second of the sabbath.* We have explained a psalm-canticle in the Preface.[1] Again, the sons of Core have been frequently mentioned.[2] Now let us see the significance of *at the second of the sabbath.* We must interpret the sabbath as the synagogue or gathering of the Jews which appeared to observe the sabbath. The second of the sabbath is the Catholic Church. So the words of this psalm are assigned to priests for the instruction of the Christian people. There is no doubt that the sons of the cross[3] can be regarded as such, and we know by the clear light of reason that they came second in time after the synagogue.

Division of the Psalm

Since the devoted people had to be taught about the faith and the ranks of the Church, the words of this psalm are rightly assigned to the holy priests, who in the first section speak praises to the Lord because He has extended His Church, and because He has shown to all earthly kings the power of His majesty. In the second section they give thanks for the Lord Saviour's coming, advising the people that there will be bishops to allot ranks in the Church, so that God the Lord Saviour who guards His servants with perennial protection can be acknowledged.

Explanation of the Psalm

2. *Great is the Lord, and exceedingly worthy of praise in the city of our God, in his holy mountain.* We must consider how these words mount by fixed stages in their marvellous arrangement. This figure is called *emphasis;*[4] first he called the Lord *great,* and then *praiseworthy* was added, but so that you would not think that He is to be praised modestly, he appended *exceedingly.* Such praise has no limit or end, but is perpetually enhanced by its diligence. So He is great because He made all things with power, and praiseworthy because He made them beautifully and wonderfully. But it is not sufficient to have said that the Lord Father is exceedingly worthy of praise; they had also to proclaim where He was to be praised, *in the city of our God,* the Catholic Church. There is a city which does not belong to our God, like the devil's Babylon where God is not worshipped but blasphemed with a quite execrable madness. This was why the place for the Lord's praises had to follow, so that none would think that He was to be proclaimed amidst heretical superstitions or in the synagogue of old. Then he added: *In his holy mountain,* so that you would have no doubt where the Church which he mentioned was set. The holy mountain is Christ the Lord, the Foundation and Head of His Church. This is the holy mountain of which the prophet Daniel says: *The stone grew and became a great mountain, so that it filled the whole face of the earth.*[5] Let us ponder the fact that the great Lord here means the Father, but the great Son likewise does not go unmentioned. As Paul says of Him when writing to Titus: *Looking for the blessed hope and coming of the glory of the great God and our saviour Jesus Christ.*[6] We read that the holy Spirit too is great. In the book of the kingdoms Scripture says that the Lord remarks to Elijah: *Behold, the Lord will pass, and the great and strong Spirit.*[7] So the Arians[8] in their mad persuasion must blush;

who, pray, is less than the others, as we read that Father, Son, holy Spirit are all great?

3. *Mount Sion is widening the joys of the whole earth: the sides of the north, the city of the great king.* So that you should not assume that the mountain previously mentioned was a place, he says that it confers joys on the whole earth. Who is this mountain but the Lord Christ, who could extend beneficial joys through the entire Church in the world? Take *earth* here in the good sense; it signifies just men who obtain abundant and eternal rewards. *Mount Sion,* as we have often remarked, designates the Church, which according to the interpretation of its name is filled by the power of holy contemplation.[9] *The sides of the north* denotes unfaithful people among whom the devil's wickedness reigned, for the devil himself said: *I shall set my throne to the north, and will be like the most High.*[10] But because sinners held in subjection by the devil have through God's pity been converted, Mount Sion and the sides of the north—that is, the Jewish nation and the peoples of the Gentiles—have become the city of the great King, in other words, the Catholic Church, known to be the gathering of the entire world. She is the second of the sabbath named in the psalm-heading. Princes of the earth are also called kings, but God alone can truly be called the great King. This mention of Mount Sion and the subsequent addition of *the sides of the north, the city of the great king,* is the figure known as *exergasia,*[11] when something is baldly stated, and then cleverly and more broadly explained.

4. *In her ranks shall God be known, when he shall receive her.* Here is revealed the future occasion of the great Judgment, when the Lord receives His Church and will himself be recognised in her ranks, that is, in the holiest and best-tried of her members. God shall be known —in other words, His power and virtue will be manifest—when the Church through His generosity will be revealed as offering Him her blessed ones, when according to the level of their merits the holy people will be set at His right hand, as Paul states: *Star differeth from star in glory: so also is the resurrection of the dead.*[12] She is received into eternal blessedness when enduring joys are granted her. God is recognised there—that is, His power and virtue are manifest—when He bestows on His Church with varying distinctions such rewards as will never end or perish. We here believe what is afforded us there in clear vision.

5. *For behold, the kings of the earth assembled themselves, and they were of one accord.* These are the sides of the north mentioned earlier. Though they came with conspiratorial intention to oppose God, many of them are known to have believed. By *kings of the earth* are meant here the Jews' leaders whom Herod banded together and asked where the Lord Christ was to be born. They aptly and in harmony said that according to holy Scripture He would certainly be born at Bethlehem. So they *assembled themselves* to declare what they had read, and *were of one accord* because all declared the one opinion.

6. *They saw and then they wondered, they were troubled, they were moved. They* are the Jews who told Herod that the Lord would be born in Bethlehem. They had seen what they had read in prophecy, and it was inevitable that wonder should arise from such great fame. But this wonder was not fickle or idle. *They were troubled,* because they knew that they were sinners; *moved,* because they deserved to discover such great majesty. We say that those who we attest have believed are *moved.*

7. *Trembling took hold of them there, pains as of a woman in childbirth.* The subsequent order of events has been most beautifully preserved. They say that first they saw, then they wondered, then they were troubled, and finally they were smitten with trembling. It is harsh fear which leads men to tremble, for the mind is inevitably wave-tossed if its body is resultantly seized by trembling. This condition was not enough in so important a matter. Repentance immediately followed, in which pains tortured them as if they were mothers in childbirth. That pain which we know has been imposed on women as punishment for sin is indeed oppressive. But the phrase, *in childbirth,* allows us to believe that fruit will emerge from humble confession.

8. *With a vehement gust breaking in pieces the ships of Tharsis.* Here the effect of the Lord's birth is expounded. Some have sought to explain *the vehement gust* by reference to when Herod, troubled for his kingdom, sent the Magi to behold the King who had been born, and to report their discovery back to him; but when they did not return to him he was naturally moved by a vehement gust, and shattered the ships from Tarsus in Cilicia[13] which were thought to have

secretly carried the Magi we have mentioned back to their native region. This is what lying kings[14] are wont to do. When they cannot gain their desires, they hasten to harm and torture the lowly. Observe the growth of the narration from its beginning to this high point.

9. *As we have heard, so have we seen in the city of the Lord of hosts, in the city of our God.* The survey of all that happened at the Lord Saviour's birth is now complete, so there follows the apt conclusion that what was seen confirmed what had been earlier prophesied. The word *so* carefully expresses the reliability of the occurrence; everything definitely took place as had been promised. *In the city of the Lord of hosts* was appended since there the truth is heard and all that was promised is beheld. *In the city of our God* is repeated so that you may realise that this is the Catholic city alone, to prevent the title being claimed by assemblies of heretics.

God hath founded it for ever. So that you do not regard God's city as transient, he says that the Church, which alone is truly called the Lord's city, is established for ever. Let Christians rejoice and exult with total, heartfelt joy when they hear that the city in which they have no doubt they are firmly anchored has been founded by the Lord. Though shaken by the storm of this world, they rightly do not fear what they know is transient. As Paul says: *The sufferings of this time are not worthy to be compared with the glory to come that shall be revealed in us.*[15]

10. *We have received thy mercy, O God, in the midst of thy temple.* The holy priests have passed to the second section, in which they exult with great joy of heart. *We have received* ought not to be interpreted as embracing everyone, because not everyone has believed. It refers only to Catholics who have followed His commandments. *Mercy* signifies the Lord Christ, who took pity on the errant world. For this reason alone He wished to be seen, so that every believer could be forgiven. It is a suitable title, a certain promise, that He who is truly pronounced Saviour and Redeemer should be called Mercy. The spokesmen wish *in the midst of thy temple* to be interpreted as the synagogue which He had come to deliver. But when that people did not show belief, the Gentiles were summoned and obtained Mercy's gifts. *In the midst of thy temple* was added so that the wickedness of

unbelievers should be more sternly rebuked. They were contemptuous of following Him whom they had undoubtedly seen in
their midst.

11. *According to thy name, O God, so also is thy praise unto the ends of
the earth: thy right hand is full of justice.* We believe without doubting
that God's name is to be adored through the whole world. Possibly
some do not know how He is to be worshipped, but there is no-one
who does not believe that he is subject to the name of God. So the sons
of Core say that just as reverence for Your name extends over the
whole earth, so too in the Church, which stretches over the entire
world, the devotion of praise is offered to You. Next comes: *Thy right
hand is full of justice,* indicating the place where these men are to be
set, for all who shall obtain eternal rewards come to His right hand. So
His right hand is full of justice, for those who by His gift have merited
to be just are received on that side.

12. *Let mount Sion rejoice, and the daughters of Juda be glad because of
thy judgments, O Lord.* Mount Sion indicates the Catholic Church,
known through the interpretation of the name to have been established for the people's contemplation.[16] It is desired that it rejoice, for
by His gift it will possess eternal joys. *The daughters of Juda* means all
holy women, for the species of just women is revealed by Juda, because the Lord Christ is descended from that tribe through the issue of
the flesh. They ask that these daughters too be glad, to show that the
Lord's Church will rejoice in persons of both sexes. They add: *Because of thy judgments, O Lord;* this is the cause of their great joy. They
are glad because of the Lord's judgments by which they know that
they will attain eternal blessedness.

13. *Surround Sion, and embrace her: tell ye in her towers.* After the
devoted priests have made mention of both sexes, they come to the
orders in the Church, which surround God's house with loving devotion. *Surround* suggests the manifestation of her glories, *embrace* the
love which enfolds the Lord's name in the recesses of men's hearts.
The following words are: *Tell ye in her towers,* so those who obey the
holy orders must not cease from pious converse. Since God's city is
the Church, the towers in it are aptly sited as heights and defences
against heretical foes. But because they were urging them to spread
the tidings to unbelievers lingering outside the Church, they say that

the preaching must be done not from houses or porticoes but from high towers from which the people outside can hear.

14. *Set your hearts on her virtue, and distribute her orders, that ye may relate it to another generation.* That the faithful's souls in hearing this joy and exultation may not grow torpid and a little slack, they say that their hearts are to be set on the virtue of the Church, that is, on charity, the virtue which nothing can excel. As Paul teaches: *There remain faith, hope, charity, these three; but the greatest of these is charity.*[17] He who orders her ranks by separate appointments distributes the orders of the Church, for in the Church there are readers, subdeacons, deacons, priests, bishops.[18] Though there is one Church, it contains offices marked out by variety of distinctions. So the devoted priests advise that these offices be distributed so that the Lord's great tidings can be preached in another generation. *Another generation* means the Christian people, known to come second after the Jewish people, which the Lord chose first.

15. *That this is our God unto eternity and for ever and ever: he shall rule us for evermore.* This is what they wished to relate to the faithful through the orders of the Church, as happens today. It is a short but comprehensive statement: *This is our God.* They mean Christ, indicating Him with their finger as if He were present. This figure is called *idea,* in Latin *species,*[19] when we arouse emotion by setting what will happen before our eyes, so to speak. *This* is an articular pronoun used when someone is indicated with outstretched hand. Here is revealed the One who was willing to appear before bodily eyes, of whom the prophet Jeremiah likewise said: *This is our God, and there shall be no other accounted of in comparison with him.*[20] Next comes: *Unto eternity, and for ever and ever.* This is uttered against those who idly dreamt that their gods were transient humans—Mars, Mercury, Saturn and the rest who are to be termed portents rather than divinities. So they maintain that the Lord Christ is to be proclaimed as immortal, the everlasting God who is most powerful and without limit, who continually protects and defends those who believe in Him. Also introduced is: *He shall rule us for evermore.* He shall rule us in particular because Christ Himself is properly and truly called our King. *Evermore* signifies without end, since He guards for a glorious eternity those whom He accepts beneath His rule, so long as they do not diverge from Him.

Conclusion Drawn From the Psalm

These fatherly and priestly words have sounded in our ears so that they may strike us on every side, and we may deserve to be guided to the right path. What great care, good King, You show to men, on whom You deign to bestow so manifold a cure in the shape of Your commands! You are not content to say once what You refuse to permit men to fail to know; You warn and teach them on every side, and You make our faith cry out through the spokesmen who are introduced, so that the possibility of ignorance seems wholly excluded. Your holy Job rightly says: *What shall I do to thee, keeper of men?*[21] You warn us what we ought to seek, You grant us what we cannot ourselves merit.

COMMENTARY ON PSALM 48

1. *Unto the end, a psalm for the sons of Core.* The words of this heading, as has often been remarked, all draw us to the Lord Saviour. It is He who is indicated by *the end*; it is Him we understand by the sons of the cross;[1] He is undoubtedly announced through the psalm. So we rightly feel that His voice will come forth, since His glowing words are presaged by so many signs.

Division of the Psalm

Throughout the psalm the words are those of the almighty Son. In the first section He states the nature of His future message or future gifts to the faithful at the time of His incarnation. In the second part He tells the foolish and mindless the great things to come. The third section states what is in store for the just and for the wicked. The fourth warns the faithful not to fear the rich men of the earth, because they lose all their power with their lives.

Explanation of the Psalm

2. *Hear these things, all ye nations: give ear, all ye inhabitants of the world.* The whole creation without exception is urged to come and

listen, because God is good without regard to persons. He does not wish to benefit a few and to disregard and neglect others, so long as they seek Him with a pure heart. Secondly, the whole world must listen to this mystery of the Lord's incarnation because the blessing extended to all equally demanded the ears of all. Next comes: *Give ear, all ye inhabitants of the world.* At this point they are more earnestly urged to grasp the words more devotedly and to place them in the recesses of their memory. By *nations* we must understand pagans, by *inhabitants of the world* the Christians and the just, who know that their dwelling in the world demands their not being involved in its wicked errors. Note too how the good Teacher has roused the enthusiasm of all to listen, so that the guilty man unwilling to benefit himself may be restored to Him.[2] Rhetoricians by adapting this to their profession make judges attentive when they promise that they will tell new or important tidings.

3. *All ye that are earthborn, and you sons of men, both rich and poor together.* In His zeal the Lord continued so that all might gather to hear, and so that none might believe that He would say anything of little account. By the earthborn we are to understand sinners who pursue earthy vices. They are rightly considered as representatives of Adam the first man, for he is said to have been not the son of man but the very first man. In contrast to this is the phrase, *Sons of men;* we must understand by this phrase the just who attain Christ's lot, for Christ too is proclaimed Son of man. Remember that He is always set against Adam, and rightly, since what perished through Adam was saved at Christ's coming. Next follows: *Both rich and poor together.* See how the statement promised earlier shines out, for the phrase, *rich and poor together,* is spoken of Christ the Lord. He is rich because He is God, poor because He is Man. As Paul has it: *Be mindful of the grace of our Lord Jesus Christ, that being rich he became poor for your sakes, that through his poverty you might be rich.*[3] So the preliminary announcement rightly heralded great things, since such outstanding and salutary words were following. The explanation of the previous phrase is brief: *rich* has reference to earth-born, because the wealthy man is known to have countless sins, and *poor* corresponds to *Sons of men,* who are poor in the confines of this world so that they may obtain the riches to come in their fullness. As the gospel says: *Blessed are the poor in spirit, for theirs is the kingdom of heaven.*[4]

4. *My mouth shall speak wisdom: and the meditation of my heart prudence.* He refines on what He began earlier, that he will speak of no human but of a divine wisdom and prudence. That wisdom is the Lord Christ, of whom Paul says: *But we preach Christ, the power of God and the wisdom of God.*[5] Solomon too attests that he knows wisdom and instruction, and understands the words of prudence.[6] *Wisdom* refers to the declaration of the divine mysteries, *prudence* to instruction in praiseworthy manners; and so the whole of God's word is shown to teem with these virtues. From this point onward He has embarked on His future narrative by first describing in marvellous compass the nature of His words, so that all may seek with longing what they feel is promised in such a proclamation.

5. *I will incline my ear by way of simile: I will reveal my plan on the psaltery.* After the true Preacher has said that the power of His eloquence is embraced under these two standards, He turns to how the precepts can now be accepted by the human race. He promised that He would incline His ear to ascertain if His devoted people were carrying out His preaching. But observe that the holy Teacher spoke of a simile. A simile is an imitation of something real, so that through the Lord's kindness we may perform with pious emulation what has been set before us as an example. But that most lucid of instructors wished to entice all men to fulfil His commands for their salvation, so he said that He was revealing His plan on the psaltery, that is, He would declare the commands of His Godhead by means of the holiness of His own body, so that He could be seen teaching not so much by word as by example, for as we have often said[7] the psaltery is a beautiful image for the Lord's body. Just as the sound of the psaltery comes from the top, so the Lord's incarnation celebrates commands from heaven.

6. *Why shall I fear on the evil day? Shall the iniquity of my heel encompass me?* This verse is to be read as question and answer; He is saying that the whole of His prophetic account of the future will find Him unafraid. This figure is called *Question and answer,*[8] when an enquiry is first made, and a suitable reply follows. He asks: *Why shall I fear?,* in other words, Why shall I be disturbed by fearful thoughts? *On the evil day* means on the day of the Passion, which was evil for the Jews but good for the faithful; it is the one who is gnawed by recollection of sins who ought to fear life's end. But Christ could not fear

death, for He had no sins of any kind. He says: *Why shall I fear on the evil day? Shall the iniquity of my heel encompass me,* as usually happens to sinners so that their final days are cut off by an accursed end? But others have suggested that the verse must rather be referred to His members, since His holy incarnation is preeminently perfect.

7. *They that trust in their own strength, and that glory in the abundance of their riches.* These words are a continuation of the previous verse, and must be joined to it; men such as these are encompassed by the iniquity of their heel, for they presume on their own strength when seen to put their trust in their own powers, being physically strong and outstanding in mental faculties and eloquence of tongue. But after He has spoken of their inner attributes, He now comes to the riches which are an external accession and through which their human standing is most greatly puffed up; for it is rare for a rich man to realise that he shares his lot with poor men. Such men must fear death, for they refuse to abandon worldly things, and their consciences attest that they fear punishment for their sins.

8. *Does our brother not redeem, and shall man redeem? He shall not give to God his ransom.* After speaking of sinners whose iniquity encompasses their heel, He passes to the outstanding nature of the healing. These words too, *Does our brother not redeem?* are to be spoken with surprise. That brother is the Lord Jesus Christ, for He said in the gospel; *Go, tell my brothers;*[9] and in a psalm; *I will declare thy name to my brothers.*[10] If He who shed His precious blood did not redeem, will man—that is, Adam, who wounded the human race by the fault of his transgression—redeem? *He shall not give* expresses denial, for no offering, no ransom can square the account for the Godhead's deigning to redeem us.

9. *Nor the price of the redemption of his soul: and he has laboured for ever.* The first part of the verse is attached to the previous statement: man when freed will not pay to God his ransom or the price of the redemption of his soul. The price is the equivalent value of something; what will man give as the price, since he has received all that he has to offer? Next comes: *And he has laboured for ever.* He refers to the faithful here, for though they cannot pay the price of the redemption of their souls, they none the less labour for ever in performing what avails them to obtain the rewards of eternal life.

10. *And he shall live unto the end, since he shall not see destruction.* He

still speaks of those who labour for ever. Since they live unto the end, that is in the Lord Saviour, they shall not see destruction, for though they die in the body, they are enriched with the gift of eternal life. Others think that these verses are to be applied to sinners. They say that those condemned to perpetual vengeance labour for ever. They will live in this world as their end, for they despair of freeing themselves from it, and live degenerately. Readers can choose which interpretation to follow; my view is that up to this point the faithful have been discussed, and now we are to hear what the unfaithful will suffer.

11. *When he shall see the wise dying, the senseless and the fool shall perish together, and they shall leave their riches to strangers.* He passes to the second mode of His teaching, in which He says that sinners will perish together with those who are wise in this world; and He pronounces that their riches which they greatly loved are to be left to foreign heirs and not to their own, a graver affliction. Thus they would not enjoy the possession of the riches which had prompted them to commit all their sins, nor would they rejoice in their kin as heirs. As Solomon says: *They could not rejoice in their sins.*[11] It is the sinner who shall see that the wise of this world are not rescued from death; among them the Athenian Solon, the Spartan Philon, Aristippus[12] and the rest who flourished with the most renowned glory of secular wisdom. He sees them perish one and all, though he reckoned them participants in divine wisdom.

12. *And their sepulchres shall be their houses for ever: their dwelling-places to all descendants and generations: they will invoke their name in their lands.* The ostentation of the wealthy dead is being described; they build tombs for themselves of splendid construction, extending over wide areas. We see some mausoleums gleaming with the finest marble; built as they are of massive masonry, they are regarded as houses that will last. Then He turns to their dwelling-places, which are buttressed by copious resources so that they endure in abiding beauty for long generations and lineages. He appends mention of the ritual which relatives usually conduct for their dead kin, when with foolish superstition they invoke the name of the dead *in their lands,* that is, in their tombs; and they believe that what they are seen to raise in memory of the dead is of benefit to them.

13. *And man when he was in honour did not understand: he is compared to senseless beasts and is become like to them.* He still speaks of

those who flourished with honour in this world; though the sinner is honoured in his lifetime because he bears the image of God, he is rightly said not to understand his dignity when he performs deeds which appear to diverge wholly from the Creator. Next comes: *He is compared to senseless beasts and become like to them.* The simile cited here befits madmen, for persons who do not understand that they bear God's image are aptly compared with senseless beasts. Since they do not show the reason which they gained by the commands and instructions of the Lord, they have rightly forfeited it as being unworthy of so great a gift. Once you take from a man the contemplation of God, he becomes nothing but a senseless beast through his empty presumption and his pride doomed to fall. But though these words, *And man when he was in honour did not understand,* are said of mortal men, they can be understood also of the apostate angels who were expelled from heaven, for they too failed to understand their distinction when they were convicted of arrogance towards their Creator. *Man* is used to describe also the devil, as the Lord attests in the gospel: *And the hostile man that oversowed the cockle is the devil.*[13] This is the tenth type of definition, which the Greeks term *hōs tupō* and the Latins *veluti,*[14] when the association with some object is such that it seems applicable not only to the thing mentioned but also to others. We have already encountered an example of this in Psalm 35: *Men and beasts thou wilt preserve, O Lord,*[15] for the Lord constantly preserves not only these but also all other things.

14. *This way of theirs is a stumbling-block to them: and afterwards they shall bless with their mouths.* The various points which have been listed are now gathered into a single heap like scattered seeds of grain, for following upon the previous verses comes a generalisation, *This way of theirs.* We must interpret *way* as the life in which we walk in this world in the tracks of our actions. He is not reticent about the effects of this way on evil men. It is precisely a stumbling-block, that is a prick and a pain, to those who espouse it, for the sinner achieves nothing for his own safety, but torture is the outcome of his activity. Next comes: *And afterwards they shall bless with their mouths.* The habit of sinners is being described here. After they have achieved the aspiration of their most wicked plans, they then give thanks to the Godhead since they have attained their wish. But they in their utter wretchedness do not realise that He originates only successful aspira-

tions which are holy. *They shall bless* not with their hearts but their mouths, the source of hypocritical utterances for the most part. As Isaiah says: *This people with their lips glorify me, but their heart is far from me.*[16]

15. *They are laid in hell like sheep, and death crops them: and the just will prevail over them in the morning.* He comes to the third part where He says that the just and the wicked are to get their due according to their merits. Eternal death feeds on sinners, who are laid in hell, for just as sheep after the loss of their wool continue to exist, so the substance of these men is undiminished, and death continually finds a part of them to torture with pain. *Crops* is a metaphor adapted from mules, which do not tear out grass by the roots but bite off the tops of the blades. There follows: *And the just will prevail over them in the morning. Prevail over* means overcome. This is precisely the lot of the blessed at the resurrection, that they prevail over the wicked. In this world sinners prevail over the just, but at the Judgment the just will in every way prevail over the unfaithful. *In the morning* is the equivalent of saying, "At the first light of day when the glory of the resurrection dawns"; for then the brightness of blessedness is revealed, and that day begins which is ended by no night.

And their resources shall decay in hell, and they have been driven from their glory. He is still describing the unhappiness of sinners, whose resources decay like putrefying rags. What help will riches lend to the dead, or what will man's presumption avail those who have passed on, who lose all the things that delighted them here, and who succumb to the eternal punishment which they thought they could never suffer? Next comes: *And they have been driven from their glory,* that is, from the world in which they boasted, or from those possessions in which they waxed presumptuous, beguiled by an unhappy fate. So the rich man was told in the gospel: *Fool, this night thy soul will be taken from thee: and whose will those things be which thou has provided?*[17]

16. *But God has freed my soul from the hand of hell, when he shall receive me.* After the faults of sinners have been described, a declaration promising salvation is rightly introduced; so just as human frailty has been laid low with terror, so it may be assisted to rise by the hope of a reward to come. This is appropriate whether the Lord Christ

refers to Himself or whether He speaks as He often does on behalf of His members. For in His descent He freed His own soul from hell, but simultaneously the souls of the people who with devoted spirit believed in His coming. *From the hand of hell* means from the power of the devil, who before Christ's coming held souls in subjection.

17. *Be not thou afraid when a man shall be made rich: and when the glory of his house shall be increased.* The fourth section of the psalm emerges from the mouth of Truth so that a most wholesome medicine may be administered to us; for this is the one complaint throughout the world: why do those men who we know are strangers to the Lord's worship flourish in this life? But this has been promised to sinners; and so the holy Teacher addresses true Christians, bidding them not fear the rich men of the world—for as a rule the moneyed man is an object of fear when greedy men are thought to serve him. *Dives* (rich man) derives from *divus* (divine one)[18] who is believed like God to lack nothing. We must interpret *man* here as the wicked man who makes himself an object of terror to those under him as he spurns the rights of justice. Next follows: *And when the glory of his house shall be increased.* Understand with this: *Be not afraid*; this figure is called *apo koinou* or in common, when earlier words go with later ones. Observe how everything favours the rich man. It was of less account to become rich, because one often finds this in business-men and mean types; but he added: *And when the glory of his house shall be increased,* that is, thronged with distinctions, with possessions, with all the praises of men, so that he thinks nothing lacking to him except supreme power. Note that He spoke of *his house,* so that not only the man himself but also all his connections seem to flourish with great ostentation. But a fine explanation now follows of why these men must not be feared.

18. *For when he shall die he shall not have all these things, nor shall the glory of his house descend with him.* Here the reason is given why the man who is glorious in the world is not to be feared. Why should we fear the rich man when he dies poor? That stumbling-block of ours is not his for ever, and he can take with him only what can make him burn. You admire his consummate elegance and costly garb in this world, but how tawdry he will appear in your eyes in the next! He did well to say that dead sinners *descend;* He means into yawning abysses,

into the deepest pit, without their worldly glory, their crowd of
clients, their array of jewels. The house which you admired remains in
its entirety, but he takes with him the huge burdens which you did
not see.

19. *For in his lifetime his soul will be blessed: and he shall praise thee
when thou shalt do well to him. Will be blessed* does not mean here
achieving sanctification, but winning the flattering words of degenerate men; the phrase is used to describe the tongues of lackeys who in
gossip and feasting often wish their patrons well, praising their souls
not for any good works but for providing fine dishes. Next comes: *He
shall praise thee when thou shalt do well for him.* Evil men bless God
when they obtain temporal goods, whereas the good man praises the
Lord even when afflicted by a mass of misfortunes, as Job and the
other saints did. So the Father is told: this sinner will praise You, but
only when You do well to him; if he suffers a contrary experience, he
never stops blaspheming. So this tendency found quite often in
wicked men is to be avoided. Let us praise the Lord with dutiful heart
at all times, for He is always achieving our salvation in periods of both
ill-fortune and good fortune.

20. *He shall go into the generation of his fathers: and he shall not see
light for ever.* Those who imitate very evil fathers will be condemned
together with them, so He says that sinners have gone into the generations of their fathers. By their fathers he means not so much physical
progenitors as those whose manners they have imitated. As He says to
unbelievers in the gospel: *You are of your father the devil.*[19] He added:
He shall not see light for ever, for sins overshadow and remove from
sinners the light of wisdom. So he said: *He shall not see light for ever,*
for even in this world no rays shone on him since his guilty heart was
shrouded in the mist of error; likewise he shall not see it for ever
because he has not deserved to obtain it through the fault of his wickedness in this world. For *the true light which illumines every man that
comes into the world*[20] is the Lord Christ, and only saints are allowed to
see Him in His divinity.

21. *And man when he was in honour did not understand: he hath been
compared to senseless beasts, and made like to them.* After forewarning
us with these necessary words He ended this most beautiful psalm by

balancing repetition of this verse.[21] He wished the sinner to abandon his evil way of life after realising from repeated rebukes that his foul condition was branded.

Conclusion Drawn From the Psalm

This psalm is to be read repeatedly and stored in the treasury of the memory, for He warns us at the outset that we must listen to it with our hearts' ears. Christ Himself attested its merit, since He earnestly urged that men listen to it in all quarters of the world. It contains all that pertains to contemplative and moral instruction. As that notable verse promised: *My mouth shall speak wisdom, and the meditation of my heart prudence.*[22] Holy Truth has unfolded to us what He promised; may He now make His precepts become sweet and cleave fast to our hearts.

COMMENTARY ON PSALM 49

1. *A psalm for Asaph.* Asaph was the son of Barachiel. We read in Chronicles[1] that he was chosen as one of the four teachers of cantors to play psalms to the Lord on musical instruments. In accord with the meaning of his name he deserved to be cited in this heading not as the author of the psalm—we have made this point about others—but as an outstanding musician, so that he could tell us something through his name. The sense of this name, which is always full of mysteries for the Jews, points to the synagogue,[2] which speaks in this psalm. But here we must understand it as the faithful synagogue of the Lord, which both believed that Christ would come and embraced His coming with exultant anticipation. In it were numbered the patriarchs, prophets, Nathaniel, and also the apostles and all who believed with pure devotion. We must clearly realise that this psalm prophesies both the first and the second coming of the Lord. Psalms 95 and 97 are known to proclaim the same tidings, so the unbelieving Jews are utterly de-

prived of any excuse, for they do not accept what the very synagogue attests. What then do they worship, if they spurn the words of the synagogue, which they claim to revere?

Division of the Psalm

In the first section the faithful synagogue, which now comprises the Christian people, speaks of the first and second coming of the Lord Christ. In the second part Christ the King himself speaks. He warns the people that they should abandon cattle as sacrificial victims, and instead offer a sacrifice of praise. In the third section the devoted synagogue already mentioned speaks afresh, ascribing to sinners their wicked deeds.

Explanation of the Psalm

The God of gods, the Lord hath spoken: and he hath called the earth, from the rising of the sun to the going-down thereof. So that no individual should believe that the Lord's incarnation is to be accorded but modest importance, His power is foretold beforehand, so that the debased nature of all unbelief may be removed. *Gods* is the title accorded to men who in their goodly life receive the grace of the heavenly Majesty; in His words of another psalm: *I have said, You are gods, and all of you sons of the most High.*[3] They are called both sons and gods because grace, not nature, grants them both titles. The God of gods is the Lord Christ; with the Father and holy Spirit He is truly called God of gods, though the title is not wholly appropriate to the Godhead because the human tongue cannot, as we have already said, indicate the height of the Godhead beyond this. *Deus* (God) in the Greek language means fear,[4] and since He alone is to be feared the word attained the role of a title. We read in Exodus: *My name Adonai I did not show them.*[5] From this we are to realise that the name is secret, and is known to have been revealed not even to chosen ministers. So He spoke through prophets, through apostles, and more powerfully through His own mouth.

Next comes: *And he hath called the earth.* We must interpret earth here as the human race clearly scattered through the whole world. Because of that which it inhabits, it is said to be inhabited; otherwise how could He have called that which could not hear? This figure is called *metonymy*,[6] when what is contained is given the name of what contains it. The psalmist added: *From the rising of the sun to the going down thereof.* By the course of the sun he points to the whole world, for its brightness rises and sets over the whole earth. The advent of the holy incarnation achieved this so that the devoted Physician could attract all nations, wounded by base errors, to the healing which is belief in Him. As Christ Himself said; *Come to me, all ye who labour and are burdened, and I will give you rest.*[7]

2. *Out of Sion the loveliness of his beauty.* Here Jerusalem is meant. It is within this city that the mountain gleams like gold metal on pure hearts. The apostles on leaving the city announced through the whole world Christ's lovely beauty. As Isaiah says: *The law shall come forth from Sion, and the word of the Lord from Jerusalem.*[8] It is a revered city, a holy hill-top; we can rightly call that notable dwelling of our King the earth's citadel. Observe how fittingly we are instructed. In the previous verse the synagogue had said that Christ the Lord was summoning all nations; now she also points to the place from where His teaching flowed over the bounds of the whole world as from a clear and most rich stream. The words of the gospel are in harmony with this verse, which begins from Jerusalem and traverses all nations, for Christ began to be proclaimed from there.[9] His lovely beauty is known, as another psalm attests: *Thou art beautiful above the sons of men.*[10] We explained sufficiently in that place why He is called uniquely beautiful.

3. *God shall come manifestly, our God, and shall not keep silence: a fire shall burn in his sight, and a mighty tempest shall be round about him.* After the synagogue of the faithful has said much about the first coming, she passes to Christ the Saviour's second coming, which by the figure known as *idea*[11] she describes with marvellous imagery in the form of different similes, so that He seems to be present rather than soon to come. By saying that He shall come manifestly, she shows that He was not clear to all at His first coming, for His majesty was hidden by the cloud of the flesh. As Paul says of the unfaithful: *If they had known it, they would never have crucified the Lord of glory.*[12] He will indeed come manifestly, when He is not to be nailed to a cross, but to judge the world. The word *manifestly* is adopted from sacrifices when the whole day was made available for celebration; the word derives

from *a mane dies festus* (festive from the early morning).[13] She repeats *God* with *our* so that the unfaithful may not believe that they share Him; for the God of Christians is the God of gods who shall both come manifestly and not keep silence. He is silent only when this world runs its course, when He does not condemn blasphemous and sacrilegious words by a harsh sentence, but sustains sinners towards the healing of conversion. He will not be silent when He says to the wicked: *Depart into eternal fire which was prepared for the devil and his angels.*[14] So elsewhere He says: *I have been silent, silent: surely I will not be silent for ever?*[15]

As for what follows: *A fire shall burn in his sight,* it is the splendid coming of the great Judge already mentioned which is being described with mystical power; for fire is said to move forward, so that the man who is straw fears that he will blaze. She added: *And a mighty tempest shall be round about him.* The tempest is not driven by winds nor roused by savage storms; rather a forceful breeze arises through divine power, so that the Lord's threshing-floor is aired by the pronouncement of His justice. Then He separates the corn from the chaff, in other words, the good from the wicked. This adjudication is rightly called a tempest, for it will come unexpectedly, and with extreme speed will snatch men up to hear His decision. *Mighty* is also aptly added. We are given to understand the extent of its strength by the fact that with the speed of a moment it weeds out the whole human race according to its merits. As Paul says: *In a moment, in the twinkling of an eye, at the last trumpet: for the trumpet shall sound, and the dead shall rise again.*[16] *A mighty tempest shall be round about him* is a quite apt observation, for the just will take their seats in judgment with Him, as the gospel promises.[17]

4. *He shall call up heaven and earth to judge his people.* He will certainly do this at the Judgment. The earth is perhaps reasonably said to be called up, situated as it is known to be in the lowest region; but how did He call heaven upward, when it is already above? The fact is that we must interpret *heaven* here as every just man, and earth as every sinner; for the just man with the Lord's help purifies himself by spiritual life while the sinner grows foul with the earthly nature of his vices. Note that at His first coming He had summoned all without distinction, so that once instructed they should amend themselves in this world; as He says in the gospel: *They went out into the ways and*

gathered together all they found, both good and bad.[18] But at the end of the world He calls up heaven, that He may now separate the just from the wicked, that they may no longer be mixed together as here in mingled dwellings.

5. *Gather ye together his saints to him, who dispense his testament before sacrifices.* Christ's synagogue now addressed the angels, who at the end of the world will by their service gather the saints from the whole earth, as Scripture says; for the Lord states in the gospel: *He shall send his angels, and they shall gather before him all the nations, and he shall separate them one from another, as the shepherd separates the sheep from the goats.*[19] Next comes: *Who dispense his testament before sacrifices.* We say that those men dispense the testament who by good deeds reenact the precepts acknowledged in the course of the Testament, such as receiving guests, giving alms, devoting oneself to charity. Clearly this is more acceptable to the Lord than the sacrifice of cattle, so that worthy deeds are offered to Him instead. Or as some would have it, this can be understood of the Jews in an ironical or taunting sense, when she scoffingly praises what is cheap, as if she were saying: "Gather before the Lord those slow to perform their holy duty, and who instead do impious deeds, and who because they celebrate their customary sacrifices to the Lord think themselves worthy of sanctification."

6. *And the heavens shall declare his justice: for God is judge.* She refines on her earlier statement, intimating by *the heavens* the just man to whom is granted the task of disseminating the divine word. She added: *For God is judge,* as if to say, "For He cannot be deceived, and knowing as He does all things clearly, He distinguishes without error." The claim is made truthfully and peculiarly of God; nothing is refused Him, nothing is suppressed before Him, no deed escapes Him, nothing on which He sits in judgment is hidden from Him.

7. *Hear, O my people, and I will speak, O Israel, and I will testify to thee: for I am God, thy God.* We have come to the second section, in which Truth himself now speaks in His own person. God does not wish His words to be received to no purpose—as Scripture says,[20] the swine should not scatter pearls—so He says to the people: *Hear,* that is, listen with devotion. We say that people hear when they fulfil what is enjoined. As Scripture has it: *He that has ears to hear, let him hear.*[21] *My people* denotes the crowd of the committed. With the words: *And I*

will speak, understand "words of profit. If you do not hear them, the result is my silence at your death." Israel, as we have frequently said, means "seeing God." "So if you see Me, do not neglect to hear Me, for seeing Me implants obedience in the listener." Testifying means giving testimony; the Lord will do this especially at the Judgment, when He will examine the deeds of each of us. Then He will give testimony to His faithful, when He will say: *I was hungry, and you gave me to eat,*[22] and words such as this. Next comes: *For I am God, thy God.* This is what with earnest entreaty He warned the people to hear, for He was in general the God of all alike, of the willing and unwilling, and in particular of those who love Him with unsullied hearts. When He says: *Thy,* He shows that the people were faithful to Him. The repetition *God, God* strengthens the mind, so that words may not slip away through being uttered only once. The phrase, *I am,* belongs to the divinity. It does not change with time, but is always there, and remains eternal. So the reply to Moses was: *I am who am,* and again: *He is who has sent me.*[23] But we must first investigate why God alone claims this term which denotes essence for Himself. When it was spoken, there were angels, heavenly creatures, and all earthly creatures as were decreed to exist. But because He is the only uncreated and eternal nature which did not begin in time and subsists as one divinity in three Persons, God alone is rightly said to be, for He needs no-one for His existence, but ever abides by the strength of His own power. In it there is another mystery; a single syllable, *sum* (I am), is embraced by three letters, so we are taught that the holy Trinity is one God.

8. *I will not reprove thee over thy sacrifices, but thy holocausts are always in my sight.* The famed Teacher and most perfect Educator wishes to divert the Jewish people from the things of the flesh, and to guide them to the mysteries of the spirit, and so He says that sacrifices of cattle are not to be sought. He attests that if a man were utterly to forgo the sacrifice of animal victims, he is not on that count to be reproved. He states that instead those holocausts are to be offered in His sight which are bestowed on holy altars with humility of heart. *Holocausts* means sacrifices which, after the offering, were burnt by fire applied from above; in Latin the phrase is *tota incensa,* wholly burnt. When Christ came, He spurned them because He was the true Victim. There is another holocaust which the Lord proclaims is al-

ways in His sight; this is when our minds are fired with divine love and boil away their sins in affliction, and like that holocaust burn and consume all their faults by torture of the body.

9. *I will not take calves out of thy house, nor he-goats out of thy flocks.* Through this verse and the two which follow He briefly recounts what He proclaims He is rejecting. This figure is called *brachylogia*[24] or brief statement, when we embrace several points in a few words. In case the human mind should hasten back to the old sacrifices on hearing the word holocaust, He explicitly rejects that former custom so that we may interpret in a spiritual sense what was previously introduced in simile. But when He rejects these two types of victim, He indicates that all sacrifices of early times are to be wholly excluded. The whole is signified by the part.

10. *For all the beasts of the woods are mine, the cattle on the hills and the oxen.* He gave the reason why He does not expect from His people the sacrifice of animals in these words: "I do not seek from you what I know is mine. Perhaps the poor man does not possess an animal because he could not catch one, or was unable to feed one." Instead He seeks an upright faith and devoted praise which all can offer through His mercy, even those blessed with no earthly possessions. It is in this sense that He recounts the rest of His list. He adds: *The cattle on the hills and the oxen,* so that no-one should put faith in the availability of these, and should disregard his conscience believing that by sacrifices he can expiate the sins of a wicked mind. This verse can be understood in another sense: the beasts of the wood represent pagans living in the most fierce superstition in the forests of this world, the cattle on the hills are the simple persons in the Catholic Church who are known to dwell on the summit of faith, and the oxen point to the apostles and prophets who toil continually in the fields of the Lord. So by means of these allusions appropriately set before us, He prefigures the Catholic Church which is to be assembled from different parts of the world.

11. *I know all the fowls of the air: and with me is the beauty of the field.* Do not take *I know* in the sense of our feeble knowledge which when occasion offers gets to know something there and then. The Lord knows the whole creation before He made it; everything which could have come into existence did so in His presence. Who can know all the fowls of the air except the Majesty alone? With this short verse

He embraced all things, for He knows all the fowls of the air, and can assess their number. He claimed to have the beauty of the field truly with Him because He is wholly everywhere. As the prophet says of Him: *I fill heaven and earth.*[25] But we must interpret this in a spiritual sense. Fowls of the air represent the wondrous heavenly virtues such as angelic powers, which in a spiritual sense rush across with swift motion according to their holy will. The beauty of the field represents the Gentiles who were to believe in Christ the Lord; this is truly beauty, for the world's entire glory is properly interpreted through the agency of man.

12. *If I am hungry, I will not tell thee: for the world is mine, and the fulness thereof.* The God of gods, as we have often observed, deigns to express His will in terms of human habits for our understanding. So He says He is hungry though He feeds all bodies and though contemplation of Him is the sweetest food and satisfying refreshment of all spiritual substances. Next comes: *For the world is mine, and the fulness thereof.* Here He rebukes superfluous solicitude, and gives His reason: "Why should I seek from you the sacrifices of cattle, when the whole world is known to be mine?" *The fulness thereof* refers to the diversity of creatures. So human concern must cease to give thought to unnecessary sacrifice of cattle; the Godhead prefers us to offer Him an upright heart in which we are known to have erred, so that what was previously foul with errant sins may become most pure with the cleansing that brings salvation. And remember that by these references He indicates the number of the predestined, which is to be filled out not merely from the synagogue of the Jews but also from the Gentiles.

13. *Shall I eat the flesh of bullocks? Or shall I drink the blood of goats?* In how many ways He deigns to give an account of His will! How will unnecessary things be welcome to Him? Does God eat bullocks' flesh or drink goats' blood? But the rejection of these can avail us when the needy receive them, when the hungry man eats and the thirsty man drinks. God in the person of the poor accepts what He does not allow to be offered Him in sacrifices.

14. *Offer to God the sacrifice of praise: and pay thy vows to the most High.* Up to this point He has mentioned what He rejects; now He states what He demands. The words of the statement are few but clearly wide in meaning. Who offers the sacrifice of praise except the

person distanced from earthly vices, the person who dies to the world to become a victim for Christ? The Lord is not pleased if a base individual sings His praises; undoubtedly He looks for an act worthy of approval, not a melodious voice. So let us sacrifice to the Lord by praising the wisdom with which He orders all things, the kindly love with which He spares sinners, the courage with which He conquers the devil. The term sacrifice is not applicable solely to the slaughter of cattle, but also to every offering which wins favour for us as a pious presentation. He too makes vows to the most High who makes preparations for them by making such sacrifices as the kindly Lord enjoins. He added: *Thy,* so that you would not chance to look for external things—a rich goat, a fat steer, and the rest which mental reasoning realises are externals; *Thy* has reference to the heart's secret lying in the recesses of the soul; this is not sought externally. Poor and rich possess it equally, the needy man is richer in it, and by it the humble of heart is much more exalted. But let us examine this more carefully, for here too we find a type of language which general eloquence does not deploy. God says: *If I am hungry, I shall not tell thee;* there is no change of speaker, and a little later He says: *Offer to God the sacrifice of praise,* and in the following verse He has added: *But to the sinner God hath said....* The sequence of our normal speech required Him to say: "If I am hungry, I shall not tell thee," and the rest; "Offer to me the sacrifice of praise"; and "I have said to the sinner, why dost thou declare my justice?" Though as one and the same Person He speaks of Himself, He seems to interweave a second spokesman in His words, and this is rightly counted among the peculiarities of divine Scripture.

15. *And call upon me in the day of thy trouble: and I will rescue thee, and thou shalt glorify me.* After stating the kind of sacrifice which appeased Him, He now promises the reward of that offering. He orders: *Call upon me,* so that none would set hope in earthly consolation, in which all things are transient and consolations feebler. *In the day of thy trouble,* that is, when another afflicts you, not when you are nettled that an enemy has escaped you. For our trouble is that which arises out of fear for our own salvation, not that provoked through fear of our bodily possessions. As Paul says: *For the sorrow that is according to God worketh penance steadfast unto salvation: but the sorrows of the world worketh death.*[26] *I will rescue thee.* In other words, 'I will free you with the utmost speed, since you are engulfed by the

devil's supporters', *And thou shalt glorify me:* "You must declare me great for ever, for I am freeing you from punishment, and shall set you in blessed rest." Some wish to refer this verse, so rich in boundless promise, to the closing stage of our life, when the soul as it passes from this life is disturbed by the struggle with unclean spirits; we read that the soul of Moses was impeded in this way.[27] See what small things the Lord asks of us, and what great things He will afford us!

16. *But to the sinner God hath said: Why dost thou declare my justice, and take for granted my testament in thy mouth?* We have come to the third part, where Asaph, the devoted synagogue, again speaks. And because the Lord had earlier said that He could accept men's praises in place of sacrifices, she is anxious that sinners should not trust in this promise and say: "Praise alone and not deeds that win approval are known to have been enjoined on us." She makes this statement with all the inevitability of reason, and prevents from presuming to sing God's praises those whose disfigured conscience could be an obstacle. This figure is called *percunctatio* (enquiry); it does not trouble to await a reply from the other person.[28] Wicked men are forbidden from presuming to take part in conversations with God. But ponder more deeply the fact that this is said about the sinners described below; she says of them: *Understand these things, all you that forget the Lord.*[29] But the divine clemency does not forbid the converted and repentant to utter praises. It is the hard of heart, who do not cease from their wicked crimes, who are prevented from declaring the Lord's justice, that is, from uttering even in general speech anything about that Majesty, for the mouth which presumes to declare the Lord's justice must itself be just. It follows that unworthy presumption should not handle His Testament either, so that holy and revered words do not appear to be able to emanate from a wicked and blasphemous mouth. As Scripture has it elsewhere: *Praise is not seemly in the mouth of a sinner.*[30] *Testament* refers to both the Old and the New, for when one is mentioned indeterminately both are being cited. This verse can also refer to heretical teachers presuming to teach God's law, for *taking for granted* suggests the presumption of the uncommitted. It does not seem that she was forbidding believers to read Scripture when she deigned to issue a warning to sinners in particular.

17. *Seeing thou hast hated discipline and hast cast my words behind thee.* She begins to take count of those to whom God's word is known to be forbidden; that man hates discipline who grumbles with wicked presumption at justified correction, and does not wish the Lord to punish him for his sins. We obtain salutary cleansing if we love more the means of our correction. It is better to be afflicted here for a short time than to be condemned at the Judgment. In addition, he who despises divine commands, and does not keep in view what is appropriate always to behold, casts the words of God behind him.

18. *If thou didst see a thief, thou didst run together with him, and with adulterers thou hast been a partaker.* He who forbids lesser crimes condemns much more greater ones. What is theft by comparison with murder? Or adultery compared with sacrilege? We must assume that He appears to have forbidden all sins with the prohibition of these two. This figure is called "the whole from the part,"[31] and is known to be employed both in this psalm and earlier. He rebukes the sinner for running with the thief; that is, for joining him in the shared intention of committing a crime, so that the crime which the thief could perhaps not achieve alone he perpetrates with his help. We must carefully examine the words: *With adulterers thou hast been a partaker.* If by a gift of money or by advice or praise he renders help to an adulterer so that by this means he attains his desires, he undoubtedly shares in the adultery. If a man has the opportunity, but does not recall the sinner from evil, he becomes a partner in the sin, because we owe this obligation to charity, not to allow ourselves or others to perish.

19. *Thy mouth hath abounded with wickedness, and thy tongue fashioned deceit.* First she rebukes sinners for theft and adultery; they are now further accused of wickedness of heart and craftiness of tongue. We must interpret *mouth* here as the thought of the heart, because she is to speak next of the tongue. The wickedness of our thoughts abounds when the human mind advances in the delights of this world and proceeds through different varieties of sinning with wicked intention. Next comes: *And thy tongue fashioned deceit.* This must be understood in many senses. He who praises falsely deals guile; he who advances malevolent designs behaves with similar wickedness; and finally all that is not true and simple is the outcome of guileful man-

ners. The expression *fashioned* is most appropriately used because it is the custom of deceivers to order their falsehoods in such a way that they coax the ears of listeners with a certain charm of words. So we shall read in Psalm 54: *They have softened their words smoother than oil, and they are darts.*[32]

20. *Sitting, thou didst speak detraction against thy brother, and didst lay a scandal against thy mother's son.* Sitting is the posture of one who lingers, so the blame is more pronounced because he has not slipped into detraction of his neighbour through the operation of some chance, but has settled into extended obloquy of his brother. *Brother* here we must interpret as all who are close in the flesh, for she is to speak later of our spiritual kin. But notice the curse with which this sin is condemned, so that he who has involved himself in such wickedness can be accounted among the greatest sinners. As the apostle James says: *He that detracteth his brother, detracteth the law and judgeth the law.*[33] Next comes: *And didst lay a scandal against thy mother's son.* The mother's son refers to the offspring of the Church, to which we are joined in brotherly love through the birth of regeneration. So the person who lays a scandal against his brother is he who devises heretical sins or other traps by which the innocent person can be caught. Of such people the man of wisdom says: *He that speaketh sophistically is likewise hateful.*[34] The word *lay* was apt because of the traps set in ambush and concealed by verbal cunning, so that simplicity off its guard may be caught by hidden bonds.

21. *These things hast thou done, and I was silent. Thou didst devise iniquity, thinking that I shall be like to thee. I shall reprove thee, and set it before thy face.* Observe how she gathers here in one sentence the more diverse statements made earlier. She says that when sinners were busy at work, the just Lord not unfairly postponed His judgment, so that time for conversion could be found while the punishment of condemnation was in abeyance. But she explains what belief arose in those wicked minds from the Creator's kindness. She says: *Thou didst devise iniquity, thinking that I shall be like to thee.* This is the tendency of mortals: whenever we allow evils to be committed and fail to resist them openly, we seem to be in sympathy with them through similarity of character. She now maintains that the wicked man has this view of

the Lord, that because He postpones judgment the crimes of men are thought to have pleased Him. But a just sentence is pronounced on this debased understanding. Earlier He said that His words were cast behind the sinner's back; now He says that by the opposite fate each person's sins are to be set before his face. Through this statement we know the nature of the judgment to come: every sinner will see before him what he thought had slipped by through the mercy of oblivion. What unbounded apprehension and fear beyond reckoning, that men should see the things which they know are the cause of their journey to eternal punishment!

22. *Understand these things, you that forget the Lord, lest he snatch you away and there be none to deliver you.* Here there is an *apostrophe* or turning towards those sinners who she earlier forbade to recount the Lord's praises. She says: *Understand,* that is, faithfully obey. So that you might not think that this was addressed to all sinners, she added: *You that forget the Lord.* It is the sinner who prays and punishes himself by self-abasing satisfaction who does not forget the Lord. So she has shown in small compass the persons of whom this is said. It is a boundless sin, intolerable negligence, to forget the Lord who bestowed on us our souls, who feeds our flesh and protects the faithful from all adversity. It is certainly madness not to remember Him who is clearly always present with us. But who are they that forget the Lord but those who despise His commands with wicked presumption? Next follows: *Lest he snatch you away, and there be none to deliver you.* When the devil snatches us, there is One to deliver us unto salvation; but when the Lord drags a man to punishment, there is none who can free the condemned one, for the very author of sins is condemned to eternal torture.

23. *The sacrifice of praise has glorified me: and there is the way in which I will show him the salvation of God.* This is posited against those who though unworthy presumed to sing the praises of the Lord. *The sacrifice of praise has glorified me*—not that which wicked men sing, but that which a pure heart is wont to offer. The Lord is honoured by that sacrifice of praise which has been consecrated by purity of faith and worth of deeds. There follows: *And there is the way.* By *the way* He means the most blessed psalmody. He explains where this path leads

with the words: *I will show him the salvation of God.* This is the splendid path which leads to the Creator of heaven and earth, but this way which is cited is trodden not by feet but by saintly minds. If we walk it with pure hearts it leads us to Christ, and it becomes for us that ladder which led those who mounted it to heaven.

Conclusion Drawn From the Psalm

This would be a most profitable psalm if only the Jews' wickedness were willing to recognise it. Initially it discussed the incarnation of the Lord. Further, the Saviour himself warns that His devoted people must abandon cattle as sacrificial victims, and discharge the sacrifices of the heart; and He forbade the sinner who did not believe in Christ to proclaim the Godhead. Next He records the nature of the sacrifice of praise which is to be offered. Finally, He revealed how the sinner is to be judged. Why, you Jews, do you still act foolishly? Why do you not fear your own death? Listen to the synagogue as she proclaims the Lord's incarnation and the future Judgment. Believe that He whose coming was foretold has already been seen. The remedies which you seek are not far off. The next psalm absolves you, if you hasten to the rewards of repentance. Why do you cut yourselves off from the universal remedy? That which frees us saves you too. Let us say together: *Have mercy on me, O God, according to thy great mercy.*[35] Seek baptism, take the flesh which you crucified, drink the blood which you shed. A holy confession can absolve the sin which unholy prayers clearly committed.

COMMENTARY ON PSALM 50

1–2. *Unto the end, a psalm of David, when Nathan the prophet came to him after he had sinned with Bathsheba.* It is worth examining this psalm a little more carefully, so that we may deserve to learn through the Lord's kindness the deep mysteries of its power. Because the king and prophet prostrated himself in making humble satisfaction, as the history of the Kings attests,[1] and because he rebuked his sin and was not ashamed to confess it publicly, the most holy Fathers decreed that he was worthy to be honoured as a specially consecrated type. For blessed Jerome among others points out that Bathsheba manifested a type of the Church or of human flesh, and says that David bore the mark of Christ;[2] this is clearly apt at many points. Just as Bathsheba when washing herself unclothed in the brook of Cedron delighted David and deserved to attain the royal embraces,[3] and her husband was slain at the prince's command, so too the Church, the assembly of the faithful, once she has cleansed herself of the foulness of sins by the bath of sacred baptism, is known to be joined to Christ the Lord. It was indeed appropriate in those days that the future mysteries of the Lord should be manifested by a deed of this kind, and that what men considered a blameworthy act should be shown to point in a spiritual sense to a great mystery. For God also ordered the prophet Osee to take a harlot to wife[4] so that it might become clear that the Church of the Gentiles, befouled by its sins, would be cleansed by union with the Lord. We find that this was enacted in figure also by Judah and his daughter-in-law Thamar;[5] as Paul says: *All these things happened to them in figure.*[6] Augustine, in the books which he wrote against the Manichee Faustus,[7] discussed this typology of David and Bathsheba amongst other subjects most carefully. So this and any other parallel was of great service to the world, because though he sinned he was to make such satisfaction, and thus humanity won eternal salvation from the transient wound of one man.

I ask you, how great was the blessed man's humility in acknowledging his fault when he showed such constancy in making satisfaction after he was pardoned? That sin of adultery is shown to have been foreign and uncharacteristic, since it was lamented with such concentration of mind. The sudden confession of the thief attracts us; we rejoice that Peter's tears were quickly in evidence; the short-lived humility of the publican we find charming.[8] But David with his more prolonged attempt to wipe away his sins afforded all men a chance to absolve themselves. He ensured that his tears, running down the faces of people who came after him, are dried with no lapse of time. Let us note also the prophet's humility. An inner voice terrified that prince's heart and he directed his anger at himself, for he knew that the rebuke by which he was blamed was just. Then that ruler over huge nations became his own harshest torturer, demanding from himself a punishment which he could scarcely have borne at another's command. It is the common practice to excuse one's own sins with specious explanations, but this most powerful king elected instead to accuse himself in the sight of all. He whose judgment the people had been accustomed to fear pronounced himself guilty. So he deserved absolution from the Lord because he did not defend his faults. It is in most joyful times that we must chiefly be on our guard against sins. When persecuted by Saul, he who had sinned in the security of his kingdom practised many virtues. We are instructed by this that we ought not to seek happiness in this world, since we make more progress in affliction and we sin more in good times. We must remember that in this psalm the status of the argument is that called "concession"; in this the defendant does not defend his action by argument, but simply asks pardon.[9] There is no doubt that this can be seen as a general rule in the penitential psalms.

Division of the Psalm

We observe that this psalm is fashioned in a most appropriate arrangement with five sections. Just as all sins are gathered under the five senses, so the evil incurred can be expiated by the same number of headings. The first is satisfaction, consisting of the most perfect humility. The second is trust in the Lord's mercy; it is always profitable for the faithful to possess this. In the third is embodied the plea that the Lord may divert His gaze from the psalmist's sins, and that instead the holy Trinity may gaze on him with mercy. In the fourth he appends the message that all sinners should be roused more and more towards a longing to make entreaty in the hope that such great wickedness may be pardoned them. In the fifth part is mentioned the cause of the Church, which was to be built through his seed at the Lord's coming; at this point he rejoices and promises that steers will be offered at his altar. Thus the pious supplication is concluded, and the joys of salvation to come are announced.

Explanation of the Psalm

3. *Have mercy on me, O God, according to thy great mercy of heart. And according to the multitude of thy tender mercies blot out my iniquity.*

When that most powerful king, an outstanding victor over many nations, heard himself rebuked by the prophet Nathan, he did not blush
to confess his sins openly or have recourse to the harmful excuses to
which men hasten in their utter shamelessness. He at once prostrated
himself with salutary humility, offered himself to God, and repentant
in his prince's purple made entreaty with holy tears. The faithful
servant does not cling to brash denials, but quickly realises the faults
which he has committed. What a marvellous beginning! By saying to
the Judge: *Have mercy on me,* he is seen to have removed the need for a
trial. These words are not disputed, but always heard in an atmosphere
of calm. This is the only means by which we can be defended when on
trial without opposition. He sought the mercy of heart which he could
not define, but which he felt was in every way greater than his sins.
Who could be competent to explain its extent, as the most holy Fathers have said? God removed the Creator of the world from heaven,
and clothed its Founder in an earthly body; He made coequal with
mortal man Him who remains equal to the Father in eternity, and for
us clothed the Lord of the world in the form of a servant, so that the
Bread itself endured hunger, the Fountain of life thirsted, Strength
was weakened, and all-powerful Life suffered death. In short, what
greater mercy of heart could there be than that for us the Creator
should be created, the Controller should be the servant, the Redeemer
sold, the Exalter humbled, the Life-giver slain? This was the great
mercy of heart which the holy man could not explain, but he readily
believed that he was absolved through that mercy which he already
knew could free the human race. As for the words, *Have mercy on me,
O God, according to thy great mercy,* this is the mode of argument from
etymological connection;[10] mercy proceeds from the Fount of the
heart's mercy. Next comes: *And according to the multitude of thy tender
mercies blot out my iniquity.* What could the Lord fail to give, when He
was begged to show pardon in accordance with His own nature? The
extent of God's kindness overtops any dimension of sins; no sin could
prevail against an appeal for the aid of such great mercy. This argument is called "from the greater to the lesser";[11] the Lord's mercy is
much the greater, though our sins seem great. So he prays for the
abundance of fatherly love in all his sins, since through the prophet
Nathan he had obtained forgiveness for his present wickedness, and
thus deserved additionally to escape the sins which he remembered

having committed at other times. With the greatest prudence he wanted no trace of sinning to remain, for only those whose entire sins are expunged are enrolled in the book of life.

4. *Wash me everywhere clean of my injustice: and cleanse me from my sin.* He must be carefully cleansed, for he is stained with the poison of wicked deeds. He who is spotted by the contamination of darkness is not washed clean without care. *Everywhere* means on all sides, at every point, so that the Lord might pardon also the sins which He knew had been committed earlier. A person can be washed in such a way that he is not absolutely clean; but he added: *Cleanse me,* so that no impurity could remain in him. This washing, which removes the stain of sins so as to make what is foul whiter than snow, is seen to denote the purity of baptism which brings salvation. By this all sins, both original and personal, are so cleansed that it restores us to the purity in which we know the first Adam was procreated. Would that we could preserve the dignity of that great gift so that sins should not sprout again and blacken us! So the prophet, as he prefigures sacred baptism, begs to be cleansed of his injustice, so that once relaxed in his untroubled state he may not seem to be indifferent once he is pardoned. We ought to take the greatest precautions that our circumstances do not become subject to punishment. As Solomon says: *Only at his death will a man be praised.*[12]

5. *For I recognise my iniquity, and my sin is always before me.* The prophet is aware that the Lord's love is such that He does not cease to be just as well, and he appropriately introduced justice into his plea so that his request would be more readily heard through the incorporation of justice. He knows that sin must be punished, but says that the Lord must spare him because he confirms from his own mouth that he is condemned. As Solomon puts it: *The just man is his own accuser at the start of his speech.*[13] So let us observe that he says: *I recognise.* The sins which we commit with knowledge are graver; those which we do in ignorance are not. Alternatively, all can know their sins, but the only persons known to acknowledge them are those seen to condemn them by personally cursing them. Perfect repentance lies in avoiding future sins and lamenting those of the past. Initially after his sin, when the prophet questioned him, David replied that the man who coveted

the poor man's ewe not belonging to him was worthy of death; at that time David did not believe that his sin should be lamented. But now as he prostrates himself and utters suppliant groans, he regrets that the sins stand before him like some shadow of a ghost. He added: *Always*, because he continually sees the sin, even when he closes his eyes. This regular contemplation of his sins reveals the perseverance of devoted supplication. Next time we look at such things with the mind's eye, we regret having done them. The Lord said in the previous psalm: *I will reprove thee and set thy iniquity before thy face.*[14] This is what the most holy man did to himself when he said: *And my sin is always before me.* He was right to seek forgiveness, for he seemed to have observed the shape of the judgment to come. This figure is called *procatalepsis* or anticipation,[15] for David fears the most grisly appearance of his sins as though already on trial at the coming judgment.

6. *To thee only have I sinned, and have done evil before thee: that thou mayst be justified in thy words, and mayst overcome when thou art judged.* Here a second example of a meditative syllogism appears; we have already mentioned this at Psalm 20.[16] The proposition of it is: "The Lord is justified in His words, and he overcomes when He is judged." To this is joined as conclusion the statement earlier set down, *To thee only have I sinned, and have done evil before thee.* It is clear that the custom of the ancients allowed this practice without censure in the expression of syllogisms.[17] Now let us return to explanation of the words. If one of the people errs, he sins before God and the king; but when the king errs, he is answerable only to God, for there is no man to judge his deeds. So the king rightly says that he has sinned to God alone, for only God could have investigated his conduct. And because he knew that God is everywhere, he rightly lamented that he had done evil before Him, and rebuked his own lunacy for not fearing to sin in the presence of so great a Judge. The words of the Lord are rightly said to be justified, for undoubtedly His words are always fulfilled. As He Himself says: *Heaven and earth will pass away, but my words will not pass away.*[18] Next comes: *And thou mayst overcome when thou art judged.* God's justice is so great that He wishes to be judged in company with men. He Himself says: *Judge between me and my vineyard,*[19] and elsewhere; *My people, what have I done to thee, or in*

what have I molested thee? Answer thou me.[20] This is why the prophet
now confesses that the Lord has such justice on His side against him
that He is totally victorious at the Judgment. As Jeremias says: *You
shall say to the Lord our God: to you is justice, but to us confusion of our
face.*[21] David was reflecting that he had been made a king from being a
shepherd, that he had received a people under his dominion, and that
he had done wrong without thought for his honour. So it was inevitable that the prophet should be worsted in a judgment conducted by
another, for he was seen to have been defeated by his own examination. Some commentators refer this to the Lord's Passion, when He
was judged and He prevailed, and after being condemned freed
the world.

7. *For behold, I was conceived in iniquities, and in sins did my mother
bear me.* Here the odium of the sin is reduced, since his personal
offence is compared to wrong-doings at large, and so the very number
together with the confession of sins roused the pity of the good Judge.
So the sense is this: "I need not mention that I have committed the sins
of which I am accused, for it is already clear that I was conceived in
iniquities springing from original sin, so that I had incurred sins before commencing my life." This argument is called "from anteced-
ents."[22] It is not unprecedented that the man conceived in iniquities
and born in sins should do wrong. What is humbler and simpler than
to confess all our sins, when we are accused of one? So it seems right
that he was readily pardoned, for after being granted forgiveness he
strives to demonstrate his guilt in many ways. Let the Pelagians[23] listen
to this, and feel acute shame that they oppose the clear truth. How can
it be that at any age, however young, we do not need to be pardoned,
since we enter this world burdened with the weight of sins? Job too
proclaims this in similar words: *None is pure before thee, not even the
child who is one day old upon the earth.*[24] Paul the chosen vessel says this
among similar things: *We were by nature in time past children of wrath,
even as the rest.*[25] Again Paul says: *By one man sin entered into this
world, and by sin death: and so death passed upon all men, in whom all
have sinned.*[26] Moreover Truth Itself attests this in the gospel with this
definitive statement: *Amen, amen I say to you, unless a man be born
again of water and the holy Spirit he cannot see the kingdom of God.*[27] So I

ask, why are children excluded from God's kingdom, since they cannot be blamed for the wrong committed? It must be that they are kept in subjection to original sin; before they commit personal sins they are known to carry with them the sins of the first man. There are other most certain proofs of this, and so the wantonness of men should not devise for themselves sacrilegious errors.

There is also the Pelagians' second wickedness, for they so attribute free will to their human powers that they believe that they can devise or enact some good of their own accord without God's grace. If this were possible, why should the prophet say: *My God, his mercy shall prevent me?*[28] When you hear that you have been forestalled by the Lord's mercy you are given to understand that nothing of your own devising occurred first. In another psalm too he says: *Unless the Lord build the house, they labour in vain who build it.*[29] He also says: *By the Lord are the steps of a man directed: and he shall like well his way.*[30] In another place too the psalmist attests: *The Lord lifteth up them that are cast down: the Lord looseneth them that are fettered: the Lord enlighteneth the blind.*[31] Since you hear that the Lord prevents, builds, directs, lifts up, loosens and enlightens when no merits anticipate Him, what do you see has been initiated as your own except that by which you can be justly condemned by reason of your pride? But perhaps you claim that the prophet Isaiah approves of free will in these words: *If you will be willing and will hearken to me, you shall eat the good things of the land.*[32] Again, Ezechiel says: *Make to yourselves a new heart and a new spirit.*[33] Again, we read: *Today if you shall hear his voice, harden not your hearts.*[34] But you interpret these and similar passages most perversely, believing that men take the first step of their good intentions of their own accord and subsequently obtain the help of the Godhead, so that (to express the matter sacrilegiously) we are the cause of His kindness and He is not the cause of His own. How then will those words of John be true: *Of his fullness we all have received, and grace for grace?*[35] Or how can that grace be termed gratuitous, if the speed of some good work precedes and anticipates it? Listen to Paul, who by his truthful preaching rebukes that most false belief of yours: *Who hath first given to him, and recompense shall be made him? For of him, and by him, and in him are all things.*[36] Again Paul says: *From him is both to will and to accomplish, according to his good will.*[37] The apostle James says: *Every best gift and every perfect gift is from above, coming down from the Father of lights.*[38]

Another much more heinous absurdity attends you. If the beginning of our good intention came from ourselves, we would be laying the foundation on which the Lord could build; no sound mind certainly can approve that. So cease to maintain what you cannot fulfil. It is those whom the Lord makes to listen who obediently listen, those who accept the Godhead's gift who yearn with profit. Once the nature of the human race was spoiled, the Lord both granted that part of free will which brings salvation and permitted its action by His fatherly love. Through the divine benevolence these things have been taught at greater length by blessed Augustine, by the most learned Jerome, and by Prosper to general accord.[39] But the accursed heresy seen to be wholly opposed to our salvation has forced us to touch on them.

8. *For behold, thou has loved truth: the uncertain and hidden things of thy wisdom thou has made manifest to me.* Just as in the previous verse he proved through our common sin that no man is excepted from transgressions, so again here by his confession he begs to obtain help, because in confessing his sin he has spoken the truth which the Lord God demands more than sacrifices. God does not take delight in our punishments, but seeks confession of our transgression. As Scripture has it: *I desire not the death of the sinner, but that he be converted and live.*[40] *The uncertain things* are those which cannot be distinguished at all, but are gathered together under the cloak of ambiguity; *the hidden things* are those which the eye cannot see and the human mind cannot judge. He not only says that these two have been revealed to him, but proclaims that they have been clarified, so that what seemed difficult even to grope for came to him clearly by a declaration. Observe that in a splendid definition he unites the gifts conferred on him. By saying: *The uncertain and hidden things of thy wisdom thou hast made manifest to me,* he reveals what the prophecy is. He added another burden to his guilt, so that his sinning continually increases as he recounts his blessings. So the uncertain and hidden things are those which God revealed to him when He showed forth His Son; first, so that the psalmist would acknowledge that He had a Son; secondly, so that he would

know that He would come from his seed to take flesh; thirdly, so that he would foretell the coming events of the Passion, and proclaim the glory of the resurrection. It is because of this that he says that he ought not to have sinned, since he has deserved to acknowledge such tidings. What sacred simplicity! Who could have devoted such pains to his own defence as the psalmist bestowed on his self-accusation! This line of argument is entitled *a causis*,[41] for he says that after the bestowal of so many kindnesses he ought not to have committed such sins.

9. *Thou shalt sprinkle me with hyssop, and I shall be cleansed: thou shalt wash me, and I shall be made whiter than snow.* In the previous entreaty he was bent low, but for this second part he relies on the Lord's mercy and stands erect, so that he should not seem to have despaired of the almighty Lord's clemency, a sin greater than all others. Though hyssop is a tiny plant, its roots are said to penetrate the heart of rocks;[42] it is also known to be good for a person's internal wounds.[43] In Leviticus it was dipped in sacrificial blood and sprinkled seven times on the body of a leper,[44] revealing that stains of sins could be effectively removed by the precious blood of the Lord Saviour. This is the simile with which he entreats that by his prophecy he may be acquitted, that he may deserve the gifts of absolution through the saving blood of Christ, in whose coming he believed with devoted heart. By hyssop he denotes the mysteries we have mentioned; they not only wipe away stains, but also show the superiority of the soul as it regains its brightness whiter than snow. There is no whiteness superior to snow to be found in bodies, but he used the phrase, *whiter than snow*, because the spiritual soul gleams much more than cleansed bodies. This figure is called *hyperthesis* or exaggeration,[45] when by our statement we seek to transcend something universally known. An example is that already mentioned at Psalm 17: *And he flew, he flew upon the wings of the winds.*[46]

10. *To my hearing thou shalt give joy and gladness: and the bones that have been humbled shall rejoice.* At this point devoted confidence in the Godhead is now revealed. He says that he will hear what will redouble his joy and gladness. The joy implies absolution, the gladness enduring rewards. The joy and gladness he shall hear is that promised to those who are forgiven: *Come, blessed of my Father, possess ye the king-*

dom which was prepared for you from the beginning of the world.[47] Next comes: *And the bones that have been humbled shall rejoice*—understand "when the tidings mentioned have been heard." This argument is called *a consequentibus*,[48] for when these tidings have been heard joy must inevitably follow. By *bones* are meant the supports of the mind, which were inevitably utterly humbled until this penitent could be absolved. He used the word *humbled* because of his awareness of his fault; this always makes men humble for their profit.

11. *Turn away thy face from my sins, and blot out all my iniquities.* He passes to the third section, asking the kindly Judge not to gaze at his sins which seem reprehensible even to himself. You must ponder here the contrasting injunctions most splendidly offered. If we turn away our faces from our sins, it is harmful, because we forget and neglect what we ought to cleanse with unbroken tears; but if the Lord does not turn away He destroys, because He judges the sins on which He gazes. So elsewhere too the prophet prays: *Turn not away thy face from me, and I shall be like them that go down into the pit.*[49] And rightly, for if we are gazed upon we are absolved by the mercy of the Saviour. As the gospel says of Peter: *And the Lord gazed at Peter, and going outside he wept bitterly.*[50] Next comes: *And blot out all my iniquities.* David was summoned to face blame on two charges, but he most prudently prays and begs on behalf of all his sins. He knew that he had committed very many more than those with which the immediate process of justice charged him, and so by a salutary abridgement he asked to be absolved through a single pardon of all of which he could be accused. The phrase, *blot out*, means forgive, for all our sins are listed, so to say, on tablets when they are enclosed within the divine awareness.

12. *Create a clean heart in me, O God: and renew a right spirit within my entrails.* We must carefully investigate these verses word by word, so that the sense can shine out more clearly for us. By *create* we mean establishing something new, so that what did not exist seems to come into being. How then are we to say that David did not have a clean heart before he sinned, when the Lord said of him: *I have found David the son of Jesse a man according to my own heart, who shall do all my wills?*[51] Here *create* must be understood as "restore to its state before its fall." So the prophet asks that a clean heart be created in him, such

as could not possibly have been stirred to repent its guilt when impelled by its sins, but which once established in constancy could not change its goodly plan of life. This will be the dispensation to holy men in particular after the resurrection. But this penitent who was eager for good things and fired with love for the future reward demanded that what could accrue in time to come should be granted him now.

A right spirit means the Son of God, the Word, of whom it is said in another psalm: *The rod of thy kingdom is a straight rod.*[52] He rightly called Him a spirit because of the nature of the Godhead, for we read in Scripture: *God is spirit.*[53] *Renew* is used by the figure of *hypallage;*[54] not that the Son Himself was to be renewed, but that He could through grace renew David, who had aged with sins. He it is who renews us, for when we have laid aside the senility of the old man, He transforms us to the new gifts of His regeneration. Just as we were old through Adam, so we are renewed by the kindnesses of Christ the Lord.[55] As Paul says: *Stripping off the old man with his deeds, put on the new, which was created according to God.*[56] He added: *Within my entrails,* the place from which he knew that the hateful sin of adultery emerged. He sought a remedy from both regions since he had sinned in both. Observe the liveliness with which he longs to be forgiven, so that you may understand that he wished to commit no such sin any more. Just as limbs which have been severed cannot assemble into their previous structure, so past sins cannot return to him who is truly repentant. Some people prefer the explanation known to be propounded elsewhere: the prophet begs God to create a clean heart in him, asking for nothing other than he had, and begging that it become clean, which it already was, for we say that to create means also to renew. Elsewhere we read of the faithful: *Behold, there is now a new creature,*[57] not with reference to some other being previously non-existent, but to a new brightness which had come forth in that which already existed.

13. *Cast me not away from thy face, and take not thy holy spirit from me.* That man is cast away from one's face who is rejected as unworthy of healing; and what is the sick man to do if he withdraws from the cure? He knew that soundness of mind and illumination of wisdom

came from His face, and he believed that if he were doomed to expulsion from the Lord's face, he would be consigned to the enemy. He wanted only his person to be gazed upon, for he cried earlier that his sins should not be witnessed. What a prophetic mind, so outstanding after committing human errors! He said nothing about power, and made no treaty whatsoever about his feelings; he asked only that the spirit of prophecy, which the king regarded as superior to all else, should not be taken from him. Similarly the prophet Jeremiah attested his power with the words: *The Lord put forth his hand and touched my mouth, and said to me, Behold, I have given my words in thy mouth. Lo, I have set thee over the nations and over kingdoms, to root up and pull down, and to waste and to destroy, and to build and to plant around.*[8] So he rightly sought that what he knew was a possession more splendid than all riches should be preserved for him. Observe that he did not say, "Grant me," as if he did not have it, but, *Take not away*, doubtless since a prayer of such a nature and intensity could be realised only through the holy Spirit.

14. *Restore unto me the joy of thy salvation: and strengthen me with a perfect spirit.* He returns to the Son of God, whom he called, *Thy salvation*, to reveal that it was Christ, at whose birth salvation came to the nations. What was previously known to a few only because of their outstanding faith became well known to the whole world. So when he says: *Restore unto me the joy of thy salvation*, he is pointing to Christ, in the contemplation of whom he was joyful even in his very tears; he feasted on the gift of his prophecy during the fasting of his repentance. He said *Restore* because he had felt some diminution of grace, for a person distances himself from that saving grace in so far as he indulges in blameworthy communion with men. When he says: *Restore unto me the joy of thy salvation*, he was aware that he had undoubtedly lost the grace of the holy Spirit, which human frailty cannot possess when it sins. Next comes: *And strengthen me with a perfect spirit.* That most holy king and wondrous prophet did not think it an outstanding task to proclaim laws to subjects and to subdue foreign nations in war; he wholly removed himself from these in thought, and more earnestly sought to be endowed with a perfect spirit, rather than be kept at the helm of the kingdom. *Strengthen*

me—he meant "lest I sin again, lest I desert you in fickleness of soul." Let[59] us not regard it as vain that this holy man, glowing with brightness of heart, named the Spirit a third time; it was surely because he was devoted to the undivided Trinity, and demanded that it should grant him pardon. For the Spirit in the essence of divinity is Father, Son, and holy Spirit, and is rightly called one God; but in the distinction of Persons there is peculiar to the Father the fact that being by nature without a beginning, He begot the Son before time began. Peculiar to the Son is the fact that by nature He was begotten of the Father. Peculiar to the holy Spirit is the fact that He proceeds from Father and Son.[60] Their consubstantial eternity and power, by an indescribable love and by their joint working, perform all that they wish in heaven and on earth. But though these things are known to us in actuality as inexplicable and incomprehensible, some of the Fathers posit a parallel from physical and existent objects on these lines: in the sun we find three properties. The first is the bodily substance itself, which is the sun; then its brightness which abides in it; and thirdly the heat which reaches us from its brightness.[61] If any such parallel can be devised for so important a topic, I think it is to be assessed as follows. The bodily substance in the sun gives us some understanding of the Person of the Father in the Trinity; the brightness in it can be a parallel to the Person of the Son in the Trinity—as the apostle says: *The brightness of his glory;*[62] and the heat in the sun is equivalent to the Person of the holy Spirit in the Trinity; as we read in Scripture: *Who hides himself from his heat?*[63]

Another example, this time from things incorporeal, is provided by the soul, which is known to be made in God's image and likeness; the soul is itself an incorporeal and rational substance, in which are present understanding and life. If it is not sacrilegious to say so, we can understand the Person of the Father in the Trinity as the substance in the soul. The Son in the Trinity can be visualised as the power and knowledge in the soul, for the Son is the power of God and the wisdom of God. And the property of life-giving in the soul can be equated in the Trinity with the holy Spirit, through which the work of life-giving in many places is proclaimed as fulfilled. As the apostle Peter says in his letter: *Put to death in the flesh, but enlivened in the spirit;*[64] and again Paul says: *The letter killeth, but the spirit quickeneth.*[65] And in the gospel the Lord says: *It is the spirit that quickeneth, for the flesh profiteth nothing.*[66] The three things which we have mentioned are never found individually and separated, though our understanding can visualise them as differentiated. But they are naturally so united that when one of them makes its appearance the three are always in evidence together. Thus through these parallels some idea of the truth of so important a matter is revealed. These and similar matters are discussed by the Fathers, but our weakness of the flesh prevents a clear understanding of them at the present time. They will be able to be understood much more clearly when saints behold the Godhead in His majesty. Anyone wishing to obtain fuller knowledge should continually read the books on the Trinity of saints Hilary, Ambrose, and Augustine,[67] for this subject is as long as it is important for the purposes of discussion. Blessed Jerome too has clearly and briefly discussed the Trinity in the context of this psalm when he was writing against heretics.[68]

15. *Let me teach the unjust thy ways: and the wicked shall be converted to thee.* He embarks on the fourth part of his entreaty, showing here the glory that will accrue to the God who spares, once his prayer is heard. The result of converting another from unfaithfulness is that he too is won over and wholly cleansed. As Scripture says: *He who causeth a sinner to be converted from the error of his way, saves his soul from death and covers a multitude of sins.*[69] There are two types of teacher; the one instructs by example, the other is known to warn sinners by words alone. In this passage we find that both are observable. So what he says is: If the prophet were spared, the greatest hope of forgiveness would be granted to the wrongdoer; for who would not accede to conversion when the king and prophet afforded an example of pardon granted to him? Or this second lesson can be grasped, that once freed from total destruction he was able to proclaim to the nations the great and diverse works of the Lord which the words of the next psalms reveal. He also promises gainful profit; because the Lord had pardoned one, many wicked men were shown to be won over through that individual. This is said not to boast but as prophecy through the power of foresight; for how many have entreated the Lord with these same

words, and been freed of their guilt and happily rid of the debts which they had incurred?

16. *Deliver me from deeds of blood, O God, thou God of my salvation, and my tongue shall extol thy justice.* From deeds of blood—the plural seems used here in contravention of the Latin language, but since it is contained in the Greek versions the translator is wholly praiseworthy, for he preferred to defy secular usage rather than depart from the truth set down. If he had said, "from blood," he would perhaps have seemed to denote a single sin, but by writing the plural he makes a clear confession that there are many. We can label this an idiom of divine Scripture. This figure is called *exallage,* or change; it is used whenever gender or case is changed in an unusual way.[70] So the prophet seeks to be delivered from the faults of the flesh, so that now he may cease sinning in this frail condition of ours. *Blood* is used here to denote the human body, for it is known to be the most important of the body's liquids. As Peter is told in the gospel: *Flesh and blood has not revealed it to you.*[71] *God of my salvation* means the Lord Saviour, through whom salvation is granted to pious believers. He further added: *My tongue shall extol thy justice;* in other words, "If you deliver me from deeds of blood"—interpreted as from sins—"my tongue will justly seek your praise." This is because of what was said in the previous psalm: *But to the sinner God hath said: Why dost thou declare my justices?*[72] Once he was absolved, he could rightly pronounce the reason why the divine law exonerates the sinner. Some people are apparently exercised why after his sin was forgiven he said: "I shall extol your justice," and did not more appropriately say: "I shall extol your fatherly love"; for he who has prayed to be mercifully forgiven ought to thank His paternal love. But if you ponder the matter with deep reasoning, it was also the function of divine justice that He should listen to one who cried to Him, spare one who entreated Him, and lift up one who made confession of his sins. Alternatively, these two attitudes are always combined in judgment by the Lord. As the psalmist is to say in Psalm 100: *Mercy and judgment I will sing to thee, O Lord.*[73] We shall explain this more clearly in its proper place.

17. *O Lord, thou wilt open my lips: and my mouth shall announce thy praise.* He proclaims that the prophet's lips which have been sealed

through his sinful condition would be opened through the kindness of forgiveness. The mouths of those who are in the dock are condemned; as Isaias puts it: *Woe is me, because I am unclean, because I am a man and have unclean lips, and I dwell in the midst of people that have unclean lips.*[74] By *mouth* is meant the hidden region of the heart, from which God's praise is efficaciously sung. So he rightly proclaims after the forgiveness of his sin that his lips will be opened, and that his mouth can announce the praise of the Lord.

18. *For if thou hadst desired sacrifice, I would indeed have given it: but with holocausts thou wilt not be delighted.* The humble suppliant knows that he is guilty through the visitation of sin, and he suggests that as king he could easily have offered sacrifices of cattle, which at that time were still being offered as expiation of sins, if the Lord had been pleased to receive holocausts. His words: *But with holocausts thou wilt not be delighted,* denote the sacrificial rites through immolation of cattle which were to be rejected with the Lord's coming. So it is clear that the prophet is wholly transported in mind to the Lord, so that he does not believe that his guilt is to be expiated by the sacrifices customary at that time, but instead by the offering which he next describes.

19. *A sacrifice to God is an afflicted spirit: a contrite and humbled heart God does not despise.* After mentioning the sacrifices which God rejects, he now speaks of those which He demands. The sacrifice which we offer to God is the spirit of pride slain by the humility of confession; it is not blood which wells out, but streams of tears pour down. When this spirit is joyful, it binds us, but when it is afflicted before God it absolves us. By the fifth type of definition, which in Greek is called *kata tēn lexin* and in Latin *ad verbum,*[75] he explains what is the more acceptable sacrifice offered to God, an afflicted spirit. There follows the certain promise of this statement, by which pardon is not now sought for himself, but promised to those who prostrate themselves before God: *A contrite and humbled heart God does not despise. Contrite* means sorely afflicted by the toils of repentance; *humbled,* that is, before God, so that the heart which had earlier been proud through arrogance became devoted through holy confession. Note how the order of events has been preserved. The heart could not have been humbled if it had not become contrite through

repeated affliction. His statement, *God does not despise,* has now the authority of a holy promise, proclaimed rather than requested, for it is certain that God does not despise such offerings, just as He is known to have rejected earlier sacrifices. We must, I think, investigate the fact that often in the divine Scriptures *heart* stands for understanding. The gospel has: *From the heart come forth evil thoughts.*[76] The apostle Peter says to Simon: *Thy heart is not right in the sight of God.*[77] Isaiah too attests: *Hardened is the heart of this people.*[78] And in Psalm 4: *How long will you be dull of heart?*[79] In Psalm 7: *The searcher of hearts and reins is God.*[80] In this psalm too he earlier said: *Create a clean heart in me, O God,*[81] so that it may be clear to all without doubting that the source of our thoughts is there, and that good and evil are drawn from there. The seat of thought is that tiny part of the body with the appearance of fire, so that it is rightly placed in the position from which good counsel can come to us.

20. *Deal favourably, O Lord, in thy good-will with Sion, that the walls of Jerusalem may be built up.* The fifth and remaining part is begun, in which the trouble of disasters is laid aside, and mindful of God's pledge he joyfully asks that what the Lord had deigned to promise should come to pass. So he begs that since the synagogue, set beneath the Law, has sinned, Sion, the Catholic Church, which succeeds it may by Christ's grace be strengthened. So the words here, *Deal in thy good-will with Sion,* imply that the mountain had not then been fashioned. Realise that by it is signified the Church, by which the world could undoubtedly have been adorned. That region is the patroness of all lands; that city of the mighty King bears the representation and name of the heavenly fatherland. Who would presume to claim that you are bounded by place, when you are known to have filled the boundaries of the whole world with the most holy faith? If you wish to infer a historical context, it perhaps points to the times of Theodosius, when his consort Eudoxia, that most religious of women, extended the deserving city and crowned it with a superior encirclement of walls.[82]

21. *Then shalt thou obtain the sacrifice of justice, oblations and holocausts: then shall they lay calves upon thy altar.* Often very holy men make some request in such a way that the promise of a vow is also

attached to it. For example: *What shall I render to the Lord for all the things that he hath rendered to me? I will take the chalice of salvation, and I will call upon the name of the Lord.*[83] Likewise here the Father is told: *Then shalt thou obtain the sacrifice of justice,* in other words, the most glorious Passion of Your Son, who offered Himself as a sacrifice for all men so that the world might obtain the salvation which it did not deserve through its own works. There is a very fine statement here of why the Passion of the Lord is to be revered as the sacrifice of justice. Next comes: *Oblations and holocausts.* This phrase now refers to faithful Christians who were to believe after the coming of the Lord, so it indicates that the hearts of living men, and not the limbs of dead cattle, are to be sacrificed. Fire which is itself destructible destroyed the second, whereas the fire of life racks the first. The cattle were at once reduced to ashes, whereas men's hearts bring the flames of affliction to our souls for a time, but lead them to the eternal joys of a pleasant Paradise. Next comes: *Then they shall lay calves upon thy altar; they* means the priests, when the Catholic Church has been built up by the Passion of the Lord. Since he has earlier said: *With holocausts thou wilt not be delighted,*[84] we must investigate why he has here in turn promised that calves will be sacrificed. These words are expressed by the figure of allegory, which says one thing but means another. He used the word *calves* either for innocents full-grown who are in the first flush of youth and whose necks are known to be strangers to the yoke of sin—he retained the word *calves* to show that the practice of the Law now past foreshadowed events to come—or he holds out promise of those preachers of the gospel whose image the evangelist Luke took on with the form of a calf. They were not to assault the air with lowing, but to fill the world with proclamation of faith in the Lord. Alternatively we are to interpret calves as those who offered their lives as victims of sweetness on sacred altars. Father Augustine, during a discussion of those gospel figures, says somewhere[85] that the Lord Himself is a calf who offered himself as a victim for the salvation of all. So whether the word is to be understood of young adults or preachers or martyrs, the prophet was able to pledge to the altar of the Lord the calves which he knew were appropriate to the Christian religion.

Conclusion Drawn From the Psalm

A most sweet psalm has flowed forth, coming down from a bitter stream of repentance. But what tears are we to believe that the people of Israel shed, when their prince lamented with such affliction? Who would not have wept when he wept? Who would not have grieved and groaned when the king in place of a bejewelled diadem wore ashes on his head, and was hoary with dust and not age? He was unwilling to appear adorned externally when he knew that he was most foul within; he was more handsome in his grime, for he rejected the pomp of the world in his sinful state. The sorrow of one heart was a sufficient corrective for the body-politic, when he incurred the charge of madness by presuming to be joyful. Happy indeed three and four times over is that state in which a secular lord won the merit of repentance before God, and the heavenly King received the glory of crucifixion!

This is the reason why, though seven psalms of penitents are taught in the book,[86] it has become customary in the Church that whenever pardon for sins is sought, the Lord is entreated through this one, and rightly. First, because in no psalm is such virtuous humility—an attitude particularly necessary for penitents—displayed, that a powerful king, set on a prophet's pedestal, hastened to lament his sins as the most abject of men; second, because after the promise of forgiveness he bound himself with such constraints of tears as if he had not been forgiven at all. The type of entreaty chosen was most restrained and appropriate, such as every truly wise generation should seek and could hasten to achieve on the spur of the moment. Nothing involving difficulty is stated here, as it is in the other penitential psalms. For example, in Psalm 6: *Every night I will wash my bed: I will water my couch with my tears.*[87] Nor does it contain what Psalm 31 states: *Thy hand was heavy on me: I was turned in my anguish while the thorn was implanted.*[88] Nor the words of Psalm 37: *My sores are putrefied and corrupted because of my foolishness.*[89] Nor the statement in Psalm 101: *For I did eat ashes like bread, and mingled my drink with weeping.*[90] Nor the phrase in Psalm 129: *Out of the depths I have cried to thee, O Lord.*[91] Nor that in Psalm 142: *For the enemy hath persecuted my soul: he hath brought down*

my life to the earth. He hath made me to dwell in darkness as those that
have been dead of old, and my spirit is anxious within me.[92] Once he has
been rebuked by the prophet and terrified by the recognition of his
sin, the king begs the most indulgent Judge that through His mercy he
may be cleansed and wholly purified of the foulness of all his sins.
Like an exemplary master, the Lord in other cases has imposed stern
modes of satisfaction on stronger men, and has permitted to the weak
these modest ones; and our loving mother the Church has rightly
chosen the second, to entice her sons by every means to the grace of a
most conciliatory confession.

Perhaps a further meaning is to be grasped here: that the psalmist
said in this psalm: *Let me teach the unjust thy ways, and the wicked shall*
be converted to thee,[93] because he foresaw that in the future people
would through this psalm seek the gifts of most abundant repentance.
Let us see clearly why it is permissible for us to repeat this psalm in
frequent meditation without its preventing us from seeking ecclesiastical privileges, whereas if it is recited by a priest over us with a vow of
repentance, we are rightly forbidden by the canons to advance further,
since pardon is being granted us in the Lord's person.[94] Whatever we
obtain in Christ's name ought to comprise a judgment both inviolable
and definitive. So an individual can practise repentance regularly by
himself, but when bestowed through a priest it does not permit us to
seek further ecclesiastical distinctions.

The number of this psalm is not otiose. It has reference to the year
of the jubilee, which among the Jews dissolved old contracts and
obligations, and which in Leviticus the Lord ordered all dwellers on
earth to call the year of remission.[95] The number also refers to Pente-
cost, when after the Lord's ascension the holy Spirit came on the
apostles, working miracles and imparting the gift of charisms. So too
this psalm, which is given the number 50, if recited with a pure heart,
looses sins, cancels the bond of our debt, and like the year of remission
frees us through the Lord's kindness of the debts of our sins.

NOTES

LIST OF ABBREVIATIONS

ACW	Ancient Christian Writers
Adriaen	M. Adriaen, ed., *Magni Aurelii Cassiodori Expositio Psalmorum* (CCL 97 and 98, Turnhout 1958)
Boylan	P. Boylan, *The Psalms* (2 vols., Dublin 1921)
CCL	Corpus christianorum, series latina
DACL	Dictionnaire d'archéologie chrétienne et de liturgie (Paris 1907–53)
DTC	Dictionnaire de théologie catholique (Paris 1903–50)
DHGE	Dictionnaire d'histoire et de géographie ecclésiastiques (Paris 1912–)
GCS	Die griechischen christlichen Schriftsteller der ersten drei Jahrhunderte (Leipzig 1897–)
A. H. M. Jones	A. H. M. Jones, *The Later Roman Empire* (2 vols., Oxford 1973)
LSJ	Liddell-Scott-Jones-McKenzie, *Greek-English Lexicon* (Oxford 1940)
L. W. Jones	L. W. Jones, *An Introduction to Divine and Human Readings by Cassidorus Senator* (New York 1966)
Martin	J. Martin, *Antike Rhetorik* (München 1974)
MG	*Patrologia graeca*, ed. J. P. Migne (Paris 1857–66)
ML	*Patrologia latina*, ed. J. P. Migne (Paris 1844–64)
OCD	The Oxford Classical Dictionary[2] (Oxford 1970)
ODCC	The Oxford Dictionary of the Christian Church[2] (Oxford 1974)
O'Donnell	J. J. O'Donnell, *Cassiodorus* (Berkeley and Los Angeles 1979)
PSt	Patristic Studies
Rev. Ben.	Revue bénédictine (Maredsous 1884–)
RhM	Rheinisches Museum für Philologie

Rogerson-McKay   J. W. Rogerson and J. W. McKay, *Psalms 1-150* (3
                  vols., CUP 1977)
Schlieben   R. Schlieben, *Cassiodors Psalmenexegese*
                  (Göppingen 1979)
van der Vyver   A. van der Vyver, "Cassiodore et son oeuvre,"
                  Speculum 6 (1931) 244 ff.

INTRODUCTION

1. The family background is detailed at *Variae* 1.3 f. and in *Anecdoton Holderi* (ed. Usener, Bonn 1879). For lively accounts in English, see T. Hodgkin, *The Letters of Cassiodorus* (London 1886); L. W. Jones, 3 ff.; O'Donnell, ch. 1. For the social and political background, A. H. M. Jones, 246 ff.; S. Krautschik, *Cassiodor und die Politik seiner Zeit* (Bonn 1983).

2. On the career and tragic end of Boethius, see H. Chadwick, *Boethius* (Oxford 1981); J. Matthews, "Anicius Manlius Severinus Boethius" in *Boethius* (ed. M. Gibson, Oxford 1981) 15 ff.

3. Ed. Th. Mommsen, MGH Auctores antiquissimi xii. There is a selective summary of the letters in English, trans. Hodgkin (n. 1).

4. For further detail, see O'Donnell, chs. 2–3.

5. For the fragments of the *Laudes,* see MGH Auctores antiquissimi xii, ed. Traube; Mommsen edited the *Chronica* and Jordanes' *Getica* in the same volume.

6. See Preface to the *Institutes* (n. 14); discussion, O'Donnell, 182 f.

7. Text edited by J. W. Halporn, *Traditio* 16 (1960) 39 ff; revised in CCL 96.503 ff.

8. Both these assumptions have their difficulties. His possible presence at Squillace has been doubted because there was no full set of Augustine's *Enarrationes in psalmos* there (*Inst.* 1.4), and Cassiodorus had systematically used this work in composing his *Expositio* during these years. Rome on the other hand was hardly a congenial retreat, being embroiled in the struggles between the Ostrogoth Totila, who captured the city twice, and the Byzantine leader Narses. But pope Vigilius remained there until January 545, and Cassiodorus could have likewise stuck it out. For his study of Albinus, see *Inst.* 2.5.10; see at Ps. 81(80).4 for the inference that he was reading works on music at this time.

9. For Vigilius' letter, see ML 69.49. For detail of the Three Chapters controversy, see O'Donnell, 169 ff.; for Zacchaeus' presence in Constantinople, see O'Donnell, 133 n. 1. The date of Vigilius' arrival, see Van der Vyver, 244 ff.

10. For the date of 555 or later, see Cappuyns, DHGE 11,1406 ff.

11. See *Variae* 12.15, *Inst.* 1.29, 1, 3. Modern literature: P. Courcelle, "Le site du monastère de Cassiodore," *Mélanges d'archéologie et d'histoire de l'École Francaise de Rome* 55 (1938) 259 ff., and "Nouvelles recherches sur le monastère de Cassiodore," *Actes du cinquième Congrès internationale d'archéologie chrétienne* (Rome 1957) 511 ff.

12. See G. Ludwig, *Cassiodor über den Ursprung der abendländischen Schule* (Frankfurt 1967) 69 ff.; J. B. de Besselaar, *Cassiodorus Senator* (Antwerp 1950) 158 ff.

13. The view of A. Franz, *M. Aurelius Cassiodorus Senator* (Breslau 1872) is controverted by van der Vyver (n. 9 above).

14. Text edited by R. A. B. Mynors (Oxford 1937). For a suggested date of c. 562, see P. Lehmann, *Erforschung des Mittelalters*[2] (1959), 41 ff.

15. See P. Courcelle, *Late Latin Writers and their Greek Sources* (trans. Wedeck, Cambridge, Mass. 1969) 377.

16. *Inst.* 1.8; *De orth.* (ed. Keil, *Gramm. Lat.* 7) 144.

17. Donatus' two books of *Artes* and Sacerdos' grammatical treatise are to be found in Keil, *Gramm. Lat.* 4.355 ff. and 6.427 ff.

18. See ML 70.1309 ff.

19. For the dedication, see *Preface*, §7; for the identification, Schlieben, 5.

20. For the suggestion of a second edition, see van der Vyver and Cappuyns (n. 10).

21. Schlieben, 99 ff.

22. Schlieben, 40–63.

23. See at Ps. 27(26), Concl.

24. I draw attention to such detailed dependence on Augustine in the commentary on the initial psalms, but have not thought it necessary to continue to document this throughout.

25. I.4.

26. See Index 2.

27. At *Inst.* 1.1.4 after mentioning Hilary, Ambrose, Jerome and Augustine, he states that he has gathered Augustine's commentaries on twenty psalms, but no Greek works are mentioned other than that of Athanasius.

28. Origen is cited at Ps. 64(63).9; in his *Institutes* he states that he

has read Origen's homilies on the Octateuch, but there is no mention of those on the psalms.

29. 1.4.3.

30. Jerome's remark to Damasus (ML 29.526c) is concerned with the gospels; for the comment of Augustine, see *De doctrina christiana* 2.22.

31. See R. Loewe, *Cambridge History of the Bible* II, III.

32. H. F. D. Sparkes, *Cambridge History of the Bible* I, 513 ff., and E. F. Sutcliffe, *CHB* II, 84 f. Loewe (n. 31) believes that the "Roman" psalter predates Jerome.

33. At Ps. 34(33).8 Cassiodorus has the reading *immittet angelum Dominus*, which Augustine rejects in favour of the 'Gallican' version; again, at Ps. 135.16 the phrase *qui eduxit aquam de petra rupis* does not appear in Jerome's translations. See B. Fischer, *Bibl. Zeitschr.* NF 6 (1962), 57 ff.; and for a review of the secondary literature on the problem of the texts, U. Hahner, *Cassiodors Psalmenkommentar: sprachliche Untersuchungen* (Munich 1973), 7.

34. E.g., at Ps. 141(140).6.

35. See Appendix A for Cassiodorus' varying citations of identical verses.

36. The fundamental treatment is that of H. de Lubac, *Exégèse médiévale* I (Paris 1959) 139 ff., 373 ff. Earlier bibliography in ODCC *s.v.* "Exegesis."

37. See Ambrose, *Comm. Ps. 36: omnis scriptura divina vel naturalis vel mystica vel moralis est.*

38. See, e.g., ACW 40.280 and 320.

39. *Pref.* p. 35; Schlieben, 107 ff.

40. See Index 3 for a full citation of these images; Schlieben, 138 ff.

41. Text edited by P. de Lagarde in CCL 72.

42. See at Ps. 114(113 A).7 and at the beginning of Ps. 133(132).

43. Jerome, *Ep.* 107.12; *Preface*, p. 41.

44. *Preface*, p. 41.

45. See Ps. 14(13).1, 7; 53(52) Concl.; 59(58).7, 13; etc.

46. For Cassiodorus' condemnations of Donatists and Pelagians, see Index 3.

47. Adequate summaries of these Christological and Trinitarian heresies can be found in DTC and ODCC; for Cassiodorus' refer-

ences, see Index 3. The treatises of Boethius can be conveniently consulted in the Loeb edition; for further discussion, see H. Chadwick (n. 2 above), 175 ff.

48. See at Ps. 3 Concl.

49. Psalms 2, 8, 21(20), 72(71), 82(81), 108(107), 110(109), 139(138).

50. Psalms 7, 27(26), 34(33), 144(143).

51. Psalms 3, 16(15), 28(27), 31(30), 57(56), 64(63).

52. Psalms 22(21), 35(34), 55(54), 69(68), 109(108).

53. Psalms 17(16), 86(85), 90(89), 102(101), 142(141).

54. First coming: Psalms 19(18), 80(79), 85(84), 97(96), 118(117); second coming: 50(49), 96(95).

55. Church's love: Psalms 42(41), 84(83); sacraments foreshadowed: 78(77), 105(104).

56. Psalms 6, 32(31), 38(37), 51(50), 102(101), 130(129), 143(142).

57. Psalms 74(73), 79(78), 137(136).

58. Psalms 105(104)–107(106), 111(110)–119(118), 135(134), 136(135), 146(145)–150.

59. Psalms 120(119)–134(133).

60. Partial alphabet: Psalms 25(24), 34(33), 37(36), 145(144); whole alphabet: 111(110), 112(111), 119(118).

61. *Conferences* 14.12.

62. Ps. 150.6.

63. *Inst.* Praef. 4; 2.1.

64. See at Ps. 2.2.

65. See *Preface*, p. 38 f. and Ps. 24(23).9.

66. A. Reifferschied, "Mitteilungen aus Handschriften," RhM 23 (1868) 127 ff.

67. See *Inst.* 2.8–10.

68. *Inst.* 2.1; 2.2.10. The earlier two are not mentioned, but Tryphon repeatedly appears in Martin's citations of unusual figures exemplified by Cassiodorus. Martianus Capella is not usually regarded as a direct source (Cf. J. R. S. Mair, *JTS* 26.2 (1975) 419), but see 90 n. 2, 129 n. 7.

69. See Appendix B.

70. See Cicero, *De inventione*, 1.27 ff.; Quintilian, 4.1.1 ff.

71. Appendix B.

72. *Inst.* 2.3.15 f.; full list of citations of arguments in Appendix B.

73. See I above, *ad fin.*

74. *Inst.* 2.4.7.

75. *Inst.* 2.4.8.

76. See Ps. 8 Concl.; 71(70) Concl.; 90(89) Concl.

77. Ps. 96(95).13; 97(96).4.

78. *Inst.* 2.5.10.

79. Ps. 81(80).4.

80. See Ps. 72(71).5 and 148 Concl.

81. See Ps. 71(70) Concl.; 104(103) Concl.; 136(135).9; 147(146,147). For Augustine's condemnations, see *Conf.* 4.3.4, 5.3.3 ff.; *De doctrina christiana* 2.21.32.

82. See Index 3 *s.v.* Scripture.

83. A fuller list in L. W. Jones, 53 f.

84. Adriaen, *Praef.* V.

85. ML 92.849c.

86. See the fuller accounts in Adriaen and Jones (nn. 83–4), to which I have appended mention of Aquinas (see *ST* 1a, 24.1; 2a2ae 17.7, 77.4, 83.1, etc.).

87. CCL, vols. 97–8.

PREFACE

1. For the biographical background, see the Introduction, pp. 1 ff.

2. For the circumstances of composition of the *Expositio Psalmorum,* see the Introduction, p. 3.

3. As is explained in the Introduction (p. 7), the influence of Augustine's *Enarrationes Psalmorum* is pervasive throughout the individual psalm-commentaries. The most recent edition is in the CCL vols. 38–40.

4. This quotation, ascribed to Virgil by Asconius Pedianus in Donatus' *Vita Vergilii* 46, becomes proverbial; see Macrobius, *Sat.* 5.3.16. Cassiodorus may have taken it from Jerome's *Hebr. Quaest. in libro Geneseos* 5.11.

5. Cassiodorus is referring here to his own speculative interpretations.

6. This threefold division is found in the eighth-century Durham ms. (B II 30); see R. A. B. Mynors, *Durham Cathedral Manuscripts*

(Oxford 1939) 21; R. A. Bailey, *The Durham Cassiodorus* (Jarrow Lecture 1978).

7. See Cassiodorus, *Inst.* 1.4.4. This section ("I have divided . . . by the community") is presumably added in the second recension of the *Expositio* made for the monks at Vivarium; see A. van de Vyver, *Speculum* 6 (1931) 271 ff.

8. Song 4.12 f.

9. Apoc. 22.16.

10. On this phrase as a likely addition in the second recension (n. 7 above), see G. Morin, "L'ordre des heures canoniales dans les monastères de Cassiodore," *Rev. Bén.* 43 (1931), 148 ff.; also M. Cappuyns, RTAM 15 (1948) 216 n. 19. The office of Prime does not seem to have been known to Cassiodorus, but appears first in Caesarius of Arles and in Benedict. See O. Chadwick, *John Cassian*[2] (Cambridge 1968) 75.

11. Ps. 139(138).11 f.

12. Ps. 71(70).22.

13. Ps. 89(88).16.

14. Ps. 47(46).10.

15. Cf. Acts 8.27 ff.

16. Matt. 13.19.

17. Jerome, *Ep.* 22.8 (= ACW 33.141).

18. The treatise is dedicated to Pope Vigilius; see M. Cappuyns, DHGE 11 (1949) 1370; O'Donnell, 134.

19. Origen cited by Rufinus, *In Iudic.* 5.2 (GCS 30.493).

20. Ps. 119(118).103.

21. 1 Sam. (1 Kings) 16.13.

22. Matt. 22.45.

23. Jerome, *De princ. Marci* (ed. Morin, 326).

24. Mark 1.10.

25. Ps. 51(50).13.

26. Jerome, *Comm. in Ezech.* 35.1; the phrase occurs twenty-five times in Ezech. 6–38.

27. 2 Kings (4 Kings) 4.27.

28. 1 Cor. 7.25.

29. 1 Cor. 7.12 and 10.

30. 2 Cor. 11.17.

31. John 1.33.

32. Wisd. 1.5.

33. 2 Peter 1.21.

34. 1 Cor. 14.3 f.

35. 1 Cor. 14.32.

36. Cf. 1 Par. 25.5 f.

37. 1 Par. 6.31 suggests that David entrusted the supervision of temple-music to these three families of Asaph, Idithun (or Ethan), and Core (or Heman). See Boylan, 151.

38. Cassiodorus here attaches himself to Augustine's traditional view (see n. 41 below) rather than to Jerome's acute scholarship, echoed by Hilary.

39. Apoc. 3.7.

40. Matt. 22.43 f.

41. See *De civ. Dei* 17.14; *En. Ps.* 9.35.

42. These senses of the proximate and the final ends are taken over from Augustine (see *De civ. Dei* 19.1) and become a commonplace in the medieval schools (see Aquinas, *ST* 1a2ae, 1.5).

43. Rom. 10.4.

44. The work of Jerome is untraced. The term *psaltērion* was used in the Greek Septuagint for the aggregate of the psalms, and the term was made popular in the west by Jerome. It is also the Greek word for the psaltery, the twelve-stringed musical instrument (see Josephus, *Antiq.* 7.12).

45. John 3.31 f.

46. Cf. Dan. 3.5 ff.

47. Cf. 2 Par. 9.11.

48. Ps. 3.

49. Ps. 63(62).

50. Ps. 93(92).

51. Ps. 39(38), etc.

52. Ps. 34(33).

53. Ps. 81(80), etc.

54. Matt. 5.18.

55. Jerome, *Ep.* 28.2 (= CSEL 54.228).

56. Augustine, *En. Ps.* 4.4 (= ACW 29.44).

57. Jerome, *Tract. de Ps.* 89 (CCL 78.118 f.). See Ps. 41(40).14, 72(71).19, 89(88).53, 106(105).48. This was the mode of division in the

Jewish tradition, accepted by the earliest Christian exegetes from Origen onward; see R. Devreesse, *Les anciens commentateurs grecs des psaumes* (Rome 1970) ch. 1.

58. Acts 1.20; cf. Hilary, *Tract. super Ps. 1, Instructio* 1 (= CSEL 22.3).

59. Ps. 2.2.

60. Ps. 21(20).3.

61. Ps. 2.7.

62. Ps. 110(109).3.

63. Ps. 22(21).2.

64. Ps. 69(68).6.

65. Tyconius the Donatist theologian in his *Liber regularum* (c. 380) propounded rules for the interpretation of Scripture, some of which Augustine incorporated in his *De doctrina christiana* (III, 42 ff.). Cassiodorus refers again to Tyconius at *Inst.* 1.9.3, intimating that some parts of his work are not to be rejected.

66. See Augustine, *En. Ps.* 44.22.

67. See the Introduction, p. 9.

68. The symbolic sense of numbers in the psalms and in Scripture generally exercised Cassiodorus greatly as they did Jerome and Augustine before him; see the Introduction, p. 17.

69. Matt. 7.29.

70. Ps. 119(118).50 and 107.

71. 1 Cor. 4.20.

72. 2 Tim. 3.16 f.

73. Jerome, *Praef. in Job* (ML 28.1140 ff.).

74. For discussion of *fastucium,* see G. Mercati, *Biblica* 29 (1948) 282 ff.

75. Heb. 4.12.

76. Ps. 19(18).5.

77. James 3.9.

78. This is the frequently voiced claim (see, e.g., the comments of Augustine cited in the next paragraph and the remarks of Cassiodorus, *Inst. praef.* 6 and 1.4.2) that the rhetorical and literary devices found in Greek and Latin literature were anticipated in and borrowed from the Old Testament. Cicero's *Topica* is a summary of Aristotle's treatise of that name.

79. Augustine, *De doctrina christiana* 3.40.

80. *Locutiones in Heptateuchum* (CCL 33.379).

81. Cf. 1 Cor. 3.18.

82. Cf. Gen. 42.23.

83. Exod. 3.14.

84. This sentence is clearly an addition inserted in the second recension; see n. 7 above.

85. I.e., among the biblical books.

86. Athanasius, *Ep. ad Marcellinum* 11 (= MG 27, 24A).

87. So earlier Jerome, *Ep.* 107.12. In his *Inst.* 1, Cassiodorus surveys the Octateuch, Kings, Prophets and Psalms (1.4), the fourth book in this sense of the O.T.

88. Sabellius was a third-century Monarchian who believed that the three Persons were not distinct, and thus that the Father was crucified on Calvary; see G. Bardy, DTC 10.2204 ff.

89. On Arius, see J. Quasten, *Patr.* 3.7–13; J. H. Crehan, CDT 1.134 ff.

90. On the Spirit of life in the Manichean system, see J. J. O'Meara, *The Young Augustine* (London 1954) 72 ff. Cassiodorus' remark betrays a certain ignorance of Manichean teaching.

91. Song 6.9.

92. Actually earlier at 4.1 ff.

93. Song 7.8.

94. Again earlier at 4.10 f.

95. Song 1.1 f.

PSALM 1

1. John 8.25.

2. The reference is to Jerome, *Hom. on Psalm 1*, rejecting the view that Christ is the happy man: "The psalm cannot refer to the person of the Lord, but refers in general to the just man" (CCL 78.3), and to Hilary (ML 9.249 f.). Cassiodorus prefers Augustine's view (CCL 38.1) that Christ is meant.

3. Ps. 116(114–115).11.

4. Job 14.4 offers the closest similarity to this text.

5. Verecundus, *Comm. in Cant.* 2.4; cf. Isa. 64.6.

6. 1 Peter 2.22.

7. John 14.30.

8. Heb. 4.15 f.

9. This image of the gate with keys is Jerome's; see n. 2.

10. Rom. 5.19.

11. For the definitions, see Cassiodorus, *Inst.* 2.14.

12. Ps. 5.5.

13. "The notional"; see Cicero, *Tusc.* 1.57, and n. 11 above.

14. Ps. 72(71).18.

15. Euclid, 1 def. 2; Boethius had published a Latin version of Euclid, and Cassiodorus followed this in his *Institutiones* in the section on geometry; see P. Courcelle, *Late Latin Writers and Their Greek Sources,* 350 ff.

16. Cf. Isidore, *Orig.* 10.22, wrongly suggesting that *beatus* is formed from *bene auctus;* Cassiodorus suggests *bene aptus.*

17. Ps. 144(143).15.

18. So Lactantius, *De opificio Dei* 12.16.

19. Actually Zach. 6.12.

20. Ps. 40(39).8.

21. This is an echo of Augustine's commentary at this point.

22. Matt. 23.2.

23. Again echoing Augustine.

24. "Subjoining"; see the references to the grammarians in LSJ.

25. John 14.30.

26. Ps. 37(36).27.

27. The categorical syllogism (as opposed to the hypothetical) has propositions and conclusion consisting of statements with subject and verb. At *Inst.* 2.3.12 and 18, Cassiodorus praises the *Peri Hermeneias* attributed to Apuleius; in that work the terms predicative (= categorical) and conditional (= hypothetical) are extensively used of propositions.

28. Augustine is again the source here.

29. Ps. 40(39).9.

30. Ps. 78(77).2.

31. The suggestion is taken over from Jerome's homily (CCL 78.5).
32. 1 Cor. 10.31.
33. Cf. Ps. 119(118).32 f., of which this is a paraphrase.
34. Cf. Varro, *L.L.* 6.6 for this bizarre suggestion.
35. Luke 24.43.
36. See Quintilian 8.3.77, etc.
37. John 4.10.
38. The interpretation is Augustine's.
39. So Varro, *L.L.* 5.37.
40. Matt. 24.35.
41. Apoc. 22.1 f., also quoted by Jerome here (CCL 78.7 f.).
42. Phil. 2.9.
43. Apoc. 5.11 f.
44. See Martin, 119 ff.
45. *De doctr. chr.* 4.4.
46. Apoc. 20.9 f.
47. He is referring to the face, which is a plane.
48. Titus 1.16.
49. The sentence echoes Jerome's commentary.
50. John 3.18.
51. 1 Cor. 15.51.
52. Ps. 32(31).1.
53. 1 John 1.8.
54. A point made earlier in Augustine's commentary.
55. Matt. 25.12.
56. Gen. 3.9.
57. See Varro, *L.L.* for these strange etymologies.
58. See n. 57.
59. Ps. 50(49).23.
60. Cf. Isa. 41.27, 51.17, 62.12.
61. Cassiodorus has in mind the One of Neoplatonism, the indivisible Unity which is the Maker of the forms; see J. M. Rist, *Plotinus* (Cambridge 1967) ch. 3.
62. Rom. 11.36.
63. Cassiodorus here echoes the treatise of Nicomachus of Gerasa (ed. Hoche, p. 84); see also Boethius, *De geom.* (ed. Friedlein, 397).

64. *Introd. Arith.* (Hoche, p. 84), also used by Boethius in his *De Arith.*

65. Wisd. 11.21.

66. This translates *drama;* Cassiodorus repeatedly envisages the psalms as dramas, allotting different sections to different spokesmen.

PSALM 2

1. This is the reading at Acts 13.33 in codex Bezae (on which, see *The Cambridge History of the Bible* I, 355); the Vulgate has *in psalmo secundo.*

2. On the psalm as musical instrument, see *Preface*, p. 30 f.

3. See Jerome, *Hebrew Names* (CCL 72.135).

4. Augustine, *Tract. in Joann.* 78.3 (= CCL 36.524).

5. On the figure of the question, cf. Quintilian, 9.2.6 ff., and Martin, 284 f.

6. Ps. 119(118).84.

7. Jer. 14.22.

8. On rhetorical figures, see Cicero, *De Or.* 3.149 ff.; Quint. 9.1.4.

9. Augustine, *Locutiones in Heptateuchum, passim* (= CCL 33.381 f.).

10. Acts 4.27, cited also by Augustine *ad loc.*

11. Herod the Great (37–4 BC) was king when Christ was born, and to him is ascribed the slaughter of the Innocents. It was his son Antipas who was responsible for the beheading of John the Baptist.

12. John 5.23.

13. Cf. Matt. 11.30.

14. Ps. 19(18).2.

15. So also Augustine, *ad loc.*

16. On metonymy, Martin, 268 ff., with references.

17. Referring to "laugh" and "deride" in the preceding paragraph.

18. Augustine makes the same point.

19. "Change" or "substitution," here referring to change of spokesman.

20. John 9.19.

21. Matt. 2.2.

22. Sion is identified with Mt. Hermon (Deut. 4.48), and is there-

fore rendered as "lofty peak"; presumably the sense of "contemplation" found in Augustine, *ad loc.*, and later in this treatise is a development of this sense.

23. Cassiodorus seems to regard *spécula*, "watch-tower," as the same word as *spēcula*, "little hope."

24. Ps. 110(109).1.

25. Matt. 3.17.

26. Cf. Acts 13.33.

27. See Augustine, *ad loc.*, and Boethius, *Trin.* 4.

28. Actually Exod. 3.14.

29. Isa. 53.8.

30. Cf. Rom. 11.36.

31. Heb. 1.3 ff.

32. Arianism is naturally an immediate issue for Cassiodorus as the religion of the Ostrogoths and of Theoderic; see Introduction, p. 12.

33. The echoes of the study of Aristotelian logic being conducted in Cassiodorus' day are strong here; cf. D. Ross, *Aristotle* (London 1949), ch. 2.

34. The definition is close to that of Boethius in *Contra Eutychen* II.

35. Exod. 4.23.

36. Again echoing the Aristotelian categories; see n. 33 above.

37. John 16.15.

38. We shall note how puerile are many of the etymologies such as this, proposed or accepted by Cassiodorus.

39. Matt. 28.18.

40. Phil. 2.10.

41. With reference to the next words of the verse.

42. Ps. 45(44).7.

43. The mistaken etymology echoes Servius, *ad Aen.* 4.242.

44. Roman rhetoricians recognise three types of speech: the formal or epideictic (e.g., a funeral oration), the judicial or forensic, and the deliberative, a speech of advice delivered in the political arena. The three types are discussed by Quintilian at III, 7 ff.

45. In the deliberative genre, the useful and honourable are stock motifs; see Cicero, *De Inventione* 2.156; Quintilian, III, 8.10 ff., who subdivides them into subsidiary motifs and adds a third, the possible.

46. See the third paragraph below.

47. 2 Cor. 4.8.
48. The fanciful derivation follows Varro, *L.L.* 5.21.
49. John 14.6.
50. Cf. Phil. 2.13.
51. See the Conclusion to Psalm 1.
52. Luke 24.39.
53. Acts 1.11.
54. Cf. Zach. 12.10.
55. Matt. 5.8.
56. Athanasius, the scourge of Arianism, emphasised the doctrine of the two natures especially in his *De incarnatione* (ed. Cross, London 1939). Hilary, "the Athanasius of the West," likewise condemned the heresy in his *De Trinitate*. Ambrose was continually embroiled in the Arian controversy; his treatises and his hymns are full of anti-Arian doctrine; see Homes Dudden, *The Life and Times of St Ambrose,* (Oxford 1935), 189 ff. For Augustine's condemnation, see e.g. *De Trin.* 5.3 ff. Jerome's attacks are found primarily in his letters; see J. N. D. Kelly, *Jerome* (London 1975) *passim.* The chronological order of the catalogue suggests that Cassiodorus has in mind Cyril of Alexandria (see J. Mahé, DTC 3.2476 ff.) rather than Cyril of Jerusalem.
57. *Conc. Chalced. actio* 2; for bibliography, see ODCC *s.v.* "Chalcedon, Council of."

PSALM 3

1. Cf. 2 Sam. (2 Kings) 18.9.
2. So Augustine, *ad loc.*
3. The timeless drama of Job encouraged commentators to date it early, especially given the absence of reference to the Jewish legal and religious systems. But no-one nowadays would date it before the fifth century before Christ.
4. So also Augustine here.
5. Ps. 35(34).12.
6. A less common term for *anaphora,* the repetition of a word or words at the beginning of each phrase.
7. Matt. 27.42.

8. So also Augustine.
9. *Enchir.* 30 ff. (= ACW 3.37 ff.).
10. On *auxesis*, see Martin, 153 ff.
11. Rom. 8.35.
12. See Martin, 303.
13. Rom. 5.3 ff.
14. Cf. John 17.1.
15. John 12.28.
16. Ps. 36(35).7.
17. John 10.18.
18. Cf. Luke 23.1 ff.
19. A false etymology.
20. Matt. 27.42.
21. 1 Tim. 1.15.
22. Cf. Gen. 26.20 ff.
23. Prov. 22.20.

PSALM 4

1. So earlier Augustine, *ad loc.*
2. Rom. 10.4.
3. 1 Cor. 10.11.
4. See Boylan, 12: "The phrase (sc. *In finem*) seems to have arisen from a misreading or misunderstanding of the Hebrew *lamᵉnasseah*, 'for the choir leader.' . . . The inscription apparently implies that every poem to which it is prefixed belonged in a special way to the official collection of songs which would be in charge of the chief singer."
5. See the *Preface*, p. 30 f.; also Ps. 147(146–147). 1 below.
6. Song 1.1.
7. Song 8.5.
8. Song 6.8.
9. Not in the handbooks, but see the references in LSJ.
10. 1 Thess. 5.17 f.
11. Job 27.5.
12. 2 Tim. 4.8.

13. Ps. 7.4.

14. Luke 12.47.

15. Cf. Luke 12.48.

16. Isa. 2.8 f.

17. Ps. 86(85).2.

18. Prov. 16.32.

19. Echoing Augustine's comment on this passage.

20. The reference is to Augustine, who inspires the rest of this paragraph.

21. See Varro, *L.L.* 5.162: *ubi cubabant, cubiculum.*

22. Ps. 149.5.

23. See *Preface*, p. 33. Cassiodorus marked the division in his manuscript. He is here following Augustine, who remarks: "The diapsalm placed at this point may quite well suggest the transition from the old life to the new."

24. Rom. 5.5.

25. Ps-Chrysostom, *In ven. crucem* (MG 50.819A).

26. "Question"; see Martin, 285.

27. Eph. 4.30.

28. 1 Cor. 1.18.

29. John 6.41.

30. Ps. 23(22).5.

31. Ps. 23(22).5. The whole section is adapted from Augustine.

32. The suggested etymology is echoed by Isidore, *Differentiae* 1.247.

33. John 14.27.

34. Cassiodorus interprets *idipsum* as the Neoplatonist One, but Boylan, 14, explains the sense of the Hebrew as "at once."

35. Its number being identical with the four gospels.

36. Appended appropriately here because Cassiodorus knows them as the four cardinal virtues; see Ambrose, *Super Lucam* 5 (ML 15.1738).

37. As the square of two, four represents perfect reciprocity and is identified with justice; see Guthrie, *History of Greek Philosophy* I (CUP 1962) 213.

PSALM 5

1. The identification is taken over from Jerome, *Tract. de Ps. 5* (CCL 78, 12), and Augustine, *En. Ps.* 5.1.

2. Matt. 5.4.

3. Ps. 2.8.

4. The point is made more explicitly by Augustine.

5. See on Ps. 2.1, 4.1 above.

6. See on Ps. 4 in the Division of the Psalm.

7. Eph. 5.27.

8. Gal. 4.6, also quoted by Jerome (CCL 78, 13).

9. The suggested connexion of *auris*, ear, with *auditus*, sound heard, is made also by Lactantius, *De opificio Dei* 8.8 (CSEL 27.29).

10. In Quintilian's definition, *rerum coniuncta diversitas* (9.3.38); cf. Martin, 305.

11. Augustine made the same point here.

12. Sabellius (likewise cited by Augustine here), the third-century modalist Monarchian, believed that the Persons were not distinct, but reflected a succession of modes of actions.

13. The condemnation of Arius' subordinationist teaching on Christ's Person came at Nicaea in 325; Arianism was still alive in Cassiodorus' day in Italy.

14. John 14.6 (taken over from Augustine). Christ as king is intermediary between God and men.

15. Deut. 6.4.

16. So also in Jerome (n. 8).

17. Ezech. 18.21 f.

18. 1 Kings (3 Kings) 17.1.

19. See above on Ps. 1, Division of the Psalm.

20. Isa. 45.19.

21. Zach. 12.10.

22. So also Jerome, *Hom.* 2.

23. The point is made also by Augustine at *En. Ps.* 3.9.

24. As Jerome remarks, "*et ordo verborum mysterium est.*"

25. John 2.19.

26. See on Ps. 1.3 above.

27. Augustine at *En. Ps.* 5.13 similarly says that the words are a prophecy rather than a curse.

28. 2 Cor. 3.5.

PSALM 6

1. See on Ps. 4.1 above.

2. See Jerome, *Tract. de Ps. 7* (CCL 78.20); Augustine, *En. Ps.* 6.1 (= ACW 29.61), and refs. in next note.

3. Hilary, *Comm. Ps.* Instr. 13 f. (= CSEL 22.12); Ambrose, *Expos. Luc.* 7.6 (= CCL 14.217); Augustine, *Serm. Domini in monte* 1.12 (= ACW 5.20 f.).

4. Amos 5.18.

5. Soph. 1.4.

6. Ps. 90(89).4.

7. The resurrection can be regarded as having taken place on the eighth day because Christ rose from the dead on the eighth day after Palm Sunday. Sermons on the resurrection are sometimes called by the Fathers "On the Ogdoad," and Ambrose at *In Luc.* 7.123 can say: "In the number eight the resurrection is accomplished."

8. This list of the seven means of forgiveness goes back to Origen; see the discussion of O. D. Watkins, *A History of Penance* (London 1920) 136 f.

9. Cassiodorus marshals the argument according to Classical theory, in which the speech is divided into exordium, statement of the case, narration, proof or correction, and conclusion.

10. In the exordium, the orator may begin *a propria persona,* or *ab adversariis,* or *ab re ipsa;* one sees here Christian adaptations of the Classical motifs.

11. This is the equivalent of the Classical *katastasis* or statement of the case.

12. The *narratio,* the facts of what happened, is the third part of the speech.

13. *Correctio* seems to be used here in the sense of self-correction or *metanoia;* the equivalent of the *probatio* in the Classical speech.

14. Mal. 3.2 f.

15. Eccli. 18.23 f.
16. On the *concessiva deprecatio*, see Martin, 41; also n. 47 below.
17. Isa. 43.26.
18. Apoc. 3.19.
19. Nathan; cf. 2 Sam. (2 Kings) 12.1 ff.
20. Ps. 50(49).21.
21. John 16.8.
22. I.e., between Son and Spirit.
23. Deut. 68.23.
24. Ps. 2.5.
25. Soph. 1.15.
26. Zach. 1.3.
27. Isa. 38.18.
28. Phil. 2.10.
29. Wisd. 5.3.
30. The etymology is bizarre.
31. John Chrysostom, *De compunctione* (MG 47.393 ff.).
32. Another fanciful derivation.
33. Ps. 107(106).26.
34. Ps. 51(50).9.
35. Actually Jos. 1.8.
36. Ps. 102(101).10.
37. Neither suggested etymology is valid.
38. This is the *a victu;* cf. Cicero, *Inv.* 1.35.
39. Ps. 126(125).5.
40. Mark 8.33.
41. Cf. Mark 8.33.
42. Matt. 5.7.
43. See n. 44 on Ps. 2.11 above.
44. This form of argument (*coniectura*) is discussed at Quintilian 7.2.1 ff.
45. *Finis* here is the alternative form of *definitio* (the orator must define the point at issue). See Martin, 31 ff.
46. See Quintilian 7.4 and Martin, 36 ff.
47. *Concessio*, admission of guilt, is a subdivision of the *status qualitatis* or nature of the case; see Quintilian, 7.4.14, and Martin, 40.
48. The number of this psalm, 6, is regarded as the perfect number. See Martianus Capella, 7.745: *hexas a paribus impar et ab imparibus par, unde et perfectus nominatur.*

49. According to Hebrew chronology, the history of Israel up to the capture of Jerusalem (586 BC) was divided into 4 eras. The fifth spans the intervening period up to Christ's birth.

50. Sermon 352 (= ML 39.1549 ff.).

PSALM 7

1. Cf. 2 Sam. (2 Kings) 15.32 ff.

2. *En Ps.* 7.1.

3. The derivation is offered by Jerome, *Tract. de Ps. 7* (CCL 78.21). The right hand is the pledge of friendship and trust, so the title is apt for one who looked to his friend's safety. Augustine renders as "the propitious" (ACW 29.75).

4. Cf. Augustine, *ad loc.*

5. At Quintilian 8.3.44 *allegoria* is rendered by *inversio*. See Martin, 262 ff.

6. Echoing the definition of Boethius, *Contra Eutychen* 3, adopted by St Thomas Aquinas at *S.T.* 1a2ae 29.1.

7. Not in the handbooks.

8. 2 Sam. (2 Kings) 18.5.

9. Cf. 1 Sam. (1 Kings) 24 and 26.

10. Cf. Ps. 1.4, also evoked by Augustine at this point.

11. Boethius (see ML 64) composed an extant work on the hypothetical syllogism. At *Inst.* 2.3.18, Cassiodorus recommends Marius Victorinus as an authority on the hypothetical syllogism; see the next note.

12. The reference is to Aristotle's *Prior Analytics*, translated by Boethius (ML 64.639 ff.). Marius Victorinus, the celebrated fourth-century convert from Neoplatonism, wrote a *De definitionibus* (ML 64.891 ff.).

13. So Augustine, *ad loc.*

14. Matt. 26.32.

15. Ps. 22(21).17 f.

16. John 3.13.

17. Ps. 18(17).11 f.

18. Ps. 11(10).5.

19. John 19.30. Cassiodorus here seems wrongly to identify *consummare* with *consumere;* but Augustine reads *consummabitur* for *consumetur* in this verse, so it is more likely that there is confusion between the two readings.

20. Rom. 14.4.

21. Ps. 19(18).13.

22. Augustine interprets as 'thoughts and pleasures'.

23. John 16.15.

24. Augustine also interprets the sword as Christ coming in glory.

25. Eph. 6.17.

26. The interpretation is Augustine's.

27. See Jerome, *Psalt. iuxta Hebr.* 7.14 (ML 29.134). The codex Palatinus has *operatus est.*

28. Luke 23.21.

29. Matt. 7.20.

30. Prov. 26.27.

31. Dan. 20.

32. Matt. 11.25.

33. This is a Christianised version of Cicero's famous definition at *De inventione* 2.163: *patientia est honestatis ac utilitatis causa voluntaria ac diurna perpessio rerum arduarum ac difficilium.*

34. The idea is a traditional one in Basil, Ambrose, Augustine and Jerome, all of whom are mentioned by Cassiodorus in his section *De Octateucho* at the beginning of *Inst.* I.

PSALM 8

1. See on Ps. 4.1 above.

2. This is taken over from Augustine, *ad loc.*

3. Heb. 1.13.

4. Phil. 2.6.

5. Phil. 2.9.

6. This is not the usual sense of syllepsis; see Martin, 300.

7. Donatists are joined with Jews here because of their belief that sacraments conferred through the *traditores* at the time of the Diocletianic persecution were invalid, and that thus the Donatists alone com-

posed the true Church. Though the schism was condemned in the
early fifth century, it rumbled on until the eighth; see W. H. C. Frend,
The Donatist Church (Oxford 1952) 305 ff.

8. Ps. 108(107).6.

9. Matt. 21.16.

10. 1 Peter 2.2.

11. So also Augustine, *ad loc.*

12. John 5.23.

13. Isa. 66.1.

14. Cf. Exod. 31.18; Augustine is the source of what follows.

15. Isa. 40.12.

16. Ps. 72(71).7.

17. Eccli. 27.12.

18. 1 Cor. 15.41 f.

19. Gen. 1.1.

20. See above on Ps. 4.7.

21. Ps. 36(35).8 f.

22. Cf. Ps. 19(18).6.

23. John 1.14.

24. Phil. 2.7.

25. Heb. 2.8.

26. Ps. 97(96).7.

27. See Cicero, *De inventione* 1.80 ff. for the division of *argumenta*
into four *probabilia* and three *necessaria*, which are *complexio, enumer-
atio, simplex conclusio.*

28. John 21.17.

29. This is adopted from Augustine.

30. So Varro, *L.L.* 5.75.

31. The sea is more appropriate than rivers because its extent suggests the wide-ranging researches of philosophers.

32. Cf. Matt. 11.30.

33. Apoc. 1.8.

34. The hymn, *Intende, qui regis Israel* (see Walpole, *Early Latin
Hymns* [Cambridge 1922] 50 ff.), is authenticated as Ambrosian not
only by this passage but also by fifth-century commentators. The
stanza evokes Ps. 19(18).6.

35. Cf. Gen. 6.18.

36. Cf. 1 Sam. (1 Kings) 16.10 f.

37. Cf. Gen. 17.12.

38. Philolaus (born c. 474 BC) is credited with the doctrine that the earth is formed from the cube; see W. K. C. Guthrie, *A History of Greek Philosophy* I (Cambridge 1962) 267, 329 ff. Cassiodorus probably found the reference in the *Introduction to Arithmetic* of Nicomachus of Gerasa, which was translated into Latin by Apuleius and exploited by Boethius in his *De institutione arithmetica.*

PSALM 9 [PSS. 9 AND 10]

1. See Psalm 3.1; Augustine has made the same point here.

2. John 8.36.

3. See Quintilian, 8.6.18 ff., etc.

4. Cf. 1 Sam. (1 Kings) 18 ff.

5. The parallel is taken over from Augustine.

6. *Idea* more usually refers to the general character of a speech (see Martin, 338 ff.).

7. Here the Origenist view of *apokatastasis* proposed at *Princ.* 3.6.1 ff. is opposed.

8. The word seems to have been German in origin; see TLL *ad loc.*

9. Ps. 7.13, cited also by Augustine.

10. Matt. 25.34.

11. Cf. Matt. 19.28.

12. Matt. 25.41.

13. Ps. 50(49).15.

14. This meaning of Sion is adopted from Augustine.

15. Prov. 1.16.

16. Matt. 25.41.

17. Isa. 66.24.

18. These words, cited in the Septuagint, are noted also by Augustine.

19. This second etymology is correct.

20. Luke 21.19.

21. Cf. Rom. 2.4.

22. Antichrist is likewise introduced at this point by Augustine.

23. The Hebrew text regards vv. 22–39 as a separate psalm (= 10), in spite of the alphabetic arrangement of the whole; the Massoretic text and hence the Revised Version followed suit; hence the different numeration from the Vulgate.

24. See verse 11 above.

25. 2 Thess. 2.4.

26. Dan. 11.36.

27. Ps. 119(118).1.

28. See Quintilian, 9.3.99; Martin, 262.

29. Wisd. 2.25.

30. Quintilian, 6.2.29; Martin, 165.

31. Matt. 24.24.

32. So Varro, *L.L.* 5.92, of course wrongly.

33. Mark 13.32.

34. Cf. Hilary, *Tract. Ps.* 9.1 (= CSEL 22.75), *De Trin.* 9.58 (ML 10.327 ff.); Augustine, *En. Ps.* 9.1 (= CCL 38.57), *De Trin.* 1.12 (= ML 42.836).

35. John 21.17.

36. John 16.15.

37. Above, 2.5.

38. Gen. 22.12.

39. Matt. 25.12.

40. Acts 1.7.

Psalm 10 [Ps. 11(10)]

1. So Augustine, *ad loc.*

2. The word in Greek is κοινώνημα, found in the general sense of "communication" in various authors but not listed as a figure in the handbooks.

3. 2 Cor. 2.16.

4. 1 Cor. 3.17.

5. Reading *mente* for *re* in CCL, which I cannot translate.

6. The words are etymologically connected; see Jerome, *Tract. de Ps. 10* (CCL 78.361), citing Varro.

7. Ps. 23(22).5.

8. The incorrect etymology is adopted from Varro, *L.L.* 5.127.

9. Macrobius, *Saturnalia* 5.21.18.

10. Ps. 34(33).17.

11. The comparison is made by Jerome earlier in *Tract. de Ps. 10* (CCL 78.355).

12. Cf. Luke 19.12 ff., also cited by Jerome.

13. The Pythagorean concept of the perfection of the number ten, the aggregate of 1, 2, 3, and 4, was adumbrated in the treatises of Boethius on arithmetic and music (see H. Chadwick, *Boethius* [Oxford 1981] ch. 2) and becomes a common feature in Christian-Platonist thought.

14. The etymology is false.

PSALM 11 [Ps. 12(11)]

1. "Gathering"; cf. Quintilian, 8.4.26; Martin, 158.

2. See Quintilian, 5.14.1 ff.; Martin, 102.

3. Actually James 1.8.

4. Acts 4.32.

5. Apoc. 13.5.

6. Cf. Alexander Rhetor, *De figuris* 1.25.

7. John 14.9.

8. So Augustine, *ad loc.*

9. Matt. 7.29.

10. Martin, 230.

11. See Isa. 11.2. The seven are specified as virtues by Gregory, *Moralia* 1.27; the term Gifts is a twelfth-century innovation. See E. D. O'Connor, *Aquinas, Summa Theologiae*, Blackfriars edn. vol 24 (London 1974), 5.

12. Prov. 2.13.

13. Gen. 16.10.

14. Cf. Matt. 20.1 ff.

15. See ML 51.770. The attribution to Prosper is disputed; G.

Morin, *Rev. Bén.* 31 (1914), 156 ff., regards it as the work of Quodvult-deus, the pupil of Augustine. But see P. Courcelle, *Histoire littéraire des grandes invasions germaniques*² (Paris 1964) 102 ff.

PSALM 12 [Ps. 13(12)]

1. 1 John 4.16.
2. Ps. 119(118).81.
3. So Augustine, *ad loc.*
4. "Dwelling on"; see Martin, 338, 342.
5. Rom. 5.5.
6. Gen. 15.6.
7. So Augustine, *ad loc.*
8. Augustine does not make this distinction in his *En. Ps.*, but doubtless Cassiodorus derives it from his other works. In *Contra Faustum* Leah and Rachel are types of action and contemplation (see ML 42.432), and in his commentary on John's gospel Augustine so depicts not only Martha and Mary but also Peter and John. The chief formative influence on medieval discussions of the two lives is Gregory the Great (see *Moralia* 28 in ML 76.467). There is a full discussion by J. Aumann in the Blackfriars edition of Aquinas, Vol. 46, App. 2: "Historical Background."

PSALM 13 [Ps. 14(13)]

1. See Ps. 53(52) Concl.; 59(58).7, 13 ff.
2. This fanciful notion is taken word for word from Varro, *L.L.* 6.47.
3. So Augustine, *ad loc.*
4. Matt. 15.24.
5. See Martin, 268.
6. Gen. 22.12.
7. Matt. 25.12.

8. The whole of verse 3, subdivided by Cassiodorus into five parts, is an insertion from Rom. 3.12–18. "The passage from *Romans* seems to have found its way into the text through the carelessness of some copyist, or possibly the insertion is due to the fact that St Paul's texts depict so fully the character of the fool" (Boylan, 45).

9. Ps. 5.11.

10. See above in Ps. 1, Division of the Psalm.

11. John 3.19.

12. The mistaken etymology is also found in Servius, *Ad Verg. Aen.* 1.688.

13. 1 Cor. 2.8.

14. Cf. John 11.48.

15. Ps. 22(21).2.

16. See above, Ps. 5 Concl., Ps. 8 Concl.

PSALM 14 [Ps. 15(14)]

1. Ps. 1.1 f.

2. See Martin, 285.

3. The whole section is fanciful. *Tabernaculum* is merely a diminutive of *taberna,* hut or cottage.

4. See Josephus, *Jewish Antiquities* 3.6. At *Inst.* 1.5.2 Cassiodorus described how a certain Eusebius visited him. Though blind he was able to describe the *tabernaculum templumque Dei,* which Cassiodorus then had painted in his *Pandecte corporis grandioris.* On the paintings in Cassiodorus' manuscripts, see Mynors' edition of the *Institutiones,* xxiii. Bede, *Hist. Abbatum* 2.16, claims to have seen them. (A pandect is a gathering of writings, here referring to the bible considered as a collection of different books; see *Inst.* 1.12.3.).

5. Matt. 21.13.

6. Cf. Matt. 26.63.

7. John 15.15.

8. Luke 23.34.

9. Matt. 26.23.

10. Matt. 4.7.

11. See at Ps. 1.4.

12. John 15.14 f.

13. Again a false etymology.

14. Ps. 132(131).11.

15. Luke 1.73.

16. Matt. 25.24 and 27.

17. John 10.11.

18. With a play on the holy Innocents.

19. See Martin, 300. But the statement seems cryptic. Does Cassiodorus mean that "He who does these things shall not be moved" implies further that "He who does not do these things shall be moved"?

PSALM 15 [PS. 16(15)]

1. It is clear from this paragraph that Cassiodorus takes *ipsi* as nominative, whereas the dative ("To David himself") is the normal rendering.

2. John 19.19; cf. Augustine, *ad loc.*

3. See the initial discussions of Psalms 2 and 7 above.

4. See earlier on Psalm 3.

5. Texts in Martin, 291.

6. Though this seems to be an echo of the fifth-century controversy between Augustine and Julian of Eclanum, the heresy had to be condemned again at Orange in 529; see R. Hedde-E. Amann, DTC 12.675 ff.

7. The influence of *De praedestinatione sanctorum* attributed to Augustine (see ML 44.959 ff) is notable here as elsewhere in Cassiodorus' commentary.

8. He is referring to the designation of God as a human person with functioning parts of a human body; see at Ps. 7.9, 11(10).5.

9. The mistaken etymology is repeated from Ps. 11(10).7.

10. Heb. 5.8 f.

11. Cf. Num. 34 ff.

12. The derivation is false.

13. Acts 1.26.

14. Ps. 109(108).6.

15. See paragraph 7 above.

16. See Martin, 286.

17. Apollinaris, friend of Athanasius and bishop of Laodicea c. 360, taught that there was no human soul in Christ, but rather the God-head. His teaching was condemned at Constantinople in 381. Texts in H. Lietzmann, *Apollinaris von Laodicea und seine Schule* (Tübingen 1904).

18. Matt. 26.30.

19. John 10.18.

20. Ps. 30(29).10.

21. By multiplying the number of the senses with the three Persons of the Trinity, we obtain the number of the psalm.

PSALM 16 [Ps. 17(16)]

1. Varro, *L.L.* rightly connects *oratio* (prayer) with *os* (mouth), but the addition of *ratio* is otiose.

2. Ps. 16(15).8.

3. In the Vulgate the sense is combined with the following phrase.

4. Job 5.7.

5. Ps. 91(90).11–12.

6. See Quintilian, 9.3.23; Martin, 266.

7. Matt. 10.22.

8. See Augustine, *ad loc.*

9. "Image"; see Martin, 119.

10. The words are unconnected.

11. Martin, 119.

12. John 13.27.

13. John 19.6 f.

14. John 8.44.

15. See 9.7. He seems to refer to his later comment at Ps. 35(34).3. The word, originally German, first means a long-handled spear, but in Christian Latin usually means a sword.

16. Cf. Cassiodorus, *Inst.* 2.14, adopted from Marius Victorinus, *De definitionibus.*

17. Ps. 5.6.

18. Gen. 4.16.

19. Ps. 31(30).20.

20. Cf. Lev. 7.

21. Matt. 27.25.

22. John 14.20 and 10.

23. Cyril of Alexandria, *Ep.* 45.1.6 (MG 77.232), with variations from the Greek text.

24. The sixteen canonical prophets; cf. ODCC *s.v.* "Prophecy."

PSALM 17 [PS. 18(17)]

1. Isa. 9.6.

2. Cf. 1 Sam. (1 Kings) 31.

3. Cassiodorus allots the verses as follows: 1–16 the psalmist, 17–32 the Church, 33–46 Christ, 47–51 the Church.

4. John 14.21.

5. There is no basis for this etymology.

6. See above, Ps. 17(16).13.

7. Cassiodorus appears to have forgotten his earlier suggestion that the prophet speaks throughout verses 1–16.

8. Ps. 51(50).7.

9. See above at Ps. 9.5.

10. Phil. 2.7.

11. Ps. 91(90).13.

12. See *Ad Her.* 4.44; Martin, 264.

13. Ps. 51(50).9.

14. So Jerome, *Hebrew Names* (CCL 72.63).

15. Ps. 80(79).2.

16. See Martin, 301.

17. Ps. 19(18).3. (but hardly *coniunctio* in the same sense), 22(21).2.

18. The passage may have been taken over from Cassian, *Contra Nestorium* 7.30.1 (= CSEL 17.388). The work of Chrysostom has been lost.

19. Cf. Prov. 1.6.

20. The Latin would then mean "within His encompassing."

21. 1 Cor. 13.12, cited also by Augustine on this psalm.

22. John 12.28 f.

23. Matt. 3.17.

24. 2 Cor. 2.16.

25. The whole of this section is adapted from Augustine.

26. This too is taken over from Augustine.

27. Acts 18.6.

28. The Latin is *salvum me fecit;* the masculine is attributable to the fact that the psalmist speaks.

29. John 15.16.

30. See above, Introduction VI.

31. Reading *tibi* for *sibi* in CCL.

32. 2 Tim. 4.8.

33. James 1.17.

34. Lev. 19.2.

35. Ps. 24(23).4.

36. Isa. 42.1.

37. In *Inst.* 2.15 f., Cassiodorus lists these *topica* or grounds of argument. Among the external arguments (*argumenta extrinsecus*) he distinguishes the *ex persona* as here, the *ex naturae auctoritate*, and the *ex temporis auctoritate*.

38. John 5.35.

39. Luke 11.33.

40. Ps. 118(117).27.

41. Ezech. 39.29.

42. I.e., the sentence would read, "The way of my God is undefiled."

43. For the *para prosdokian* (which I read for the *paraprosdoxia* of CCL), see Quintilian, 9.2.23.

44. Jer. 23.29.

45. Ps. 42(41).2.

46. So also Augustine, *ad loc.*

47. Phil. 2.9.

48. Matt. 27.25.

49. Matt. 13.42.

50. The phrase *vexilla crucis* calls to mind the hymn of Cassiodorus' contemporary Venantius Fortunatus, *Vexilla regis prodeunt.* That hymn, however, commemorates the arrival of the relic of the True Cross at Poitiers in 567, a date too late for influence on this passage.

51. Isa. 52.15.

52. Isa. 6.10.

53. See Martin, 290 ff.

54. John 8.44.

55. Matt. 22.16.

56. The verb is cognate with *mens*, but the suggested fusion of *mens* and *ire* is fanciful.

57. So also Augustine, *ad loc.*

58. Cf. Gen. 32.25.

59. The comment, taken over from Augustine, derives from Matt. 15.2.

60. Matt. 21.9.

61. 2 Sam. (2 Kings) 1.14.

PSALM 18 [PS. 19(18)]

1. The suggestion is adopted from Augustine's Second Discourse (= ACW 29.183).

2. Cf. Psalm 50(49).16; but the words have been adapted to the present passage.

3. Ps. 50(49).5.

4. Ps. 148.5.

5. This too is found in the discussion of Augustine; see ACW 29.187.

6. This is the fifteenth of the *argumenta* listed by Cassiodorus at *Inst.* 2.15, taken over from Marius Victorinus' Commentary on Cicero's *Topica.*

7. Ps. 42(41).8.

8. More commonly, the term is used to denote an alternative means of expression; so Quintilian, 9.3.12 ff.; see Martin, 298.

9. *sponsus*, bridegroom, is derived from *spondere.*

10. Ps. 1.1.

11. See Augustine at ACW 29.189.

12. Cf. Acts 2.3.

13. Deut. 6.4.

14. He means by "six verses" the six statements in verses 8–10.

15. The seventh in the catalogue of definitions reproduced from Marius Victorinus at *Inst.* 2.14.

16. Matt. 5.17.

17. 1 Cor. 14.20.

18. 1 Tim. 6.13.

19. Rom. 8.16.

20. 2 Tim. 4.8.

21. Reading *decet* for *docet* of CCL.

22. Amos 5.18.

23. Above, Ps. 6 Concl.

24. "Climax"; see Martin, 255.

25. 1 Cor. 2.9.

26. Eccli. 18.30.

27. Ps. 51(50).5.

28. Ps. 32(31).5.

29. This too is taken from Augustine; ACW 29, 194.

30. Eccli. 10.15.

31. Ps. 50(49).16.

32. See Augustine (ACW 29.195).

33. Cf. Luke 13.11 ff.

PSALM 19 [PS. 20(19)]

1. See Martin, 277 ff.

2. Cf. Gen. 27.1 ff.; Augustine, *ad loc.*, expresses the idea summarily.

3. John 16.7.

4. On the diapsalm, see the *Preface*, p. 33; it is likewise indicated by Augustine here.

5. See Martin, 298.

6. On the Roman triumph and the lesser ovation, see R. Payne, *The Roman Triumph* (London 1962); H. S. Versnel, *Triumphus* (Leiden 1970).

7. See Martin, 256.

8. Prov. 24.16.

9. Martin, 107 ff.

PSALM 20 [PS. 21(20)]

1. John 17.10.
2. Ps. 72(71).2.
3. Matt. 27.37.
4. Luke 22.15.
5. See Martin, 301.
6. Ps. 132(131).15.
7. Gen. 16.10.
8. Ps. 135(134).6.
9. Above, *Preface* p. 33.
10. Matt. 3.17.
11. See Martin, 262.
12. John 17.1.
13. Cf. *Ad Herennium* 4.17; Quintilian, 9.1.27.
14. Ps. 140(139).14.
15. Cf. Luke 23.38.
16. Eccli. 2.11.
17. Ps. 18(17).31.
18. See above, 1.2, 7.6.
19. See Martin, 102 ff.
20. Rom. 5.10.
21. Above, n. 11.
22. Matt. 25.41.
23. Cf. John 11.50.
24. Reading *amphibolia* for *amphibologia;* see Martin, 241 f., 262.
25. John 10.18.
26. The first two are Psalms 2 and 8.
27. Not Hebrews but 1 Cor. 15.28, the *lapsus memoriae* demonstrating that Cassiodorus frequently cites from memory rather than from particular versions of Scripture.
28. The heresy of Eutyches, condemned at Chalcedon in 451, was to maintain that there was only one nature in the bodily Christ. The heresy was attacked in Boethius' *Contra Eutychen* (date about 512).
29. That is, by the doctrine of one nature, but human not divine as claimed by Eutyches.
30. Nestorius, condemned by the Council of Ephesus in 431, proclaimed the doctrine of two persons in Christ.

PSALM 21 [PS. 22(21)]

1. John 20.1, taken over from Augustine's First Discourse.
2. Phil. 2.10.
3. Usually the part from the whole (see Martin, 270), but Quintilian, 8.6.19, includes under this heading "what follows from what precedes."
4. Cf. Augustine (n. 1).
5. Statius, *Thebaid* 3.661.
6. 1 Cor. 2.8.
7. Cyril of Alexandria, *Ep.* 17 (MG 77.113B), citing Heb. 2.9 initially.
8. Ambrose, *De incarnatione Domini* 5.36 (ML 16.862 ff.).
9. John 19.11.
10. Matt. 26.39.
11. Ps. 61(60).6. The idea expressed here, implicit in Augustine's discussion of this psalm (see n. 1), is more fully explained in his *Ep.* 140, which Cassiodorus has read, for he cites it in paragraph 29 below.
12. 2 Cor. 5.21.
13. Cf. 2 Cor. 12.7–9.
14. Cf. Job 2.1–6.
15. Matt. 3.17.
16. Ps. 86(85).2.
17. The Fathers regularly interpret the name Israel as 'seeing God'; see the texts cited at ML 61.838.
18. This is the third of the fifteen types of definition taken over from Marius Victorinus, *De definitionibus*, in Cassiodorus, *Inst.* 2.3.14.
19. Rom. 8.32.
20. John 20.17.
21. "Repetition"; see Martin, 303.
22. "Abasing"; Martin, 153, exemplifies a different use of the figure.
23. 1 Cor. 1.27.
24. Cassiodorus' source for the parthenogenesis of worms is probably Augustine, *Ep.* 140.21.
25. Gen. 1.31.
26. Cf. 1 Sam. (1 Kings) 26.20.
27. Matt. 13.25.
28. See n. 3 above.

29. Matt. 27.42.

30. Matt. 27.40.

31. On irony, see Martin, 263 ff.

32. Matt. 27.43.

33. Ps. 19(18).6.

34. Luke 1.35.

35. Matt. 26.39.

36. Ps. 90(89).4.

37. "Anticipation"; see Martin, 277 f.

38. Augustine designates the bulls as the ringleaders, and the calves as "dissolute ruffians."

39. Luke 23.31.

40. See above, 3.4.

41. Ps. 51(50).17.

42. Matt. 10.16.

43. So Augustine, *ad loc.*

44. Cf. Mark 15.38.

45. John 13.34.

46. Actually 2 Cor. 5.17, but cf. Isa. 65.17.

47. John 10.18.

48. Matt. 27.45, 51.

49. Augustine, *Serm.* 350.1 (ML 39.1533).

50. 1 Cor. 1.23.

51. On the Arians and the topicality of the heresy, see Introduction VI.

52. 1 Cor. 1.24 f.

53. 1 Cor. 1.21.

54. John 19.23.

55. Matt. 16.18.

56. Matt. 27.35.

57. Cf. Lev. 16.8; of the two buck-goats, one was to be sacrificed and the other prayed over before being dispatched into the wilderness.

58. Cf. Num. 26.55.

59. Cf. Jos. 18.10.

60. Cf. Jonas 1.7.

61. Prov. 18.18.

62. Cf. Acts 1.26.

63. Eph. 1.11.
64. Actually Col. 1.12.
65. Apoc. 5.5.
66. 1 Peter 5.8.
67. Heb. 2.10–12.
68. Matt. 28.10.
69. Matt. 12.50.
70. See n. 17 above.
71. So Augustine, *ad loc.*
72. Augustine, *Ep.* 140.66 (CSEL 44.212).
73. Tob. 12.12.
74. Matt. 6.8.
75. Dan. 10.2 ff.

PSALM 22 [PS. 23(22)]

1. "A gathering together"; see Martin, 307.
2. Ps. 119(118).103.
3. So Augustine, *En. Ps. ad loc.*
4. 1 Peter 2.2.
5. Eph. 5.27.
6. Hab. 3.19.
7. Deut. 6.5.
8. Jos. 1.5.
9. Lam. 4.20.
10. Ps. 45(44).7.
11. Gen. 32.10.
12. Exod. 12.11.
13. Heb. 12.11.
14. The words are etymologically connected. Cassiodorus has in mind the annual festivals of the ancient Roman calendar.
15. 1 Cor. 11.29.
16. 1 Cor. 10.21.
17. Cf. Gen. 8.11.
18. Ps. 45(44).8.

19. Isa. 51.17.
20. John 4.13 f.
21. Ps. 84(83).5.
22. See Martin, 276.
23. See Martin, 257.

PSALM 23 [Ps. 24(23)]

1. Ps. 23(22).6.
2. Heb. 6.19.
3. Not in Martin.
4. Ps. 110(109).4.
5. Matt. 5.34 f.
6. Matt. 5.38 f.
7. This line of argument is based on the person concerned, as against *a propria persona*, in which the speaker discusses his own situation, or *ab adversariis*, where the comment is on opponents, or *ab re ipsa*, where the topic itself is discussed.
8. Ps. 67(66).2.
9. See Quintilian, 8.6.65; Tryphon, *Trop.* 1.10 (see Martin, 309).
10. Varro, *L.L.* 5.32: . . . *qua in oppidum portarent, portas.*
11. "Of what kind"; above on Ps. 22(21).4.
12. Cf. John 18.6.
13. "Doubling of words"; see Martin, 302.
14. 1 Sam. (1 Kings) 2.30.
15. For this claim that the Classical rhetoricians derived rhetorical figures and techniques from biblical literature, see Introduction VIII.

PSALM 24 [Ps. 25(24)]

1. John 1.47.
2. Jer. 1.5.
3. Job 2.3.

4. The likelihood is that the two missing letters (Waw, Quoph) and their verses have fallen out; see Boylan, *ad loc.*

5. *Ep.* 30 (= CSEL 54.243 ff.).

6. Lam. 1–4.

7. "Representation of character"; see Martin, 291.

8. Ps. 27(26).14.

9. "Redoubling of words"; see Martin, 301 ff.

10. Ps. 24(23).7–10.

11. Varro, *L.L.* 5.35, a reasonable suggestion.

12. The derivation is probably *se-* and *meare*, with the meaning of a side-road.

13. Presumably a derivation from Greek *kuklos* (circle) is being suggested.

14. The etymology is essentially correct.

15. See Martin, 254 f. As Quintilian, 8.3.83, states, the meaning is deeper than the words convey.

16. Luke 18.19.

17. Matt. 5.45.

18. Ps. 34(33).9.

19. Matt. 5.4.

20. Cf. Augustine, *ad loc.*

21. The Catharistae are the Manichean sect condemned by Augustine, as described by him at *De haeresibus* 38 (CCL 46.306), and are not to be confused with the later Albigensians.

22. 1 Cor. 2.9.

23. Ps. 139(138).22.

24. Israel is regularly interpreted by the Fathers as "seeing God"; see Ps. 22(21) n. 17.

25. Eph. 5.27.

26. Cf. Apoc. 4.10 f.

PSALM 25 [Ps. 26(25)]

1. See Augustine's First Discourse on Ps. 35(34).1 (= ACW 30.186), where these two meanings of the name David are suggested.

2. 2 Tim. 4.8.

3. Matt. 6.13.

4. Gen. 22.1.

5. Deut. 13.3.

6. Matt. 6.13.

7. John 14.6.

8. At *Inst.* 2.3.15, Cassiodorus summarises, probably from Marius Victorinus' commentary on Cicero's *Topica,* the Aristotelian *loci* on which arguments are based. The *Ex contrario* is the sixth of these.

9. 2 Peter 3.16.

10. Phil. 3.20.

11. For this derivation, see Paul. ex Fest. p. 29 Müller; Servius, *Ad Verg. Ecl.* 5.66.

12. Isa. 4.3.

13. 1 Cor. 3.17.

14. See Martin, 294.

15. 1 Kings (3 Kings) 19.18.

16. Ps. 6.9.

17. Ps. 18(17).26 f.

18. Cf. John 5.2; I propose the reading Solymis for the Salomonis of CCL.

PSALM 26 [PS. 27(26)]

1. Cf. 1 Sam. (1 Kings) 16.13.

2. Cf. 2 Sam. (2 Kings) 5.2.

3. The earlier messianic psalm is Ps. 22(21).

4. "Proof by demonstration"; see Martin, 103 ff.

5. See Ps. 25(24).7.

6. Ps. 4.2.

7. See Martin, 303 ff.

8. Perhaps Juvenal, *Satire* 10 ("The Vanity of Human Wishes"), is in Cassiodorus' mind here, though similar themes recur in Boethius' *Consolation of Philosophy.*

9. Cf. Ps. 118(117).22; Matt. 21.42.

10. Ps. 34(33).9.

11. Exod. 14.15.

12. Matt. 5.8.
13. John 14.6.
14. I.e., the O.T. books.
15. For the four senses of Scripture, of which the first is the historical, cf. H. de Lubac in n. 36 to the Introduction.
16. Matt. 2.20.
17. Exod. 4.19.
18. Cf. Quintilian, 3.6.46 and 66; Martin, 243.
19. James 1.5.
20. Cf. Wisd. 11.21.

PSALM 27 [PS. 28(27)]

1. See n. 1 to Ps. 26(25).
2. Psalms 3 and 16(15) are in Cassiodorus' mind.
3. The etymology is fanciful.
4. Heb. 1.5.
5. Matt. 26.39.
6. Cf. Dan. 6.10.
7. Cf. Matt. 5.17.
8. Matt. 6.9.
9. Cassiodorus here attacks the Arian doctrine that Christ did not have two natures, and that the nature of the Son was bestowed on Him by the Father, and that this took the place of the soul in the historical Jesus.
10. John 3.2.
11. Matt. 25.34.
12. Matt. 25.41.
13. Luke 6.38.
14. Luke 25.34.
15. See Martin, 277 ff.
16. Ps. 4.6.
17. Isa. 11.1.
18. Matt. 25.34.

Psalm 28 [Ps. 29(28)]

1. A tabernacle is properly a tent, which can serve as dwelling for men on military expeditions; here the expedition is against the vices of the flesh.

2. Of the three main types of oratory (deliberative, judicial, demonstrative), the third is used for epideictic or formal occasions; see above, Introduction VIII.

3. 2 Peter 1.21.

4. The seven gifts of the holy Spirit are listed at Isa. 11.2.

5. John 1.12.

6. So Augustine, *Enarr. in Ps., ad loc.*

7. The derivation is fanciful.

8. "Frequent repetition" of a word; cf. Martin, 276.

9. 1 Cor. 3.16.

10. Cf. Deut. 9.10.

11. Ps. 69(68).2.

12. Apoc. 17.1, reading *meretricis magnae quae sedet;* the harlot signifies Babylon.

13. So Augustine, *ad loc.*

14. In Latin, *vox Domini in virtute.*

15. Esth 13.9.

16. James 4.6.

17. Ps. 104(103).16.

18. Matt. 3.17.

19. This description of Christ as a son of unicorns, or as identical with the unicorn, is to have a long literary history. In the *Physiologus* we find the story that the unicorn or rhinoceros can be captured through the charms of a maiden, with whom it sports innocently; the animal thus becomes a symbol of chastity, and so of Christ. See T. H. White, *The Book of Beasts* (New York 1954) 20, quoting the ms. Harl. 4751: "Our Lord Jesus Christ is a unicorn spiritually, about whom it was said, And he was beloved like the son of unicorns."

20. Cf. Num. 20.1 ff.

21. Matt. 3.3.

22. See Pliny, *H.N.* 8.32, an account of how stags by their venomous breath entice snakes from their lairs and devour them.

23. Cf. Isa. 11.2 f.

24. Matt. 3.17.

25. Acts 9.4.

26. Acts 13.2.

27. This is probably Ps-Augustine, *Contra Varimadum* 3 (ML 62.411 ff.). See Adriaen's n., citing Morin, *Rev. Bén.* 31 (1914–19) 238, and Fischer, *Biblica* 23 (1942) 154.

28. Cf. Cicero, *Tusc.* 3.3, *consentiens laus bonorum.*

29. Matt. 28.19.

30. John 14.27.

31. For the *De Trinitate* of Didymus, see MG 39.3 (on the authorship, see L. Doutreleau, SC 83 (1962) Introduction). Presumably the reference to Ambrose is to *De fide* or *De spiritu sancto* or both.

32. Presumably another condemnation of Arianism; see Introduction VI.

Psalm 29 [Ps. 30(29)]

1. Matt. 28.18.

2. Matt. 26.68.

3. Matt. 27.40.

4. Cf. Matt. 27.35.

5. See Martin, 268: the definition is not appropriate in this instance, where the one word in Latin bears an extended sense.

6. John 15.16.

7. Cf. Ps. 37(36).8 f.

8. See above, n. 8 to Ps. 26(25).

9. John 1.14.

10. Col. 2.9.

11. Ps. 45(44).3.

12. John 5.26.

13. The ninth type of *argumentum* at *Inst.* 2.3.15; Cassiodorus has drawn the list from Marius Victorinus' Commentary on Cicero's *Topica.*

14. Ps. 16(15).10.

15. Mark 16.15 f.

16. See Martin, 249.

17. Phil. 2.9.
18. Matt. 3.17.
19. Rom. 6.9.
20. Ps. 35(34).18.

PSALM 30 [Ps. 31(30)]

1. See n. 2 to Ps. 28(27).
2. A true derivation.
3. Isa. 53.7.
4. Luke 23.46.
5. Phil. 2.7.
6. See Ps. 1.2 and n.
7. See above, Introduction VI.
8. The etymology is baseless.
9. John 14.30.
10. Cf. Matt. 7.14.
11. Matt. 26.38.
12. "Vivid description"; see Martin, 289 ff.
13. Jer. 17.5.
14. The words are not etymologically connected.
15. John 9.16.
16. John 8.48.
17. Zach. 13.7.
18. Not in the handbooks, but see n. 18 to Ps. 35(34).
19. Col. 2.9.
20. Ps. 12(11).9.
21. Ps. 116(114, 1–9; 115).16.
22. John 14.6.
23. Ps. 34(33).9.
24. Matt. 11.25.
25. "Gathering together"; see above, n. 2 to Ps. 12(11).
26. Matt. 5.8.
27. For the Church as tabernacle, see above, n. 1 to Ps. 29(28).
28. Reading *desperavi* (CCL *speravi*).
29. The derivation is fanciful.

30. Matt. 3.17.
31. Matt. 27.46.
32. John 15.14 f.
33. Eccli. 10.15.
34. See Quintilian, 8.5.11, and Martin, 257.
35. The image is appropriate because the Commentary (like Augus-tine's Third Discourse on this psalm; see ACW 30) makes much of Christ's marriage with the Church.
36. Cf. Gen. 41.46.
37. Cf. Luke 4.23.

PSALM 31 [PS. 32(31)]

1. For the true meaning of *intellectus* (= Hebrew *maskil*, didactic poem), see Boylan on Psalm 42(41).
2. Ps. 19(18).13.
3. See paragraph 8 below.
4. Reading *quia . . . qui* (CCL *qui . . . quia*)
5. So Cicero, *Inv.* 2.94: *concessio, per quam non factum ipsum proba-tur ab reo, sed ut ignoscatur id petitur.*
6. The psalm is visualised as a speech of defence in a court of law, in which the conventional structure contains an exordium followed by narration, the facts of the case.
7. See *Preface*, p. 33.
8. Cf. Luke 18.13.
9. "By removal of the opposite"; see *Inst.* 2.3.14.
10. Jerome, *In Oseam* 2.8.14 (CCL 76, 90).
11. Acts 9.4.
12. John 8.11.
13. Job 2.3.
14. John 1.47.
15. 1 John 1.8.
16. A bizarre etymology.
17. For the texts, see Martin, 41.
18. Cf. Ps. 6.6.
19. Above, Ps. 3.8.

20. The derivation is fanciful.
21. Above, Ps. 7.1.
22. Ezech. 18.28.
23. Above, Ps. 1.2.
24. "In common"; see Martin, 300.
25. Luke 11.9 f.

PSALM 32 [PS. 33(32)]

1. Matt. 5.11 f.
2. Phil. 4.4.
3. John 16.22.
4. Eccli. 15.9.
5. See p. 31.
6. In fact *cithara* is a Greek borrowing.
7. Job 1.21.
8. The point is taken over from Augustine verbatim.
9. Exod. 20.3 f., 7, 12 ff. Again Cassiodorus follows Augustine.
10. Ps. 56(55).12.
11. Luke 2.14.
12. Ancient rhetorical theory recognised three types of speech, the *deliberative* (appropriate for political assemblies), the *judicial* (for forensic cases), and the *demonstrative* (for formal occasions, such as funeral-speeches). See Quintilian, 3.4.14.
13. "By the word"; n. 16 to Ps. 17(16) above.
14. Luke 7.50, describing how Christ rewarded Magdalen for anointing his feet.
15. I.e., its nature; see *Inst.* 2.3.14.
16. Isa. 14.16.
17. Isa. 46.10.
18. Jer. 33.25.
19. "appearance" or "notion"; see Cicero, *Acad.* 1.30.
20. Ps. 51(50).11.
21. Ps. 143(142).7.
22. The Pauline texts (Rom. 8.28–30, Eph. 1.3 ff.) were resumed and discussed by Origen in his *De principiis*, and later by Augustine in his

De praedestinatione sanctorum (ML 44.959 ff.), a work with which Cassiodorus must have been familiar.

23. Ps. 19(18).6.

24. The *ab adiunctis*, the seventh *argumentum* listed at *Inst.* 2.3.15.

25. Matt. 5.6.

26. Translated in the Douai version as "waiteth for," but literally "beareth with."

27. Luke 21.19.

PSALM 33 [PS. 34(33)]

1. Cf. 1 Sam. (1 Kings) 21.13 and Augustine's First Discourse on this psalm (ACW 30.144).

2. Cf. Jerome, *Hebrew Names* (CCL 72.61: *pater meus rex*).

3. Following Ps. 7 and Ps. 27(26).

4. Cf. Ps. 25(24); Cassiodorus does not take into account Ps. 9 and 10 (9.22–37) and Ps. 11 (10).

5. The sixth or vau-verse is wanting, as in Ps. 25(24); see Boylan, *ad loc.*

6. See above at Ps. 25(24).1.

7. The derivation is unfounded.

8. On *enargeia* (not *energia*), see Martin, 288.

9. 1 Cor. 11.27–29.

10. 1 Tim. 6.16.

11. John 1.9.

12. Augustine in his Second Discourse claims that the Vulgate has the correct reading, and condemns the version approved by Cassiodorus; see ACW 30.170.

13. John 6.54.

14. Matt. 9.6.

15. Cf. Horace, *Odes* 3.24.62 ff.

16. Rom. 8.28.

17. "*Ex contrario*"; cf. Cicero, *Top.* 11, and Boethius, *In Top. Cic.* (ML 64.1065 ff.).

18. *Argumentum* is formed from *arguo*, of which *argutus* is the perfect participle.

19. Cassiodorus here again draws on Augustine's Second Discourse (ACW 30.177 f.)

20. Matt. 25.34.

21. "pattern" or "example"; see Martin, 262.

22. Again derived from Augustine's Second Discourse (ACW 30.180).

23. Matt. 5.3.

24. Luke 23.43.

25. For the further influence of Augustine's Second Discourse, see ACW 30.182.

26. See ACW 30.185.

27. Cf. Luke 16.24 and ACW 30.184.

28. Cf. Exod. 1.5.

29. Augustine, *Enchiridion* 84 ff. (= ACW 3.82 ff.)

PSALM 34 [PS. 35(34)]

1. Above, e.g., n. 1 to Ps. 26(25).

2. Matt. 5.44.

3. So Varro, *L.L.* 24, but the words are unconnected.

4. Eph. 6.16.

5. The suggestion is fanciful. Varro derives *scutum* from *secutura*, an equally wild suggestion.

6. See earlier at Ps. 17(16).13. Initially it means a German spear; in Christian Latin usually a sword. I have emended *dolus* (guile) to *dolo* (pike) here, since at 17(16).13 Cassiodorus says that one of the meanings of *framea* is *contus*, pole or pike. The metaphorical sense of divine punishment is often attested.

7. Ps. 17(16).13.

8. Ps. 142(141).5.

9. Mark 8.33.

10. Jer. 23.12.

11. See Martin, 294.

12. Matt. 22.61.

13. John 2.19.

14. Matt. 26.64 f.

15. Matt. 26.60 f.

16. Cf. Mark 11.13 f.

17. Cf. Matt. 25.32 f.

18. Fortunatianus, *Rhet.* 3.9, speaks of *meson* (moderation) as one of three types of utterance.

19. The etymological connection is fanciful.

20. Cf. Matt. 4.2.

21. Isa. 58.6–9.

22. Matt. 10.12 f.

23. In fact these "ablatives" are datives.

24. Cf. Servius, *Ad Aen.* 1.577, 2.283, etc.

25. Luke 12.66.

26. Matt. 27.41 f.

27. "Etymology"; the source is Cicero, *Top.* 2.10: *notatio, cum ex vi verbi argumentum aliquid elicitur.*

28. This alternative explanation, together with the chaff image in the next section, is taken over from Augustine; see ACW 30.217 f.

29. Above, Ps. 7.18; Augustine's *Confessions* stress this double sense.

30. Matt. 22.16 f.

31. John 11.50.

32. Luke 23.31.

33. "Energetic repetition"; cf. Herodian, *De figuris* (Spengel, *Rhet. Graeci* 3.99).

34. Apoc. 13.5 f.

35. The first is Ps. 22(21); others are 55(54), 69(68), 109(108).

PSALM 35 [PS. 36(35)]

1. Phil. 2.7 f.

2. Isa. 42.1.

3. The distinction between the two types of sinner, including the quotation from *Wisdom*, is taken over from Augustine (see ACW 30.223 f.).

4. Wisd. 9.15.

5. The erring philosophers are the Epicureans.

6. Again the formulation of Augustine (see n. 3 above).

7. The argument *ab ingenio* is one of the *argumenta extrinsecus* (see Inst. 2.3.16).

8. This is Augustine's interpretation.

9. Ps. 4.5. So Varro, *L.L.* 5.162, 8.54.

10. "A gathering together"; see Martin, 307, and Ps. 11.2 above.

11. Again following Augustine.

12. This too is Augustine's interpretation.

13. The rhetoricians define the *genus demonstrativum* as the speech of praise or blame (e.g. a funeral-oration), as distinct from the judicial and deliberative types; see Quintilian, 3.7.1 ff.

14. See Jerome, *Psalt. iuxta Hebr.* 36.7 (ed. de Sainte Marie, 52).

15. Rom. 11.33.

16. So Augustine (see ACW 30.240).

17. This is also the thought of Augustine (ACW 30.242).

18. Isa. 12.3.

19. A development of Augustine's thought (ACW 30.244).

20. John 1.9.

21. John 1.5.

22. The *a genere* is the second of the fifteen argumenta cited by Cassiodorus at *Inst.* 2.3.15.

23. Eccli. 10.15.

24. Matt. 25.41.

PSALM 36 [Ps. 37(36)]

1. The Vulgate does not contain the Hebrew alphabet as the Hebrew version does; the sixteenth letter omitted is Ain.

2. See at Ps. 25(24).1.

3. The seven—25(24), 34(33), 37(36), 111(110), 112(111), 119(118), 145(144) —are listed at Ps. 25(24).1.

4. See above, Ps. 1.2.

5. "Expression of character"; see Quintilian, 9.2.58, etc., and Ps. 16(15).1.

6. 1 Cor. 12.31.

7. So Varro, *L.L.* 5.108, but the words are unconnected.

8. Quintilian, 5.10.4 ff., defines it as "the argument by which we

seek to prove something," but notes that others define it as the definite conception of a thought in at least three parts, in other words a syllogism. The definition here clearly diverges from Quintilian's. See also Ps. 27(26).1.

9. James 2.20.

10. Gal. 5.17.

11. Rom. 7.24.

12. Col. 3.4.

13. Cf. Quintilian, 8.6.67, and Ps. 6.7 above.

14. Rom. 12.12.

15. *Nequam* is actually *ne aequam*, "not just."

16. Hyperbaton ("leaping over," cf. Quintilian, 8.6.62 ff.) means the transposition of a word or words from the natural position to a later point in the sentence for elegant effect. Here Cassiodorus is suggesting that verse 9 logically follows on from 7, with 8 interposed.

17. There is no such etymological connection.

18. The etymology, which may be correct, is taken from Varro, *L.L.* 5.116.

19. Luke 6.38.

20. The *e contrariis*; see above, Ps. 26(25).4, 30(29).6, etc.

21. Normally an example *simpliciter* (cf. Quintilian 5.11.1).

22. Ps. 41(40).2.

23. Cf. Matt. 5.6.

24. "Additional effect." Quintilian, 8.3.88, calls it "repetition of the same truth."

25. *A coniugatis*, the first in the list of proofs at *Inst.* 2.3.15.

26. Usually *diaphora*, difference.

27. Ps. 142(141).6.

28. Cf. John 14.6.

29. 1 John 2.18.

30. Matt. 27.46.

31. Matt. 5.10.

32. Ps. 1.2.

33. Gal. 6.8.

34. Wisd. 5.8 f.

35. For the false etymology, see Varro, *L.L.* 5.21.

36. 1 Thess. 4.16.

37. "Depiction of character"; cf. Quintilian, 9.3.99.

38. Ps. 56(55).13.
39. See above, Ps. 34(33).4.
40. Joel 2.20.
41. John 14.6.
42. Ps. 23(22).4.
43. Sedulius, *Carmen Paschale* 1.349.

PSALM 37 [Ps. 38(37)]

1. Ps. 32(31).1.
2. Ps. 51(50).5.
3. So Augustine, *En. Ps.* 37.5.
4. This is the third of the penitential psalms; see on Ps. 6.1.
5. "Expression of character"; see above on Ps. 37(36).1.
6. Job 1.1.
7. Prov. 9.8.
8. Job 19.11.
9. Augustine, *Ench.* 33 (= ACW 3.41 f.).
10. See at Ps. 6.2.
11. Cf. Nah. 1.9.
12. See Ps. 7.14, where "arrows" is said to denote the apostles.
13. Job 6.4.
14. Job 7.21.
15. Job 30.17.
16. For the motif of necessity in the *narratio* of a Roman speech, see Quintilian 3.8.22.
17. "Depreciation"; see Martin, 153, and Ps. 22(21).7.
18. This is of course a fanciful suggestion.
19. Job 17.1.
20. Job 42.3.
21. Job 7.16.
22. *De anima* (CCL 96.503 ff.).
23. Another false derivation.
24. A fanciful etymology.
25. Compare Cicero, *De amicitia* 20: *est enim amicitia nihil aliud*

nisi omnium divinarum humanarumque rerum cum benevolentia et caritate consensio.

26. Job 4.5.

27. Job 19.17.

28. Job 19.13.

29. Job 2.9: *dic verbum in Domino.* The Vulgate rendering, *Benedic Domino,* was interpreted ironically by Jerome and other Fathers.

30. Reading *alter* for *alteri* in CCL.

31. Job 3.26.

32. See paragraph 9 above.

33. Job 13.15.

34. Dan. 3.17 f.

35. Ps. 13(12).5.

36. Gal. 6.1.

37. Job 7.20.

38. "Emphatic utterance," but here equivalent to climax; see Martin, 255 f., and Ps. 25(24).7 above.

39. Job 2.9.

40. Job 6.30.

41. Job 42.7 f.

42. Isa. 14.13 f.

PSALM 38 [PS. 39(38)]

1. Ch. 2.

2. See Jerome, *Hebr. nom.* 1.11 f.; Augustine, *En. Ps.* 38.1.11 f.

3. James 3.8, 5.

4. Eccli. 28.28 f.

5. In this bogus etymology Cassiodorus ignores the different quantities of *sĕra* and *sēro.*

6. Matt. 7.6.

7. 2 Cor. 5.17.

8. Gen. 1.26.

9. 2 Cor. 4.16.

10. 2 Cor. 4.16.

11. Cf. Ps. 22(21).6, 17(16).12, 118(117).22.

12. Augustine, *De diversis quaestionibus* LXXXIII 51 (CCL 44A.78).

13. 1 Tim. 6.10.

14. Ps. 19(18).13 f.

15. See 27(26).1. Quintilian (5.14.14) says that there is no difference between the syllogism and the *epichirema* except that the syllogism deals with true facts, the *epichirema* with credible ones.

16. The connection with *os* is clear enough (cf. Varro, *L.L.* 6.76), but *ratio* is irrelevant.

17. Luke 7.48.

18. Ps. 35(34).3.

19. Matt. 25.34.

20. Cf. Varro, *L.L.* 5.33: *peregrinus a pergendo* (actually from *per* and *ager*).

21. Ps. 39(38).4.

PSALM 39 [PS. 40(39)]

1. "Etymological relation," the first in the list of arguments at *Inst.* 2.3.15.

2. "The notional," see above, Ps. 1.1.

3. A fanciful derivation.

4. The eight Beatitudes; Matt. 5.3.

5. Cf. Deut. 33.

6. Matt. 6.24.

7. On the pantomime, the solo dancer who portrays mythological or historical themes, see E. J. Jory, *British Institute of Classical Studies* 28(1981) 147 ff.

8. Cf. Matt. 14.29.

9. Cf. Dan. 3.24.

10. Throughout this section Cassiodorus echoes Augustine's condemnation of the attraction of spectacles in the *Confessions* 3.2, 6.8.

11. 'A change-over' of spokesman; see Martin, 296 ff. Christ is allotted this verse, but the Church the next.

12. Heb. 10.10.

13. I.e., the distinction between sacrifice of cattle (Heb. 10.8) and the sacrifice of Christ.

14. Ps. 51(50).19.
15. Ps. 1.1.
16. Ps. 1.2.
17. Ps. 1.3.
18. Ps. 1.3.
19. Ps. 1.6.
20. John 19.9 f.
21. John 14.6.
22. Luke 2.29 ff.
23. Luke 11.13.
24. Luke 4.21.
25. Ps. 22(21).10; cf. Matt. 27.46, Mark 15.54.
26. Acts 9.4.
27. Luke 22.61 f.
28. Mark 8.33.
29. So also Varro, *L.L.* 6.43: *cogitare a cogendo dictum: mens plura in unum cogit unde eligere possit.*
30. So Quintilian, 8.6.54, etc.; see Martin, 263, and Ps. 22(21).9.
31. Job 1.21.
32. Matt. 3.17.

PSALM 40 [PS. 41(40)]

1. Cf. Gen. 7.12.
2. Cf. Exod. 34.28.
3. Cf. 1 Kings (3 Kings) 19.8.
4. Cf. Matt. 4.2, Mark 1.13, Luke 4.2.
5. Eccli. 3.33.
6. Above, Ps. 7.6.
7. Above, Ps. 1.1.
8. Luke 6.30.
9. Untraced.
10. Matt. 25.40.
11. Luke 9.80.
12. "Abundant connection"; see Martin, 305.
13. John 15.20.

14. John 11.48.
15. John 11.50.
16. John 19.12.
17. John 10.18.
18. Cf. Mark 14.45, Matt. 26.49.
19. John 6.71.
20. Cf. Mark 14.20, Matt. 26.23.
21. John 2.19.
22. John 1.14.
23. Phil. 2.10.
24. See *Preface*, p. 33 f., where Jerome is cited as advocating a five-book division in his *Commentariolus in Ps. 40*; Hilary of Poitiers, *Tractatus super psalmos* (CSEL 22.3) opposes this view.
25. Acts 1.20.

Psalm 41 [Ps. 42(41)]

1. Of the three Levite families entrusted by David with the care of temple-music, the Hemanites were descendants of Core; see 1 Par. 6.31.
2. So Jerome, *Tract. Ps.* 84.1 (CCL 78.102); Augustine, *En. Ps.* 41.2.13 (= CCL 38.460).
3. Jerome, *Hom. 92 in Ps. 41* (ed. Morin, p. 410; *Fathers of the Church*, tr. Ewald, p. 243).
4. "Comparison"; see Quintilian, 6.3.59, etc.
5. This is the 14th argument listed in Cassiodorus' *Inst.* 2.3.15.
6. Matt. 5.6.
7. Matt. 5.5.
8. Ps. 103(102).1.
9. Ps. 146(145).2.
10. Ps. 43(42).5.
11. Lam. 4.20.
12. So Augustine, *En. Ps.* 41.12 (= CCL 38.469).
13. Deut. 4.47 f.
14. So Augustine, *loc. cit.*

15. See Quintilian, 8.3.59. The figure gets its name from the mixed population of Sardis.

16. Ps. 36(35).7.

17. Eccli. 35.26.

18. "Question"; see Martin, 285, and Ps. 2.2.

19. Cicero, *Inv.* 2.150. This statement is an echo of the familiar claim by Christian apologists that secular learning was derived from the Hebrew scriptures. See *Preface*, p. 38.

20. 2 Cor. 7.10.

PSALM 42 [PS. 43(42)]

1. This is the definition of Cicero, *Inv.* 2.163: *fortitudo est considerata periculorum susceptio et laborum perpessio.*

2. John 8.12.

3. John 14.6.

4. Cf. Exod. 26.

5. Exod. 25.40.

6. The proposed etymologies are fanciful.

7. Ps. 42(41).12.

8. 2 Cor. 7.9.

9. On the two last, see n. 1 to Ps. 39(38) and n. 1 to Ps. 42(41).

10. Cf. Num. 33.1 ff.

11. Cf. Matt. 1.17.

12. Reading *anima fidelis* (CCL *anima fideles*).

PSALM 43 [PS. 44(43)]

1. For this interpretation of sons of Core, see at Ps. 41.1 above.

2. This will be one of the *argumenta extrinsecus* mentioned at *Inst.* 2.3.16.

3. Cf. Deut. 2.32 ff.

4. Cf. Jos. 6.20.

5. Cf. Gen. 32.24 ff.

6. Gen. 32.28.

7. "Intensification by repetition"; see Martin, 157 f., and Ps. 25(24).7.

8. Heb. 11.38.

9. Matt. 10.23.

10. Above, Ps. 27(26).3.

11. Ps. 22(21).8; cf. Matt. 27.39, Mark 15.29.

12. Rom. 8.35.

13. Another "extrinsic" argument (see n. 2 above).

14. In classical Latin *obliviscor* is followed by the genitive, but in scriptural Latin the accusative is found; Cassiodorus does not try to explain why.

15. The derivation is mistaken.

16. Gen. 22.12.

17. Clearly derived from Quintilian, 8.6.34: . . . *quam recte dicimus abusionem, quae non habentibus nomen suum accommodat quod in proximo est.*

18. Ps. 121(120).3.

19. Ps. 51(50).19.

Psalm 44 [Ps. 45(44)]

1. Matt. 3.17.

2. John 1.1.

3. Mark 10.18.

4. "Praise of beauty"; cf. Quintilian, 3.7.12.

5. Isa. 53.2 f.

6. Augustine, *En. Ps.* 44.7.

7. Song 1.4.

8. Cf. 2 Cor. 5.19.

9. Song 4.3.

10. "Praise of power."

11. Matt. 10.34.

12. Eph. 6.17.

13. Gen. 49.10.

14. Cf. Gen. 24.2.
15. Song 3.8.
16. Ps. 14(13).2.
17. Ps. 19(18).6.
18. Arianism; see above, Introduction VI.
19. John 17.10.
20. "Praise of the judgment."
21. Ps. 110(109).2.
22. See Boethius' translation of Aristotle, *Categories* (ML 64.198B).
23. Song 1.3.
24. Jerome, *Ep.* 65.14; Augustine, *En. Ps. 44.23.*
25. "Description" or "conception"; see Martin, 262, and Ps. 9.26.
26. Song 1.1.
27. For Babylon: "confusion," see on Ps. 135(134).11.
28. Cf. Song 1.4.
29. Song 3.6, 6.9.
30. Cf. 3 above.
31. Cf. 5 above.
32. "Bounding over words"; cf. Quintilian, 9.3.91, and Ps. 37(36).9.
33. Song 1.3.
34. Cf. 10 above.
35. Cf. Exod. 39.1.
36. Cf. 7 above.
37. John 6.44.
38. Cf. 10 above.
39. The term *tonans,* "the Thunderer," for God is taken over from Classical poetry.
40. Jerome, *Ep. 65,* written in 397; see J. N. D. Kelly, *Jerome* (London 1975) 212.

Psalm 45 [Ps. 46(45)]

1. See above, Ps. 42(41).1.
2. See above, Ps. 1.2.
3. Cf. Cassiodorus, *Inst.* 2.3.14.

4. 2 Cor. 7.10.

5. Acts 13.46.

6. "Comparison"; cf. Cicero, *De oratore* 3.117, and Ps. 1.3 above.

7. John 4.13 f.

8. John 1.14.

9. Matt. 16.18.

10. The play between *susceptor* ("protector") and *suscepit* ("took on") is difficult to reproduce in English.

11. The word *prodigium* is derived from *prodicere*, to foretell.

12. This figure is normally used of turning aside to address a person or persons directly, but it can also describe a change from one subject to another; see Quintilian, 9.2.38.

13. See 9 above.

14. Rom. 11.25 f.

15. John 14.27.

Psalm 46 [Ps. 47(46)]

1. *Iubilare* is a word of Hebraic origin; Varro, *L.L.* 6.68, connects it with the exclamation *io*. Cassiodorus' suggestion is fanciful.

2. See Martin, 249, and Ps. 7.4 above.

3. Apoc. 19.10.

4. Matt. 27.37.

5. Isa. 52.7.

6. Cf. Gen. 25.30 ff.

7. Acts 1.11.

8. *Epembasis* is similar to *anaphora*, repetition; see Ps. 3.3, 22(21).6 above.

9. Paphos in Cyprus was a prominent centre of Aphrodite-worship. Ares-Mars was considered to have a Thracian origin (Farnell, *Cults*, 339 ff.), and Jupiter (= Zeus) was said to have been born in Crete.

10. Cf. John 2.20.

PSALM 47 [PS. 48(47)]

1. See *Preface*, p. 32.

2. Above, Ps. 42(41).3–6.

3. For the sons of Core as "sons of the cross," see above, Ps. 42(41).1. Throughout the discussion of this psalm they are equated with the priests who are spokesmen.

4. "Rhetorical stress"; see Quintilian, 9.2.64, and Ps. 25(24).7.

5. Dan. 2.35.

6. Titus 2.13.

7. 1 Kings (3 Kings) 19.11.

8. On the Arians, see above, Introduction VI.

9. Sion is regularly interpreted in the Fathers as "contemplation"; see, e.g., Augustine, *En. Ps.* 2.5 (= ACW 29.26).

10. Isa. 14.13 f.

11. "Adorning"; see Martin, 228.

12. 1 Cor. 15.41 f.

13. The reference in the verse is actually to Tharsis, the Spanish Tarsessus, visited by Phoenician merchant-ships.

14. Has this any application to Cassiodorus' earlier experience of the Gothic kings?

15. Rom. 8.18.

16. See n. 9 above.

17. 1 Cor. 13.13.

18. For the gradual establishment of these orders in the Church see J. T. Lienhard, *Ministry* (Message of the Fathers of the Church 8, Delaware 1984); N. Mitchell, *Mission and Ministry* (Message of the Sacraments 6, Delaware 1982).

19. Above, Ps. 9.5.

20. Bar. 3.36.

21. Job 7.20.

PSALM 48 [PS. 49(48)]

1. On this interpretation of the sons of Core, see above, Ps. 42(41).1.

2. Reading *ipsi* for *ipse* in CCL.

3. 2 Cor. 8.9.

4. Matt. 5.3.

5. 1 Cor. 1.23 f.

6. Cf. Prov. 1.2 f.

7. Cf. *Preface*, p. 31.

8. Cf. Aristotle, *Poetics* 1456b, and Ps. 114(113A).5.

9. Matt. 28.10.

10. Ps. 21.23.

11. Wisd. 10.8.

12. Solon (c. 600 BC) was renowned as lawgiver, poet and sage at Athens. Philon is presumably the Academic philosopher cited by Augustine in the *Contra Acad.* (= ACW 12); though he came from Larissa not Sparta. Aristippus is the famed Cyrenaic philosopher.

13. Matt. 13.39.

14. "For example"; cf. Cassiodorus, *Inst.* 2.3.14.

15. Ps. 36(35).7.

16. Isa. 29.13.

17. Luke 12.20.

18. Cassiodorus quotes from Varro, *L.L.* 5.17: *dives a divo, qui ut deus nihil indigere videtur.*

19. John 8.44.

20. John 1.9.

21. Cf. 13 above.

22. 4 above.

PSALM 49 [Ps. 50(49)]

1. Cf. 1 Par. 6.39.

2. His name means "one who assembles the people"; it is prefixed to twelve of the psalms.

3. Ps. 82(81).6.

4. The Greek *deos* (fear) has no etymological connection with *deus*.

5. Exod. 6.3.

6. Above, Ps. 2.5.

7. Matt. 11.28.

8. Isa. 2.3.

9. Cf. Luke 24.47.
10. Ps. 45(44).3.
11. Above, Ps. 9.5.
12. 1 Cor. 2.8.
13. A bizarre etymology.
14. Matt. 25.41.
15. Isa. 42.14.
16. 1 Cor. 15.52.
17. Cf. Matt. 19.28.
18. Matt. 22.10.
19. Matt. 25.31 f.
20. Cf. Matt. 7.6.
21. Luke 8.8.
22. Matt. 25.35.
23. Exod. 3.14.
24. Martin, 338, and Ps. 87(86).6.
25. Jer. 23.24.
26. 2 Cor. 7.10.
27. Jude 9.
28. So Cicero, *De oratore*, 3.203.
29. See 22 below.
30. Eccli. 15.9.
31. *Synecdoche;* above, Ps. 9.2.
32. Ps. 55(54).22.
33. James 4.11.
34. Eccli. 37.23.
35. Ps. 51(50).3.

PSALM 50 [Ps. 51(50)]

1. Cf. 2 Sam. (2 Kings) 12.13.
2. The passage of Jerome is lost.
3. Cf. 2 Sam. (2 Kings) 11.2 ff.; reference to the brook of Cedron is added from 2 Sam. (2 Kings) 15.23.
4. Cf. Osee 1.2 ff.
5. Cf. Gen. 38.11 ff.

6. 1 Cor. 10.11.

7. *Contra Faustum* 22.7 (= CSEL 25.691 ff.).

8. Cf. Luke 23.40 ff., Matt. 26.75, Luke 18.10 ff.

9. An almost word-for-word citation of Cicero, *De inventione* 2.94.

10. "A coniugatis" (Cassiodorus, *Inst.* 2.3.15).

11. Cf. *Inst.* 2.3.15.

12. Eccli. 11.30.

13. Prov. 18.17.

14. Ps. 50(49).21.

15. See Martin, 277.

16. See at Ps. 21(20).8.

17. That is, with the conclusion preceding the proposition.

18. Matt. 24.35.

19. Isa. 5.3.

20. Mich. 6.3.

21. Bar. 1.15 (the prophecy is traditionally ascribed to Jeremias).

22. *Inst.* 2.3.15.

23. See above, Introduction VI.

24. Cf. Job. 14.4.

25. Eph. 2.3.

26. Rom. 5.12.

27. John 3.3–5.

28. Ps. 59(58).11.

29. Ps. 127(126).1.

30. Ps. 37(36).23.

31. Ps. 146(145).7 f.

32. Isa. 1.19.

33. Ezech. 18.31.

34. Ps. 95(94).8.

35. John 1.16.

36. Rom. 11.35.

37. Phil. 2.13.

38. James 1.17.

39. Augustine, *De gratia et libero arbitrio* (ML 44.881 ff.); Jerome, *Dialogi contra Pelagianos* (ML 23.495 ff.); Prosper, *De gratia Dei et libero arbitrio* (ML 51.213 ff.).

40. Ezech. 18.32.

41. "From causes," the 11th of the 15 arguments listed at *Inst.* 2.3.15.
42. Perhaps an inference from 1 Kings (3 Kings) 4.33.
43. Cf. Celsus 1.3.22.
44. Lev. 14.6 f.
45. Cf. Quintilian, 9.1.29, and 18(17).11.
46. Ps. 18(17).11.
47. Matt. 25.34.
48. "From what follows"; the 9th argument at *Inst.* 2.3.15.
49. Ps. 143(142).7.
50. Luke 22.61 f.
51. Acts 13.22; cf. 1 Sam. (1 Kings) 13.14.
52. Ps. 45(44).7.
53. John 4.24.
54. Here in the sense of "interchange"; cf. Quintilian, 8.6.23, and Ps. 14(13).2.
55. Cf. Eph. 4.22 f.
56. Col. 3.9 f.
57. Cf. 2 Cor. 5.17.
58. Jer. 1.9 f.
59. The whole of the passage from here to the end of 14 is cited by Theodulf, *De spiritu sancto* (ML 105.274 f.).
60. Cf. Boethius, *De Trin.* 1 and 5.
61. This passage is cited by Abelard, *Theol. Christ.* 1.5.
62. Heb. 1.3.
63. Ps. 19(18).7.
64. 1 Peter 3.18.
65. 2 Cor. 3.6.
66. John 6.64.
67. Hilary *De Trin.* (ML 10.25 ff.); Ambrose, *De fide* (ML 16.527 ff.); Augustine, *De Trin.* (ML 42.819 ff.).
68. The treatise has not survived.
69. James 5.20.
70. Cf. Quintilian, 9.1.35, and Ps. 2.7, 19(18).5, 40(39).6.
71. Matt. 16.17.
72. Ps. 50(49).16.
73. Ps. 101(100).1.
74. Isa. 6.5.
75. "Word for word"; cf. *Inst.* 2.3.15.

76. Matt. 15.19.

77. Acts 8.21.

78. Isa. 6.10.

79. Ps. 4.3.

80. Ps. 7.10.

81. Ps. 51(50).12.

82. Eudoxia, wife of Theodosius II, emperor in the east 408–450 AD, lived in Jerusalem for many years before her death in 460, and was responsible for strengthening the city's fortifications. See H. Leclercq, DACL 14 (1939) 166 ff.

83. Ps. 116(114.1–9; 115).12 f.

84. Ps. 51(50).18.

85. Augustine, Sermons 4.21 (= ML 38.45).

86. See above on Ps. 6.

87. Ps. 6.7.

88. Ps. 32(31).4.

89. Ps. 38(37).6.

90. Ps. 102(101).10.

91. Ps. 130(129).1.

92. Ps. 143(142).3.

93. Ps. 51(50).15.

94. A reference to the practice of public penance, in which the sinner was excluded from communion, required to undergo a period of self-humiliation, and precluded from ministry. See Amman, DTC s.v. "Penitence"; J. N. D. Kelly, Early Christian Doctrines, 422 ff.

95. Cf. Lev. 25.10.

APPENDIX A: VARIANT CITATIONS OF THE TEXT OF THE PSALMS

The purpose of this list is to demonstrate that though Cassiodorus basically employs a text of the *Vetus Latina*, he not infrequently quotes from other versions, notably Jerome's "Gallican" Psalter, the version in the Vulgate, and Jerome's Hebrew Psalter. These are indicated by Gall. and Hebr. respectively. Some of the variants are doubtless explicable by Cassiodorus' citing from memory or paraphrasing. The left-hand column indicates psalm and verse; the right-hand column shows the variant where he quotes that psalm and verse at other points of the commentary.

2.8	postula a me	5.1	pete a me
4.2	in tribulatione	27(26).3	in tribulationibus
4.3	usquequo	51(50).19	quousque
6.7	lacrimis	119(118).36	lacrimis meis (Gall., Hebr.)
8.8	boves	150.2	boves universas (Gall.)
19(18).7	nec est qui se abscondat	51(50).14	quis se abscondit
22(21).12	discesseris	119(118).150	discedas
22(21).20	aspice	140(139).8	respice
23(22).4	etsi ambulem	37(36).39	si ambulem
23(22).5	poculum tuum	11(10).7	calix tuus (Gall. calix meus)
24(23).7	vestras	108(107).11	vestri
28(27).5	destrues illos, nec	110(109).6	destrues eos, et non (Hebr.)
30(29).7	ego autem dixi	104(103).29	ego dixi
31(30).20	perfecisti	17(16).14	perfecisti eam
32(31).4	in aerumna dum confringitur mihi spina	51(50)	Concl. in aerumna mea dum configitur in spina (Gall. dum configitur spina)
32(31).8	in quibus	73(72).22	quibus (Gall.)
36(35).7	iudicia tua	104(103).3	iudicia Domini

583

37(36).23	dirigentur	51(50).7	diriguntur
37(36).25	egens	129(128).1	egentem
37(36).35	super cedros	73(72),18, 129(128).8	sicut cedros (so Gall.)
41(40).2	in die mala	37(36).19	in die malo
42(41).2	cervus desiderat	127(126).1	desiderat cervus (Gall.)
45(44).7	virga recta est	23(22).4	virga aequitatis (Gall. virga directionis; Hebr. sceptrum aequitatis)
45(44).8	oleo laetitiae	23(22).5	oleo exultationis (Hebr.)
45(44).8	prae consortibus tuis	89(88).21	prae participibus tuis
50(49).15	et magnificabis me	9.10	et glorificabis me
50(49).21	statuam illam	6.2	statuam illa
51(50).5	peccatum	19(18).13	delictum
69(68).2	Deus	29(28).3	Domine
69(68).16	neque urgeat	55(54).24	neque aperiat 142(141).8 non urgeat
74(73).2	in quo habitasti (Hebr.)	105(104).26	in quo habitavit in eo (Gall. in quo habitasti in eo)
74(73).8	omnes sollemnitates (Hebr.)	74(73).18	omnes dies festos (Gall.)
80(79).8	Domine, Deus virtutum	104(103).58	Deus virtutum (Gall.)
83(82).5	venite, disperdamus . . . et non memoretur	83(82).13	venite et disperdamus . . . et non memorabitur
84(83).3	concupiscit et deficit	65(64).5, 119(118).81	concupivit et defecit
84(83).5	in domo tua, Domine, in saeculum saeculi	23(22).6, 111(110).1	in domo tua in saecula saeculorum (Gall.)
85(84).11	complexae sunt se	72(71).3	osculatae sunt se (Gall. osculatae sunt)
89(88).22	auxiliabitur ei . . . non nocebit eum	139(138).5	auxiliabitur illi . . . non apponet nocere ei (Gall.)
90(89).4	mille anni ante oculos tuos tamquam dies hesterna quae praeteriit	6.1	ante conspectum eius mille anni sicut dies unus 22(21).12 mille anni ante oculos tuos, sicut dies hesternus qui praeterivit
95(94).6	ante eum: ploremus ante Dominum	142(141)	Concl. coram Domino: ploremus ante Deum
95(94).5	fundaverunt	19(18).2	finxerunt
95(94).5	et aridam	119(118).73	et aridam terram
101(100).1	misericordiam et iudicium	119(118).156	iudicium et misericordiam
102(101).10	tamquam panem	51(50)	Concl. sicut panem
104(103).16	quas plantasti (Hebr.)	29(28).5	is quas Dominus plantavit (quas plantavit Gall.)

104(103).19	in tempora	104(103)	Concl. in tempore
107(106).16	portas aeneas	108(107).11	portas aereas (Gall., Hebr.)
110(109).7	bibet	124(123).5	bibit
119(118).81	in salutare tuum	13(12).1	in salutari tuo
123(122).4	abundantibus	119(118).153	abundantium
127(126).1	laborant aedificantes	51(50).7	laborant qui aedificant (Hebr. laboraverunt qui aedificant)
139(138).8	tu illic es	119(118).151	ibi es (Hebr. ibi es tu)
143(142).3	in obscuris	51(50)	Concl. in obscuro
143(142).7	velociter exaudi me, Domine: defecit	104(103).29	exaudi me, Domine, quoniam defecit
143(142).7	similis ero	51(50).11	ero similis
148.5	quia ipse dixit . . . ipse mandavit	102(101).26	quoniam ipse dixit 118.73 dixit . . . mandavit

APPENDIX B: ARGUMENTS, DEFINITIONS, SYLLOGISMS, TYPES OF SPEECH

Arguments (cf. *Inst.* 2.3.16f.):

ab adiunctis,	33(32).18
ab antecedentibus,	51(50).7
a causis	51(50).8
a concessione	6.2, Concl.; 32(31).1; 51(50).1
a coniugatis,	37(36).20; 40(39).2; 51(50).3; 118(117).18; 119(118).154; 132(131).15; 144(143).6
a consequenti(bus),	11(10).2: 30(29).8; 51(50).10; 58(57).12
ex contrario,	26(25).4; 30(29).6; 34(33).11; 37(36).16; 58(57).2; 119(118).113; 138(137).6
a dictis factisque maiorum,	44(43).2
a differentia,	119(118).163
ab enumeratione,	8.8
ab eventu,	74(73).11
a forma	45(44).3
a genere,	36(35).13
ab ingenio,	36(35).4
a laude rei laesae,	74(73).2; 94(93).6
a maiore ad minus,	51(50).3; 102(101).8
a minore ad maius,	42(41).2; 82(81).6
ab necessitate,	32(31).4; 38(37).6; 127(126).1
a persona,	24(23).5; 105(104).5
a potestate,	45(44).3
a prole,	45(44).17
a rebus ipsis,	20(19).9
a specie,	45(44).12
a tempore,	102(101).14
a tormentis,	44(43).18
a victu,	6.9

Definitions (cf. *Inst.* 2.3.14);

2 (Ennoematike/notio), 1.1; 14(13).3; 40(39).5; 41(40).2; 80(79).2; 81(80).11; 104(103).3; 146(145).6

3 (poiotēs/qualitativa), 22(21).4; 24(23).8; 33(32).5; 106(105).3; 119(118).2

4 (hypographike/descriptionalis), 80(79).14

5 (kata tēn lexin/ad verbum), 17(16).13; 33(32).4; 46(45).2; 51(50).19; 57(56).5; 68(67).16; 72(71).17; 84(83).6; 86(85).5; 96(95).5; 119(118).129; 139(138).21; 140(139).10; 145(144).3

7 (kata metaphoran), 19(18).8

8 (kat'aphaeresin tou enantiou/per privantiam contrarii), 1.1; 32(31).1f.; 86(85).8; 94(93).20

9 (kath' hypotypōsin/per quamdam imaginationem), 73(72).1

10 (hōs typō/veluti), 49(48).13

12 (kat'epainon/per laudem), 18(17).2; 68(67).7; 86(85).15; 89(88.8); 111(110).7; 112(111).1; 136(135).9, 21

13 (kat'analogian/iuxta rationem), 82(81).6

14 (kata to pros ti/ad aliquid), 89(88).27

Syllogisms, arts of logic, Pref. p. 38; 32(31).11; 39(38).7ff.; 42(41).6, 12; 43(42).5

—Categorical, 1.2; 31(30).8; 32(31).11; 37(36).1; 46(45).2: 53(52).1f.; 61(60).5; 91(90).1; 97(96).10; 121(120).1; "purest and chief of syllogisms," 150.6

—Enthymematic ("mentis conceptio"), 21(20).8; 51(50).6, 81(80).3; 94(93).10; 111(110).9; 141(140).1

—Epichirema (rhetorical syllogism), 27(26).1; 37(36).2; 39(38).12

—Hypothetical, 41(40).2; 63(62).7; 71(70).1; 101(100).2; 131(130).1; 139(138) Concl.

Types of speech (see 2 n. 44):

—Deliberative, 2.11; 73(72).17; 77(76).6

—Demonstrative, 29(28).1; 33(32).4; 36(35).6; 52(51)Concl.; 74(73).12; 87(86) Concl.; 89(88).16f.; 93(92).1; 96(95).5; 114(113).12; 135(134).1

—Judicial, 6 Concl.

APPENDIX C: SUGGESTED
ETYMOLOGIES IN THE TEXT

adolescens/adolere, 68(67).28
ager/agere, 107(106).38
altare/altitudo, 26(25).6
altare/altae arae, 43(42).4
altare/alta res, 43(42).4
amicus/animi aequus, 38(37).12
angulus/genu, 118(117).22
animus/anemos, 124(123).3
animus/anaema, 124(123).3
aper/asper, 80(79).14
apes/a pedibus, 118(117).12
aqua/a qua, 124(123).5
argumentum/argutus, 34(33).11
aries/a fronte ruens, 29(28).1
arma/arcere, 35(34).2
atrium/ater, 135(134).1
auris/auditus, 5.2; 102(101).3;
  115(114).2
aurum/aura, 72(71).15

barbarus/barba rus, 114(113).1
bipennis/pinnus, 74(73).6

caelum/celare, 114(113).24
calix/calidus, 11(10).7; 16(15).5;
  75(74).9
calumnia/capitis alumna,
  119(118).134
campus/capacitas, 132(131).6

canes/canere, 59(58).7
captare/captiose tractare,
  94(93).21
caput/capere, 110(109).6
carcer/arcere, 142(141).8
caro/carus, 78(77).39
catuli/callere, 104(103).21
causa/casus, 73(72).13
cicatrix/caecus, 38(37).6
circum/circuitus, 31(30).14
cithara/cita iteratio, 33(32).2
cogitatio/cogere, 40(39).15
collis/colere, 114(113).4
columba/cellae alumna, 55(54).7
consilium/consulere, 1.5; 55(54).6
convallis/cavata vallis, 60(59).8
cubile/cubare, 4.5; 36(35).5

daemones/di manes, 96(95).5
decem/decus, 11(10) Concl.
delictum/linquere, 25(24).7
dentes/demere, 3.8
deus/deos, 22(21).2; 50(49).1;
  94(93).1
diligo/de omnibus eligo, 18(17).2
dives/divus, 49(48).17

eripe/rapere, 31(30).2
erudire/rudis, 2.11

esca/edere, 78(77).31
fides/quod fiant dicta, 78(77).36
flamma/flagellum, 106(105).18
fons/fovere, 68(67).27
frenum/fero retinendo, 32(31).9
fructus/frui, 1.3; 107(106).38
frumentum/frumen, 4.8
funes/funera, 16(15).6

gemitus/geminatus luctus, 6.7;
    38(37).10
gens/genus, 2.9; 79(78).1
gladius/clades, 37(36).15
gratia/gratis data, 84(83).12

hereditas/herus, 2.9; 16(15).5;
    78(77).62
hircus/hirsutus, 66(65).15

ianuae/Janus, 74(73).5
idolum/ipsum dolum, 97(96).7
ieiunium/inedium, 35(34).13
infernum/inferre, 9.18
insula/in salo, 72(71).10
iter/terere, 1.5
iubilare/iuvare, 47(46).2; 81(80).2
iudicium/iuris dictum, 37(36).30;
    72(71).2
iurare/iure orare, 89(88).4;
    119(118).106; 132(131).2

lac/liquor, 119(118).70
lacus/latere, 28(27).1
lamenta/intra lares monumenta,
    78(77).63
latus/latere, 91(90).7
laus/laurea, 34(33).2
lectus/electus, 6.7

lex/ligare, 1.2
limus/ligans humum, 69(68).3
locuples/loca plura tenens,
    65(64).10

manifestus/mane dies festus,
    50(49).3
mansueti/manu sueti, 25(24).9;
    37(36).11
mare/meare, 104(103).25
mensa/mensis, 23(22).5
meridies/medius dies, 55(54).18

nares/gnaritas, 114(113).15
necessitas/in nece, 31(30).9
nomen/notum, 72(71).17
nox/nocere, 1.2

obturare/tus, 58(57).5
occasus/horarum casus,
    107(106).3
oculus/ocior lux, 6.8
oculus/occultus, 6.8
odium/oris repudium, 139(138).22
olus/olla, 37(36).2
oratio/oris ratio, 17(16).1;
    39(38).13; 86(85).1
ostium/obstare, 141(140).3

pactio/pax, 119(118).158
palma/pacis alma, 92(91).13
palpebrae/palpitare, 11(10).5;
    132(131).4
patria/patris atria, 96(95).7
pauper/a paululo lare, 9.35
pax/parcere or pascere, 122(121).7
pennae/pendere, 55(54).7

peregrinus/pergens longius,
    39(38).13
pessima/pessum data, 34(33).22
portae/portare, 24(23).7; 69(68).13
portio/pars, 119(118).57
portus/portare, 107(106).30
prodigium/porro dicere,
    46(45).9; 78(77).43; 105(104).27;
    135(134).9
profanum/pro fano, 89(88).40
profundum/porro fundum,
    130(129).1
pupilla/pusilla, 17(16).8;
    109(108).12
pusillus/pugnus, 37(36).10;
    54(53).9
psalmus/psauein, *Pref.* 31

retia/retinere, 141(140).10
ructare/rumpere, 119(118).171
ruina/repetens ima, 32(31).4;
    91(90).6

saeculum/in se, 61(60).7; 74(73).12
scabellum/scandere, 110(109).1
scitus/scire citus, 73(72).11

semita/semivia, 25(24).4
sera/sero, 39(38).2; 147(146
    + 147).13
servus/servare, 119(118).122
simulacrum/simulatio sacra,
    97(96).7
sol/solus, 104(103).22
spes/stabilis pes, 40(39).5
sponsus/spondere, 19(18).6
stagna/stare, 107(106).35

tabernaculum/taberna-
    cenaculum, 15(14).1
terminus/ter minus, 2.9
terra/terere, 2.11; 37(36).29

venenum/venae, 14(13).3
vertex/vertere, 7.17
via/vehere, 1.5; 25(24).4
via/violentia, 44(43).19
vinea/vites, 80(79).9
vir/vires, 1.1
virga/vi, 2.10
virtus/viriditas, 140(139).8
volucres/volatus, 8.9
vultus/velle, 31(30).23

APPENDIX D: FIGURES
OF SPEECH AND THOUGHT

aetiologia (causae redditio), 16(15)9; 56(55).13; 61(60).6; 95(94).3; 96(95).4; 101(100).3; 114(113).9; 139(138).10; 143(142).8

allegory (inversio), 7.1; 32(31).9; 51(50).21; 53(52).1; 59(58).7; 68(67).18; 98(97).8; 100(99).2; 105(104)Concl.

amphibolia (dictio ambigua), 21(20).12

anacephaleosis (recapitulatio), 114(113).21

anadiplosis (congeminatio dictionis), 24(23).9; 25(24).4; 122(121).3

anaphora (relatio), 27(26).3; 44(43).15; 53(52).2; 118(117).6; 124(123).2; 129(128).2

anastrophe (perversio), 24(23).5; 53(52).5; 62(61).2; 86(85).7; 87(86).2; 131(130).1

antiptosis (casus pro casu), 35(34).14

antiphrasis, 56(55).2

antiprosopon, 79(78).7

antisagoge (contradictio), 12(11).5

antistathmesis (recompensatio), 126(125).5

antonomasia (vice nominis) 68(67).13

apo koinou (a communi), 32(31).11; 49(48).17; 84(83).4; 89(88).3; 136(135).4

aposiopesis, 18(17).46

apostrophe (conversio), 21(20).6; 46(45).11; 50(49).22

astismos (urbana dictio), 99(98).1

auxesis (augmentum), 3.4; 69(68).5; 74(73).7; 79(78).4; 106(105).22; 135(134).7

brachylogia (brevis locutio), 50(49).9; 87(86).6

cacozelon (mala affectatio), 106(105).14

catachresis (abusio), 43(42).23; 75(74).11

tapeinosis (humiliatio), 22(21).7; 38(37).6; 69(68).6; 90(89).4; 102(101).10
tautologia, 21(20).3; 67(66).8
topothesia (loci positio), 125(124).2

zeugma, 15(14).5

INDEXES

I. OLD AND NEW TESTAMENTS

599

2. AUTHORS

Abelard, 581
Adriaen, M., 5, 20, 521, 559
Albinus, 517
Alcuin, 19
Alexander Rhetor, 541
Amann, E., 544, 582
Ambrose, 6 f., 9, 68, 283, 537; *Comm. in Ps.*, 519; *De fide*, 581; *De incarn.*, 217, 551; *De Trin.*, 506; *Hymns*, 116, 538; *Super Lucam*, 89, 532, 534
Apuleius, 16, 526, 539
Aquinas, Thomas, 20; *S.T.*, 521, 536
Aristotle, 102; *Categories*, 575; *Poetics*, 578; *Prior Analytics*, 536
Asconius Pedianus, 521
Athanasius, 518, 545; *De incarn.*, 68, 530; *Epp.*, 40 f., *De libro psalm.*, 8
Augustine, *passim*; *Conf.*, 521, 570; *Contra Acad.*, 578; *Contra Faustum*, 493, 580; *De civ. Dei*, 30, 523; *De diversis quaest.*, 392, 570; *De doctr. Christ.*, 38, 53, 519, 521, 527; *De gratia et libero arbitrio*, 500, 580; *De haeresibus*, 555; *De praedest. sanctorum*, 544, 562 f.; *De Trin.*, 506, 530, 540, 581; *Enarr. in Ps.*, 23 *& passim*; *Enchiridion*, 70, 335, 378, 531, 564, 568; *Epp.*, 232, 551, 553; *Locutiones in Hept.*, 36, 59, 525, 528; *Sermones*, 89, 99, 226, 510, 536, 552, 582

Ps-Augustine, *Contra Varimadum*, 282, 559
Aumann, J., 542

Basil, 537
Bede, 19; *Hist. Abbatum*, 543
Benedict, 522
Besselaar, J. B. de, 518
Boethius, 17; *Aristotelis Cat.*, 575; *Contra Eutychen*, 12, 63, 529, 536, 550; *De arith.*, 528, 539; *De geom.*, 527; *De Trin.*, 529, 581; *Top. Cic.*, 563
Boylan, P., 531, 543, 555, 561, 563

Caesarius of Arles, 522
Cappuyns, M., 518
Cassian, John, 4, 14, 520, 546; *Conferences*, 14 f.; *Contra Nestorium*, 546
Celsus, 581
Chadwick, H., 517, 520, 541
Chrysostom, John, 78, 181, 546; *De compunct.*, 95, 535
Cicero, 16; *Academica*, 562; *De amicitia*, 568 f.; *De inventione*, 16, 422, 529, 535, 537, 538, 561, 573, 580; *De oratore*, 528, 579; *Topica*, 258, 286, 330, 548, 556, 559, 563, 565; *Tusc. Disp.*, 526, 559
Courcelle, P., 518, 526, 542
Cyril of Alexandria, 530; *Epp.*, 546, 551

3. GENERAL INDEX

Abimelech, 324 f.
Abraham, 27, 124, 150, 368, 462
abysses = Testaments, 420
Achimelech, 269
Achis, 324
Adam, 49, 51 f., 55, 113, 245, 268, 353, 355, 391, 393, 471, 473, 496
Agapetus, 2
Albinus, senator, 1
alphabetic psalms, 13, 246 ff., 324 ff., 357 ff.
allegory, use of, 9 f.
Alleluia-psalms, 13
Antichrist, 125 ff.
Apollinarius/Apollinarists, 12, 165
archer = heretic, 136
Arians/Arius, 12, 41, 62, 83, 92 f., 214 f., 282, 299, 464 f., 557
Aristippus, 474
arithmetic, 116
arrows = apostles, 106; = evangelists, 182; = Christ's words, 444; = devil's powers, 378
Asaph, 29, 479, 488
Ascension, 114
asp/asps = Jews, 152
Athalaric, 2
Augustus, 457

Babylon, 160, 272, 448
Barabbas, 220
Barachiel, 479

Bathsheba = type of Church, 493
beasts = men of pleasure, 114
beasts of woods = superstitious pagans, 485
beds = thoughts of aggressive men, 76; = physical pleasures, 95
Belisarius, 2
belly = memory, 294 f.
Benedict, 3
Bethlehem, 196
birds = proud men, 114
Boethius, 1, 517
bones = mental strength, 295, 307, 333, 340, 422; bones of Christ = apostles, 223, 226
bow = divine commands, 136; = O.T. and N.T. 136; = ambush of infidels, 457
bowels of Christ = Church, 223
bridechamber = Virgin's womb, 196

Cades, 281
Caiphas, 411
Calvary, 415
calves = Jews, 222; = innocents, preachers, martyrs, 510
Candace, 26
canticle, meaning of, 31, 73, 176; expresses joy/grief not repentance, 388
canticle-psalm, 32
cassia = redemption by baptism, 446